THE GOLDEN BRIGADE

The Untold Story of the 82nd Airborne in Vietnam and Beyond

Robert J. Dvorchak

A KNOX PRESS BOOK
An Imprint of Permuted Press
ISBN: 978-1-63758-469-9
ISBN (eBook): 978-1-63758-470-5

The Golden Brigade:
The Untold Story of the 82nd Airborne in Vietnam and Beyond

Permuted Press, LLC
New York • Nashville
permutedpress.com

Published in the United States of America
1 2 3 4 5 6 7 8 9 10

Dedicated to the 227 All Americans of the 82nd Airborne Division who perished in Vietnam, the 1,100 who were wounded and their brothers in the Golden Brigade who have preserved their memory. All The Way!

Table of Contents

Prologue: Last Man's Club ... i
Chapter 1: Unexpected Letter ... 1
Chapter 2: Changing Times ... 3
Chapter 3: America's 9-1-1 ... 17
Chapter 4: Who Are You Guys? ... 29
Chapter 5: Joining The Fight ... 37
Chapter 6: First Blood ... 41
Chapter 7: Street Without Joy ... 47
Chapter 8: Where It's Worst ... 51
Chapter 9: Hell Breaks Loose ... 61
Chapter 10: Stand Down ... 75
Chapter 11: Life Saver ... 81
Chapter 12: Deadliest Day ... 85
Chapter 13: A Friend And Hero ... 95
Chapter 14: The Lazy W ... 103
Chapter 15: A True All American ... 111
Chapter 16: Doc Dillon ... 115
Chapter 17: Sorry About That ... 117
Chapter 18: The Three Villes ... 123
Chapter 19: The Ambush ... 129
Chapter 20: Road Guards ... 135
Chapter 21: Golden Gloves ... 139
Chapter 22: Suicide Attack ... 143
Chapter 23: Toughest Letter ... 149
Chapter 24: Hell's Hamlet ... 155
Chapter 25: Joe Tentpeg ... 163

Chapter 26: Airborne Shuffle 173
Chapter 27: Legs 177
Chapter 28: Conde Arrives 191
Chapter 29: Operation Mot 197
Chapter 30: Epiphany Hill 209
Chapter 31: Typhoon Tested 215
Chapter 32: Home Boys 221
Chapter 33: Golden Sword 225
Chapter 34: Night Rider's Star 233
Chapter 35: New Ground 241
Chapter 36: Murray's Journey 245
Chapter 37: Thanksgiving 249
Chapter 38: Helping A New Guy 253
Chapter 39: 'Tis The Season 257
Chapter 40: Christmas Without Joy 265
Chapter 41: Stronger Than War 269
Chapter 42: Two-Way Vision 275
Chapter 43: Death From Above 281
Chapter 44: Death Down Below 285
Chapter 45: Mike Foxtrot 295
Chapter 46: Water And Blood 305
Chapter 47: An Act Of Love 317
Chapter 48: Baptism By Boat 321
Chapter 49: Supporting Roles 327
Chapter 50: Conde's Crew 333
Chapter 51: Grim Friday 341
Chapter 52: One Family's Grief 347
Chapter 53: Of Their Own Accord 351
Chapter 54: Dead Ducks And Loose Ends 355
Chapter 55: Lost In The Woods 359
Chapter 56: Golden Promise 365

Chapter 57: Birthday Without Joy 369
Chapter 58: Random Fate 373
Chapter 59: Small Doses 379
Chapter 60: Dear John And Other Lunacy 385
Chapter 61: Moonstruck 391
Chapter 62: Dogs Of War 399
Chapter 63: Delta Diary 403
Chapter 64: Last Blood 413
Chapter 65: Unkindest Cut 419
Chapter 66: Reckoning 429
Chapter 67: Resolution 437
Epilogue: Golden Devotion 445
Index 449
Photo Credits and Acknowledgments 471
About the Author 473

PROLOGUE
LAST MAN'S CLUB

I found the beginnings of this story the way a genealogist discovers an overlooked branch of a family tree. It was there all along but had been orphaned by history as a bough best forgotten. Even those who were part of it never spoke of it. Yet it remained alive because part of their code compels them to remember their fallen brothers. As part of a unit that fought in Vietnam, they had each other's backs in the crucible of war and will have each other's backs until the day they die. It wasn't just any unit either. Their identity stems from the battle flag of the 82nd Airborne Division, the renowned Army organization that considers itself family and lives by the motto *All The Way.* Despite everything ever written about Vietnam and the Baby Boomers who came of age in the 1960s, their sacrifice and the way they have honored their comrades has never been fully acknowledged. They are as proud to be part of their parent organization as any generation that ever served. More than a missing chapter of Airborne history, they hold within their hearts an untold piece of Americana.

The back story began with the 100th anniversary of the founding of the division, one of the best known but least understood clans in the world. It's not a family one is born into but rather one in which a place is earned, the bond of shared sacrifice having the same cohesive quality as a bloodline. From far and wide, even from overseas, comrades-in-arms made a pilgrimage in 2017 to the Rosen Centre Resort Hotel in Orlando, where the only thing thicker than the August humidity of central Florida was the pride of those who regard the 82nd Airborne as their parent organization. Hats, shirts and vanity license plates bore the family crest of a Double A patch that stands for All Americans.

The coat of arms originated in World War I when it was noted that the original members of the 82nd Division came from every state in the country. The All Americans spent more consecutive days on the front line than any other Army unit in that war to end all wars. Its most famous character was Sergeant Alvin York, a sharp-shooting Presbyterian elder from Tennessee who was awarded the Medal of Honor for single-handedly overcoming an entire German battalion. York's motivation for fighting and killing was to put an end the fighting and killing, the eternal paradox of war.

A generation later, the Airborne tab was added when the division became the first Army unit trained to reach World War II battlefields in gliders or under the canopy of parachutes. The All Americans made four combat jumps in the bloodiest war in history, the third of which was the night drop into Normandy ahead of the amphibious landings on D-Day. They also fought in the climactic Battle of the Bulge, during which one grizzled All American said of the German advance, "I'm the 82nd Airborne, and this is as far as the bastards are going to get." Within months, division commander James Gavin accepted the surrender of an entire German army in the war's final days. The Airborne acquired the additional title of America's Guard of Honor, so named because General George S. Patton said the division's honor guard was the best he had ever seen. Insiders refer to themselves as the Brotherhood of the Silk, except females now jump and parachutes are made of nylon, but the Family of Synthetic Fabric doesn't have the same poetic ring. By whatever name, they are the best soldiers in the world. Just ask one of them.

A third crop of All Americans, the sons of the Greatest Generation, got the mission of Vietnam, and their story was obscured the politics and policies surrounding America's most unpopular war. At the time, the 82nd Airborne was America's 9-1-1 force, a combat unit that was ready, willing and able to respond on a moment's notice to any emergency anywhere in the world and capable of parachuting out of airplanes, if necessary, to take the fight to the enemy. The Pentagon had no plans to send the Airborne to Vietnam, but an emergency in the form of the Tet Offensive forced the hand of decision-makers.

By happenstance, I was in Florida to have dinner with retired three-star general James H. Johnson Jr., the former division commander who was the first one out the door during a combat jump into Panama in 1989 and who led the division when it drew the original line in the sand in the ramp up to Operation Desert Storm. As a New York City-based war correspondent with The Associated Press, I had witnessed war at the foxhole level with the 82nd Airborne and published a journal about that experience entitled *Drive On: The Uncensored War of Bedouin Bob and the All Americans.* Having read the book, the general wrote me a letter saying that it was first-rate history. He also called me the Ernie Pyle of the 82nd Airborne, a reference to the famed war correspondent who told the story of World War II from the point of view of the infantrymen who fought it. A writer could have no higher praise, and a man could have no higher honor than to be called a brother by an Airborne paratrooper. For me, it felt like a long overdue welcome home.

In retirement, Johnson was also the Honorary Colonel of the association representing the 505th Parachute Infantry Regiment, known by the motto H-Minus because it jumped in before everybody else. He invited me to speak at the regiment's business meeting in one of the hotel's hospitality suites. As humbling as it was to talk about the life-changing experience of going to war with the 82nd Airborne, I said that my time with them was the most meaningful episode of my professional life. The All Americans were the most colorful characters, and the people with the most character, that I ever met.

At the same time, inside a brotherhood within a brotherhood, the dwindling survivors of a last man's club attended to their own business in the same room. In a quaint custom, they had already set aside a pricey bottle of Woodford Reserve Kentucky Straight Bourbon so that the last living member could make a final toast to the sacrifices of his deceased comrades. The amber-colored spirits, along with a ceremonial sipping glass, were encased in a custom-made wood cabinet adorned with handles and hinges hammered out of melted shell casings and gun barrels. This last man's club represented the Golden Brigade, the name given to the 82nd Airborne in Vietnam.

What's more, the members of the Golden Brigade Association, with money from their own pockets, were in the process of creating something to remember them by. The concept was a Legacy Bowl, an oversized silver chalice adorned with gold inlets and 15 goblets representing the subordinate units that were like the spokes inside the wheel of the brigade. The plan was to unveil the bowl at a 2018 reunion marking the 50th anniversary of the unit's deployment to Vietnam. Their big event, named Operation West Point, would be held at the U.S. Military Academy.

The elements seemed like the stuff of stardust—graying soldiers in their golden years planning a golden anniversary for a Golden Brigade tested in the hellfire of Vietnam. Yet, as Jim Johnson pointed out, the story had never been fully told in context, and that I would be the best person to gather the names, dates and places for this branch of the family tree. He, more than anyone else, set the story in motion.

The first question was whether the Golden Brigade was some sort of Army irony, like the guy who has the nickname Lucky because he had the last lottery number in the last draft ever held. No, the survivors said, the name was authentic. They had even trademarked the phrase: All They Touched Turned To Gold. That's a splendid sentiment, but Vietnam and the Midas touch are seldom mentioned in the same sentence. Still, the precious yellow metal is renowned for its ability to survive the harshest of acid tests. Gold is what remains after caustic solutions dissolve away all the rocks hiding the treasure.

The next question was whether Vietnam veterans would want to re-open the internal scars associated with the war. The answer was that the time had come to tell it. They weren't asking for anything. They didn't think they were owed anything. But five decades after the fact, having reached the age of average male life expectancy, they agreed to talk. Otherwise, they would take their experience to their graves.

"We are in that stage of our lives where our ranks grow thinner with each passing year. We're dying off. We didn't talk about Vietnam except among ourselves. It's time to tell it now before we're all gone, even if some of it is painful," said Richard O'Hare, an amateur historian who shepherded the Legacy Bowl project. "This was the seminal event in our lives. These men saved my life. I had their backs. They are my brothers. The valor—I saw it with my own eyes."

The very existence of the Golden Brigade Association, which was formed while the unit was still in Vietnam, speaks to the Shakespearean bond of brotherhood. It's why men who experienced deprivations and danger gather together, not so much to revel in war stories but to relate to each other in a way nobody else can.

"It's a need. I perceive it as a need. You need to feel that cohesion again," O'Hare said. "People say we weren't joiners, but nobody asked us to join anything. We were looking for a home. We didn't have a home because nobody really wanted us. We were the orphans, the bastards, the red-headed stepchildren."

As a child of The Sixties, just slightly younger than most of them, I felt an instant connection. My oldest brother was wounded twice within 10 days in Vietnam while serving in the Air Cavalry Troop of the 11th Armored Cavalry Regiment, and he was spit on when he came home. I was also drafted into the U.S. Army, but the war was over by the time I took the oath of enlistment, and I never left the States. Of all those who say they got a raw deal during that era, the worst was reserved for those who held up their end of the contract and did their duty as they saw fit. Having once gone to war with the All Americans, I was also aware of the disconnect between what really happens and what is remembered.

One reason that so little is known about the 82nd Airborne in Vietnam is that their war began as a classified mission, then morphed in a 22-month slog in two major areas of operation. What's more, the unit operated under the control of larger military units who required extra firepower but gave little recognition to the 82nd Airborne, the very definition of what the Army calls a bastard brigade. Returning soldiers fought an additional battle on the home front when they were greeted with scorn or the cold slap of indifference. The rebellious segment of the sex, drugs and rock 'n' roll generation likes to say that those who can remember the Sixties weren't really there. Those who went to Vietnam can't forget, no matter how hard they tried. A fly on the wall at a gathering of Vietnam veterans might overhear one say to another, "How was Vietnam to you last night?" Or if asked when exactly they were in Vietnam, survivors might answer, "Last night." The war lives in their subconscious and surfaces in their sleep.

"A lot of people think the 82nd Airborne wasn't even in Vietnam. Our story gets lost. This was our Battle of the Bulge," said Paddy Barry, a retired lieutenant in the New York City Police Department who was then chairman of the Golden Brigade Association.

The man in charge of planning for the 50th reunion, Barry balked at having his name in a book, but he agreed to talk as a way of honoring the 227 All Americans who died in Vietnam.

"Those 227 are our Forever Young," Barry said. "If you look at our casualty list, you'll find cooks, clerks, typists, you name it. Everybody fought."

The names of those killed are listed on the 82nd Airborne Vietnam Memorial at Fort Bragg, North Carolina, home of the Airborne and Special Forces. The monument predates the Vietnam Memorial Wall in Washington, D.C., where those 227 are among the 58,300 names etched in black granite. But more than just numbers or names, the All American casualties were flesh-and-blood human beings ranging in age from 18 to 43, from the lowest rank of private to lieutenant colonel. They were 5-foot-6 and 6-foot-5, from big cities and small towns no one's ever heard of. Some weren't even U.S. citizens. One of them, Staff Sergeant Felix Modesto Conde-Falcon, was posthumously awarded the Medal of Honor, the country's highest award for valor, 45 years after he was killed fighting to save the lives of his men. His name is flecked with gold on the Fort Bragg monument, and his gilt-edged story deserves to be told.

This book is also a tribute to unsung heroes—the mothers, fathers, siblings, wives and children who lost loved ones and paid the dearest price demanded by war. If there is one thing everybody can agree on about Vietnam, it's that those who died should be remembered.

Two years' worth of research began with an invitation from Richard O'Hare to visit his Virginia home, where two American flags flank the entrance to a driveway marked with a sign saying Proud Veteran. His house sits on a secluded lot where acorns can be heard falling from the oak trees, and deer, squirrels and hummingbirds proliferate on the premises. With a vanity license plate that reads 82ABVN, O'Hare had gathered so much military memorabilia that it takes two man-caves to store it all. He keeps a two-volume history of the 82nd Airborne in Vietnam, each written by a different military author and each covering different years. Both volumes helped provide a timeline, but both are incomplete.

O'Hare also had the foresight to videotape interviews with two key officers before they passed away—Richard Seitz, who commanded the 82nd Airborne in 1968, and Alexander R. Bolling Jr., the commander who took the combat punch of the 82nd Airborne to Vietnam in the form of its Third Brigade. Both provided inside information essential to the story.

"Our leaders were veterans of World War II, Korea and earlier tours in Vietnam. Without them, I am convinced our casualty rates would have been double," O'Hare said.

O'Hare also kept maps of South Vietnam with its different war zones. In a war without front lines fought against a foe who blended in with a population Americans fought to keep free, O'Hare preserved the locations of the brigade's major fire bases built in a country about the size of Florida.

"Vietnam was like no other war," O'Hare said.

More details emerged a few months later when the Golden Brigade and the 82nd Airborne Division Association honored its dead at Arlington National Cemetery on Veterans Day of 2017. Led by the flashing lights of a police escort, former paratroopers and veterans of the division performed their annual rite of laying wreaths at All American monuments, including one for the Golden Brigade. Its plaque, dedicated 24 years earlier, is inscribed with the same words adorning the Vietnam monument at Fort Bragg: "Nothing is dearer than life, but nothing is more precious than to live it in freedom."

Flowers were also placed at the Vietnam Veterans Memorial Wall. In doing the honors for the Golden Brigade, Rick Dalton of Illinois made a special effort to look up the name of Benjamin Perry Benton on Panel 34 West, Row 31.

"I don't care if I ever have my name written in a book, but I want people to remember him," Dalton said. "He took over my squad when I was wounded, and I always felt guilty about coming back alive. I think about him every day. Whenever I reach a point where I don't feel like doing something, I think of him and I keep going."

Then at Christmastime, in keeping with the Vietnam veterans' pledge that no generation should ever be forgotten, the Golden Brigade Association donated gift cards to those in the 82nd Airborne currently deployed.

Contributing to this story are declassified documents and after-action reports, along with personal letters, journals and diaries. Information was gleaned from sources available online, especially the records kept by those who founded the Vietnam Memorial Wall and its Wall of Faces, which puts images next to the names of the fallen. Photo albums were a time machine back to the days in the field. The main source for the good, the bad and the real of Vietnam came from scores of interviews with those who were there.

"I owe it to the guys who were killed. Here's the last opportunity I may get," said John Szczepanski of East Chicago, Indiana, who was wounded twice in Vietnam before embarking on a career in human resources with the Indiana-based White Lodging hotel company. His mission to honor fallen brothers continued for more than five decades.

Others figured it would be therapeutic to unburden themselves of memories they bottled up. War is a different experience for everyone, but ask anybody who's ever been to war, it is so intense that not a day goes by without some reminder of it.

"It's time to get it out of your system. The worst thing you can do is hold it in," said Frank Cunane of Gloucester City, New Jersey.

Les Museus of Brainerd, Minnesota, expressed similar feelings.

"I buried it. When it comes back, it comes back in pieces. If you would have asked me 20 years ago to be part of a book project, I would have thrown the request in the trash," said Museus, the father of three sons. "We were ostracized anyway when we came home. I was totally ignored. Nobody cared. But maybe people should know what it was like. It does you good to talk."

Life for those who fight for it has a flavor the protected will never know. An unvarnished account, as told through the eyes of those who saw Vietnam for what it was, has a way of shattering stereotypes.

Putting the story in context requires a trip back in time.

Chapter 1
UNEXPECTED LETTER

Nothing other than the peace and joy of the holiday season was on Richard Conde's mind on the final day of 2004. A savory aroma wafted from the kitchen, where his wife Terri, expecting the imminent arrival of their first child together, prepared his favorite dinner of spaghetti and chicken. Opened packages lay beneath the fresh-cut Christmas tree in the living room of their ranch-style home, situated on a cul-de-sac adjacent to a pasture in central Texas. Bathed in the sparkle of holiday lights, Richard opened the front door for a 50-step walk to his mailbox. Then an unexpected letter set in motion a series of events that changed his life in a heartbeat.

In the mail was an envelope from an unknown person with a return address that Richard failed to recognize. It was from Leslie Hayes in Kentucky, and the first thought that flashed through his mind was that it might be a female admirer from his past. He tucked the envelope into his back pocket, and while his wife put the finishing touches on the evening meal, he went into the bedroom to read a two-sentence, one-paragraph sheet of paper. Leslie (Les) Hayes wrote that he was with Richard's father the day Felix Modesto Conde-Falcon was killed in combat in Vietnam 35 years earlier. If Richard wanted to know more, he was welcome to respond.

Just like that, a portal opened to the past. Richard was three years old when his father died, too young to have any memory of him. All that he knew from his mother, who was left to grieve her loss while raising Richard and a younger sister, was that his father was a good man. Richard was aware that his father was in the Army from the granite headstone placed in the Rogers Cemetery in Bell County, Texas, but not once could the son recall asking any questions about his father. A child growing up in the aftermath of Vietnam knew little more than a stigma existed about war and the soldiers who fought it. Still, without being consciously aware of it, a void had existed for decades inside Richard's heart. In trying to bury his past, Richard had felt alone, lacking a father's guidance and denied a relationship his childhood friends took for granted. But the letter, as succinct as it was, uncorked a flood of emotions that had been bottled up.

Returning to the kitchen, Richard picked up the phone, and with trembling hands, dialed the number provided. On the receiving end, Leslie's wife Diane heard him say, "Hello, this is Richard Conde." With that, a Niagara of tears burst forth.

"You don't know how many years we've searched for you," Diane said, sobbing. "Les is at work right now, but he has so much he wants to tell you. He's just going to flip out. Your father was his platoon sergeant. He just had to find you."

After talking for a spell, they arranged for Richard to call Les the next day. A catharsis that had been a long time coming would take a long time to complete. In the process of meeting his father for the first time, Richard was also about to discover that he also had a second family he never knew existed, a family that lives by a code of remembering the fallen even if everyone else wants to forget. His journey of discovery meant getting to know his father's unit, the Golden Brigade of the 82nd Airborne.

To uncover every precious detail, a trip back in time was necessary.

Chapter 2
CHANGING TIMES

Blessed with the freedom of choice enjoyed by every U.S. citizen, an ambitious young man who could throw, catch and hit a baseball began The Sixties with the dream of playing in the major leagues. At a time of Camelot and the Cold War and the dawning of the Age of Aquarius, Felix Modesto Conde-Falcon was willing to uproot his life in the pursuit of his happiness.

Honored to have his father's surname and his mother's last name in the hyphenated form of Hispanic tradition, Felix was born in the town of Juncos in the eastern part of the U.S. territory of Puerto Rico. Known for its sugar cane and tobacco fields, Juncos was a hotbed of baseball, a game introduced by American troops stationed on the island following the Spanish-American War. The town fielded its own team in the Puerto Rican amateur league, and its best known product was Roberto Clemente, a Hall of Fame right fielder and humanitarian who donned his first baseball uniform in organized competition playing for a team named after Ferdinand Juncos. Although four years younger than Clemente, Felix and every other native son idolized Clemente for the grace, skill and tenacity he needed as a pioneer that earned him a place in on the biggest stage in American baseball. Pride swelled when Clemente and the Pittsburgh Pirates beat the New York Yankees in the 1960 World Series. If Clemente could shatter barriers, a stocky, left-handed hitting catcher decided to give it his best shot too.

With his uncle Angel Falcon serving as his guardian, Conde bid farewell to his island home and ventured to Chicago for a tryout with the White Sox. The organization's talent evaluators, however, told him he lacked the right stuff. But having already made up his mind to remain on the mainland, Conde figured his next best chance of achieving the American dream was to enlist in the U.S. Army. At a recruiting station in Chicago, on March 30, 1962, Conde signed his name on the dotted line and went off to basic training at Fort Knox, Kentucky. The commander-in-chief was John F. Kennedy, who had challenged a new generation of Americans to ask not what their country could do for them, but what they could do for their country. The president had also pledged that America would pay any price, bear any burden, meet any hardship, support any friend and oppose any foe to assure the survival and success of liberty. And locked in a space race with the Soviet Union, Kennedy challenged the country to land a man on the moon and return him safely to Earth by the end of The Sixties.

Baseball still played a major role in Conde's life when he was stationed at Fort Hood outside of Killeen, Texas. A rancher named Lorenzo Layton was looking for players on a summer team he sponsored in a recreational baseball league in nearby Cameron, and an acquaintance mentioned that he knew some soldiers who would be eager to play when off-duty. Among them was Felix Conde, and when this field general wasn't looking out on the diamond through his catcher's mask, his eye was drawn to a young woman working at the concession stand. Her name was Lydia Layton, daughter of the team's sponsor. Teammates noted that Conde spent an inordinate amount of time buying soft drinks or snow cones between innings. "Hey, Conde, you're up," someone would say, and the flirting would momentarily cease.

Cupid's arrow found its mark. In due time, on a Fourth of July, Conde asked Lorenzo Layton for his daughter's hand in marriage. The father said no, but love found a way. Conde convinced Lydia to elope, asking her to meet him at a gas station across from a bowling alley near her home. Lydia's brother, Brigido, volunteered to drive her if that's what she really wanted. The couple exchanged vows in a civil ceremony, but wanting everything to be just right, they later remarried in a Catholic church.

Not long afterwards, Conde was transferred to Fort Bliss near El Paso, where he served as a drill sergeant training civilians to become soldiers. Lydia was pregnant by that time, and a complication arose. Her water broke early, and she was hospitalized two and a half months before her due date. A doctor at Fort Bliss told Conde he could either save the mother or the unborn child, but he couldn't save both.

Forced to make a decision no husband ever wants to make, Conde told the physician, "No, you're going to save them both."

The doctor couldn't promise anything.

"It's gonna be both or you better not come through that door," Conde told him flatly.

Lydia delivered a son, and both survived, just as her husband had willed. They named him Richard, but he was known as Rico.

"Rico was the miracle baby," said an aunt, Stella Gonzalez. "He was so tiny that Felix could hold him in one hand, like a ball inside a catcher's mitt."

Eleven months later, the Condes welcomed a daughter, Jeannie, into the fold. A half a world away, the American Army was fighting in Vietnam…

Alexander R. Bolling Jr. was a career officer from a military family who was sent to Vietnam in 1962 as one of President Kennedy's advisors assessing a civil war in Southeast Asia. Known as Bud to distinguish him from his namesake and Army father, Bolling always said with pride that he wasn't born, he was issued. Soldiering was so ingrained in his family's history that his earliest childhood desire was to join the Army. Fifteen of his ancestors, the embodiment of the rugged Minute Man, were among the American colonists who fought the War of Independence against the British. A graduate of the U.S. Military Academy at West Point, Bolling was commissioned as a second lieutenant in 1943, smack in the middle of World War II. His father, a veteran of World War I, was a general commanding a division at the time. Shortly after D-Day,

Bud Bolling crossed Omaha Beach into Normandy with follow-on forces. After fighting his way across France, Bolling saw combat in the Battle of the Bulge, during which he was wounded by his own artillery and was taken prisoner by the Germans. He escaped and was captured again, then escaped once more to make his way back to American lines. He reconnected with his father, who gave him a week to regain the 40 pounds he had lost as a prisoner before giving his son command of an infantry company. After the war, Bud Bolling stayed in the service. A scholar/soldier, he spoke five languages and taught German to cadets at West Point before his assignment to South Vietnam, the lower half of a divided land that was a simmering cauldron of political, military and religious complexity.

Situated on the eastern edge of the Indochina Peninsula, Vietnam had a rice-growing culture that emerged thousands of years Before Christ. Once ruled by emperors and dynasties, it had also been dominated for a thousand years by China, its northern neighbor, until the population rebelled. Then about the time of the American Civil War, Vietnam was colonized by France, which subjugated the people and harvested its natural resources until Japan ruled the country in World War II. After the Japanese surrender, France tried to re-establish control by force of arms but suffered a military defeat following a nine-year conflict known as the First Indochina War. International powers divided the country into North and South at the 17th Parallel in 1954, with elections slated in two years to allow the country to determine its own fate. At the time, America was ensnared in the Cold War with the Soviet Union, and the vote would surely favor the Communist factions. With U.S. consent, the election was cancelled by South Vietnamese leader Ngo Dinh Diem, a Catholic in a Buddhist-dominated land. Diem's forces were fighting a civil war against insurgents known to history as the Viet Cong, who were allied with Ho Chi Minh's army in the North. American advisors had been dispatched to assess South Vietnam's ability to stand on its own but were not supposed to engage in combat.

In his advisory duties, Bolling traveled the length and breadth of South Vietnam, often without a military escort. He was a frequent visitor of Hue, which rhymes with suh-WAY and was once Vietnam's imperial capital. This jewel of a city existed along the north and south banks of the Perfume River, so named because flower petals that fell along its northward path to the South China Sea gave it an aromatic fragrance in the autumn of the year. The Old City on the north bank featured canals, moats, walled palaces, pagodas, Buddhist temples and elaborate urns holding the cremated remains of Vietnam's emperors. The New City on the south bank housed Hue University, where students clad in white attire furthered their education. Ho Chi Minh once studied there, but Hue always thought of itself as a cultural and religious enclave, equally aloof from Communist ideology and a Saigon government aligned with the West. One of the city's Buddhist monks, protesting against what he considered to be Saigon's corrupt and oppressive regime, doused himself with gasoline and burned himself alive. Still, when Bolling left for home in 1963, he thought Vietnam was in his rear view mirror for good.

"I never thought I'd see Vietnam again except as a tourist," he said.

Then came what Bolling believed to be the tipping point for American involvement. Sensing that Diem had lost his grip on the country, the U.S. supported a coup by South Vietnamese army generals. Diem was assassinated in the regime change, which created a power vacuum. His country may have suffered from his strong-arm tactics, but he kept a lid on things. When no effective leadership emerged to replace Diem, North Vietnam sent in regular army troops to bolster the southern insurgents.

"If Diem wasn't assassinated, I really believe there never would have been a U.S. combat soldier in Vietnam. Lots of people made decisions based on no knowledge of the local situation," Bolling said.

Three weeks after Diem was killed, President Kennedy was assassinated in Dallas.

Consideration had been given to sending American combat troops into Vietnam ever since the French were defeated at the battle Dien Bien Phu. To find out what such a commitment would entail, Army Chief of Staff Matthew Ridgway dispatched a team of military experts to get basic information. No stranger to war, Ridgway was the commanding general of the 82nd Airborne Division when it did parachute assaults into Sicily, Salerno and Normandy. He also knew the Far East. During the Korean War, Ridgway rallied U.S. forces at a critical point and subsequently replaced Douglas MacArthur as overall commander of that war. Into Vietnam he sent engineers, communications specialists, medical officers, logisticians and combat veterans. The conclusions were that Vietnam was practically devoid of facilities to support a western army. Telecommunications, highways and railways were almost non-existent. Port facilities and airfields were totally inadequate and would require a tremendous engineering and logistical effort. At the same time, a land of rice paddies, jungles and rain forest was well suited to guerilla warfare at which the Far East soldier is a master. Intervention would require a large ground force. Supply lines would stretch halfway around the world. Jungle heat and tropical diseases would exact a heavy toll. Ridgway concluded that sending U.S. combat forces to Vietnam would be a tragic adventure, that the civilians who control the military would be tempted to think only of the immediate objective while ignoring the realities on the ground. His findings, which were included in his autobiography *Soldier*, reached President Eisenhower. The idea of intervention was shelved, at least temporarily.

However, General Maxwell Taylor offered a different opinion to a different president. A former artillery officer in the 82nd Airborne and the commander of the 101st Airborne Division in World War II, Taylor succeeded Ridgway as Army Chief of Staff and later served as military advisor to President Kennedy. Sent on his own fact-finding mission to Vietnam, Taylor recommended the introduction of a U.S. military force, writing that Southeast Asia was "not an excessively difficult or unpleasant place to operate. While the border areas are rugged and heavily forested, the terrain is comparable to parts of Korea where U.S. troops learned to live and work without too much effort." Taylor's conclusions were used to green-light America's eventual decision to send ground forces to South Vietnam.

At any rate, Bolling's next posting was the Pentagon, and he could list the exact amount of years, months, weeks and days that he polished his seat with his backside in that job. Bolling had wanted to command a large unit of troops ever since he earned his ring at West Point, describing himself then as "a runny-nosed butter bar," or second lieutenant. His ideal job opened up in December of 1966 when he was assigned to the 82nd Airborne Division as commander of the third of its three combat brigades, ready to respond to any military emergency outside of Vietnam…

Bud Bolling's favorite people were sergeants, the backbone of the U.S. Army or any army for that matter. One in particular was Gordon (Duke) Dewey, the non-commissioned officer in charge of military intelligence in the Third Brigade. Bolling always smiled at the memory of Dewey making a hard landing during a proficiency jump in front of a Marine officer. Duke cracked his back on that jump, and the officer asked if he was hurt.

"Not in front of any damn Marine I ain't," Dewey growled. In truth, his back injury from that day bothered him all his life.

Raised in an orphanage outside of Boston, Duke Dewey shined shoes to earn pocket money. One day, a customer with unique footwear sat down and changed Dewey's life. Decked out in his dress uniform, the man wore Airborne jump boots.

"From that day on, I wanted to be a paratrooper," Dewey said.

To realize his dream, Dewey joined the Army and volunteered for jump school, parachuting five times to earn his Airborne wings. The Army's elite, paratroopers are as physically fit as champion athletes, toughened up on marches, runs and obstacle courses. Trussed into a harness, a paratrooper defies death by stepping into the roaring wind, day or night, carrying a 70-pound pack and a weapon. A system of hooks and straps opens the parachute with a shock that feels like being hit across the shoulders with a club. What follows is the brief silence of floating until contact with the ground, which has been described as leaping from the top of a railroad car traveling at 35 miles per hour onto a hard clay road. Once on the ground, and usually surrounded, paratroopers form up to take the fight to the enemy. Little wonder the job attracts its share of characters. Having earned his wings, Dewey advanced to Special Forces.

Like Bud Bolling, Dewey served as an advisor in South Vietnam. At one point during his time there, insurgents overran a South Vietnamese force, and emergency assistance was requested from two South Vietnamese Ranger battalions that the U.S. had outfitted and supplied. Those battalions were a ghost force, however. "They didn't exist, except on paper," Dewey said. Corrupt commanders pocketed all the money earmarked for soldiers' pay, support and rations. In Dewey's mind, the ghost battalions exemplified the dysfunction, corruption and ineptitude within the South Vietnamese Army. He had a gut feeling about the quagmire that followed.

"You could see it coming," Dewey said. "I figured we'd be there 10 years supporting those sons of bitches."

Dewey developed a special bond with Bud Bolling. "He would get on you if you got out of line, but he was a soldier's soldier. I would have done anything for that man," Dewey said. Although he never said it out loud, he thought of his commanding officer as the father he never had, and the Airborne was the family he never knew…

College football provided the crowning achievement of Jim Littig's athletic life. A native of Portland, Oregon, and the son of a prize-fighter, Littig was a 240-pound defensive lineman on the University of Utah team that beat West Virginia in the 1964 Liberty Bowl. The first major college football bowl game played indoors, the Liberty Bowl was televised nationally on December 19 from inside the Atlantic City Convention Center on the New Jersey shore. That championship ring was a memorable send-off when Littig graduated and began a career in the Army. Having participated in the Reserve Officer Training Corps program, Littig was commissioned as a second lieutenant and entered the Army's infantry officer training school. He then attended the three-week jump school at Fort Benning, Georgia, and advanced to Ranger school, a combat leadership course that tests participants physically and mentally during the toughest training a solider can get. The Army sent him to Fort Bragg, where he joined the 82nd Airborne Division as a member of its Third Brigade.

In a quirk of history, the Atlantic City Convention Center was also the site of the 1964 Democratic National Convention that nominated Lyndon Baines Johnson as its presidential candidate. LBJ campaigned on promises of a Great Society and a War on Poverty, but his legacy became Vietnam, even though he expressed reservations about sending combat troops there. In a phone conversation with a national security advisor that was made public 33 years after the fact, Johnson said: "It looks like to me like we're getting into another Korea. It just worries the hell out of me because I don't see what we can ever hope to get out of there with once we're committed. I don't think it's worth fighting for, and I don't think we can get out. And it's just the biggest damn mess I ever saw." On the campaign trail, Johnson said: "We are not about to send American boys nine or ten thousand miles away from home to do what Asian boys ought to be doing for themselves." He sent them anyway in March of 1965, with the stated intent of preventing South Vietnam from being overrun by outside forces. He did so without a formal declaration of war or the full call-up of reserve units to active duty. He wanted to wage a limited war. The reality was that the enemy gets a vote on how it fights…

Youthful wanderlust motivated Canadian Richard Davidson to begin a journey that landed him in the Third Brigade of the 82nd Airborne. A French-speaking native of Montreal, Davidson had a boyhood desire to see the world. One day, while hitchhiking in New York state, he was taken into custody as an undocumented visitor. As Davidson wriggled out of that legal jam, he was advised that if he wanted to travel, he should earn some money instead of living a life of vagrancy. If he really wanted to see the world, he should join the U.S. Army. With a goal of making a better man of himself, Davidson enlisted at Albany, New York, on May 9, 1965, without even knowing what Vietnam was.

During basic training at Fort Dix, New Jersey, Davidson began the rite of passage from civilian to soldier. Like every trainee, he was shorn of his hair and civilian clothes to be issued dog tags and uniforms colored in the shade of green known as olive drab. With no formal schooling in English, he learned a new and colorful language from his drill sergeants, for whom every other syllable was an F-bomb and mother was half a word. He was also taught discipline, survival techniques and how to fire the Army's weapons. Having been given his choice of Army careers because he was a volunteer, Davidson opted for the Airborne. His wings qualified him for the extra $55 a month paid to paratroopers.

Seeing the world began with a trip to the Dominican Republic in 1965, when the Third Brigade of the 82nd Airborne was the tip of the bayonet in a joint force of paratroopers and Marines. Set against the backdrop of the Cold War, the mission was to protect American lives and to prevent a Communist takeover. Codenamed Operation Power Pack, it was overshadowed by Vietnam and is largely lost to history. Although the original plan called for a parachute drop, planes loaded with paratroopers landed to the east of Santo Domingo in the wee hours of April 30. The Airborne secured a vital bridge and established a corridor for a link-up with Marines who had landed to the west. To show the locals that American forces were in full control, the 82nd Airborne Division Band marched along what was called the All American Expressway. During the operation, the division suffered its first combat deaths since World War II. Ultimately, 13 of the 27 Americans killed in action were paratroopers. The All Americans even sunk a ship that rebel forces were using as a staging area. Using the firepower of the 106-millimeter recoilless rifle mounted on a jeep, a paratrooper sent the SS *Santo Domingo* to the bottom. While the fighting was over in a relatively short time, security forces remained until September of 1966. As an indication of how America as a whole thought about its military, the number one song on the Billboard charts in 1966 was Sgt. Barry Sadler's *Ballad of the Green Berets.* It out-performed all the hits produced by rock artists, Motown groups and the mop-haired musicians of the British invasion.

Power Pack was already in progress when Richard Davidson joined the effort. While billeted at a place called Camp Hutchinson, named for a paratrooper who had been killed in the operation, Davidson said his buddies passed the time by leaping out of second-floor windows to simulate airborne drops and the parachute landing fall. "Usually it was after they had a few drinks under their belts," Davidson said.

He returned to the States by sea aboard the Navy's Landing Ship Tank (LST) 1171 and reported back to Fort Bragg. Considered a blip on the radar screen at the time, Operation Power Pack was officially recognized as a campaign in 1992…

The military career of Richard Seitz had come full circle by March of 1967 when he was promoted to command the 82nd Airborne. A native of Leavenworth, Kansas, Seitz intended to run his family's ice cream and dairy business in the Midwest before war led him on a different path. Commissioned as an officer through the Reserve Officer Training Corps program at Kansas State College, Seitz was at Fort Benning when the first test platoon of a revolutionary kind of warfare was created. Volunteers from the infantry donned plastic football helmets, strapped on parachutes and leapt out of an airplane over a drop zone. If he was going to be in the Army, Seitz figured Airborne was the way to go. His first company commander was James Gavin, an 82nd Airborne legend who wrote the book on the best use of Airborne troops in battle. Gavin had once noted: "Show me a man who will jump out of an airplane, and I'll show you a man who will fight." As for Seitz, he did a combat jump into southern France and also fought with the 82nd Airborne in the Battle of the Bulge. A generation later, he was a staff officer at Army headquarters in South Vietnam before he was called home to lead the 82nd Airborne Division. His troops were the cream of the Army, but the division was badly under strength. Many graduates of jump school were filling the combat needs of other Army units in Vietnam. "It was a very turbulent time," Seitz noted…

On June 7, 1967, the newest class of second lieutenants received their rings and tossed their hats into the air upon graduation from the United States Military Academy at West Point. This group of leaders in character was well aware that the fighting in Vietnam had begun during their academy years, when it was drilled into their heads that the history they learned was made by the people who taught them. William Westmoreland, a former West Point superintendent who commanded U.S. forces in Vietnam, had visited the cadets at one point, saying: "Like your brothers before you, you will march to the sound of the guns."

Michael Hood, one of the Class of 1967, said all of his classmates had kept an eye on Southeast Asia. "We talked about Vietnam constantly," said Hood, who grew up in Fort Worth, Texas and enrolled in his first military school at the age of 10. A free spirit who was a member of the West Point cheer squad called the Rebel Rousers, Hood had left his mark at West Point. "I was No. 1 in my class," he deadpanned, "for the number of hours I spent walking the yard for disciplinary reasons."

Robert Murrill was also part of that class and was a member of the parachute team. Other classmates were James Adams, Ronald Frazer, Dean Risseeuw and Thomas Schwartz. All of them were destined for slots in the 82nd Airborne…

The Third Brigade was on alert status in July of 1967, ready to go anywhere on a moment's notice, when an emergency call reached headquarters. In keeping with the secretive nature of Airborne missions, Paddy Barry remembers that mouthpieces were taken out of the pay phones so that no one could call out. Paratroopers were locked down before drawing weapons, ammunition and combat gear. Then they were trucked to the Green Ramp connecting Fort Bragg to Pope Air Base for the boarding of transport planes, mission undetermined and destination unknown.

Barry came from Manhattan's Yorkville neighborhood, where the Irish were among the ethnic groups who used their fists to protect their turf. Drafted into the Army on June 14, 1966, he volunteered to become a paratrooper as a way of following in the jump boots of his father, who had participated in each of the 82nd Airborne's campaigns from North Africa to Berlin in World War II.

"My dad was livid when I got drafted. He said he fought so that I wouldn't have to," Barry said.

Barry recalled that his flight was in the air for something like eight hours. Then from his window seat, he looked out to see a city on fire. The order came for troops to load their rifles. Subsequently, a second order was given to chamber a round but to keep the safety on. Locked and loaded, troopers were finally told to fix bayonets so that they were ready for anything when they hit the ground.

"We must be in Berlin," Barry thought to himself.

Actually, his plane landed at Selfridge Air Force Base in a suburb of Detroit. The Motor City had been set ablaze in one of the worst race riots in the nation's history. The destination struck him as odd.

"The 82nd Airborne doesn't invade the United States," Barry said.

The spark of Detroit's unrest came in the wee hours of Sunday, July 23. City police raided an unlicensed bar where 82 African Americans celebrated the return of two local soldiers from Vietnam. Police decided to arrest everyone present, and while they were arranging transportation, a crowd gathered outside. Tensions that had simmered for decades boiled over. Fights broke out between citizens and police. Bottles were thrown. Shots were exchanged. Fires were lit. By mid-afternoon, flames rose above the city skyline. Nationwide, there were 159 race riots in what became known as the Long Hot Summer of 1967, and the worst of the unrest was felt in Michigan's largest city, famous for making automobiles and producing Motown music. The unrest lasted five days, resulting in 43 deaths, 1,189 injuries, 7,200 arrests and 2,000 buildings destroyed. In response, the Michigan National Guard was called up to assist police, but it had no training on quelling civil disorder. When federal help was requested, President Johnson turned to the 82nd Airborne, whose ranks were filled with soldiers who had seen combat in Vietnam.

Bud Bolling was playing bridge at home the evening of July 23 and, as is common with the Airborne, was scheduled to be up at five o'clock the next morning to run with his troops. Then the call came to go to Detroit. For the first time since the Bond Marches of the Great Depression, federal troops had been called up for domestic duty.

Although the Airborne has established procedures on how to respond to a crisis, the White House insisted on doing things its way. As one example, ammunition was taken off a plane so that more troops could board.

"It was a terrible, chaotic deployment. The worst ever," Bolling said.

Richard Seitz sent troops in the same order he would if this had been a mission to a foreign country, but without the artillery.

Upon landing in Detroit, Bolling led a convoy of military trucks, jeeps and civilian buses to a command post at the Michigan Fairgrounds before getting down to the business of containing the raging disturbance.

"Where's the hottest spot? Where's the worst trouble?" Bolling asked.

He was given the whole east side of the burning city, and Bolling proceeded to Southeastern High School to set up shop. The police had established a presence there, but all the blinds were pulled down. An officer with the National Guard was also on duty, but when the Airborne arrived, he skedaddled. "He said, 'Thank God you're here.' Then he disappeared. No briefing on the situation at all," Bolling said.

The White House's point person was Cyrus Vance, a former Secretary of the Army and deputy Secretary of Defense under LBJ.

"What do you need?" he asked Bolling.

"I need two helicopters in that field tomorrow," Bolling said, pointing to the high school's football gridiron.

"Do you want tanks too?" Vance asked.

"No. We'd never use a tank against American citizens," Bolling replied.

Bolling also told the police officers present: "Raise these shades. If someone wants to take a shot at me, I'll stand in the window."

Into a burning city went the Airborne on July 25. Because firefighters and policemen took sniper fire on emergency calls, paratroopers rode along as protection on fire trucks and in squad cars. Military helicopters flew over the city as part of the show of force. Soldiers with Detroit roots were sent into trouble areas to gather intelligence. Under orders from General Seitz, troops had their chin straps buckled on their steel pot helmets, with rifles loaded and bayonets fixed, whenever they were in eyeball contact with residents. Soldiers were also told to look their best by breaking out starched uniforms on patrols. They couldn't help but notice exhausted National Guardsmen sleeping in the streets with sidewalk curbs as their pillows.

Two incidents were reported of paratroopers receiving and then returning fire. The word on the street was that rioters had broken into an armory because troops heard the chatter of machine guns, and it wasn't coming from their weapons. Detroit had the look, sound and feel of a war zone. But in quick order, any shooting was silenced.

"Outside an apartment building where there were a lot of people sniping, Bolling got on a bull horn and told people that if they didn't take action to curtail the shooting that the 82nd Airborne would do it for them. The sniping stopped," Seitz said.

Archie Carpenter, one of Bolling's battalion commanders, said looters were confronted coming out of a pillaged liquor store at one point. One man brandished a handgun and pointed it at a squad of paratroopers. It was a bad decision. The man was shot dead by a trooper who had just returned from Vietnam. An inquiry determined the use of force was justified. Word spread on the street that pointing a loaded weapon at an Airborne infantryman was a death sentence.

Most of the rioting ended without gunfire. Troops merely did their daily physical training with the usual Airborne flare, sounding off with cadence while running.

"We were singing, *'I wanna be an Airborne Ranger, live me a life of guts and danger…'* And every time a left foot hit the ground, we'd shout, 'Kill!' That word gets out fast," said Paddy Barry.

"That military appearance made all the difference," added General Seitz. "The thing that really impressed the citizens was how good these soldiers looked. They looked like All American, Jack Armstrong types ready to take on anybody. There was some taunting, however. Our black soldiers were called Oreo cookies—black on the outside but white on the inside."

City dwellers eager to see the restoration of peace welcomed the paratroopers.

"There was an article in paper that we were living off C Rations, so this woman shows up at my command post and asks how many men I had. I told her 1,900, and she says she has 1,900 bowls of chicken noodle soup. We had food coming out the wazoo. The locals offered to do our laundry. You couldn't buy a haircut. They put on shows to entertain us. The city just adopted us. There was nothing but respect," Bolling said.

As calm returned, paratroopers moved to Chandler Park and erected pup tents. Duke Dewey, the intelligence sergeant, told some gullible supply officer that troops needed to obtain a supply of rock salt to prevent an infestation of something he called "canvastherm," an imaginary bug that feeds off canvas tents. The unsuspecting officer set about making calls for rock salt until a higher-ranking officer caught on. "You've been had. There ain't no such thing as canvastherm," the chastened officer was told. It pays to be on one's toes when in the presence of the Airborne.

Another twist was the welcoming of the tent-dwelling troops by Detroit's females. "We got overrun by women," Dewey said. "They were tired of being cooped up."

Having served as a firewall, the Airborne began returning to Fort Bragg on July 28 and completed the move by the next day. Switchboard operators began receiving calls from Detroit women for Joe Tentpeg and Private Messkit, which were the *nom de guerres* of paratroopers. Thus, closed one of the most unique episodes in Airborne history…

For one cohort of Baby Boomers, 1967 was the Summer of Love. Free spirits left home for San Francisco, the epicenter of a counter-culture movement led by the long-haired Hippy and the Flower Child. Richard O'Hare left college too, not to go to San Francisco with a flower in his hair, but to join the Army and become a paratrooper.

A native of Brooklyn whose Irish-Catholic family moved to the Long Island community of Franklin Square, O'Hare had an extended family that fought in World War II and who routinely gathered for Sunday dinner. While the women sat in one room, the men congregated in another to tell stories over a beer or two. Children were to be seen and not heard, and if he remained quiet, O'Hare heard tales that were part of family history. As a boy, he had grown up with a collection of toy soldiers, ships and planes, which he engaged in mock battle by using firecrackers as special effects. From the time he had turned 10, O'Hare collected comic books of G.I. Joe and religiously watched the weekly television show *Combat!* about a squad of infantrymen waging war against the German Army. O'Hare's father served in the Seabees, the name given to the U.S. Navy's Construction Battalions, and an uncle had jumped into Normandy with the 101st Airborne Division. He also remembered the sermons by a priest who had been a chaplain in World War II. Although the rules of civilization hold that it is illegal and immoral to take another human being's life, the priest preached that is justifiable to kill in war when a citizen/soldier is defending his country and protecting his family.

O'Hare was no stranger to the social changes going on around him. The oldest of five children, he saw the Beatles in concert at Shea Stadium when he was a student at Sewanhaka High School. He was also fully aware that his country was at war in South Vietnam, and earlier in 1967, heavyweight boxing champion Muhammad Ali was among those draftees who refused induction into the Army. O'Hare followed his own path. Six weeks after his 19th birthday, O'Hare put down his books at Hofstra University and enlisted on July 17, much to his father's chagrin.

"My father was so proud of me going to college. He was heart-broken when I told him I joined the Army, but the decision had already been made. I wanted to do my part just like he had done," O'Hare said.

His motivation for boarding a bus to basic training at Fort Jackson, South Carolina, was to join the fight against Communism. On the heels of the Korean War, confrontations with the Red menace with led to incidents such as the Bay of Pigs, the Berlin Crisis and the Cuban Missile Crisis, during which time American school kids were taught to hide under their desks in the event of a nuclear attack. The war in Vietnam was sold to the American public as necessary to stop Communism, because if South Vietnam fell, other nations in Asia would fall like dominoes.

O'Hare had the job title of infantryman, or in the argot of the Army, his Military Occupation Specialty was Eleven Bravo, also known as Eleven Bang Bang or Eleven Bad Ass. Following advanced training at Fort Dix, New Jersey, O'Hare went to jump school. He ran constantly, even through the mess hall. A soldier would pick up a tray, have food ladled onto it and then wolf it all down on his way out the door without ever sitting down. To keep everybody in the proper frame of mind, the Airborne song *Blood On The Risers* was played over loudspeakers. Borrowing from the melody of the *Battle Hymn of the Republic*, the song includes the refrain, "Gory, gory what a helluva way to die." Jumping out of an airplane amplifies what soldiers call the pucker factor, when the anal sphincter muscles tighten up during times of stress.

"If you're not scared, you're crazy," O'Hare said.

The Army has a certain benchmark that it expects of all soldiers, but paratroopers are expected to exceed the standard, even in the way they dress. Soldiers who lack wings on their chests are known derisively as legs.

O'Hare was selected to attend officer candidate's school. Before a spot opened up, however, his orders took him to Fort Bragg. During orientation, the new arrivals were shown the movie *The Longest Day,* which featured John Wayne as an 82nd Airborne battalion commander jumping at night into Normandy to liberate the town of St. Mere Eglise…

Joe Mays had received his diploma from Texas Western College, best known as the school that fielded five African American starters who beat an all-white Kentucky team in the 1966 NCAA basketball finals. As classmates started careers as doctors, nurses, lawyers, teachers, engineers and accountants, Mays asked himself: "What would John Wayne do?"

He enlisted in the Army to become an officer and a paratrooper, following in the footsteps of a father who had served in the 82nd Airborne. He remembers instructors at Officer Candidate School drilling the notion into his head, "If you don't pay attention or if you fall asleep in class, you will die in Vietnam." When he completed his five training jumps at Fort Benning, the jump school commandant, who had graduated with his father from the course in August of 1943, pinned his father's wings onto his chest.

Mays signed in with the 82nd Airborne on Christmas Eve of 1967, just weeks after his father wrote a letter for the front page of *The Army Times* newspaper. In passing the torch from one generation to the next, it read:

"So now you have arrived at the point toward which all of your past years' activities have been directed. I offer you my congratulations. If you choose to remain in the Army, you will be respected and looked up to by most people of all walks of life. But you will also suffer many hardships, moments of self-doubt and recrimination, and will be reviled and looked down upon by some members of our present society. There has always been a segment of our civilization who are honestly opposed to the military. No matter how unjust it seems, you will be asked to defend the rights of these people. You will be granted some power. Use it wisely. If ever there was a key to leadership, it is the word and act of loyalty. Loyalty to your country, loyalty to your superiors and in particular, loyalty to your men. Don't be soft, don't quibble, don't vacillate and be soft-hearted when you know you are right. Make sure you establish rapport and friendship with every man in your command, a willingness to meet with him and talk with him and listen to his problems. Most officers learn quickly to listen to their superiors. A great many of them never learn to listen to their subordinates and so

alienate the very soldiers upon whom your success depends. Today's Army is so complex and technical that you can never know everything. Ask your men to show you how to keep your M-16 clean and operable and ask them to show you how to fire the M-60 machine gun. They will respect you and you will probably learn some things that only they know. Be proud, but be humble. Be humbly grateful that you were born in the greatest country in the world, that you were reared a God-fearing Christian, that you received a good education at a school that I know you love and that you have attained the status of an officer in the U.S. Army. Can you do this while maintaining a sense of humor? Life without surcease from its enormities can be a depressing existence. You must be able to laugh at yourself and with others. It is not uncommon for moments of humor to crop up in the gravest situations. Don't be overly impressed with yourself, but maintain your true perspective. Good luck in the arts and practices of being a paratrooper. I, too, traveled that same route 25 years ago and remember with nostalgia the heart-in-the-throat approach to the door, the wild tumultuous exit, the exhilarating feeling of the wind in your face, the quiet and wonderful solitude of the descent, the reality of the ground transmitted through the shock of landing and the tremendous sense of accomplishment that you are just a little bit above the ordinary soldier. Love, Dad."

As 1967 drew to a close, the Johnson administration was publicly optimistic about Vietnam, saying that the war had reached a cross-over point because the Communists were dying faster than they could be replaced.

"We are inflicting greater losses than we are taking," President Johnson told the nation in a televised speech on November 17. "We are making progress."

Four days later, William Westmoreland told Congress: "I am absolutely certain that whereas in 1965 the enemy was winning, today he is certainly losing."

Ellsworth Bunker, the U.S. ambassador to South Vietnam, echoed a sentiment that the French had used in 1954 before their defeat in Vietnam. "There is light at the end of the tunnel," Bunker said. His words morphed into an overworked phrase that the light belonged to an oncoming train.

Meanwhile, James Gavin, the former commander of the 82nd Airborne, returned from a fact-finding trip to Vietnam to tell congressional leaders that America's strategy was ill-conceived. The use of conventional tactics in an unconventional war convinced him the effort was futile.

"We are in a tragedy," Gavin said.

Chapter 3
AMERICA'S 9-1-1

Barely three weeks into the watershed year of 1968, the 82nd Airborne was alerted to strike back against Communist aggression in an Asian hot spot with a forbidding climate. The crisis was in North Korea, which had seized the USS *Pueblo* on January 23 and parked the intelligence-gathering ship at Wonson harbor. One of the 83-man crew had been killed when North Korean gunboats fired on the ship. The captain and the rest of the crew were blindfolded, beaten and imprisoned. For a unit trained to be combat ready in just such emergencies, the mission was to parachute into harm's way to rescue them. On call to be the first in was Bud Bolling's Third Brigade.

Anxiety levels spiked across Fort Bragg as troopers were locked down. One of the busiest soldiers on post was Robert Murrill, a second lieutenant who was fresh out of West Point and Ranger school. While he aspired to be a platoon leader in a rifle company, Murrill was the brigade's supply officer, filling a slot normally occupied by a major. Being relegated to such a role prompted him to protest to Colonel Bolling, who told him that the immediate need was in supply. In fact, the colonel ordered Murrill to go to the latrine to wash out his ears so that he could hear better. Murrill smartened up and did what was needed.

Given the time of year, a major concern was the harsh Korean winter. During the Korean War, American troops suffered frostbite, and engines froze solid as temperatures plunged to as low as 30 degrees below zero. For the *Pueblo* operation, winter gear from strategic stockpiles was distributed, including parkas, mittens and oversized thermal footwear that the troops called Mickey Mouse boots for their cartoon-ish appearance. The motor oil in all the vehicles was changed to a type better suited for arctic conditions.

Then, just like that, the White House aborted the mission.

"I didn't mind too much. There are lots of bad guys in Korea. It's cold. And I can't drive a ship," Bolling said.

Among the troops who were relieved by the cancellation was Gerald Kennedy, whose Airborne roots were planted by family members who had built the jump towers at Bragg and who has five family members buried at Arlington National Cemetery. A one-time enlisted man who rose in the ranks to command the brigade's Military Police unit, Kennedy said: "It was a suicide mission, you can't drop us into a place like Korea and expect us to come out alive. I was glad that was over with."

Diplomacy dragged on for 11 months before the crew was freed. The North Koreans kept the *Pueblo* as a war trophy.

The Airborne resumed its role of being the Army's strategic ready force. Then South Vietnam erupted in flames when the twin forces of the Viet Cong and the North Vietnamese Army launched a country-wide offensive on January 30-31. The attacks coincided with the lunar new year of Tet, the beginning of the Year of the Monkey. Breaking a truce that was in place for the Vietnamese to honor their ancestors with celebrations and fireworks, Communist forces attacked nearly every major city and military base in South Vietnam. They even reached the grounds of the U.S. Embassy in Saigon. After 35 months of ground combat, America's war strategy had just gone sideways. Although most of the attacks had been absorbed and North Vietnam's goal of inciting the civilian population to rise up had failed, the Communist flag still flew over the imperial capital of Hue, and Marines were under siege at an outpost called Khe Sahn. Overall commander William Westmoreland was most concerned about the threat posed in the area below the Demilitarized Zone, the man-made line that separated North and South. In his judgment, a setback in the three northernmost provinces of South Vietnam was conceivable but not probable. In papers classified as top secret, Westmoreland requested immediate reinforcements in the form of the 82nd Airborne and a regiment of Marines. In fact, he thought the best course of action would be to have the Marines do an amphibious assault from the South China Sea and then put the Airborne ashore through the beachhead because the U.S. military lacked the helicopters needed to transport the paratroopers onto the battlefield. The assault, codenamed Operation Durango City, was earmarked for April. In communications dated February 8 and February 11, higher command agreed with Westmoreland's request, but the timetable was pushed forward and the amphibious landing was scrapped. Instead, Airborne troops would enter the country aboard cargo jets. Although the nation's first civilian 9-1-1 system was about a month away from being operational, the military version was up and running. The Airborne was needed to race into a country in flames, and the Third Brigade was the unit on call.

On the Sunday morning of February 11, Bud Bolling was on the golf course. Fortune favored the colonel in his match that day with a civilian friend, and he was up $2.50 in bets on the 11th hole. Then a messenger driving a red scooter approached with an urgent message ordering Bolling to report immediately to division headquarters. He never did collect on his wagers. Within minutes, he was at headquarters. Everything was so hush-hush that not even the duty officer knew what was going on, and duty officers always knew the score. Entering General Richard Seitz's office, Bolling sensed a tension that was thick enough to cut with a dull bayonet.

"I just got a call from the White House," Seitz told him. "Bud, you're going to Vietnam."

The oxygen was momentarily sucked out of the room.

"Sir, I've been to Vietnam. I want to stay with my troops in the brigade," Bolling responded.

"I didn't say you were going alone. This is a national emergency. Your brigade leaves as soon as we get the official orders," Seitz said.

According to an old Airborne saying, when the green light pops, the bullshit stops. In an eye-blink, everything was all business. Still in his golf attire, Bolling hurried to brigade headquarters. The paperwork for all pending matters on his desk was boxed up and set aside. He gathered his key subordinates and flipped the switch that began the organized chaos of assembling three battalions of infantry along with combat engineers, motorized cavalry, artillerymen, helicopter pilots, military police, intelligence experts and the communications specialists needed for all of them to talk to each other. The immediate challenges were time and distance. When Bolling got his first chance to race home and change into uniform, evening had arrived. His wife Fran was asleep, and since he was forbidden to discuss specifics anyway, he left a note saying he was on an alert. A long time passed before he saw that house again.

The official order, classified as top secret, arrived from the Joint Chiefs of Staff at 5:30 p.m. on Monday, February 12. A brigade task force of approximately 4,000 paratroopers was to deploy on a temporary basis, which under Army regulations meant three months. Movement would be by air. The force was to be in place no later than February 26, with the remainder of the division ready to follow. To protect security, no public announcement was made. Media interviews were banned.

A thousand things happened at once. Motor oil in the brigade's vehicles was changed again to a viscosity that would function better in a tropical climate. Supply officers were given access to stockpiles of jungle boots, light-weight uniforms, ammunition, weapons, extra canteens and the food needed to sustain the troops. From the start, Seitz had told Bolling that every asset in the division was his for the taking. Bolling took everything that was combat-ready. He later said that he took the whole division with him, even though it was organized under a single brigade commanded by a colonel rather than a division led by a two-star general.

In the whole of the U.S. Army, the Airborne was the only combat-ready unit that could be sent immediately to Vietnam. Still, a classified document at the time described the division's readiness as marginal, not because of the quality of its soldiers or the quality of their training, but because the unit was at half strength. It was an appalling indictment of those in overall charge of the military. The Third Brigade had roughly 2,000 troopers able to go on the mission, half of what was required. Instead of having three platoons per rifle company, some companies were down to two platoons or less. At the same time, seven of the brigade's 13 rifle companies were commanded by second lieutenants rather than captains, and some battalions were commanded by majors instead of lieutenant colonels. While those young officers had the right stuff for the most part, they lacked experience. What's more, the brigade had roughly 200 artillerymen available, half the number required to do the mission. To make up for the shortfalls, fill-ins were taken from the other two brigades and folded into Bolling's command.

An estimated 80 percent of the division's troopers had already fought in Vietnam with such Army units as Special Forces, the Sky Soldiers of the 173rd Airborne Brigade, the Screaming Eagles of the 101st Airborne Division and the jump-qualified brigade of the 1st Cavalry Division. They had been placed in the 82nd Airborne to act as the country's strategic reserve while serving out their remaining time in the Army. Some soldiers had been back from Vietnam for less than a month. Ultimately, it was decided that anyone who had been back in the States for 30 or more days and had 30 days remaining on their enlistments would deploy. The best the Airborne could come up with was 3,670 troops.

"We had platoons where the men didn't know each other's names. These poor guys, you wonder what they were thinking," Bolling said.

Troops learned their fate in various ways. Richard Davidson, the French-speaking Canadian, remembers a cool February night when he was walking by the orderly room in his barracks. He overheard his company commander talking on the phone about an alert. Davidson was ordered not to mention it to anyone.

"I was a little scared but mostly surprised. I kept it a secret, but I told the guys to get a good night's sleep because they would need it. They kept asking me what was up, but all I could say was, 'Sorry, man. You'll find out soon enough.' Then I racked out," Davidson said. "Someone came in at 3:30 in the morning and shouted, 'Everybody up! Fall out in 15 minutes.' "

When the word came to assemble, Davidson had a decision to make. His time in the Army was nearly over, and nobody was sure if he had to go.

"My commanding officer called me into his office and said, 'You may not have to go.' He told me to give it an hour and return with my answer. Thinking about all the training I had, and having lived with my buddies for a year and a half, I gave him my answer right then and there. 'I'm going, sir. I can't leave these guys. It's a point of personal honor for me to go to war with them.' He said, 'OK, get ready to move out like the others.' My company only had enough men to form a platoon. We turned in our winter gear, and there was no longer any doubt. Vietnam it was. Half of the fellows around me had already been there. The word was half or one-third of us would not be coming back. I wrote a postcard home, trying to convince my parents that I would be all right, but I waited until the last minute to send it. I did not want to worry my parents sooner. That whole week was a confusing one."

Suffice it to say that the troops who had served their one-year tour of duty in Vietnam weren't thrilled at being ordered back. Among the fillers was John Frances Plunkard, 20, of Frederick, Maryland. In his youth, Plunkard was in a Boy Scout troop named after Francis Scott Key, the poet who penned the words to *The Star-Spangled Banner*. A natural athlete who played baseball and ran track at Frederick High School, Plunkard found his biggest fame on the football team. His accuracy as a place-kicker was so renowned that he was called the man with the Golden Toe. Plunkard enlisted in the Army six months after ground troops had been committed to Vietnam, and he was sent there too after completing all his training. On May 19, 1966, while serving in the 173rd Airborne, Plunkard's platoon suffered heavy casualties during a fierce firefight. He killed two enemy soldiers and forced others to flee while saving the life of a wounded comrade. Plunkard dragged the wounded man to safety, an act of valor for which he received a Bronze Star. Two days later, Plunkard was wounded when an enemy rocket slammed into his unit's position. Jagged metal shards ripped into his arms, legs, hip and the back of his neck. The recipient of a Purple Heart, he spent two months in a hospital before reporting back to combat. While recovering from his wounds, Plunkard penned a letter that was published in his hometown newspaper, The Frederick News-Post. In that letter, he voiced frustrations about Vietnam. War had never been formally declared, yet he and his brothers-in-arm were engaged in mortal combat against a foe that was fighting to the death. Nobody knew who the enemy was until he was shot at.

"This is the craziest war I believe any country could get in. The only word I can say to even come close is the word HELL because that's just what it is," Plunkard wrote. "The things you go through and see just drive you to hate with a passion. If we would only declare war, I think every American over here would put more effort in it. The way everybody thinks is, why should we fight when nobody has even declared war? I think the reason we're still here is to save face. We're in too deep to pull out now.... You know, when I first came over here, I had pity on these people but now that's all gone. After I've seen my best friends get all shot up and killed, I've changed tactics. They tell us to hold your fire until fired upon, but now I'm gonna drop the first person I see in black P.J.s whether it be man, woman or beast. I hate to talk like this, but if you could go through what I've seen in the past two months, you would agree, I'm sure."

With eight months left in the Army, Plunkard was engaged to be married and had just purchased a new Dodge Dart. Despite any personal misgivings, there was never any doubt that Plunkard would honor his Airborne contract. He made a positive first impression on his new company commander, St. Elmo P. (Step) Tyner, a West Point graduate from Carmel, California, who was named for the patron of the sea.

"If I had been casting a recruiting commercial, (he) would have a featured spot. Everything about his appearance and behavior bespoke 'professional,' " Tyner said.

One comrade who had a special bond with Plunkard was Gordon Day, a Mohawk Indian. Schooled in the ways of the warrior, Day learned about the natural world from a spiritual leader in the Long House at Kahnawake, a tract of land straddling Canada and New York that was set aside for the Mohawk Nation. Members of Day's tribe were known as the guardians of the Eastern Door long before Europeans arrived in North America. In colonial times, his ancestors fought the French, the British and the Americans, and tribal members say with fierce pride that they were never defeated. Members of Day's family had also fought in the American Civil War. His grandfather served under General John (Black Jack) Pershing against Poncho Villa in Mexico and again with Pershing's Allied Expeditionary Force in World War I. His father fought the Japanese as an infantryman with the Old Breed of the 1st Marine Division at Guadalcanal. The Mohawk reputation of being fearless was burnished when members of the tribe's White Wolf Pack embraced the dangerous occupation of ironworkers who built the bridges and skyscrapers of New York City. From the time he was 15, Day had worked as one of those sky walkers until he was drafted into the Army in 1966 and then volunteered for the Airborne. Married and the father of three kids, Day had entered a death pact with Plunkard long before the callout.

"If one of us failed to return, the other would look up his family," Day said. "We cut the inside of our thumbs with a knife and pressed them together. I told Johnny, 'From this day on, we are brothers. My blood is running through you. Your blood is running through me.' He would check on my family. I would check on his."

Now part of the deployment, Day was handed an M-79 grenade launcher, a weapon that looked like a sawed-off shotgun which could lob grenades or fire buckshot. He had never pulled the trigger on one before.

Another filler who joined Plunkard and Day in the same company was Jimmy Barnes of Hammond, California. Barnes had also shed blood for his country in Vietnam, having been shot in the left hip in 1965 while serving in the 1st Cavalry Division.

"We weren't enthusiastic about having to go back. You'd have to be crazy to want to go back to Vietnam. I had three months left in the Army, and I even called my congressman. The choice was either to go or lose all honor. We took our medicine and got ready to go," Barnes said.

Other congressmen called division headquarters to inquire about the fairness of sending soldiers back to Vietnam after they had just returned. The standing orders of the All Americans, however, took precedence. The standard reply to such inquires was: "This is the 82nd Airborne Division. Everybody in this division is committed to go anywhere in the world at a moment's notice. There's a war going on. We make no apologies for sending people to fight as ordered."

Andrew Blais of Barrington, New Hampshire, was assigned to Plunkard's fire team. A draftee who had volunteered for the Airborne, Blais was a French-speaker who had just finished a mission with the Airborne in Africa.

"There was some bitching by the guys who had only been back from Vietnam for a month or two. The feeling was, 'Jesus Christ, enough! We did our part.' Then it became, let's go do the mission. Do your job. Get it done. When we got the job done, we could come home. We didn't see it as deploying for a tour in Vietnam. This was a three-month mission to disrupt and stop the Tet Offensive. The soldiers in the 82nd are freedom fighters. They fight for the oppressed. They just didn't know the politics of it," Blais said.

Mark Robertson of Concord, North Carolina, was a Cherry, an Army term given to those doing something for the first time. The son of a pilot who supplied planes to the

Russians on the Eastern Front in World War II, he had volunteered for the draft and had a chance to go to Officer Candidate School with a specialty in armor, which meant he would be protected by 55 tons of steel in a tank. Instead of waiting for an opening, however, he volunteered for jump school.

"Nobody will admit this, but we were all just young kids, scared as shit with something to prove to our fathers and to ourselves. We needed those wings to prove our manhood. I grew up on Audie Murphy and John Wayne movies. At the time, my life was kind of idyllic. Bragg was close to home, and it didn't look like we were going anywhere. I figured I'd serve out my time and that would be it. I even asked my mom if I should volunteer for Nam. She told me, 'Don't you dare do that.' Forty-eight hours later, I was on my way to war. It taught me a valuable lesson. Never assume that things are going to work out the way you think," Robertson said. "Going back to Nam was a shitty deal for the guys who had just been there, but it was great for a Cherry like me. I didn't know my ass from a hole in the ground. They had experience, and a lot more of us would have died if it wasn't for them. Paratroopers are tough as nails. Sure, we fought each other at times. But when the chips are down, everybody does their remarkable duty. Going into combat was a duty I had to do. I wanted to go to Vietnam. I wanted my folks to be proud of me."

Rich O'Hare's wait for an opening in Officer Candidate School abruptly ended with the orders to deploy. Six weeks removed from jump school, he was on his way to Vietnam and would eventually be placed in the cavalry unit.

"They opened up the warehouses and issued us jungle boots, jungle fatigues and a steel pot combat helmet with the paratrooper chin strap. I got my brand new M-16 right out of the box. We were cut off from communicating with the outside world, and boom, just like that, away you go," O'Hare recalled.

O'Hare had never loaded or pulled the trigger on an M-16, which could fire semi-automatically or shoot 20 rounds in 3.2 seconds if the selector switch was on full auto, a setting known variously as Rock 'N' Roll or John Wayne. He had been trained on the M-14 rifle, and he would have to learn how to sight in and clean the new weapon on the fly. The inner barrels of the newest M-16s, which became the infantryman's standard rifle in Vietnam, were coated with chrome to make the weapon more reliable. Because of the heat and pressure generated by the automatic weaponry, the barrels in older versions tended to corrode and cause jams, which was a bad thing for a soldier in life-or-death combat.

Just about the time the official order arrived at division headquarters, fresh-faced Second Lieutenant Mike Hood was having an off-duty beer at the Officer's Club. A Special Forces officer mentioned that something was afoot with the 82nd Airborne, so Hood returned to the living quarters he shared with four other guys.

"One of my roommates who had his bags packed said that he had been called out. I go into the house and everybody's gone but me. I called my company but didn't get through until one in the morning. They asked me where I've been and said they had been trying to reach me. So I report, and they asked me if I wanted to go to Vietnam. I said, 'Sure.' We were so cranked. Being in the Army but not being in Vietnam was like having a law degree but not practicing law," Hood said.

Needing every soldier it could muster, the brigade even mobilized characters who came with the warning: "Break open only in time of war." They had been confined for various peacetime infractions.

"We opened up the stockade," said Jim Littig, who was going off to war just five days after he had arrived at Fort Bragg. Placed in charge of the Long Range Recon Platoon, Littig said: "Throughout 1967, it looked like the war was over, and I thought we were going to miss it. It turns out that the enemy was just gathering stuff for the 1968 offensive. I saw it as an opportunity."

The Fayetteville jail was opened up too. Bob Murrill, now the commander of the headquarters company in one of the battalions, bailed out a soldier who had been arrested for some violation of civilian law. It was not unusual for a paratrooper to get into a scrape at some den of iniquity such as Rick's or Bottom's Up on Hay Street, which was known as Combat Alley before civic leaders cleaned it up.

"He needed to join us on our journey. I doubt that he considered this a better resolution of his situation, however," Murrill recalled.

Among the characters in the unfolding drama was James Sanner, an ordained Catholic priest from Erie, Pennsylvania. He had reported to Fort Bragg as a chaplain the day of the deployment order. A man of God who was headed off to war, Sanner volunteered to become a chaplain after reading an article in a Catholic newspaper that the military had a shortage of priests. With 50 hours of flight time in a Cessna, he figured he might draw the Air Force. The powers that be slotted him for the 82nd Airborne.

"I didn't even know what the Airborne was," Sanner said.

Sanner reported to jump school on January 6, 1968. Just four days into the program, while he was spit-shining his boots to the Airborne standard, Sanner received word that his father had passed away. He returned home to oversee funeral arrangements, then resumed training at Fort Benning. Being a priest wasn't the only thing that made him stand out. He was 34, and just about everybody in his group was 18 or 19. When the time came for the first of five training jumps, Sanner was asked if he would hear confessions from those in line.

"That first jump? Oh, wow. I could see out the door that we were flying in an oval pattern. There must have been some problem over the drop zone. The jump master finally gave the command to stand up, hook up and shuffle to the door. You follow the man in front of you, put your knees in the breeze, count one one-thousand, two one-thousand as the chute deploys. You check your canopy to make sure it fills. As you approach the ground and get to tree top level, you tuck your chin, get your feet pointed, and make the parachute landing fall. I did four more jumps to become Airborne qualified. They asked me if wanted them pinned on or if I wanted blood wings, which is where they pound the wings into your chest. I told them to pin them on," Sanner said.

At Bragg, he was scheduled to make, in his words, his Cherry jump with the 82nd Airborne. But while having dinner with the division chaplain, Sanner caught images on TV of jets bombing the walls of the Imperial Palace of Peace in Hue. When the chaplain said he would help him pack, Sanner replied, "Pack for what?" The reality of the priest's situation sunk in. "Holy smokes," Sanner said. "When they started passing out the mosquito netting, I knew we were going to Vietnam."

Meanwhile, even as men and equipment were assembling, the first flight was set to leave about 24 hours after the official orders had been cut. Colonel Bolling and 20 or so members of the advance party crossed the Green Ramp to the adjoining Pope Air Force Base to await their ride.

In the group was Command Sergeant Major John Pearce, the highest-ranking enlisted man in the unit and a combat veteran who had previously served in Vietnam. The recipient of the Silver Star, the nation's third highest award for valor, Pearce had also shed blood for his country. He carried the brigade's flag—a red, white and blue swath of cloth that served as a powerful symbol of the unit's identity. Emblazoned on it was the crest of the All Americans and the number of the Third Brigade. No matter where they were going or how long they might be in combat, the individual soldiers were unified under that flag and their All American shoulder patches.

The brigade, a French word that means "those who fight," was also christened with a new name. As the group gathered in a waiting room, intelligence sergeant Duke Dewey had a flash of inspiration. He recalled the words a three-star general had once spoken about Bolling's unit during the Detroit deployment.

"Bud, everything your brigade touches turns to gold," said John Throckmorton, a former commander of the 82nd Airborne.

If the unit had the Midas touch, then Dewey figured it should be called the Golden Brigade. The name stuck the whole time it was in Vietnam. An official stamp that would appear on subsequent paperwork carried the name Golden Brigade. Even the Big Army, which assigns numbers to all its units, came to recognize the name.

At the same time, division commander Richard Seitz visited the departing group to wish it Godspeed. Bolling was asked how his wife was taking the developments, but given the hush-hush nature of the deployment, Fran Bolling was in the dark about what her husband was doing, where he was going or how long he would be away.

"She thinks I'm going on a training mission," Bolling told the general.

With that, Seitz dispatched a detail to locate Mrs. Bolling. On the eve of Valentine's Day, she was getting her hair done at a local beauty salon when she was whisked away to say goodbye to her husband.

"When they brought her down, she had a box of mints that she gave me. She said Happy Valentine's Day, and off I went," Bolling said.

That first group boarded a C-141 Starlifter, the Air Force's first jet-powered transport plane. Four Pratt & Whitney engines throttled up, and the silver bird rumbled down the runway and into the sky, heading toward the sound of the guns in Southeast Asia.

The second Starlifter to take to the air was loaded with 99 soldiers and 10 disassembled helicopters, the flying machines that became the symbol of the Vietnam War. The ranking officer was James Zinchuk of Boston, Massachusetts, whose father had flown aboard B-17 bombers in World War II. Zinchuk had enrolled in the Reserve Officer Training program at Boston University and was destined to fly.

"The ramp was still down. The division band was playing *The All American Soldier*, and General Seitz came aboard. He said, 'Congratulations, lieutenant, you're taking the 82nd Airborne to war for the first time since World War II.' I saluted and said, 'Airborne.' We had to resolve things like what color cover to wear on our helmets, and everybody's jump strap had to be on left hand side although half of them were originally on the right," Zinchuk said.

Having been called out on the mission, Lieutenant Keith Bell of Denver, Colorado, followed procedures and loaded up a propeller-driven cargo plane with the equipment needed to fight a war. Then he had to unload it all and repack it in a jet plane the Airborne was using for the first time on such a large scale. "The Air Force guys said we were flying in a Starlifter. We had made training jumps from them before, but we had never taken them on a mission," Bell said. Lots of things were being done for the first time.

General Seitz worked tirelessly with his staff to make sure no detail was overlooked. Any trooper who had not already done so made out a last will and testament, something that is standard operating procedure in the 82nd Airborne. Then late into the night at the end of a long week, he got a call from the White House. President Johnson wanted to send off the troops in person. He was due to arrive on Saturday, February 17.

"I had just come home from the Green Ramp, took off my boots and had a cold beer at 12:45 a.m. The president would arrive at Pope that afternoon and be on the ground for 40 minutes. It's a good thing we didn't have more time to prepare. I probably would ordered a fresh coat of paint on everything at Bragg," Seitz said.

The commanding general put his boots back on and went back to work. He arranged for the division band to be present for the playing of *Hail to the Chief*, and a public address system was set up on a flatbed truck from which the president would speak.

During his 53-minute flight from Washington, LBJ had a bowl of chili aboard Air Force One, according to the White House log. He was accompanied by Army Chief of Staff Harold K. Johnson and assistant commandant of the Marine Corps Lewis W. Walt. A glitch in the sound system caused a short delay. Then the president walked to the microphone, cleared his throat and began speaking in his Texas drawl at 5:08 p.m.

"Wherever you are, wherever you go, each of you knows that you have with you always the devotion, the concern, the prayers of all those dear to you and to whom you are very dear," the president began. "As you depart once again to answer the call from afar, I come here today as your president to tell you that on your journey the hearts of this nation and the hopes of men in many nations fly with you and will follow with you until this duty is done. It is never easy for men to leave. It is never easy to ask men to leave home and happiness for duty far, far away. But the duties of freedom have never been easy. For your nation, for all of its people, those duties may become more demanding, the trials may become more difficult, the tests more challenging, before we or the world shall know again that peace on this planet is once more secure."

In his remarks, Johnson repeated the reasons he had sent troops to Vietnam in the first place—to prevent the Communist North from taking over the South by force of arms. America and its leaders were the ones seeking peace, he insisted, and the enemy was bent on pillage and aggression. The foe's immediate goal was to shake the government of South Vietnam to its foundation, to shake the confidence of its population, to destroy the will of America to see the war through. It was the enemy who had shown, in Johnson's words, that terrorists can strike and can kill without warning before the forces of order can throw them back. America's response must be unwavering resolution in the face of ruthless attacks. Each departing paratrooper was a symbol of America's will and commitment.

"There has never been a finer fighting force wearing the American uniform than you," Johnson said. "I believe—I know—that you will serve the cause of freedom just as your forefathers served it. You will serve it with bravery, you will serve it with skill, you will serve it with devotion. We are proud of you. I came here to speak on behalf of all America, and to tell you that you are our finest because you are Airborne."

For those in the ranks, Airborne was a charged word. Upon hearing the president say it, paratroopers shouted the response they gave with gusto whenever a commander uttered it: "All the way, sir!"

Although Seitz insisted the response was spontaneous, Mike Hood and others say the troops had practiced saying it something like three times before the president arrived.

After his speech, Johnson boarded a transport plane filled with paratroopers to bid them farewell on their journey. The Air Force crew chief in charge of the Starlifter told him: "Make it quick. We're moving."

Using the aircraft's public address system, he made another short speech. Again, the crew chief encouraged him to wrap things up. Not even the commander-in-chief could disrupt the timetable of an Airborne unit heading off to war.

"Sir, you got to get off. We're moving," Johnson was told.

After departing the plane, LBJ changed his schedule. Since Fort Bragg was home to Womack Army Hospital, he wanted to visit with soldiers who were recovering from wounds suffered in Vietnam. At hand was an old Chrysler sedan that served as a commander's vehicle, and with General Seitz sitting in the back seat between the president and the Army Chief of Staff, the group moved out. Someone was smart enough to call ahead, and a doctor in a white lab coat had the elevator waiting to take the president to the seventh floor. Johnson stayed for 30 minutes or so.

At one point, Seitz relayed story that was recorded in the president's daily log about a trooper who had been Absent Without Leave for 24 days. When the AWOL soldier learned his unit was moving out for Vietnam, he called to say he was returning to duty. He said he had been to Vietnam before and wanted to return with his fellow soldiers. Another soldier with one day left in the Army re-enlisted for six months because he said he belonged with the men in Vietnam and wanted to do his part.

During his time at Bragg, Johnson took time to shake hands with troops awaiting departure. Among them was Lieutenant Colonel John G. Jameson, commander of the 1st Battalion of the 505th Parachute Infantry Regiment. Because his battalion was the last of the three to deploy, Jameson then took his troops back into the field to make sure everyone was proficient with the new rifles that had been issued. Jameson had also received word from those who had already landed in Vietnam to take as much as he could with him, especially practical items such as sandbags.

Also shaking hands with the president was Thomas Locastro of Shannon, Mississippi, who had reported to the 82nd Airborne the day before Valentine's Day. A combat veteran who had already merited a Purple Heart, Locastro had served in Vietnam the previous year with the 101st Airborne Division. Among the wounds he suffered was a head shot, which had required months of recuperation in an Army hospital. Recently married, he had to tell his new bride that he was leaving her to go to Vietnam again. She didn't have a driver's license and would have to stay with the wife of comrade who was also deploying. Locastro described his encounter with the commander-in-chief in a journal he had purchased from the Post Exchange.

"The president said to us, 'You're my soldiers. You're the best of the best. You're the finest troops in world,' " Locastro wrote. "They always lie, you know, just to get you to do something for them, and to bail them out of some shit they've gotten themselves into."

Chapter 4
WHO ARE YOU GUYS?

C-One-forty-one on the strip, sixty-four killers on a one-way trip. Mission undetermined, destination unknown. Don't even know if we're ever coming home. – Airborne cadence.

Even without parachutes, the 82nd Airborne jumped into war with both feet, uncertain as to what exactly it was up against but with a general sense that kill-or-be-killed combat awaited. Just what kind of person picks up his weapon, packs everything he needs on his back and then flies off to the other side of the planet to fight a war?

"Crazy people," said Duke Dewey, the sergeant who had given the Golden Brigade its name.

There is that. The All Americans have historically come from all walks of life in every corner of the United States, but it's an inside joke that the characters in the 82nd Airborne have one thing in common beyond their motivation and dedication—they all share the same mental disorder. According to Airborne lore, the question of sanity was raised when the Army first started looking for soldiers who would jump out of perfectly good airplanes in flight and hit the ground running to take the fight to an enemy that had them surrounded. A doctor would look into a candidate's left ear while a second doctor would peer into the right one. If they could see each other through the empty space, the Army had itself a candidate to become a paratrooper. One company commander, upon reaching the ground on a training jump, described it this way: "We're all here because we're not all there," pointing to his cranium. Paratroopers are a special breed of bad asses defined by the Airborne saying: For those that jump, no explanation is necessary; for those that don't, no explanation is possible.

"We knew we were going right into the thick of it," Dewey said. "Look, the 82nd Airborne is the greatest fighting unit in the world. I love that division. They're the fighting-est bunch of bastards ever. Paratroopers know one thing and one thing only. We're shock troops. Our creed is Airborne All The Way. From the day you go to jump school, there's a constant drilling into the psyche that works in your brain. It's a mindset. It grows on you. That's who you are. I'm a professional solider. That's what I do. If you have the balls to jump out of an airplane, you'll fight. I've been with guys at the end of a 20-mile march in full gear who got into a fist fight over a pound cake in a C Ration pack. A few minutes later, they were friends again, like nothing had happened."

Travel time is a moment of peace for a soldier. It allows for moments of reflection and mental preparations ahead of the danger. The experienced ones use the time for practical purposes.

"You go to sleep," Dewey said. "You get all the sleep you can because when you get there, there won't be much chance of getting any rest."

Nobody appreciates sleep more than a soldier.

Bud Bolling was off to war for the first time since he commanded a rifle company a generation ago. This was bigger than the advisory role he had five years earlier in Vietnam, bigger than the Detroit deployment and bigger than brigade-sized exercise like a recent proficiency jump on Vieques Island in Puerto Rico. He settled in on the journey with these thoughts in mind: "I had the best troops in the world. We could do anything. The 82nd was coming to save the day."

Bolling also knew something the pilots were unaware of. Before the unit left, an old friend who had also been an advisor in Vietnam called with some inside scoop. He said the destination would be that place where they had been with a mutual friend in 1963. Without mentioning the name Hue, Bolling knew he was headed for the old imperial capital where urban combat was still raging.

The way things worked, paratroopers boarded their aircraft and the pilots then opened sealed orders informing them of their destination. The first stop on this mission was Elmendorf Air Force Base in Alaska, where the Starlifter refueled. On the next leg, the pilots opened their orders to fly to Yokota Air Base on the Japanese island of Honshu for another refueling. For the final part of the odyssey, orders were unsealed to land at Chu Lai, some 100 miles south of Hue.

"That's not close enough. You want to go to Da Nang," Bolling told the pilots.

"Da Nang is closed. It's still under attack," he was told.

If that major air base was closed, the situation was worse than Bolling thought. Arriving in Chu Lai at 11 a.m. local time on February 15, Bolling planned to show the flag. The brigade's colors were unfurled so that he and the advance party would have a proper welcome when the clamshell doors opened at the rear of the plane. Living up to the Airborne code that the officer is first out the door, Bolling walked down the ramp and put his combat boots on the tarmac.

An Air Force corporal greeted him by saying: "Who the hell are you guys?"

Somebody high up on Westmoreland's staff had neglected to tell the people on the receiving end that 3,670 paratroopers and 2,300 tons of equipment were en route. There's always the five percent who don't get the word.

"We're the 82nd Airborne, and I got a surprise for you, corporal. Every 90 minutes, there's going to be a plane arriving for 10 more days," Bolling said.

Following the advance party were 160 flights of Starlifters, plus six turboprop C-133 Cargomasters ferrying the heaviest loads, such as the brigade's artillery pieces and bigger trucks. The air movement was like a giant, stretched-out Slinky. The lead element landed, with the coils of the spring closing in behind it.

Dean Risseeuw of Milwaukee, Wisconsin, may have been the youngest person on that first flight. A 1967 graduate of West Point who was in charge of the brigade's personnel section, he had only made one proficiency jump, also known as a Hollywood jump, with the 82nd Airborne at Bragg.

"The colonel was so disappointed that there was no one there to greet us. No one knew we were coming. It all happened so fast. We stored the brigade colors again, marched off the plane and stood off to the side until the colonel got things sorted out," Risseeuw said.

Chu Lai was the in-country headquarters of the Army's 23rd Division, known as the Americal. Bolling took off to find its headquarters. Outside the office of Nels Parson, the Americal's chief of staff, Bolling encountered an orderly wearing the All American shoulder patch. The orderly professed surprise when told the 82nd Airborne was on the ground.

"The 82nd Airborne is in Fort Bragg," he said.

"We're here now," Bolling responded.

To sort out the confusion, calls were made to the appropriate commands to verify that the Airborne was inbound. On the fly, arrangements were made to receive the force and find places for them to bed down.

"I don't think anybody slept that first night," Bolling said.

Confusion still reigned as the second flight touched down. James Zinchuk had the men under his command off-load the brigade's helicopters, parking the disassembled flying machines off to the side of the runway.

"An Air Force colonel drove up in a jeep and asked, 'What are these things doing on my runway? Tow them or I'll wreck them.' I put a crew to work to reassemble the helicopters and went off to the Post Exchange to get a case of beer as an incentive to the guys who were putting the rotors back on," Zinchuk said.

Things got even more interesting that night.

"I was laying in my bunk when I heard this weird noise. It was like ka-bunk, and then ka-boom. We were being mortared. Nobody told us where to go, so we just rode it out," Zinchuk said.

John Lukas of Lynnfield, Massachusetts, had a similar experience his first night. A draftee, Lukas had volunteered for the Airborne while he was taking basic training at Fort Dix, New Jersey. While recruits were seated in the post theater, two sharp-dressed paratroopers, standing 6-foot-5 with rows of medals and jump boots marched in. From that moment, Lukas wanted to be 6-foot-5 too. When the Third Brigade deployed to Detroit in 1967, Lukas went along, sleeping right off the runway at Selfridge Air Force Base while wondering what was wrong with the picture of paratroopers being deployed to an American city.

"Every time the dial spun around, the Third Brigade seemed to be on alert status," Lukas said.

Having flown from Bragg to Chu Lai, Lukas racked out in one of those General Purpose military tents. During the night, incoming rounds began to explode. Somebody out there was trying to kill him, and a canvas tent offered next to nothing in the way of protection.

"Nobody told us what to do in the event we got rocketed. Everybody was running around like crazy. We ran into a bunker that was a Marine communications center. They told us we couldn't stay, but we had nowhere else to go," Lukas said.

Meanwhile, Richard Davidson said his journey to Vietnam began when he snuck away from a secure hangar at Pope Air Force Base to call his mother in Montreal from a pay phone.

"We were supposed to stay in this restricted area, but this meant nothing, for death would be worse than any punishment they might give us for leaving," Davidson said. "At Pope, a minister or a priest talked to us. There were Bibles to take if we wanted one, and coffee and doughnuts were available too. We were on standby. Departure time at any minute. Groups of men were leaving on different planes, day and night. Then my turn came, right after 3 o'clock in the morning. On board, I was invited up to the cockpit and sat in the pilot's seat, which was spare, of course. The airmen treated us real well, as if they were giving us our last living wish. I had butterflies constantly. We never knew what the future reserved for us. When I got to my seat, emergency rescue procedures were given in case of a crash at sea. There was snow in the mountains in Alaska. In Japan, they told us not to take our weapons off the plane, for this would violate some law or treaty. On the final leg, I was thinking about what I said to my mother when I tried to convince her that I was going to return. We played cards to take our minds off of nothing and everything. That got boring. About half hour before we were to land, they gave us our ammunition, grenades and all sorts of gear. What scared me most was when they said we might be bombed on landing. They won't even give us time to land. What the hell kind of landing zone are we going into? We might have to fight our way off the plane, so get off fast and move out. They dropped us off and then took off. It was sticky and hot. We moved by truck through an area that had barbed wire on each side. It looked like a prison camp. The whole division area was confused, with men running back and forth. Everyone was asking all sorts of unanswered questions."

Paul Headley, a farmer's son from south New Jersey who joined the Army to see the world, was among the veterans returning to Vietnam. As a member of the First Brigade of the 1st Cavalry Division, he had already served one tour and was being sent back.

"The Cav was one of those units that always seemed to get into it. They'd walk out the door and get into a fight. I'm not a religious man, but during that first year, I remember feeling, 'God, get me out of this, and I'll go to church every day.' I was assigned to the 82nd Airborne when I got back. When we were alerted, they took the speakers out of the phones so we couldn't call out, put barbed wire around the barracks and placed guards at the exits. When we got to Japan, I was able to call my mom to say I wouldn't be coming home. I figured I was a dead man."

Making peace with oneself is part of a soldier's lot. If you accept the fact that you're already dead, you can do your job without having to worry about what might happen. When the ramp came down at Chu Lai, the tropical humidity and the smell of Vietnam took Headley back in time.

"It was like I never left. The United States was a place I had visited for a short period of time," Headley said.

Richard Underwood of Lubbock, Texas, was a second lieutenant commanding a platoon in a rifle company on his way to war for the first time. He had been one semester away from receiving his diploma from Texas Tech University when he ran out of money and became eligible for military service. A buddy who had been in the Special Forces unit with recording artist Barry Sadler advised him: "If you go, you might as well get the best training you can get. That sounded like an adventure to me, so I volunteered for the Airborne, took Ranger training and signed up for Officer Candidate School."

On the way over, Underwood came to grips with the burden of command. "I was thinking about my life and the 43 other guys I was responsible for. That's a pretty heavy weight. All of the guys in my platoon had been to Vietnam before with the 1st Cavalry Division. They were flowing us in. The only reason they didn't send the whole division was they didn't have enough people. When we landed, a pilot with a sense of humor says: 'Welcome to Chu Lai. The temperature is 82 degrees, with light to moderate ground fire.' All you could hear was magazines being loaded into rifles. The ramp went down, we got off, the ramp went up, and the pilot took off. They didn't want those C-141s on the ground long. Colonel Bolling made a joke apologizing for a band not being there to greet us. We got to the side and reported for duty."

As the officer in charge of a 44-man platoon, West Pointer Michael Hood strapped himself into a sling seat in a Starlifter for the three legs of the flight. Only he and his platoon sergeant, Sherman Hussey, had never been in combat before. Everybody else had served at least one tour in Vietnam. He remembered a moment at Bragg when he found Sergeant Hussey cleaning the latrine on the day President Johnson flew down to see them off. "He thought that president might have to use the latrine, so he wanted to make sure it was spotless," Hood said.

When Hood's flight approached Vietnam, an announcement was made that the destination was Chu Lai. "The guys who had been to Vietnam before let out an audible, 'Oh, no' because they knew that was a hotter part of the country," Hood said. "No matter what, they were a wonderful bunch of guys. The ammunition was passed out. They loaded their rifles. I had no clue what to expect. We ran off the aircraft."

Within a year, only Hood and one other soldier from that flight was standing. Everybody else in the platoon had been killed or wounded.

Joe Mays, a platoon leader in the same company as Hood, wore his father's jump wings on his uniform. There wasn't much in the way of talk on the trip over, but not much had to be said. "I knew what I saw on their faces. We were going to war," Mays said. Because music was a big part of his generation, Mays kept a play list of his favorite songs from 1968. Two of them were by the rock group Steppenwolf: *Born To Be Wild* and *Magic Carpet Ride.* Either one was appropriate for the flight over.

Bob Murrill's journey deviated slightly in that it went not to Alaska but to Honolulu, Hawaii. During a 24-hour layover for refueling and maintenance, he had a chance to visit his sister Peggy. She was there because her husband was assigned to the nuclear submarine USS *Daniel Boone,* which at the time was docked at Pearl Harbor. Back on the plane, as the ranking officer on his aircraft, he opened the sealed orders to confirm what everyone knew in their hearts. They were headed to Vietnam.

"I didn't feel fear at this time. I did, however, feel a lot of anxiety—not knowing what would lie ahead and whether I had done enough to prepare for it. Being with these men pumped me up. They were ready for the task ahead, and I knew I needed to make them believe I was too," Murrill said. Five of Murrill's uncles had served in World War II, including one who served in a crack unit of Rangers under Colonel William Darby. Darby once said that commanding such men was like driving a team of high-spirited horses. "No effort was needed to get them to go forward. The problem was to hold them in check," Darby said.

James (Doc) Slavin of Waterbury, Connecticut, was a man dedicated to saving lives, not taking them, but being aboard a flight bound for Vietnam was right where he wanted to be. A 1966 graduate of Yale Medical School, he joined the Army right after his internship. "I wanted to be a paratrooper. I wanted to go to war for my country," Slavin said.

A battalion surgeon, Slavin was well aware of the Airborne spirit. On his first crack at jump school, he had washed out and failed to get his wings. Still, he was assigned to a medical platoon at Fort Bragg. "A sergeant there told me, 'You may be the best doctor in the world, but if you ain't Airborne, you ain't shit.' I got a second chance at jump school and got my wings," Slavin said.

The Starlifter that carried him to Vietnam developed a fuel leak but made it to its destination.

"They were passing out ammo just before we landed when the pilot says, 'I'm not even going to turn the engines off. I'll be at Clark Air Force Base in two hours.' Then he took off and was gone," Slavin said.

Tom Wallace of Coudersport, Pennsylvania, had been studying forestry at Penn State University when he joined the Army. After boot camp, advanced training and jump school, he was assigned to the First Battalion of the 508th Parachute Infantry Regiment of the Third Brigade. He had never fired an M-16 and saw one for the first time when it was handed to him right out of the box from Colt Industries. His squad leader and some comrades gave him a crash course on the weapon.

"Of the 10 guys in my squad, seven of them had already served in Vietnam. That was a big plus for the rest of us. If we had all been new like me, there would be a lot less of us around to talk about it," Wallace said. "They passed out ammo on the plane before we landed at Chu Lai. The pilot didn't even shut his engines off as we went down the ramp. You started wondering what was going on. We're not crazy. The 82nd Airborne is a cross section of America willing to fight for what we believe in."

A military deployment offers little in the way of in-flight entertainment, but two sergeants, Claud Dunn of Louisville, Kentucky and Phil Cronin of Boston, Massachusetts, brought along their own stash of drinks.

From the time he had entered the Army in 1964, Dunn wanted to be a paratrooper. "I wanted to join the Army to see world. In the recruiter's office, I saw a poster of a paratrooper standing in the door preparing to jump. That looked interesting. I said, 'Sign me up.' The recruiter said I'd get an extra $55 a month too, and I can imagine them thinking, 'Man, we got a live one today.' I was 19 years old and on a career path of becoming Airborne infantry. You gotta have something special in you to be Airborne. Crazy, maybe. Definitely different."

As the planes were being loaded at Pope, Dunn and Cronin were sent on an errand in their jeep. After completing the task, Dunn asked his buddy how much money he had with him, and the two pooled their resources for a stop at the liquor store. They stashed their unauthorized cargo into a duffel bag, and their jeep was the last piece of equipment loaded onto their flight. While in the air, the two soldiers asked permission to sit in the vehicle because it was going to be a long flight. They cracked open a bottle.

"We didn't know if we were gonna live or die. If I was gonna die, I was gonna die happy," Dunn said.

Cronin had no qualms about the mission. "It was my job. That's all. I was doing what I was ordered to do," he said.

Rich O'Hare had never been in a Starlifter before boarding one in the middle of the night to leave for Vietnam. With a row of vehicles strapped down along the center of the plane, he was one of six troopers aboard the aircraft. Although the jet was pressurized, it was unheated and uncomfortable. The four jet engines were noisy enough to make him half-deaf too. The plane was equipped with a crude precursor of a microwave oven, and the crew heated up TV dinners for him and his comrades. During the usual banter on the way over, guys talked about where they were from and where they went for basic training. One buck sergeant who had served a year in Vietnam with the 173rd Airborne Brigade noted that he still carried shrapnel in his testicles from his first tour.

"The big question was what it was going to be like on the other side," O'Hare said.

When he landed at Chu Lai, an Air Force enlisted man posed the same question that was asked of Bud Bulling: "Who the hell are you guys?"

Vietnam was like stepping into a giant, roofless greenhouse. The tropical air was hot and humid to the point of being soupy. A peculiar odor assaulted the nostrils, starting with the aroma of chlorophyll from all the vegetation and the smell of mildew common in such an environment. Hints of jet fuel, gun powder, salt water, fish, human excrement and death added to the mix. Being inside this bubble came with a sense of being on edge, a feeling that lasted every second a soldier was in Vietnam. In this surreal realm, the lid of civilization had been ripped off to expose an alternate universe. What the soldiers had left behind became known as The World. The only way back to The World was to go through whatever was ahead.

Chapter 5
JOINING THE FIGHT

Once on the ground, Bud Bolling set out to receive his marching orders while the rest of his brigade was completing its journey. In a borrowed helicopter, he and five staff officers flew north to the big U.S. military installation at Da Nang. There to greet him was the commanding officer of the 101st Airborne Division, Major General Olinto M. Barsanti, a Nevada native of Greek ethnicity who had been wounded seven times in World War II. Under the chain of command at the time, the Golden Brigade was under the operational control of the Screaming Eagles.

The arrangement had historical significance. After the 82nd became America's first Airborne division, the Army essentially split the unit in half to create the 101st Airborne Division. Brother units from the start, the two divisions did combat jumps together in Normandy and Holland, then were both rushed to the front during the Battle of the Bulge. Now they were together again, but not without smoothing over some of the friction common in sibling rivalries. With the Distinguished Service Cross, five Silver Stars and seven Purple Hearts counted among his decorations, Barsanti was a proven warrior. He also had a hot temper that was not among his better qualities.

"Where have you been?" Barsanti asked.

"I just got off the plane." Bolling replied.

"You're part of my outfit now. When are you going to put the 101st shoulder patch on?" the general asked.

Preserving the identity of the All Americans was foremost in Bolling's mind, and he wondered how division commander Richard Seitz would have reacted.

"I looked at this major general, and I'm just a colonel, and I said: 'I'll wear that 101st patch anywhere on my uniform, including my right hip pocket, but that 82nd patch goes on my left shoulder.' Never again did he ever say anything about the Screaming Eagle patch. We were always the 82nd Airborne. We came here as a fighting unit, and we would stay together as a fighting unit," Bolling recalled.

That red, white and blue patch is a sacred symbol that distinguishes the All Americans from other units. It doesn't weigh much, but it's weighted with history and tradition. In fact, Bolling would demand that his troops wear the flashier, colorful version instead of opting for a subdued patch that would blend in more easily with the jungle surroundings. "I wanted to let these people know who was killing them," the colonel said.

Bolling was given the name Night Rider as his radio call sign because he had flown all night to reach Vietnam.

In the meantime, overall commander William Westmoreland and his second in command, Creighton Abrams, the cigar-chomping, hard-charging World War II veteran, had arrived in Da Nang to greet the new arrivals. Bolling knew Abrams from his days at West Point.

"I'll bet you didn't think we'd serve together again so soon, did you, Bolling?" Abrams said by way of greeting.

"No sir, but I'm delighted to be here," Bolling replied.

All the brass went into a conference room. Speaking first, Westmoreland provided an update of the offensive mounted by Mister Charles, his catchall word for the Viet Cong and North Vietnamese Army. Standing in front of a map, Westmoreland made big sweeps with his hand, while outlining what was needed to counter the attacks. Sitting silently, Bolling mused that he only had about 2,000 actual trigger-pullers to cover the wide swath indicated by Westmoreland, but he held his tongue while waiting to hear from Abrams, whose name would later be attached to the Army's main battle tank.

"Bolling, we got to get your outfit up north as fast as we can, but we don't know how to do it. We're losing a C-130 a day trying to relieve the siege at Khe Sahn," Abrams said, referring to the fighting being done by two Marine regiments, Army troops and the South Vietnamese Army at a combat base to the west.

Bolling replied: "There's a road that I had been up hundreds of times as an advisor."

The reference was to Highway One, an artery that ran the length of Vietnam mainly on a course parallel to the eastern coast. The problem was that the enemy had cut the highway in 86 places, and the road was closed to U.S. convoys.

"We'll open it," Bolling said as an audible gasp filled the room.

Abrams directed the Americal Division to provide Bolling with 75 trucks, which was a major sacrifice for a division commander to make. The trucks were allotted, and a plan was formulated to move the All Americans by road. But first, Barsanti requested an immediate airlift of a portion of Bolling's brigade to join his troopers and the Marines in the battle for Hue.

"I want a battalion up here right now," Barsanti barked.

The assignment was given to the 650 men in the three rifle companies of the 2nd Battalion of the 505th Parachute Infantry Regiment, commanded by Major Jake Privette. The battalion spearheaded the movement to Vietnam, and it was the first to complete in-country orientation. As a practical matter, Privette asked how he would feed his men, and fate did him a small but important favor. One of the officers in the 101st Airborne was Louis (Rip) Collins, who had escaped the same German prison camp with Bud Bolling during World War II. Collins promised the All Americans they would have what they needed, and he delivered. Personal relationships overcame the flaws in the supply system. The machinery was set in motion to move Privette's battalion as soon as possible. Six C-130 Hercules cargo planes were scrounged up from the Air Force to get them to Hue.

"This was not a super smooth operation," Bolling said.

As an aside, after that big brass meeting broke up, Bolling intervened on behalf of some Special Forces soldiers who had been confined on suspicion of smoking marijuana. In truth, they had been burning citronella, or lemongrass, to repel the malaria-carrying mosquitoes that flourished in Vietnam. The stuff has a similar aroma to marijuana, but after assuring Bolling that they weren't smoking weed, Bolling had them released on his authority.

Speed was of the essence in the bloody battle for Hue. The Marines, operating under a command structure known as Task Force X-Ray, had overall control of the battle and did the fighting within the city. Reinforcements provided to them were three battalions of the 101st Airborne and the battalion from the Golden Brigade. The Marines assigned the Army units to take up positions south and southeast of the city.

Barely a week after leaving Fort Bragg, the All Americans headed north at 9 o'clock in the morning on February 22. The battalion's last elements landed the next day.

Among the troopers rushed forward was James T. Greene of Jamestown, Tennessee. A year after he had become an Eagle Scout, Greene joined the Army when he was 17. His enlistment papers were signed by his father, a Navy veteran of World War II who had been wounded while serving aboard a minesweeper. Even though his signature allowed his son to join early, the elder Greene told him: "You don't know what you're getting into." The young soldier volunteered for the Airborne to get the $55 a month in jump pay and was originally assigned to the 101st Airborne. When that unit deployed to Vietnam, however, 17-year-olds were banned from going, and he was transferred to the 82nd Airborne. He had just turned 18 when the All Americans deployed to Vietnam. Now here he was, not old enough to vote, on the firing line outside a burning city as Marines engaged in savage house-to-house combat against a foe determined to make the Americans pay with blood for every step.

"If you're a young kid, 6-foot-2 and 140 pounds, nothing is too hard," said Greene, who had an older brother serving in the Navy at the time. "I was young and dumb. I wanted to go."

With his comrades in Bravo Company, Greene took up station at a bridge that spanned the Perfume River and connected the Old City and the New City of Hue. Communist forces were retreating along a waterway called the Phu Bai Canal, and a group of them was spotted trying to flee. Troopers dropped their packs and gave pursuit, leaving Greene and a buddy behind to guard the equipment. This was straightforward, fast tempo infantry work. Get the bad guys before they get you.

"These were the guys who had been shooting up the Marines. Our job was to stop them from escaping," Greene said. "I heard shooting, and our guys got seven of them. They killed them right then and there. It was real. You just never hear about us being up there in the history books."

Chapter 6
FIRST BLOOD

Cobbling together a single brigade by borrowing heavily from the two sibling units in the 82nd Airborne Division posed a problem. Soldiers ordinarily bond with each other during months of training together and living in the same barracks. It's what helps make the Army a team. A guy knows his job and has a reasonable expectation of what to expect from the guy to the right and to the left. However, unit cohesion was strained going into Vietnam because troops were just getting to know each other. In a letter to William Westmoreland dated February 20, Lieutenant General Robert H. York of the XVIII Airborne Corps, the umbrella organization that the 82nd Airborne belonged to, noted that team-building was necessary before troops went into combat.

"To form this brigade, the rest of the division had to be stripped down to cadre strength. Well over half the personnel came from the other two brigades. Since this was done only a couple of days before their movement date, they have not had an opportunity to work together as a team," York wrote.

Westmoreland acknowledged the need for team-building. In his return letter, Westmoreland said it was anybody's guess how long the brigade would stay, but he hoped to have to back in the States by late summer or early fall.

According to standard operating procedure, newcomers to Vietnam participated in what was called Proficiency Training, or P School. It was a chance for soldiers to adjust to the heat, humidity and dampness of Vietnam. Classes were held on the rules of war outlined in the Geneva Conventions, even though hostile forces felt no need to abide by international treaties. Nuances were explained about the two types of foe to be encountered, a civilian insurgency called the Viet Cong that blended in with the local population and the professional soldiers of the North Vietnamese Army, who were experts at concealment. The toughest challenge for American troops was the inability to know who was an enemy until they were shot at. Hostile forces were called by various names, including the bad guys, Victor Charlie, Mister Charles, gooks, dinks, slopes, slants or zipper heads, a term left over from the Korean War. Orders were direct—kill or be killed. Rifle ranges were available to instruct troops on how to fire, zero in and clean the M-16 rifle for those who had never shot one in anger before.

For 80 percent of the Golden Brigade who had been to Vietnam before, much of the orientation at the Americal Division's combat training center outside of Chu Lai was a refresher course. For the soldiers setting foot in the country for the first time, it was an eye-opening education.

As part of the program for troops to get acquainted, special attention was paid to finding and avoiding unseen killers in the form of booby traps, which had been expertly planted to kill the unsuspecting at random. Just as improvised explosive devices bedeviled American troops in future wars, booby traps and land mines were a nightmare in Vietnam. Those indiscriminate and carefully concealed killers were placed everywhere and anywhere, just waiting to be triggered. They ranged from sharpened punji sticks dipped in animal urine to explosive devices such as Chinese-made grenades set to explode through trip wires. Booby traps caused more American casualties in Vietnam than any other source.

The learning process had its own risks, a point driven home when a trooper in the 82nd Airborne was killed during orientation on Leap Day, February 29. That first casualty, Staff Sergeant Joe Rodriguez, 30, of Tucson, Arizona, wasn't supposed to be in Vietnam. He broke the rules to get there.

A platoon sergeant who had been part of Operation Power Pack, Rodriguez was married and the father of five. According to battalion commander John G. Jameson, Rodriguez was on a temporary duty assignment in Florida when the 82nd Airborne received its emergency orders for Vietnam. Rodriguez called in and wanted to deploy too, but the guidance was for him to stay put because it was only supposed to be a three-month mission. However, Rodriguez was such a dedicated All American that he left Florida without permission, meaning he was technically Absent Without Leave, a punishable offense under the Uniform Code of Military Justice.

"If he hadn't have gone AWOL from Florida, he wouldn't have been the first guy killed," Jameson said.

At P School, Rodriguez was in the field on maneuvers with his unit, Charlie Company of the 1st Battalion, 505th Parachute Infantry Regiment. With him was Paul Headley, the farm boy from New Jersey who had known Rodriguez from his first days in the 82nd Airborne. Although the two men had formed a tight bond, their relationship got off to a bumpy start.

Headley, who was two pay grades below Rodriguez, was returning to Vietnam after serving a 12-month tour of duty with the 1st Cavalry Division. Among the awards he had received was the Combat Infantryman's Badge, a coveted medal adorned with the image of a Minute Man musket. The CIB is earned by a soldier with an infantry occupation who has practiced his profession in a war zone. When Headley reported for duty at Fort Bragg, Sergeant Rodriguez made it a priority to test his mettle.

"He didn't like me. I had a CIB, and those 82nd guys liked to measure themselves by how many jumps they had made. Before you know it, we got into a fist fight in his office. He broke my nose," Headley said.

A short time later, Headley was in formation when Rodriguez found fault with the way Headley was wearing his uniform, which in the Airborne has to be perfect.

"He asked me if I wanted to go to his office again, and I went in first. I hit him. Hit him with a fire extinguisher too. Split his lip and gave him a black eye," Headley said.

A contentious relationship between an enlisted man and the sergeant who has immediate command of him can make for a miserable existence, but Headley had passed a test by standing up for himself and fighting back. Subsequently, when Rodriguez challenged his men over some perceived infraction, he offered to fight anyone in his platoon who disagreed with him.

"That Headley, he's not afraid to visit me inside," the sergeant said. Respect had been earned.

"We wound up being friends," Headley said. Such good friends, in fact, that Headley presented a gift to his sergeant before they headed to Vietnam together. Headley's godfather raised German Shepherds back in New Jersey, and Headley asked for a pup to give to Rodriguez's son.

In the early afternoon of the hot, sunny day of February 29, Headley and Rodriguez were working in close proximity as Charlie Company made a coordinated movement across some jungle terrain. The idea was to use a compass to reach an imaginary line on a map by a certain time, just like the company might have to do in combat. A glitch developed during maneuvers. Troops had fallen behind schedule in the tangled undergrowth, and the company commander urged Rodriguez and his men to pick up the pace.

"Joe was being told to hurry up, and as we were moving, we spotted some Viet Cong who were running," said Headley, who carried the 25-pound M-60 machine gun that provided combat punch to his squad. "I had been through this shit before on my first tour and urged him to be cautious, because those guys could lead us into a trap."

Rodriguez continued to move up, and Headley's worst fears were realized. The sergeant inadvertently entered an area that had not been cleared. He triggered the unseen tripwire on a booby trap and was mortally wounded.

"He died in my arms," Headley said. "I always felt guilty about what happened. Maybe I should have been able to convince him not to move ahead so fast…"

Just 19 days shy of his 31st birthday, Rodriguez was subject to a grim procedure for those killed in Vietnam. He body was placed inside a body bag, then into a metal transfer case to be flown back to the States. A military escort accompanied the body to a funeral home in his hometown of Tucson, Arizona. There, his flag-draped coffin was lowered into a grave at Holy Hope Cemetery. He was decorated with the Combat Infantryman's Badge he so coveted and was also awarded a Purple Heart.

Years later, Paul Headley looked up Joe Rodriguez's name on Panel 42 East, Line 9 of the Vietnam Memorial in Washington, D.C. He also located the son who had been given the German Shepherd pup in the course of telling the family how their father died. In time, a day care center at Fort Bragg was named in honor of the Golden Brigade's first combat loss.

News of Rodriguez's death rippled through the ranks, especially since it came on a training exercise designed to prepare incoming troopers for combat in Vietnam,

"That was a rude awakening," said Richard Underwood, a second lieutenant who led the second platoon of Charlie Company. "Somebody we know just got killed. This is for real. For the guys who had been to Vietnam before, it was a reminder. It was particularly somber for me and the new guys. Sergeant Rodriguez was a great, great individual. Everybody liked him. His nickname was Rock, and the memory I'll always have is of him kissing his five kids goodbye when we were leaving Bragg."

Chaplain James Sanner was pressed into an unwelcome but necessary duty for the first time. Rodriguez was a Catholic, and the priest anointed his body according to the rites of the Catholic faith. Years later, Sanner also looked up the sergeant's name on The Wall in Washington, D.C., spending half a day there processing what he didn't have time to do in Vietnam.

As an aside, Rodriguez wasn't the only trooper who was listed as AWOL but ended up in Vietnam, according to Robert Anderson, who ultimately served in the Golden Brigade as a supply officer.

"When we first got called out, I would have a manifest saying there supposed to be 98 personnel on a flight to Vietnam, but my count would show there were actually 106 on the plane. The situation was confusing because some were assigned to go and then the guidance was changed to say they didn't have to. The result was that we had guys who were classified as AWOL or deserters because they were supposed to be at Bragg when, in fact, they were fighting in Vietnam. Some of them got shot up and were earning medals. It all got straightened out later, but it was kind of embarrassing," Anderson said.

Meanwhile, the company commander who ordered Rodriguez to speed up his patrol was not long for the job. He was sacked by Colonel Bolling, who did not countenance incompetence. Charlie Company now needed a new captain.

Back in The World, February 29 was the last day on the job for Secretary of Defense Robert McNamara, a former Ford Motor Company executive who was one of the Whiz Kids in the Kennedy and Johnson administrations. A veteran of World War II, he had played such a major role in the escalation of the war that Vietnam was called McNamara's War, and a line of defense made up of motion detectors and listening devices below the Demilitarized Zone was called the McNamara Line. A numbers cruncher, McNamara was responsible for using body counts as measure of progress during the prosecution of the war, figuring that there were a limited number of enemy fighters and that a war of attrition would convince the enemy to abandon its cause. He also advocated a program under which low I.Q. individuals would be drafted for duty in Vietnam. They were called McNamara's Morons and, predictably, performed poorly. By late 1967, McNamara had privately concluded the war was un-winnable. He advised President Johnson to freeze U.S. troop levels, stop the bombing of North

Vietnam and turn over the war to the South Vietnamese. He never voiced his concerns publicly, however. Over time, he had come to accept the fact that a second attack on a U.S. ship in the Gulf of Tonkin, a 1964 incident that was used as a reason to go to war, never happened. In his 1995 memoir *In Retrospect,* McNamara said of the decision-makers who committed combat troops to Vietnam: "We were wrong, terribly wrong. We owe it to future generations to explain why." He noted that not every problem has a military solution, and that "military force—especially when wielded by an outside power—cannot bring order in a country that cannot govern itself." Real power, he concluded, was knowing when not to use it. McNamara became president of the World Bank. He was the only Secretary of Defense to be removed from his job during time of war until Donald Rumsfeld.

Chapter 7
STREET WITHOUT JOY

Although 75 trucks had been provided by the Americal Division, some elements of the Golden Brigade still lacked a ride north from Chu Lai to the outskirts of Hue. The 82nd Airborne has historically been long on combat power but short on logistics, and the Long Range Recon Platoon had no means to travel. The LRRPs (pronounced Lurps) were a provisional unit serving in an exploratory role within the Airborne. Based on a British concept of having stealthy troops serve as the eyes and ears of the larger force, each brigade in the division had its own recon element. When the callout came for Vietnam, the LRRPs from the other two brigades joined those from the Third Brigade. The solution for finding transportation fell to Sergeant James Dale Dillon of Jacksonville, Florida. A medic who was known to his comrades as Doc, Dillon had served two previous tours in Vietnam with the Special Forces, and he was a good man to know in this part of the world.

"He was the sort of guy who could get anything from anybody. He knew everybody," said Jim Littig, commanding officer of the recon platoon.

Dillon and another sergeant set out on what is known as a midnight requisition and made their way to the Americal's motor pool. Dillon found an unattended jeep, a three-quarter ton truck and a workhorse known as the deuce-and-a-half because it could haul two and a half tons of cargo. The locks were cut off the target vehicles, and using his free-hand artistic skills, Dillon painted the markings of the 82nd Airborne on their bumpers. All were driven back to the staging area.

"It was obvious he had done that before," Littig said. "The Americal knew that we had stolen them, but they couldn't do anything about it."

Doc Dillon was also the type of scrounger who procured the tiger-stripe camouflage jungle fatigues for the recon platoon.

Meanwhile, the Golden Brigade assembled a convoy. As tents and supplies were loaded onto trucks, a monsoon rain drenched the troops. Like they say in the Airborne, if it ain't rainin', we ain't trainin'. Duke Dewey loaded up a footlocker with liquor that was available in Chu Lai, figuring it could be used as snake bite medicine when the unit reached its destination.

Under the plan, the troops would move up Highway One in three separate serials of 150 vehicles each. Each serial would take two days to complete the trip, first from Chu Lai to Da Nang for an overnight stay at a Marine base, and then through the treacherous Hai Van Pass to another Marine installation at Phu Bai just south of Hue. Troop B of the 17th Calvary Regiment, comprised of jeeps outfitted with recoilless rifles and machine guns, would lead the way to open the road. Vehicles were to remain 50 meters apart. The speed limit was set at 20 miles per hour on the open road, and half that through villages and hamlets. Jeeps, trucks and vans would be in contact by radio, and those in charge would report in at designated checkpoints. The vehicle in the lead of the column was adorned with a red hood panel. The trail vehicle had an amber panel. The markings allowed commanders hovering above in helicopters to keep tabs. With the exception of cargo carriers, all canvas was removed from vehicles, including the ones carrying the troops. Windshields and tailgates were down. An assistant driver rode shotgun in the cab of each truck. Sandbags were emplaced in the trucks as extra protection for the troops, who were provided with armored vests. Weapons were carried at the ready, and each soldier had a supply of ammo, two canteens and rations. Drivers were to follow the tracks of the vehicle in front of them to minimize the chance of striking land mines. Contingency plans were in place for stretches of the road that had bridges or were likely ambush sites. Color codes were established for smoke grenades—white to mark enemy positions, and red, green, violet or yellow for friendly positions. Medevac procedures were reviewed.

"Every soldier was prepared to fight the whole way. Hell, we were fighting the minute we stepped off the airplanes," Bud Bolling said.

On the morning of March 3, designated as D-Day, the first serial pulled out of Chu Lai. Although rain had fallen the night before, the convoy stirred up a cloud of red dust. Vietnam was the only place on the planet where it could be raining and dusty at the same time. The vehicles rumbled through several villages before reaching Da Nang at 6:30 p.m. without incident. Enemy rockets slammed into the base that night, but the overhead cover inside the wire prevented casualties.

The second leg of the trip was more harrowing. Because a blown bridge had to be repaired, the convoy was delayed in Da Nang until one o'clock in the afternoon. Then the convoy started out over the Hai Van Pass, a 12-mile section of serpentine road. For natural beauty, it rivals the coastal highway through Big Sur in California. Still, it was the most dangerous stretch of road in Vietnam even in peacetime. Built in the only place in the country without a coastal plain, the pass was where the mountains of the Annamite Cordillera ran right up to the waters of the South China Sea. Also known as the Pass Through the Clouds, it is often shrouded in mist. At its highest point is a gateway of stone built by an ancient lord, and the structure stands as a national historic relic. Old concrete bunkers built by the French also dotted the crest. In ancient times, Chinese invaders who used war elephants as early versions of tanks were loathe to venture south of the Hai Van Pass, where the twists and turns serve as a barrier to any land army. Danger increases if an enemy plants booby traps through the bottleneck or hides in the brush to take potshots.

The third vehicle in the procession was a gun jeep driven by Reid Lyon, who once aspired to be a drummer in a studio band in Los Angeles. Lyon was born in Tokyo, where his father served on Douglas MacArthur's staff. He grew up on a farm near the Potomac River before moving to Charlotte, North Carolina. When his musical ambitions failed to pan out, he joined the Army and volunteered for the Airborne because he had always been fascinated by paratroopers.

"The view from the Hai Van Pass was breath-taking, but it was also nerve-wracking. Precarious. Coming down the far side was when we kept getting sniped at. I was a Cherry. We never stopped, but we returned fire," Lyon said.

Troop commander Dennis Malcor, whose call sign was Yellow Leg, rode in a gun jeep driven by Mark Robertson. Just as it crested the top of the mountain, the jeep took fire from an ambush site.

"I heard the rounds coming in. I could hear them whizzing by. I'm sure I looked like I had seen a ghost. It was hairy," Robertson said.

Malcor got on the radio to Colonel Bolling, who was hovering overhead in his command helicopter.

"Night Rider, this is Yellow Leg. We're taking fire," Malcor said in a calm voice.

"When you take fire, you return fire," Bolling replied, giving the authorization to shoot back.

Malcor unlimbered his jeep's 106-millimeter recoilless rifle and fired. He then secured the large-bore gun and got back into the jeep.

"Hey man, that was some close shit," Malcor told Robertson. With that comment, Malcor's standing went up in his driver's estimation.

Paddy Barry, riding in the back of a truck, said two wheels of his vehicle were actually off the road and dangling over open air at one point. Under the orders of march, if a vehicle went over the side of the road and tumbled down toward the sea, troopers were supposed to toss a live grenade into the fuel tank to destroy it, thereby denying the enemy of its use.

"We had a saying over there. If we go down, we all go down together," Barry said.

Richard Davidson sat on the protective vest he had been issued. Sitting on a flak jacket afforded some protection against the possibility of getting his manhood blown off if his truck struck a land mine.

Andrew Blais said that his part of column stopped when it took sniper fire, and troops got out of the truck. That's when he heard Sergeant Johnny Plunkard yell, "Stop! Don't go any further."

With the benefit of wisdom acquired on his earlier combat tour, Plunkard had spotted a trip wire on booby trap.

"That was the whole idea, for the sniper to get us away from the trucks. It was a teaching moment and a valuable lesson for me. I said to myself that I'm going to stick to this guy like glue. It wasn't the last time Johnny saved my life," Blais said.

Despite receiving mortar and rifle fire, cavalry troopers and the brigade's Military Police kept the road open.

John Therrien's part of the convoy had cleared the pass and was proceeding down the far side when it was ambushed. Therrien positioned his gun jeep and opened up with the recoilless rifle. As he told his comrades, the fight against the North Vietnamese Army was different from fighting guerrillas.

"We weren't fighting farmers. These were professional soldiers who had disciplined fields of fire," Therrien said.

As the convoy neared its final destination, bombed out villages carrying the scars of war came into view. This stretch of Highway One was named the Street Without Joy, or *La Rue Sans Joie,* the title of a 1961 book about the French in the First Indochina War. The Vietnamese troops who defeated the French had fortified a string of villages along a line of sand dunes and salt marshes between the highway and the South China Sea. Each village had small pagodas, temples and tombs, which offered ideal concealment for launching attacks. The villages were spaced 200 to 300 yards apart and were surrounded by bushes, hedges, bamboo trees and small fences, which rebel forces had augmented with an interlocking system of trenches and tunnels, underground arms depots and first-aid stations. The wet ground was unfavorable for the large scale use of tanks, and the few roads through the area were mined and sabotaged. A Frenchman with a sardonic sense of humor had come up with the name Street Without Joy. The French likened their war to a dog being attacked by fleas. The dog may be bigger and more powerful, but with so much area to defend against pests, the dog gets tired of scratching. Or as one of the French soldiers said, "We've been in the shit so long we can no longer smell the stink."

In his journal, Tommy Locastro mentioned the damage done to the villages. "Very hot trip. Most of the towns on the way destroyed. War is really bad for these people," Locastro wrote.

At any rate, despite the delays from harassing ambushes, all three serials made the 119-mile trip from Chu Lai to Phu Bai without a single casualty or without losing a vehicle. The brigade had pulled off a movement that was thought to be suicidal.

Phu Bai was a U.S. military base that had been rocketed and attacked during the Tet Offensive. Located seven miles southeast of Hue, it was originally the site of an Army intelligence post that monitored enemy radio traffic. Then the Marines turned it into a tactical operations center, complete with an airfield for attack jets. It was also home to elements of a Navy Construction Battalion, or Seabees. Upon reaching it, the All Americans rested at a sand dune area east of the airfield and shared the chow and foxholes of the battalion that had flown north to fight outside Hue.

The cavalry element that included John Lukas halted at a spot about 500 yards northwest of the Seabees installation at Phu Bai.

"There were about 135 of us who occupied the high ground. We had taken some sniper fire during the trip from Chu Lai, but we were joking among ourselves that it was just the Marines who were pissed off we were there," Lukas said.

Chapter 8
WHERE IT'S WORST

The area where the paratroopers got off the trucks was the narrowest part of South Vietnam. The swath of land was about 30 miles wide from the South China Sea to the mountains marking the border with Laos in the West, yet every type of surface feature in the country was evident. The coastal plain was home to the country's only major highway and its series of side roads, along with a crisscrossing network of rivers, streams and canals. The flat ground was dominated by grids of rice paddies cultivated by peasants living in villages, some of which were pacified and some of which were controlled by Communist forces. Also situated on relatively flat ground were temples, ancient tombs and other structures of religious significance. Plainly visible in the West were the mountains covered with triple-canopy rain forests. The mountains marked the border with Laos, but the dividing line was rather porous. The North Vietnamese moved men and supplies through a natural conduit called the A Shau Valley, which was the first exit off the Ho Chi Minh Trail that snaked around the Demilitarized Zone. Then they used the waterways, or a secondary road named Highway 547, as infiltration routes. Opposing forces did not face each other along a front line. Enemy forces were everywhere and nowhere, all at the same time. The Airborne's mission, like the mission in any war, was to close with the enemy and kill them.

To the Vietnamese, the area was known as Thua Thien Province, the home of the smoldering ruins of Hue and its environs. On U.S. military maps, which divided South Vietnam into four tactical zones, it was I Corps. The Marines controlled operations within its confines.

In keeping with military courtesy, Bud Bolling sought out the highest-ranking officer at Phu Bai and reported to a Marine brigadier general. His immediate task was to find a location for a base camp that would serve as headquarters. The conversation included a simple question.

"Where are the bad guys? Where is it the worst?" Bolling asked.

Using a map as reference, the general pointed to a relatively open patch of slightly elevated ground northwest of Phu Bai and south of Hue. It was smack in the middle of hostile territory that concealed those who had taken Hue and then made the Marines pay for every yard in the fighting for its recapture. What better place for the Airborne to build its home?

"Duke Dewey said it was a danger zone. Code Red. I don't know where he got his intelligence, but he was right," Bolling said.

As Dewey said, invoking the words of an officer from the 101st Airborne that were spoken in a previous war, "We're paratroopers. We're supposed to be surrounded."

Accompanied by a combat engineer who swept the ground with a hand-held mine detector, Bolling walked 500 yards to the northwest toward a spot that was occupied by his cavalry unit. Into this turf, the brigade's battle flag was planted.

"We're starting here," Bolling proclaimed.

Building a camp required much more equipment and supplies than the Golden Brigade had brought from Fort Bragg, however.

"The Marines had a big supply depot and told us that if we needed anything to let them know, and what we needed most were mines and concertina wire. They gave us anything we wanted, for which I am eternally grateful to the United States Marine Corps. The Marines fed us too. It was the last good food we had for a while," Bolling said.

Lacking earth movers and construction equipment, Bolling worked out a deal with the Seabees. In exchange for the loan of their bulldozers, Bolling offered to trade captured enemy weapons he intended to be in possession of soon. The blades of the heavy machines shaped the land, plowed some roads and dug holes for protective bunkers. Clouds of dust arose over a ground devoid of trees. Troops began the manual labor of filling sandbags for protection, assisted by a local workforce in the form of refugees who had been made homeless by war. As suspected, some of those locals were hostile agents secretly marking key positions.

Although it was as Spartan as any Army camp erected in the field, a miniature city rose from the ground within days. The town hall was the brigade's tactical operations center, a fortified bunker that became the nerve center of operations. Bolling's residence was a hexagonal, two-man tent that had been brought from Fort Bragg. Also built were a helicopter pad, artillery position, motor pool, supply depot and ammo dump. The Military Police set up shop in a shallow valley, building protective bunkers next to two tents sardonically named Alcatraz and Sing-Sing. The sanitation department began with a bank of four-hole outhouses for calls of nature, which came with increased frequency as the brigade's soldiers subsisted on C Rations and took their malaria pills, the side effects of which were loose bowels. The settlement's perimeter featured guard posts with interlocking fields of fire. Claymore mines, named after a Scottish medieval broadsword that cut down enemies in swaths, protected the edges of the encampment. Triggered by hand, a claymore could violently expel rows of steel pellets, each pellet about the size of a pea. It worked like a remote-controlled shotgun, and the gadget came with a helpful tip: Front Toward Enemy. Filling gaps in the defenses was a field expedient called fougasse, or 55-gallon drums filled with thickened gasoline that could be detonated with a claymore. Fougasse worked like a flame-thrower against any force that tested the camp's defenses.

"There wasn't a single thing there, but within two or three hours of our arrival, we began building the camp," said Gerald Kennedy of the Military Police unit. "We had to scrounge for everything. We were rolling thieves. All we had was what we brought over on our backs. We built a prisoner of war compound and strung wire around it. The guard towers on the perimeter were 30 to 40 feet high and made out of sandbags. It looked like a penitentiary."

Tom Ladwig, the brigade's chemical officer, said the place had its own aroma. "I never smelled anything like that in my life. It was like a mix of rotting food and sewage. I can still smell it," he said.

One little-known brigade asset was operational the same day the bulldozers carved out a cavity in the ground. It was the radio intelligence unit of the Army Security Agency, which began monitoring the radio frequencies to seek out any transmissions of hostile forces. The intel unit called its home The Hole, which was surrounded by concertina wire and protected by two guards on station 24 hours a day, seven days a week. A warning sign went up that said: "Do Not Enter. You Will Be Shot."

"Ninety-eight percent of the infantry guys never knew we were there, but we were active the first day. The engineers dug us a hole about 100 feet up the hill from the chopper pad. When the colonel would get out of his helicopter, the first place he came to was my hole," said J.V. Stephenson, the sergeant in charge of the 358th Army Security Agency Company.

Underground, and with generators providing power for lights and equipment, Stephenson's crew marked a map with color-coded pins when radio signals were intercepted. Enemy units could be identified by their call signs or the type of radios they were using. Once pinpointed, the hostile forces could change frequency and Stephenson could still track them.

"The radio is just like a fingerprint," Stephenson said.

A settlement needs a name, and this one memorialized Sergeant Joe Rodriguez, the trooper killed by a booby trap in Chu Lai. A hastily made sign at Camp Rodriguez hailed it as the home of the Third Brigade of the 82nd Airborne Division. Also printed out was this biblical reference: Greater Love Hath No Man Than to Lay Down His Life For His Country.

On the northern boundary of Rodriguez was Camp Eagle, home of the 101st Airborne. Both camps were roughly elliptical in shape.

With zero chance of having anything resembling a field hospital, Jim (Doc) Slavin took steps to erect an aid station.

"We tried to dig a hole for one, but the ground was like cement. Every time we hit it with a pick, we hardly made a dent. I gave 10 bucks to one of the Seabees with a bulldozer, and he dug us a great hole. It was the best position in the whole encampment," Slavin said.

As it turned out, 80 percent of the medical supplies brought over by the brigade had surpassed their expiration dates and were useless. Getting new medical supplies was no easy task. A single brigade was hardly at the top of the priority list in the Army logistics system, which had a half million troops to supply. Such a unit is known in the Army as a bastard brigade.

"We had a horrible time getting supplied. We had to beg and steal everything. We had to steal it or buy it," Slavin said.

Meanwhile, Creighton Abrams flew in for a meeting.

"What do you need the most?" the general asked Bolling.

Bolling lacked experienced commanders for five of his rifle companies and had no one capable of handling mail through the Army Post Office (APO) system.

"I need five captains quick, and I need an APO even faster. My men need to get their mail," Bolling replied.

"You'll have the APO this afternoon," Abrams promised.

A captain qualified to run the postal operation was dispatched from Saigon. But upon reaching a village along Highway One just outside Camp Rodriguez, he was ambushed and killed before he handled a single letter. A replacement was needed to get the mail flowing.

While Camp Rodriguez offered next to nothing in the way of amenities, infantry life was even more primitive. On the first day the camp was operational, Lieutenant Richard Underwood and his top sergeant connected two shelter halves to make a rudimentary tent, just the way the Army had trained them. They could have saved themselves the trouble.

"I never slept in it once," Underwood said. "We got the word that we were moving out. We went out on ambush and stayed in the field the whole time."

In a conventional war, the brigade's three infantry battalions would have moved to the front and taken a position on the line. In this war, the battalions started on the outskirts of Hue and then fanned out to the east, northwest and west. One of the brigade's top priorities was to block the enemy's flow of supplies and troops coming through from the mountains, which Bolling described as his open left flank.

As of March 8, the brigade was taking part in what was known as Operation Carentan, named after a D-Day objective in Normandy. If they weren't patrolling, troops were guarding both ends of the two bridges spanning the Perfume River. Hue's battle scars were still fresh. The equivalent of two infantry divisions of NVA had snuck into the city, some of them wearing women's garb to blend in with the civilian population. It took 25 days of fighting to evict them, but not before 4,000 civilians died and more than 100,000 residents were uprooted from their homes. Three-fourths of the city's houses had been damaged or destroyed. The electrical grid and water systems had been knocked out. Sporadic fighting continued even after the Communist flag had been taken down.

In one instance, Andrew Blais was pulling bridge security on Johnny Plunkard's fire team.

"Across the bridge, we saw Marines scurrying around getting mortared. You could see the explosions. Then this guy in a jeep gets about one-third of the way across the bridge when he gets hit. He's losing control, veering all over the bridge and everything goes in the river. It stayed afloat for a little while, then it sank. That's when I heard Sergeant Plunkard say, 'Cover me!' "

Plunkard shed his boots, removed his shirt and set his weapon down before diving into the river to swim toward the jeep. His rescue attempt was unsuccessful, so he continued to swim to the far bank. Climbing out of the river, he cut his foot on something in the mud and walked back across the bridge to where he had left his fire team.

"He bandaged his foot and said, 'OK, let's go.' He was the bravest man I ever met. Who in the world runs toward mortar fire?" Blais said.

Tommy Locastro remembers his company setting up outside the north gate of The Citadel, which had been the scene of some vicious fighting.

"Right near us, Marine bodies were stacked like cordwood. There must have been 200 of them. To get into the Citadel, the Marines were going into a little hole in the wall. We told them to back up. We'll blow a hole through the son of a bitch, and we hit it with a recoilless rifle," Locastro said.

Lieutenant Joe Mays and his company stood guard on the eastern bridge over the Perfume River. The gravity of the situation was broken by one of those moments in which soldiers find humor.

"The fighting was still going on, and we had permission to light up anything on the north side of the river and engage anyone on the south side of the river if they engaged us first," Mays said. "We had a private first class named Arthur Hudson of New York City who was the radio operator, and he looked green. He told me that he hadn't pooped for two weeks. When I asked why, he said that he knew that as soon as he dropped his pants, a VC was going to shoot him in the butt. So, I got about six guys to make a circle around Hudson and stand guard. He was finally able to relieve himself."

Mays' company later moved out to the area east of Hue where it guarded a fuel line leading from a Navy installation on the coast to a fuel depot in the Imperial City.

"We could hear explosions in the night that didn't sound like weapons. It turns out the local villagers tapped into the line and used the fuel for their stoves and lanterns. The problem was it was JP4 jet fuel, which doesn't work very well in stoves but does cause explosions," Mays said.

One of Richard Davidson's first duties was pulling guard duty at night on one of the bridges.

"We had put out some trip flares. The NVA would tie empty tin cans to the tails of dogs and send them across the bridge. The dogs would trip the flares and the whole place would light up," Davidson said.

Davidson also recalled digging a hole for protection in case his position was attacked. His shovel had only dug a few scoops of dirt before unearthing a grisly discovery. "The spot was the grave of a kid who had been killed. I didn't know it was a grave. I was a Cherry," he said.

Another time, while on patrol, Davidson was walking along a five-foot high fence when bullets began impacting all around. "I jumped over that fence like a bird on the wing," he said.

Some troops patrolled the rivers in boats supplied by the Navy. Some sights were downright extraordinary.

Duke Dewey remembered a time when he and Colonel Bolling were flying over the smoldering ruins of Hue. Down below on the Perfume River was a guy water skiing behind a Navy vessel called a PBR for Patrol Boat, Riverine. They went down to investigate and discovered it was Captain Wesley Ford, the staff officer in charge of the Golden Brigade's planning section.

"He was a character," Dewey said of Ford. "He had been in Special Forces, and this was his third tour in Vietnam. He didn't give a damn. Wes was something else. He used to fly around in his helicopter playing *The All American Soldier* on the loudspeaker."

Meanwhile, on March 11, troopers in the cavalry unit were ordered to form up in their area of Camp Rodriguez. Their mission was to go into a secure section of Hue to pick up a load of ammo at a Marine post and then escort it back to Phu Bai. It meant they had to drive up and down Highway One in the dark.

At two o'clock in the morning, with unit commander Dennis Malcor in the lead jeep, the first platoon of B Troop exited the base camp through a village called Gia Le and turned left onto Highway One. Under a shroud of fog that made it seem darker than it was, the vehicles moved without lights. Drivers strained their eyes to follow the vehicle in front. Thirty minutes into the trip, the convoy came to a bridge leading into Hue.

"Three vehicles went across. When the fourth one tried, all hell broke loose," said Reid Lyon. "Everything lit up. Green tracers were everywhere. I felt a jolt. My steering wheel was shot off, but I still had it in my hands. The vehicle rolled into a ditch. Normally, in an ambush, you pull the jeeps over to the side of the road in a herring bone pattern so that you can use the recoilless rifle, but we couldn't deploy it. Sergeant Larry Morning put a boot on me and kicked me out of the jeep to get me out of the line of fire. He started throwing grenades. We were taking fire from the right and left. Mortars came in, then rockets."

The shooting roared unabated for 15 minutes. The aroma of gun powder hung heavy in the damp air. Just behind Lyon, a sergeant on his second tour in Vietnam was hit. Troopers dragged him 50 yards or so up to the bridge. With no medic on the mission, Lyon put a tourniquet on the wounded man's left leg.

"I was terrified. I lost my Cherry," Lyon said. "In hindsight, the round that hit my steering wheel had just missed me. After the fact was when I got really scared. That was an intense time."

John Lukas, who was Malcor's driver, felt a searing pain in his wrist from a small but jagged piece of metal. It took a moment to realize he had been hit.

"I yanked the piece of shrapnel out and burned my fingers at same time," Lukas said. "The medics told me later I did a good job."

Just as suddenly as it started, the firing ceased. The column proceeded to pick up the load of ammo, then rolled to Phu Bai to complete the mission. Lyon's jeep was towed to safety, with him still carrying the displaced steering wheel.

Elsewhere, out in the field, the infantry discovered signs of just how brutal, savage and bloody the fight for Hue had been.

Lieutenant Keith Bell was leading a platoon on patrol west of Hue when a horrible smell assaulted his nose. One whiff of a decomposing human body makes an indelible impression on the senses.

"Talk about stench. In this little swale was a shallow mass grave. The NVA had executed hundreds of people. Some of the bodies were only half-buried. We put up a perimeter around it, and Colonel Bolling came out. It was investigated as a war crimes site. The dead included government officials, school teachers and South Vietnamese soldiers. My initial reaction was that Communists are not nice people," Bell said with soldierly understatement.

In another battalion's area, a mass grave containing nine civilian bodies was discovered. The hands of the dead had been tied behind their backs. Each had been shot in the back of the head. Then a third large grave was found. More than 100 civilians and South Vietnamese soldiers had been dumped inside. Many of them were buried alive.

In all, crudely dug pits around Hue held 3,000 civilians, 600 of which were still alive when they were buried. Clues to what happened were found in documents seized in a later operation.

Prior to the Tet Offensive, a ring of spies acting on behalf of the Viet Cong, some of which were students at the University of Hue, compiled lists of government officials, professors and students who were labeled as tyrants or puppet personnel of the Saigon government. When the city was attacked and occupied, Ho Chi Minh's freedom fighters rounded up anyone who failed to adhere to North Vietnamese doctrine. What followed was a murderous rampage that constituted one of the worst atrocities of the war.

Around the same time, another war crime occurred near Chu Lai where the 82nd Airborne had landed and was processed in by the Americal Division, and this one involved U.S. forces. On March 16, at a complex of hamlets known as My Lai, elements of the Americal Division said they were given orders to shoot anything that moved.

Although it would take 20 months for photos of the atrocity to surface, the death toll included 504 men, women and children. Second Lieutenant William Calley, a college dropout who served a platoon leader, was charged with murder and was the only officer convicted of playing a direct role in the massacre. Eleven others were charged, but the cases against them fizzled out or they were acquitted.

Back at his headquarters, Colonel Bolling studied the tactics of the hostile forces around him. It was a generally held belief that while American firepower ruled during the day, Charlie owned the night. Bolling, or Night Rider as he was known, refused to cede anything to the foe. He planned to take the night away from Charlie.

"That's when the bad guys are out. If they won't fight in the daytime, that's unfair, but we'll play their game," Bolling said.

Night ops were a staple of Long Range Recon, but they didn't have to venture out very far to make contact. Hostile forces were trying to get back to their sanctuaries in the west to lick their wounds or to regroup for future attacks. Hunter/killer teams were formed to intercept them, and the teams did just what the name implies.

"I was out there hunting. We were going to hunt them down and kill them. I'm a professional soldier. It was my job. I'm doing what I was trained to do. This was where I belonged," said Jim Littig, who around his neck wore a pinkie ring that belonged to an uncle who fought in World War I. "We didn't have any trouble finding the enemy. We knew where they were."

Littig's group had an international flavor. One soldier on his team had fought in the 1956 Hungarian uprising against the Soviet Union. Another had been at the Bay of Pigs in an unsuccessful invasion of Cuba. One was a native of Ethiopia who fought with the Egyptian army in a Middle East war. A couple of others had seen fighting in the African Congo. They had all gravitated to the 82nd Airborne because they viewed it as the best fighting outfit in the world.

According to the tactics taught in Ranger School, ambush teams would move to a location, and then to throw off the enemy, they would go to their actual ambush site to be in position by 10 o'clock at night. Teams were equipped with the precursor of night vision goggles called the Starlight scope, which intensifies the ambient light of stars to enable the user to see in the dark. Other senses, such as hearing and smell, became heightened.

"The jungle will tell you when the enemy's coming. It gets real quiet," Littig said.

The biggest bang on ambush was provided by the claymore mine.

"We'd get two to six kills on some nights," Littig said. "There was a degree of excitement from the adrenaline rush, the intensity. You had the sense you were in combat, but it was remote. When you're 21, you think you're bullet proof. If it's going to happen, it's going to happen to someone else. Success was when you didn't get your people killed."

In his unit, combat engineer Paddy Barry learned to link four claymores together with grenades and detonation cord. On a night ambush, this so-called daisy chain would explode in sequence.

"Barry, you are to killing what Picasso was to painting," his commanding officer told him.

That was fine by Barry.

"We're the 82nd Airborne. We weren't over there to play tiddlywinks. We were there to arrange a meeting between the enemy and his Maker," he said.

The first major engagement to test that fighting spirit was near.

Chapter 9
HELL BREAKS LOOSE

When Captain Paul Davin was assigned to the 82nd Airborne as a company commander, he was unaware that his predecessor had been removed from his post following the death of Sergeant Joe Rodriguez. It didn't matter. He clicked with the unit right from the start.

Originally from Reading, Pennsylvania, Davin had begun his military career in 1956 with the Marine Corps, spending four years, seven months and three days in that branch of the service. He was tattooed with the Marine logo but decided to transfer to the Army, earning his jump wings before being sent to Vietnam for the first time in 1966 with the 101st Airborne.

"The first time I got shot at, I was scared. I was laying on ground, wishing I didn't have buttons so I could get lower. I was trying to crawl into my helmet," Davin said.

On that first tour, he received a Bronze Star. He also came down with malaria and was given a ticket back to The World. But dissatisfied at being back in the States when there was a war going on, he returned to Vietnam with the 173rd Airborne Brigade.

"I had to be there," Davin said.

Then word came that the 82nd Airborne needed company commanders, and Davin found himself inside a tent at Camp Rodriguez with several other replacement officers.

"I met Colonel Bolling for the first time, and he asked if I wanted a rifle company. I hesitated a second before answering because I didn't know if I could handle that shit. Before I could say a word, he said, 'OK, you got Charlie Company.' I answered back, 'Airborne!' The 82nd was the only unit I ever clicked with. All of my platoon leaders were fantastic. All of the guys in the unit were great," Davin said.

As the commander of Charlie Company of the 1st Battalion of the 505th, Davin arrived just as the first pitched gunfight was at hand between the 82nd Airborne and the twin forces of the North Vietnamese Army and the Viet Cong. Aggressive patrols by two battalions of the 505th had already made sporadic contact in an area north of Camp Rodriguez and east of Hue. Villages and hamlets dotted a landscape was flatter than beer on a plate, with individual rice paddies defined by earthen dikes or thin lines of scraggly trees.

The 1st Battalion, commanded by Lieutenant Colonel John G. Jameson, patrolled along a secondary road known as Highway 552, which ran east out of Hue toward the coast. A command post had been set up in an abandoned schoolhouse at Phu Vang, a village that had paid a bloody price during the Tet Offensive. All of the teachers from that school had been assassinated by Communist forces seeking to impose their ideology on the local populace. Part of the school's roof had been destroyed by bombs.

South of the road, and running roughly parallel to it, was a canal that reeked of death. The stench came from the bloated corpses floating in its muddy brown waters. To the south of the canal was a tributary of the Perfume River, which lost so much pace on its northern path that it branched off to form the Song Dai Giang River. That waterway followed a southeasterly course to the sea.

The 2nd Battalion, commanded by Major Jake Privette, pushed up from south of the waterways in a reconnaissance in force, an offensive operation designed to find and test an enemy's strength. Privette's battalion was assisted by a Viet Cong defector who now worked for the Americans. In the local language, he was a Hoi Chanh, meaning one who has returned to the fold. As two rifle companies walked the ground, the defector abruptly and ominously dropped to a prone position.

"Jake and his men hit the ground too," said Bud Bolling, who surveyed the area from above in his helicopter. "Then all hell broke loose from the canal."

From Bolling's chopper, a smoke rocket was fired to mark the spot where the shooting had erupted. The smoke was a visual signal meant for the brigade's Forward Air Controller, who was overhead in a single engine, propeller-driven observation plane. The controller's call sign was Gimpy, so named because he walked with a limp as the result of a sprained ankle.

"I'm popping yellow smoke. Gimp, do you see it?" Bolling radioed. "There's something bad along that canal."

Gimpy acknowledged and fired a smoke rocket to mark the target for a couple of F-4 Phantom jets providing close air support. The fast movers released 750-pound bombs from their bomb racks, right on target. Not only did the violent explosions obliterate the position, but a large group of soldiers was flushed from their hiding places. On a dead run over open terrain, they scurried along earthen dikes that were part of the paddy system. One of the biggest challenges of the Vietnam War for the American military was to find and fix a stealthy enemy who preferred hit-and-run tactics. Now the enemy was in full view, presenting a target rich environment.

"I was astounded by how many were in there. Hundreds of people wearing pith helmets were running single file along dirt paths between the rice paddies," Bolling said.

From his perch 50 yards off the deck, Bolling pointed down to his door gunner behind the trigger of an M-60 machine gun. The commander took a split-second to size up whether the fleeing horde was friend or foe.

"The last thing we wanted was headlines in The New York Times saying that the 82nd Airborne shoots up South Vietnamese army," Bolling said.

The South Vietnamese Army wore American jungle fatigues and steel pot helmets. The force on the run was dressed in different garb.

"There had to be two or three hundred of them. As they reached this little town, they'd disappear, which told me they had an underground escape route. I decided to take a chance. I told my gunner, 'Have at it.' You can imagine an American soldier who's never fired a shot in anger and the adrenaline that's flowing through his belly," Bolling said.

And then, pffft. Nothing. The weapon jammed. The gunner tried several times to clear it, but the weapon refused to spit out bullets. It's the first rule of Murphy's Laws of Combat: what can go wrong, will.

"He couldn't get it going," Bolling said. "That was lesson No. 2 or 3 upon my arrival. Test fire the machine guns after we take off. Not long bursts. But from then on, I wanted to see bullets going out."

As daylight faded, and as more air missions and artillery strikes were ordered, Bolling halted his ground patrols. They lacked the means to cross the waterways surrounding the pocket anyway. Back at headquarters, he and his staff hatched a plan to sweep the area the next day. In a two-pronged movement, Alpha and Charlie Companies from the 1st Battalion would move along Highway 552 while two companies of the 2nd Battalion would push up on the southern bank of the canal. On the map, the secondary road was delineated by alternating rectangles of red and white in a pattern that looked like a stick of candy. The forthcoming action became known as the Battle of the Candy Stripe. Troops called it the Battle of the Schoolhouse. By any name, it was a three-day engagement of brutal, savage, chaotic fighting that began on March 20.

"That place was infested with bad guys," Bolling said.

Tommy Locastro humped the radio for Paul Davin's company and was always within arm's length of the commanding officer. The 25-pound radio was called the PRC-25, or the Prick 25, and was vital in calling in firepower. Because of the radio's importance, hostile forces considered it to be a priority target. In an act of defiance, Locastro placed a pennant on his antenna that said: Fuck Ho Chi Minh.

"We were cowboys," Locastro said with a tone of resignation.

To prepare for what might be a long day, Locastro fixed himself a lunch. He bought some French bread on the black market from a Vietnamese woman, then rummaged through a pile of C Rations for peanut butter and jelly to make sandwiches.

Also briefed on the plan was Alpha Company, which included Lieutenant Mike Hood and roughly three dozen infantrymen in his third platoon.

"They said we're going to go in and sweep this area, and there are no good guys in there. They said, 'Look, shoot anything that moves,' " Hood recalled. In the retelling, Hood said the rules of engagement made him think of the orders given to the Americal Division's William Calley at My Lai. "They told us that, but we knew the difference," said Hood.

In the wee hours of the morning on March 20, or zero dark thirty in Army lingo, Charlie Company proceeded down the Candy Stripe to secure a village. Visibility was minimal in the inky darkness. Richard Underwood's second platoon was on point when the heavy rattle of Chinese-made machine guns erupted from the village. Mortar rounds rained from the sky as part of the ambush.

Charlie Company's troopers instinctively returned fire. Then they realized that their foe had forced the villagers out in front of them as human shields. In a brutal act designed to exact the bloodiest price possible, hostile forces had herded civilians into a crossfire.

"All hell broke loose," Underwood said. "I can still see the sight of a mother carrying a baby in her arms, with a chunk of flesh torn out of the baby's arm."

As he returned fire, Tommy Locastro realized that he had shot an old woman who ran right into his field of fire. One of the tragedies of any war, but especially this one, was that civilians got caught between competing forces hammering away at each other with rapid fire weapons.

"I felt so bad. I prayed the Our Father over her, but I had to keep going. All hell was breaking loose," Locastro said.

Veteran machine gunner Paul Headley joined the fight. He and his crew eliminated a machine gun that was firing at his comrades.

"It was still dark when they opened up on us. Green tracers were going everywhere. This machine gun was firing, and I saw the sweep of tracers coming toward me. I got tangled up in the wire, but I got the guy. I'm a country boy. I always was a pretty good shot. Still am," Headley said.

Artillery was called in. Then as the barrage lifted, troopers moved into the village while the enemy force withdrew south across the canal. The shooting continued from the flank.

"My medic was treating a little child with a leg wound when we began taking fire from the south bank of the canal. We could see them shooting at us. I was scared shitless," Underwood said.

Any sane person confronts that flash of fear when forces with murder in their heart are intent on killing, but those in the Airborne infantry learn to put fear aside and continue the mission. Underwood called for support.

"That was the first time I called in artillery. That was the first time I shot anybody," Underwood said.

One of the enemy dead, retrieved later, was an insurgent in black pajamas carrying an M1 rifle, the standard weapon of American infantry in World War II. Only then was it determined that she was an 18-year-old girl fighting for the Viet Cong.

In the meantime, Alpha Company disembarked from its trucks and set out on foot down the Candy Stripe. Mike Hood remembered it this way:

"We got out there about three o'clock in the morning and started moving down this road to the east. We were walking along the road, as you see in the movies, guys on each side and me in the middle. We start getting hit by mortar and small arms fire.

I fell down in the middle of the road, and I'm trying to talk on the radio with one ear in the dirt. My machine gunner was near me in this little ditch. We started taking fire from the wood line, and he raised up to return fire. With his back pressed against my right ear, he got hit. He was my shield. We scrambled around and everything, and then it was like it just stopped. This is really crazy. And we got up and started moving down the road again. We got toward our area because it was starting to get daylight."

The machine gunner survived his wounds and awaited evacuation while Alpha Company found cover in a cemetery. Finding safety in a graveyard may sound creepy, but a cemetery was one of the safest places in Vietnam because it provided protection. In the Buddhist tradition, graves are marked with a dome representing a tortoise shell. Each grave is two or three feet in height and four to six feet long, and each dome is surrounded by an ornamental wall of cement. The whole collection of 20 or more domes is encircled by another cement wall, about three feet in height and a foot thick. No sacrilege was meant in occupying a graveyard. Metaphorically, the dead protected the living.

Then first platoon moved south toward the canal in an attempt to flank the force that had opened fire on Charlie Company. Leading the platoon was James R. Adams, who graduated with Hood from West Point just nine months earlier. On the radio net, Adams was identified as One-Six, one being his platoon and six referring to his status as the unit's leader.

"All of a sudden, you just hear a roar. That's what it sounds like. It sounds like a roar. It doesn't sound like boom, pop, pop. It's a steady roar. And I remember saying, 'They got ambushed.' People are yelling on the radio. You could hear across the net that One-Six is down," Hood said.

Adams and his men ran smack into a company-sized ambush. The opening burst cut down one soldier, who was out in the open. In a spontaneous reaction, Adams left the safety of his position to retrieve the wounded man. He was fatally shot in the attempt, becoming the first graduate of the West Point Class of 1967 to be killed in action in Vietnam. He would be recognized with a Silver Star, the nation's third highest award for valor, but there was more to his story in this battle.

Alpha Company commander David O'Donnell, a lieutenant who was designated Alpha-Six, was hit in the shoulder. Despite his severe wounds, he was able to call in artillery and air strikes, bringing the supporting fires extremely close to his men. O'Donnell had to be evacuated, and in the line of succession during the heat of battle, Mike Hood assumed command. It was his battle now.

"So, I've got to figure out what the hell is going on, because we're all lying face down in the cemetery. These guys were in this little tomb next to me, and this guy with a machine gun was next to me. I said, 'Okay, I'm moving forward.' So, I started to make my way out of these mounds. And I remember as I jumped over the first one and laid down, the machine gunner says, 'Well, there goes another Six.' I remember that as plain as day. Anyway, I got up and realized that my classmate was killed in action, and the company commander was down, and the platoon was just decimated. One guy was still out there who was wounded, and the NVA just kept shooting him in the legs. In the early stages, we took a tremendous amount of casualties of people trying to assist people or rescue people. That's a huge discipline, but this was a rough situation. I got to where everybody was and was able to call in air strikes. It was a very rude awakening, an intense baptism. It wasn't really my first baptism, but this time they put my whole head in. Before they just poured a little cup of water. This time was the full immersion," Hood said.

The brigade's helicopters, subject to a heavy volume of fire, attempted to evacuate the wounded and the fallen. Battalion commander John Jameson was over the scene in a helicopter piloted by William Summers, who requested and was granted permission to try an extraction. Using his three years of helicopter experience, Summers landed his bird in a hot landing zone. The most seriously wounded were whisked away for emergency medical care. Other pilots followed Summers' lead, and within minutes, all of the wounded were out. In the fog of war, however, James Adams was inexplicably left behind, and according to the Airborne creed, no one gets left behind.

"The big deal was to account for everybody. So, we got all that done. We withdrew. We got back to our area. I got a call from our battalion commander. He said, 'Can you account for all your Sixes?' And I said yes, affirmative, because everybody had been told (Adams) was on the chopper list. Well, the bottom line was we had left one out there, and it was my classmate. It took us three days of intense combat to get back to where we were that morning," Hood said.

Elsewhere in Alpha Company, Lieutenant Joe Mays' platoon advanced into the firefight. It was nothing like the combat depicted in war movies. One of the men crawling up on his elbows and knees toward the gunfire was Sergeant Joseph J. Cassidy Jr., a team leader from Philadelphia who had previously served a tour in Vietnam with the 101st Airborne.

"My platoon started moving up when Sergeant Cassidy was shot in the face and killed. It was the first time that I have experienced death under those kind of circumstances, the first time I lost a man. I think that is the day that my guys and me became men. We were no longer boys. Platoon leaders are responsible for the lives of their men, but when they're shooting at you, you can't keep them from hitting one of your guys. Their bullets kill too. I'll never forget Cassidy. He was one of my guys. I live in Virginia, and every time I go to the Vietnam Memorial in Washington, D.C., he is the first name I go to," Mays said.

Cassidy, 21, received the Silver Star for his valor. His brother and four sisters mourned his death at his burial at Beverly National Cemetery. A brother-in-arms, Kenneth Taylor, didn't know Cassidy had been killed until 25 years later. He posted condolences on the message board for the Vietnam Wall of Faces: "He was one of the most fearless people I ever met. He said, 'I love the Army. You can do push-ups any time you want, and they actually pay for it.' To this day, when I remember his face, I feel great loss. He was just a fellow American who would do anything for his country."

Roughly eight hours after the shooting started, and in the midst of all the mayhem, Mike Hood and Alpha Company were ordered to take up positions along the Candy Stripe. His troops covered the movement of Charlie Company, which was given the task of crossing a 30-foot wide cement bridge over the canal to eliminate the guns on the far side.

The third platoon, company headquarters and one squad of the second platoon had crossed the narrow span when automatic weapons opened up on them from three sides.

Unable to maneuver, Captain Davin called in more artillery. The supporting fire was ineffective, however, because friendly and opposing forces were almost intermingled. Davin and Locastro took cover in an enemy trench.

"Those Vietnamese trenches were dug for smaller soldiers. I jumped in one, or in front of one, and Locastro was on top of me. It was a hell of a way to spend an afternoon when the shit is hitting the fan. You ask yourself if you're ever going to get out of this place," Davin said.

The peanut butter and jelly sandwiches that Locastro had made were now smashed in his pockets. He thought to himself, "I'm going to get killed following this guy."

Paul Headley's machine gun jammed as he crossed the bridge, but he cleared the weapon and got it going. He nailed one enemy soldier hiding behind a Buddhist temple.

"Another guy was hiding behind some bodies, and he would fire sporadically. This little guy was pretty crafty. I got him right in the head," Headley said.

Among those pinned down was Canadian Richard Davidson.

"As we were going over the bridge, everything opened up. You could see the fires coming out of the muzzles. I saw two guys get hit by a mortar round. Another guy took three bullets to his shoulder, stomach and knee. One guy was hit loading a magazine and lost his fingers. I always carried two magazines in my helmet, and somehow, they fell to the ground. As I bent over to pick them up, rounds started impacting right in front of me. If I hadn't stopped, I would've been killed," Davidson said.

Davidson also lost contact with a squad mate and buddy, Leo Gunning of Potsdam, New York, who was nowhere to be seen.

"I kept yelling, 'Leo, Leo!' He didn't answer," Davidson said. "It turned out that he ducked into a spider hole and was too close to the enemy to answer. He got confused during the fray and didn't know which way was back. When he did make it later, I was so happy to see him."

From his position, Davidson saw jets swooping in. Canisters were dropped that ruptured upon hitting the ground and then ignited into a hellish mass of orange flame that sucked the oxygen out of the air. It was napalm, developed in World War II by a Harvard professor and first tested on an athletic field near Harvard Business School.

Napalm got its name from the combination of the chemical agents—naphthenic acid and palmitic acid—that thickened the fuel into a jelly-like mass. The stuff stuck to a surface, in some cases a human body, and kept burning. Napalm had been used extensively against the Japanese in World War II and was most effective against bunkers, caves and tunnels.

"We were only a couple of hundred feet away. The napalm sent balls of flames 300 feet into the air. We were so close that I felt a burn on my skin and face," Davidson said.

During the melee, machine gunners became critically low on ammo. Battalion headquarters sent a crew into Hue to get more, and they happened across Lieutenant Gerald Kennedy, whose Military Police unit was guarding a house occupied by some Catholic nuns. Kennedy had extra ammo in his jeep, and he headed off to the battle site.

"These guys were frantic. They needed ammo. We scrounged up what we could and took off. We stopped at battalion headquarters, and they told us we needed to get it up to the guys. Well, how do we get there? They said to take the road until you come to a dirt trail. On the way, we could hear gunfire. They didn't alert us about that. The closer we got, the louder it got. Firing became more intense. We drove another 200 to 300 yards, unloaded the ammo and they asked us if we could get more. Then we saw a jet rolling in and we witnessed a napalm run. That stuff burns everything in its path," Kennedy said. "We take off, still under fire, and a mortar round goes off about 10 to 15 meters on the left side of the jeep. It was loud. All three of us felt the concussion. We were lucky."

Having made this emergency ammo run under harrowing conditions, Kennedy, his driver and the machine gunner were put in for Silver Stars. But he said the unit of the 101st Airborne that was in charge of decorations downgraded it to three Bronze Stars. "We made do," Kennedy said. "We were all there together with one job."

The entrenched enemy force was too powerful for one or two companies to subdue. At 4 o'clock in the afternoon, all elements were directed to break contact and return back across the canal to reach battalion headquarters. The withdrawal was no less dangerous than the initial charge.

Paul Headley received the Bronze Star for helping the wounded get out of the trap. Because he spoke French, Richard Davidson was placed in charge of a blindfolded prisoner. While crossing the bridge, both he and the POW were knocked into the canal but managed to make it back. Under fire, Tommy Locastro made it back too.

"They were shooting everybody who crossed the bridge, so I crawled across the bottom of the canal with my radio on. Bullets kept coming at us. I made it to the far side and crawled up the muddy bank," Locastro said. "It was insane. Don't ask me how I didn't get whacked."

In addition to James Adams and Joe Cassidy, killed in action the first day at the Candy Stripe were: Private Eugene Small, 23, of Palatka, Florida, recipient of the

Silver Star; Specialist William Goodheart, 21, of Brooklyn, New York; Private First Class Willie Grant Jr. of Los Angeles, California; and Sergeant Abelardo Vera, 24, of Brownsville, Texas.

In the March 20 entry of his journal, Locastro wrote: "One hell of a day. Almost got killed. Lost six people and a lot wounded. Enemy was everywhere. BAD DAY. Could not run across bridge so had to swim under it. What a mess it was. I was so tired after all day and night. Fighting started at 2 a.m. and stopped at 7:30 p.m."

To keep the enemy forces from melting away, the area was pounded all night by artillery, attack jets and helicopter gunships.

Meanwhile, when the original ambush touched off a day-long battle, Bravo Company of the 1st Battalion was alerted to move from its location on an island in the Perfume River to reinforce Alpha and Charlie.

"They asked for volunteers, but there was no need to. We're the 82nd Airborne. We're a band of brothers," said Gordon Day. "I'm an Indian, but I'm closer to the guys in the 82nd than I am with people in my own tribe. About 75 of us saddled up. I've never met a braver bunch of young men in my life. They talk about the Greatest Generation, but they better never forget these kids. They were great too."

Day was his company's troubleshooter. Wherever he was needed, he went, often taking the point. On one occasion, he witnessed a napalm strike and marveled at the accuracy of those doing the bombing.

"The best pilots in the world are Marines. They take basic training, just like the grunts," Day said.

But Day had pushed too far forward. As the billowing mass of flame ignited, he pressed his face into the dirt, but the exposed half of his face was seared, and one eye was burned shut. The napalm also scorched his lungs.

At another point, Day and his unit came across a bunker, and one of his comrades was about to heave a grenade into it when Day screamed for him to stop.

"I heard a baby cry. I had kids, so I know what a baby sounds like at two o'clock in the morning. Sure enough, there were six women and a baby in that hole," Day said.

Day and his blood brother, John Plunkard, also took out a machine gun position. Day was grazed on both thighs by a machine gun round that was a half-inch in diameter.

In a letter to his family written on March 21, Johnny Plunkard gave a summary of the first day of fighting:

"Yesterday, A Company ran into a regiment size of NVAs not more than a mile from their camp. C Company went to help, and both got pinned down so we were called to go help. They got hit at 4:30 by mortars and we got there about 7:00. We got our asses tore up. I think we had 9 killed and 30 some wounded. It lasted 13 hours and was continuous. We pulled back last night about 5 p.m. I captured five prisoners yesterday and beat the hell out of 2. I think one of them won't make it. I could care less. I thought for sure that we were goners. We got cut off from the platoon while we were checking a bunker. They hit us from three sides and the platoon pulled back about 75 yards. I guess they thought we were dead, but we fooled 'em. We laid up there for almost four hours. I've never been so scared in my life. We counted 20 NVA dead, but I know there's more. I saw some awful things yesterday. Guys getting shot in the legs, stomach and head…I was so scared last night that I couldn't sleep. They bombed and had artillery in there all night. We're supposed to go in there this afternoon again. My nerves are shot to hell. I can't stop shaking. I guess everybody else is the same way. Looks like I'm gonna have nightmares again—bad ones like everybody else here."

From Bud Bolling's point of view, March 20 went down as follows: "The 1st Battalion did a tremendous job on horrible terrain. We were up against maybe 800 to 900 people. The enemy at times was as close as four feet away. This was not like the hill to hill fighting in Korea."

One of the brigade commander's duties was to attend a nightly staff meeting at headquarters of the 101st Airborne at Camp Eagle. There, Bolling was asked for a body count.

"The biggest fake ever perpetrated by mankind is the body count. Lots of people blamed Westmoreland for it. General Westmoreland would never have dreamed up anything like that. It wasn't the kind of person he was. Besides, he didn't do too well in math when he was at the Citadel or West Point. That would've been the last thing he thought of. It galled me to see him get the blame. That was McNamara, another Whiz Kid. He was really intelligent, but as the world knows, we killed the entire population of North Vietnam four times over!" Bolling said with an emphasis on overstatement.

He figured his troops had killed scores of enemy that day, but nobody was in a position to count bodies. Besides, the NVA and Viet Cong dragged their dead from the battlefield and tried not to leave anyone behind. In the Buddhist tradition, a corpse cannot be reincarnated if it's not buried properly. At any rate, Bolling was greeted by a staff officer.

"What's your body count?" the officer asked.

"I don't know. I saw three or four, maybe as high as 10," he replied.

"Give me a body count."

"Three."

"I can't tell that to General Barsanti. He'll kill me."

"Tell him I gave it to you."

"Can you give me a commander's estimate?"

"The commander's estimate is a whole bunch."

On the second day, a two-pronged assault was planned along the northern and southern banks of the canal. If an Airborne unit makes contact, it is taught to maintain contact and press the attack. In the Airborne, the infantryman is the weapon.

A regrouped Alpha Company would move south of the Candy Stripe to sweep east on the north bank of the canal. Bravo Company of the 508th Parachute Infantry

Regiment, which had been held in reserve, would cross a different bridge and attack east on the south bank. This time, tanks and an armored cavalry platoon on loan from the 101st Airborne would provide additional support.

As dawn broke on March 21, Bravo Company took fire from a bunker before it could cross the bridge, and one of its troopers fell dead. In what was less than ideal tank country, the metal monsters slogged across the marshy ground. A round from a tank's main gun eliminated the fire coming from an enemy bunker. The tank was too heavy to cross the bridge, but Bravo Company moved across one platoon at a time to get into position.

Troops quickly discovered the reason for the fierce opposition. The enemy had built a fighting trench, reinforced with bunkers and overhead cover, that extended for more than three miles along the entire length of the canal. Every 300 yards or so, escape trenches had been dug perpendicular to the main position. For much of the day, artillery and planes pounded the fortifications.

It may have been the jet age, but one aircraft that troops came to appreciate was the Air Force Skyraider. Powered by a piston engine, the single-seat airplane was optimized for close air support and had been in service since 1945. Its top feature was its ability to do more than zoom over a battlefield.

"I always liked the Skyraiders. They could loiter over a target," said Tom Wallace, the former forestry student at Penn State University.

Those listed as killed in action from Wallace's Bravo Company that day were Sergeant Charles Edward McGee, 22, of Marks, Mississippi, and Staff Sergeant Ronald Clifford Fransen, 21, of Eagle Bend, Minnesota. Alpha Company lost Gilbert Hernandez-Carrion, 27, of New York City. He is buried at the Municipal Cemetery in Manati, Puerto Rico.

At one point, circumstances allowed Charlie Company commander Paul Davin to eat a meal from a tray perched atop his jeep. An armored personnel carrier rumbled by, carrying the body of a trooper killed in the fighting. The corpse had been mutilated by the wounds of war.

"That was the only time I ever puked. This kid was just all shot up. I went through his pockets for personal effects and removed a ring from his finger. I gave it to the First Sergeant to make sure it got back with the body," Davin said.

The number of enemy dead was unknowable. Again, Bolling was unable to provide a definitive body count when he reported to 101st Airborne headquarters.

"You're relieved," General Barsanti barked.

"OK, I'm relieved. Where do I go?" Bolling replied.

The flash of temper quickly passed.

"No, you're not relieved," Barsanti said. But he insisted that the Golden Brigade start providing better numbers.

The rifle companies engaged in the fighting at the Candy Stripe took up night defensive positions. Troops formed a circle with guards posted all night in the event of a counterattack.

On March 22, the push to the east began anew. To extract the wounded, the helicopters buzzed over the area. One was flown by Chief Warrant Officer Thomas Purser, the most experienced pilot in the brigade. He landed under heavy fire, and the bird's occupants left the aircraft and stayed on the ground to allow five wounded men to be flown to an aid station. For his valor under heavy fire, Purser was awarded the Distinguished Flying Cross.

Bolling's primary mission that third day was retrieving the body of James Adams. The brigade still lacked a Graves Registration officer, who would have been tasked with the job of recovering a fallen soldier and preparing him for the final journey. The Golden Brigade took care its own.

In the effort to retrieve Adams, Bolling placed a demolitions expert aboard his helicopter. An established enemy tactic was to sabotage a body with booby traps, which would inflict damage on those who came to get it. For support in what might be a hot landing zone, Bolling also enlisted the services of a tank that would provide support on the ground.

"We had to fight back to find Jim Adams' body. The plan was to fly into fire, throw the body on the helicopter and get out of there fast to take it to the hospital," Bolling said.

The body was found wrapped in a poncho liner and was recovered without incident. A Boy Scout and an outdoorsman, James Robert Adams, 23, of Bartow, Florida, originally attended the U.S. Air Force Academy before enrolling at West Point. Older than his fellow cadets, he was on the boxing team at the academy. One of his tactics was to invite opponents to wade in before he unloaded his thunderous left hook.

After graduation but before deployment to Vietnam, he had married a nurse at the academy hospital. Now Barbara Adams was a war widow. An astrologist, she had told him that he would come home alive if he made it past March 15. The stars did not align in his favor, however.

Adams is buried in the cemetery at West Point. Of the 335 West Pointers who died in the Vietnam War, Adams was the first of the Class of 1967 to die in combat. The words of the academy's alma mater echo through the years: "And when our work is done, Our course on Earth is run, May it be said, 'Well done: Be Thou at Peace.' "

The oldest daughter of his sister Patti named her son James Adams Stewart in his honor. His legacy lives on in a new generation.

The Candy Stripe had cost nine All American lives, all of them clustered together on Panel 45 East on The Wall. More than two dozen soldiers had been wounded. For that price in blood, Barsanti got his body count. After action reports noted that the Golden Brigade had killed 109 hostile forces, captured six prisoners, destroyed a base camp, eliminated a fortified trench and captured four tons of rice.

Late on afternoon of March 22, with the dead recovered and the guns having fallen silent, the brigade was ordered to move to their next mission. They were relieved by an element of Marines.

Mike Hood remembered turning over the terrain to a Marine company, which was commanded by an officer who had graduated from the U.S. Navy Academy the year before he left West Point. Hood briefed the Marine officer before moving on.

"So we left. We're going north. Two days later, the chaplain came to see me and asked if I remembered that group of Marines. I said, 'Sure.' He said the kids that went in there had just got in the country. They put 50 men in my sector where I had 20. They took three mortar rounds that night and took 27 casualties," Hood said.

For Joe Mays, giving up the ground his troops had just fought so hard to take went against the grain of conventional warfare. It happened all the time in Vietnam.

"In Officer Candidate School, we were taught that you don't win a war until you occupy the land. If I knew then what I know now…," Mays said. "It's easy to say now why we didn't win that war. We didn't really understand the Vietnamese people. Most westerners think of life as linear. You're born, go to school, get a job, get married, raise a family and you die. Most Asians see life as circular. A lot of them believe you come back again. If it's their time to die, it's their time. If it's not their time, nothing's going to happen to them. We don't have a clue about how those people think. Ho Chi Minh said the North will just keep coming, that we will get tired of this war before they do. Could we have defeated them if we went north? We'll never know. We never elected to send ground troops into the North."

Meanwhile, in a letter written on March 23, John Plunkard told his folks:

"Well, we got our first big firefight over with under our belts. We took a hell of a beating, but we gave one too. Yesterday, we went back after a body we had to leave when we pulled back. I actually had to hold back the tears. It hurt like hell to see something like that. I think everybody else felt the same too. There were so many NVA bodies I didn't even bother to count. We're still set up down the road from the village, and when the wind blows this way, you can smell the dead. It's so bad that every time I open a can of C Rations, I gag. Hell, I'm losing weight like mad because of this. My pot gut is fading fast. Guess I'll have to put something on my nose so I can eat or I'm going to starve to death. I don't know how long we'll be set up here, but I hope it's not much longer. Last night I took my fire team to the water point all night. They think the gooks are gonna try and knock it out sometime soon, along with the bridge. I'm glad it wasn't last night."

Hell had indeed broken loose. It was as if the forces of the underworld were freed from eternal damnation to roam the Golden Brigade's sector of Vietnam. At Camp Rodriguez, the fallen were remembered in a ceremony called Empty Boots, in which a soldier's rifle is stuck into the ground with a bayonet between his combat boots, and his combat helmet is placed atop the butt of his rifle. Many an infantryman with wings on his chest prayed to Michael the Archangel, the patron saint of paratroopers, to care for the dead. According to legend, Michael was the winged warrior who descended into Hell to battle Lucifer's legions. More solemn ceremonies and more encounters with Hell would follow.

Chapter 10
STAND DOWN

The soothing blue waters of the South China Sea had a curative quality. The saltwater killed off ringworm, jungle rot and other tropical pests that attack a human host. The waters also healed the nicks and cuts a soldier endures while crawling through the bush. The gentle motion of the waves, as comforting as a mother's heartbeat, calmed nerves after a life-or-death battle. Tommy Locastro experienced such a setting the day after Charlie Company's intense fight at the Candy Stripe. The adrenaline that floods through a man's system begins to wane. The fear a soldier puts aside creeps back into the consciousness.

"It's the day after when you get the heebie-jeebies and your hands start to shake," Locastro said.

From the crucible of combat, Charlie Company was moved to a Navy facility known as Col Co Beach for a rare stand down. Troops were served hot meals cooked in Navy kitchens, and given the benefits of Navy know-how when it comes to building camps, troops could watch movies projected onto an outdoor screen.

In a journal entry of March 22, Locastro noted: "Nice morning and a real fine place with everything, even movies. Good food. Lobster and all. Navy always has good food. Hope I never leave this place."

Richard Davidson also appreciated a day at a sandy beach after the Hell he and his comrades had just gone through.

"We were there a day or so to lick our wounds and reorganize," Davidson said.

Davidson had been wearing a Buddhist necklace he picked up somewhere along the way, but he gave it away to one of the locals. He replaced it with a Catholic item called a scapular that his grandmother had mailed him. Made of two patches of cloth linked together with strings, the scapular assures the wearer that he is protected by God's grace, and that even if one under such protection is killed, he will not burn in the fires of Hell. Because it is made of cloth, a scapular also had the practical advantage of not making noise. Davidson thought of it as his way of putting his life in the hands of a higher power.

"I'm sure God protected me because of that," Davidson said.

Lieutenant Colonel John G. Jameson, commander of the 1st Battalion of the 505th, recalled that the installation at Col Co Beach even had cold milk and ice cream. In the tropics, the Navy found a way to convert reconstituted milk into ice cream.

"The Seabees said they were glad to see us. The Marines who had been there before had a contest to see who could go the longest without a shower, and they all won," Jameson said with a wry touch of humor.

The battalion commander also recalled the time he retrieved a vehicle that the Marines had pilfered.

"Somebody stole the chaplain's jeep. I was in the air and landed the chopper when I saw it. It still had the 82nd's markings on it. I said to this lieutenant, 'I gotta take that jeep back.' He says, 'I can't let you do that.' The next sound I heard was the charging handle sliding back on an M-16. My Command Sergeant Major Jerry Mitchell says in a calm voice, 'We're taking the jeep.' That was that. We got our jeep back," Jameson said.

The stand down ended too quickly. The company was transported back to the sights and sounds of a Third World country that served as a backdrop to war.

Locastro remembered a time when he and one of the medics, Raymond "Doc" Johnson of Hamilton, Ohio, went to a village to patch up some civilians, and following normal practice, handed out candy to the kids. "The VC had killed a lot of people and tortured others. Spent all night putting them back together. Doc is a fine person to these people," Locastro said.

One scene made a lasting impression on Davidson. Riding in a truck loaded with G.I.'s, he remembered seeing a group of villagers slaughtering a water buffalo on the side of the road. They collected the beast's blood in buckets to use in their meals, then divided the butchered animal.

The roads were always packed with displaced civilians, whose homes in Hue or in the surrounding villages had been destroyed by war. The pathetic lot had no place to stay and no place to go. With their economic system shattered by conflict, the civilians eked out an existence as sellers on the black market. They sold their wares to those who had money—the American soldier.

All kinds of goods were available. Little girls sold cans of Coca-Cola that were available in the field almost as fast as they could be pilfered from the supply docks of nearby shipping ports. The profits from these sales were often shared with the Viet Cong, which completed an ironic circle in which Americans were financing the war against themselves.

Villagers sold food such as loaves of bread and steamed rice, a welcome change from Army rations. One French influence on the Vietnamese culture was that the locals became experts in making baguettes. The local entrepreneurs also offered everything and anything that would appeal to an American teenager in his hormonal prime—pornographic pictures, sexual favors, booze and marijuana.

Davidson recalled one man offering a bottle of Vietnamese booze for $20. A paratrooper offered half that, and when the man wouldn't come down in price, the soldier swiped the bottle without paying a cent. The sequence led to an incident at a brothel run out of a tent just off Highway One.

Davidson was back in the company area when a lieutenant ordered him to go find two sergeants, one of which happened to be the guy who swiped the jug of alcohol. One of the first places he looked was the brothel, where the world's oldest profession did a brisk business.

"There were a couple of Australian soldiers who were playing cards with the whores. The pimp who ran the place was up the road somewhere. One of the Australians, who thought the whores were cheating at cards, fired his weapon in the air. Our sergeants were in the back room. One of them ran out and loaded his grenade launcher and was going to fire. The pimp came running in, and there was stand-off. I didn't say nothing to nobody. I just convinced our guys to get out of there because we were going on another mission," Davidson.

Another time, one of Davidson's buddies bought five joints of something for $10. Davidson, the friend and another buddy smoked whatever it was while they were still on stand down. Whether it was opium or marijuana or something else, Davidson took part and remembers being embarrassed at the effect it had on him. He vowed never to smoke reefer in the field, something that became an unofficial code of conduct.

"We couldn't take that chance with drugs in a combat zone," Davidson said.

Officers such as Bud Bolling and plenty of enlisted men swear they never once saw a drug in Vietnam. In a combat unit, soldiers were almost always on missions and had neither the access nor the desire to purchase the stuff. But no history of Vietnam could be authentic without the acknowledgement that reefer was available.

"It was cheap, easy to get and potent," said Tommy Locastro.

In his journal, he mentioned smoking pot, but that was only at a base camp. "The code was simple. Don't get messed up in the field. If you're in a rear area, do your thing," Locastro said.

Marijuana was as much a part of the Baby Boom generation as rock music. In fact, the musicians of the day thought of the mind-changing substance as an alternative to booze and was something that made the music sound better. If it existed in the civilian world, it existed in the microcosm of military life.

Captain James Slavin, a battalion surgeon, told an anecdote about how he smoked marijuana by accident. There were two Special Forces teams located near the 82nd Airborne, and one day, one of the Green Berets asked to borrow the doctor's jeep. When he returned, he volunteered that he had gotten his hands on some weed and asked Slavin if he wanted any. Slavin could have turned the solider in and have him locked up in the stockade for possession of an illegal substance. Instead, he took a joint and put it into his pack of unfiltered Lucky Strike cigarettes.

"I'm smoking two packs a day at the time. Then we get word of an officer's call, and while I was waiting inside the tent, I pulled a smoke from a pack and lit it up. I'm sitting there by myself, and an officer comes in and asks, 'Who's smoking pot in here?' It dawned on me that I lit up the wrong cigarette. I thought any second now that he would tackle me from behind. He was a guy who carried a baseball bat as a swagger stick. I put it out, and he never said another word," Slavin said.

Lieutenant Joe Mays said he knew of only one person who smoked marijuana in Vietnam. That was his brother, who was stationed at the sprawling Bien Hoa military base outside of Saigon.

"He told me he did," Mays said. "But I do believe that our guys self-policed themselves and didn't use any drug in the field. You had to be able to count on the guy to your left or to your right."

John Lukas of the cavalry unit steered clear of the stuff himself but knew that it was around.

"It was available, but it was more available in Bragg than in Vietnam," Lukas said.

Mark Robertson, also in the cavalry unit, said the first time he saw marijuana was at jump school at Fort Benning.

"One of the guys had a joint that he got in the mail. He lit it up as a challenge to see if we could handle this stuff, but there were 10 of us, so I don't think anybody got much of a high," he said.

Robertson also said that some of the combat veterans who returned to Vietnam with the 82nd Airborne got hold of the local product soon after arriving at Chu Lai. They called the stuff *dien cai dau* cigarettes, which was pronounced dinky dow and was the local word for crazy.

"The fairy tale story isn't necessarily the truth. There were juicers who drank beer and whiskey, and there were heads who smoked pot," Robertson said. "Vietnam turned me off to beer. The stuff they gave us tasted like melted aluminum after the cans made the journey by ship across the ocean and then sat outside in the sun. Smoking was mostly a social thing. You could chill out, listen to music or celebrate with your buddies because we made it through another day. It was never done on duty. Always at base camp. One time the sergeant came around and said, 'Guys are smoking dope, and we have to put a stop to it.' I told him I'd help in any way I can. I was higher than a kite at the time."

Soldiers who did partake used it for the same reasons marijuana was legalized 50 years later for medicinal purposes in 22 states and for recreational purposes in eight states. The active ingredients of a substance that grew in the ground settled nerves. In an environment of butchery and savagery, where an individual survived from minute to minute, it was an outlet that took the edge off. They weren't all saints. Never claimed to be. But they weren't all sinners either. They were 19-year-olds trying to survive in an alternate universe that was not of their making. Without the mandatory drug-testing in today's modern Army, it's impossible to say how many soldiers smoked pot in Vietnam. But in a combat unit like the 82nd Airborne, machine gun teams were not manned by

Cheech and Chong either. Marijuana use certainly didn't approach the levels of college students smoking dope back in The World.

Anyway, by the beginning of April, Charlie Company moved to a location northwest of Hue to support operations of the 101st Airborne. The area was defined by a system of waterways and canals around the Song Bo River. Intelligence reports noted that the hostile forces were regrouping for another attack on Hue, and the waterways were their access routes.

One thing that stayed with Richard Davidson was a conversation he overheard involving his buddy, Leo Brent Gunning.

"He had called his mother and told her he had a premonition that he was going to die and wasn't coming back. I gave him shit for it. You don't say something like that to your mother," Davidson said.

Chapter 11
LIFE SAVER

Andrew Blais found refuge under Sergeant John Plunkard's wing as their rifle company kept up the daily slog of combing the ground for signs of the enemy. Plunkard protected him on more than one occasion.

"Our mission was to get into contact, contact, contact. Fight them until they disperse. We were always moving. I never dug a fox hole in Vietnam. Just move, move, move, and sleep on the ground. And I always slept with my rifle across my chest with two bandoliers of ammunition," Blais said. "I'd ask John, 'How come it's always us that has to go on these missions?' He said, 'It's our turn. That's all.' I was scared shitless, but I said to myself, 'I gotta do what I gotta do.' "

Blais carried his dog tags in his pocket rather than around his neck. The metal tags were shiny and noisy. Instead, he too wore the Catholic scapular and thought of it as spiritual protection.

"I was the point man as we were entering this village. There was a narrow patch over a stream that was maybe 20 to 30 feet wide. My eyes are ahead. Then I heard John say, 'Stop! Stop!' He spotted another freaking trip wire. That guy saved my life again," Blais said.

"Another time, we were in an abandoned village. There was a two-story building, which was unusual in a village of single story huts, and it had a commanding view of the countryside. I thought to myself it would be a good place to hole up, to be dry for one night."

Plunkard insisted that the squad take up positions elsewhere.

"All of a sudden, a big firefight breaks out. John says I'm going to take a look, and when he said something like that, he was gone. Turns out, the enemy had charged that building. They thought we were in there. That could have been me. John then explained that the reason you don't go up on the second floor is you can't get out. This guy was saving my life," Blais said.

One time, Plunkard's fire team guarded a trail at night. In the inky darkness, eight to 10 enemy soldiers went by.

"You couldn't see your hand in front of your face. I could have reached my hand out and tripped them. We radioed it in, and five to 10 minutes later, the artillery was blasting. That really shook us up. We were in a low spot. All I remember was that one round actually flipped me on my back. I had drops of blood coming out of my ear from the impact. Couldn't hear anything. John snuck around and took out another gun.

That's how brave he was. In the middle of one firefight, he tapped me on my helmet and signaled to lower my fire. I was shooting high."

Another time, the fire team was out on night patrol.

"I'm in the back this time, and somehow, I fell and tumbled off the trail. The squad kept going and now I'm all alone. A strange calmness washed over me. I wasn't going to run. I said, 'This is the 82nd Airborne, they ain't leaving me behind.' I never lost faith in them. Sure enough, 15 minutes later, they came back for me."

Jimmy Barnes had a fire team in the same squad, and he and Plunkard had become fast friends. Barnes had been shot in the left hip during his previous tour in Vietnam with the 1st Cavalry Division, and Plunkard had been wounded in the hip during his previous tour with the 173rd Airborne. While each of them had played high school football, their bond was their hip wounds.

"You get a hot round put through your ass and it dawns on you that you could get screwed up over here," Barnes said.

Plunkard made a strong impression on Barnes.

"He was fearless. He was John Wayne. I was Sergeant Rock," Barnes said. The latter was a reference to Sergeant Franklin (Frank) John Rock, a fictional character depicted in DC Comics books. A civilian who hailed from the two-fisted steel town of Pittsburgh, Rock was the battle-hardened leader of Suicide Squad in Easy Company. Sergeant Rock shot down German fighter planes, lobbed grenades with unerring accuracy and had a sixth sense about World War II combat.

Barnes remembers the time Plunkard voiced a desire about confronting a Soviet-made jet flown by a North Vietnamese pilot.

"I wish a MiG would come down and strafe us," Plunkard said.

"Why would you want that?"

"I've been to Red-Eye school."

A Red-Eye was an early version of a surface to air missile system that an infantryman could carry. The precursor of the Stinger missile, it gave the infantryman a way to bring down an enemy aircraft. Even though Plunkard didn't have a Red-Eye with him, he would have welcomed the chance to use one in combat.

During his first tour, Barnes fought North Vietnamese troops in the Central Highlands and gained a measure of respect for their tenacity and their tactics. His opinion changed in the fighting outside of Hue.

"I could see fighting in the mountains, their troops against our troops. But fighting in villages with all those civilians around? I lost all respect for them. They didn't care how many people got killed, and they made us look like the bad guys," Barnes said.

Barnes recalled coming across an occupied bunker. He pulled the pin on one of his grenades and was about to toss it inside when he heard a baby cry. Inside were 18 women and kids. He put the pin back in the grenade.

The strangest sights could be seen in the villages.

"I saw a baby who was dressed in a shirt but didn't wear underwear. When it would take a shit, the mama-san would call over one of the village dogs and have it lick the baby's bottom. These people were almost in the Stone Age," Barnes said. "Look, the guy behind the water buffalo just wanted to plow his rice paddy and feed his family and be left alone. The worst thing I ever saw was an old guy in a rice paddy with his leg shot off. He was holding up his identification card crying, 'No VC. No VC.' I asked myself, What the hell are we doing over here?' "

One of the All Americans who fought shoulder-to-shoulder with Plunkard, and who was mentioned in his letters home, was his Mohawk blood brother Gordon Day.

"John was like the little brother I never had," Day said.

On March 26, Plunkard wrote a revealing letter home on what it was like to be in this environment and the insanity of this war:

"Received your letter this morning. Our mail situation hasn't been the best in the world, but it's better than none at all. We're still here at this schoolhouse. It's beginning to look like a mud hole. For the past 48 hours, it's done nothing but rain. I'm in a bunker now with about six inches of water in the bottom. We've got sandbags and ammo boxes in here so we can stand on. A lot of good it does. We're still wet as hell. My feet have turned white and shriveled all up. None of us have taken a bath for two weeks now and talk about stink! If I were to take my fatigues off, they'd stand up by themselves. They've got so much mud and grime on them. You can almost see mold forming on them, ha ha.

"I wish I could write to you more often, but there's nothing to write about except the fighting and we're doing so much of that let alone write about it. All I can say is it's worse now than it was the last time I was here and steadily increasing…I did a terrible thing yesterday. I shot another gook—a woman. Day spotted her and when we tried to stop her, she turned around and ran. We had been receiving small arms fire all day from where she came from. I yelled for her to stop in Vietnamese, but she kept on going. I know she heard me. We fired a warning shot, but she kept going so I had no alternative but to drop her. I hope she never felt it. I feel bad as hell about it cause she had no weapon, but our orders were to shoot anybody who ran. The third squad got a man with a NVA weapon. The bastards are on the other side of a canal and there's no way we can get to them without getting an ass whipping. They're dug in too well. Artillery and air strikes don't affect them at all."

Meanwhile, April 1 marked the beginning of Operation Carentan II. The mission was still the same—to take the fight to the enemy—but the focus of the effort had shifted to the northwest of Hue.

Plunkard's company received orders to move to the east side of the Song Sia River. One tributary that branched off from the main waterway was the Song Bo River, a meandering flow that hostile forces used as a conduit. On a map, the serpentine

Song Bo looked like the loops of a letter in the alphabet. The Airborne called it the Lazy W.

John Plunkard wrote another letter home on March 31 and mentioned the movement:

"Dear Mom, Dad and Joe:

"Well, today was payday. It seems like everybody's morale came up better. I know mine did. For the past two weeks, it's gone from bottom to rock bottom. We'll be pulling out tomorrow. We're going on the other side of Hue. I think we're gonna act as a blocking force. There's supposed to be an NVA division moving towards Hue. From all reports, Hue is supposed to get hit hard again."

Back in The World on March 31, President Lyndon Johnson stunned the nation in a televised speech. Six weeks after ordering the Golden Brigade to Vietnam with a promise to support them until their duty was done, Johnson announced his personal withdrawal from the war he had escalated. Having once said the Air Force "couldn't bomb an outhouse without my approval," Johnson ordered a partial bombing halt over North Vietnam and said the United States was open to peace talks "to discuss the means of bringing this ugly war to an end." But in LBJ's own words, wars are easier to get into than get out of. In his televised speech, Johnson also announced that he was terminating his re-election bid, saying, "I shall not seek, and I will not accept, the nomination of my party for another term as your president." It was called LBJ's renunciation speech or his withdrawal speech. Historian Doris Kearns Goodwin called it Johnson's abdication. Johnson had told her the real reason for sending U.S. troops to Southeast Asia: "If I left the war and let the Communists take over South Vietnam, then I would be seen as a coward and my nation would be seen as an appeaser."

Chapter 12
DEADLIEST DAY

Richard Underwood and his second platoon in Charlie Company were patrolling five miles northwest of Hue along a river plain dotted with villages. One day, in the calm of the early afternoon, troops took advantage of a chance to rinse off layers of grime, grunge and sweat while being ever mindful of the blood-sucking leeches that abounded in tropical wetlands.

"We had stopped by a river. We didn't get a bath every night, so we went skinny dipping," Underwood recalled.

Just as Underwood's men were putting their jungle fatigues back on, word came to saddle up. Charlie Company, just weeks removed from the fierce fight along the Candy Stripe, had orders to load onto a string of helicopters to set up a blocking position around a village. For the record, the place was called Ap Nam Phu, located on the west bank of the northward-flowing Song Sia River, but few knew it by name.

"It was just another village to us," Underwood said.

The plan was for Charlie Company to land north of the village and set up a blocking position. Then a company from the 101st Airborne would push up from the south the following morning. In the previous three days, using the same cordon and clear tactics, the Screaming Eagles had fought a series of engagements in the same general area. With the support of air strikes and artillery barrages, they had counted the bodies of at least 38 North Vietnamese soldiers, discovered an abandoned field hospital and seized several tons of rice.

The date was April 4. What might have been any other Thursday became the bloodiest single day for the Golden Brigade in Vietnam, a day remembered for 10 Gold Star families and eight Silver Stars.

While Underwood's men loaded up for an air assault, the other two platoons of Charlie Company assembled from different locations to consolidate into a single entity. Third platoon boarded helicopters at Fire Base Geronimo, named for the last Native American chief to surrender to the U.S. Army and the name shouted by World War II paratroopers when they jumped from a plane. Among them was 19-year-old Salome Beltran, all 5-foot-2 and 115 pounds of him.

"We knew there was a possibility of contact, but every day was bad. It was 24 hours a day, seven days a week," Beltran said.

A native of Watsonville, California, Beltran was the oldest of 11 children and the grandson of Spanish immigrants who had first settled in Texas and used mule power to eke out a living delivering firewood. Beltran's father had encouraged him to serve his country,

"Nobody in my family had ever been in service. My dad said, 'Junior, I want you to join the Army, to give something back for the privileges we have to be Americans.' It was the best thing I ever did," Beltran said. An Army sergeant later encouraged him to become a paratrooper, and given that Beltran was making $79 a month as a soldier, the extra $55 a month in jump pay sweetened the deal.

Aboard the chopper, with blades pounding out their rhythmic thumps while the wind rushed through the open doors, Beltran performed a ritual he did before every mission. He prayed the Hail Mary.

Meanwhile, Tommy Locastro remembered being in and around Camp Evans, a place built by the 101st Airborne near an old French fort. He wrote in his diary, "A lot of shit around here. A lot of North Vietnamese regulars. We're in an old French camp. Here we are 15 years later, still fighting the same people. What brains does it take to know we shouldn't be here?" Then, serving as radio operator for Charlie Company's commander Paul Davin, he loaded onto a helicopter that was headed for Ap Nam Phu.

As the first ones in, first platoon touched down in a dry rice paddy about 150 yards north of the village. A thin line of trees separated the village from the rice fields, and earthen dikes lined the ground to separate one paddy from another. The platoon deployed and moved forward, but in what would later be seen as an oversight, the artillery of the 101st Airborne neglected to prep the area with its big guns. The concealed enemy allowed the platoon to get close, then sniper shots and a later volley of gunfire erupted from the tree line, followed by the grumble of a machine gun on the left flank. Within moments, first platoon had dead and wounded all over the ground, according to machine gunner Paul Headley.

"That's a day I'll never forget. There were 30 of us spread out over an area the size of a football field in rice paddies that were laid out in a pattern like you see in cranberry bogs. The village was straight in front of us. They opened up. It was like organized chaos. We split up. There was firing back and forth. Everybody was seeking cover. A shot hit me and knocked me down, but it hit me in the canteen, so I was OK," Headley said.

Platoon leader Larry Kocher was less fortunate. An enemy bullet struck the rucksack in which the lieutenant carried his signal flares, and the pack ignited. As Kocher raised up to remove the burning pack, a bullet ripped through the back of his arm and shredded his triceps muscle.

His radioman, Private First Class Robert Joseph Moore of Morristown, New Jersey, was shot through the throat and fatally wounded. He was identified later by what he wore around his neck—a scarf with a floral pattern that his girlfriend had sent him for luck. Moore, 20, had kept the radio going long enough under such chaotic conditions that he received a Silver Star.

Two medics rushed forward to aid the wounded. Both were killed by enemy forces ruthless enough to know that a unit's morale would plunge if the care-providers were hit. One was Specialist Daniel Guardado, a 21-year-old draftee from Santa Ana, California. The other was Specialist Raymond Junior Johnson, 22, of Hamilton, Ohio, who had hoped to become a doctor when he returned to The World. Both of them received the Silver Star for attempting to treat wounded comrades while under fire.

Meanwhile, Paul Headley opened up at what was shooting at him.

"We were behind a dike, and there was this guy shaking like a dog trying to pass peach pits. He went nuts. He was saying, 'Fire, fire!' I wondered why he wasn't firing. Kocher was right next to me. I said, 'Sir, you better get the hell out of here and have that wound treated.' He wouldn't leave us. He wanted to stay with his men to direct the battle. One of the commanders was above in a helicopter and was telling him over the radio, 'Move up. Move up.' I heard Kocher tell him, 'Why don't you come the fuck down here if you want to fight this battle?' It was a crazy mess," Headley said.

The air snapped with bullets, and the cacophony of battle was in full roar when Richard Underwood's platoon touched down in a hot landing zone. His first thought was, "Holy shit. They're shooting at us." As his men advanced, Underwood shifted them to the right to avoid going up the backs of Kocher's platoon.

"We started moving forward. There was this berm on the edge of the village that started out at maybe six to seven feet tall and then sloped down to maybe eight inches of dirt. I said to myself, 'OK, you're in charge. You're the leader. You gotta do something.' I was more or less reacting, but I had good training. I spread my guys out and set up a perimeter. We had to suppress the fire. I shot back too, mainly out of frustration. I was just hoping I could hit one of those little bastards. One of my men, a big guy named Jessie Tabor, dove for a spider hole that was too small for him to fit into. Then a round went right between us, and we both squeezed into that little hole. We have wounded everywhere, so we started calling in medevacs."

Meanwhile, the helicopter carrying Tommy Locastro made a big bank to the left and set down in a cemetery east of the village.

"First and second platoons were getting slaughtered. I jumped off the skid into the shit. You could see bodies out there but didn't know if they were alive or not. The way the Army trains you, the only way to get out of a firefight is to run into it and eliminate the fire. We all started dragging bodies out. You could hear that thunk, thunk, thunk, of bullets hitting legs. They kept shooting the bodies," Locastro said.

The company command post was eventually established in the graveyard. Communication with the platoons was gone because their radiomen had been hit, and Locastro had the only established radio. Captain Paul Davin called in a fire mission for an artillery strike, which was dicey because the opposing forces were now so close to each other. An urgent call for helicopter gunships was also made.

At the same time, Salome Beltran's slick landed fresh troops. The plan dissolved the moment the bullets started flying.

"We were supposed to set up a blocking position and wait for them. Instead, they were waiting for us," Beltran said.

Bullets travel in a straight line, yet the dirt around Beltran's boots was boiling up. That told him the shooters were firing from elevated positions.

"Shoot the tops of the trees! Shoot the trees!" he remembered saying as he pushed forward. "There was lots of yelling and screaming. We didn't need or wait for permission to fire. What made me move up? You can't stop in a rice paddy. You'd be a sitting duck. Besides, we're Americans. We have to continue on. You get fatalistic about it. Do whatever it takes. Do it right. Get them before they get us. That's training. You don't even think about it, but that doesn't mean you're not scared."

The grand goal of the war to protect South Vietnam's freedom dissipated in the noise and chaos of a bloody melee. In reality, soldiers fought for their lives, and for the lives of their brothers to the left and to the right. Then one act of barbarity made a bad situation worse.

Jerry Shain, a sergeant from Cromwell, Kentucky, who was on his second tour, got separated from his buddies. He was surrounded and captured. His blood-curdling screams for help could be heard as he was being hacked to death with machetes wielded by North Vietnamese soldiers. A white-hot rage ignited inside the paratroopers.

"If you eat, shit and sleep with these guys every day, you get tight. And you get really pissed off if they kill one of your friends. We had a saying that we would all go in together and all come out together," said Paul Headley.

Added Salome Beltran: "You get so mad you lose your fear. We were just pissed off. A lot of the fighting was *mano-a-mano,* hand-to-hand. We were looking for some payback."

Firing as he advanced, Beltran rushed forward to start dragging back the bodies of the fallen. He leaped into a bomb crater and landed atop a wounded man, who told him to stay down. The advice saved Beltran's life because gunfire erupted on the flank seconds later. After gathering himself, Beltran moved forward again to reach the wounded. When he returned to the crater, the soldier inside it had died. For his actions in disregarding his own safety to retrieve the dead and wounded, Beltran was awarded the Silver Star.

"I didn't do anything more than a lot of other guys did. There were a lot of brave guys that day. Lots of guys didn't get enough credit, but we weren't thinking about who got credit. You don't have time to think. We were just pissed off," Beltran said. "The real heroes are the ones who didn't come back to their families, and the real heroes are the mothers and fathers, brothers and sisters, aunts and uncles, and grandparents who would never see them again. I loved these young men. They were my friends, my brothers. We were all willing to die for our country. That's why we do it. We love America. If I had a chance to do it again, I would."

Also in Beltran's platoon was Richard Davidson, who had four days left on his enlistment. In soldier's slang, he was a short-timer, a single-digit midget. Yet deposited onto a battlefield and upon hearing a faint voice cry for help, he moved forward too.

Crawling to avoid being hit, Davidson reached his platoon leader, Lieutenant Daniel Ragsdale, and the officer's radioman. Both were shot through the head. Although Ragsdale miraculously survived, his head wound robbed him of the memory portion of his brain. The radioman was killed instantly. As Davidson pressed on, he spotted an enemy soldier in a spider hole off to the side and tossed a grenade. Upon reaching a fallen comrade, Davidson failed to find a pulse, but he starting to drag the man back anyway. In a matter-of-fact tone, Davidson noted that the soldier was African American.

"He was a brother. We're the 82nd Airborne. Our blood is the same color," Davidson said.

In his attempt to evacuate the soldier, Davidson was shot. A round ripped through his right buttock, then penetrated the thigh and exited at the right groin. What's worse, another bullet smashed his left testicle, grazed his penis and hit his left thigh. As he agonized on the ground, Dave, as he was known, looked up to see his buddy, Leo Brent Gunning, crouched over him.

"Don't worry, Dave. I'll take care of you. We got in this together, and we'll get out together," Gunning told him.

Davidson blurted out, "Get down!" Before he got the second syllable out, a slug from an enemy rifle struck Gunning's head, the contents of his skull spilling onto Davidson. Gunning's premonition of death had been realized.

Two sergeants ran up to retrieve Davidson. As they did so, a mortar round exploded. Each of them was hit by 30 to 40 pieces of shrapnel while a shard of jagged metal lodged in Davidson's right arm. As daylight faded, medical assistance was urgently needed all over the field.

One helicopter gunship, piloted by Gerald Frye, fired on enemy positions until his ammunition was exhausted. Captain Davin got patched through to him on the radio and told him about the wounded. While green tracers filled the air, a flashlight was used to guide the chopper down to the ground. Amazingly, Davin recognized the pilot as a man who had shared a pitcher of beer with him a year earlier at the Officer's Club in Fort Riley, Kansas. "I told him I was going to Vietnam, and he said he was too. I said, 'Maybe I'll see you there,' but I never expected it to be under these circumstances," Davin said. "He landed in the dark to pick up our wounded. This guy risked his ass and saved a lot of guys' lives. He should have gotten the Medal of Honor."

A medevac helicopter did arrive, but it overshot its landing area and set down between Charlie Company's command post and the enemy. The chopper was shot full of holes and the pilot was hit, but the co-pilot was able to take off and whisk the wounded back to an aid station.

Among those flown from the battlefield was Larry Kocher. Although his wound was not in a fatal area, he had lost so much blood while staying in the fight that he went into shock. He died at the aid station.

"The worst part of it, and it tears me up to this day, was Kocher had a Corvette, and I had a Corvette. He was a hell of a guy. We were all just kids," Paul Headley said.

A native of West Milford, New Jersey, the 22-year-old Kocher was barely five months removed from being commissioned as an Army officer. He was survived by his wife, Karen. For his valor on the field that day, Kocher was posthumously awarded the Silver Star.

To stand its ground through the night, Charlie Company set up a night defensive position. Having run low of ammunition, troopers paired off and lay back-to-back. Some fixed bayonets. Orders were to stick anything that moved.

"That was a shitty night," Captain Davin said.

Hardly anybody slept. Enemy soldiers could be heard sneaking around in the dark. Proof of their activity was confirmed the next morning. One dead enemy had a .38 Special handgun, which was a firearm that belonged one of Charlie Company's dead. The trooper carried the handgun in his backpack, which meant the NVA soldier who stole it from his dead body had paid with his life too.

In one attempt to retrieve a fallen brother, one soldier in Richard Underwood's platoon crawled out to the body of Private First Class Michael Lee Farmer of Atlantic City, New Jersey. Farmer, 20, had been walking point when the battle erupted, and he was among the first to fall. "Somebody had a nylon rope, or Ranger rope. They tied the rope to Farmer's web gear and tried to pull him back, but the only thing that came back was his harness. It was that deadly," Underwood said.

Farmer's body was recovered at daybreak. A veteran of a previous tour in Vietnam, he was survived by his mother, two brothers and a sister. Farmer, an African American, also received the Silver Star.

Also, among those killed that awful day, and also a recipient of the Silver Star, was a cook who had been pressed into service as an infantryman because Charlie Company's strength had been depleted in previous engagements. He was food service specialist James Guerdon Signett, 18, a graduate of Indian River High School in Chesapeake, Virginia.

The oldest member of Charlie Company to die in that fight was 29-year-old Staff Sergeant Robert Gerald Elgin of San Francisco, California. The Silver Star he received was posthumously awarded to his two daughters, Kathy and Tina.

Shortly after dawn, the men of Charlie Company retrieved the rest of their dead. Some of the fallen had their throats cut. Surprisingly, there were survivors. Ron Belliott of Long Beach, California, had originally been listed as missing in action. He had fought until he fired his last bullet and then hid from the enemy during the night. A surfer, he was found alive by troopers in the 101st Airborne who swept the village in the morning.

Another man had spent a long night alone. He was a crewman on a helicopter who was ejected from his aircraft when one of its skids clipped a monument in the graveyard.

When the shooting stopped, the forces inside Ap Nam Phu had melted away. Charlie Company gathered up all its dead, wrapping the bodies in ponchos and placing them in a row to await evacuation.

"I didn't want to look because I knew I'd be looking at them the rest of my life," said Captain Davin.

In the confusion of battle, some villagers had been hit.

"One hooch took a hit from one of our grenade launchers, and a girl who was maybe 10 years old was wounded. One of the medics fixed her up. We gave her family some money. Said we were sorry. Then we moved out again," David said.

According to the after action reports, one dead NVA was found in the village and 24 others were subsequently discovered in a fresh grave. Other accounts differed. Some survivors of the battle said the villagers had already stripped the dead NVA soldiers, and body parts of others blown away by artillery or the gunships littered the ground.

"We took an ass whipping, but we gave back more than we took. Horrible things happen in war, but I'm proud of what I did that day," Salome Beltran said.

An exhausted Tom Locastro had fallen asleep that night between the bodies of the two dead medics. He remembered being kicked in the boots by his company commander.

"Are you alive, or are you dead too?" Captain Davin asked.

"I'm alive," Locastro answered.

Playing over in his mind were the details of the battle, of hearing Jerry Shain getting chopped up, of the effort to push forward to get to the dead and wounded.

"Nobody was going to let their buddies lay out there. You don't even think about it. You knew most of them. It would be a dishonor or a disgrace to leave them," Locastro said.

In his journal, Locastro wrote: "A terrible day and hope to see no more like it again. Fifty percent alert all night. Got the rest of the bodies this morning and move into a bad village. Found all kinds of shit. Blew up all the bunkers. Sure was a waste of lives for both us and them. All this isn't worth the high cost of lives."

Locastro also wrote down the names of the dead: Larry Kocher, Bobby Moore, Michael Farmer, Jerry Shain, Junior Johnson, Danny Guardado, Leo Gunning, Jim Signett and Bobby Elgin. Years later, he looked up the names on the Vietnam Veterans Memorial in Washington, D.C. They all appeared on panel 48 East, and Locastro named the fight of April 4 as the Battle of 48 East.

Richard Underwood, whose platoon started out with a swim in a river and ended up in a bloody fight, was once asked what award he received that day.

"I walked out alive. At the time, it felt like a whole lot. And it was," Underwood said.

When the guns at Ap Nam Phu fell silent, Charlie Company was whisked away to another area for another mission.

"If you're a grunt, you go where they tell you to go," Underwood said. "We just kept going. Never got enough rest. Never got enough sleep. You do your job. Do your mission. Drive on."

Units of the Golden Brigade even adopted a saying as their unofficial slogan: "Take two salt tablets and drive on." Troops also began carrying one rifle round in a pocket as a last resort. If they ever found themselves in the predicament that befell Jerry Shain, they would use that last bullet to avoid being chopped to death.

Also, on April 4, in another area northwest of Hue, Jim Littig's Long Range Recon unit prepared to set up a night ambush. It had been operating along a major trail that the North Vietnamese used to escape from the environs of Hue through the lowlands toward their mountain sanctuaries in Laos. This part of the trail had small hills on each side, just the kind of terrain that Rangers learn is best for setting ambushes. The enemy's pattern was to wait for cover of darkness before lighting out for the triple canopy cover of the rain forest, and Littig's unit had been productive, routinely killing two to four or five enemy a night with claymore mines. On this night, a hot meal of Army hash had been choppered out, and Taher Fahti Ghais chowed down. Holding the equivalent rank of corporal, he then took the point to lead an ambush team toward the position it wanted to be in by 10 o'clock. On the way, Ghais was shot three times in the chest by a sniper.

Littig and his medic, James (Doc) Dillon, rushed to the soldier's side to administer mouth-to-mouth resuscitation. Littig could taste the Army hash as he tried to revive him.

"I couldn't eat beef hash for years," Littig said.

The first member of Long Range Recon to be killed in action, Ghais was the 10th soldier in Golden Brigade to die on April 4. He may not have even been a U.S. citizen, but he died as an All American. A native of Addis Ababa, Ethiopia, Ghais had once fought with the Arabs against the Israelis in one of the Mideast wars. His brother, Ahman, said he was a graduate of Victoria College in Cairo and came to America to study aeronautical engineering at Boston University in Belmont, Massachusetts. Taher wanted to become a pilot, but the Air Force rejected him because of a vision issue. A U.S. Army recruiter promised him a chance to fly helicopters if he became a paratrooper, so he enlisted. Taher deployed on his first tour to Vietnam with the 173rd Airborne and later served with the 101st Airborne, during which time was shot in the shoulder and received a Purple Heart. He was training recruits at Fort Dix, New Jersey, before he pulled some strings to join the 82nd Airborne. When the Golden Brigade received its orders to deploy, Ahman Ghais went to North Carolina to see his brother off and to collect his belongings. He never saw his brother again. Taher Ghais, who is buried in Belmont Cemetery in Massachusetts, is also listed on Panel 48 East on The Wall.

Back in The World, April 4 was the day Martin Luther King was assassinated. The civil rights leader, who had marched for racial equality while preaching non-violence, was gunned down outside his room at the Lorraine Motel in Memphis, Tennessee. His killer fired a Remington Gamemaster rifle out of the window of a flophouse 80 yards away. King's death triggered the deadliest wave of social unrest since the Civil War. Race riots erupted in more than 100 cities. One of the worst was in Washington, D.C., where disorder raged within two blocks of the White House. To quell the disturbance, what was left of the 82nd Airborne was again called up for domestic duty. While some All Americans were fighting a war in Southeast Asia, the rest were tasked with keeping the peace at home.

The quest for racial equality was an issue that defined much of the Sixties, in society as a whole and in the military in particular.

Hollis Crowder of Batesville, Mississippi, grew up a black man in the American South. In the region where slaves once picked cotton on the plantations of white masters, a segregated society still existed a century after the Civil War. Separate water fountains were designated for use by whites and coloreds. On road trips, Crowder recalled family members bringing along a mason jar in the car as a portable toilet because blacks couldn't use the restroom at white gas stations. Blacks also had to go around the back of a white restaurant to get a hamburger.

Crowder, who had two uncles who were veterans of World War II, still wanted to serve his country as a paratrooper. He enrolled in the Reserve Officer Training Corps in high school and his first year of college.

"Serving my country was something that I was going to do, and I wanted to be in an Airborne unit. My thinking was there was a strong possibility of going to Vietnam. I was going to be the best prepared and serve in the best fighting unit I could," Crowder said.

He had already committed to the Army up when word of King's murder reached his college campus in Nashville.

"I remember that night. Some fires had been lit. Someone with a BB gun was trying to shoot out a streetlight. Students were shouting, 'They killed Martin! They killed Martin!' It was a pretty tough time. People were asking me, 'Why are you going to Vietnam to fight for someone else's rights when you don't have those same rights here?' I told them, 'We may not have all those rights yet, but we're not slaves anymore either. Somebody had to fight for that.' My father always used to say, 'Freedom isn't free. Somebody has to pay the price for it,' " Crowder said.

The Army wasn't exempt from racial friction. Up until the Korean War, blacks served in segregated units. When integration became policy, soldiers accepted it the same way they accepted getting up at five o'clock in the morning.

"In the Army, we all had the same haircut and wore the same clothes. Everybody had the same name—Maggot. We were all one. We were all maggots, brought together at the same time in the same place. We pulled for each other. That's a bond that civilians can't connect with," Crowder said.

As a radio operator in Alpha Company, Carl Bludau of Victoria, Texas, said race was irrelevant in Vietnam. "We spent tons of time in that jungle. We were tight. Ain't no blacks, whites or browns in the field. It's just us. All we had was each other. We had to learn how to get along," he said.

Willie Rivera of the Bronx, New York, served in the cavalry unit and described it this way: "I don't care who you are, what religion you are, what color your skin is or how you dress. The only thing that matters is, when the bullets are flying, do you have my back. That's the brotherhood."

In Vietnam, Paddy Barry first heard of King's death and the rioting when he went to a medic to get two stitches in his hand. "We're better off over here," the medic told him. "They're shooting people back home."

Chapter 13
A FRIEND AND HERO

Fifty years to the day that Richard Davidson was wounded at Ap Nam Phu, he was on a mission to honor the man whose last act was trying to save his life. On a drizzly, 37-degree morning, Davidson had driven down from Montreal with his wife and a contingent of Canadian Vietnam Veterans of Quebec, who left their motorcycles at home and rode in cars because of the inclement weather. The group formed up in the parking lot of the Price Chopper Grocery Store in Potsdam, New York, to connect with family and friends of Leo Brent Gunning. A police escort led the procession to Gunning's grave.

"Leo was my best friend and a real hero. He gave me his last breath. He gave his life trying to save mine. It's my duty and my honor to be here on the 50th anniversary." said Davidson, wearing a black jacket emblazoned with a large red, white and blue All American patch on the back and Airborne wings with a Combat Infantryman's Badge on the front.

Although the day was dedicated to Gunning, his story couldn't be told without the details of Davidson's journey. One of the loose ends of Vietnam, or any war, was the fate of the wounded. Comrades who carried a wounded man to a helicopter for an emergency flight to an aid station might never see the bleeding man again or know if he lived or died. Davidson was one of those medical metaphors—hastily bandaged, never again whole, faced with a long recovery but never forgetting the fallen.

Having lost a lot of blood, Davidson was in and out of consciousness from the moment he left the battlefield. He does remember being at an aid station with Sergeant Carlton Walls, who had ignored his own wounds to bandage up Davidson.

"We had a pact among ourselves that if we lost a vital body part, we didn't want to come back. We had a .45 (sidearm) available if we wanted to take matters into our own hands," Davidson said.

The way Walls remembered it, Davidson had asked for the firearm, which would have been a plausible request for one who had been so badly wounded. Davidson has no memory of making the request. The ordeal that followed would have been impossible if he lacked the will to live. In fact, Walls just assumed that no one could have survived such severe wounds and figured that Davidson had died until the two of them met 42 years later at a reunion of the Golden Brigade Chapter of the 82nd Airborne Division Association in Dallas, Texas. After their reunion, Davidson presented Walls with one of his two Purple Hearts.

"You never thought that I survived," Davidson wrote in a letter to Walls. "I am personally honoring you, Carlton, for your bravery in saving my life. I remember both you and the other sergeant receiving shrapnel wounds. You both should have also received the Purple Heart. Carlton, I am now sharing my Purple Heart for your bravery and wounds." The letter was written on November 1, 2010.

Recovery was long and arduous. At one point, Davidson recalled being in a hospital next to a ward of wounded prisoners of war, who were watched over by a guard carrying a handgun.

"I wanted to take the handgun and kill them all. That's how much hatred I felt," Davidson said.

He never acted on his feelings, however. He was flown to a military hospital in Japan, where he was on the operating room table for 12 hours as doctors removed his shattered testicle and patched him up. During recovery, he came across Daniel Ragsdale, the lieutenant who had been shot in the head and who Davidson had assumed was dead. Ragsdale's left side had been paralyzed by the wound.

"I remember him telling me, 'You're a good man, Dave.' That kept me alive all these years. That was better than getting a Silver Star," Davidson said.

Somewhere along the way, Davidson received a letter from Ollie Rasmussen of Sidney, Montana, one of the members of his platoon in Charlie Company. It read: "I thought we would get out together until you started stopping bullets. It's good Ragsdale is going to be OK…I've got to try to get straightened out. Right now I'm a mess. I haven't shaved since I got out. My hair is long, and I'm either half drugged or drunk, but I laugh a lot…I just happened to think of something quite funny. Remember when you were carrying the cross-eyed gook across the canal by the schoolhouse and fell in while he was blindfolded? I'll bet that was a hell of a surprise. That makes me laugh every time I think about it."

Despite being shot in the buttocks, thigh, testicle and penis, Davidson counted his blessings.

"Mine was a million dollar wound. It was all flesh but didn't hit a bone or didn't hit an artery. I was alive," Davidson said.

Davidson also remembers being asked by another wounded man to shoot him in the leg so he wouldn't have to return to Vietnam, a plea that went unfulfilled.

To receive additional care, Davidson was flown from Japan to Philadelphia, Pennsylvania, for treatment at Valley Forge Hospital, where the worst of the wounded from Vietnam occupied ward after ward under care administered by the Veterans Administration.

"There were guys with holes in them. Torn up bodies. All kinds of wounds. One guy who needed skin grafts had his arm sewn to his chest to regenerate more skin," Davidson said.

At Valley Forge, which was the home of George Washington's winter camp in the darkest days of the Revolutionary War, Davidson underwent another operation on July 17, 1968. Extensive healing and rehab followed, along with volunteer work in the finance section of the 22nd Surgical Hospital at Valley Forge, work that earned him a letter of appreciation. Five months after his final surgery, he was released from the hospital and given an honorable discharge from the U.S. Army.

War protesters who had turned against the soldiers fighting in Vietnam did not have a concentrated presence in Canada. Even if they had, Davidson would have ignored them.

"I'm not concerned about stupidity," Davidson said. "My family was there to meet me. They were glad I was safe. I did my duty with honor and respect the best I could, risked my life to save my buddies and they risked theirs to save mine. That carried a lot of weight. I am very honored to have served. I'm very honored to have served in the 82nd Airborne because it's a very special organization."

His war was over long before the Golden Brigade returned, before all U.S. forces had withdrawn from Vietnam by 1973, before Saigon fell to the forces of the North two years later. His take on those events? "No more Americans will die," he said.

Like many returning war veterans, Davidson found himself in a state of hyper-alertness, as if a switch had been turned on in his brain and he couldn't turn it off. He had trouble sleeping at first too. Still, he picked up his life as best he could and got married. Doctors had restored the function of his wounded manhood, and he fathered a son and a daughter. He has been blessed with five grandchildren. Neither his first marriage nor his sexual function endured, however.

"You live with it. You learn to adjust," Davidson said.

To deal with internal wounds, Davidson tried to forget Vietnam.

"I never talked about it. It was bad enough to live it," Davidson said. "It's human nature that we remember the good times and forget the bad ones. It's better for your mental health."

His overriding takeaway from Vietnam? "Nothing could ever be as bad as that. I cherish how peaceful we live here. I thank God for our beautiful country. I have no regrets in going but do have regrets for the pain," he said.

Canada never officially entered the war, and individual Canadians who served in the U.S. military technically violated a 1937 law that made it illegal for Canadians to go to war in the armed forces of any foreign state. Davidson was unaware of the law, but it wouldn't have stopped him. While some 30,000 Americans dodged the draft or deserted to Canada to avoid service in Vietnam, a roughly equal number of Canadians joined American forces during the same period. Many of them served in Vietnam.

On more than one occasion, Davidson was asked why a Canadian would volunteer for the Airborne. "What are you doing here? People are going the other way," he was told.

Recognition of Canadian veterans took time. It wasn't until 1989 that the Canadian Vietnam Veterans of Quebec erected a monument, a slab of granite flanked by two blocks of marble. The monument is located in Melocheville, Quebec, about 20 miles outside of Montreal.

In 1995, the Canadian Vietnam Veterans Memorial, also known as The North Wall, was erected in Windsor, Ontario. It bears the names of 147 Canadians who died serving in Vietnam with the U.S. military along with these words: "As long as we live, you shall live. As long as we live, you shall be remembered. As long as we live, you shall be loved."

At some point, Davidson procured a newspaper clipping, now faded, of Leo Gunning having received a Bronze Star with V device and oak leaf cluster for his valor. The citation read: "Moving with the third platoon, Specialist Gunning went forward to aid a sister platoon that was pinned down by heavy mortar and automatic weapons fire. As his platoon engaged the enemy with suppressive fires, he crawled forward over open ground under heavy enemy fire to reach the lead platoon. He continued to advance under fire and retrieved a wounded soldier, dragging him to safety. Specialist Gunning once again exposed himself attempting to evacuate another casualty. As he was dragging the fallen soldier to safety, he was mortally wounded. Specialist Gunning's personal bravery and devotion to duty were in keeping with the highest traditions of the military service and reflects great credit upon himself, his unit and the United States Army."

Davidson had once before made a pilgrimage to Potsdam, a community of 18,000 residents located in what New Yorkers call The North Country, where cars and trucks share the roads with horse-drawn Amish buggies. He came to visit Gunning's grave and to console Irene LaBrake Gunning, whose son had called home before he died to say that he wasn't coming back alive. Davidson shared the burden of grief with Mrs. Gunning by telling her what a great soldier and friend her son had been.

Davidson had a similar message on April 4, 2018. When the police escort arrived, those assembled in that parking lot fell in behind the flashing lights to drive through the town, which is bisected by the Raquette River on its northward path to the Saint Lawrence River.

A procession of 40 cars drove to Garfield Cemetery, where two color guards holding American flags stood in the rain to greet the mourners. In a leafy section of a graveyard that conjured up images of colonial New England, the crowd assembled at the Gunning family plot.

Davidson carried two wreaths of red and white carnations adorned with the crest of the 82nd Airborne Division. One was for Gunning's mother.

"We mustn't forget our mothers," Davidson said.

The second wreath was for Leo. Davidson planted the flags of Canada and the United States in the cemetery soil. Brothers don't always have the same last name or even have the same nationality. Just as he began to speak, the rain subsided.

"Leo, we've come here to pay our respects. I asked you to make the weather better, and you did," Davidson said.

A brief but heartfelt eulogy included remarks about how Leo Gunning was a history buff who told stories to his comrades about the Battle of Hastings and other historic military campaigns.

"We were a good bunch of guys," Davidson said. "We had our good times too. Leo and I smoked our share of pot."

Davidson also carried a copy of the Candle Prayer, which reads: "Almighty God, our heavenly father, who on this earth fills our human canopy with the breath of life and carries us into your presence on the wings of your spirit, surround the souls of our departed comrades with your heavenly presence. O God, in whose hands are the living and the dead, we give you thanks for the good example of these, your servants, who were willing to dedicate their lives to the service of our country. Grant to them your merciful protection that the good work which you have begun in them may be perfected in the world to come. Bless and comfort all who grieve this day, and may we ever remain loyally steadfast to the highest ideals for which many have died and by which we all should live. This we ask in the name of our Lord. Amen."

After the graveside visit, family and friends adjourned to the Frank Barclay American Legion Post 74 for a reception. Davidson bought the first two rounds of drinks, bringing along glasses etched with the logo of the Golden Brigade. He also furnished a bottle of Black Velvet, a Canadian whiskey, and proposed a toast.

"Here's to Leo, and the 82nd Airborne Division. All The Way!" Davidson said before clinking glasses with a visitor.

In a separate room were tables and folding chairs for those partaking of salad, sandwiches, pizza and a cake decorated with the All American logo. Pictures of Gunning were placed on a table, along with the American flag that was draped over his coffin in 1968.

Tributes flowed for several hours, a reminder of a good life snuffed out and the personal price paid by the Irish Catholic family of a soldier slain in war. Gunning's sister Colleen, an Air Force veteran, recalled how the news broke her mother's heart.

"When he died, she just gave up. She quit trying," Colleen said. "My mother loved to read. Leo loved history. He was a good brother—loyal, quiet, introspective. He didn't make friends easily, and he didn't suffer fools gladly. He didn't even go to his high school graduation. He didn't want anybody to make a fuss over him. He didn't want the attention."

Yet the family found solace in the fact that Leo had friends who loved him as much as they did, and the line of cars for a memorial service 50 years after the fact was the very definition of respect.

"Our family is very big on respect. I'll never forget all his family and friends being there for him," Colleen said.

Gunning's brother Steve traveled all the way from Broken Arrow, Oklahoma, to attend. He related how their father, a World War II veteran, had died when the brothers were young.

"Leo was the oldest son. My mom worshipped him. We looked up to him like he was a god. He was a father figure to me," said Steve, a Navy veteran. "He was gifted. He loved to express his thoughts in writing. History especially. He had the gift. That's the sad part. It did break my mom's heart when he didn't come back."

It was not lost on Steve Gunning that someone who served with his brother so many years ago would make such a thoughtful gesture by returning on the 50th anniversary, a golden anniversary in the annals of the Golden Brigade.

"What they went through no one can understand," Steve said. "The guys fighting that war did what they thought was right. They did it out of sense of duty to themselves. They watched your back, you watched theirs. Nobody can pretend to understand what it was like over there. It was out of their control. But an experience like that, when it's you versus the rest of the world, draws them that much closer."

Peter LaBrake Reynolds, a first cousin of Leo's on his mother's side, said it was in keeping with Gunning's character that he died trying to save a wounded buddy.

"That was Leo. He was just that kind of guy. I idolized him. He was like my big brother. This is a small town, where everybody knows everybody else. It was overwhelming to see that line of cars going to the cemetery to honor him," Reynolds said.

"I was there the day he called home to tell his mother about his premonition. I can't give you details, but he said, 'I'm coming home in a box.' Leo was laid out in the parlor of my grandmother's house. My father was a World War II vet, and that was the only time I ever saw him cry. He said Leo died way too young," Reynolds added.

Stories were told about Leo being a solitary man who liked to walk in the woods. He did some hunting with his father, but more often than not, he used his .22 rifle for target practice rather than for shooting living creatures. In one anecdote, Leo and a friend were out shooting at cans when his buddy shot and killed a bird. Leo admonished him and sent him home.

"We were surprised when we found out he was in Vietnam. It was hard for us to imagine him being over there fighting," Reynolds said.

Among the people who said words over Leo's grave, and who took part in the event at the Legion Hall, was John Smith. He and Leo were classmates at Parishville-Hopkintown Central High School, and Smith had served in Vietnam with the 173rd Airborne.

"My best memory was that of Leo in English class. We were given an assignment to write a 500-word essay, and the rest of us were counting all the words. Leo didn't have to struggle. He wrote seven or eight pages, and the teacher asked him to read it in class. You could have heard a pin drop as he shared his essay," Smith said. "He kept a journal in Vietnam. Had it been printed, I have no doubt it would have been a best seller."

As a paratrooper himself, Smith understood the unbreakable bond shared by the men who had fought in Vietnam, especially in close-knit combat units like the 82nd Airborne.

"You can't explain it. For those who went, no explanation is necessary. For those that don't know, no explanation is possible. They are brothers forever," he said.

When the time came to leave, Richard Davidson gathered up his Canadian friends for the three-hour drive back to Montreal. Way back in the Sixties, he had started his adventure to make himself a better person and to see the world. Given his physical and internal scars, and given the fact that he had lost buddies like Leo Gunning, he was asked if it had been worth it.

"We learn from everyone we meet in life," Davidson said. "There are lots of good people in the world, and some bad people too. The good people have to do the right things to make this a better world to live in."

The weather turned colder and windier later in the afternoon. A storm whipped up over the Great Lakes. By nightfall, a silent shroud of snow blanketed Leo Gunning's hometown and Garfield Cemetery. No scene could have been more peaceful.

Chapter 14
THE LAZY W

Gordon Day developed a tight relationship with First Sergeant Louis Pigeon, the highest ranking enlisted man in Bravo Company of the 1st of the 505. Like Day, Pigeon had Indian blood in him, and the common denominator made for an instant bond.

"Pigeon was 6-foot-6 and came from Oklahoma. He had served in World War II, Korea and a previous tour in Vietnam. I told him I didn't want any favoritism, so give me all the dirty jobs and the dangerous jobs," Day said.

Accordingly, Day walked the point on April 5 when Bravo Company saddled up and headed out for a trouble spot along a river plain that housed a village complex, just the sort of spot that the North Vietnamese Army coveted for concealing troops and storing supplies.

The probability of contact was high. The day before, which was the same day as Charlie Company's bloody engagement just to the northwest at Ap Nam Phu, a South Vietnamese Army battalion had fought a hostile force on the same ground Bravo Company was moving toward. Located five miles from the Imperial City, the hotspot was a thumb of land situated between the east bank of the Song Sia River and the western arm of the Lazy W. In such a tight area, the ability to maneuver was restricted, a fact underscored by the loss of three of the five tanks the South Vietnamese unit had taken in there.

One of Bravo's walking wounded, Andrew Blais, was deemed unfit for the operation. Although he wasn't ailing bad enough to be evacuated from the field, he was physically unable to take his place on Sergeant John Plunkard's fire team. Blais suffered from dysentery, an intestinal malady that befell him when he drank water from a stream to slake his unquenchable thirst in the tropical heat. In addition, his hearing was shot, and his ears had bled after an exploding artillery shell fell so close it knocked him over on his back and shattered his ear drums. Blais balked at being left out. After all, Bravo Company's motto was: No one falls out; no one gets left behind.

"I can't leave you guys," Blais said in protest.

That's when Billy Flint, the machine gunner in his squad, told him in no uncertain terms: "You're going to stay back. If you're too stupid to listen, I'll kill you."

Over his objections, Blais was placed at an aid station. Also there, awaiting evacuation, were the bodies of the fallen from Ap Nam Phu.

"I stared at them. I kept thinking to myself that they're asleep and they'll move any minute now. They didn't," Blais said. "One of them was (Taher) Ghais. And when

I hear people saying unflattering things about Muslims, I say to myself, 'I fought alongside one, and he was a brother.' Anyway, replacements came in with the ammo. In hindsight, I thought of it as divine intervention that I didn't go with the company."

What bothered Blais the most was that he was the point man in his fire team, and if he couldn't go, another man would have to take his place. Sergeant Plunkard took on the job of walking point, and that was the last time Blais saw him.

"I've always felt guilty about that," Blais said.

That day, the 100 or so men of Bravo Company conducted a reconnaissance in force to probe what they were up against. To their front was a large stream or canal that ran perpendicular to the arm of the Lazy W. A hump-backed concrete bridge spanned the waterway and led to an interconnected series of dwellings.

With third platoon providing cover, Bravo Company began crossing the bridge. Second platoon, the company command group and half the first platoon made it across. Then a Russian-made rocket, similar to ones the Red Army used against the Germans in World War II, screamed out of the sky.

"I was in a rice paddy when, out of the corner of my eye, I saw some black object coming overhead. A rocket landed right in the middle of the command group and exploded," recalled Sergeant Jimmy Barnes.

A 15-man squad that included Gordon Day and John Plunkard had their own vantage point as they approached a schoolhouse and a six-foot high row of hedges.

"Not a single window was broken in the schoolhouse. I looked over and saw our reflection, like we were staring back at ourselves," Day said. "I heard an explosion and everybody at the command post was down. I thought headquarters section was gone. I didn't think any of them were alive."

Another rocket exploded, lifting Day into the air and depositing him on the other side of the hedges and into an enemy trench.

"I got tossed like you might throw a toy soldier. I like to think it was the hand of God that picked me up. I hit the quick release on my pack and grabbed the .45 from my shoulder holster," Day said. "The NVA opened up on us. Plunkard was with the squad, keeping everybody's heads down. We were surrounded. The only way we were going to get out of there was to fight our way out. Paratroopers are the meanest and toughest fighters there are. It takes a certain man to jump in low into the middle of a battle and break your way out so that others will follow you. Your eyes become like a devil. What we needed most was covering fire and a radio."

The company commander, Captain St. Elmo P. (Step) Tyner, and five men around him were hit but still alive. Tyner gathered himself and radioed for artillery support. At the same time, the enemy sprung an L-shaped ambush, opening fire from the front and the flank.

"The NVA were well dug in and concealed; and were placing effective fire from two directions. Those of us north of the canal were pinned down. The bridge that the remainder of the company would have to cross to reinforce us was the humped type common in Asia, and I could see NVA machine gun bullets grazing its deck. But the other two platoons could support by fire, and they did with a vengeance until, in groups of two and three, our isolated troopers managed to withdraw over the exposed bridge to the relative safety of the canal's south bank," Tyner recalled.

Not that it was easy. Day remembers crossing the bridge under fire.

"I still have bits of concrete in my face from the bullets that were impacting around me. There were so many acts of bravery that nobody got any recognition for," Day said.

Tyner was evacuated by helicopter, and Lieutenant Charles Posey, an African American who was Bravo's executive officer, assumed command. He was about to lob a smoke grenade to mark targets for an air strike.

"I stopped him. We had six more men in there. He said, 'You better hurry up and get them out. We're going to light up the whole area,' " Day said.

Just after the men made it back, aircraft dropped canisters of napalm that erupted into pillars of orange flame.

At the end of a furious and chaotic day, the company established a night defensive position in a graveyard. As plans were being made to resume the attack the next day, John Plunkard wrote a letter to his folks and summarized the day:

"This won't be a long letter because I don't have time to tell you everything that's happened since we moved. All I can say is that we're in the shit up to our ass. We made a sweep through a village this morning and ran into about 160 or more NVA and got pinned down for an hour. They hit us with a .57 millimeter recoilless rifle and wounded four people, none real serious, but it knocked the hell out of about 10 people besides. I think we're going back in tomorrow. We found a gook who looks like he's been dead about three days, and he was loaded down with AK47 ammo. The maggots and flies have done away with most of him. We're set up in a cemetery right now," he wrote.

"We just got news that C Company had (nine) killed and 15 wounded last night. There must be a regiment or larger force in this village with a casualty report like that. I hope to hell I soon get to come home. I don't mind it as bad this time as I did last time, but I'm scared all the time. I've got to worry about myself and the men under me in my fire team. Before I can rest, I've got to see that they're OK."

The letter was his last.

Jimmy Barnes made his own preparations before the attack resumed on April 6.

"I gave my wallet to one guy. Gave watch to another guy. I wanted my parents to have them if I didn't come back," Barnes said. "The last time I talked to Johnny, I said, 'Plunk, we're going to get it today.' His face was beet red. He knew."

Bravo pushed forward along the same route leading to the bridge. A company of South Vietnamese soldiers supported them on the left, and a company from the 101st Airborne took up a position on the northern bank of the Lazy W to seal off any escape routes. Three charges pushed the enemy back, but with their backs now to the river, the North Vietnamese soldiers made a desperate stand from a trench behind the hedges.

At one point, Plunkard led his team toward the yard in front of the schoolhouse, the windows of which were now shattered.

"He went right, and I went left. I glanced over and saw him go down. I kept yelling, 'Plunk! Plunk!' He never answered," Barnes said. It would take three more days of bloody fighting to find out for certain what happened to him.

Meanwhile, arriving on the field to coordinate the movements of the infantry units was Major Joseph Cincotti, the officer in charge of operational planning for the 1st Battalion. A man of unquestioned courage, Cincotti was so tough that he actually chewed broken glass, but he had to be kept on a tight rein, according to battalion commander John Jameson.

While moving around on foot, Cincotti personally encountered some NVA troops in trenches. He killed all that he saw but was wounded by a rocket explosion. Evacuated to an aid station, Cincotti was later visited by the battalion commander, who wasn't sure if he should decorate Cincotti for his valor or bring charges against him for landing on the ground in violation of regulations. He chose the former, and Cincotti was awarded a Silver Star.

Louis Pigeon, Bravo's top sergeant, was also hit while assisting the wounded. The company's losses of key personnel kept piling up.

One particular act of valor was attributed to Sergeant Ronnie Harrell, who received the Distinguished Service Cross for what happened that day. Jimmy Barnes said Harrell was right behind Plunkard just before Plunkard was hit. According to the unit history, two platoons of Bravo were pinned down by heavy fire, and Harrell maneuvered to strike the enemy's left flank. After he ran out of ammo for his own weapon, Harrell grabbed an AK-47 from a dead North Vietnamese soldier and fought on alone. Enemy forces were between him and his platoon, which was under heavy fire and taking casualties. As he made his way back to his unit, he killed five enemy soldiers in a trench. Subsequently, he rallied a squad and destroyed a machine gun nest. Harrell and his comrades overran other positions that were pinning down second and third platoons. Upon seeing a wounded radioman out in the open, Harrell pulled the soldier to a safe place and used the radio to report his progress to the company commander. Time and again, he ignored his wounds and rushed into the open to pull back the wounded.

As dusk approached, illumination rounds fired by the artillery made it seem like daylight. Units maneuvered in the ghostly light while other guns targeted the NVA positions.

"As the wounded came back, I kept asking what was going on," said Andrew Blais from his spot at the aid station. "I asked about Johnny, and someone said he was gone. He took a spray across the chest. Everyone in my fire team was gone too. I felt very guilty because I wasn't with them. John Plunkard was the bravest man I ever knew, and a true All American. You can have your John Waynes. They're nuts. He wasn't nuts. He was just a brave man. I felt like a lost soul for the rest of my time in Vietnam,"

Upon learning that his blood brother had been hit, Gordon Day took the news especially hard.

"They tell you in command school to only make acquaintances, not friends, so it won't hurt as much if they get hit. But we were all in it together. It's pretty hard not to get to know everybody. It's hard to talk about John. He was the kid brother I never had," Day said.

Troopers reached company headquarters to report what happened to Plunkard and to say his body was still on the battlefield.

"Billy Flint threw down his machine gun and told the company commander, 'Plunkard's hit bad. We gotta get him.' We tried, but it would have been suicide to go back in there right then," Barnes said.

Bravo's losses that day included Sergeant First Class Clifton Walker, 39, of Butler, Georgia, and Private First Class Walter Edward Joyce Jr., 18, of Somerville, Massachusetts.

For the next two days, the battle raged without interruption. Supported by air strikes and artillery, troopers fought for every inch of ground against a determined resistance. The enemy's trench system was so well built that American firepower, as overwhelming as it was, had little effect. The ground was also honeycombed with spider holes. From these camouflaged foxholes, enemy soldiers pushed up with their helmets to raise the lids and fire at troopers.

"We were in there for five days total. It was back and forth. Confusing. Mass insanity. The troops we were up against were the ones that had taken Hue. They were so expert in camouflage. You could walk right up to a spider hole and never know it was there. Those holes were triangulated too. They covered each other. It's a miracle me and my fire team made it back," Jimmy Barnes said. "The only thing I ate in those five days was a can of peaches, and I couldn't keep even that down. I threw that up. If you think you're going to die any minute, you have no appetite. There was a point where I broke. I started crying and screaming and shaking. I had to ask one of the guys to hit me to get me out of shock. The world's smallest book is about war heroes from Hammond, California." Even a soldier who saw himself in the image of the fictional Sergeant Rock had a breaking point.

Meanwhile, Paul Davin's Charlie Company, fresh off the fight at Ap Nam Phu, arrived as reinforcements. His unit was held up momentarily at a waterway, where steep banks and deep water discouraged a crossing on foot. Having arrived on scene in his helicopter, Colonel Bud Bolling told Davin he had to get across.

"The next thing I know, they airlifted in an aluminum rowboat for us to use. We were in the Navy again," Davin said.

The stream was crossed.

"Paul was a fearless company commander," Bolling said.

At one point, Bolling got a message from headquarters of the 101st Airborne that the commanding general wanted an update on the fighting.

"Hurry up and finish the battle because we have to have a report at the staff meeting," Bolling was told.

"Just tell him we're fighting out here and if he wants to join us, we'll give him some tea," Bolling replied, his voice tinged with sarcasm.

At a later point, troops had fought their way into the village and confiscated a telephone switchboard at what had been the headquarters of an entire NVA battalion. Enemy forces were so entrenched that they communicated by telephone instead of using radios. Bolling figured its capture would impress his superiors.

"I go down to get the switchboard and took it to the next staff meeting," Bolling said. "I said, 'Here's a battalion switchboard, General, compliments of the 82nd Airborne Division.' I get the same story. 'How many did you kill?' "

Finally, on the fifth day, a helicopter landed at Bravo Company's command post, and an officer emerged to get a first-hand account. Jimmy Barnes thought it was the battalion commander. Others thought the officer was from the 101st Airborne and may even have been the commanding general. At any rate, Bravo's senior sergeants told him the enemy's defenses were impregnable. Four days of pounding had failed to dislodge the enemy from its trenches. To which the arriving officer said: "You're paratroopers. You're going to take that position even if it comes down to the last man. All they can do is kill you."

When the officer left, the lieutenant who led Barnes' platoon tried to rally his troops.

"Hey, they're going to make us take that position anyway. We might as well do it," the lieutenant said.

Also, on the fifth day, Barnes said a radio message was intercepted from the North Vietnamese commander.

"He said his troops keep killing these Americans, but they keep coming. He also said his forces were out of ammo, and that he was willing to stand and die to the last man," Barnes said.

Bravo Company's ranks had now shrunk to 44 able-bodied men, a number usually associated with a single platoon. In advance of the final charge, they fixed bayonets, converting their assault rifles into spears, the kind of weapons used in the Stone Age.

"Guys just looked at each other," Barnes said. "Damn, a bayonet charge against automatic rifles? A bayonet was a weapon of last resort. They always tell you not to bring a knife to a gunfight. It reminded me of that line from the movie Pork Chop Hill: 'You're gonna go down in history as the last bayonet charge ever.' They called in artillery that was landing 75 to 100 yards in front of us. It was whistling through the corn. We were scared shitless."

At mid-morning of a bright, hot day, the final charge began—past the yard in front of the schoolhouse, through a little gully where the enemy was waiting in spider holes and toward the hedge row.

"We busted right through the hedges and into the trench. There was an entrance to a big tunnel. I tossed a grenade, but they were gone. They had been ordered to leave instead of fighting to the last man. If they had been there, they would have mowed us down. We were low on water, and I must have been dehydrated. I thought I was going to pass out. I was so glad to get out of there. It's like you can't believe you're alive," Barnes said.

Not long after taking the position, the troops were told Bravo Company was pulling back. Barnes told Lieutenant Posey that he, Billy Price and another solider were going to find Plunkard, no matter what.

"I know what it's like to be out there alone. I didn't want his family to go through the ordeal of thinking he might still be alive," Barnes said.

In the schoolyard, near a water well, was an area of loose dirt. Digging with his hands, Barnes found Plunkard's body lying face down in a shallow grave. His helmet and rucksack were gone. Troopers proceeded with caution because the NVA had been known to booby-trap the bodies of dead G.I.s with grenades, so that if someone came to retrieve a corpse, the grenade would explode and add to the number of casualties. Plunkard's comrades tied a rope to one of his legs and pulled him out.

"I was so shook up. He was my best friend. I patted him on the back before they put him in a body bag and choppered him out. That really took the wind out of our sails," Barnes said.

From the sturdiness of the trenches and the ferocity of the fight, it became apparent that a sizable NVA force had occupied the area. A unit of the 101st Airborne killed a battalion commander and captured his satchel of documents, which confirmed his unit was part of the 803rd NVA Regiment. The Screaming Eagles killed more than 80 enemy trying to flee the pocket.

The Golden Brigade's after-action reports noted that the unit had trapped and destroyed another battalion of the same regiment. It had the switchboard to prove it.

Once again, troops were ordered to the next assignment, leaving the ground that had been paid for in blood. Hostile forces snuck back in.

"Here's the quandary of Vietnam. One week later, we went back to that same area to set up ambushes. It was total insanity," Jimmy Barnes said.

Chapter 15
A TRUE ALL AMERICAN

The first word to reach Frederick, Maryland, informed the Plunkard family that John was missing in action. A subsequent notice confirmed the family's worst fears. Their loved one had been killed in battle.

"I came home on school bus and walked into the house. My father, mother, sister and his fiancé were there. I just knew. By the look on their faces, I knew," said younger brother Joe Plunkard, who was 12 years old at the time.

The remains of John Francis Plunkard, 21, were flown to the Department of Defense Mortuary at Dover Air Force Base in Delaware and placed in a flag-draped coffin. For the final leg of his journey, he was escorted home by Michael Glines of Modesto, California, the soldier whose life John had saved when they served together in Vietnam with the 173rd Airborne.

During two days of viewing at the M.R. Atchison & Son Funeral Home, John Plunkard was remembered as a member of the Francis Scott Key Boy Scout Troop, the Frederick Lions Midget football team, the Araby and Linden Hills softball team and the Frederick High School football team, where he was known as the kicker with the Golden Toe. An employee of the Frederick Lumber Company before he had volunteered to join the Army and become a paratrooper, he had been killed in action as a member of the Golden Brigade of the 82nd Airborne. He was posthumously awarded the Silver Star.

The funeral was held on Saturday, April 27. Officiating were the Rev. Donald W. Bracken, pastor, and the Rev. W. Merval Weaver, pastor emeritus, of the United Presbyterian Church.

One of the pall bearers was Blaine Smith, who was John's high school classmate and a sergeant in Mike Company, 3rd Battalion, 7th Marine Regiment, 1st Marine Division. Smith's final tribute came from the Bible verse of John 15:12: "Greater love has no one than this, that one lay down his life for his brothers."

Also, among the all-military pall bearers was childhood friend and Purple Heart recipient Randy Weddle. He and John had been inducted together in the Washington and Lee Post 5 of the Disabled American Veterans in April of 1967. Others who carried the coffin were Sergeant Gerald Green, Corporal Darrell Taylor, Staff Sergeant Al Duncan and Corporal Craig Roderick.

Military honors were provided by the Honor Guard at nearby Fort Detrick. Bugler Charles Mollick sounded the 24 haunting, poignant notes of "Taps" at the grave in

Mount Olivet Cemetery. John L. and Frances Everhart Plunkard bade farewell to their son.

The family kept John Plunkard's memory alive with annual notices in the local newspaper. One such item appeared on a Christmas Eve: "He gave his life for the medals he won. But what can we pay for a great son? The boys he saved, for the life he gave, I hope are home on Christmas Day. Mom, Dad, Ann and Joe."

Seven years after his brother's death, Joe Plunkard joined the Army and earned his own jump wings, serving in the 504th Parachute Infantry Regiment of the 82nd Airborne, the same unit that his older brother had once served in. His induction in February of 1975 qualified him as a Vietnam Era veteran.

"I just figured I should serve," Joe Plunkard said. "I saw him jump from a C-119 at Indiantown Gap once. That kind of impressed me. I wanted to be a grunt."

The most enduring eulogy came in the form of a letter written to Joe Plunkard by Step Tyner, the former commander of Bravo Company who had been wounded at the Lazy W and who retired from the Army as a lieutenant colonel.

"Your brother was the one whose loss I most keenly felt. Of course, he was a likable young man, but my acquaintance with him was professional, and I had come to regard John as a potential platoon sergeant. The pain of losing such an exemplary leader was in part assuaged by pride in both the nature and the degree of his heroism…What your brother did was to rescue a number of wounded soldiers from an open area, cut off from the rest of the company, and organize them into a defensive position where they were able to hold until friendly forces effected a link-up. His last energies as a living mortal were expended in saving lives, not in taking them, and my impression from what eye witnesses recounted to me is that, but for John, the others would have died or, perhaps worse, been taken prisoner by the NVA," Tyner wrote.

"John's achievements in his brief but active lifetime are a source of pride to all of us who knew him, but must be especially gratifying to you and your Airborne family. John was not just an American, he was All American, performing arduous duties with quiet competence and certain moral conviction. He was neither a thrill-seeker nor a bloody killer nor a reckless fool as some war heroes are made out to be. Rather, he was the quiet hero with a strong core of compassion, giving his last measure of devotion on behalf of his fellow troopers. Mortally wounded, he did not fall out. Seeing others in danger, he did not leave them behind. To my judgment, an Airborne trooper can hope for no finer epitaph. I will never forget the impression John made on me. I know you must miss him. In different ways and to differing degrees, all of us who knew him do," Tyner added.

Although he was wounded and away from the battlefield when Plunkard was killed, Tyner said a recommendation for the Distinguished Service Cross was made. Tyner believed that more than a Silver Star was merited, and Joe Plunkard kept up efforts to have the Department of the Army review the records.

Gordon Day lived up to his part of the death pact he had entered into with John Plunkard. Although it took some time to find the family because he had the wrong name of Plunkard's hometown, Day looked up the family and mourned with them. Day also christened a son as John Lee Day in honor of his blood brother. In all, five offspring of friends and family are named John in Plunkard's honor. A barracks at Fort Detrick in Maryland was named after him too.

The Dodge Dart that he had purchased before going back to Vietnam was restored by his brother Joe. The car has a place of honor in a family garage.

In 2017, Joe Plunkard approached some local officials about the possibility of having a bridge named after his brother. He submitted the paperwork and lobbied on behalf of the project, even picking out a suitable location.

Fifty years after John Plunkard's death in Vietnam, a sign went up on that part of Maryland Route 355 that spans Interstate 70. The bridge is one-quarter mile from where John grew up and a half-mile from where he is buried. It was the first time the state of Maryland had dedicated a road or a bridge to a Vietnam veteran who had been killed in action.

"All infantry units are tight, even the legs. The Airborne takes it up a notch. The bond is there," Joe Plunkard said.

The official dedication came on September. 21, 2018. A reception followed at the American Legion in Woodsboro, Maryland. Among the 75 or so people in attendance was Andrew Blais, who traveled from New Hampshire to salute the leader of his fire team one last time. Blais, 71, had fathered nine children and has 22 grandchildren and two great-grandchildren.

"I had to have kids, and I wanted them to be good, because if they did well enough, maybe God will forgive me," said Blais, who became a Mormon after the war. "I owe my very existence to this man. He was the bravest man I ever knew, and a true All American."

Blais never had the opportunity to say goodbye to the man who had saved his life more than once. At the dedication, he corrected the oversight.

"I had a chance to spend a quiet moment at his grave. We talked," Blais said.

John Plunkard's name is on Panel 48 East, Line 54 of The Wall.

Andrew Blais noted that a traveling exhibit of The Wall once came to the University of New Hampshire near his home. He went to look up the name of his hero.

"The college kids were playing Frisbee and moving about on campus. It struck me in a poetic sense. The names on this wall are people who were mostly college age. These kids have no idea what kind of sacrifice they made," Blais said.

Chapter 16
DOC DILLON

The customized license plate on Jim Littig's car is YADO68, a nod to a bloody hill in Vietnam and the year he and his Long Range Recon Platoon were there. Every time Littig drives to his lobbyist office in Washington, D.C., or takes the family on vacation or pays tribute to the Golden Brigade's fallen at Arlington National Cemetery, he is reminded of that place and his medic, James (Doc) Dillon.

Yado was the name of a piece of high ground north and west of Hue, located on the west side of Highway One not far from where the fighting at the Lazy W River took place. Rising above the coastal flats, Yado Hill looked over an escape route that fleeing enemy forces used to get out of Hue en route to their sanctuaries in Laos. Their method was to start moving around 10 o'clock at night under cover of darkness and then scurry away to reach safety before the sun came up. Yado Hill provided enough cover to conceal Littig's men during the day, and it was an ideal place for setting up claymore mines at ambush sites.

For eight straight nights beginning on April 1, 1968, the element had sprung ambushes that killed three, four or five enemy soldiers a night. Recon troops were in position again on April 9, and Doc Dillon was among those waiting in the vegetation. He carried an M-14 rifle and a .45 caliber sidearm, and he wasn't hesitant about using either weapon. In the Airborne, even the medics were bad asses.

Dillon was older than every trooper on that mission, even Lieutenant Jim Littig. Married and the father of a daughter, he had turned 31 on April 5. In addition to his skills at finding transportation and supplies for his unit, he was wise in the ways of Vietnam from his previous two tours in the Special Forces. In the early days of the Golden Brigade's deployment, Dillon attached a piece of medical equipment to Littig's web gear.

"I was a new second lieutenant, and he taped a green can to my gear that contained a blood expander. He told me, 'I may not always be able to get to you, so you have to learn to do this yourself.' He was just a good-hearted, even-keeled guy," Littig said.

Dillon was a living, breathing incarnation of the three rules of war for a combat medic: 1) good men will die; 2) not even Doc can change Rule 1; 3) for his brothers, Doc will die trying to change both Rule 1 and Rule 2. He had worked feverishly to save the saves of men torn up in combat. Even when he couldn't save a life, he always gave his best effort.

On the night of April 9, the noises of the night ceased ominously. Enemy forces had entered the kill zone of the ambush. Littig routinely tied the detonator for the claymores around his wrist, so he didn't have to fumble around for it in the dark.

"We set off the claymores, even the ones up in the trees, and got four or five them. Then all Hell broke loose. You never know how many of them may be coming up the trail," Littig said.

The point element was the vanguard of 70 to 80 North Vietnamese soldiers headed for Laos. When the claymores went off, the hostile forces deployed into battle formation.

"They were maneuvering on us. They got some grenades in on our position. Doc Dillon was killed. Me and my platoon sergeant were hit with grenade fragments," Littig said.

The ambush team pulled back to a predetermined safe spot and called the artillery, which had been zeroed in on the area ahead of time. Once the shells started exploding, the bad guys lost their appetite for the engagement and withdrew.

"They wanted to get out of there anyway. They didn't want to fight. They broke contact after about 20 to 30 minutes. They wanted to get out of the flats and into the jungle before daylight," Littig said. "We were evacuated at 10 o'clock the next morning."

Sergeant James Dale Dillon of Jacksonville, Florida, took his last helicopter ride back to a temporary morgue. His body was flown home for burial with full military honors at Marietta National Cemetery in Georgia. His name is etched into the black granite on Panel 48 East of The Wall.

The organization that built The Wall also set up a web site to honor the fallen. In 2008, a remembrance for Doc Dillon was left on the Wall of Faces by his granddaughter, Amanda Cornelius, who had joined the Air Force to serve her country. It read:

"Grandpa: We never met but I know your daughter to be a good lady. You would love her. Thank you for the inspiration and memories. I have been told stories of you being remembered as wild, crazy, enjoying life and full of love. Your service and dedication were an inspiration. As a granddaughter, I now serve currently in the U.S. Air Force. I will always remember you and hope one day to meet you at the Pearly Gates. Thank you, Grandpa, God bless, and we will always remember."

Littig recovered from his wounds and subsequently became the executive officer of Alpha Company in the 2nd Battalion of the 505th Parachute Infantry Regiment. There were more bloody days ahead with his new outfit.

His way of remembering Doc Dillon is his license plate: YADO68.

Chapter 17

SORRY ABOUT THAT

One catchphrase borrowed from pop culture and repeated by troops in Vietnam came from a TV show called *Get Smart,* a parody on secret agents that centered around a bumbling character named Maxwell Smart. He shrugged off gaffes and missteps by saying, "Sorry about that." The line always got a laugh. In Vietnam, when something didn't go as planned or accidents happened, the same phrase was applied.

"We said 'sorry about that' so often that General Westmoreland himself issued a ban against using it," said Duke Dewey.

No problem. Troops adapted by translating the phrase to Vietnamese. The result was *xin loi* or *sin loi,* which was a disguised way of saying the same thing as Maxwell Smart. The expression was a way of making sense of the senseless, and it had endless applications.

Having served in Special Forces as an advisor on an earlier tour in Vietnam, Dewey taught valuable lessons about the way things really worked to unsuspecting junior officers.

"Ninety-nine percent of the officers we had there were good," Dewey said.

The others? They learned the hard way.

Take, for example, the episode of the Seiko watch that Dewey sold to an inexperienced, fresh-faced lieutenant who got on his wrong side. The Japanese-made Seiko time piece was an icon of the Vietnam War. Prized by the grunts as a status symbol, the dark-faced watch with the luminescent dials served the practical purpose of keeping reliable time, day or night, in the field. As with anything in huge demand, the watches proliferated on the black market, where it was up to the buyer to beware. Counterfeits and knock-offs abounded. Accordingly, Dewey sold a fake Seiko to a runny-nosed, butter bar lieutenant for something like $20.

"Not long afterwards, he looked me up and said, 'Something's wrong with the watch. It doesn't keep good time.' I told him that those Seiko watches were made in Japan, and his was keeping Japanese time," Dewey said. "Some major tracked me down and told me one of his lieutenants was walking around with a bad watch. He told me to give the guy his money back. I never did find the guy though."

Sorry about that.

In another caper involving a young officer, Dewey made sure a lieutenant's workspace always had a full supply of items that looked and tasted like the tropical chocolate bars that came in a brown wrapper and were found in Army rations. If the pile started to dwindle, Dewey was quick to replenish the stock.

"Some officer asked him about all those candy bars, and he told him that Sergeant Dewey made sure that he had 10 to 20 of them on his desk at all times. The officer asks him, 'Are your bowels kind of loose?' The lieutenant answers, 'Yes, sir. It's our diet and the climate of Vietnam, I guess.' Then the officer says to him, 'Do you know you're eating Ex-Lax?' The guy was slow," Dewey said.

Sorry about that too.

Tropical chocolate bars were a story unto themselves. Their taste was affected by the fact that they were laced with additives that made them less likely to melt in the heat of Southeast Asia. American soldiers wanted to be like their fathers who handed out chocolate in World War II to the jubilant inhabitants of liberated towns who greeted them as heroes. With tongue planted firmly in cheek, veterans of Vietnam say that when they passed out tropical chocolate bars to the locals, the taste was so unappealing that the peasant kids threw them back.

Meanwhile, Captain Dickie Keaton of the Military Intelligence Detachment worked closely with Duke Dewey in trying to figure out what hostile forces were planning.

As background, Keaton was commissioned as an Army officer through the ROTC program at East Tennessee State University, and after spending some time in a combat unit, he had gone to the Army school that teaches intelligence gathering. In early 1968, he was selected to go to Vietnam to do military work while he wore civilian clothes. He happened to arrive just after the Tet Offensive began, and he was assigned to the 82nd Airborne instead. At Camp Rodriguez, he supervised a crew tasked with staying one step ahead of the enemy.

"I had really good soldiers. They were college grads and volunteers. All of them wanted to be James Bond," Keaton said.

Living conditions were downright primitive until the world-class scrounging ability of the Airborne made things better. A sergeant showed up at Keaton's headquarters in an Army truck that had had all the identifying markings painted over. It was bound for the big Navy supply depot in Hue where all kinds of equipment was stockpiled for use by the Marines. The sergeant gave Keaton a shirt that identified him as a lieutenant in the 9th Marines, and off they went. At the supply depot, the sergeant produced the paperwork to requisition two General Purpose medium tents, items that were sorely needed at Camp Rodriguez.

"He told the supply officer what we needed and said we were in a hurry because I had to be somewhere," said Keaton, who passed himself off as Lieutenant Schmedlap.

The caper resulted in the Airborne receiving two tents, along with poles, ropes and pegs. Then they beat it out of there before they were caught. Both tents were erected at

Camp Rodriguez in plain view of the route Colonel Bud Bolling took to get from the flight pad to his headquarters.

"Glad to see the supply system is working," the colonel told Keaton. Much later, Keaton confessed to Bolling that the tents had been pilfered. Bolling didn't mind. The tents made living conditions better for his troops.

One of the tents was used as a dining facility, its canvas providing at least some cover when it rained. The second one was set up as a day room, or a primitive lounge for off-duty troops. There was enough space in it to place a small refrigerator. Troops could stop in for a relatively cold drink. In addition to soft drinks, they could also get a cold beer, with a limit of two beers per soldier per day. If anyone abused the privilege, Keaton said he would remove the refrigerator and reassign any offender to a line company in a different outfit.

Then Duke Dewey entered the picture. With his connections in the Special Forces, Dewey learned that a contingent of Green Berets had gone to Hong Kong to have maintenance done on a C-130 Hercules cargo plane. The plane came back fully loaded with all kinds of goodies, and Dewey approached Keaton with an idea.

"Dick, could you use a movie?" Dewey asked Keaton.

"Sure, we could show it in the day room. It could be a morale boost for the men," the captain replied.

The movie was known at the time as a stag film, or the Sixties version of adult entertainment. A projector was found, and a sheet was hung between two tent poles to serve as a screen. The refrigerator was stocked with soft drinks and beer, and some munchies were scrounged up for the snack bar. By word of mouth, troops found out about movie night.

"I'm sitting in headquarters, and here comes the chaplain. 'I heard you have some movies,' he said. I replied, 'Yes, but not the kind you'd be interested in.' He said, 'Oh,' and went back to his quarters," Keaton laughed.

Sorry about that.

The show went on as soldiers found a respite from the stresses and strains of war, thoroughly entertained at the absurdity of the scenes. The audience even asked for an encore.

"We ended up having to show it twice," Keaton said.

At the same time, the tent that served as the camp mess hall had all kinds of functions, including one as a place of worship. Chaplain James Sanner conducted religious services there, at least until a resourceful first sergeant traded a jeep for a real chapel with an actual cross on it. But in another example of Airborne resourcefulness, the sergeant later spotted that jeep in a village. The vehicle was unattended, and he brought it back to base camp. It still had the markings of the 82nd Airborne on it. All in the service of the Lord, or as the motto of the chaplain's corps says, *Pro Deo et Patria*, for God and Country.

On Sundays, Sanner presided over services in the field by taking a helicopter around to all the fire bases. The helicopter was provided by Colonel Bolling.

"We'd go to all the mountain tops. There would be maybe seven separate services. On one Sunday, I had nine," Father Sanner said.

During the week, a driver would take the chaplain out to the field in a jeep to care for the spiritual needs of the soldiers. On such occasions, Sanner would hold the driver's rifle for him just in case, even though chaplains weren't supposed to carry weapons.

Depending on the circumstances, his altar might be stacked ammo crates, C Ration boxes or the hood of jeep. During services, Sanner donned a cloth vestment called a chasuble that draped over his fatigues. It's the outermost garment used in services and rites. The one he brought with him from the States was white and stood out like a neon sign in the bush. A battalion commander cautioned that the white could be seen a mile away and made Sanner a perfect target for snipers. The chaplain wore it anyway, but the first chance he got, he had one made out of a cargo parachute and then got a green one from home.

"We'd stop at checkpoints on the bridges or hit the smaller camps and have Communion for those who wanted it. Soldiers would come out of the woods for that," said Sanner, who wore a medal of St. Michael the Archangel with his dog tags. "I'd hear confessions too. Someone would say, 'I shot into the bush and I think I shot someone.' And I'd say, 'That could be. It's not a sin. We're at war. This is part of war.' "

The paratrooper spirit made a lasting impression on Sanner.

"There was just something special about the 82nd Airborne. You could feel it and see it in the way they dressed and the way they comported themselves. Their spirit is really something. They were always respectful. Yes, they're known for their coarse language, and often times I'd hear someone say, 'Watch it. Here comes the chaplain.' What stood out most for me was how young they were. They were just kids."

One time, Father Sanner was invited to celebrate Mass at the Seabees installation at Phu Bai. He drove to the camp, where being resourceful themselves, the Seabees had built themselves a first-rate mess hall and a club with a bar. The air-conditioned club served as Sanner's altar that day, and he brought along his sacred cloth and his chaplain's kit of religious relics. The Seabees sprung a surprise on the chaplain.

"Under the plexi-glass were all the centerfolds from Playboy magazine," Sanner said, laughing at the memory. Well, the job of the chaplain is to nurture the living, care for the wounded and honor the fallen. If bringing soldiers to God and God to soldiers meant placing an altar cloth over the revealing photographs of Playmates, so be it.

Glenn McGhie of San Fernando, California, also had a story to share that was biblical and bawdy, just like the Airborne itself. In civilian life, McGhie had served overseas on a Mormon mission, and he and his wife were expecting the birth of a child. Then his number came up in the draft, and he entered the Army in October of 1967. Six months later, he was in Vietnam and assigned to Charlie Company of the 307th

Engineers in the Golden Brigade. McGhie spent six weeks or so out in the field, but when his superiors found out he could type, he became the company clerk, a sort of Radar O'Reilly. Among his new duties was to find movies to be shown as entertainment for off-duty troops at Camp Rodriguez.

"We had a surplus of generators for some reason, and I sold or traded them to get movies and the projector. I took what I could get. I was lucky to have that job," McGhie said.

Available in the supply chain were TV shows converted to film or first-rate movies like *The Good, The Bad and The Ugly.* One time, he got his hands on a reel of *The Green Berets*, featuring John Wayne as a Special Forces officer operating in Vietnam. The movie screen was a piece of plywood erected on a flatbed trailer in an area of rolling hills, a location that lent itself to an outdoor theater. It also happened to be within sight of the prisoner of war compound, a holding pen that was rimmed with barbed wire.

"Most of the time, you're not even aware the POWs are there, but from behind the wire, they'd watch the movies too. One of the scenes in *The Green Berets* is when a Special Forces camp gets overrun. Well, the POWs are standing and cheering at this, so our guys start booing and hissing. Later on, when John Wayne and his guys take the camp back, our guys jumped up and cheered while the POWs were hissing and booing," McGhie said.

It was good duty, but McGhie said the audience was a demanding one. He'd have to change reels in the dark for some movies, and the audience would shout out catcalls during the slightest delays.

Anyway, First Sergeant James Wallace asked McGhie if he might be able to bring in a live band for entertainment. McGhie worked his magic, and a Vietnamese rock group with electric guitars and a drummer filled the bill. The first sergeant was so impressed that he asked McGhie if he could find an exotic dancer. It took some doing, but through his network of contacts, McGhie got in touch with an enterprising performer from the Philippines who brought her act to Vietnam. She traveled with her own retinue of bodyguards and entertained at various camps in South Vietnam.

"When the first sergeant asks you to do something, you do everything in your power to keep him happy," McGhie said.

Well, the striptease artist performed to the music of a Richard Strauss opera based on the biblical story of Salome, who danced erotically for her uncle, King Herod, and as a reward, asked for John the Baptist's head on a platter. Her music was *The Dance of the Seven Veils.*

"She was built like a brick outhouse. I was supposed to take pictures and was sitting up front. Just at the point when she removed her last piece of clothing, a guy jumped up right in front of me. All I got was a picture of the back of the guy's head," McGhie said.

Sorry about that.

Chapter 18
THE THREE VILLES

Tommy Locastro had received his orders to return home from the emergency deployment to Vietnam. One of his best buddies had already left the combat zone, and Locastro had been assigned non-combat duty while he awaited transportation on what soldiers called the Freedom Bird, or any plane that flew back to The World. Having survived Charlie Company's battles at the Candy Stripe, Ap Nam Phu and the Lazy W River, Locastro was eager to get back to the bride he left behind. He had done everything he was asked to do on what the Big Army called a temporary assignment.

"So happy to leave this rotten place," Locastro noted in his journal. He had been away on Easter Sunday, marked the one-year anniversary of being wounded on his first tour on April 23, came down with a touch of dysentery or some other tropical ailment and checked off each day as one closer to going home.

But Bud Bolling still had a war to fight. Even as the number of the dead and wounded had depleted the ranks of the Golden Brigade, Bolling was losing men who, under Army policy, were returning home. With that in mind, Bolling summoned a group of 15 to 20 soldiers, including Locastro, to his headquarters. He wanted to know if any of them would stay in the fight before going home.

"I'm going to ask you the worst thing a commander can ask. I'm short people. Will you volunteer to go back on the line?" Locastro remembered the brigade commander as saying.

"Everyone in the tent snapped to attention and shouted the Airborne response: 'All The Way, Sir'! It brought tears to his eyes," Locastro said. "It's not bravery. It's being responsible to friends. You want to protect them as much as they protect you."

In his journal, however, Locastro gave voice to his inner feelings. "Well, Colonel Bolling said back to the front again…I must be nuts to go back to combat again." He rejoined Charlie Company in the 1st of the 505 just as the next fight was on the horizon.

In Alpha Company, platoon sergeant Sherman Hussey was free and clear too. His duty was done. But when word came at the end of April that his company was needed for a combat mission, Hussey volunteered.

"He came to me and said, 'I'm going with you. I have to go with you,' " said company commander Mike Hood. "I should have just said no. My biggest regret is that I didn't talk him out of it. The guy was home free. He shouldn't have been there."

Elsewhere in Alpha Company, medical specialist James Ray Fedro of Fort Worth, Texas, was pressed into service again because of a fateful set of circumstances. Fedro,

20, was a short-timer and should have been out of the field. Medics, however, were a precious and rare commodity. James (Doc) Slavin, the battalion surgeon, had 36 medics when he arrived in Vietnam. Within a few weeks, however, battle deaths and wounds had reduced that number to about 15. Ideally, each company should have had a medic for each platoon, but there just weren't enough to go around. When replacements did start to dribble in, issues arose with the new guys. According to Slavin, one replacement from a post in Germany barely lasted his first day in the field. Overweight and poorly trained, the guy went out with a platoon on patrol. The tropical heat and the pace of maneuvers took their toll, and two soldiers actually had to assist the medic during the operation. "He almost died out there," Slavin recalled. To replace the replacement, Fedro was sent back into the field.

"He was taking the spot of a guy who was unprepared. If people are going to count on you and you can't deliver, it puts everybody at risk," Slavin said. "Medics need two things: morphine and a set of balls." In his private photo collection, Mike Hood has a grainy black and white snapshot of Fedro and another medic, Paul Nance, carrying a wounded trooper from the field.

All of these threads became interwoven on May 1 when a stream of peasants, lugging only what possessions they could carry, fled their dwellings in three interconnected villages on the south side of Highway One just two miles west of Hue. Displaced men, women and children were part of the joyless procession. A lack of activity in the rice fields provided another clue that something was awry.

In questioning the mass of humanity, a recon platoon learned that North Vietnamese troops had taken over the villages and forced out the inhabitants. After reporting the situation to headquarters, the recon unit took up a blocking position outside the northernmost village. Two rifle companies were ordered to investigate. Charlie Company, which had spent the night in defensive positions just two kilometers to the west, moved out. Alpha Company pushed up from the south.

"We were in there the day before. Kids were working the fields with water buffaloes, guiding them with sticks. But on this day, the kids were gone. The buffalo were all loose. You get this eerie feeling that something's going to happen. Then all hell broke loose," said Tommy Locastro.

Captain Paul Davin, commander of Charlie Company, raced up when the guns began to shoot. "When it first started, we were running. We left our gear to get in the fight," he said. Mike Hood had said of Davin: "Best company commander I ever saw, hands down."

Approaching across open rice paddies, the point element of Charlie Company surprised several daydreaming enemy soldiers and killed them.

"We saw three of what appeared to be enemy. I said to the element, make sure they're bad guys. I took the first shot," Davin said.

When first platoon entered the upper hamlet, machine guns and rifles opened up with an intense stream of fire, wounding two troopers who were evacuated in the battalion commander's helicopter. Second platoon took sniper fire from the center hamlet and returned fire as it deployed to attack. To support the ground troops, Davin called in an air strike.

At the same time, Mike Hood's Alpha Company advanced on the southernmost hamlet, named Bon Tri. Unit spirits were high. Using ink pens, troops had written "Hood's Rangers" on their shirts.

"We start to move into the village, and we start taking sniper fire. So, we deal with that, and we move a little bit further and we find NVA packs and grenades. People had left and run. So, I begin to call in artillery fire and walk through the village. I put two platoons side by side, and I bring the third up around to my right. All of a sudden, it hits the fan again. What we had done was walk into a regimental headquarters. They were trying to get away, and they were jumping out of little foxholes and trying to grab guys' weapons. It was truly a melee," Hood said.

Hood radioed for close air support, and moments later, an attack jet whooshing along at 800 feet above the ground was inbound with its payload.

"Get everybody down. It's coming in hot and heavy," the pilot radioed back.

During the course of the fight, a total of 21 air strikes were called in. At the time, the number was a record for most air strikes in a single ground engagement in South Vietnam, Hood said. In addition, ground troops were supported by the big guns of a navy battleship stationed in the South China Sea. The shell from one of its nine 16-inch guns weighed about the same as a Volkswagen Beetle, and the projectiles could be tracked with the naked eye on their arc through the sky.

"We were bringing in air strikes. Charlie Company was bringing in air strikes. We were in there intermingled with the enemy, and they're still firing mortars, and we're trying to locate them. It was a pretty big affair. The bottom line is, we got the situation stabilized," Hood said.

In the chaos, two troopers were killed. Three others were missing in action and later found to be killed. Fifteen troopers were wounded. Among the dead was Sherman Hussey, who had volunteered for the mission. Hussey was survived by a wife and two daughters, one of whom later posted an online tribute: "When you were killed, part of mother died also." Fedro, the medic who wasn't supposed to be in the field, was also slain. One of Fedro's friends back in The World later posted that Fedro would not have been drafted if his ex-wife hadn't reported their divorce to his local draft board.

"Unfortunately, I lost my sergeant. Every senior leader I had was killed or wounded. The senior aid man, which was his first day, was killed. It was a rough day. It was a much longer day than the 20th of March," Hood said.

The cacophony of noise from bombs, shells, mortars, machine guns and rifles was almost continuous. Joe Mays, a platoon leader in Alpha Company, was wounded during the fray. He called it a day like no other.

"It was the worst day of my life, not because I was wounded, but because a lot of good young men died," Mays said.

Mays gave this account of the battle: "All of a sudden, mortar rounds started exploding all around us. We took cover, but then we were engaged by the NVA with small arms fire while the mortar rounds kept coming in. Several of my men were injured and killed. The firefight seemed as if it would never end. I was pinned down near a tree with one of my guys wounded and one of them dead. I had been hit with mortar shrapnel in my arm and leg. I could see the NVA less than 50 meters away. At one point, I reloaded my M-16, picked up another M-16, put a new magazine in it, put both the weapons on rock 'n' roll, stood up with a rifle in each hand and shot all forty rounds in just a few seconds. We were still getting mortared and shot at. I am not sure exactly what happened next, but I think Hood's platoon and first platoon moved near us and continued to engage the NVA. By then our artillery started coming in and we eventually were able to disengage."

Extracted by helicopter, Mays was taken to an aid station to have his wounded leg and arm patched up. Then he got caught up in the fog of war. He considered himself fortunate to have survived and didn't think his wounds were that serious. After downing some food, he re-entered the fight.

"I left the hospital, found my M-16 and saw a helicopter that was going back to the area of the firefight. I got on it and shortly thereafter rejoined my platoon. In the meantime, the brigade hospital reported that I had gone AWOL. I guess I forgot to tell them that I was going back to be with my guys. I just left. I didn't tell anybody," Mays said.

The record got straightened out in due time. A wounded officer who returned to the battlefield was absolved of having been perceived to be in violation of military law. Mays processed the episode by recalling the words of his paratrooper father to look for a flash of humor in the darkest of circumstances. When Mays recounted the story, he laughed.

Mays also recalled a conversation with his father after he returned to The World. "My father said that the difference between his war and my war was that he was told you get to go home when you the war is over. He was in it for three years. An individual's commitment in Vietnam was 12 months, regardless of the outcome."

Meanwhile, Alpha Company's sweep flushed enemy soldiers out into the open and into Charlie Company. That stealthy enemy rarely stood and fought, electing to hide in camouflaged holes and trenches or blending into villages to conceal their presence. This time, the rifles and machine guns of Charlie Company took dead aim.

"It was a real turkey shoot," Tommy Locastro said.

At the end of a grueling day, Alpha Company began settling in for the night when Frank Butner Clay, the assistant division commander of the 101st Airborne, arrived by helicopter for a situational report.

"We were consolidating our position just before dark and this commander from the 101st flies in and asks what's the situation. His call sign was Eagle Eye. I point out everything to him and told him we were going to secure the area with ambush sites. He got up to leave and said, 'Thank you, Captain.' One of the kids said to him, 'Hey, sir, he's just a second lieutenant.' He turned around and said, 'When you're running the ship, you're the captain.' It was what I needed to hear at the moment," Hood recalled. "I had six KIA and 20 wounded. That was 40 percent of company."

In addition to Hussey and Fedro, the casualty list included Sergeant Paul Nance Jr., who was just 30 days shy of his 24th birthday and was the only son of Paul and Helen Nance. He had already served one tour in Vietnam and had been married for six weeks before he got called out with the 82nd Airborne to return to war. An alumnus of North Carolina Wesleyan College, he gave a couple of shot glasses to a classmate on the last day of school and said, "We'll have a drink when I get back." He never got to have that drink. Nance was one of five alumni of that school who were killed in Vietnam. Their names are on a plaque outside the school's tennis courts, which were dedicated in 1997. "Paul Jr. was a caring, fun, hard-working and thoughtful person. He loved the outdoors and spent many happy hours on the Pamlico River in Washington, N.C. His parents never really got over his death. We all still miss him," said a cousin, Susan Nance Sautter, in an online post.

Also killed that day were two privates first class, John Runyon Neary II, 21, of Odessa, Texas, and James Sherwood Allport, 19, of Marlowe Heights, Maryland, who was buried in Arlington National Cemetery.

In 2015, veteran Carmine Francis Renaud left this tribute to Allport on the Virtual Wall of Faces: "Jimmy, I sometimes have moments to reflect, and I will tell you that you are always with me. I will never forget when we lost you, Paul and Sherman. I thought the guilt of survival would go away, but it never does. I would trade a year of tomorrows for one yesterday to be with my brothers. We stand alone together."

The names of the Alpha Company troopers killed on May 1 are together forever on Panel 53 East of The Wall.

Another member of Alpha Company was killed on May 2 by fratricide, although no details are available how it happened. He was Private First Class Errol Michael Barrimond, 21, of New York, N.Y. He was later buried at San Juan Public Cemetery in Tunapuna on his native island of Trinidad in the Caribbean.

At the cost of six All Americans killed and 20 wounded, another enemy unit had been rendered ineffective and would pose no further threat to Hue. A prisoner told the intelligence units that the three villages had been taken over by a battalion of the 90th

Regiment of the North Vietnamese Army. A sweep of the battlefield produced 128 enemy bodies.

On May 2, Tommy Locastro was among those who policed the three villages. The nauseating odor of burnt human flesh filled his nostrils during a search that uncovered more enemy weapons. He slept in a temple that night, pondering the events and reflecting on his own survival.

"I don't know if it's about bravery or being responsible to your friends. You just do what you have to do. Sometimes I feel guilty about making it. Why wasn't I killed? Why them?" Locastro said.

For his part in the battle, Mike Hood was awarded the Silver Star in an action that became known as the Battle of the Three Villes.

"These were dreams. You never even consider something like that. Before this action, I got a letter from Glynn Hale, my roommate at Bragg. I'm real excited. It was my first letter. But he apparently put a letter meant for another friend into my envelope. It began, 'Dear Shit Head: I guess you've heard that damn Hood is already in Vietnam. Worse yet, he's had his picture in the papers back here, and there's rumors of him receiving some decorations. Just can't stand it. I can hardly wait to get there.' "

Hale did three tours in Vietnam. A generation later, he was the commander of the Third Brigade of the 82nd Airborne in Desert Storm. Hood returned the favor and wrote him a letter saying not to start the war without him. The fight was over before Hood got there.

In a letter written 32 years after the Three Villes, Bud Bolling wrote: "Of all the troopers I know, I can think of no one who saw more combat that Mike Hood…He started out as a platoon leader in the initial tough fighting we encountered upon arrival. Needless to say, he was ultimately made a company commander."

Hood never forgot Hussey, who had been in the Army since the days of the Korean War. In May of 2017, on his way to All American Week at Fort Bragg, Hood took a side trip to Carthage, North Carolina. He visited the cemetery where his sergeant shared a plot and a common tombstone with his wife, Shirley Mae. She died 17 months after her husband was killed.

"It was rough. A lieutenant could not have asked for a better platoon sergeant. He was a leader," Hood said. "A day hasn't gone by that I haven't thought of Hussey."

Chapter 19
THE AMBUSH

Artillery officer Rene Georges Baumann was described by his peers as a capable fighter who put it all on the line to do the job he was trained to do. He had been on the first flight over with the Golden Brigade and was the fire control officer when the artillery section recorded the brigade's first confirmed kill on February 28 while it was acclimating to Vietnam.

"We were at the top of our game technically as artillerymen," said Thomas Meeker, who had roomed with Baumann in Fort Bragg for five months prior to the deployment. "We were using a lot of artillery. Just blowing everything away."

Yet an aura of mystery surrounds Baumann, who at 26, was older than the other second lieutenants in his unit. Although he was an All American fighting America's war, he wasn't a U.S. citizen. Not yet anyway. His motivation for serving in the Army was to speed the process of naturalization, which helps explain why a native of Switzerland who grew up in the shadow of the snow-capped Alps was fighting in the tropics of Southeast Asia with the 82nd Airborne.

"Rene was the one guy I was closest to," Meeker said. "He was a good paratrooper, a good soldier. Capable. He was quite serious about his job, but he could relax when he was off duty. He was jovial then. Always had a smile on his face. He had some connection to Walnut Creek, California, but nobody knew quite what it was."

Baumann had already served one tour of duty in Vietnam as a jump-qualified sergeant in the 101st Airborne Division. He then extended his enlistment to earn his commission from Officer Candidate School as an artillery specialist. Prior to that, he had served in the army of Switzerland, a country known for its chocolate, precision watches and military neutrality but nonetheless a country that fielded a force to protect its borders.

While in Vietnam at the end of April in 1968, Baumann had been summoned to the U.S. Embassy in Saigon to address his citizenship application, and he expected to be naturalized within a few months. On his return to the field, Baumann was attached to a rifle company in the 1st Battalion of the 508th Parachute Infantry Regiment. As a forward observer with the Red Devils, he was the man on the scene who determined the map coordinates for the big guns to zero in on, and he adjusted that fire so that the rounds fell where they did the most damage. One characteristic of the King of Battle, as the artillery is known, is that it doesn't have to hit directly. Anything within 25 yards of an exploding shell would be subject to the shock waves and the spray of hot metal shards whistling through the air.

In the early days of May, Baumann and the Golden Brigade received a new mission. With the security of Hue having stabilized, the 101st Airborne shifted its focus to the A Shau Valley, the natural conduit that Communist forces used to come and go into South Vietnam. To support operations in the A Shau, a significant artillery position and staging area for troops was built atop a hill in the jungle. Called Fire Base Bastogne, it was named for a place that became a big part of Screaming Eagles history during the Battle of the Bulge in World War II. Bastogne was about 22 miles west of Hue and accessible overland along a road known as Highway 547. Two fortifications were built along its length to guard against ambushes. One was Fire Base Boyd, located on the western side of the west branch of the Perfume River and just north of the Nam Hoa Bridge. Boyd originally was a rock quarry that provided gravel for construction crews. Between Boyd and Bastogne was Fire Base Birmingham, or Hill 90, named for a trooper in the 101st who drowned trying to rescue a comrade who was taking fire while trying to cross a river in 1967. Located on the front edge of the western mountains, Birmingham was used as a staging area for helicopter assaults or for the insertion of recon teams. It was the responsibility of Baumann's unit and three other rifle companies of All Americans to keep Highway 547 open to convoys delivering ammunition and supplies beyond Boyd and Birmingham all the way out to Bastogne.

Although it was called Highway 547 coming out of Hue, it was little more than a two-lane, washboard road the closer it got to Bastogne. The jungle grew thicker too, and to beat back the undergrowth, U.S. planes sprayed the sides of the road with Agent Orange, one of a number of herbicides used during the war that later were determined to cause cancer and other harmful side effects. When the jungle growth died, flame-throwers were called in to burn away the dead vegetation. Specially modified armored bulldozers called Rome plows cleared both sides of the road to keep ambushers at bay. It was still hostile country, however, and there had been enough shots exchanged to indicate an enemy force was lurking.

As it turned out, with a convoy scheduled to move on May 5, a perfect ambush had been set up by the K10 Battalion of the 22nd Regiment of the North Vietnamese Army. Along a roughly mile-long stretch of Highway 547, enemy soldiers placed pits for mortars and rocket launchers on the north and south sides of the road. Land mines that could be detonated from a command center were planted. Machine gun nests were set up at critical spots. And once the deadly trap had been sprung, escape routes had been mapped out for the ambushers to melt away into the undergrowth before they could be detected. The only thing capable of disrupting those carefully made plans was the 82nd Airborne.

Guarding against ambushes on one section of the road was the 1st Battalion of the 508th, with Rene Baumann serving as forward artillery observer in Charlie Company. The company commander was Captain Afton Watts, 31, of Austin, Texas, who had been stationed in Germany before volunteering for Vietnam. With 10 years of Army service under his belt, he was less than three months away from becoming a civilian. As he made preparations for the May 5 mission, one of his troops heard him say: "Just 51 days left."

The fourth platoon of Charlie Company drew the assignment of protecting the westernmost edge of their area of responsibility. A machine gunner on the point set up his weapon, and to maximize his field of fire, he directed his assistant gunner to move forward to clear away some brush. As the solider went about his task, he was cut down by a burst of enemy fire. The machine gunner spotted the three enemy soldiers who had killed his assistant. One long volley from his M-60 killed them all. What's more, the chance exchange triggered a major fight.

Upon hearing the gunfire, the NVA figured the convoy had entered their trap. Mortars shells fired from a hill to the north began raining down on the first platoon. Other mortars joined in from south of the road, dropping rounds onto the third platoon.

As the mortar fire intensified, there was an officer's call to determine the best response. Captain Watts prepared to move his command post to a better location from which to coordinate the fight. Just then, a shell landed in the midst of his command element. Killed in addition to the captain were his radio man and the company's chief medic, Specialist 5 Ernest Payne, an African American from Baton Rouge, Louisiana. At the same time, Rene Baumann was fatally shot through the throat.

First Sergeant Frank Zappala raced forward and killed three NVA who had fired on the command element. With no other officers around, he took command and ordered the company to assault the ambush positions in hopes of pushing the enemy into the open.

A hurried call for assistance was answered by Alpha Company. Moving from the southwest, it broke out of the jungle roughly 600 yards from where the opening shots were fired. Captain Jack Hayman ordered his troops to drop their rucksacks and double-time it to the sounds of the guns. Rushing along the tree line near the road, Alpha Company hit the enemy in the flank and was met with stiff resistance. After two attempts failed to break through, Hayman dispatched his first and second platoons, with Lieutenant Gary Hall in command, to swing north around the enemy.

Hayman maneuvered his remaining two platoons south, attempting to get around the enemy's right flank and envelop the force. Encountering opposition along the way, the platoons finally found the rear of the enemy position and cut off the escape routes. Hayman's troops established a skirmish line and waited.

Meanwhile, the first and second platoons got behind the enemy but were pinned down by intense and accurate mortar fire from a piece of high ground known as Hill 66. They held there as Zappala and Charlie Company assaulted the mortar position and killed 26 hostile forces.

Hayman then radioed Hall to attack with his two platoons. After two unsuccessful attempts to break through, Hall's men achieved the desired result on their third try. It was a turning point.

Unable to hold its ground, the North Vietnamese battalion fled toward its escape routes. Helicopter gunships and air strikes strafed them as they ran, increasing their panic. With two platoons of Alpha Company in hot pursuit, the NVA ran smack into the waiting muzzles of Captain Hayman's element. The ambushers had become the ambushed. Machine guns and rifles threw up a wall of steel that left enemy dead stacked in heaps. Caught between four platoons of troopers, the NVA charged piecemeal against the Americans in a futile attempt to break out. Captain Hayman personally killed seven NVA in the engagement.

In the heat of the battle, Sergeant Henry Trotty of Lieutenant Hall's element broke into a jungle clearing and confronted three enemy soldiers manning a mortar. He charged, killing two of them with his rifle and finishing off the third with his bare hands. After destroying the mortar ammunition, Trotty picked up the tube and brought it back with him. He asked that the weapon be sent back to the 82nd Airborne Division Museum at Fort Bragg. For his extraordinary actions, Trotty was awarded the Distinguished Service Cross, the nation's second highest award for valor.

Meanwhile, Hall's two platoons linked up with Hayman's force, and the wounded were evacuated. Late that afternoon, both Alpha and Charlie Company of the Red Devils linked up with Captain Paul Davin's Charlie Company of the 1st of the 505, which had already seen its share of firefights in earlier engagements. The three companies were preparing to move to night defensive positions when 10 exhausted enemy soldiers stumbled out of the jungle and tried to attack. All were cut down.

Following the brief but vicious encounter, Davin's company moved to its night defensive position, with Private First Class Richard Herbert posted as a guard on the company perimeter. In the darkness, he heard people speaking Vietnamese.

"There were three of them, only ten feet to my front when they stopped," Herbert said in an after-action report. "There were only two small bushes between us. I aimed at the NVA who was doing all the talking and opened up."

Captain Davin and Private First Class Andrew Campbell, who was Herbert's squad leader, came on the run to see what the shooting was about. The three walked to the front of Herbert's post and found one NVA body and two blood trails. The dead NVA had a pistol and documents that indicated he had been a company commander.

After the battle, enemy bodies were counted. In their failed attempt to ambush a convoy, more than 100 NVA were killed.

Seven All Americans paid the price in blood that day. In addition to Watts, Baumann and Payne, losses included Private First Class James Nathan Carroll III, a supply clerk from Cincinnati, Ohio, and Private First Class Thomas George Brocker of San Jose, California, from Charlie Company. Killed from Alpha Company were Second

Lieutenant Gary Arnaldo Guasp of Brentwood, New York, and Private First Class Max Edward Nimphie Jr. of Fenton, Michigan. All of them are together on Panel 55 East of The Wall.

"May 5 was a traumatic day," said Tom Meeker.

The convoy that was supposed to be targeted did not move on May 5. It proceeded the next day to Fire Base Bastogne and delivered its vital supplies without incident.

As an aside, the hill from which the North Vietnamese had fired their mortars onto Highway 547 was eliminated as a future threat when it was denuded of vegetation. Cargo planes dropped Agent Orange onto the hilltop, killing all of the jungle growth. Then came the next step. Tom Ladwig, the brigade's chemical officer, said he was aboard a helicopter that flew over the hilltop. Inside were 55-gallon drums of napalm wired to thermite grenades.

"I pulled the ring on the grenades as the barrels went out. When the napalm hit the ground and spread, the grenades exploded and ignited a fireball," said Ladwig.

On other occasions, the brigade's chemical unit would drop tear gas onto an area suspected to be hiding the enemy. The idea was to smoke them out in the open and then rain down artillery on their position. This practice wasn't foolproof, however. Ladwig remembers the time tear gas was dropped at 10,000 feet but dispersed too early. "None of it ever hit the ground," Ladwig said. Another time, planes sprayed the jungle with diesel fuel, and a follow-on flight was supposed to drop white phosphorous grenades to set the fuel on fire.

"One grenade hit the side of the helicopter and came back in. We had to scramble to get it out of there," Ladwig said. "The vegetation was so green and wet; it didn't burn anyway."

Meanwhile, Tom Meeker kept alive the memory of Rene Baumann. Meeker, whose father was a career officer in the National Guard in California, enlisted in the Army in the summer of 1965 with the idea of receiving a commission. "I wanted to do something I couldn't do as a civilian," he said. After basic and advanced training, he earned his wings at jump school and was then posted to the John F. Kennedy Special Warfare Center at Fort Bragg, where he was assigned to Echo Company of the 7th Special Forces Group. From there, he enrolled in Officer Candidate School with an emphasis in artillery and joined the 82nd Airborne in August of 1967. Then came Vietnam.

"Being in the military changed my life. First of all, I grew up. I don't think you can go back to being a kid or go back to being like the people our age who didn't go to Vietnam. You're more focused, more serious. You take more responsibility. Have a better understanding of relationships. When the country called, I was there. I was personally fortunate. I wasn't traumatized by Vietnam whereas some people were. It was just something I did. It's common for all wars. The old men start it, and it's the younger people that fight. They shouldn't be there. They should be growing up back home. Now they're growing up during a war," said Meeker, who retired as a lieutenant colonel.

Through the years, Rene Baumann remained in his thoughts.

"I often think about him. His story is pretty awesome," Meeker said.

At one point, assisted by computer searches, Meeker made contact with Raymond Froidevaux, who was a year younger than Baumann but grew up in the same Swiss village of Columbier. Situated on the banks of Lake Neuchâtel, it had a population of under 5,000 residents.

"We were in the same school but in different classes. After class, in his free time, René would play marbles in the public garden of the village with other friends," Froidevaux recalled.

Baumann's mother received word that her son was missing in action, and shortly thereafter, she got news that he was dead. Although some records mistakenly indicate that Baumann was buried in Walnut Creek, California, his remains were taken to Switzerland in a flag-draped coffin. He was cremated and buried in the cemetery of his home village.

A few years after his death, Mrs. Bluette Baumann gave all the mementoes of her son to Froidevaux. These included the American flag that covered his coffin, his military awards and letters of condolence from U.S. officials. One medal was the Bronze Star for valor. The citation, written on stationery carrying the logo of the 101st Airborne, read: "His initiative, zeal, sound judgment and devotion to duty have been in the highest traditions of the United States Army and reflect great credit on him and on the military service."

One letter was from four-star general Ralph Haines, acting chief of staff of the U.S. Army in Vietnam. Dated May 21, 1968, it read: "Although I know that words cannot lessen your sorrow, I hope you will find consolation and gain strength from the thought that your son served his Nation with courage and honor. You can indeed treasure the thought that your son was noble among men in that he gave his life that free men might live."

Another letter came from President Johnson. Dated June 3, 1968, and written on White House stationery, it said: "This nation will be forever indebted to his bravery and selfless devotion. I pray that your pride in your son's dedication will give you strength at this time."

Lastly, there was this August 4, 1968, correspondence from General Creighton W. Abrams. It said: "Rest assured that we who remain here in Vietnam will continue our efforts to bring peace to this troubled land so that your son's sacrifice will not have been in vain."

Froidevaux promised Bluette Baumann that he would go to Vietnam to see the ground where his boyhood friend had died. True to his word, Froidevaux and his wife visited Hue and then the highlands off Highway 547 where Baumann was killed.

Some loose ends remain about Rene Baumann. Not every question can be answered. Although he never became a U.S. citizen, he died and was buried as an All American.

Chapter 20
ROAD GUARDS

Keeping the road open to the A Shau Valley was a vital but dangerous mission for the 82nd Airborne. Highway 547 was the main supply route for moving ammo and fuel out to Fire Base Bastogne to support combat operations, and every trip along its route was an adventure. Combat engineers swept it every morning with devices designed to detect mines and roadside bombs, which Mister Charles routinely planted to disrupt traffic. On one occasion, the Golden Brigade's cavalry unit escorted a fuel convoy on a harrowing trip through the jungle, this time at night.

The mission fell to Captain William R. Porter, commander of B Troop of the 17th Cav, after he was summoned to brigade headquarters. Having been commissioned as a second lieutenant through the ROTC program at the University of Maine in 1966, Porter had gone through basic officer courses and jump school before being assigned to the headquarters staff of the 82nd Airborne. The first time he had been shot at was in the Detroit riots. He was part of the emergency deployment to Vietnam and the movement up the Hai Van Pass. Now, Colonel Bud Bolling assigned Porter the task of escorting a convoy from Camp Eagle past Fire Base Boyd and Fire Base Birmingham to Bastogne.

"It was nothing unusual, nothing any different than what we ordinarily had to accomplish," Porter said in a 1989 interview with the ROTC Unit at the University of Maine, where he was a history professor. "And I said, 'Fine. When do I pick up my convoy, tomorrow morning?' And (Colonel Bolling) said, 'No. You pick it up tonight.' And I looked at my watch, and I said, 'Tonight?' And he said, 'Yes, I want you to pick it up tonight.' And I said, 'Now wait a minute. You want me to move a convoy down there at night, down through the thick jungle all the way around this road, and my responsibility for the last month or so was to clear the road with the engineers to make sure that the mines emplaced overnight by the enemy were cleared so we could use the road in the daytime?' We had a little bit of discussion because I didn't think it was too wise, but it was very clear the boss said do it. So I said OK."

Only then did he learn that the night trip involved five fuel tankers—each loaded with 10,000 gallons of flammable liquid—that were needed for a helicopter assault into the A Shau Valley. Normally, a truck would have a driver and a companion riding shotgun, but Porter ordered the driver go it alone. He wanted to avoid unnecessary casualties.

"I don't need another person on that vehicle, because if that vehicle hits a mine, it's going to go up. When you provide a lucrative target, and any of those tankers goes up along the narrow road, you would never be able to turn the other ones around. You would never be able to go forward," Porter said.

In the dark of night, with one of the 17th Cavalry's three platoons providing security, scouts in their gun jeeps led the way. Although Porter did not want the convoy stretched out for miles, he did space the five tankers a few hundred yards apart. That way, if one was destroyed, the other four would still be intact.

"Then we turned all of our lights off, and we traveled down the road at night just as quickly as we could," Porter said. "You could probably hear your heartbeat. The place had seen much fighting, and I know there wasn't one person there who wasn't afraid, but they kept moving very quietly."

Miraculously, the convoy and its precious fuel rumbled along without incident. Within 800 yards of their destination, the Cav escorts radioed the guards at Bastogne that they were approaching.

"We just picked up the phone and said, 'Open the gates. Here we come.' And we turned our lights on, and we drove the vehicles that last half mile just about as fast as you could possibly go. We didn't want them to shoot us up thinking we were sneaking in," Porter said.

The trucks made it safely, and the escorts stayed at the fire base that night. None of them knew how critical the mission had been until afterwards. They just knew it was dangerous.

"The average soldier says, 'What are you doing to me? You're trying to kill me. Why am I going on this convoy? This is dumb. It can wait until tomorrow.' Even myself, when I was first told to do it, I didn't fully understand the impact. I questioned the mission because it didn't make sense, but then when I was told that it was important and I needed to do it, I saluted and I drove on and did my mission," Porter said.

The helicopters assaulting the A Shau Valley lifted off at first light and got into a major engagement with an NVA regiment. The night convoy may have been a minor trip in the totality of things, but the 82nd Airborne had delivered essential supplies.

Porter retired from the Army as a colonel and routinely attended the reunions of the Golden Brigade Association, the leadership of which was once under his command.

"They were good soldiers then, and they're good people now," Porter said.

Highway 547 had significance to others as well.

On the cusp of the 50th anniversary of the Golden Brigade's deployment to Vietnam, Paddy Barry asked fellow veteran Claud Dunn if he had any regrets.

"No. No regrets. I went to war for my country. I served with the best fighting outfit in the world. I lived up to my responsibilities as a man," Dunn told him.

But the more he thought about it, Dunn said there was one thing. Having been wounded in Vietnam, he was issued the paperwork and the citation for a Purple Heart, but he had never received the actual award. Nothing more was said, and Dunn put the matter aside.

Dunn's wounds were suffered on May 14, 1968, during an ambush along Highway 547. He had spent the previous night celebrating his 25th birthday, which is how he remembered the date. Dunn was part of a mission that day to provide security for the combat engineers sweeping the road for mines, and Paddy Barry was one of the engineers.

"Stuff happened over there that would have normal people up all night. We rolled over and went to sleep," Barry said.

Monsoon rains had washed out the road in places, and a natural culvert formed in the stretch that Dunn was patrolling. He was in a gun jeep equipped with a 106-millimeter recoilless rifle, the big bore gun that was essentially an artillery tube mounted on four wheels.

"All of a sudden, they sprung an ambush on half our people. I saw what was happening, and from down in the culvert, I unlocked the gun," Dunn said.

The weapon can deliver a world of hurt. One of the shells it fired was called a fleschette, which had eight separate containers, each filled with 1,000 steel darts. Stabilized by tail fins, each one-inch long dart resembles a miniature arrow. When fired, the 8,000 darts in each round sound like angry bees in flight, which is why the shell was called the beehive round.

After the first shot left the barrel and the darts buzzed through the air, there was silence. Then the enemy guns began barking again.

The loader chambered another beehive round and yelled "Up!," which meant the gun was good to fire again. Dunn let fly with another round. Then another, and another, and another.

"After six rounds, you were supposed to let the barrel cool, but I fired 13 times. I said to myself, "I ain't letting them mothers kill me,' " Dunn said. "The gun was glowing red. It caught the loader's shirt on fire. So, we all scrambled to take cover under the jeep. AK rounds were going through the jeep engine. I had to crawl over the barrel to get out, and as I was lying there, I felt something on my backside. I thought I must've caught something sharp getting out of the gun jeep because I was bleeding. The loader checked me out and said, 'You're hit.' I had been shot through the buttocks. One bullet made four holes. You could have put a steel rod through my ass and hang me up to dry."

A medic who rushed over to Dunn couldn't withhold his laughter.

"I don't know why you're laughing. This shit hurts," Dunn said.

The medic replied in a deadpan tone, "You're the first guy in the history of the Airborne to be shot running away."

Dunn, too, laughs at the memory.

"The medic gave me a shot of morphine. I know why people get addicted to that stuff. It numbed me right up," Dunn said.

The healing process took three months before Dunn could return to duty. The citation and paperwork were put through for the Purple Heart, an award that originated in 1782 with George Washington and the Continental Army as the Badge of Merit. It became the Purple Heart through the efforts of General Douglas MacArthur in 1932. According to the National Purple Heart Hall of Honor near West Point, MacArthur was the first recipient of the award. In Dunn's case, he never did get the actual medal to go with his paperwork.

"When I got back home, I just got on with my life. I didn't want anybody to think I was calling attention to myself," Dunn said.

Then in April of 2017, Dunn was told to bring the authorizing certificate to Fort Bragg during All American Week, which traditionally is the third week of May when the division welcomes back all former paratroopers and those who went to war with the 82nd Airborne. This occasion was extra special because the Third Brigade honored all those who fought in Vietnam under its battle flag.

With steak, hamburgers and hot dogs on the grill for the Third Brigade Combat Team's annual picnic, Vietnam veterans assembled once more. The main speaker was Dunn, a retired command sergeant major who still fit inside his dress uniform the way the Airborne wears it—with his trousers bloused, or tucked, into his Corcoran jump boots.

In his brief remarks, Dunn said with a laugh: "If it wasn't for the 82nd Airborne, the Marines wouldn't have anybody to look up to." He spoke about the hellish conditions in Vietnam—the mosquitoes, leeches, heat, rain, rice paddies and jungles. He also recalled how returning soldiers were called baby killers and spit on. A standing ovation followed his remarks.

Fifty years after Dunn shed blood for his country, the Purple Heart was pinned onto his chest.

"It was the greatest day of my life," Dunn said.

Chapter 21
GOLDEN GLOVES

Willie S. Manuel may have served the shortest amount of time of any soldier in the Golden Brigade, but in the 18 or so hours that he lasted, he experienced one of the more unique battles in Vietnam—a fist fight at an ancient temple housing the cremation chamber of a long-dead emperor.

A replacement who was trained as a supply clerk, Manuel arrived at the command post of B Troop, 17th Cavalry on the evening of May 18. He reported to First Sergeant Marion Foster and platoon leader Lieutenant Doug Caton, unsure of what duties awaited.

"I'm a clerk, and I'm near sighted," Manuel told them.

"Oh, don't worry about not being able to see things in the distance. We'll put you right up front," Foster replied dryly.

Foster meant it facetiously. A native of the coal mining region of northeastern Pennsylvania, Foster was a grizzled leader who was seen as a father figure to the troopers under his charge. He was a veteran of the battle of Pork Chop Hill in Korea and had spent a previous tour in Vietnam with the 173rd Airborne. His attempt at humor failed to elicit a laugh from a nervous Cherry, however.

As it happened, the cavalry unit got mortared that night, and troopers scrambled for safety.

"We got Manuel to a bunker. He was shaking like a leaf. He was scared to death. That was a long night for him," recalled Caton.

Caton had attended law school at the University of Virginia and got drafted in 1966. After receiving his commission in Officer Candidate School, Caton wanted to receive the best training possible by becoming an Airborne Ranger, but he was sent to Vietnam before he could check every box on his dream sheet.

"I never got to Ranger school. I went to the real Ranger school in Vietnam," Caton said.

On May 19, after the mortar attack, the cavalry mounted up for a mission to provide security in their gun jeeps. Troopers were also on the lookout, as always, for places where the bad guys might be hiding. They were traveling on Highway 549 about two miles southwest of Hue when they came to an emperor's tomb.

"We were on a search and destroy mission when we went to this temple area. We saw a Viet Cong sentry asleep on the top of a crypt and went to investigate. As it turned out, this whole cemetery was undermined by tunnels and loaded with underground warehousing for rice and arms," Caton said.

The sentry ran into a courtyard outside a structure that was the size of a small house and surrounded by a 20-foot high stone wall. A single doorway provided passage inside. Buddhist monks were on the grounds, their stone silence masking the trouble that awaited. The first to arrive at the portal was Specialist John Therrien, with Manuel in tow.

Therrien told Manuel to guard the exit, ordering him to shoot anything that moved. He then entered and began circling around a cremation furnace, described as a half of a beehive laid on its side with holes in its bottom to make for a hotter fire. Along the way, Therrien caught a fleeting glimpse of the VC, who was running for his life. Therrien tried to catch him from behind, but the enemy soldier finished his circuit first. He spotted Manuel at the door and fired a shot that smashed Manuel's arm. Having committed the cardinal sin of dropping his rifle, a bleeding Manuel dashed to where he thought the rest of the platoon would be. Now he was being pursued by the VC.

"I saw Manuel was running. He was scared shitless," recalled Richard O'Hare, who was the 60-gunner on that mission. "He was screaming, 'They're all over the place. I don't know what I'm doing here. I don't belong here. I was trained as a supply clerk.' "

Therrien had heard the shot that wounded Manuel and raced to see what had happened. As he rounded the furnace, he encountered a second VC who had come out of hiding. Therrien killed him with his rifle, then resumed his pursuit.

The fleeing enemy soldier realized that Therrien was behind him. He veered off onto another pathway, and as he ran, he glanced back over his shoulder. Just then, he came face-to-face with Specialist Don Murphy, who was coming forward with the rest of the platoon. Both startled soldiers eyed each other for a split second. Murphy was armed with a grenade launcher, a weapon that was of little use in such confined quarters. So, he tossed the weapon at the VC, who froze for a moment as he was bringing his rifle into firing position. Murphy grabbed the assault rifle with his left hand and then threw a punch with his right, hitting his opponent in the jaw and knocking him out. From then on, he was known as "One Punch Murphy." The unconscious prisoner was dragged outside the tomb.

Accompanied by Sergeants Franklin D. Fritz and William Hoffay, Therrien went back in for a closer look. The three troopers pitched several hand grenades as a precaution but saw nothing of significance. Fritz began probing the brick floor of the temple with his bayonet. The search had just about concluded when Fritz's bayonet discovered a passageway that had been difficult to spot in the darkness. It led to a tunnel.

"Fritz pries open the door, and here comes this gook with a rifle, ready to start shooting. Fritz smashes the door down on his head and away he disappears," said Richard O'Hare. "We talked about tossing grenades but figure that there may be a bunch of explosives down there. Our interpreter who was along on the mission convinces them that it is now or never to surrender, and out they come without their firearms. Fritz went down and pulled out their weapons."

By now, reinforcements had arrived.

"I heard over the radio net that the platoon was in contact. We got there just as it was wrapping up. It must've been five minutes," said Mark Robertson of B Troop. "When the floor opened up and a VC came out, Sergeant Fritz clocked the guy. He was known as KO Fritz after that. A couple more VC came out, and one ran right into the arms of Hoffay,"

The punches were reminiscent of a Golden Gloves boxing contest staged back in The World. The slugfest also served a metaphor for the fighting spirit of the All Americans, who will fight a foe until Hell freezes over and then fight on the ice. To this point, troopers had exchanged gunfire in rice paddies, in village complexes and in the jungle. Now they could lay claim to having fought with their fists in an emperor's temple. The engagement became known as The Donnybrook. The body count was one, with four enemy taken prisoner. Five rifles, a rocket launcher and various documents were captured. Intelligence later confirmed that Troop B had eliminated one of three VC squads still operating in its area.

Manuel was evacuated to an aid station and then flown to a hospital in Germany. He survived his wounds but was never heard from again.

"I never knew his name or where he came from. When it happened, all we knew was that the Cherry got shot. Never saw him again. That was his first and only day with us," Robertson said.

Chapter 22
SUICIDE ATTACK

Helicopter pilot James Zinchuk flew so many missions he qualified for 18 Air Medals. He transported commanders who controlled operations from the air, brought the wounded back to aid stations, flew supplies out to the troops, spotted for the artillery and dropped tear gas and motion sensors into the jungle. With a perspective gained above the deck, he also saw sights of war he couldn't un-see. One time, he retrieved a soldier who foamed at the mouth from heat stroke. Then, during the recovery of an enlisted man who had drowned and washed up on the shore of the Perfume River, he watched overhead as the dead man's arms were pulled from his torso by those who had reached him. The soldier was listed as killed in action because it would be too problematic to explain how a drowning victim came home with both arms detached. One sight he could never get out of his mind was when a soldier loaded all his gear onto an air mattress to cross a waterway, then slipped below the surface and never came up. He once flew a mission over the A Shau Valley, 50 feet off the ground at a speed of 50 knots, with a Vietnamese ally using a loudspeaker to encourage the bad guys to surrender. Then the door gunner opened up because he thought he saw somebody moving on the ground, which defeated the purpose of encouraging the enemy to come out and to give up. It was all part of Vietnam, as were the nights at Camp Rodriguez when Zinchuk might unwind from the stresses of missions by watching a movie on an outdoor screen. One such night epitomized the lunacy of Vietnam.

Scheduled to take Colonel Bud Bolling up on a mission the next morning, Zinchuk donned a T-shirt, shorts and sandals before finding a spot in front of a screen the engineers had set up on the bed of a flatbed trailer. The feature was *Khartoum*, an action flick about the British army defending an outpost in the Sudan against a horde of radical Muslims. At the point in the movie when the attacking Arabs begin firing their cannons at the British stronghold, Zinchuk heard an explosion behind him.

"I said to myself, 'What's this? Is this movie in stereo?' Then I caught the tail end of a B40 rocket crashing into the base, and I dove for a bunker," Zinchuk said. "It was like you see in the movies. Sandbags were collapsing. Dirt was coming in. Guys were crying for their mothers. One guy with an M-16 emptied a mag out the doorway. I asked him, 'What the fuck was that?' He said, 'I was just testing it.' Then I said, 'Let me out of this fucking hole.' I ran to the flight line, where we at least had M-60 machine guns on the ships. I remember yelling, 'Don't shoot! Lieutenant Zinchuk coming in! Don't shoot!' "

Don Carson of the Military Police unit was watching the same scene from *Khartoum* at his own location when fact became stranger than fiction.

"All around us, things were exploding. About 45 of us crammed into a bunker designed to hold 30. Then we ran to the jeeps to start plugging holes in the perimeter," Carson said.

On the night of May 20-21, the base camp of the 82nd Airborne and Camp Eagle of the 101st Airborne came under attack. Rockets had fallen inside the wire on previous occasions, but they were mainly an annoyance. This was different. Not only was a shower of Soviet-made rockets raining down, 100 specially trained attackers called sappers had breached the defensive wire. For them, it was an act of desperation. They had no other recourse but to try to kill the All Americans who had been killing them, even if it was a suicide mission. Carrying satchel charges, the shadowy figures dressed in loin cloths sought out targets to destroy, blowing themselves up in the process. After-action reports indicated the attackers were doped up on opium or some other drug that provided chemical courage. Once the sappers did their dirty work, a battalion of North Vietnamese regulars was poised to follow up with a ground attack.

The way combat engineer Paddy Barry remembered it, the entertainment that night was an episode of the TV show *Combat!* "One of our guys saw green streaks going through the air and thought they were fireflies. Fireflies hell. They were tracers from enemy rifles," said Barry. "There were real bullets coming through the screen. Mortar fire was being exchanged inside our wire."

The assault actually began with diversionary attacks on two outposts set up on the high ground west of Hue. As rockets roared through the night sky on their deadly arcs, troopers at Fire Support Base Boyd and Fire Support Base Panther II buttoned up. Rich O'Hare was at Panther II in a bunker that faced Camp Rodriguez.

"The pucker factor was at its highest because we thought we'd be in the soup pretty soon. The artillery fired nonstop, and we were locked and cocked," O'Hare said.

Ten minutes after those attacks, sentries from the 1st Battalion of the 508th reported movement to their front along the triple row of razor wire protecting the perimeter of Camp Rodriguez. A general alarm was sounded, and base camp awakened to a fight.

Three sapper teams charged forward. One team killed three guards from the 101st Airborne and broke through the southernmost point of Camp Eagle. A second team penetrated halfway along the southern wire. The third element broke through into the area of Camp Rodriguez where prisoners of war where housed in an enclosure.

Gerald Kennedy and the Military Police were off-duty at their own area. Their two tents, Alcatraz and Sing-Sing, were set up in a little valley next to a creek that was full of leeches.

"We were off by ourselves, and we had our own movies. That night, a stag flick was showing. Then we got hit," Kennedy said.

Troopers dashed to a bunker they had built between the two tents. Having withstood the initial rocket barrage, they regrouped and emerged to take up the fight against the suicide forces running about with explosives strapped to their bodies.

"When we came out of the bunker, the porn flick was still running. You're running for your damn life and that movie was still playing," Kennedy said with a tone of amazement.

The chaos and confusion lasted for hours. According to one estimate, 800 rockets slammed into Camp Rodriguez. Firefights broke out all over the grounds.

An urgent call for air support was answered by a gunship known as Puff the Magic Dragon, officially an AC-47 cargo plane that was modified into a deadly weapon and was especially useful in defending bases against night attacks. Capable of orbiting a target for hours, Puff had three motorized Gatling guns. The guns spit out 100 rounds per second and could put a bullet into every square yard of a football field in 10 seconds. Every fifth round fired a red-glowing tracer, and the volume of fire was so great that a solid red curtain, like the fire coming out of a dragon's mouth, was visible. Puff was also known by the generic name of Spooky.

"Spooky was above us for the longest time. There was just a steady stream of red coming down. It was just unreal. They were lifesavers," Gerald Kennedy said.

Reid Lyon was at Fire Base Panther I, located five kilometers from base camp. From the high ground, he witnessed the attack and the response.

"The solid stream of red coming from Spooky's Gatling guns looked like a Death Ray," Lyon said.

Inside the wire, commanders asked for illumination rounds that could shed light on the darkened landscape. One mortar tube from B Troop of the cavalry unit fired more than 150 illumination rounds, turning night into day until the sun came up. Combined with artillery bursts that performed the same task, the man-made light exposed the attackers. Troopers in their underwear emerged from their bunkers to open fire.

During the attack, casualties began to pile up at the battalion aid station inside the Camp Eagle, and the All Americans scrambled to assist. Lieutenant Carroll Guthrie of the brigade's Headquarters Company, accompanied by two jeeps manned by Military Police, escorted several ambulances from the Golden Brigade's medical company. To relieve crowded conditions, they evacuated some wounded troopers and transferred them to the Golden Brigade's facilities. Along the way, a chaplain from the 101st Airborne stopped them and said more medics and firepower were desperately needed along the wire.

Guthrie raced toward the perimeter. As he and his troops approached the camp boundary, they heard wounded men shouting for help. One trooper went back for an ambulance, backed it up to the perimeter and loaded up four severely wounded men.

Moments after four troopers of the 101st Airborne were whisked to the aid station, two more wounded were found and evacuated in a gun jeep driven by Specialist

Anthony Coor. Coor dropped off the two men, then picked up additional machine guns and ammo before speeding back to the perimeter. Under Guthrie's direction, the All Americans secured the gap in Camp Eagle's wire for 90 minutes until troops from the Screaming Eagles relieved them. Their actions not only prevented more sappers from entering but sealed off the escape routes of the enemy combatants.

"I remember waking up to sirens and incoming rounds. I ran down to the bunker at the Tactical Operations Center. Colonel Bolling came running across from his quarters," said Tom Ladwig. "They had penetrated the wire and blew up a couple of bunkers in the 101st's area. Carroll Guthrie was amazing. He even took the prisoners we had in the enclosure and put them in a shelter."

Guthrie was decorated with a Silver Star. It was pinned on by Major General Olinto Barsanti of the 101st Airborne.

The fight became personal in a hurry. Ignoring the explosions going off around them, All American troopers hunted down and killed off the trespassers. At dawn, smoke still rose from the compound. Five troopers from the 101st Airborne had been killed and 35 others wounded. Several members of the Golden Brigade were wounded but none fatally.

Although Bud Bolling and his command group were unscathed, the colonel's quarters were hit too. During the melee, fresh holes shredded the canvas of his two-man hexagonal tent. In fact, for the time he was headquartered at Camp Rodriguez, the tent that Bolling had brought with him from Fort Bragg had 474 holes in it.

Bolling found shelter in the bunker beneath the Tactical Operations Center, and mortars and other weapons were set up on the roof. "They're not getting the Old Man!" Duke Dewey said in rallying the defenses.

The close call made an indelible impression on Chaplain James Sanner. A shell had whistled through his tent and hit the cross adorning its interior. The first chance he got after the sapper attack, he and his tent-mate requisitioned a .45 caliber sidearm from the armory and kept it in their quarters. In Vietnam, even a priest needed more than the grace of the Almighty to defend himself.

"I wasn't supposed to have a weapon. It was for our own safety in case things got really bad," Sanner said. "If those sappers would have turned right, they would have come right into our camp."

The bodies of 54 sappers were found in an around the wire. One of them was a familiar face. He was a Vietnamese man who cut hair inside Camp Rodriguez. Secretly, he was working for the Viet Cong. While acting as a barber, he marked the location of key bunkers ahead of the attack.

When dawn broke, Jim Zinchuk saw another incredible sight as he prepared to take Colonel Bolling up in his helicopter.

"On the road between the helicopter pad and the Tactical Operations Center, there were 35 NVA bodies. A bulldozer was getting ready to push them into a hole. That was something," Zinchuk said.

Camp Rodriguez, the home of the 82nd Airborne, became a burial ground for the sappers who died trying to overrun it.

Security was the responsibility of the 101st Airborne that night. As things settled down, Military Police interviewed those who had been in the guard towers to determine about how the sappers breached the wire. Don Carson said the investigation determined that marijuana had been smoked.

"On the perimeter, there were four soldiers on watch and four off in the guard bunkers through the night. We found out that someone was smoking weed when the sappers opened the wire and came running through," Carson said. "Weed leads to complacency, and complacency leads to death."

In addition to bulldozing a common grave for the dead attackers, combat engineers were given three follow-up missions, according to an after-action report. More coils of wire were added to strengthen the perimeter of Camp Rodriguez. In addition, a new battalion-sized fighting position was constructed astride the most likely avenue of approach to the base camp, providing the brigade with its own guard post. It was completed in five days. Engineers also built a 5.4-mile section of road from base camp to a Seabees position to the south, allowing for speedier movement of reinforcements in the event of a repeat. The road was open in a week.

Chapter 23
TOUGHEST LETTER

Before the 82nd Airborne left for Vietnam, Bud Bolling knew Ronald Frazer as more than just one of the junior officers under his command. Like Bolling, Frazer had received his class ring from West Point during a time of war. When Frazer was posted to Fort Bragg as an Airborne-qualified second lieutenant, he and his fellow newcomers were invited to Bolling's home.

"The colonel wanted to get to know all of his lieutenants. He had three data points on each man in brigade—what state they were from, what was their hometown and where they had gone to college," said West Pointer Dean Risseeuw.

Ron Frazer also began a courtship with Bolling's daughter, Kathryn.

"It got serious very quickly. They were engaged to be married, or at least there was the understanding they were going to be wed," Risseeuw said.

In Vietnam, Frazer had already distinguished himself in a May 4 action outside of Hue while his unit was under the operational control of the 101st Airborne. Major General Olinto Barsanti had personally presented Frazer with a Silver Star for valor.

After Captain Afton Watts had been killed during the ambush along Highway 547, Frazer took command of Charlie Company in the 1st of the 508. At the age of 22, he was commanding an infantry company of All Americans less than a year after leaving West Point.

Frazer's company had the mission of securing a section of Highway 547 leading to the A Shau Valley. The company operated out of Fire Base Boyd and guarded the Nam Hoa Bridge over the Perfume River. South of the road was a mountain located 15 miles southwest of Hue. Known on the map as Nui Ke, or Hill 618, the cone-shaped peak was covered with gnarly brush and trees. It was the highest ground between the coastal plain and the mountains along the Laotian border, and it provided a commanding view of the countryside. Enemy forces, which had built fortified bunkers and observation posts atop the mountain, used it as a base.

Frazer's company was inserted by helicopter on May 24 between Highway 547 and Nui Ke, where elements of the 90th NVA Regiment of the North Vietnamese Army were hiding. A firefight erupted and spilled over into the next day. The citation of Frazer's second Silver Star provided the only known summary of what happened:

"His company came under heavy attack by an enemy force of unknown size. Unhesitatingly, Lt. Frazer moved through bullets and rockets to reach his lead elements and assist them in locating enemy bunker positions to their front. During the initial fighting, several of his men were seriously wounded and his point elements were becoming confused because they could not pinpoint the enemy positions. Lt. Frazer, with complete disregard for his own personal safety, moved forward with his machine-gun teams and pointed out targets to the gunners. Again, exposing himself to intense small arms and machine gun fire, he moved across to his maneuver element and led them to the flanks of the enemy bunkers. This enabled his men to inflict heavy casualties on the enemy, but the fire from the enemy bunkers became so intense that they were forced to pull back to their original starting point. Lt. Frazer reorganized his men and started back on a second attempt to take the enemy bunkers when he was mortally wounded by enemy machine gun fire. His personal bravery and devotion to duty were in keeping with the highest traditions of the military service and reflect great credit upon himself, his unit and the United States Army."

Among the members of Charlie Company who died in the fighting with their company commander were Corporal William McNamara Levendis, 21, a field wireman from Vienna, Virginia; Staff Sergeant Jamie Villalobos, 27, of Ecorse, Michigan; Private First Class Joseph Passavanti, 20, of Park Forest, Illinois; Private First Class Bernard Francis Yarbinitz, 22, of Johnstown, Pennsylvania; and Private First Class John Harrison Anderson Jr., who had turned 20 a month earlier, of Wellsville, Pennsylvania. Fifteen other members of the company were wounded. The NVA suffered 23 dead.

Dean Risseeuw remembers hearing the bad news from Colonel Bolling, just as he had learned that West Point classmate James Adams was killed at the Candy Stripe.

"We got the word to pop smoke for Night Rider, and the colonel emerged from his helicopter. He said, 'I have some bad news. Ron Frazer was killed,' " Risseeuw said. "He was crying. He was asking, 'How am I going to tell Kathy? How am I going to tell my wife?' I had never seen a colonel cry. He was devastated."

Of the two letters Bud Bolling wrote on Ron Frazer's behalf, one contained his condolences to Frazer's parents, retired Army Major Lloyd D. Frazer, who was the former principal at Lincoln High School in Cambridge City, Indiana, and Lewesa Frazer, a career school teacher.

Bolling also wrote to his daughter, telling Kathryn that Frazer died doing what he was trained to do, serving his country in time of war. She took the news hard. The gallant young Army officer she hoped to marry was gone. He had died while serving under her father, who she felt was supposed to be protecting him.

Born at Fort Sumner, New Mexico, Frazer was the second oldest of eight children. He was in the fifth grade when he saw the movie *The West Point Story*, which inspired him to be a cadet. A member of the National Honor Society and class president in his junior and senior years at Lincoln High School, he was an outstanding wrestler and linebacker on the football team. To go with his rugged athletic looks, he was known for his sense of humor and wore an ever present smirk.

He was survived by seven siblings: Mrs. Darlene Keihn of Muncie, Indiana; Pamela, a student at Earlham College; sisters Theresa and Carole at home; and brothers James, Jeffrey and Stephen at home. Also surviving were paternal grandparents, Mr. and Mrs. James H. Frazer of Williamsburg; and maternal grandparents Mr. and Mrs. Joseph Thornburg of Blountsville.

Frazer was buried in the West Point Cemetery.

Bob Murrill, who at the time was the executive officer of Frazer's battalion, was tasked with a tough writing assignment of his own. He wrote to John and Viola Anderson of Wellsville, Pennsylvania, to console them about the loss of their son, John.

Mrs. Anderson wrote back to say how much she appreciated his words, and that John's personal belongings had been shipped home. She closed with her prayer for "our boys" in Vietnam: "That the war will soon be over; and our loved ones will all be home safe and sound. God bless you and all the boys. May He keep all of you in his loving care."

A draftee who had been in Vietnam for less than a month, Anderson occupies a place of distinction on the Vietnam Veterans Memorial. For visitors approaching the west side of The Wall, Anderson's name is the first one etched onto Panel 70 West, Line 1.

May 25, 1968 was a noteworthy day in the whole of Vietnam. Eighty-nine Americans were killed that day, making it the bloodiest day of what would be the bloodiest month of 1968. A total of 2,403 Americans were killed during May. For the entire year, a total of 16,592 American lives were lost, making it the bloodiest year of the Vietnam War. That same year, U.S. troop levels peaked at 549,500.

It has been said that the opposing sides in Vietnam never understood each other. U.S. forces were engaged to keep the Communist North from taking over South Vietnam, which they did by inflicting as much damage on the enemy so that at some future point they would no longer be able to sustain the fight. On the other hand, the North Vietnamese fought to prolong the war as long as possible so that the Americans, who were viewed as successors to the French as occupiers of the homeland, would grow weary of the struggle and withdraw.

At the end of May, Ho Chi Minh told the National Assembly in Hanoi: "It is better to die than to be a slave. There is nothing more precious than freedom and independence."

The words on the Golden Brigade commemorative coin and the monuments to its dead are: "Nothing is dearer than life, but nothing is more precious than to live it in freedom."

Meanwhile, the mission of dislodging hostile forces from Nui Ke Mountain was assigned in June to Alpha Company of the 2nd of the 505. The unit was commanded by Captain John Kapranopoulos, who was on his second tour in Vietnam and was known variously as Captain K or The Greek. A native of New Hampshire, he wore black-framed Army eyeglasses and a protective black glove on his left hand. Having been hit by shrapnel on a 1965 tour in Vietnam with the 173rd Airborne, Captain K had spent a year in Chelsea Naval Hospital in Boston, Massachusetts, battling an infection and having his hand rebuilt by a Navy doctor. Although he could have qualified for a medical discharge, Captain K opted to stay in the Army as long as he could serve in an Airborne unit.

"I liked the infantry. I liked the closeness of an Airborne unit. I told them if they guaranteed I could stay on jump status, I'll volunteer to go to Vietnam," Kapranopoulos said.

His dedication and combat experience were a good fit for a rifle company in the 82nd Airborne.

"I was very fortunate to have very good platoon leaders. The troops were outstanding. I loved every one of them. It was an outstanding group of hard-working, dedicated young men. I was proud to be the commander of that company." Kapranopoulos said.

The captain's radio operator was Texan Carl Bludau, who thought the world of his company commander. "We were called Cold Steel Alpha, and he called me Blue Steel, because it's the toughest steel there is. It may bend but it never breaks," Bludau said.

Taking the high ground promised to be a tough assignment. In fact, Jim Littig, who had healed from wounds suffered the night Doc Dillon was killed and was now serving in Alpha Company, took a precaution familiar to soldiers on the eve of battle. He wrote a letter home to his parents and the girl he had been dating, just in case.

"I thought I was going to be killed. My element was supposed to take up a blocking position on a ridge line that should have been given to a larger force," Littig said.

The battle for Nui Ke began with an awesome display of firepower. The mountain was bombed by wave after wave of attack jets, and artillery units concentrated their guns on an area about the size of two football fields.

Platoon leader Keith Bell said the top of Nui Ke was obliterated.

"I don't think there was a tree standing on the peak of that place," Bell said. "The recon platoon went in first and rappelled out of helicopters. My platoon was next. We found a battalion-sized base camp and a bunch of uniforms and equipment, but the occupiers had fled. We got mortared that night with seven or eight rounds."

One spot where the helicopters touched down was called Landing Zone Greek as a nod to Kapranopoulos. He and his men had taken the high ground.

Back in The World, President Lyndon Johnson had decided to change commanders in Vietnam. William Westmoreland was to relinquish his role as head of Military Assistance Command, Vietnam to become chief of staff of the Army. His replacement was West Pointer and World War II veteran Creighton W. Abrams. In a letter dated March 23, LBJ noted that Robert McNamara had stated that Westmoreland was "the best man to lead the Army," and that in his new post in Washington, Westmoreland would serve as "my strong right arm." Abrams, who had been Westmoreland's deputy since May of 1967, changed strategy in his prosecution of the war. He de-emphasized body counts as a measure of progress and shifted the military focus to bring security to South Vietnam by eliminating the Viet Cong, thereby denying the infrastructure that supported the North Vietnamese army. Abrams officially assumed command on June 10, 1968.

Chapter 24
HELL'S HAMLET

Bud Bolling once likened the task of clearing out the bad guys to what Elliott Ness and The Untouchables did in cleaning up the organized crime syndicates in Chicago during Prohibition. Federal agents did take down crime bosses like Al Capone, but how did they know when they had all the henchmen? Criminal organizations survived and continued their enterprises in the underworld as long as they didn't call attention to themselves. The sapper attack against Camp Rodriguez and other enemy activity, such as the nightly planting of land mines on the roads used by the Golden Brigade, meant the bad guys were still around.

One brazen confirmation of enemy presence was a sign posted outside a village west of Camp Rodriguez. It said: "Danger Airborne Troopers, Go Home—Do Not Go Any Further or You Will Die!" The village was Thon Chau Chu, which was situated at the edge of the coastal flats and nudged up against the jungle and elephant grass. The place was located off a secondary road designated as Highway 546, and it happened to be along the route the All Americans used to haul supplies from their base camp to Fire Base Boyd. Every morning, combat engineers cleared the route with mine sweepers, and every night, Charlie would plant more mines and improvised explosive devices. The cycle was more than a nuisance. It was a threat to life and limb.

To eliminate the threat, B Troop of the cavalry unit was dispatched to Thon Chau Chu. Although village elders and other inhabitants were interrogated, they failed to divulge any useful information. The locals were caught between two deadly forces. On the one hand, the Viet Cong and North Vietnamese considered the place as a haven to store food and recruit civilians to their cause, and they had built a series of concealed bunkers and escape tunnels for their purposes. They threatened to kill anyone who cooperated with the Americans and their South Vietnamese allies. On the other hand, the Americans would question the villagers and demand to know, under threat of harm, where the bad guys were. It's like the old Asian adage: When the elephants collide, the grass suffers.

A flash point came on May 27 when Platoon Sergeant Abron Griffin brought hot chow from base camp to feed a platoon that was searching Thon Chau Chu and the adjoining hamlet of Thon Nguyet Bieu. Griffin's vehicle detonated a road mine. He was wounded and evacuated. Subsequently, a platoon led by Lieutenant Anthony Bennett of Cottonwood, Arizona, was supposed to walk through the village to clear it. The platoon was fired upon by several snipers.

"I was on the right flank. I heard six AK-47 rounds, then I heard Steve Kline screaming. He was maybe 20 yards away and had been hit through the neck. Next to him was Don Beatty, who was hit square in the chest and died instantly," said platoon member Reid Lyon.

Meanwhile, Mark Robertson and his cavalry unit were operating out of Fire Base Panther I. Mainly, he and his fellow troopers would go out on nightly ambushes in four-man teams. Each team had a Starlight scope and took up positions about 75 yards apart on a trail. In addition to setting up their claymore mines, the teams would link 10 hand grenades with detonation cord. In what troops called a daisy chain, the grenades were wired to explode at the same time.

"It's kind of insane when you look back on it, but it made sense at the time. We'd open up with the claymores, and they'd jump off trail to the other side, right into the hand grenades," Robertson said.

Robertson had been through Thon Chau Chu a number of times without incident, so it was unsettling to hear over the radio that cavalrymen had been killed and wounded.

"I'm at Panther I, and I hear Lieutenant Bennett say over the radio that Beatty was killed, and Steve Kline was shot. You're not supposed to do this, but Bennett spelled out the name using each letter, B-E-A-T-T-Y. I was really pissed off when I heard the news. There was so much anger about our guys being killed. Beatty was a guy I was really close to. He had been to Nam before, and he had a Zippo lighter engraved with Long Range Recon Patrol. He befriended me. He was a really cool guy," Robertson said.

Beatty, 25, was a sergeant from Rochester, New York. Back in The World, his infant daughter, Cindy, was left fatherless. She was too young to have any memory of her father, but she kept him alive through the stories she heard about him. Nearly 50 years after Beatty was killed, Cindy posted an online tribute. She wondered how her life would have been different and how unfair life is sometimes. She hoped to see him in the afterlife, to hold him and hug him like she never had the chance to do. She invoked the words familiar to little girls who grow up fatherless: "I hope you are proud of me and what I have made of my life."

After the fatal shots were fired, the platoon moved on foot toward a line of scraggly trees. Unable to locate the exact source of the snipers, the platoon called for artillery and air strikes. Sniper fire was temporarily silenced.

The following day, Lyon's unit worked the same area but came in from a different direction. When the cavalry's first platoon was targeted by a barrage of rockets and automatic weapons, Lieutenant Bennett maneuvered his men and surrounded the location. His gun jeeps fired 50 rounds of high explosive and fleschette rounds while attack jets and helicopter gunships concentrated their fire on where suspected enemy positions were marked with smoke. When the shooting stopped, two platoons on foot swept the area. That night, an ambush team stayed behind in the hamlet and spotted a mortar firing from nearby Chau Chu. The team called in an artillery strike on the position.

On May 31, the first and second platoons of B Troop again swept the hamlet of Nguyet Bieu. Lieutenant Bennett's men came across signs that a squad had camped in a clearing the night before. As he led his men forward, Bennett, 22, was targeted and killed by a burst of gunfire, complete with that sickening thud a bullet makes when it hits a human being. Reid Lyon described it as a sound similar to a wooden paddle striking a mud puddle.

"We were sweeping toward this high ground. You couldn't see 10 yards because the vegetation was so thick. Then all hell broke loose," Lyon said. "The lieutenant was a brave man and a great officer. It was kind of a shock. Very sad. He was leading from the front as he assaulted a bunker."

The son of Worthy Lee and Lucresia Simpson Bennett, the lieutenant had attended Mingus Union High School near his hometown in Arizona and was a graduate of the Officer Candidate School (Armor) at Fort Knox, Kentucky. Every year, Reid Lyon stops to reflect on his name at Panel 62 West of The Wall. Gerald Kennedy of the Military Police Company also left this online tribute to Bennett: "Tony, I will always remember your extreme sense of humor, your outgoing personality and your professionalism as an officer."

After Bennett fell, the troops pulled back and marked their location with smoke grenades. To answer the emergency call for close air support, attack jets swooped in.

"They were so low you could see the rivets on the planes. They did the job. A 500-pound bomb at low altitude is actually dropped behind you before the bomb wings snap open to slow them down. They hit the tree line to our front. Then came the napalm. It cooked everything," Lyon said.

Fellow cavalryman James Klein described what it was like.

"I could read the captain's name on the F-4. He was firing his cannons, and the spent 20-millimeter casings were dropping on my head. A FAC comes in and marks a target with rockets. I look up and see two contrails. A jet makes a 90-degree bank, blasting away, and then the napalm canisters drop off the wings. I hit the dirt. You could feel the heat in your chest when it ignited. The trees bend in, and then snap back. All the oxygen is sucked out of the air. We used napalm like it was going out of style," Klein said.

There was a close call at the position occupied by Mark Robertson's platoon, which was mistakenly targeted by the Forward Air Controller, or Gimpy FAC.

"When Bennett got killed, that pissed people off. He was a pretty cool dude," Robertson said. "We were engaged in a firefight, and air support was coming in. Gimpy came down and fired a targeting rocket right in the middle of all of us. Guys started popping smoke to mark us as a friendly position. Everybody popped smoke of all different colors. It looked like Mardi Gras. An F-4 pilot came in on an attack run, saw our smoke and waved his wings as he sped off. He figured it out," Robertson said.

B Troop's recoilless rifles and mortars, positioned on the hills overlooking the hamlet, also blasted the area. In the aftermath, troops discovered two dead Viet Cong and a number of blood trails indicating other guerrillas had been killed or wounded before being dragged off.

"As we pushed through, we captured this shell-shocked NVA captain. It was weird. There were two Americans wearing khaki pants and white shirts, working with a South Vietnamese unit that interrogated him. They were brutal," Lyon said.

The civilian clothes were giveaways that the Americans were with the Central Intelligence Agency, which had agents working in concert with a Provisional Reconnaissance Unit. The PRU was a paramilitary organization of Vietnamese civilians and some former Viet Cong who had defected to the side of the South.

"They told me to take prisoner away. I had him by the arm, and he was trembling violently. I tried to comfort him as best I could and dropped him off at the command post," Lyon said. "The prisoner pointed out where the other NVA were in the tunnels. There was a scraggly line of trees, but you couldn't see any bunkers. It's amazing how industrious those guys were."

Actually, the enemy had built two separate bunkers in the tree line, but they were so well entrenched that bombs and shells failed to eliminate them. Finally, on June 1, a breakthrough came when a chieftain from a nearby village had a change of heart and agreed to show the location of a tunnel complex. He volunteered to lead one of Troop B's elements to point out a site that was near the area of the previous day's engagement. Accompanied by an interpreter, he joined a foot patrol led by Lieutenant Douglas Caton.

"All of a sudden this guy pops out of a spider hole behind us and starts shooting," said Richard O'Hare, who was on that patrol.

The chieftain was killed instantly. The interpreter was wounded and went down. A bullet grazed Lieutenant Caton's combat helmet. Another shot wounded another trooper. The entire patrol was in jeopardy of being wiped out by a gunman shooting into their backs, and it was only a matter of seconds before O'Hare was targeted. Then a trooper named Jimmy Connors, who was off to the side, shot the assassin dead. It was the first time Connors had killed a man.

"He changed after that. He was religious guy. He became very quiet. More withdrawn," O'Hare said.

Meanwhile, more attack jets were summoned. F-4 Phantoms whooshed in and targeted the spot that the slain chieftain had pointed out.

"We were pinned down in the elephant grass. I'm a 19-year-old Cherry with my face in the mud when I saw Lieutenant Caton standing in the midst of whizzing machine gun bullets, pointing the way to the bunkers for the jets. The jets were so low I could see the pilots. They had already gone by when out of the corner of my eye, I saw these canisters tumbling through the air. It was napalm. I said to myself, 'Oh my God, I am going to die right now.' It hit with a pha-whoom, and I felt the heat on my face. It sucked all air out of my lungs, and those bunkers were a-goner," O'Hare said.

Directing a jet on an attack run while under fire was nothing new for Caton, but he downplayed his role in the fight.

"That wasn't the first time or the last time," Caton said. "I did my job like everybody else. I accomplished my mission and protected my men."

John Therrien witnessed a napalm strike score a direct hit on the tunnel entrance.

"There were times when I had bullet holes in my uniform, but none of them touched me. I knew my Father in heaven was taking care of me," Therrien said. "I ain't afraid to die. I've been on borrowed time for 50 years now."

Troopers later found the incinerated bodies of the forces that were trying to kill them. The burnt corpses were called "crispy critters," a knock-off of a name for a breakfast cereal.

The deeper the cavalrymen probed, the more they learned that the Chau Chu complex was a regular food supply point for hostile forces who frequently occupied the village. The area was honeycombed with a series of well-concealed tunnels and bunkers, which allowed enemy forces to hide or melt away. Close calls were common.

"I was sitting on a mound taking a break when this shard of shrapnel is coming right toward me. It was slow enough that I could see it. I moved my head instinctively to the right, and it went by with a 'whoosh.' It laid me back," said Reid Lyon.

Before one final sweep was made, Chau Chu was cordoned off by four rifle companies—two from the 2nd Battalion of the 505 and two from the 1st Battalion of the 508th. Troop B captured a suspect who confessed to be a Viet Cong. The prisoner showed them supply locations and tunnel entrances. Five Viet Cong were killed trying to escape, and four were captured. Nine weapons and six tons of life-sustaining rice were seized. Bravo Company of the 2nd of the 505 listed two troopers as killed in action, including Specialist Jerry Michael Stone, 20, of Lockhart, Florida.

The mission accomplished, Reid Lyon's unit was pulling out of Chau Chu when he caught a glimpse of something that stayed in his memory. It had nothing to do with the chaos, noise and death surrounding the Golden Brigade's fight in the Hamlet from Hell, however. In the company of American agents in their khaki pants, members of the South Vietnamese paramilitary unit beheaded five Viet Cong. Their heads were impaled on pikes, which were then stuck into the ground. This act of barbarity, similar to ones the Viet Cong had engaged in during their struggle, was meant as a direct warning to the bad guys—stay away or the same thing will happen to you. History shows that fights between brothers are the most vicious. This civil war between the North and the South, with the Americans in the middle, had a ferocity all its own that flew in the face of the rules of war.

Anyway, the road mining incidents subsided. As a consequence of the Tet Offensive, the Viet Cong had broken their cover to assist the North Vietnamese Army in the hopes of inciting the general population of South Vietnam to rise up and join their cause. There was no uprising, and the Viet Cong was eliminated as a coherent fighting force. But U.S. troops still had to be on guard because more guerrillas joined the Communist cause. Like Bud Bolling had mused, how do you know when you have cleaned out all the bad guys.

Beheadings weren't confined to Thon Chau Chu either. West Pointer Bob Murrill mentioned an incident that happened at a different place and a different time while he commanded a rifle company in the 1st of the 508. He wrote in his recollections about Vietnam:

"One afternoon, I was given orders for my company to provide perimeter security around a Vietnamese village while a unit of the Army of South Vietnam (ARVN) combed thru the village looking for Viet Cong. This was a normal operation, conducted to interdict Viet Cong guerrillas hiding within the populace. Two platoons of my company left at zero-dark-30 the next morning, so we could be in position by first light. It wasn't long before several suspects were rounded up and brought to a central location for interrogation. I was standing near that area speaking with the ARVN Commander—a Vietnamese infantry major. As we were talking, I heard a 'Whack!' I turned around and saw that one of the ARVN interrogators had cut the head off one of the prisoners with his machete. I grabbed the ARVN major and said, 'You will take that soldier into custody and I am going to immediately report this incident to my headquarters.' I was ordered at once by our battalion executive officer to leave that location with all my troops. No U.S. troops would be involved in any situation like this. We pulled back until extraction helicopters arrived. I am not aware how or if that ARVN major handled the incident. There was so much animosity between North and South Vietnam military forces that both sides occasionally participated in atrocities."

Meanwhile, Douglas Caton experienced the personal loss of a brother, who was a medevac pilot in the 101st Airborne. Gerald Lewis Caton, a warrant officer with the 326th Medical Detachment whose call sign was Eagle Dustoff, was shot down and killed on August 17, 1969, less than a month into his tour of duty. He was the co-pilot in an OH-6A helicopter adorned with Red Cross markings when he went down with his ship. Buried at Arlington National Cemetery, he was remembered as a funny, compassionate, talented, gentle man.

"In Vietnam, we lost the cream of the crop of a whole generation of able young men. To me, that was the big loss. It was a terrible waste," said Douglas Caton, who stayed in the Army and retired as a major general in the reserves.

"I came back with both arms and both legs, so I was fortunate. The experience gave me credentials I wouldn't have otherwise," he added. "In the big picture, Vietnam was a little bump in the road. It's forgotten. I don't think people care one way or another. The only people that won were the Vietnamese. The only problem with history is people don't learn from history. Like somebody once said, history is just one goddamn thing after another."

Back in The World on June 5, Democratic presidential candidate Robert F. Kennedy was shot by an assassin inside the Ambassador Hotel in Los Angeles following his victories in the South Dakota and California primaries. He was pronounced dead 26 hours later. The perpetrator was Palestinian immigrant Sirhan Sirhan, who shot Kennedy three times with a .22 caliber Iver-Johnson Cadet revolver. In his bid for the presidency, Kennedy viewed the war in Vietnam as un-winnable. He advocated a bombing halt of North Vietnam and the gradual withdrawal of U.S. and North Vietnamese troops. On the campaign trail, he said the deepening swamp of Vietnam was "like sending a lion to halt an epidemic of jungle rot," and he said the South Vietnamese government was an ally in name only that would not last a day without the efforts of American arms. Kennedy was buried in Arlington National Cemetery near his brother John.

Chapter 25
JOE TENTPEG

The toughest fight was the one without a name, a battle that began the minute a soldier arrived in Vietnam and lasted until he boarded the Freedom Bird for the flight home. The daily slog stressed out a person physically and mentally, but the unrelenting pace was difficult to translate into a movie scene.

"Every war has its different challenges," said Pete Trusko, a lieutenant who led the weapons platoon and was later commander of Charlie Company in the 1st of the 508. "Vietnam was a very beautiful country. You'd think to yourself that when the war was over, it would be a great tourist destination. When somebody is trying to kill you, it's just not as attractive as a postcard. It was rough. Very surreal actually."

Trusko attended the University of California at Berkeley, a hot spot of anti-war sentiment. He chose to serve his country and joined the 82nd Airborne Division in time for the Detroit deployment and the emergency order to Vietnam. The infantryman's homeless existence was accentuated by a condition called the pucker factor, when the anal sphincter muscles tighten up as a reaction to danger.

"Every day was the same. One day bled into another. We were out in the field constantly, cruising for a bruising, looking for trouble. There was a pucker factor of 10,000. It was balls to the wall and hope you didn't get zapped," Trusko said. "It was just hot, hot, hot, so hot and humid that occasionally guys would crash and burn and have to be medevaced out. It seemed like it rained all the time. Everybody was hot and bothered. We wore the same clothes until they fell off. The jungle was so thick that one day it took us 13 hours to go one klick (kilometer). With just a compass and a map, we kept track of where we thought we were according to landmarks like hills and rivers. There were times we got so close to the enemy that we could smell the rice cooking. You could literally see bullets coming at you without ever seeing who fired, or Mister Charles would drop three rounds down a mortar tube for Uncle Ho and then *di di mau* it (run away in a hurry). It got to the point where you could hear that dunk, dunk, dunk sound of a mortar being fired, estimate distance and direction, and then return fire before their first round hit. It was a very comforting sound to hear our outgoing against some son of a bitch trying to kill you. We'd get to our remain overnight spot, set up the claymores and some trip flares. We had rotating guards in two-hour shifts. It sucked to be on guard duty. I would sleep with my back against a tree, leaning on my ruck with my rifle across my lap. My favorite weapon was the hand grenade. There's no arguing with a hand grenade. I carried four on my ruck.

Then we'd do it all over again. Same shit, different day. War is hell, but actual combat is a motherfucker."

This was the realm of Joe Tentpeg, a generic name derived from a piece of wood that was driven into the ground to anchor the entire Army structure. On the one hand, Joe ranked at the bottom of the pecking order and drew the dirtiest, most thankless jobs. Although most often thought of as a pawn, Army infantrymen are the Queen of Battle, the most versatile piece on the chessboard. Joe Tentpeg was the guy in the field with rotting feet and a parched throat and an empty belly, and yet the entire rest of the military, in theory if not in practice, existed to support him. In previous wars, he was known as G.I. Joe, or Doughboy or even the Minute Man, the guy who took up a rifle to fight for freedom or to defend his home. He was also called cannon fodder, ground-pounder, foot-slogger, dogface, line doggie, trigger-puller, bullet-stopper, life-taker and heart-breaker.

In Vietnam, Joe was a grunt—the sound that a man makes when he slings a 70-pound pack onto his back or the noise that an animal makes when it roots around in the mud. The title was a badge of honor because a grunt can hack it beyond the limits of human endurance. In later wars, infantrymen came up with the phrase "embrace the suck"—to consciously accept or appreciate something that is extremely unpleasant but unavoidable in doing one's job. The embrace occurred daily for Joe Tentpeg, who referred to his surroundings as the field, the boonies, the bush or the shit.

During World War II, journalist Ernie Pyle lived with the grunts and loved them. "They have no comforts, and they even learn to live without the necessities," Pyle marveled. Among his other insights into the brotherhood, which he likened to a spouse that tolerates no divorce, was this: "Such companionship finally becomes a part of one's soul, and it cannot be obliterated…There is no sense in the struggle, but there is no choice but to struggle. We are in it up to our necks, and everything is changed, even your outlook on life. They are bound to be different people from those you sent away."

For starters, Joe Tentpeg was never dry. It was either raining or he was sweating, or both. He smelled like a wet dog, and the infantry is so tight-knit that they knew each other's smells.

"We all stunk but being dirty has its advantages. After a while, even the mosquitoes won't bite you," said Richard O'Hare. "It was the same for everybody. It's kind of like growing up poor. You make do with what you have and not cry about what you don't. The human being is a damned adaptable creature. Besides, we had it better than the guys on the other side. Plus, the South Vietnamese physically beat their soldiers."

The tropical heat and humidity sapped energy and drained bodily fluids. Daytime temperatures flirted with 100 degrees, while the maximum and minimum humidity levels were 99 percent and 42 percent respectively. Escape from the broil was possible only in the higher elevations.

"It was cold as hell in the mountains. You could see your breath at night. My best friend was my jungle sweater. It could get wet and still keep you warm," said Keith Bell. "The 82nd Airborne has some pretty dedicated people. We were instilled with a pride in our country. When given a job, you do it to the best of your ability. I'm proud to have done it."

Infantryman Tom Wallace shivered in that cold too, at least when he wasn't marveling at the conditions in a Third World country where villagers survived without electricity and plowed their rice fields using water buffalo.

"Your capacity to adjust to those conditions is greater than you think. You don't realize how dirty you can be and still live. What couldn't even be imagined doing a year before you do routinely. It became a part of you. Eventually, it becomes a job. You do what you have to do, just like what Ernie Pyle wrote about," Wallace said.

In many photos from Vietnam, guys are shirtless. Not only did a wet T-shirt become a heat trap, the cotton cloth was needed to clean rifles and weapons. The necessity of a working rifle trumped the need for regulation appearance. Guys also gave up wearing their Army-issued boxer shorts. Wet underwear trapped heat and invited crotch rash. Joe Tentpeg went commando in more ways than one. When constantly wet, green Army socks contributed to the condition known as trench foot. Joe Tentpeg carried dry socks in his rucksack or just stopped wearing them.

Grunts carried everything they needed to survive in their packs, which routinely weighed 70 pounds or more. In addition to food and water, soldiers hauled bandoliers of ammunition and 100-round links of extra bullets for the machine gun. Like desperados from the Wild West, they crisscrossed these items over their torso. Also, part of the individual load were first aid kits, trip flares, claymore mines, detonation cord, smoke grenades, hand grenades, perhaps a sidearm and either a bayonet or big-bladed knife. A poncho liner, which was a kind of quilted blanket made of cotton and synthetic fibers, doubled as a quick-drying item to sleep on or something that provided shade from the sun. The most versatile piece of gear was the Army-issued green towel, handy for wiping away sweat or keeping mosquitoes from buzzing around the head and ears. If moistened and wrapped around the neck, the terry cloth acted as coolant. A towel could also cushion the weight of weapons or gear that dug into the shoulders. In a pinch, a soldier might cover himself with a towel to sneak a cigarette in the dark. On breaks, soldiers would stoop over at the waist to shift the weight off their shoulders. Every extra ounce added to the burden, but the grunts still managed to lug around an empty ammo box to hold their letters from home and the writing materials needed to write back. The standard radio was the PRC-25 or Prick 25, which weighed 25 pounds, not counting spare batteries and an optional extra-long antenna.

Radioman Carl Bludau carried so much in his pack that he had his own ritual when his column would stop. "I used to lean against a tree and slide down just to sit. To get back up, guys would have to help me," he said. "The regulations were for us to be out for no more than 28 days and then have two days at a fire base. My first time in the field, our company was out for 50 days. Our little brigade just seemed to be involved in something every day. Nobody could hump with the 82nd Airborne. They couldn't do it."

In the clothing department, jungle fatigues would rip, rot or plain disintegrate in the field. The Army's answer was to fly out new clothes every three weeks or so. Along with ammo and rations, duffel bags of fatigues would be kicked out of helicopters. The Golden Brigade's supplies came through the 101st Airborne, and the re-supply of clothing was another reason why troops called themselves orphans. Gordon Day said the uniforms were actually the laundered hand-me-downs of the Screaming Eagles, who kept the new stuff for themselves. The sense of being a bastard unit was sometimes captured in print. One battalion commander, Lieutenant Colonel Herbert B. Winkeller of the 2nd of the 505, wanted the camouflage helmet covers of his men to read: Boston Blackie's Bastards. The practice was short-lived. Winkeller was in command for 15 days in April before he was wounded by a sniper.

Footwear rotted away too. Jungle boots had a steel shank in the sole to protect against punji sticks. A hole covered by a screen was placed on the side of a boot to let out water, but the holes weren't big enough to be effective and the screens were often ripped out.

Paradoxically, in a place that was always soggy, fresh drinking water was scarce. Joe Tentpeg would have given just about anything for a gulp of clear, cold, sweet drinking water that people back in The World take for granted. Water was sometimes flown into the field in rubber bladders, which made it taste like it came from an inner tube. The amount of water needed to ward off dehydration was too heavy to carry for longer missions. Soldiers scrounged for what they needed in the rainwater that pooled in bomb craters. In the act of filling canteens, guys would joke about whether they were a skimmer or a dipper. The least hazardous water came from the bottom of a pool but still had to be treated before consumption. The Army issued water-purification tablets called Halazone or iodine pills to kill pests in the water. Soldiers would add the pills and swish their canteens until they dissolved. The additives did nothing to enhance the taste, especially when water had the same temperature as the tropical air. Then again, Joe Tentpeg was so thirsty that he had no choice but to gulp hot water laced with additives.

"Halazone water tasted like crap," said Keith Bell. "We drank it."

Water from streams or rivers required treatment too. The closest thing to fresh water was rain collected from ponchos or the large leaves of the local vegetation.

The staple of Joe Tentpeg's diet was the World War II-era Meal, Combat, Individual, or C Ration. These were pre-cooked meals that came in cans roughly the size of a can of Campbell's Soup. The Army calculated that Joe Tentpeg needed 3,600 calories a day to be effective in a combat zone, and there were 12 different dishes available, from beefsteak to spaghetti. It didn't take much time in the field to develop menu fatigue, however, and nothing merits more growl time in the ranks than Army food. Joe Tentpeg's names for a can of grub opened with a P-38 can opener were downright colorful. Beans with frankfurters were better known as beans and baby dicks. One particularly despised meal was lima beans and ham, also known as beans and mothers, with mothers being half a word. The flatulence-inducing can of chopped ham and eggs earned the nickname High Explosive. Hardened crackers were called John Wayne cookies. Desserts such as pound cake or cans of peaches were prized. Fruit cake was not. Some C Rations were older than the guys eating them. Also included with the ration packs were cigarettes, matches, chewing gum, instant coffee, cream, sugar, salt and a plastic spoon. Toilet paper was provided, but Joe Tentpeg claimed it was of such poor quality that it couldn't wipe a spider's butt. The cigarettes came four to a pack and were provided by Camel, Chesterfield, Kent, Lucky Strike, Marlboro, Pall Mall, Winston, Kool and Salem. Non-smokers traded them for better food.

Although meals could be eaten cold, they were least distasteful when heated. For a heat source, Joe Tentpeg used a small cube of the plastic explosive known as C4. Although C4 exploded violently when detonated with a blasting cap, it would burn like sterno when lit with a match. In a pinch, a can of oily peanut butter could be lit to heat a meal. With ingredients taken from C Rations, creative recipes for pizza or toasted cheese sandwiches helped add variety. Sticky buns, for example, could be made by adding jelly and a packet of sugar to a can of bread. Just cover with a canteen cup and heat over a flame.

Ideally, commanders sought to provide at least one hot meal a day, but that wasn't always possible. However, even the hot chow that made it out to the field in a Mermite can wasn't always seen as an improvement.

"It tasted just like mom used to make—only she didn't take a dump in it before she served it," Rich O'Hare said jokingly.

Under such primitive conditions, mail was a godsend. Packages from home delivered hot sauce, Hickory Farm sausages, cookie dough and Kool Aid packages to flavor canteen water. A tin of chocolate chip or oatmeal raisin cookies might be reduced to crumbs by the time it arrived from the States, but they were luxurious crumbs. Joe Tentpeg shared everything with his brothers-in-arms, even his letters. Salome Beltran's parents couldn't write English, so his buddies let him read their letters from home.

Bathing was a distant memory. In the field, Joe Tentpeg might take a one-quart shower—pouring a canteen over his head; or using his steel pot helmet as a wash bowl. Because it always rained, a soldier might lather up in a downpour, only to get stuck with a layer of soap on his skin if the rain stopped abruptly.

The environment was an enemy in and of itself, right down to the peculiarities in Vietnamese soil. Called laterite, it was reddish clay rich in iron and aluminum. When dry, it was as hard as a brick and turned to dust under the weight of heavy traffic. When wet, it was as slippery as elephant snot and clumped onto boots, tires and vehicles.

The closest comparison to the jungle environment was the climate found on larger islands during the Pacific campaigns of World War II. A verdant tropical ecosphere is an outdoor laboratory for diversity. The combination of heat and overabundant moisture encouraged super-sized growth. The mahogany and teak trees that flourished in the triple-canopy rain forest were so large that it took three men with outstretched arms to surround a single trunk. The climbing plants in the gnarly undergrowth would snag backpacks and were called let-me-go vines. Other thorns also grabbed hold of clothing and equipment, thus becoming a wait-a-minute bush. Using a machete, Joe Tentpeg sometimes hacked his way through fields of head-high elephant grass, the leaves of which had razor-sharp edges that shredded uniforms or cut into the skin. Each bloody cut acted as a dinner bell for pesky critters out for a meal.

Creatures included centipedes with a nasty sting that grew up to 24 inches long. The environment was home to all kinds of snakes, from 10-foot long cobras and fat pythons to venomous bamboo vipers, also known as the two-step snake, because a guy who got bit might only be able to take two steps before keeling over. Actually, the two-step snake wasn't that deadly, but the medics had no anti-venom for the poison in their fangs. Spiders were everywhere, especially the hairy ones that were as large as a man's hand. One soldier, when confronted by a spider at the entrance to a bunker, actually threw a grenade inside to eliminate the menace. There were bees the size of a fist, angry hornets, venomous scorpions, aggressive red ants with a nasty bite and fat flies that gorged off dead bodies. The Vietnamese rat, a hardy rodent that grew to the size of a puppy, proliferated in every area that soldiers operated in.

Then there were the blood-sucking leeches. Some of these vampires of the jungle thrived in waterways. Others lurked in trees, sniffing out their prey by sense of smell or by feeling vibrations. The slimy globs had a natural anesthetic that enabled their mouths to latch onto their prey and an anti-coagulant to encourage the flow of blood. An engorged leech could swell to the size of a man's thumb. Joe Tentpeg dealt with this nuisance by burning the leeches off with bug spray or the tip of a lit cigarette. Nearly everyone experienced or knew of a guy who had a leech attach to their manhood, making removal a bit more delicate. In one after-action report, mention was made of a leech that actually attached to the tip of a soldier's penis. No medevac was available, so the soldier had to ride out an awkward night before he could be flown to the rear for treatment.

Other creatures of the rain forest made Joe Tentpeg feel as if he were being mocked by the enemy. One night noise sounded like *fah-CUE,* repeated every 15 seconds or so. It was called the Fuck You Bird, but it turned out to be a lizard broadcasting its mating call.

On the other hand, microscopic pests delivered misery in inverse proportion to their size, like the mosquitoes that thrived in the watery environment. Clouds of the pesky buggers boiled up from the elephant grass in swarms so thick that they blotted out the moon. Repellant was issued, but the oily stuff irritated the eyes and lips. The insects would attack like dive bombers in those vulnerable areas. A mosquito bite would bleed when scratched, and the fresh blood attracted new mosquitoes. Mosquitoes also transmitted malaria, which was more than a nuisance that would land a guy in the hospital in a bed of ice as doctors toiled to reduce fevers. Malaria was a serious ailment, which is why soldiers swallowed two types of malaria pills—a large orange one and little white ones. Malaria could be a killer. Among the All Americans who died from malaria were Sergeant John Babinsack of Freeport, Pennsylvania, and Private First Class Joseph Harold Thomas of New York City.

In addition, microscopic pests contributed to such afflictions as ring worm, trench foot and amoebic dysentery. An intestinal disorder might have Joe Tentpeg running to a crude seat at an outdoor latrine, or he might be confined to a hospital until the pests he had ingested were killed off. The medical staff never could diagnose some maladies, so the term fever of unknown origin came into vogue.

"That conflict brought out the best and worst in people," said James (Doc) Slavin, who said the most common ailment for a soldier in Vietnam was diarrhea. "I had a senior sergeant come to me with a note saying he had a bad back and would be out of action for three weeks. He obviously wrote it himself. Then I had one specialist who was pulled out of the field by three or four guys. I took his temperature, and it was 106. I told him he was really, really sick, but he wouldn't go to the hospital. He said, 'I'm the machine-gunner in my squad. If I don't go back out, they won't have a machine gun.' Imagine a 19 -year-old with that kind of attitude."

One of Joe Tentpeg's most unpleasant duties was the disposal of human waste that accumulated in the 55-gallon drums placed under the seats of the latrines at fire bases and the main camp. If the smelly filth wasn't burned regularly, maggots by the millions would emerge from it. The Army's answer was to incinerate the waste in a practice the troops called Frying the Breakfast or Shit Burning Detail. Because the stuff in the drums was runny, diesel fuel or mogas (motor vehicle gasoline) was added and ignited. It could take hours to burn and required frequent stirring. The unforgettable stench was Vietnamese perfume. Although most enlisted men hated the burning of human waste, Manuel Ramos in a Cavalry platoon often volunteered for the duty. When Richard O'Hare asked him why, Ramos replied: "It gets me out the field." One man's odious chore can be another man's salvation.

A rare luxury in the field, especially in the first few months, was a transistor radio for listening to the Armed Forces Radio Network. But at a firebase, Joe Tentpeg might have a chance to listen to some music. His favorite disc jockey was Chris Noel because she was empathetic to his plight. The antithesis of Jane Fonda, she entertained troops by playing a Beatles song about the sun coming up in the morning. Upon hearing it, Joe Tentpeg knew he had made it through another night.

In short, Joe Tentpeg existed day to day, hour to hour, minute by minute. When he was low on ammo, that was his immediate need. When the bullets were flying, staying alive was his only concern. Only when he got a few minutes of down time did he think about cold beer, clean clothes, new boots, a hot shower or decent chow. He could talk with his buddies about anything or everything, never letting on how terrified he was in the last fight. A prime topic of conversation were the women back home. A cheesecake photo of an American model in the military newspaper Stars and Stripes evoked all kinds of troop talk. Another main topic of conversation was the time left before going back to The World, summarized in the familiar expression: "I'm so short I could walk under a snake's belly."

It was not unusual for a soldier to keep a diary of this surreal existence, putting pencil to paper to describe how hungry he was, how he longed for a home-cooked hot meal, how exhausting it was to shoulder a 70-pound pack but how he kept going because he didn't want to let his buddies down, how the monsoon rains turned mountain trails into slippery slopes, how homesick he was when he thought of his mother and the girl he left behind, how pretty the Vietnamese village girls looked. Even Joe Tentpeg's counterpart kept a journal. One was found on the body of Tran Ninh Nguyen, a North Vietnamese soldier who journeyed from Hanoi down the Ho Chi Minh Trail around the Demilitarized Zone and into Laos before infiltrating into South Vietnam. Translated for Bob Murrill, the journal held a universal truth. Although opposing sides are out to kill the other, foot soldiers share the same misery and the same will to drive on lest they let down their buddies.

A sample of Tran's entries:

– "Rain falls strongly. The road is very muddy and slippery. March for three straight days. It seems to be the biggest hardship and difficulty I ever underwent. Sometimes I almost cry for slipping and falling down, but I still try to follow my friends to reach the objective."

– "Sometimes I have the feeling I am on the moon. Sometimes I feel I am at the bottom of the sea."

– "Sometimes enemy aircraft bomb the place we had just left. Sometimes I feel that I cannot walk anymore, but I still do my best. At those times, I remember my family and my friends from the North."

– "The more we underwent hardships, the more the indignation increases against the enemies."

Tran also carried a poem provided by the National Liberation Front, the political arm of the Viet Cong. It said in part: "They held the knife and cut our dear country into two parts, but our singing has endured. The gunshots from the South seem to pierce my heart. We can only look and cry at how our country is divided. Our country put rifles in your hands in order that you protect the Motherland. Your hearts have held the blood of a lot of people who had gone before us. Though the swords are close to your neck, you focus on the way forward. You advance and you don't know how to surrender. If one of us falls down, a hundred of us get sad and angry. A few comrades of mine already died, but their hands still held the flag when dying…We will kill all enemies and destroy all their installations…I seem to see your victory on the liberation flag. Your way is full of sunlight, of freedom and truth, to the promise of a beautiful future."

The poem was called "To the Liberating Solider." The Airborne song salutes the All Americans as "soldiers of liberty."

Tran's last journal entry was June 29, 1968, while he was in Hue. He was killed two months later in a jungle firefight.

Chapter 26
AIRBORNE SHUFFLE

Time had expired on the order that sent the 82nd Airborne on its temporary, three-month assignment to Vietnam. While individual troopers had been going home in dribs and drabs, the larger fate of the Golden Brigade had yet to be determined. The inside word was that all those who came over in response to the Tet Offensive would return to Fort Bragg to be replaced by those in the division who were still in the States. The august minds in the Department of the Army had other ideas, however. Congress turned a deaf ear to William Westmoreland's request for an additional 200,000 troops, which he proposed as a way to counterattack after the Tet Offensive failed to achieve any of its military objectives or incite a popular uprising. Existing units would have to do the job, and the Big Army wasn't about to send the 82nd Airborne home. An announcement on May 1 sealed the Golden Brigade's fate in a complex reshuffling.

While the majority of the paratroopers in the original deployment were to return to Fort Bragg, the brigade's colors and its commander would remain. Paratroopers who elected to stay formed the nucleus of the brigade, but the unit was slated to be reorganized as a new entity—a separate light infantry brigade with more soldiers and more firepower. Replacements would fill the manpower needs, and the fundamental nature of an Airborne unit was changed.

Of the 3,650 personnel who went to Vietnam, 2,513 or nearly 70 percent were back home by July 31. Most of them had served a previous tour in Vietnam. In other cases, enlistments had run out and soldiers were returning to civilian life. The brigade's future would be built around the 1,137 troopers who elected to stay, but even those men qualified for leave because they had deployed in such a hurry. A total of 2,947 replacements were needed by the brigade.

If such a shuffle happened in peacetime, it would take months just to fill out the paperwork. This reorganization was done on the fly during time of war. The 82nd Airborne name was retained, and all replacements wore All American shoulder patches. However, for the first time since World War II, the unit lost its jump status.

Tangible changes included bigger and more powerful artillery pieces. Armored personnel carriers replaced gun jeeps in the cavalry unit. A support battalion was created. Each battalion would expand from three companies to five.

Creighton Abrams personally delivered word of the complex restructuring to Colonel Bud Bolling, who lobbied successfully to remain in country as commander of the unit. Bolling endorsed the plan of granting leave to the troopers who elected to stay.

"Sir, most of my guys left the motors running in their cars. I think they ought to get two weeks back home," Bolling said.

This transition period was called The Lull because the unit did more patrolling than fighting. The lowest assigned strength for the brigade occurred on June 11, when the unit was at 46 percent of its authorized numbers. After-action reports described it as a time of turbulence, but the task was accomplished.

Among those eligible to take the Freedom Bird home was Tommy Locastro. He received the word on May 11 to leave his battalion and report to the big air base at Bien Hoa, where he was scheduled to board a departing flight six days later. While Locastro was quartered in a barracks at Bien Hoa, the base was hit. Three soldiers from another unit were killed and 14 wounded in a rocket attack.

"One rocket hit two or three barracks away. It vaporized a tent. From then on, I slept outside my barracks on a cot," Locastro said.

The duffel bags of departing troops were shredded, dispersing some of the medals and combat awards packed inside. Incredibly, some of the awards were stolen by garrison soldiers who never left the base camp.

"There was some pilfering going on. That was a sick ass feeling, seeing people take awards that they weren't entitled to," Locastro said. He wrote in his journal: "Hell, let me get out of this damn place. Please."

As it turned out, Locastro's trip home was delayed by three agonizing days. He finally boarded a flight at 9 o'clock in the morning on May 20, leaving Bien Hoa for a hop to Japan on his way back to The World.

"I am very glad to have made another tour in Vietnam. Now the long ride home again. But I really don't mind at all because on the other end my wife Jan is waiting," Locastro wrote in his journal. He also noted: "When Charlie Company of the 1st Battalion, 505th Parachute Infantry Regiment, 82nd Airborne Division left in February, we had 203 men. In less than three months, we lost over 15 killed and 85 wounded. Fifty percent casualties. What for?"

Another trooper who got orders for home was Jimmy Barnes, who had endured the loss of John Plunkard and other buddies from his rifle company. He got the word while he was posted at Fire Base Bastogne, which he described as a series of five or six hills with different elements on different hills.

"Replacements started coming in. They didn't have jump wings, but we were just glad to get them. We didn't give it a second thought," Barnes said. "Then this sergeant yelled over to me with the eight most important words I ever heard in my life, 'Sergeant Barnes, pack your shit. You're going home.' He said it with what sounded like a touch of envy. As I walked down the hill to the chopper, mortars started coming in. If I had stopped to say goodbye to this one guy, I would have been killed," he added.

Barnes was pulled back to Camp Rodriguez before boarding a cargo plane with scores of other guys bound for home. They took a hop down to Bien Hoa to be processed out.

"They gave us clean fatigues and made us get a haircut. I was at the NCO Club drinking a beer when rockets started coming in. All the guys who had been garrisoned there dashed for cover. The incoming was landing maybe a thousand yards away. Me and the other guys from the 82nd just stood there drinking beer, watching the show," Barnes said.

His flight landed back in the States on June 4, the day before Robert Kennedy's assassination. Barnes remembered that the arrival gate had been roped off, with the parents of soldiers gathered behind the ropes.

"One guy brought home a Thompson submachine gun. He went over to the rope and told his parents, 'Here, put this under your coat.' Can you imagine something like that happening today?" Barnes said.

"One of the proudest moments of my life was when I got home. I made it out with my skin. I looked like a million bucks," Barnes added. "But no one ever asked you about it or wanted to know what it was like over there. It was a taboo subject. You just wanted to forget the whole thing. It's like it never happened. It was a crazy time."

Because his enlistment was up, Paddy Barry left too. He got back to Fort Bragg on June 3 and headed home on a weekend pass. On a stopover at Dulles Airport in Washington, D.C., anti-war demonstrators spotted his uniform and started yelling. One woman doused him with a cup of coffee. The country had changed in the time he was away. For the first time in history, soldiers were blamed for a war that had become unpopular. Shameful attitudes even surfaced in his tight-knit New York City neighborhood.

"I went down to the local bar. This guy says to me, 'Oh, you're one of those fucking guys.' I asked him what he meant, and he says, 'You know, one of those baby killers.' So I say, 'Where are you going with this? Do you want to dance?' So, he backs off and says he didn't mean anything by it. He offered to buy me a drink. I told him to take his drink and stick it up his ass," Barry said.

Barry picked up his life as best he could. He got married and joined the New York City Police Department, rising to the rank of detective over a long and distinguished career.

"My father gave me the best piece of advice ever. He said, 'Nobody owes you anything in this world,' " Barry said.

Meanwhile, Tom Ladwig also qualified to leave Vietnam. Still, the strangest feeling haunted him.

"I felt guilty ever since. Just guilt that I didn't do more. I felt like I abandoned my post. I should have stayed," said Ladwig, who had a graduate degree in chemistry and biology and had a 30-year career in the aerospace industry with Hughes Aircraft.

The home front was like an extension of battle.

"When we came home, we weren't respected. We weren't treated well at all, even at the Veterans of Foreign War posts. They'd tell us, 'You weren't in a real war,' " Ladwig said. "My parents were living in LaCrosse, Wisconsin, and my mother attended the First Presbyterian Church. One Sunday, she asked that the congregation include those serving in Vietnam in their prayers. The minister says, 'No, I can't do that. I don't agree with this war. Shame on them for being there.' Then in his sermon the following week, he repeated it. He didn't mention my mother by name but said he had turned down a woman's request for prayers for those serving in Vietnam. Needless to say, my mother moved to a different denomination."

Chapter 27
LEGS

Raised in an Irish-Catholic neighborhood of New York City, John Carney devoted the second half of his life to doing the Lord's work. He took his vows to enter the priesthood when he was in his mid-40s following a 20-year career in the U.S. Army, which included a hitch with the 82nd Airborne on the first of his two tours in Vietnam.

"People would ask me what I did before I was a priest. I would answer that I used to shoot people—and that I was good at it," Carney says with a perfectly timed pause that makes him laugh at the quizzical looks he got from those who posed the question.

Among those who attended Father Carney's 1991 ordination in his new hometown of Albuquerque, New Mexico, was Michael Hood, who once was his company commander in the Golden Brigade.

"He used to say that after serving with me, the only way he could regain his standing with the Almighty was to become a priest," Hood said with a chuckle.

Truth be told, Carney loved the Army and is proud of his service as a combat officer. Part of him was and always will be a soldier. He readily admits that he was not jump-qualified when he arrived in Vietnam in June of 1968 and was assigned to the 82nd Airborne.

"I was a leg," Carney said, using the derogatory word that paratroopers call soldiers who aren't trained to jump out of airplanes. "I was a professional solider, but as a leg, I felt like a fraud. The first chance I got when I got back from Vietnam was to go to jump school. I wear that 82nd Airborne patch fully and proudly. At the time, the guys who were part of the original deployment and who were being sent home think the war was the three months they were there. We were the Johnny-come-latelys. Any time a replacement arrives in a war zone, particularly a leader, it's kind of natural that you get looked upon differently. But in an Airborne unit? It's terrible. You get that who-the-fuck-are-you look. It was a screwed up time. It was a terrible, terrible system. The Army was creating inefficiency just trying to maintain the level of troops. There was no unit cohesion. That was one of the lessons learned from Vietnam."

Carney had been commissioned as a lieutenant in the Reserve Officer Training Corps program during his college days in Rhode Island. Although he was trained as a Ranger, he had not gone to jump school before he was sent to Vietnam. At Camp Rodriguez, he was given his All American shoulder patches with an Airborne tab and assigned as a platoon leader in Mike Hood's unit—Bravo Company of the 1st of the 505.

Paratroopers draw strength from the fact that the person to their left and to their right is also jump-qualified. They can depend on each other when the bullets are flying. One part of Airborne lore dates back to World War II when Supreme Allied Commander Dwight Eisenhower asked a paratrooper in the 101st Airborne if he liked jumping out of airplanes.

"No, sir," the nervous soldier replied.

"Well, aren't you in the wrong outfit then?" Eisenhower asked.

"No, sir. I like to be around the guys who do like to jump," the trooper answered.

Still, as hard as it might be for die-hard Airborne traditionalists to accept, that All American shoulder patch transforms a soldier, even a leg. The patch is the identifying mark of an elite unit steeped in tradition, and those who wear it accept the personal responsibility of living up to Airborne standards. So it was that Lieutenant Carney set up in the field at Fire Base Panther III, leading day patrols and night ambushes to perform the job of finding and killing the bad guys.

"I was just trying to do my job. I was totally rejected, and it hurts. You get angry, but it wasn't my call either. If you stay up front and paratroopers can tell you're not a coward, they come to accept you," Carney said.

One of the first replacements to don All American patches was Frank Cunane of West Collingswood Heights, New Jersey, just across the Delaware River from Philadelphia. A draftee, he had gone to boot camp at Fort Knox, Kentucky, and took advanced training at Fort Polk, Louisiana. Named for a Confederate general who was also an Episcopal bishop, Polk had the most realistic jungle training the Army could offer. A portion of the post was known as Tigerland, where the dense vegetation and the heat and humidity of the Deep South provided a precursor of what was to come in Southeast Asia. Cunane remembered leaving for Vietnam on the day after the NCAA basketball tournament. Lew Alcindor, later known as Kareem Abdul-Jabbar, helped UCLA avenge its only loss of the season by beating Houston and then dispatched North Carolina in the title game. Cunane watched on TV, then flew off to war on March 23.

After Proficiency School, Cunane was first assigned first to the 101st Airborne and then to the Golden Brigade.

"I'm not jump qualified. I won't even go up a six-foot ladder," Cunane said. "They told me, 'Nobody's jumping in Vietnam now. We just need bodies.' That was a comforting thought. They needed bodies."

Cunane joined the fourth squad of fourth platoon in Alpha Company of the 1st of the 508. He only was in Camp Rodriguez once. All other days were spent in the field. Although he was treated as an outsider because he was a replacement and a straight leg infantryman, Cunane said the guys who had just returned to Vietnam were glad to see replacements. That meant they were going home. Besides, after he proved his mettle in the ambush on Highway 547 on May 5, he had passed some form of acid test.

"I was 20 years old, and I'm here with the rough and tough Airborne. But all that Airborne shit went out the window after the May 5 ambush. We were all in it together," Cunane said. "There were a couple of E5s (sergeants) from the 173rd Airborne, all medaled up from their first tour, who said, 'If you want to survive this fucking place, kill everything you see out here.' We lived liked animals. My counselor told me that after that first contact, I was no longer a human being. We were savages."

During the reorganization of the Golden Brigade, Peter Henderson arrived in Vietnam with a special skill set in military intelligence. Instead of analyzing photographs of the countryside as he was trained to do, he spent the war flying two missions a day as the back seater in a single-engine, propeller-driven airplane named after a hunting hound—the 0-1 Bird Dog. Produced by Cessna for the Army and a holdover from the Korean War, the aircraft flew low and slow over Vietnam at speeds easily surpassed by hot rods and muscle cars back in The World.

The mission was to stalk enemy troops, fly ahead of convoys, mark targets and call for and adjust artillery in an aircraft that was unarmed and lacked armored protection. Sitting on his flak jacket as a shield from ground fire, Henderson carried a map board and a radio along with his M-16 rifle. There were times when the pilot would bank the plane to allow Henderson to poke his rifle out the window and empty a magazine or two at targets of opportunity. Because he was left-handed, the hot casings ejected from the weapon hit him in the face as he fired.

"We were human drones," Henderson said. "Air crews qualified for wings. I had wings, just not the Airborne variety."

A native of Clinton, Michigan, Henderson enlisted in the Army on September 25, 1967. After basic training at Fort Knox, he attended the military intelligence school, then located at Fort Holabird, Maryland. In Vietnam, he was assigned to the 518th Military Intelligence Unit and had a cot inside a tent at Camp Rodriguez. In reality, Henderson flew out of the Phu Bai airfield with the 220th Aviation Company, also known as The Catkillers. His pay grade was one below sergeant and one above private.

"At my rank, we didn't get a lot of info. Just go out, find them and kill them. Flying was a thing I loved to do. I enjoyed it as opposed to humping the way the grunts had to do. It was a little cooler up there. It was a young man's game on the ground. I was 25. Turned 26 in Nam," Henderson said.

The Bird Dog was an inoffensive looking thing compared to the jet-powered attack aircraft buzzing the battlefield. With windows surrounding the pilot and the back seater for maximum observation, it carried two smoke rockets under each wing to mark targets. Its real value was its ability to summon firepower. Henderson's radio was linked to the brigade artillery. The pilot was on an Air Force frequency as a forward air controller who could call in air strikes. The Bird Dog prowled at altitudes of 500 to

2,500 feet, and the grunts on the hilltops say they could look down and see the plane. Flying at speeds of 80 to 130 miles per hour, the aircraft provided an inviting target for enemy gunners. Henderson never wore dog tags on his missions in case his plane was shot down.

"It could get scary. A lot of those planes were lost during the war. Fortunately, the people shooting at us on the ground failed to lead us. You could see their tracers coming in behind us. That was the thing that amazed me. It was almost like World War I. We'd fly missions over No Man's Land, lots of adrenaline running, come home with a few holes in the aircraft and get patched up. Between missions, we might get a hot meal or have C Rations," Henderson said.

In addition to surveillance and providing overhead cover for convoys, the Bird Dog also provided bomb damage assessments to enlighten commanders about the effectiveness of raids.

"After B-52 strikes, you'd look for footprints and see where the enemy went. There weren't any jungles left after a B-52 strike. All you could see were craters," Henderson said. "Nobody understood unless you were there."

When replacements started to arrive, Bud Bolling's sole concern was if they were good soldiers, not whether they had jump wings. He even saved the letters from non-Airborne soldiers who said they were welcomed into the Golden Brigade by jump-qualified troops.

"It never entered my mind we might have a morale problem with legs coming in. Everybody was too busy doing things," Bolling said.

Duke Dewey, the brigade's intelligence sergeant, had similar thoughts.

"It was never an issue with us. When you have no choice but to fight, you fight. The 82nd Airborne had legs as replacements in World War II too," Dewey said. "Some of our replacements were really good soldiers. They fought like paratroopers, and paratroopers are the best in the world. We fight because you take care of your brothers. It had nothing to do with the political bullshit. We took care of each other."

In the ranks, Richard O'Hare said the replacements earned their place in the Golden Brigade as long as they knew enough to set up a claymore mine with the Front Toward Enemy and could hack it in the bush.

"They faced the same bullets we did. Their blood was red when they got hit too," O'Hare said.

That said, O'Hare also noted that the troops brought in from Germany to maintain the new armored personnel carriers didn't exactly embrace the crude living conditions in the jungle.

"They were used to living in barracks, drinking good German beer and being around German women. They had a real attitude about having to be in Vietnam," he said.

Neither the brigade nor the new men flowing in had any say on how the Big Army decided to prosecute the war. It was just the way the system was set up back then. While

70 percent of all those who went to Vietnam were volunteers, the military made up the difference through the draft, or Selective Service. It was by no means universal service. Upon reaching the age of 18, American males were required by law to register for the draft. The physically unfit were rejected, and exceptions were made for those who acquired medical excuses for things like bone spurs. In addition, deferments were granted to college students for the time they were in school. Those who could find slots in a reserve unit could fulfill their military obligation without the danger of being sent to Vietnam, because most reserve units were not mobilized. Local draft boards filled their quotas by deciding what names to call. Those chosen for service faced a two-year commitment, beginning with basic and advanced training. If Vietnam was their fate, they would be given a 30-day leave before flying off to Southeast Asia. Then a soldier would serve a one-year tour in a combat unit based on their military occupation, which in the case of the 82nd Airborne, meant lots of infantrymen. The system ended with Vietnam. It was scrapped when the military transitioned to an all-volunteer force in 1973.

Draftee John Kelsey of Camdenton, Missouri, was a replacement who contradicted stereotypes. While it was generally true that working-class kids were more likely to be drafted, Kelsey was a graduate of the University of Missouri, had worked for an accounting firm for a year and was married when his draft notice came. His boot camp was Fort Leonard Wood, Missouri, and his advanced training was at Tigerland. He was 23 when he arrived in Vietnam on April 8, 1968 and was assigned to the 82nd Airborne.

"There were about 25 of us on a night flight to Phu Bai on a C-130 loaded with cargo. I propped myself up and said the rosary," Kelsey said. "Nobody said a word. Everybody was lost in their own thoughts. I got off plane and slept in a ditch. The next stop was Fire Base Geronimo. I was the first replacement. I knew nobody. The guy I was replacing said to stay next to him all night. I remember this sergeant saying, 'Where's that fucking leg?' And the guy says, 'He's right here with me.' "

Now wearing All American shoulder patches, Kelsey went on a few tryout patrols. His M-16 rifle was replaced with the M-79 grenade launcher, for which he carried 100 rounds. On one patrol, he was part of a squad that climbed the tallest mountain outside of Camp Rodriguez.

"You have to gain trust and prove yourself," said Kelsey, whose biggest concern was being shot by a sniper. Then he was pulled back to Hue to guard the Citadel and the bridges over the Perfume River. One memory that stayed with him was the daily sight of a one-legged kid playing with a soccer ball.

In May or June, Kelsey was ordered to report to the communications bunker at Camp Rodriguez. Because of his college degree in accounting, he was assigned to the finance section, making sure the officers and the enlisted men got paid every month. His days in the bush were over, and he never took anything for granted again.

"The whole experience is seared into my mind. It was of such magnitude; it remains with you on a daily basis. There's not a day goes by that I don't spend a moment reflecting. It was a course changer. It makes you realize the value of time. The lesson for me was don't waste time," Kelsey said.

Military service was generational for Ron Snodgrass, who was originally from Chicago. His grandfather had answered the call in World War I, and his step-father was part of D-Day in the next world war. With America fighting in Vietnam, Snodgrass enlisted in Army but didn't expect the reaction he received.

"My stepfather said, 'What the hell did you do that for?' I told him, 'I thought you'd be proud.' And he says, 'I am proud. Just do your duty. Don't be a hero. When the bullets start flying, don't be the first one to stand up and start shooting,' " Snodgrass said.

In May of 1968, Snodgrass arrived at the 90th Replacement Battalion in Bien Hoa for P Training. Soon after his arrival, enemy mortars peppered the big base, sending men scurrying for cover.

"The truth of the matter is, there was no place in Vietnam that was safe," Snodgrass said. "There was a representative of the Knights of Columbus in Bien Hoa who handed out razors, soap and other items. One thing he handed out was a medal of St. Michael the Archangel, the patron saint of paratroopers. It made me feel close to home, so I wore it. I was supposed to go to the 101st Airborne, but then word came that the 82nd Airborne needed 15 or 20 replacements. There was an Army saying at the time that only three things fall from the sky—rain, bird shit and fools."

Before he knew it, Snodgrass was in Camp Rodriguez and assigned to Charlie Company of the 2nd of the 505. He was soon out on patrol on ridge after ridge in the mountainous rain forest near the Laotian border. In addition to his rifle and 300 rounds of ammo, he carried a light anti-tank weapon for use against bunkers, a five-pound block of C4 plastic explosive and two belts of ammo for the M-60 machine gun. He wasn't exactly welcomed by the Airborne infantry, but everybody adapted.

"They gave me shit at first for being a leg. They said, 'If we're out in the boonies humping and you can't keep up, we're leaving you behind.' I thought, 'Shit, these guys are bad asses.' But once you proved yourself, you were OK," Snodgrass said.

Before long, his tattered jungle fatigues were being held together with safety pins from bandoliers. A helicopter flew out a duffel bag of new clothes. The ones he got were an ill-fitting size large size, which made him look like a scare crow.

"I never tried to be anything I wasn't. When a re-supply of clothes came out, I once got a blouse with Airborne wings sewn on them. I started to cut them off with my knife, but my squad leader says, 'Leave those on. You're one of us now.' I was in the club. Any successful organization has a few guys that think outside the box. But these guys were professional officers and NCOs. They knew what they were doing. The 82nd Airborne is the best unit in the whole damn Army," Snodgrass said.

"We had a change of command ceremony once. I'm some slob in the third rank, third guy in, standing in front of the battalion guidon with all the battle streamers as thick as feathers on a chicken. I thought to myself, 'I'm standing where heroes stood.' I felt this sense of pride that I was part of the 82nd. Like any family, we had some squabbles. But we were one unit, one organization, guys fighting for one another. We looked out for each other. All that stuff about Mom and apple pie goes out the window when the bullets start flying. I was fighting for the guy next to me, and he was fighting for me. All we wanted to do was get each other home," Snodgrass added.

"Everybody got their nose bloodied little bit. We'd chopper out somewhere, hump in a certain direction and if there was no contact, we'd go back to the landing zone for another flight. On some days, we'd make three air assaults. I felt like a worm on a hook, waiting for a fish to take a bite. We were bait," Snodgrass said. "We couldn't go any farther north than the Demilitarized Zone, and we weren't authorized to pursue enemy soldiers into their sanctuaries in Laos. If you're not out there to take the other guy's territory, it's like fighting a war with one hand tied behind your back."

One time, his Army rations were a can of lima beans and ham manufactured in 1944, four years before he was born.

"I was eating stuff that was older than I was," Snodgrass said. "It wasn't a pleasure cruise. You just had to adapt."

James Klein grew up in the New York City borough of Staten Island. He never felt like he fit in on a college campus, so he volunteered for the draft because he could choose his branch of service. He picked the Army. The first time Klein was ever on a plane, he flew out of LaGuardia Airport to Columbia, South Carolina, for boot camp. After advanced training at Fort Jackson, he boarded a flight and landed at Bien Hoa.

"I looked out the window and saw clouds of black smoke. I thought to myself, 'They're under attack.' It turns out they were burning shit from the latrines. That was on Easter Sunday," Klein said.

P Training was another eye-opener.

"They fired AK-47s at us to get us used to the sound. They also put us in body bags. They said, 'If you don't listen, this is what's going to happen to you,' " Klein said.

At first, he was assigned to 101st Airborne and then joined the Golden Brigade, thinking to himself, "Oh my God, what am I doing here?"

"They needed somebody in the mess hall and offered me a job in the kitchen. I wasn't about to be a spoon," Klein said. Instead, he went out to the field with the cavalry unit, part of which was posted at Fire Support Base Panther II along with four artillery pieces.

"I was the first leg, the first Cherry in the unit. Here I am carrying a machine gun, sometimes 11 klicks out and 11 klicks back," Klein said. "It was a toy company war. We used to joke that the plastic stocks on our rifles were made by Mattel, and our plastic canteens were made by Ideal. I have told people this ever since. I can't understand how 14 months of my life can have such a lasting memory."

Also among the replacements was Donald Behm, who grew up in Palmyra, Michigan, a farming community with about 100 houses. Some of his relatives had fought in World War II, and one of his neighbors was a Korean War veteran. When his number came up, he went without hesitation.

"I owed it to my country. I felt I had a contract with America," Behm said.

Inducted into the Army on January 13, 1968, and trained at Fort Campbell, Kentucky, and Fort Lewis, Washington, Behm was offered a chance to attend jungle warfare school in Panama. When he decided not to volunteer, his first sergeant cut him orders to the jungles of Vietnam. Arriving on June 14 at Bien Hoa, Behm went through P School and was given the shoulder patches of 101st Airborne. But when he reported to Camp Eagle, he was instead assigned to the Golden Brigade, specifically Charlie Company of the 1st of the 505.

"My second day in country, we were on a company-sized operation. I'm pretty sure it was the first time I ever rode in a helicopter. From the sky, our landing zone looked like a field of mowed grass, but it was really reeds in a swamp. I jumped out and sank waste deep in muck. That was my introduction to Vietnam. They told me, 'Follow the guy in front of you. Go up that hill,' " Behm said.

Like all of the newcomers, Behm had to pass the Airborne acid test.

"I was a dumb farm boy. I had no clue what I was getting into, what a small part of the Army the Airborne was. Their first words were, 'Fucking leg. Did you bring your body bag?' I was thinking this is going to be a long tour. I was scared as hell. They looked down their noses at us. We were brutalized. We took a lot of shit at first because we were legs. We wore it like a badge after that."

The plan was to break in the new guys by having them go out on patrols without engaging in any major fights. The hill that Behm's unit was asked to climb, however, was Nui Ke, the conical shaped mountain that dominated the landscape southwest of Camp Rodriguez.

"It took us two days to climb it. The undergrowth was so thick we grabbed vines and trees to make it up. Halfway up, one guy got hit by sniper. None of us ever saw the sniper," Behm said.

A bullet hit the wounded man in the gut and clipped his kidney. As a medic pumped fluids into him, he was placed on a poncho. Behm was one of four men designated to carry him to a helicopter.

"I had a downhill corner. The blood was flowing from the poncho into my boot. That was another introduction to Vietnam. I was thinking, 'I have 360-some days more to go?' The wounded man wrote us a letter later that although they cut out a couple of feet of his intestine, he was going to be OK. Wow. A million dollar wound. It gave us a lot of hope that if he could survive that wound, maybe we could make it too," Behm said.

On the heights of Nui Ke, which had been blasted by bombs and shells, troopers found trenches, bunkers, tunnels, a generating station and even a hospital complex.

"We were up there three or four days at the most, then moved on. It was all rock, but the ingenious NVA found enough dirt to dig in. I remember there was a generator there with a naked light bulb. The medical supplies had labels that said they were made in Czechoslovakia or Hungary or some other Iron Curtain country," Behm said.

From the first mission on, Behm did what he had to do to make it through his tour. At 6-feet tall and weighing 145 pounds, Behm started carrying the Prick-25 radio. He was good at judging distances and could read a map, but the job meant carrying an extra 25 pounds of equipment, plus spare batteries. As he recalled, his company was at half strength due to casualties, attrition and personnel turnover.

"We had days where we did three separate helicopter assaults, or we just humped up and down Hilltop So-and-So in the rain forest. The east side is where the weather comes in. The western slope was like grass. It was really strange. A mahogany tree could have a trunk that was seven feet in circumference. It was 60 feet up in the air to the first branch. The canopy was so thick you couldn't see the stars at night," Behm said.

Adjusting to the exotic environment was part of the deal. Behm remembers an encounter with a centipede that was eight inches long. Those critters could sting with a poisonous bite. On 90-plus degree days, Behm would dampen his olive drab green towel and wear it around his neck to keep him from overheating. Sometimes, he wore the same clothes for a month. Some high-caliber ammunition came in crates packaged in 1941. The bullets were older than the soldiers firing them. His digestive system was once afflicted with a case of the worms. A medic gave him three pills to treat the condition, but the side effect was diarrhea.

"I remember one time we were told to dig up graves to look for hidden enemy weapons. The Vietnamese respect their dead, and we never did find any weapons. But God, digging up a rotting corpse…," Behm said, unable to complete the thought. "We went through some tough situations. I came out of it without a scratch, but I didn't know anybody else besides me in my company that wasn't killed or wounded during the year I was there. I was lucky as hell, the company good luck charm. Some guys carried an AK-47 round for luck because it was the one that had their name on it. In the infantry, it's better to be lucky than good."

Newcomer Robert Zeeman grew up in the Bronx, New York, and had earned a degree from Boston University in May in 1967. He tried unsuccessfully to get into the Coast Guard, Navy or Air Force, but they were all full. Instead, he was drafted into the Army and remembers that on April 4, 1968, all passes were cancelled just in case troops were needed to quell a race riot in Atlanta after Martin Luther King was assassinated. Zeeman was ultimately sent to Vietnam and arrived at Bien Hoa.

"In P Training, we were getting a lecture under the canopy of a parachute. The guy next to me pokes me in the ribs and say, 'Don't look now, but there's a scorpion on your thigh.' I brushed it off with the butt of my rifle, got up and stomped it," Zeeman said.

Because he wasn't assigned to a unit right away, Zeeman spent time on shit burning detail. The word of mouth among the latrine lawyers, who were the guys that heard and spread all the rumors, was that the worst possible assignment a Freakin' New Guy (FNG) could get was Up North with those crazy bastards in the 101st Airborne. Zeeman was then assigned to the Screaming Eagles and said to himself, "Shit, I'm dead." Then after being flown to Camp Eagle, Zeeman was reassigned to the 82nd Airborne.

At the base camp of the All Americans, an officer in the 2nd of the 505 noticed he could type 110 words a minute and had higher scores than anyone else on the aptitude tests. Nonetheless, Zeeman was assigned to an infantry company as an assistant machine gunner. On patrols, he wore two belts of ammo around his shoulders and carried two ammo cans.

"I'm Jewish, and we're not supposed to kneel, but when I went to a service conducted by a Protestant chaplain, I hit my knees and prayed, 'Lord, I may be in the wrong place, but please take care of me,' " Zeeman said.

Life in the boonies required adjustments.

"Guys had been out for something like seven days, and I noticed everyone really stunk. Two or three days later, it didn't matter. I stunk too," Zeeman said.

He recalled pulling guard duty at the bridges over the Perfume River. By this point, the U.S. military had placed electric cables into the water and would turn on the juice during curfew from 9 p.m. and 6 a.m. If a sampan came through, it got fried.

One time, he was bedded down in a bunker that was occupied by a battalion of Vietnamese rats. One guy decided to shoot one of the vermin, but the bullet ricocheted around the bunker. Zeeman looked up to see the beady eyes of a fat rat staring straight at him. He got a mosquito net the next day as a shield against the rats, and his father mailed him a hammock so he could sleep above the critters.

Subsequently, Zeeman's company moved west to provide security for the 101st Airborne at Fire Base Bastogne. Their big guns were assaulting the A Shau Valley, firing a round every minute.

"It was so loud, you couldn't even think," said Zeeman, who became his company's radio operator.

On one occasion, a twin-rotor Chinook helicopter was bringing in ammo and supplies to Bastogne when its sling slipped. Artillery shells spilled all over the jungle floor, and the 101st Airborne assigned Zeeman's company the mission to destroy them, lest they fall into the hands of the bad guys who could use them as booby traps.

"They always gave us the shit detail," Zeeman said. "Well, some of those shells were still in crates and some of them were loose. The lieutenant asks for the C4 to blow them up, but we only had a little bit left because we were using it to heat our rations. So, the lieutenant gets on top of the loose shells and places a claymore on top of the pile. He spliced the wires on the hand detonator and moved about 100 feet away. Whooom! The explosion was deafening. The ground shook. I thought for sure he was dead, but he survived."

Zeeman continued: "Being a grunt is a lowly profession. Basically, you get with the program, get your head out of your ass and fall in. It's complete drudgery every day. You'd hear the order to 'Saddle up.' Then you'd take two salt tablets and drive on. You'd have 75 pounds of gear on your back, not including the 26 pounds for the radio. The heat was unbelievable. There were lots of snakes and leeches and mosquitoes. I saw bees that were the size of my fist. If you took your boots off, you'd have to shake them out because centipedes liked to crawl in them, and they bit. One night, we woke up at 2 a.m., marched for three hours and then fanned out in circle. The sun started coming up, and I found myself staring at a spider's web that must have been eight feet by eight feet. It was the home of the biggest spider I ever saw in my life. I said to myself, 'I hope this thing doesn't eat me.' "

Zeeman added: "We had some good times. We had some not so good times. I was proud of everything we did. We were a good bunch of guys. Vietnam shaped the basis for the rest of my life. I would do it again. I love this country. Every day I wake up is another plus."

One person Zeeman pledged to remember was Private First Class Gerald Wayne Springer of Prescott, Kansas, killed in action on August 29, 1968. Zeeman credited Springer with preserving his sanity in the crazy world of Vietnam, and on Memorial Day of 2016, he posted this online tribute to a brother listed on Panel West 45 of The Wall: "It's been almost 48 years since I last saw you. Frankly, there is not a day that goes by that I don't think about Vietnam. It just never leaves you! I just wanted to let you know that as long as I am alive, I will honor your memory and your sacrifice. You are alive in my heart and mind."

Mike Gamble of McCalla, Alabama, a rural town near Bessemer, joined the 82nd Airborne in April of 1968. A draftee, he went to boot camp at Fort Benning, Georgia, and took advanced training at Fort Lewis, Washington.

"Those who were afraid to fight deserted to Canada. How could you face yourself when you know you're a coward? I did not want to be a coward," Gamble said.

He remembers duty at Fire Base Bastogne and patrolling the A Shau Valley.

"The toughest people in the world are infantry. It'll make a man out of you. You learn to sleep where you are, even on the slope of a hill. You level off the ground with an entrenching tool and tie yourself with a rope around a tree. One time, I woke up and this big lizard had jumped onto my chest," Gamble said. It was the Fuck You Bird.

"Look, everybody makes the same sacrifice. The suffering, living together, eating the same crappy food—that's the brotherhood. I can't explain how it happens, but we formed an unbreakable bond," Gamble said. "You learn quick that the North

Vietnamese were some of the best trained soldiers in the world. There were civilians who were friendly during the day who tried to kill you at night. You never knew who was who."

Gamble's biggest personal test came in August when he came down with malaria or a fever of unknown origin. When his temperature spiked to 104 degrees, he was taken to a hospital and placed in a bed packed with ice. Rather than taking his time to get better, he pleaded to return to the field.

"I gotta get back to my guys," Gamble told the attending physician.

"Are you crazy? Your fever is still high," the doctor responded.

"I don't care. I gotta get back with my guys," Gamble replied. "It's just a calling. We were like family. You do whatever you have to do."

In The World, a Kraft product called Shake 'N Bake was a convenient way to cook chicken. The idea was to place a thigh or a breast into a plastic bag of herbs and spices, shake vigorously to apply a coating and then bake. In the Army, which was critically short of mid-level leadership, some soldiers were selected for Non-Commissioned Officer's School, a 12-week program of training and classroom courses at Fort Benning, Georgia. Graduates were given sergeant's stripes and unofficially called shake and bakes, or 90-day wonders, by those who had to earn their rank in the field. Oklahoma native John Koons was a shake and bake.

"I was in the first all volunteer class for NCO school, and there were 200 of us enrolled. It was excellent training," said Koons, a draftee. "We were told that only 100 of us would make sergeants. The washouts would have the rank of corporal and get a 30-day leave before heading to Vietnam. We were also told that of the 100 who passed, half of us would die in Vietnam."

With three stripes on his sleeve and that prediction in his ear, Koons arrived at Bien Hoa to join other newcomers for orientation. He was 20 years old, but to younger soldiers, he was the Old Man. Incredibly, he earned his Combat Infantryman's Badge during P School.

"We were outside the wire on patrol, and we started taking fire. We thought it was all part of the training. Then the sergeant says, 'This ain't no drill. Shoot back!' They were enemy soldiers. I'm one of the few guys who got his CIB in P Training. We got rocketed too. So, we'd dive under the bed and drag the mattress over top, just like they taught us. Once you get the all clear, you then throw the mattress back on the bed and go back to sleep. We had C Rations for breakfast because one rocket hit the cooks' tent and killed them all. It was tough right from the beginning. Welcome to Vietnam."

Koons, whose uncle was an Army Ranger in World War II, was originally assigned to the 101st Airborne and shipped north to Phu Bai.

"I was already trembling. I said to myself, 'Here we go, God.' I was already writing myself off, but my attitude was to take out as many of the enemy as you can before that happened," Koons said.

At base camp, he ran into a high school buddy who was a company clerk in the 82nd Airborne. The brigade was short on mortarmen, and since Koons had some training with that weapon, he was transferred to Delta Company of the 2nd of the 505.

"One of the sergeants told me to take the Screaming Chicken patch off my shoulder and put on the patch of the Alcoholics Anonymous," Koons said. With that, he joined the Golden Brigade and went out into the bush in the villages, jungles and rain forest.

"We knew it wasn't World War II, but it was also worse than I could have imagined," Koons said. "War is hell, no matter which one you're in. It brings out the best and brings out the worst on any given day. Look, we were all flawed. But I wouldn't change a thing. I'd do it all again," Koons said.

Lieutenant Bob Murrill remembers one replacement from Minnesota known as Ink Spots because his upper body was covered with tattoos. Ink Spots was also a convicted felon. He had murdered his sister's boyfriend, but a judge said he could avoid prison if he joined the Army. Another replacement had been convicted of killing someone in the Watts riot of 1967 in Los Angeles. Murrill said they were two of his best fighters and were among the most loyal.

Some duds and non-hackers were among the replacements. But not only did the newcomers fit in for the most part, some were destined to play key roles in the history of the Golden Brigade. To say otherwise would be a disservice to those draftees who answered the call and held up their end of the contract.

Chapter 28
CONDE ARRIVES

Stanley Dodson remembers the date and the place because it foreshadowed future events. For one thing, he became a member of a brand new rifle company created out of existing units. For another, he met Staff Sergeant Felix Modesto Conde-Falcon for the first time on July 28, 1968. At the time, platoons from three companies were flown by Chinook helicopter to the pad at Col Co Beach, the Navy installation on the South China Sea.

When the brigade deployed to Vietnam, each of its three infantry battalions had three rifle companies. Under the blueprint of reorganization, each battalion coughed up an element of troops to form a Delta Company. In the case of the 1st of the 505, the first platoons of Alpha, Bravo and Charlie Companies were like individual ribs from which a brand new entity emerged. They hooked out to form the 1st Composite Airborne Amphibious Commando Company (Provisional), or more simply, the Delta Dragons. Their battalion was the Nightfighters, whose motto was Travel Light, Fight at Night. Each replacement received a Nightfighters membership card.

Dodson, then a lieutenant, took charge of the second platoon of Delta Company. Joining him was Conde, who had been serving as a spit-and-polish drill sergeant converting trainees into soldiers at Fort Bliss, Texas, before he was sent to Vietnam. The invisible hand of destiny was at work.

"I hadn't known Conde before. The first time we saw each other was on that beach," said Dodson. "I remember him saying he was from Chicago. He spoke perfect English, and I don't recall him saying anything about being a native of Puerto Rico. I had my own job to do, and I let him be the one with the hands-on approach with the troops. Our understanding was that he would do his job and bring as many of those kids back home as he could. My first impression was that he was aggressive in everything he did, including discipline. He would charge, charge straight ahead if need be, and put himself in danger to protect his soldiers. He ended up doing some great things to bring back as many of those kids as he could."

The bond formed by the birth of the Delta Dragons only strengthened as the company and Dodson's platoon carried out their mission of waging war. They were almost always out in the boonies.

"The biggest thing I ever owned in Vietnam was my rucksack," said Dodson, who spent nearly 30 years in the service and retired as a lieutenant colonel. "The only time we saw Camp Rodriguez was going in and out. We were never assigned garrison. I chose to stay in the field, and I dragged those kids with me."

Three enlisted men whose own destiny was linked to Conde and the second platoon of Delta Company were participants in the christening of the new unit. Among them were draftees Leslie Hayes of Russell, Kentucky, and Seldon (Pete) Watkins, the second oldest of 13 children who hailed from a rural community near Erie in northwestern Pennsylvania.

As the platoon's radio man, Hayes was as close to Sergeant Conde as a man could get. He was always within arm's length of his platoon sergeant in case artillery or air strikes were needed, or to make sure that higher-ups always knew where the platoon was positioned, day and night. For security reasons, call signs were changed frequently, but Conde was most often known as Night Hawk Five.

"We knew that he was married and had a couple of kids back home. He made it clear from the start that he was going to make a career of the Army. He insisted that we act a certain way, that you don't do anything stupid to get yourself or your buddies killed. He insisted that you call him Sergeant, not Felix. He was a bit of a jokester, but he much preferred that the joke be on the other guy, not him," Hayes said.

Conde was in Vietnam to fight, and it showed.

"He never knew defense. He was only offense. In a firefight, he expected you to charge," Hayes said. "If he said it once he said it a thousand times, 'There's no greater honor than dying for your country.' "

But Conde was not one of those sergeants who thinks he knows everything because he had more stripes on his sleeve. Having been trained on the M-14 rifle, Conde sought Hayes' help in learning how to tear down and clean the new M-16 he had been given.

Said Pete Watkins of Conde: "He was gung ho. He was there for a reason, and he was going to do the best he could to get that job done."

Soldiers have no say in which unit they're assigned or with whom they go into battle. The Army makes those decisions for them. But Hayes and Watkins had already formed their own bond by the time they were folded into the Delta Dragons.

Before Vietnam, Hayes was a part-time college student. His father had recently passed away and his widowed mother couldn't afford to send him full-time. Then he was drafted and inducted into the Army on November 17, 1967. Hayes went to Fort Knox, Kentucky, for basic training. After advanced individual training at Fort McClelland, Alabama, his next stop was Tigerland.

Having qualified as a sharpshooter with the rifle, Hayes had also been schooled on an armory of weapons—handgun, light anti-tank weapon, the M-60 machine gun, the Thompson submachine gun and the .50 caliber machine gun. At Tigerland, troops were issued BB guns to simulate combat.

Hayes arrived at the U.S. military base in Bien Hoa on May 12, 1968. He boarded an olive-drab bus and noticed the windows were covered with sections of chain-link fence that had been welded to the vehicle.

"What's this for?" he asked the driver.

"That's so nobody tosses a grenade inside the bus," came the reply.

"That just don't sound right," Hayes said.

Indeed, three years after ground troops were committed to Vietnam, one of the largest military installations in the country was still vulnerable to insider attacks by bad guys who blended in with the local citizenry working at the base. During three days of P Training, Hayes filled sandbags and adapted to the smothering heat and humidity. He was assigned to the 82nd Airborne, and when he informed those in charge that he wasn't jump qualified, he was told not to worry. The All Americans weren't parachuting into combat, and they needed bodies. He was then flown to join the brigade for his assignment in the field.

"It was hotter than Hell, and it rained the whole time," Hayes recalled. "I was there for two or three days before there was finally a dry day. I picked through a mound of leftover C Rations and found some peanut butter, jelly and crackers. I made four little snacks and was just about to dig in, thinking that maybe I can survive this. Then, 'ka-boom.' The skies opened up, and it started to rain again. The downpour washed away my snacks. It was heart-breaking. I cried like a baby. My first thought was, 'I have 360 more days to go?' My first night in the jungle, we were guarding Fire Base Bastogne. That's when I heard the Fuck You Bird for the first time. Just being there was a battle. But you get used to it."

At first, Hayes was his unit's point man, the guy out front who has the whole rest of the Army behind him. He tired of that duty and became a radioman. He weighed out all his gear once to find that it weighed 70 pounds, and that the Prick-25 radio weighed an extra 26 pounds, not including spare batteries. Although his gear was more than half his own body weight, Hayes figured it beat walking point.

Inducted into the Army on January 2, 1968, Watkins swore allegiance to the United States and saw his mission as fighting Communism, an ideology bent on world domination. He attended boot camp at Fort Dix, New Jersey, and took advanced training at Fort Jackson, South Carolina, before reporting to Vietnam as an Eleven Bravo infantryman. He landed at Bien Hoa in June, and he too boarded an olive-drab bus with sections of chain-link fence welded over the windows.

"They told you straight away that it was there to keep grenades from being tossed into the bus. I wondered what the hell had I gotten myself into," Watkins said.

After orientation, Watkins was standing in formation as unit assignments were called out. When he was told he was going to the 82nd Airborne, he asked the duty officer, "Why am I going to an Airborne unit? I'm not jumped qualified." The response was the All Americans weren't parachuting into combat, and besides, they needed bodies.

Tall and lanky, Watkins joined the brigade as a machine-gunner, the weapon weighing 25 pounds over and above what he carried on this back.

"When I first got to my unit, the lieutenant pointed and told me to join this group of guys. Les was there, and the first thing he said was, 'You got any cigarettes?' I had quit smoking, but I had some with me, and I gave him my smokes. Then he asked if I had any water. I needed my water to stay hydrated like they had told us. He said they were going to get re-supplied, so I shared that too. We didn't get re-supplied until the next day. I thought all these guys were veterans, and I was the FNG (Freakin' New Guy). It turned out they were only there a few weeks longer than I was. Hell, they had just got there too," Watkins said, laughing at the memory.

All the new guys came to appreciate how precious water was. In the field, troops would fill empty canteens with water from bomb craters, streams and rivers, then treat it with the Halazone or iodine tablets.

"When you're thirsty, you do what you have to do," Hayes said. "It's hard to understand water being a luxury. Vietnam is the only country in the world where you could be standing in a foot of water and there's not a drop to drink. It's also the only country in world where you could see hogs eating roasted human flesh."

Hayes once came upon a stream that looked as clean and pure as any brook in Kentucky. He filled a canteen and chugged it down. Then just upstream from where Hayes was drinking the water, his buddies found a headless enemy body with a bloated belly. Fifty years later, the story was funny.

His most useful piece of equipment was a finger-nail clipper. Hayes used it to pop blisters, pull out splinters and perform minor surgery. He wore his green Army towel all the time and never washed it once.

A rare overnight stay at Camp Rodriguez led to his most humorous memory. Showing on the movie screen that night was a James Bond flick, but the projectionist couldn't get the sound to work, no matter how hard he tried. The Airborne found its own solution.

"Two black guys got up and ad-libbed the entire dialogue. One of them even did all the female voices. We never laughed so hard in our lives," Hayes said.

On Watkins' first night in Vietnam, he was told to guard a Buddhist temple. The bad guys were known to worship there during the day, and then use the temple as a staging area for night ambushes. Watkins was posted as one of the guards to make sure they weren't around.

"The first night was the worst," Watkins said. "I had an air mattress, and I got it inflated. Every time I moved, the mattress would squeak, and I got rid of it after that. I could hear rustling too. Every time I heard something, I thought somebody was out there trying to get by us. On my first ambush, I have to admit I was scared to death. You're out there at night, straining your eyes, hearing every little noise and thinking something's about to go down. As times goes on, you learn what to expect. You get used to it. You get used to anything. When I went over, I had this feeling that there was a good chance I was not coming home. I wrote my mother and told her to tell my younger brothers to join the Navy or the Air Force. The grunts had it rough. Back home, my Mom and Dad went to church every Sunday and would pray for my safety."

Another soldier who became part of the original Delta Company was Ron Vitale of Philadelphia. He had attended Father Judge High School, an all-boys Catholic school that lost 27 of its graduates in Vietnam, more than any non-public school in the nation. Outside the school is a monument to the fallen in the form of a large granite stone in front of an American flag. It includes an engraving of Michelangelo's Pieta and an inscription from the Gospel of St. John: "Greater love than this no one has, that one lay down his life for his friends."

Vitale was drafted into the Army in December of 1967 and took training at Fort Bragg and Tigerland. In Vietnam, he found out that the new guys got the dirty jobs, like filling canteens.

"I was the Cherry, and they sent me on a water run to this village. I filled all the canteens and drank one down. No one told me about treating the water with Halazone. I got diarrhea so bad, it was shooting out of me," said Vitale.

Diarrhea was no laughing matter in the field, but it didn't get soldiers out of duty either.

"We boarded five choppers to go on a mission. While my helicopter was still hovering, my platoon leader said, 'Let's go!' I said, 'We haven't landed yet.' He kicked me out of the helicopter. When I hit the ground, I shed my pack and pulled my pants down because I had to go so bad. They told me they'd leave me behind if I couldn't keep up, so I gathered all my strength, and with the help of the medic, I got back on that patrol. I washed my pants out the best I could, but I had to wear the same ones until the next re-supply," Vitale said.

Newcomers faced an unforgiving learning curve. They took malaria pills, slathered on the insect repellant and subsisted on C Rations.

"I didn't mind the pound cake and peaches. But to this day, I won't eat fruit cocktail. I used to dream about having a cheeseburger once we got back to The World. I had 11 leeches on me once and didn't even know it. One of them swelled up to the size of a Coke can," Vitale said.

Shared misery is a glue. The worse it gets, the more a solider relies on his buddies, just as they rely on him.

"Anyone who has ever been in a war zone knows that you'll never do anything again in your life that's as impactful, as meaningful, as unforgettable," said Pete Watkins. "You look out for each other. I'm glad that I was able to serve in the 82nd Airborne."

Stanley Dodson explained the brotherhood this way: "I've been in lots of units, and you never lose that bond with guys you were in combat with. You never lose that affection for those guys. I stayed in the Army for 30 years, including five postings at Fort Bragg. I don't know of anybody in that platoon that stayed in the Army after their time was up in Vietnam. It made their experience together even more significant."

The significance came in due time.

Chapter 29
OPERATION MOT

Following one of his daily helicopter missions, Colonel Bud Bolling walked from the flight pad at Camp Rodriguez to The Hole run by the Army Security Agency. While being briefed, Bolling was told that the bad guys knew his call sign. A suggestion was made that he replace Night Rider with another name.

"No," the brigade commander said. "I want them shaking in their boots every time they hear Night Rider is in the air."

Sure enough, in August, a North Vietnamese Army unit came to fear the mention of Night Rider. All of the military intelligence experts who advised Bolling noticed a particular pattern involving the NVA's 22nd Regiment. That unit had been conducting hit-and-run engagements against the All Americans and had drawn blood on more than one ambush. Then the regiment would melt away to what it considered to be a safe haven on a series of hills about four miles southwest of Nui Ke Mountain or about 20 miles south of Camp Rodriguez. When the brigade sent helicopters over the hills, the regiment melted away until the danger had passed. In the bigger picture, analysts believed the NVA was staging for another offensive during what became known as the mini-Tet of August. After hearing the intelligence, Bolling set in motion a plan that became the 82nd Airborne's largest operation to date—an air assault by an entire battalion against an enemy base camp. It was called Operation Mot, a Vietnamese word that means No. 1, and it was a reference to the enemy commander.

"He wanted that son of bitch. He wanted that guy," said J.V. Stephenson of the radio research unit. "More than any other unit, we were looking for him."

While Mot was thought to be a code word, intelligence sergeant Duke Dewey said the NVA commander really had the last name Mott.

As planning began, the All Americans benefited from a stroke of good fortune. A corporal who served in the recon unit of Mott's regiment surrendered to the Marines on Highway One just south of Phu Bai. Once a professor at Hue University, the turncoat had been dragooned into the North Vietnamese Army. The Marines, however, failed to elicit any useful information and turned him over to the Airborne. The Professor was a godsend.

"The irony was the Marines said the guy didn't know anything. He turned out to be one of the best assets we had during the whole time. He knew where everything was," said Dickie Keaton, commander of the 518th Military Intelligence Detachment.

Instead of confining the Professor inside the POW enclosure at Camp Rodriguez, Keaton placed the corporal inside his own tent to make him feel at ease. The man was given U.S. jungle fatigues and even ate at the headquarters mess tent. He had a special fondness for ice cream, which the Golden Brigade could procure from the Seabees. A little luxury like ice cream made from reconstituted milk prompted the guy to sing like a canary.

"If you treat them with respect, you get a lot more out of them," Keaton said. "I had two interrogators, one Ukrainian and one Czech. These guys spoke everything but English, but both were on their second tours and spoke pretty good Vietnamese. We asked our prisoner if he would be willing to show us where the regimental headquarters is. He agreed."

To this point, Keaton had put together scraps of information on three-by-five cards that he kept in a shoebox. On a map, dots covered the area of NVA activity until a pattern emerged. Keaton would have given anything for a laptop computer to track the movements, but such a luxury hadn't been invented yet. Not only did the Professor point out locations, he sketched the whereabouts of command bunkers and defensive trenches. He also supplied the names and troop strength of subordinate units. On August 17, the Professor boarded a helicopter that flew over Mott's jungle headquarters.

"He was definitely scared when we put him on the helicopter. Rumors abounded that POWs were thrown out of helicopters in mid-flight, and unfortunately, some of those rumors were true," Keaton said.

The helicopter flew at an altitude of 2,000 feet, high enough to keep the NVA from thinking it was a threat. Flying over a particular ridge, the Professor pointed down and said: "It's right down there." He was so excited he almost fell out of the aircraft.

Then things got even better. An enemy combatant who rallied to the cause of the South Vietnamese was entitled to a reward if he surrendered with his weapon. In a further show of good faith, the Professor pointed down to a field where he had buried his rifle and stashed all of his personal equipment. He asked the helicopter to land. Tensions were rightfully high because it could be a trap.

"I went with him as he dug his weapon out. I was concerned that I just might get shot. The pucker factor was definitely raised. I made sure the door gunner kept us in his sights," Keaton said. "He retrieved his AK-47, emptied it and held it over his head."

For turning himself in along with his weapon, the Professor received a reward of 1,500 Vietnamese piasters, or $15 in American money. With what he added to the information the brigade already knew about Mott's regiment, a plan was formulated to soften up the area with a massive air strike. Once the battlefield was shaped, 645 Red Devils from the rifle companies of the 1st Battalion of the 508th Parachute Infantry Regiment would be inserted by helicopter.

An additional request was made of the Professor. Would he be willing to be aboard a helicopter during the battle and help direct the assaulting troops by pointing out trails and rally points? Once again, he agreed.

In a real life game of chess, Bolling had set a trap for a unit-on-unit gunfight. He was never one to allow the enemy to dictate when and where a strike would be launched. To lull Mott's regiment into a false sense of security, all activity was halted.

"I told the Old Man, 'Cease all flights,' " Duke Dewey said. "We had that guy cornered."

And although helicopter flyovers were curtailed, the commanders of the rifle companies were taken on one flight over the target area to get an idea of their landing zones and the terrain they would have to fight on. To mask their true purpose, helicopter flights were made at higher than normal altitudes and not directly overhead. Mott and his unsuspecting regiment remained smugly in a well-concealed and fortified base camp.

On the evening of August 22, the Red Devils were in their staging areas at Fire Base Birmingham, which had the best flight line for helicopters to whisk troops into battle. The first blow was supposed to have been delivered by Air Force B-52s, those Big Ugly Fat Fuckers that carried bombs by the ton in their bellies. Known as an Arc Light, a B-52 strike was so powerful that the bombs obliterated the jungle and created craters eight to 12 feet deep. Anyone even close to an Arc Light would have his eardrums shattered by the concussive blasts. This bombing mission was supposed to blast out landing zones in the overgrown jungle. The B-52s, however, were needed elsewhere and their mission was scrubbed. The battle plan was changed before the first shot was fired. Smaller fighter-bombers and attack jets were summoned as substitutes to open holes in the jungle for helicopters to land and disgorge troops. Five aircraft were assigned to blast out each of two landing zones, with their 2,000-pound bombs fused to super quick. Forward air controllers guided them on their runs.

At first light on August 23, Operation Mot kicked off. Attack jets created two primary landing zones and one alternate site. The air strikes were made in concert with an intense and deadly bombardment by the brigade's artillery, positioned four miles to the north at Fire Base Panther III. The command post for directing the battle was supposed to be atop Nui Ke Mountain, but helicopters were unable to land there because of bad weather. An alternate site was selected.

The first air assault was made by Delta Company, commanded by 22-year-old First Lieutenant Bob Murrill. Like he had before every mission, Murrill sought solace in the 23rd Psalm: "Yea, though I walk through the Valley of the Shadow of Death, I will fear no evil; for You are with me. Thy rod and Thy staff, they comfort me…" His trigger-pullers, laden with full packs, had lifted off at 7:15 a.m. under overcast skies from Birmingham. Canon shells and bombs were still exploding as Delta Company touched down at Landing Zone Brick, an abandoned fire support base that became the battalion command post. Troops called it Leech Island because of the prevalence of the pesky blood-suckers in the area, and their name for the operation was the Battle of Leech Island.

"My company was the first one in. Being the first to hit an enemy position is generally a godsend. The element of surprise is always a commander's best friend. Colonel Bolling had caught them completely by surprise," Murrill said.

Delta Company crossed a tributary of the Perfume River and headed west over a series of mountain ridges through triple canopy jungle. Contact came quickly.

"Two North Vietnamese soldiers appeared behind us. It was hard to say who was more surprised, them or us. My troops shot them and put them off the trail after taking their weapons and checking for anything our intelligence folks would want to review," Murrill said. One of the dead soldiers carried a diary that was sent to battalion headquarters and later returned to Murrill.

At 8 o'clock, helicopters delivered Alpha Company and Charlie Companies to Landing Zone Red. To the south of those two units, Captain Charles Heaukulani's Bravo Company assaulted Landing Zone Silver at 9:40 a.m. The entire airlift was completed in about three hours, and the Red Devils were operational without having a single casualty.

Infantrymen moved out with the intent of enveloping the enemy forces and then closing in on Mott's command post. The NVA still had the upper hand. It owned the high ground, and it knew the terrain.

The next day, on August 24, one squad of a Bravo Company platoon moved forward to a particular objective. Using a mountain stream as an avenue, troops had advanced about 150 meters when intense fire from automatic weapons pinned them down. The rest of the platoon answered with grenade launchers and anti-tank rockets, allowing the trapped squad to pull back. Since no progress could be made against fortified positions, Captain Heaukulani ordered his other platoons to seal off the enemy forces while he pondered his next move.

At the same time, Alpha and Charlie Companies were ordered to reinforce Bravo to exploit the contact. Although both companies were some distance away in thick jungle, they found a stream running south and followed it as a avenue of approach. At a distance that was the equivalent of the length of four football fields from Heaukulani's unit, Alpha Company made contact with an entrenched NVA force. Taken by surprise, the enemy broke and ran to the west. Three companies of Red Devils were now united and pursuing the fleeing NVA. Meanwhile, Murrill's Delta Company reacted instinctively and moved to the sound of the guns.

"The noise from the explosions and rifle fire was so loud, the brain sensory system goes into overload. On top of that, the smell of gun powder is acrid. You cannot think rationally during this chaos. You can only react as you have been trained. I recall everything being in slow motion. Adrenaline had kicked in. I saw trees around me being hit with bullets. We just kept moving forward. I also remember having a conversation with God. I said in my mind, 'God, it doesn't matter if You are three-in-one or one-in-three. You are either with me or not.' As the next few days proved, it was obvious that He was with me," Murrill said.

Murrill radioed for close air support and warned the jet drivers to be alert. The NVA's .50 caliber machine guns could shoot them down. He popped smoke to show his location, and a pilot acknowledged the color that rose through the trees. An F-4 Phantom made its bomb run, dropping its payload southwest of Delta's position. Along the way, the jet was hit by enemy fire.

"I could see through the trees that the aircraft had been hit. Trailing smoke, the F-4 turned to fly back to friendly territory. I saw two parachutes for the pilot and navigator," Murrill said.

Meanwhile, overhead in an observation helicopter, the Professor who had been of such importance in planning the battle played a vital role in its prosecution. When troops on the ground reached designated areas, he pointed out trail junctions and directed them to take the correct paths. He led Alpha Company around several enemy positions, enabling the troopers to kill nine NVA and take three suspects. Along with the Professor, those suspects then led the company to an NVA communications center, where Alpha Company troopers captured several field radio transmitters and a copy of the enemy's signal operating instructions.

The Red Devils pressed the enemy all day. Whenever troops encountered a fortified enemy position, they called in artillery to hammer it. When the shelling lifted, they resumed their attacks and took more positions. This was done several times until contact was broken at dusk. Soldiers took up defensive positions, which involved forming a circle called a night laager.

The attack resumed the morning of August 25, with Alpha and Bravo pressing westward. Along the way, numerous NVA supply points were discovered and yielded a haul of weapons, ammo and food.

Charlie Company moved south over rugged terrain to swing in behind the enemy and block any escape routes. In late morning, heading down a reverse slope, Lieutenant Jim Green's first platoon was ambushed by 16 enemy soldiers—eight of them perched in trees and eight hidden in camouflaged bunkers. The point man, Corporal Phillip Warren Weaver of College Park, Georgia, was killed in the opening burst. Weaver, a draftee who got married shortly before he deployed to Vietnam, was four days shy of his 21st birthday. Several other platoon members were severely wounded, and the entire group was pinned down momentarily. Second platoon crawled down the trail to assist. Artillery fire was adjusted and fell within 50 meters of the first platoon. Suppressing fire relieved the pressure from the snipers in the trees.

After the dead and wounded were evacuated, Charlie Company was ordered to push west along a ridge line. Within a short distance, an NVA force opened fire on them from concealed bunkers that mutually supported each other. The first three men of the point squad were killed in the opening volley, including two from New York. One was Lieutenant Raymond Krobetzky, 21, of Armonk. His men held him in the highest regard as a leader of men who would carry you or your pack if you were wounded or couldn't keep up. He was a 1965 graduate of Valley Forge Military Academy, where he commanded plebes as a first sergeant. Known by the nickname "Krobait," the blue-eyed officer was the only son of Ethel and Raymond Krobetzky. Also killed was Corporal Juan Manuel Quinones, of New York City, who would have turned 20 in less than two weeks. He was later buried at Municipal Cemetery in Yauco, Puerto Rico, his native land.

The fire fight that followed was described as Hell on earth. Troopers would drive the NVA from one bunker, then use it as a position to cover the attack against the next bunker. At one point, Charlie Company's second platoon maneuvered around the enemy's flank and overran an entire bunker complex. The element of surprise was so complete that the former occupants' noon meal of chicken and rice was still cooking. Thirty enemy soldiers had been killed at a cost of four troopers killed and ten wounded.

Meanwhile, Bravo Company was about one klick away in a valley and took an accurate barrage of mortar fire. One squad was pinned down by machine guns. Lieutenant Phillip Van Gorp immediately maneuvered the remainder of his platoon to exploit the contact. After using bazooka-like weapons and grenade launchers as preparatory fire, he ordered his men to fix bayonets for a frontal assault. According to an after-action report, the charge resulted in the "bayoneting of several NVA as they attempted to fight their way from their bunkers and killing 13 NVA while suffering only two friendly wounded and also discovering several field radios and other documents." It wasn't the last time an order to fix bayonets was given.

The fourth day of the battle was pivotal. It began as a copy of the previous day as the enemy fought delaying actions against the attacking Red Devils. With Bravo and Delta Companies driving forward, the mobility provided by helicopter paid dividends. Alpha Company was extracted at 9 a.m. and repositioned to an area about six miles to the east.

At 1 o'clock in the afternoon, Bravo Company made contact with an NVA squad. Captain Heaukulani, known as the big Hawaiian, ordered two platoons to advance using fire and movement. The enemy began to withdraw, moving uphill to the west through dense undergrowth. Combat veterans smelled a trap, and their suspicions were confirmed when heavy automatic weapons fire and Russian-made rockets suddenly filled the air. Through the noise and chaos, Heaukulani pulled his leading elements back a short distance and called for artillery and air strikes to within 70 meters of his position. He continually exposed himself to hostile fire as he moved between his pinned down elements.

At this point, Lieutenant Larry Fleener's second platoon made a flanking movement while third and fourth platoons pushed forward. Just then, a reinforced NVA company opened up. In assessing the situation, Heaukulani determined that two of his platoons were pinned down and unable to move, but the fire directed against them was mostly ineffective. If he advanced, his men would be exposed to hostile fire. The captain decided to sit tight until Fleener's platoon completed its flanking maneuver.

Undetected, Fleener's men crawled through 700 meters of thick jungle to get into position. According to an after-action report, they fixed bayonets and charged into the NVA's right flank, catching the surprised enemy off guard. Confusion spread in their ranks. Fleener's men advanced on the run to exploit the situation, tossing hand grenades and shooting from the hip as they attacked. Fleener received the Distinguished Service Cross for his actions that day. His citation read, in part: "Despite steep, rocky terrain covered with thick underbrush and sniper fire which wounded four more of his men, he succeeded in maneuvering to the rear of the hostile positions. His force was discovered by an enemy security element and began to receive a heavy automatic weapons barrage. Reacting immediately, Lieutenant Fleener directed rifle fire on the security element and, closing on the nearest bunker with two other men, silenced it with two hand grenades. Led by their valiant commander, who demolished three additional bunkers single-handedly, the platoon systematically destroyed fortification after fortification. His heroism permitted the remainder of the company to sweep forward and annihilate the North Vietnamese."

Now that Fleener had eased the pressure on the rest of the company, Heaukulani seized the opportunity to lead third and fourth platoons in a daring frontal assault with bayonets fixed. Tom Wallace was part of that charge, but he doesn't remember receiving an order to fix bayonets. He didn't carry one anyway, but he did have a paratrooper knife.

"We got a kick out of reports of a bayonet charge, but we did assault the hill. It was a thing you wanted to get over with as quickly as possible, and we did," Wallace said.

The critical part of the charge, Wallace noted, was made with hand grenades by Bravo Company's First Sergeant James L. Edwards of Memphis, Tennessee. A battle-tested veteran, Edwards had fought on Pork Chop Hill in the Korean War and had already served two tours in Vietnam—one as an advisor and a second with the 173rd Airborne. Those in the ranks called him Big Ed, but never when he was within earshot. Married and the father of four children, he had the resolute eyes and imposing physical stature of a true warrior.

Edwards had already taken charge of an unfolding situation when the third platoon, which was leading the company, was fired upon by rifles and machine guns. In the heat of battle, the point squad had gotten separated from the rest of the platoon. Almost out of ammunition, the platoon was trapped in the enemy's kill zone and was in danger of being overrun. Most of the riflemen were down to their last 20-round magazine. But accompanied by a radio operator and another man, Edwards ignored the rounds zipping past him and rescued the squad from its dire predicament.

"For at least an hour, I was exposed to enemy fire," Edwards told the Pacific Paraglide, the 82nd Airborne's in-house newsletter. "I had everyone move back except for three men. The radio operator, another man and I stayed up there throwing hand grenades. Enemy forces were fixing to assault, but we drove them back. When they pulled back, I moved back and reorganized the platoon."

At this point, Edwards spread the platoon out in battle formation and prepared to advance across a ravine defended by enemy guns.

"We started to receive heavy machine gun fire, small arms fire and B-40 rockets point blank. As we advanced at a crawl, I saw a couple of bunkers, and I jumped up and threw a couple of hand grenades, and I knocked out one bunker. The fire ceased and we started to move forward again. This time we attacked and knocked out four bunkers before we got halfway up the hill. During the whole firefight on this hill, the platoon that I led knocked out 12 to 14 bunkers. All of my 28 men were young soldiers, but they were definitely good," Edwards said.

Edwards received the Distinguished Service Cross for his actions that day. His citation read in part: "Finding the point squad out of ammunition and about to be overrun, he placed heavy fire on the communists, single-handedly forcing them back and enabling the squad to withdraw. When his comrades had reached the defensive perimeter, he crawled back and continued to expose himself to the hostile barrage for the next three hours to direct his men. When another platoon managed to reach the rear of the enemy, he led an attack, making a one-man assault on the first fortification which blocked his troops' advance and killing its two occupants with hand grenades. After he had destroyed a second bunker with hand grenades and annihilated both its defenders with rifle fire, his men stood up and overran the enemy positions."

A textbook infantry assault brought the battle to its climax. Charlie Company's troops reached vacated enemy bunkers and used them as cover for an assault on the next bunker. The relentless advance forced the NVA into the open. Thoroughly bewildered, and caught in a crossfire, the remnants of the NVA force, confident of victory only minutes before, broke and ran. Reinforcements from Charlie and Delta Companies were on the way to assist, but Heaukulani's company had taken the position by the time they got there. Several fleeing enemy soldiers ran straight into the reinforcements and were cut down. The bodies of 92 of Mott's men littered the ground.

Later that day, at 10:30 at night, Alpha Company had established night defensive positions when an NVA platoon was detected moving only a few meters from its perimeter. Another vicious firefight erupted. A call went out for artillery. The cannons were aimed to the hit grid coordinates provided to them. But during the ebb and flow of the battle, the forward artillery observer got mixed up and gave the wrong direction when he told the artillery battery to adjust its fire, according to an after-action report. In the fog of war, an errant shell killed four All Americans and wounded four others. The military calls such an incident a blue-on-blue, or friendly fire. But as Murphy's Laws of Combat notes, friendly fire isn't. It's fratricide. It's an evil that is part of any war, no matter how hard everybody tries to avoid it. It's a sickening feeling when a man is lost to enemy fire, but it's even worse when brothers are responsible for killing brothers.

Frank Cunane remembers that episode because it was such a close call for him. As the point man in his element of Alpha Company, he came to a big tree while on patrol. A tree offered something sturdy to lean up against during the night, and he figured it would be an ideal place to set up. However, he was ordered to continue up the hill. He didn't give it a second thought until later, when a medic delivered some disturbing news about a big flash and boom from their own guns.

"You know that tree where you were going to set up? That's where the artillery shell hit. That would've been you," the medic said.

"That was a sad night," Cunane said. "Then later, we heard a tiger growling in the jungle. It's bad enough somebody is out there trying to kill us, but now we have the animal kingdom coming at us. What else could go wrong?"

In addition to Weaver, Krobetzky and Quinones, among the Red Devils killed during the four-day battle were Lieutenant John Baxter, Platoon Sergeant Washington James and Sergeant Ronald Pharis, a medic. Baxter, 29, was a native of Plainwell, Michigan. James was from Shady Spring, West Virginia, and would have turned 29 in nine days. Pharis, 23, was from Lake City, Florida, and had only been in Vietnam for a month. A comrade, Sergeant Edgar Ramirez, lay next to his body the night he was hit and prayed for his soul. His older sister, Barbara Pharis Reynolds, remembered waving goodbye the day he left for Vietnam. In an online tribute posted 46 years after his death, she wrote: "My darling brother, you will always remain in my heart and will never be forgotten…I thank God that you didn't die all alone (and) that you had a brother with you." She and her grandchildren look up his name on The Wall and visit his grave in Memorial Cemetery in Lake City, where he is buried next to his parents.

Also among the Red Devils killed were: Private First Class Roger Earl Bishop of Louisville, Kentucky, a draftee who was slain on his 21st birthday and who had volunteered to walk point in place of a comrade; and Specialist 5 Vincent Allen Clark, 24, of Indianapolis, Indiana, a draftee who was killed by a mortar round.

All of the dead from the battle are listed on Panel 46 West of The Wall. All were replacements in the Golden Brigade.

Meanwhile, other troopers who were seriously wounded required medical evacuation. In one instance, several men attempted to clear an opening in the jungle for the inbound choppers. Although any movement was hazardous, medics from the other platoons made their way to scene to treat the wounded. One helicopter arrived and lowered an evacuation basket. Two of the most critically wounded were loaded. While the basket was being raised, half of the multi-stranded lift cable snapped and began to unravel. The basket started to spin as the helicopter sped away to a battalion aid station. With only moments to spare before the cable snapped, which would have dropped the wounded to a sure death, the aircraft touched down.

Mott's unit simply disintegrated. His command bunker was taken intact, and he had fled so quickly that he left behind his combat gear, personal clothing and his family pictures. Colonel Bolling flew over the jungle in his helicopter, using its loudspeaker for psychological purposes. Night Rider's message was: "Mott, we have your sports shirt. Now you can turn yourself in and be a hero or we're coming after you."

Those in the intelligence sections gave all the credit to Bolling and his infantry units for the success of the operation.

"He wiped that guy out," J.V. Stephenson said. "Those kids did their jobs. When the president called 9-1-1, they answered the call. We just gave them the info."

It took several days to appreciate what had been achieved. Among the positions that were seized were two field hospitals dug into the hills of a remote jungle outpost. One underground care center was so large that it had two levels. After two days of being gutted of its captured equipment and medical supplies, the hospital was destroyed to deny the enemy of its use.

Late in the morning of August 29, the troops of Charlie Company swept through the regimental base camp and uncovered a storage area stockpiled with weapons and tons of ammo. In addition, stacks of enemy documents were seized and whisked away for translating. Included in this treasure trove was a detailed map of Hue that listed street names and locations of safe houses that the NVA used during its reign of terror in the imperial capital. The documents also showed the residences of undercover Viet Cong agents who had been living in the city, along with the locations of VC aid stations, places to store ammo and evacuation points. All of the information was turned over to the Vietnamese National Police, who later raided all the key points and rounded up 50 hardcore Viet Cong. Another enemy document detailed the complete plan for the Highway 547 ambush that had been thwarted by the Red Devils on May 5.

"We found so much ammo, it took three days for four helicopters to haul it out of this area. We had mortar fire coming in both sides of a landing zone we set up. I was the last man off the landing zone. I made sure all my troops went out, then I went out," First Sergeant Edwards said.

Edwards and his men were subsequently given a two-day stand down, which included a steak dinner with cold beer at Camp Rodriguez.

"One of the guys asked if we were going to get to see a movie as entertainment, and Big Ed replies, 'God damn it, if I wanted entertainment, I'd go out on ambush tonight,'" marveled Tom Wallace. "He was the real deal, the epitome of a professional soldier."

To show his troopers how much he appreciated what they had done, Bolling flew out to Mott's headquarters with a finance unit. Payday was at the end of the month, and those who had done the fighting deserved to be compensated. Accompanying Bolling to photograph the occasion was draftee John Bell of Fresno, California, a combat photographer assigned to the new 45th Public Affairs Unit that Bolling had created. It was Bell's first time aboard a helicopter.

"I got the highest score at P training. They gave me a certificate and a Zippo lighter and said, 'Congratulations, you're with the 82nd Airborne.' I had never heard of the 82nd Airborne. So I said, 'Hold on, hold on. I'm not a paratrooper. I've never jumped out of a plane.' They laughed. They said, 'Nobody's jumping in Vietnam. You'll fit right in with these guys. They're crazy.' Maybe they knew I was crazy too," said Bell.

Bell snapped a picture of troopers getting paid on the very site that was once an NVA regimental headquarters. No helicopters were available to take Bell back to base camp, so he spent his first night in the jungle.

"I slept in Mott's bunker. The floor was lined with palm fronds," Bell said.

Later on, Bell overhead a radio conversation between Bolling and the troops who took Mott's hill. Bolling asked if they wanted anything. No, came the reply. They had everything they needed.

"These guys were tougher than nails. But they checked around and told the colonel, 'We'd like ice cream.' Bolling answered, 'What flavor?' The next thing you know, here comes a helicopter carrying a pallet of ice cream—chocolate, strawberry and vanilla. It had melted, so we were drinking ice cream. But that was Bolling. His guys were out there, and he was going to pay them, and he was going to bring them ice cream in the jungle," Bell said.

As successful as the operation had been, a second part of the battle had yet to unfold. Mott's men were being murdered by artillery, losing 90 soldiers in one bloody barrage. The NVA reacted by making plans for a suicide attack against the big guns located on Fire Base Panther III.

Back in The World during the last week of August, TV sets in America's living rooms were filled with bloody images of hostilities between opposing forces playing out in real time. A world away from Vietnam, this carnage occurred in Chicago, the host city of the Democratic National Convention. With Lyndon Johnson having removed himself from the running, and with aspirant Robert Kennedy felled by an assassin, Democrats nominated Vice President Hubert Humphrey inside a convention hall that was surrounded by a steel fence topped with barbed wire. In the streets, a bloody confrontation occurred on August 28 during what became known as the Battle of Michigan Avenue. An army of protesters that included college students, Hippies, Yippies and the radical Students for a Democratic Society united to voice their opposition to the Vietnam War. When protesters marched down Michigan Avenue toward the convention hall, they were met by Chicago police in riot gear and troops from the Illinois National Guard. Police fired tear gas and swung their billy clubs to break up the demonstration. Hundreds on both sides were injured, and nearly 700 protesters were arrested. A commission that investigated the ugly events concluded that it was a "police riot." The anti-war protesters had chanted, "The whole world is watching." Hanoi certainly was. If its army was failing to achieve victory on the battlefield, North Vietnam was winning the psychological war. In retrospect, Chicago was the place that guaranteed the election of Richard Nixon, who had earlier clinched the Republican nomination by promising to end the war and to restore law and order.

Chapter 30
EPIPHANY HILL

Drill sergeants looked at John Szczepanski's vowel-challenged, tongue-twister of a last name and called him Alphabets. It's pronounced shuh-PAN-ski, and even his buddies shortened it to Ski. His memory of what happened on a hill in Vietnam during one 24-hour window was as vivid 50 years after the fact as the moment when his company was overrun by suicide attackers hell bent on trying to take out a Golden Brigade artillery position. He talked about that day even though he had to open some emotional scars to do it.

A lanky, street-savvy Midwesterner from the industrial belt of cities along the southern rim of Lake Michigan, Ski was the son of a Polish father and an Italian mother. With that wise guy sense of humor of his, he told friends that he actually had a Sicilian godfather. A natural athlete who participated in track, basketball and baseball, Ski knew the streets but didn't look for trouble. His father was an Army staff sergeant and combat engineer in World War II. Several of his uncles had also served in that war, including one who gave him a copy of his journal from his time in the jungle fighting against the Japanese. His Aunt Mary had also served in the Nursing Corps. When he was drafted, Ski stepped forward without so much as a thought about skipping out.

"Every male I knew was in the military," Ski said. "When you're called by your country, you just go. I knew there was war going on, and I'd probably be sent to Vietnam at some point."

The physical part of Army training was no problem. How to handle, fire and clean weapons was something Ski learned in boot camp at Fort Leonard Wood. He also did advanced training in the heat and humidity at Fort Polk's mosquito-infested Tigerland in Louisiana. Having done well on Army aptitude tests, he was slotted for Officer Candidate School. When the time came to determine his future, however, a sergeant wearing the blue cord of an infantryman told him: "Today's your lucky day. You're going to be in the infantry. That's the Queen of Battle."

Ski was at Polk the day Martin Luther King was assassinated. "We were all called together and put on alert. They told us that if New Orleans goes up in flames, you guys are going to restore order," Ski said. "I remember walking the streets and talking with some of the guys. Was it even in realm of possibility to kill Americans?"

In Vietnam, he was assigned to the 82nd Airborne and ultimately joined Delta Company in the 2nd of the 505. "Yeah, they called me a leg at first. My attitude was,

'Okay, whatever you do, I can do too.' I was proud to be a part of the 82nd. It was an honor. I lived with them. They died with me. I did what I had to do," Ski said.

His most precious possession in Vietnam was a General Electric tape player/recorder that he carried in a waterproof bag in his rucksack, even though it was extra weight to haul around. Back in East Chicago, Indiana, his mother gathered his two sisters and his brother, along with friends, to send taped messages that were his bridge to home. Ski and his buddies from Delta Company recorded their own messages to send back.

"Those tapes took your mind off everything else. My buddies got to know my family. My family got to know my buddies. Nothing was going to happen to that cassette," Ski said.

Some of the tapes from home included Motown music. Ski was such a big fan of the Motown sound that he had rose-colored glasses like those worn by David Ruffin, the lead singer of The Temptations. And when there was some down time, Ski and his buddies got into spirited debates over which group was best—The Temptations, The Four Tops, Smokey Robinson and The Miracles or Junior Walker and The All-Stars. They sometimes sang a cappella versions of their favorite hits.

In June of 1968, Delta Company received a replacement who was from New York City but whose family came from Puerto Rico. He was David Alicea, a quiet kid who kept to himself until Ski coaxed him into joining the group discussions about music. Motown broke down barriers and helped create one of those Army bonds between people from diverse backgrounds who ordinarily would have never met.

Then on August 28, Ski and the men of Delta Company were positioned atop a high point designated on maps as Hill 46 but better known as Fire Base Panther III. The summit offered a picturesque and commanding view of the east branch of the Perfume River, which on its path of least resistance, looped around Panther III in a semicircle before resuming its northern journey.

Atop the heights was a .50 caliber machine gun, complete with a Starlight scope, that could fire on enemy sampans stealthily trying to navigate the river at night. The most powerful punch at Panther III was provided by a dozen artillery pieces arranged in two separate batteries. The big guns supported Operation Mot and the assault on a regimental headquarters about four miles to the southwest, and those cannons had slaughtered scores of North Vietnamese soldiers in the previous four days.

Ski set up in an open, grassy area, with David Alicea taking up a spot about 15 feet away. Nearby was a guy called Frenchy, a California kid who was obsessed with the fact the he would be targeted by the North Vietnamese because he spoke French. The ammo dump was on the other side of the hill but within walking distance. The battalion's artillery was behind them.

"We were spread out. We were just looking at each other, thinking this may be our last time together," Ski said. "I took off my boots to get some sleep. Then all of a sudden…"

Cold Steel Alpha Company of the 2nd of the 505 provided perimeter security for Panther III. And as daylight faded on August 28, Captain John Kapranopoulos voiced concerns to the battalion commander that something was awry.

"I had the company positioned at the crest of the hill. All my troops were dug in. I could see enemy mortars firing to different spots, landing in different areas near us. They were probing us. I even called everybody to see if any friendlies were firing, so I knew it was enemy. I told the battalion commander they were trying to zero in their mortars. He just shrugged it off," Captain K said.

His suspicions aroused, Captain K ordered a 100 percent alert that night. One of his troops also had an inkling that trouble was brewing. He was Ed Kochanski, a draftee of Polish descent from the anthracite coal region around Scranton, Pennsylvania. Kochanski's weapon was the M-60 machine gun, which he nicknamed Honey because she never let him down. While setting up for the night, Kochanski spotted some shadowy movement in the distance and deduced that enemy forces were nearby.

"I told everybody around me, 'Dig in. We're going to get hit tonight.' I was exhausted, but I dug in and got blisters on my hand while doing it," Kochanski said.

Then in the darkest hours of the night, at around 2 o'clock, a shower of 100 mortar shells and rockets hit Panther III. It was the prelude to an assault by 50 North Vietnamese sappers whose goal was to destroy the artillery pieces that had been killing their comrades, even if they had to blow themselves up in the process. Ed Kochanski went to dive into the hole he had dug. Four of his comrades were already inside.

At John Szczepanski's position in Delta Company, six Americans were killed and wounded 15 in the opening barrage.

"Something must have exploded nearby because I was in mid-air when I woke up. I knew we were under fire. I yelled over to David Alicea, 'You gotta lock and load. We're under attack!' It all happened in a short amount of time, but it seemed like an eternity. It was hand-to-hand. They were on us. We got overrun," Ski said. "I heard one guy yelling, 'My gun's jammed. My gun's jammed.' His leg got blown off."

Ski spotted one of the shadowy sappers and aimed his rifle, pausing for a split-second. If he fired, his muzzle flash would give away his position. If he didn't, the sappers would keep charging. He fired, and sure enough, he had brought attention to himself.

"I remember a flash going off. Then I heard a clink, clink, clink out of my right ear, the metallic sound of a rolling grenade. In that split second, I jumped on top of David and we started to roll. The next thing I know, there was an explosion. He took the full force of the blast. The only part of me that was exposed was my foot, and I took some shrapnel. If we had rolled one more time, I would have been the one on top," Ski said. "The concussion of the explosion blew off all his clothes. When I looked up, he was standing with shrapnel wounds all over. He was screaming, 'Ski, Ski, help me.' I said,

'I'm here. I'm here.' There is no way to describe that feeling of seeing a friend in that condition."

Alicea's wounds did not appear to be life threatening, but Ski knew that if he went into shock, the nightmare could get a whole lot worse. Instinctively, Ski cried for help.

"I was yelling for the medic, but nobody was coming. I told one of the guys to talk to David in Spanish, and I ran down in the dark to get a medic. I just reacted. I didn't hesitate. I was yelling, 'I'm an American,' so I wouldn't get shot. I found a medic, but he wasn't too interested in coming up the hill where all the explosions were going off. I told him, 'If you don't come to help my friend, I'll fucking kill you.' We went back up to where David was, but he was gone," Ski said. "It was all fuzzy. I remember choppers coming in and so many tracers in the air that it looked like a solid stream of red firing in a straight line. Then I looked down and found that I hadn't put my boots back on yet."

The sappers who penetrated the defenses scattered on their individual missions, throwing satchel charges into bunkers, ammo storage areas and gun pits. Artillery crews lowered the barrels on the big guns and loaded them with fleschette rounds, each one spewing out thousands of steel darts that made that hair-raising buzzing sound. Lanyards were pulled hurriedly to stop the suicide charge, and the blasts joined the cacophony of guns shooting in the dark. Instead of firing rounds that sailed on an arc over miles of ground, artillery pieces became giant shotguns firing directly at point blank range.

The fighting became a series of personal engagements. In one instance, Private First Class Michael Kernoelje of Battery A was attacked by three sappers. He killed two with his rifle before they reached his gun pit. The third broke through with the intent of destroying an artillery piece with his satchel charge. Out of ammo, Kernoelje leaped on the man. The hand-to-hand struggle lasted for five minutes before Kernoelje strangled the life out of his foe with his bare hands. During the fight, Kernoelje was bitten on his face and neck by his attacker.

The sappers killed one artilleryman, Private First Class Louis Charles Moore, a 21-year-old black soldier from St. Louis, Missouri, who was in Kernoelje's battery. But despite all the explosions and carnage, only one artillery tube was damaged. The remaining guns were still in working order. When the momentum of the attack was broken, surviving sappers ran back into the jungle under cover of another mortar barrage.

Daylight revealed a ghastly scene.

"There were dead bodies on ground. It was a hell of a battle. It was a pretty intense time," said Captain K. "The battalion commander arrived and didn't say a word. He didn't even look at me. He knew he was wrong."

After a sleepless night in Delta Company's area, Ski looked out at what he called a living Hell.

"Nobody was cleaning up, so I started raking up body parts," Ski said. One of the parts was an American soldier's foot.

Alicea was nowhere to be seen. Frenchy was dead, his torso so torn open that the bones of his rib cage were exposed. Using a pair of tweezers, Ski picked grenade fragments out of his foot.

"Someone told me a big black dude, who was a weight-lifter, had squeezed the life out of one sapper. There was another guy who said he hid behind the ammo boxes the whole time. You don't know what you're going to do in combat," Ski said.

Ski finally sat down on an ammo box and tried to comprehend what happened.

"All I did was gag. There was no way to describe the smell of blood, burned flesh and gunpowder. It stayed in my nostrils for years. To this day, if somebody's eating a rare steak, I start gagging," Ski said.

"Then I had what I call an epiphany. I kept thinking about the book of Genesis, when God created something out of chaos. This was the day that Genesis was reversed. Chaos was created out of something. I knew at that moment that nothing in life would ever be the same. Sitting there by myself, I was trying to digest it, to make sense of it. Everything was broken. Anything was conceivable. The depth of my soul was shattered. The next thing I remember was the lieutenant saying, 'Ski, I want you to man the machine gun.' "

At one point, a helicopter with the All American emblem on its nose landed. The passenger who emerged was the brigade commander, who touched down to survey the battlefield and to pin a Silver Star on Kernoelje, the artilleryman who killed a sapper with his bare hands.

"Hey, solider. I'm Colonel Bolling. Is there anything I can do for you?" he asked Ski.

"We have to get our mail. And I have to find my friend David," Ski replied.

Mail arrived the next day. Subsequently, a small helicopter called a Loach or what Ski called the Mosquito touched down, and a captain sought out Ski.

"I need you to come with me. We have to go to Da Nang," the captain told Ski.

The aircraft flew east to the South China Sea and turned south over the water. In Da Nang, a jeep was waiting to take Ski to a building that looked like a giant garage. About 100 feet inside, there were two openings. On one side were the naked bodies of dead soldiers stretched out on gurneys. On the other side were a bunch of boxes, stacked like drawers in a cabinet, each one containing a corpse.

"They pulled a body bag out, unzipped it and rolled back this cotton wrapping from a corpse. The smell assaulted my nostrils," Ski said. "They asked me if I knew who it was, and I said, 'Yes, that's my friend, David Alicea.' They wanted me to be sure, and I was. I recognized him immediately from his curly hair and olive skin. Then I just walked out and went back out to the field."

In addition to Alicea, members of Delta Company who were killed that day included Private First Class Daniel Jacques Bottan, 22, a draftee from Santa Paula, California;

Private First Class Allen Sevarn Dunbar, 21, of Houston, Texas; Private First Class David Vernon McCollum, 20, of Huntington Park, California; and Private First Class Robert Conroy Perry, 20, of Petersburg, Michigan. Eleven other members of Delta were wounded and evacuated.

Killed from Alpha Company was Private First Class Robert Bruce Randall, 21, of Edina, Minnesota. A private who was a field radio mechanic from Headquarters and Headquarters Company was also killed. He was Howard John Hartman, 20, of St. Clair Shores, Michigan. All of them, including Moore the artilleryman, are listed on Panel 46 West of The Wall, the same panel as the soldiers killed in the fight to take Mott's headquarters.

In the aftermath of Vietnam, burial records are nearly complete for those whose bodies were recovered and sent home. David Alicea was an exception. No record existed to indicate what cemetery he had been buried in. Undeterred, John Szczepanski embarked on a decades-long quest to find his friend's grave in order to pay his last respects.

"I would like to at least do that before I die," Ski said.

His final word on what happened on the artillery hill. "By the grace of God, it wasn't my time," Ski said.

It wasn't the last time he lost a brother in Vietnam either.

Chapter 31
TYPHOON TESTED

To thwart another attempt by North Vietnamese sappers to attack the artillery atop Panther III, the Golden Brigade inserted its cavalry unit to conduct a reconnaissance in force. As part this tripwire, Mark Robertson and a comrade manned a listening post for two nights at the base of the hill.

"It was hot as blazes. The heat was just sweltering, and we didn't have any water. Around two or three o'clock in morning, we went looking for a source of water. There was a crater from a bomb or a shell that was filled. So I dipped my canteen in and added two Halazone tabs. It was pretty nasty, but it was water. Then as dawn was just coming up, I could see we were on the edge of a tremendous field occupied by water buffalo. They had shit in the same water I was drinking. I love fresh water. Guys would get packets of Kool Aid from home to add flavor to the water, but to this day, I can't drink Kool Aid."

But too much water, not the lack of it, became a real issue on September 4. Bearing down on the brigade's area of operations was a monstrous tropical cyclone, which is a hurricane by a different name in this part of the globe. Named Typhoon Bess, the organized weather system sucked up moisture from the South China Sea and, like the heat engine it was, added strength to its winds as it surged inland. Then it stalled, dumping torrential rains and battering the landscape with sustained winds for four days. Add it to the list of indignities endured by the grunts.

Mother Nature's fury brought the war to a halt. Workhorse helicopters and other flying machines were grounded. Pursuit of the remnants of Mott's regiment was suspended. Even the North Vietnamese Army and their guerilla allies were unable to operate. It wasn't itty-bitty rain, or big old fat rain, but it was sideways rain. The downpour was so heavy that a hand held in front of the face could not be seen.

As two feet of rain fell in 96 hours, the temperature plummeted too. Troops that had become used to the tropical heat now shivered in place. Medics faced an epidemic of chest colds. Misery had reached new depths.

"Intel had the NVA moving on us, so we were on high alert. The temperature dropped to something like 60 degrees, but after what we were used to, it was bone-chilling cold. We had bunkers, but the rain was blowing sideways. There was no spot to stay dry. There was no way to get off the hill," Robertson said. "The wind was so bad the choppers couldn't get through. We were absolutely isolated. There was no way in, and no way out. Everybody was exhausted. Our supplies were low. The artillery was low on shells. We had to count ammo. The sergeants were going around asking how many mags we had."

In the real world, weather forecasters warn those in the path of a vicious storm to find shelter until it blows over. In Vietnam, the grunts rode it out in the open. No matter how low a guy's spirits would sink, he refused to give in because he knew his buddies were depending on him, just as he was depending on them.

In the hills surrounding what had been Mott's regimental headquarters, Delta Company commander Bob Murrill and his troops hunkered down behind tree trunks in the rain forest to block the fierce winds. Still, it was impossible to avoid getting drenched.

"Those extreme conditions of hard rain and powerful winds caused us to be about as miserable as I had been since Ranger School," Murrill said in his recollections. "The only protection was our ponchos, which merely kept the wind and rain from hitting our bodies directly. Otherwise, we were as cold and wet as if we were standing or sitting without outer garments. When we sat, leaned against a tree or laid down, we were constantly in muddy and running water. Nothing around us was dry. We had a limited number of small sterno cans, used primarily to heat our C Rations, that we lit between our legs under our ponchos. This provided a bit of short-term warmth, but the fumes were so bad, we had to stick our heads out of the poncho to breathe."

Survival was measured one minute, one hour, one wretched day at a time. The difference between making it or not rested on little things. Atop Panther III, platoon sergeant Marion Foster, the veteran of Pork Chop Hill in Korea, tended to his cavalrymen in his own way. From somewhere in his pack, Sergeant Foster produced a bottle of Jack Daniel's. He roamed from one miserable bunker to the next, offering a sip of whiskey just when guys needed a pick-me-up the most.

"Everybody got a shot. It warmed you up. No matter how forlorn things seemed at that moment, it told me that all things are possible. If you can get a shot of Jack Daniel's on Panther III in the middle of a typhoon, you could do anything!" Robertson said.

Foster had already done enough shepherding during his time in Vietnam that his troops saw him as a de facto father. Sometimes a father knows that a shot of booze is just what a man needs.

"These old guys could find a bottle of whiskey in the middle of the Saudi desert," marveled Rich O'Hare, who also weathered the storm with the cavalry unit. "I don't know what it was, probably bourbon, but he gave everyone a pull, and man, it tasted good!"

Foster provided sustenance too. The day before Typhoon Bess unleashed her fury, one of the South Vietnamese soldiers fighting alongside the All Americans had liberated a chicken from a village at the base of the artillery hill. Under Foster's guidance, the bird was plucked, gutted and added to a concoction of C Ration leftovers to create a chicken stew. No one is sure if the meal was cooked in a steel pot helmet or an ammo can, but

Foster served it to his men out of a long-handled canteen cup. The fact that somebody cared brings men to tears 50 years after the fact.

"He poured a little bit into each of our cups. I really enjoyed that chicken stew. It was steaming hot," Robertson said.

Through the storm, troopers stayed on guard. O'Hare and other cavalrymen dug foxholes directly to their front and surrounded them with concertina wire. Even though rainwater filled the holes, the two-man team inside had to stay alert for enemy activity. Every so often, they lobbed a grenade into the jungle.

"Each squad would have to send out two men for an hour's watch in the listening posts, 24 hours a day. You couldn't see a foot in front of you day or night, and we were authorized to fire periodically to see if any of the enemy were sneaking up on us. M-79's work great for that," O'Hare said.

When not on watch, troops tried to ride out the weather in protective bunkers, built with walls of sandbags and roofs made of perforated steel planking and plastic sheets. While bunkers offer rudimentary protection against mortars and rockets, they aren't watertight. The holes dug into the side of the hill merely served as traps for rainwater.

"Men were sleeping on cots, the floor or stretchers. I had a stretcher," O'Hare said. The reality of sleeping on an object designed to carry wounded men to an aid station is never lost on those at the ground level.

"The rain came down in buckets, and the wind howled for what seemed like days. Water ran through the bunkers, and you were cold, wet and muddy—period. I have heard it was one of the worst typhoons in a decade and just stalled over the northern part of South Vietnam. I am told that at least one bunker collapsed on another position, and they had to dig the troopers out," O'Hare added.

Just as the soldiers did, the creatures of Vietnam looked for shelter too, especially the rats.

"Now the fun starts," O'Hare said. "I came into my bunker from one of my tours just looking for a place to crash. I was exhausted as was everyone else. I turned on my flashlight with the red lens, and all I could see were rats running along the top of the ledge. Apparently, they had been flooded out of the ammo bunkers. I pulled out my .45 and was going to shoot at them when I decided that this was not a good idea. Oh, well. I guess they needed a place to go too. I collapsed on my stretcher and immediately fell asleep. At some point, I woke up to hear all this squeak, squeak, squeaking in my head. I flipped on the flashlight and rats were running all over the bunker, including right by my head."

Inside the bunker were remnants of sundry packs, which were packages filled with supplemental items such as cigarettes, writing paper, pens, soap, toothbrushes and candy. Grunts in the Golden Brigade rarely received the packs. In fact, O'Hare said this was the first and only time he ever saw one. All of the useful items had been taken, but no one had claimed the Chuckles, which were jellied candy with a light layer of sugar.

The journey to Vietnam and storage in tropical weather had hardened the Chuckles to the extent that they were just about unfit for human consumption. For vermin, it was a different story.

"I guess they tasted pretty good to hungry rats! With the daintiest of language, I got up and threw the box out in the pouring rain, and the rats, or most of them, followed," said O'Hare, the unofficial Pied Piper of Panther III.

Typhoon means to roar or to blow furiously, and Bess lived up to the name. Bridges were swept away. Roads were washed out. Structures collapsed. At Fire Base Boyd, John Carney said the sand-bagged walls of the bunkers caved in, destroying what minimal shelter the troops had.

"We were all wet and cold. My biggest memory of Vietnam was that tremendous typhoon," Carney said.

Doc Slavin was at Fire Base Bastogne, which had a fairly decent aid station despite the remoteness of its location. He had placed the flag of Ireland over the facility as his way of paying tribute to the fighting spirit of his ancestors. Typhoon Bess destroyed that flag, and Slavin had to write home to get a replacement from his folks.

All American ingenuity came into play. At Fire Base Birmingham, Sergeant Felix Conde took action to provide at least some rudimentary shelter from the storm. One man's floor may be another man's ceiling, and Conde found a practical use for an empty fuel bladder, a giant rubber device used to store gasoline in the field.

"He dragged it up the hill, cut it into appropriate pieces and placed them on the roof. It smelled like gasoline, but it was the only dry cave at Birmingham," said platoon leader Stanley Dodson.

Elsewhere at Birmingham, Ron Vitale of the Delta Dragons sought shelter from the storm in a bunker built at the military crest of a hill, which is just beneath the actual crest to provide the best sight lines while preventing anyone from being silhouetted against the skyline.

"I never saw anything like that typhoon in my life. It rained so much that the river was coming up. My bunker filled with water. I see this rat and pulled out my .45. Pow! Everybody jumped," Vitale said. "Then there was a mud slide, and the whole bunker started coming apart and slid down the hill with the concertina wire. The wind was blowing so hard it set off our trip flares. The slide also set off one of the claymores. We had to rebuild the bunker again."

Denied any possibility of re-supply, troops survived on the rations they carried in their soggy packs. One story that made the rounds involved a guy who was down to his last can of fruit cake. He had carried it around for use in an emergency. If he were ever captured an enemy soldier, he would feed it to the enemy, who would then be likely to die within six hours of consumption, or so the joke went.

Frank Cunane in Alpha Company shared an anecdote about how even the items in the sundry packs had been exhausted. "It was so bad that guys were smoking Kents.

Nobody smoked Kents. But if there aren't any Marlboros, you take what you can," Cunane said.

In Bravo Company of the 1st of the 508, Tom Wallace and his buddies rode out the storm in the jungle. Wet clothing made it seem chillier than it was.

"I don't think the word hypothermia was in vogue then, but some guys were close to having hypothermia. We were low on food. Guys were sick. The storm itself was an ordeal," Wallace said.

In the 2nd of the 505, Ed Kochanski in Cold Steel Alpha Company rustled up a wooden pallet to place on the earthen floor of his foxhole, which rapidly filled to the brim with rainwater. Bayonets were used as anchor pegs to keep ponchos from blowing away.

"It was just brutal. I stood on that pallet for days. There was a river flowing right underneath me. The rice paddies looked like an ocean," Kochanski said.

After what seemed like an eternity, Typhoon Bess mercifully moved on almost as suddenly as it had blown in. A bright sun appeared under clear blue skies, yet the landscape was unrecognizable. All of the lowlands were inundated. Swollen rivers overflowed their banks. The only things visible were the tops of hills.

"I went to sleep on a mountaintop and woke up on an island," said cavalryman Jim Klein. "It seemed like it went on forever. It was dark. I couldn't see 10 feet. The wind was strong, but the rain was worse. We were just soaked. The skin on our fingertips was white and shriveled. You think you're going to rot away. You're starving and you're scared as hell. Even Mother Nature had it in for us."

When helicopter flights finally resumed, food and supplies reached the grunts. Rich O'Hare experienced what he considered to be a miracle.

"The storm broke, and we were looking for some hot chow. The mess tent had blown down, but the troopers were putting it back up. Hot coffee was the priority, and this was just brewing when a helicopter shows up completely out of the blue. There was something white streaming off the sides. By now the sun had come out, and steam was rising from the ground. Believe it or not, the chopper was full of reconstituted milk and ice cream. Apparently, there was a plant, probably in Da Nang, that took powdered milk and reconstituted it to make it taste something like milk. They also made ice cream out of it. We all lined up and we each got a quart of milk and a quart of mushy ice cream. I think mine was chocolate. Milk was a rarity and ice cream was even rarer. We weren't used to it. Within about ten minutes, guys were retching all over the place from milk sickness—or that's what I called it. Regardless, it tasted good going down, and I didn't heave mine up. I don't remember what we did after this, but it was back to the war," O'Hare said.

Back to the war involved the final pursuit of the remnants of Mott's regiment.

"It took several days for our equipment and us to dry. Nevertheless, we immediately cleaned and oiled our weapons," Bob Murrill said.

On September 9, Bravo Company of the 1st of the 508 was moving to night defensive positions on Hill 224. As the lead element approached the crest, they were ambushed by two NVA squads who greeted them with rocket propelled grenades and machine guns. Troops took cover in a position that had been abandoned by the North Vietnamese while firepower fell on the ambushers in the form of artillery, helicopter gunships and attack jets. At dusk, a plane appeared and dropped illumination rounds all night to light up the battle area. A sweep the next morning found eight NVA bodies.

Bravo Company suffered the loss of Specialist Carrel Gorum Ealum, 20, of Fort Walton Beach, Florida. Ealum had been in the hospital and returned to the field on a re-supply helicopter the day he died. He had volunteered to take the point for what turned out to be his last patrol. The remaining Red Devils were extracted on September 12 for two days of rest.

A total of 269 soldiers in Mott's regiment had been killed and six were taken prisoner. Captured were nearly 700 individual weapons, 14 mortars and 14 rocket launchers, 19 radio transmitters, two typewriters, 1,900 NVA uniforms, 8,000 bottles of medical drugs, 15 tons of rice and 200 pounds of documents. The price in blood was 20 All Americans killed in action and 45 wounded.

Operation Mot was Colonel Bolling's master stroke, and it came just as the Golden Brigade received new orders.

Chapter 32
HOME BOYS

If one day blurs into another, a grunt can remember events as if they happened yesterday but without any memory of exactly where or when they occurred. Take, for example, the time Ed Kochanski and Alpha Company of the 2nd of the 505 were patrolling in the boonies. Troopers chopped their way through the undergrowth and climbed steep hills to find summits that had been bombed, and they occasionally came across abandoned villages.

In one such place, Kochanski liberated a machete that had a hooked-blade and a bamboo handle. It was much more efficient than the machetes issued by the Army. During a break, Kochanski lit up a Hav-A-Tampa cigar with a wooden tip, not because it was packed with high quality tobacco but because the smoke shooed away mosquitoes. Sergeant Robert Gary Owen of Gasquet, California, sat down and lit up a cigar too.

"He had been walking point, chopping his way through the jungle, and was all hot and sweaty from swinging a machete. I showed him the one I found, and he asked if he could use it. He thought it was terrific," Kochanski said. "Then we saddled up and went back on patrol. Looking back on it, I wonder every day whether it would have just been better to be quiet and sneak in just to observe."

With Owen on point and making good progress with the homemade cutting tool, he broke out into a clearing. Hostile forces were waiting in ambush. They shot Owen in the chest.

"He got slammed backwards and was impaled on a tree. He's hung up and remained upright. They kept shooting him in the chest. But because they concentrated on him, he actually saved a lot of lives," Kochanski said. "The sergeant yelled to flank out. We were firing on line, moving forward."

When the ambushers melted away, the troops finally reached Owen. All shot up, he never had a chance. His date of death was October 6. The place where he got it was in the middle of nowhere in an engagement that had no name, something that was a common occurrence in Vietnam.

"There was Gary. We were all putting him in a poncho to carry him out. Some of his blood spilled all over my shirt. I had to look at his blood on me every day for a while. We called in a chopper that came down through a hole in the trees. That's a day I will never forget," Kochanski said.

Another day he will always remember was when an unfamiliar face showed up in Alpha Company. He was paratrooper William Murray, who was new to the unit but not new to Vietnam. As part of the 82nd Airborne's original deployment, Murray had served in long range recon until he came down with malaria and was shipped home for a 30-day convalescent leave. Assigned to Alpha Company, he was just getting himself squared away. Asked where he was from, Murray said Carbondale, and Kochanski's ears perked up.

"Carbondale, Pennsylvania?" Kochanski asked.

When Murray nodded yes, Kochanski knew he had found an instant buddy.

"Hell, I'm from Scranton. We're homeboys," Kochanski said.

The two men had grown up 10 miles apart in the same region of northwestern Pennsylvania, yet they shook hands for the first time 10,000 miles from home. What they had in common was more than mere geography. Northeastern Pennsylvania is where immigrants from various ethnic groups—Irish, Polish, Slovak, Italian—had settled to perform the back-breaking, dangerous work of going underground to dig out the anthracite coal that fueled America's Industrial Revolution. Miners were housed in communities that sprouted around the various mines, and each town was built on the pillars of hard work and family ties.

"I was proud and excited to meet someone from my hometown," Kochanski said.

Murray's story began with a grandfather who labored in an anthracite processing plant and came home every day covered from head to toe with the black grime of coal dust. The family lived in what was built as a company house, and to keep the place heated in the wintertime, it would scrounge for lumps of coal to burn in their furnace. They didn't have much, but they had each other, and they got by. The dignity found in pulling themselves up by their own bootstraps had the fringe benefit of citizenship and a slice of the American dream. A young man had to learn to use his fists to survive, or he could find an outlet in sports.

By the time Murray arrived at Benjamin Franklin High School, he was stood 5-foot-8 and weighed 220 pounds. A hard-nosed lineman, he earned a starting slot as a freshman and played offense and defense. He remained in that role as a two-way player for four years. He had a different team in mind before he received his diploma, however.

"I wouldn't say we come from a military family, but my father served in the Army, and we had an uncle in the Navy. Billy just had a fascination with paratroopers," said his younger brother, Leo. "He was 13 months older than me, but we were as close to being Irish twins as you could get. If you messed with one of us, you messed with both of us."

In February of his senior year, Billy had already enlisted. Shortly after his graduation on June 14, 1967, the Army recruiter who had signed him up arrived at the house to send him off to basic training. A glitch developed, however. The recruiter had promised him a slot in the Airborne, but the Army, in its infinite wisdom, trained him to be a cook. Murray was serving meals at Fort Dix, New Jersey, as Vietnam heated up, and his idea of serving his country involved more than serving meals in a mess hall.

"He was really mad," Leo Murray said. "When he came home on leave, we went to see that recruiter. I told him that I was there when he promised my brother he could be a paratrooper. I told him that if things didn't change that I was going to call our congressman, Joe McDade. Well, something happened. Because when he got back to Dix, Billy had orders to go to jump school at Fort Benning, and he was assigned to the 82nd Airborne. In February of 1968, he was sent to Vietnam."

The details of Murray's early days in Vietnam are something he kept to himself, but Jim Littig remembers him as being part of his ambush teams. While Murray was wounded by a knife cut, his other wounds were not caused by bullets or shells. He came down with malaria, spending time in a bed of ice as doctors in Vietnam toiled to reduce the fever ravaging his body. Just as leaves were being granted to the brigade's soldiers who had deployed for the Tet Offensive, Billy Murray left for home. Arriving back in Carbondale on July 3, he had been changed by war.

"We went to a place called Newton Lake, where we used to hang out as kids and where he used to be a lifeguard. It was the Fourth of July, and a burst of fireworks went off. Billy got down on beach and actually started digging a hole to place his head in. He was shell-shocked. He was a different person. Ready to rip somebody's head off. He distanced himself from his girlfriend too. He showed me the jungle rot on his feet. I never saw anything like that in my life," Leo Murray said.

For the next couple of weeks, the brothers hung out. When the time neared for Billy to go back to Vietnam, Leo tried to talk him out of it. In his condition, Billy could easily qualify for a medical excuse.

"Billy, there's no shame in not going back. Look at yourself," Leo said.

"No, my country needs me. My men need me. I have to go," Billy replied.

Ignoring his brother's advice, Billy bade farewell on August 3 and returned to Vietnam. Ed Kochanski noticed that Murray didn't get much mail and seldom wrote home. Kochanski wrote home just about every day, and in one letter, he asked his mother to look up Murray's family. She even started to write her own letters to her son's new buddy.

At one point, Murray and Kochanski were on patrol together in the boonies. Drenched by a monsoon rain, troopers reached out to grab vines and tree limbs to pull themselves up a steep slope. The downpour had turned the laterite clay into a slippery surface, and footing was treacherous. On the left flank was a rain-swollen stream that had become a raging river, complete with waterfalls, whirlpools and deep holes.

"It rained and rained and rained. I mean, it came down in buckets," Kochanski said.

Without warning, Alexander Beard, a platoon sergeant from Mobile, Alabama, lost his footing and slid down the hill toward the stream. He tried unsuccessfully to dig in his heels and to shed his rucksack. Fellow soldiers reached out to stop his descent. Nothing worked. Beard splashed into the swirling stream and went under.

"Out of nowhere, here comes Billy Murray. He had seen what happened, took off his shirt and boots, and in he went after Beard," Kochanski said. "Maybe it was only a minute, but it seemed like a long time. I thought Billy was gone too. I thought we lost them both. Finally, Billy pops out of the water and he's screaming, 'I had him. I had him. I couldn't get him up. He was too heavy with the rucksack on.' Now Billy's gasping for air, but after taking some deep breaths, he dives down again!"

After another minute or so, Murray resurfaced, this time with the sergeant. None of his comrades could believe that Billy had done it, but they all knew this paratrooper was a powerful man. It was too late, however. All efforts to revive Beard failed. The date of his drowning was October 13. A Regular Army sergeant, he was 16 days shy of his 30th birthday. A helicopter was summoned to retrieve the body from the jungle. Beard was strapped onto a steel platform and lifted out.

"It looked like he was sleeping. I hope he went straight to heaven," Kochanski said. "And I was so proud of Billy for what he did to try to save that man's life."

Murray stuffed his feet back into his jungle boots, but he never could lace them up all the way. His legs were too thick. Then he and his comrades saddled up and resumed their trek up that slippery slope. When Alpha Company reached the top of the hill, the enemy sprung another ambush. Murray and Kochanski survived.

A different outcome awaited them on a future mission. Two buddies randomly brought together by the Army could be torn apart by war. That was also the nature of Vietnam.

Chapter 33
GOLDEN SWORD

A helicopter befitting the rank of a four-star general touched down on the pad at Camp Rodriguez, and out stepped overall commander Creighton W. Abrams. He proceeded to Bud Bolling's headquarters to share some high-level news concerning the 82nd Airborne.

"I like to come up here because you're winning the war up here," the cigar-chomping Abrams said by way of greeting. This was no courtesy call or a pat on the back for the 82nd Airborne, however. High command handed the Golden Brigade a new mission in a new location.

"I'm gonna pull you into Saigon," Abrams said.

The top priority for Abrams at this stage of the war was to put an end to the Viet Cong's practice of indiscriminately firing rockets into the South Vietnamese capital as a way of terrorizing the civilian population and harassing the U.S.-backed government. The Airborne was to establish its new home in the northwest quadrant outside Saigon, then eliminate the rocket threat with aggressive patrols while it guarded the western approaches to the city to prevent another Tet. The unit would also serve as a Fire Brigade, on call to respond to trouble spots encountered by other Army units, including those working all the way out to the Cambodian border. Saigon itself, with all of its temptations, was off-limits without special authorization.

Like a good soldier who is given an order, Bolling saluted and said, "Yes, sir." He also asked for a favor because the Army often changes commanders when it changes a unit's mission.

"Let me keep the brigade," Bolling said.

"You talked me into it. You get to stay," Abrams replied.

While some of his troops were still engaged in combat, Bolling thus had to oversee the logistical challenge of transporting 4,500 or so men to a new destination 400 miles to the south. The distance and urgency paled in comparison to the original deployment, but a Herculean effort was still needed. Planning began immediately for a troop movement that was called Operation Golden Sword.

Meanwhile, elements of the Golden Brigade were engaged in fighting between Camp Rodriguez and Da Nang along Highway One. The mission was to stop the enemy from replenishing his food stocks with rice from the coastal lowlands, and 30 North Vietnamese soldiers were killed over a three-week period in the vicinity of a village named Phu Loc.

At the same time, a two-man observation helicopter was shot down in the Phu Loc Valley west of the South China Sea and north of the Hai Van Pass. In the helicopter were an officer from the 101st Airborne and a liaison officer from the Golden Brigade's artillery unit. Both were presumed dead. The chopper had gone down in a horseshoe-shaped valley surrounded by high ground on three sides. The place was crawling with bad guys.

On the ground, Captain John Kapranopoulos and Alpha Company of the 2nd of the 505 joined forces with a company from the 101st Airborne for a combat assault into the thick jungle as close to the wreckage as possible. They worked in concert with Charlie Company of the 2nd of the 505, which was also operating in the area. Charlie Company drove through the open end of the valley from the east and passed within 100 yards of the crash site, but as an indication of how thick the undergrowth was, the wreckage was never spotted. Finding a needle in a haystack would have been easier.

Then, as it continued through the valley, Charlie Company came under fire from a heavy barrage of enemy mortars. Alpha Company had been pushing up the ridgeline that formed the lower half of the horseshoe when troopers heard the enemy mortars firing from the slope above. The company advanced cautiously, hoping to catch the mortar crews by surprise. As the point platoon neared the enemy positions, machine guns opened up on them. Several men were hit. Lieutenant Earl Hughes, the platoon leader, survived a close call when two enemy bullets deflected off the flashlight he had attached over a shirt pocket.

Captain K ordered the rest of the company to come on line with the point platoon while he called in artillery and close air support. Charlie Company moved to the sound of the guns, and coordinating with its sister unit by radio, attempted to trap the NVA. Darkness prevented the two companies from reaching each other, however. From their night defensive positions, both companies set up ambushes in an attempt to block the enemy's escape. Under cover of the night, the NVA had broken contact.

At dawn, both companies headed down the far side of the ridge in a renewed attempt to find the downed helicopter. While cutting its way through the jungle, Alpha Company discovered an NVA base camp and training area that was large enough to accommodate two battalions. Troopers seized a cache of 50 rockets, 100 pounds of explosives, 10 claymore mines, 8,000 rounds of ammunition, three mortars, construction tools and enough uniforms to outfit an entire company.

A short time after the discovery of the base camp, a platoon from Charlie Company, led by Lieutenant Keith Bell, was assigned to get to the crash site.

"We had been out for three or four days. We got into firefights two days in a row and had gotten mortared. We were in a night defensive position in this little valley when I heard about the helicopter for the first time. The company commander said, 'Bell, I want you to go to these coordinates.' It was 1,000 yards away," Bell said.

Bell and his platoon moved out. Despite slow going, the platoon finally found the observation helicopter facing upside down and tangled up in trees, but there were no bodies inside. Overhead, a command helicopter directed Bell to a little ravine about 200 yards away. Next to a stream that provided fresh water, the two officers were found hiding under a rock. Miraculously, they were alive after nearly five days of surviving smack in the middle of enemy territory. Both had suffered several broken bones and were weakened by lack of food and sleep.

"They sure were glad to see us," said Ron Snodgrass of Charlie Company. "Those two guys got to go home. I was proud of that. I'm glad we were able to help. It was written up in the Chicago papers. The story gave credit to elements of the 101st Airborne."

An evacuation helicopter was summoned, and a litter was lowered through the treetops to extract the two officers.

"Then, at night, I had to move 1,000 meters back to my company's position using only a compass and a map," Bell said. "When you walk sideways across a slope, the tendency is to drift down, but we stayed on the right course. I was proud of that."

Their mission accomplished, Alpha and Charlie Companies were pulled back to Camp Rodriguez for a two-day stand down just before they moved south to join the rest of the brigade. In appreciation for the rescue of one of its officers, the 101st Airborne sent over a case of Jack Daniel's Tennessee sipping whiskey to Bell and his men.

"I gave half of it to the platoon, distributed some among the officers and gave the rest to the First Sergeant. Getting those two men out alive was one of the proudest moments of my time in Vietnam," Bell said.

As an aside, Bell had sent some money home to Colorado with a request for a case of Coors beer, which was unavailable in Vietnam. When the brew arrived, he shared it with his men. He kept two cans for himself, wrapping them in his poncho liner and placing them in his rucksack. But during a firefight, when his pack was the only protection Bell had, the cans were riddled with bullets. It was a close call. Several rounds lodged into the poncho liner, and the beer poured out. Bell never got a drop of the golden liquid made with Rocky Mountain spring water.

As for as the move to Saigon, plans were adjusted on the fly for the Golden Brigade to pull off a three-way swap with two other Army units. The Third Brigade of the 101st Airborne, which had been operating in the south, moved up to rejoin its parent organization. Its new home would be Camp Rodriguez, which ceased to exist as a name when it was folded into Camp Eagle. A brigade of the 25th Infantry Division took over the area vacated by the Third Brigade of the 101st Airborne. After planners did some final tinkering, the Golden Brigade moved to the sprawling base at Bien Hoa, 35 kilometers north of Saigon, to receive orders.

Transport planes flew a battalion down every two weeks. First to move was the 1st of the 505 along with an artillery battery, an engineer platoon and a squad of Military Police. The battalion's home, built from scratch, was called Fire Base All American.

Headquarters for the artillery was Camp Copperhead, an abandoned missile site located about four miles northeast of FSB All American.

Following them were the 1st Battalion of the 508 along with Bolling's headquarters. Fire Base Hardcore became the new home for the Red Devils. The encampment housing the brigade's tactical operations center was built in 16 days and was dubbed Camp Red Ball.

The Military Police and the 82nd Support Battalion settled in a former French fort across the road from a village called Phu Loi, about 12 miles north of Saigon. As with any Army troop movement, the old adage of "hurry up and wait" applied.

Bill Gehron of Williamsport, Pennsylvania, who was in the Military Police unit, found out that *Harper Valley PTA* by Jeannie C. Riley was the top-rated country song back in The World. "I was waiting under the wing of a C-130 to board a flight to Phu Loi. Someone had a tape player, and that song kept playing over and over and over," Gehron said.

Phu Loi was a contested village. Military Policeman John Marcon said his unit used Starlight scopes to keep the place under observation from their guard towers.

"The village was right across the road. We could see the bodies of villagers who had been hanged by the Viet Cong," Marcon said. "We were also the Phu Loi patrol. If we got probed by five or six enemy, we'd saddle up in the middle of the night and try to engage. That's crazy. But like one of our officers said, when the general tells you to do something, you do it."

The cavalry unit, which had swapped out its gun jeeps for armored personnel carriers, would have required 40 transport planes to fly the tracked vehicles to their new destination. Instead, B Troop was scheduled to go by ship. The heavy machines were loaded onto six Navy Landing Ships, Utility (LSUs), but a harbor obstruction forced a delay. In one of the after-effects of Typhoon Bess, a thick layer of silt had been deposited into the harbor. It had to be dredged out before ships could move.

Mark Robertson had just returned from a 30-day rest and recreation leave and had been promoted to sergeant. Although he had never been in armored personnel carrier before, he was now a commander of one of the vehicles. The mechanics who came in from Germany provided a crash course on how the tracks worked.

"While we were waiting to sail, some guys went swimming. Then we got an urgent call from the harbor master saying the enemy was using a water tower on an island as an observation post and sending signals back about what was going on. The harbor master asked if we could do something about it. We said, 'Sure.' I took the demolition bag, and me and another guy put on some conical hats and took two sampans out to the island. We get there, and this water tower is about 30 feet high. I really didn't know what I was doing, but I offset the charges on two the support legs—high on one side and low on the other side. We ran the wire out while low-crawling, and I yell out, 'Fire in the hole!' The explosion makes a hell of a loud noise. The tower pitches forward. As it does, the water tank comes off and is headed right for us. We came this close to getting killed by a water tank," Robertson said.

Finally, the ships departed for a brief voyage to Da Nang, where the troops and cargo were reloaded onto a larger Landing Ship, Tank (LST), the same type that ferried men and equipment ashore during World War II. This second leg of the trip involved sailing down the Vietnamese coast to the mouth of the Saigon River.

"We paused at the mouth of the river because our commanding officer wanted an escort in case we were ambushed. We had two .50 caliber machine guns on each side of the ship. Then two attack helicopters arrived. With one Cobra flying on either side, we completed the final leg," said Jim Klein.

The 2nd Battalion of the 505th, which had taken part in the helicopter rescue, was the last to journey south. Its new home was Fire Support Base Harrison, but one of its units remained temporarily in the A Shau Valley under the operational control of the 101st Airborne. It was Bravo Company, commanded by Captain James (Tom) Hennessey.

An Army brat, Hennessey was born in Covington, Kentucky, and relocated for the first time when he was six weeks old because home is where the Army sends you. His father had been in the first graduating class of the Eastern Kentucky University ROTC program, and his father commissioned him when Hennessey was part of the 25th ROTC class. The Army was in his blood. Having already served one tour in Vietnam with the 25th Infantry Division, Hennessey volunteered to return. In August of 1968, he was assigned to the 82nd Airborne. In a brief but unceremonious welcome, Bud Bolling dropped him at Bravo Company and told him: "There's your company, Hennessey."

As it turned out, Bravo Company was chopped from the Golden Brigade and attached to a battalion of the 101st Airborne commanded by Chargin' Charlie Beckwith, a football player at the University of Georgia who became a legend in Special Forces as the first commander of Delta Force. Having served a hitch in the 82nd Airborne at Fort Bragg, Beckwith had already been wounded on an earlier tour in Vietnam. The first time Hennessey saw him, Beckwith was standing on the left skid of a helicopter and jumped off just as the chopper landed. Bravo Company spent three months under Beckwith's command, patrolling and setting ambushes in the jungles near the Laotian border.

"When you're a bastard child, you get all the shit details. We never saw a fire base. We were out in the bush whole time," Hennessey said.

Bravo Company was finally released from the 101st and trucked to the airfield at Phu Bai. The 120-man unit, which wore the dirt and sweat of the boonies, boarded a single C-130 Hercules.

"They packed us in like sardines. We landed 40 minutes later, just after dark, and I asked the pilot where we were. He said Da Nang. They had run out of crew time and had to land there. There was no one to meet us. Nowhere to go. We simply set up our poncho liners in the middle of the airfield between runways for the night. There was no need for security, so everyone got a good night's sleep. At dawn, while I was enjoying my cup of coffee, a jeep came screaming across the field and an Air Force major asked, 'Just what in the hell are you doing on my airfield?' I explained that we had been dropped off the night before and we were awaiting transportation to Bien Hoa. We were hustled aboard the first available C-130 and landed at Bien Hoa mid-morning. Put it this way. We were happy to see Bien Hoa," Hennessey said.

Well before Bravo Company rejoined the All Americans, and with the brigade's battle flag planted in its new location, the 82nd Airborne was operational on October 21. From that point on, the brigade's time in Vietnam was delineated by what it did Up North and what it would do Down South.

The chain of command was an alphabet soup of acronyms. While overall operations were controlled by Military Assistance Command Vietnam (MACV), the brigade fell under the Capital Military Assistance Command (CMAC) and worked in concert with its South Vietnamese counterpart called the Capital Military District (CMD). This section of the country was designated as III Corps, but the Airborne also was under the command of a corps-level group called II Field Force. The latter was headquartered at Long Binh, the largest military base in the country. It controlled various Army units operating in the 11 provinces surrounding the South Vietnamese capital.

One of Bud Bolling's first duties was to report to Walter (Dutch) Kerwin, the general in charge of II Field Force. The duty officer told him to take a seat because Kerwin was in a meeting.

"I sat there for two and a half hours. Finally, I went over to the chief of staff and said, 'Tell the commander I got a war to fight. Just let me know if he needs me,' " Bolling recalled. "Not once did General Kerwin ever say welcome, go to hell or kiss my foot. Nothing. He hated paratroopers. If he walked into this room, I would not say a word to him. He was one of those guys in the Army that had no leadership ability. You can put that on the record."

Bolling was shuttled to a meeting with an officer on Kerwin's staff. "Don't you paratroopers screw things up around here!" the officer said by way of greeting. Bolling was asked how he intended to fight the war in his new area of operations.

"We going to fight at night, sir," said Bolling, who had taken the night away from Charlie in the action Up North.

"Fight at night? Against those people?" he was asked.

"That's when the bad guys are out," Bolling replied.

"Are you going to do some dumb Airborne thing?" he was asked.

Bolling mulled over those words, as if taking the fight to the enemy in a war zone would somehow screw things up for Army command.

"No sir, we're going to fight at night," Bolling said.

Given the task of defending Saigon from rocket attacks, strategists plotted the maximum effective range of those terror weapons at 11 miles, and a circle was drawn to determine the rocket belt. Any weapons secretly stashed inside the belt had to be eliminated. Bolling also set out to ambush any force that attempted to infiltrate via the road and river networks. That meant establishing roadblocks along highways and bridges.

At the same time, an ambitious effort was begun to pacify the outlying villages, some of which were under the sway of the Viet Cong.

Overall, the landscape was completely different from what it had been Up North. The ground was flatter and wetter. When the brigade fired its mortars in its new area of operations, the weapon tended to sink into the muck. As a solution, mortars were placed atop old truck tires, which absorbed recoils without getting buried. Mosquitoes were more prevalent. Rivers and canals rose and fell with the tide, and operations officers consulted tidal charts to prevent Charlie from moving in on high tide and melting away on low tide. Dry ground was a rarity in a region blanketed with rice paddies. Life inside the fire bases improved, but the grunts hardly ever spent time in base camps. They were out on roving patrols and ambushing at night. The most noteworthy landmark Down South was a 3,000-foot tall extinct volcano called Nui Ba Den, or Black Virgin Mountain, but it was located about 60 miles northwest of Saigon in Tay Ninh Province. The conical peak was close to the Cambodian border, which was just as porous as the Laotian border Up North.

As a general rule, the bad guys blended in with the local population. Operating in small groups and preferring hit-and-run tactics, the Viet Cong had stockpiled weapons and rice in concealed locations along trails and streams. Stockpiles were sometimes placed in false graves inside cemeteries.

In the absence of a front line, the names of new battlegrounds emerged—the Pineapple, the Hoc Mon Bridge, the Cu Chi tunnels, the Parrot's Beak and the Angel's Wing out on the Cambodian border, the Ho Bo Woods and the Iron Triangle.

Back in The World on October 16, at the awards ceremony following the 200-meter dash at the Summer Olympics in Mexico City, gold medal winner Tommie Smith and bronze medalist John Carlos stood in black socks, bowed their heads and raised a black-gloved fist during the playing of *The Star-Spangled Banner.* The two sprinters, who said they wanted to call attention to the cause of human rights, were vilified for protesting during the National Anthem with the Black Power Salute. The U.S. Olympic Committee sent them home from the games.

Chapter 34
NIGHT RIDER'S STAR

Don Carson, the Canadian citizen who served in the Military Police unit, was assigned for a time as Colonel Bud Bolling's bodyguard. The way the brigade commander conducted the war endeared himself to his troops but caused many an anxious moment for those assigned to protect him. "He would fly to contact and run into the jungle with his 1911 sidearm," said Carson. "I'd say, 'Sir, you can't do that. Do you know how much paperwork I'd have to fill out if something happened to you?' He did it anyway. That was one reason his troops would follow him anywhere."

Salome Beltran, the Silver Star recipient from the bloody fight at the village of Ap Nam Phu, also admired the colonel. He recalled the time he was in the prone position during a firefight, sending rounds down range at what was shooting at him. Enemy snipers were present too. Out of the corner of his eye, Beltran saw a helicopter land in the jungle. An officer popped out and strode over to Beltran.

"He tapped me on the back and said, 'Go get 'em, brother.' His aides would tell him to get down, and he'd tell them to get bent. It was Bolling," Beltran said. "Then he would ask, 'Who wants ice cream?' And he'd grab one of his aides by the collar and tell him to go get some freakin' ice cream. Some captain might be gone for five hours, but he'd come back with it. There was something special about him. You could sense it. He was a wonderful man and a great leader. He reminded me of Patton."

Others saw similarities between Bud Bolling and George S. Patton, the World War II commander known for his audacity. Nobody used the phrase "Old Blood and Guts" to describe Bolling, however.

"He was Patton without the gruffness and the ego. On a scale of one to 10, he was an 11. He would size up a situation and say, 'This is the way we're going to do it.' And then he'd get it done," said J.V. Stephenson of the military intelligence section. "He knew the guards at my bunker by their first names, and he always stopped in for coffee."

Troops often flocked around him during visits to the field, according to Chaplain James Sanner.

"When his helicopter would land, the soldiers would leave the protection of the bush and come around because they liked him so much. He was really a model of what a soldier should be and how he should act. He took care of his men. He lived it with us," Sanner said. "When we first arrived at Chu Lai, he had a cot and slept there in this old building. He was always the first one up in the morning. He ate the same food we ate, even though he could've gotten better chow at the officer's mess."

Then, in the midst of packing up and moving 400 miles Down South during the mission change, the Joe Tentpegs of the Golden Brigade swelled with pride when their commander was promoted to brigadier general on October 1. Just as Camp Rodriguez was being turned over to the 101st Airborne, Night Rider took his place at the head of a formation. Wearing the bright red, white and blue shoulder patch of the All Americans on his jungle fatigues, and with his boys standing ramrod straight at attention, Night Rider had his badge of rank pinned to his collar by Melvin Zais, commander of the 101st Airborne Division.

It was a special moment for a man who had been born to be a soldier, who had followed proudly in his father's boot prints and who had led a new generation of the 82nd Airborne into combat. The ceremony lasted only a few minutes, which was all the time Bolling could spare from his schedule.

There's a reason troops refer to a commanding officer, or at least the competent ones, as the Old Man. In a unit that thought of itself as an orphan or bastard brigade, Bolling was a father figure who kept his troops functioning as a unit and focused on the task at hand. He was the first to put his boots on the ground in the emergency deployment to Vietnam. He flew to every engagement in the battles around Hue. He made sure the fallen were remembered in the Empty Boots memorial services, and he wrote those tough letters of sympathy home to the families who lost loved ones. He made sure his men got their chow and mail, and if ice cream could be served in the officer's mess, he insisted that the stuff get into the field with the troops too. Sometimes, a drink of water made all the difference to a grunt.

"All the companies in my battalion were flown out in helicopters on a big op once. It was a very hot day, maybe 115 degrees, and guys were passing out from heat exhaustion. Bolling flew in and gave water to some of the guys," said Robert Zeeman. "The amazing thing was, most field grade officers in Vietnam never put a foot on the ground. They walked on air. Not Bolling. He lived it with us."

Up North, Bolling received a Silver Star for valor after one the battles, but he was no stranger to the fear a soldier must set aside in a gunfight. In one action, his command helicopter set down to help evacuate the dead and the wounded. The volume of casualties overloaded the chopper, and the engines groaned when the aircraft tried to lift off. Bolling was confronted with one of the hairiest moments of his military career.

"The blades of the helicopter clipped the tops of the trees. I said, 'This is it. We're going to crash.' My pilot even called in a May Day, but he got it up in the air. Oh, I was really scared," Bolling said. He also accomplished the mission.

Rank does have its privileges, but Bolling balked at one the perks afforded to general officers in Vietnam. Having a star on his collar entitled Bolling to his very own air-conditioned trailer. A mobile home with two bedrooms and a bath was a giant improvement over a shredded Army tent and an outhouse, but Bolling refused the perk. It spoke volumes about the man.

"I protest. I'm a taxpayer. I disapprove of that. I'm gonna send it back," the new general told his superiors. The Big Army insisted, however, and Bolling kept his trailer.

"I took my first warm bath. It had hot and cold running water, and a refrigerator too. We used to hold staff meetings in there. They also asked me if I wanted a sedan with a little flag on it. I said, 'Heck no. We're at war. I have a jeep.' "

If the trailer was mandatory, Duke Dewey figured he'd make it as comfortable as possible for a man he thought of as the father he never had. Using his connections on the black market, Dewey procured a plush red rug for the trailer's floor.

"There was nothing I wouldn't do for that man. If he wanted champagne and pheasant, it might have taken me an hour to find, but I would have gotten it for him," Dewey said.

While driving himself and his men at a relentless pace, Bolling used the sheer force of personality to preserve the identity of the 82nd Airborne. For example, because his brigade was under the operational control of the 101st Airborne, the infantry routinely air-assaulted into battle aboard helicopters adorned with a Screaming Eagle on their noses. Not Bolling. His helicopter sported the red, white and blue emblem of the All Americans.

On another occasion, the 101st Airborne wanted to celebrate its birthday on August 16, the day that proud division was activated in 1942 after being created from the 82nd Airborne. The idea was to fly around to all the fire bases and blare paratrooper music from the loudspeakers as a way of boosting morale. One thing was lacking, however. Nobody in the Screaming Eagles had any paratrooper songs, so Bud Bolling lent them his tape. The first song that echoed over the jungles and the triple-canopy rain forest was *The All American Soldier*—the song of the 82nd Airborne.

Maybe it was because he knew the sting of battle from World War II, when he spilled blood for his country and twice escaped German imprisonment. Maybe it was because he knew what it was like to be hungry and tired and living day-to-day on the edge in an uncertain world far away from home. Maybe he was just smart enough to know that when he committed his boys to battle that some of them would bleed and die. Bolling was mission first, but he avoided wasting lives.

"It always gets me about casualties. It's how few casualties you take while accomplishing a tough mission," Bolling said.

Bolling's regard for his troops was evident before the deployment, according to Lieutenant Colonel John G. Jameson, one of the battalion commanders in the brigade. Jameson recalled a time at Fort Bragg when he and the brigade commander were riding down Longstreet Boulevard. He spotted a G.I. walking on crutches. The soldier said his first sergeant had told him to get to the hospital to treat an injury, and he was going to obey even if it meant a four-mile walk on crutches. After riding the man to the hospital, Bolling then ordered that a couple of ambulances be placed on standby at a designated area for troops needing emergency care.

"He was a super guy. A smart guy. But he had a knack for asking the right questions too," Jameson said. "He didn't harass the troops unnecessarily. He didn't suffer fools gladly either."

In Vietnam, Mike Hood and other junior officers admired the way Bolling conducted himself. "After a particularly tough fight, higher headquarters would tell him he did a good job. And he would respond, 'No, my guys did a good job.' If Omar Bradley was the G.I.'s general, Bud Bolling was Joe Tentpeg's general, always and forever," Hood said. "Everything about him revolved around taking care of his troops. His men always came first. That was his legacy. Woe be unto those who didn't care for Joe Tentpeg."

One witness to the way Bolling functioned was John Bell of Modesto, California, who had the equivalent rank of corporal as a photographer in the public affairs unit.

"This guy was the real deal. Whether it came down to strategy or psychology, he knew how to get people to work for him. He took care of people as if they were his children. He believed in giving credit where credit is due. It works with kids, and it works with hard core soldiers. His men worshipped him," Bell said. "These guys were real-life Rambos, not the Hollywood kind, but the real deal. They would do anything for him."

Even the existence of a public affairs office was an example of Bolling looking out his men. Rather than using it to further his own image, Bolling wanted photographs of his soldiers to be sent to their hometown newspapers. John Bell witnessed the magic in that.

"I was out on an assignment, and this troop came running up and asked, 'Do you remember me?' He reached into his pocket and pulled out a sweat-stained, folded up newspaper clipping with a picture of him that I had taken. This soldier told me I could have anything he had. Anything. His mother was so proud of him she bought a dozen newspapers. The whole community was proud of him. The only thing I wanted was for him to keep making his Mama proud and for him to stay safe. I realized then that if I got zapped that day and never took another picture, my time in Vietnam would have been worth it. Bolling knew what he was doing. When a man who has nothing, who has endured hardship, who has learned to be content with the very basics, when this man offers you everything he has, I have but one thing to say, 'General Bolling, sir, Airborne All The Way!' "

Bolling had a sense of humor, albeit a dry one. At one of the briefings in the tactical operations center, the pet monkey of a staff member made a ruckus.

"That's OK," Bolling said. "He's about as helpful as any of the officers in here. The monkey can stay."

Foolishness was not tolerated, whether the source was village chieftains or officers under his command.

One time Up North, Bolling was perturbed that pot shots were being fired at combat engineers who were building a road near a village. Bolling arranged a meeting with the village chief to explain that those crews were there to help. Consequences would result if any more shots were fired.

Said Bolling: "Through an interpreter, I said, 'Mister Mayor, you tell everyone in your town that the next time a shot is fired on this road, I am going to sweep it one hundred yards on each side. I'll bulldoze it. If you think I'm kidding, try me out.' The guy's eyes got real big. A couple of weeks later, a shot was fired. We left the temple and a medical clinic standing, but we knocked down every building that had housed any bad guys. We bulldozed an area exactly 100 yards on each side. We never again took another shot from that town. What we didn't know, there was a minimum of a battalion of NVA in there."

John Bell was present at the original meeting but didn't witness the bulldozing first-hand. He heard about it later.

"This was a man of his word. It was kind of biblical: 'Let your yes be yes and your no be no.' Like I said, he was the real deal," Bell said.

One health issue that often gets glossed over was the rate of venereal disease among the troops. Bolling was aware of the statistics listed in the after-action reports, and his method of prevention was to keep Joe Tentpeg away from temptation.

"If I ever saw any prostitution, that went away. If there was VD, it had to be from monkeys. We were so deep in the jungle," Bolling said.

Down South, Bolling once tried to reach one of his subordinates, but the officer was away from his duties.

"Is he in Saigon?" Bolling asked the clerk on duty. "Tell him to report to me at 0800 tomorrow with his suitcase."

Called onto the carpet, the officer was unceremoniously dismissed.

"Your men can't go into Saigon, but you did. You just ended your military career. Get out of here. I recommend strongly you resign from the Army," Bolling told him.

Bolling's name had power. When John Bell first arrived at Camp Rodriguez, there was no place to develop film. Bolling sent his driver to take Bell to the Marine base near Hue. When Bell said he was a photographer with the 82nd Airborne on an important assignment, the Marines graciously gave him the use of their photo labs. Then, with the move Down South, Bell experienced another example of Bolling's clout during the construction of a new facility.

"We were set up at Phu Loi, and I needed running water plumbed into my dark room. The request was relayed to Bolling. In a few days, a man from the Army Corps of Engineers came by. I told him I wanted the water to be filtered so I wouldn't scratch my film in the development. He just laughed and said that this would be impossible. I told him OK and asked for his name, because when I relayed the message to General Bolling, he would want to know who I talked to. I didn't have to say any more. 'Just hold on, hold on, let me see what I can do,' the guy told me. Within a week, I had my own filtered water, complete with plumbing," Bell said.

Little things meant a lot. At one meeting of the brigade's officers, the subject of hot sauce came up. "I went to see my boys in the field. They said Tabasco sauce would make the C Rations taste better. I had to apologize that they didn't have any," Bolling said. Then he turned to someone on his staff and said: "Send my boys some Tabasco sauce. Not just one or two bottles. Get them cases of it. I don't care where or how you get it. Just do it. If this is not carried out, I'll see to it that you and your friends will not be getting your steaks here at Red Ball. Do I make myself clear?"

Ice cream was a bit easier to find Down South, but it was still a luxury. Bolling continued his practice of getting it out the troops in the bush. He recalled one meeting he had with a mortar squad in the 1st of the 508, set up in a swamp. When Bolling asked what they wanted most, the answer was beer and ice cream.

"I can't bring you beer, but what flavor ice cream?" Bolling replied. "I radioed Red Ball and said to get me five gallons of ice cream—chocolate and vanilla, and some dry ice. Those were the happiest soldiers I ever saw."

Letters from home were another priority. At one briefing, Bolling told an aide: "Mail is very important to my boys. As soon as the mail arrives, get it to my boys immediately. If I find out that their mail is being delayed, I will personally be coming after your mail. Am I understood?"

Although burdened with the duties of a combat officer, Bolling found time to intercede on behalf of his troops. One example, documented in the unit history, involved Johnny Brenson. A specialist in Alpha Company of the 2nd of the 505, Brenson had come in from the field to go on a seven-day leave in the Philippines. Before he could go, Brenson had to show his ID and ration card in order to trade in his military pay certificates for cash, but he had lost his ID. At Camp Red Ball, wearing his dress khaki uniform and seemingly stuck, Brenson had a chance encounter with General Bolling.

"Enjoy your leave?" Bolling asked him.

"Not so far, sir," Brenson answered, explaining his predicament. "Wait here! We'll get your money changed," Bolling said.

The general cut through all the red tape and straightened everything out. Brenson was soon on his way to enjoy a leave made possible by a commanding officer who cared.

Bolling also made an indelible impression on another enlisted man, Arthur Kellogg of Titusville, Pennsylvania. Drafted 13 months earlier, Kellogg went to the federal building in Pittsburgh to take his physical and was immediately put on a train for basic training at Fort Jackson in South Carolina. "They didn't give you a chance to change your mind," he said with a laugh. A product of NCO school and a one-time drill sergeant, Kellogg had been hospitalized with dysentery, an ailment that caused diarrhea, cramps, headaches and fever. He figured he caught it from eating Vietnamese bread or from the squadrons of flies that landed on everything in Vietnam. He was being cared for in an Army field hospital with an 82nd Airborne patch attached to the end of his bed. He called it General Bolling's General Hospital.

In a letter home that was dated December 8, 1968, Kellogg noted that Bolling visited him and all the troopers from the brigade who were hospitalized: "He is one of the best men there could be in command of any unit. He is as common as anyone else, and he talks to you as if you were his own son. He is concerned about his men, and he will do about anything possible to make your environment better."

Finally, Bolling shared a personal story that elicited a chuckle. He was on his way to firefight just as the troops at Camp Red Ball were watching a movie being shown on a screen that was bigger and better than anything they had Up North.

"The feature was *The Green Berets*, and it was just at the point in the movie where John Wayne is ascending in a helicopter. At that very moment, my helicopter started up, and I'm taking off right with John Wayne," Bolling said.

Life imitates art. Nobody outside the 82nd Airborne may know much about Bud Bolling, but he was one the best combat officers the Army ever produced. His boys always thought of him as a rising star.

Chapter 35
NEW GROUND

Every time David Straza walks on a linoleum floor, pain shoots through the toes on his left foot. Every time the aches return, he is transported back across the years to one of the 82nd Airborne's first foot patrols Down South and the memory of Sergeant First Class George John Kendra, a 35-year-old father from the coal mining town of West Hazelton in northeastern Pennsylvania.

"It's like a time machine," said Straza. "You remember those people until the day you die. You had to have been there, I guess. We lived like dogs. We all suffered equally through the same pain and the same misery. We shed our blood. We did our jobs. We never complained, and we're not complaining now."

Inducted into the Army on January 8, 1968, Straza arrived in Vietnam at Bien Hoa for orientation. There, he met fellow Chicagoan Frank Walenga, and both were issued All American shoulder patches.

"Hey, we're not jumpers," the men said on being assigned to the unit.

"That's OK. Nobody's jumping over here anyway, and they need bodies," they were told.

Both were whisked away on the same helicopter as replacements during the Golden Brigade's reorganization. Straza was assigned to third platoon, and Walenga, who would create his own time machine in a later operation, went to fourth platoon. They would see each other on the trails from time to time.

"I went where they told me," said Straza, whose parents were of Polish and German ancestry.

Up North, Straza recalled being atop mountains that were so high he could look down at the tops of clouds. The triple canopy of the rain forest was so thick it would blot out the sun. On patrols in that environment, troops might only be able to move 100 yards in a single day if they didn't have a trail or stream to follow. When the brigade relocated Down South, troops seemed to be in the sun all day and constantly slogging their way through swamps, like the kind of terrain encountered on October 30, 1968.

On that day, Straza's squad was operating in a place called the Pineapple, named for an abandoned plantation once run by the French. The terrain, dotted with the stubble of pineapple plants, was some of the worst the Golden Brigade encountered, and it was ideal for the bad guys to conceal mortars and rockets intended for Saigon. In the search for this elusive foe and his weaponry, Straza and 10 comrades patrolled the flooded ground. Because it was new territory for Alpha Company of the 1st of the 508, platoon sergeant George Kendra volunteered to accompany the squad.

"It was in the morning," said Straza, who had just turned 20. "We had walked maybe 30 minutes. Our feet were wet. Fire ants were leaping at us from the trees. That was Vietnam."

Following standard operating procedure, troopers walked single file, with five yards or so separating each man. The point man was Michael Bush of Nathrop, Colorado.

"Bush was following the tree line, and I saw him raise his hand. That was the signal for us to halt. Then all of a sudden, it started. Bush opened up. Then they started firing back," Straza said.

An enemy round struck Bush in the arm, taking him out of the fight. Later, it was determined that another round had struck the ammo pouch on his utility belt. If the pouch hadn't absorbed the force of the projectile, he likely would have been killed. Then, as the bullets snapped through the air, Sergeant Kendra acted instinctively.

"I'll never forget. Kendra was seven feet or so away from me. He said, 'Let's go. Move up, move up, move up.' Kendra got hit right away and let out a groan. I never heard anything like it in my life," Straza said.

Instinctively following his training, Straza assumed a kneeling position, his right knee on the ground and his left leg outstretched and bent at a 90-degree angle. Using his elbow to prop up the machine gun on his left thigh and with the stock snugly pressed into his right shoulder, he had a stable firing platform. He aimed at the positions where the enemy fire was coming from, but nothing came out when he squeezed the trigger.

"My gun wouldn't go. Someone was yelling, 'Get it going! Get it going!' I said, 'I can't.' I opened the breach and saw that the gun had been hit and was disabled by an enemy round. I just couldn't get it to work," Straza said.

Still in the kneeling position, Straza resorted to his backup weapon—a .45 caliber sidearm. Just as he began to shoot back, an enemy round struck him just above his left ankle.

"I felt my leg slam back. It's sort of an adrenaline rush. It didn't even hurt at the time," he said. The shooting lasted five to seven minutes before things fell silent. The enemy force, most likely the Viet Cong, broke contact and melted away.

"The medic came up to me. I told him to take care of Kendra first. He said it was too late. Kendra was dead. A bullet went through his heart," Straza said.

A chopper was summoned to evacuate the casualties. Kendra, who had been in Vietnam for less than three months, was placed in a body bag and then an aluminum transfer case to be returned home for burial. His tight-knit hometown, located about 30 miles south of the Pennsylvania community of Wilkes-Barre in Luzerne County, mourned his loss. Established in the 19th Century to house the miners who dug anthracite coal of the ground, West Hazelton was home to a number of ethnic groups such as the Slovaks, of which Kendra was a member.

Fifty years after Kendra was killed, his son Steven posted this online message: "We all miss you. You are in my thoughts each day. I try to pass on my memories of you to my kids. Both Rebecca and Zachary know you and miss you."

Meanwhile, Straza returned to the States to mend from his wounds. He got out of the hospital in March of 1969, still limping and still suffering from permanent nerve damage but seriously contemplating a return to Vietnam.

"You get this bad feeling that you don't want to leave your buddies, and I considered going back. It just wasn't possible," Straza said.

The old neighborhood welcomed him back, and he never had to worry about taking his uniform off to avoid war protesters.

"I didn't have to go through any of the crap. I'd go down to the barbershop, and the guys told me to put my uniform on. They were behind us," Straza said. But he was aware that public opinion had turned against the war and that soldiers who sacrificed in Vietnam were symbols of an unpopular policy.

"Every guy felt it. 'Why me? What did we do?' " Straza said. "I have no regrets. Never a day goes by that I'm sorry for what I did. I did what we were supposed to do. I served with honor. I went with pride. I'll die with pride."

In his mind, his mission was to protect South Vietnam from being subjected to autocratic rule. Without intercession, the Communists would assassinate those who refused to go along or ship them off to re-education camps.

"America protects those who can't protect themselves. We went there for a particular reason. Look at what happened after we left—killing fields, genocide, re-education camps. We were there to prevent that," Straza said.

Several years after the war was over, Straza was at a campaign rally for his brother, an ex-cop running for alderman. Incredibly, he happened to cross paths again with Frank Walenga. Forever bonded by their service, they attend the reunions of their old outfit.

"We've talked about that bond of brotherhood. It's the people I served with who are important. You're as close to them as you are with your own brother. Your ass is in their hands. Their ass is in yours. We depended on each other. It's not like you can just take your ball and go home. We shared everything, even a toothbrush. That bond is unbreakable. It never goes away," Straza said.

And with each step he takes on a linoleum floor, Straza is reminded of Sergeant First Class John Kendra advancing toward the enemy, shouting "Let's go! Move up!"

Chapter 36
MURRAY'S JOURNEY

Among the new responsibilities for the 82nd Airborne was securing a bridge along a section of Highway One that ran northwest from Saigon toward Cambodia. The two-lane span, built over a canal cutting through a marshy area about 10 miles outside the South Vietnamese capital, was vital because the highway was a major supply route used by the U.S. military to shuttle men and the materials of war. The bad guys recognized its importance too. During the Tet Offensive, the bridge had been targeted in order to disrupt American convoys, which would have had to take a long, circuitous detour. The bridge and canal shared the same name as a nearby village—Hoc Mon.

Hoc Mon had a notorious reputation, beginning with the fact it was the site of a brothel or, in the slang of the times, a Temple of Negotiable Virtue. The working women who were part of the world's oldest profession sometimes left the hooch to bathe in the canal, a act of futility given that the waterway was dirtier than an open sewer. During down times, some off-duty troops used the bridge as a diving platform to leap into the canal too. One trooper snapped a picture of the wife of one of the officers firing a grenade launcher from the top of a guard tower.

Used as an infiltration route by the Viet Cong, the Hoc Mon canal was covered in thick vegetation on both banks. In order to hamper enemy movements, the banks were sprayed with Agent Orange or some other defoliant, and when the undergrowth died, flame throwers were brought in to burn it back.

The Hoc Mon Bridge remained open to civilian traffic, with checkpoints set up to deter enemy infiltrators. These checkpoints produced some remarkable sights, like the time when Ed Kochanski's unit stopped a bus to check ID cards.

"Off the bus come these nice looking Vietnamese girls with their beehive hair dos. They moved to the side of the road and took a dump, wiped themselves and got back on. Talk about a Third World country," Kochanski said.

Guard duty turned deadly serious on November 16, however. Kochanski and Billy Murray, the two homeboys from northeastern Pennsylvania, were on duty that day. One standard operating procedure for sentries was to toss a grenade periodically into the Hoc Mon Canal just in case any enemy used the waterway as cover in an attempt to blow the bridge. In Alpha Company of the 2nd of the 505, the sergeant who was in charge of procuring grenades from the supply chain opted for a field expedient for some unknown reason. Instead of requesting more grenades, he rigged explosive charges made of a quarter stick of TNT attached to a piece of detonation cord that was five or six inches long. The hitch was a soldier would have to light a fuse attached to a chunk of dynamite and then throw it into the water.

"I had just gotten off my watch, and Murray was next up. He asked if he could borrow my helmet because he had left his in the bunker," Kochanski said.

"I was walking away when all of a sudden—Boom! I hear this loud explosion. Billy had lit a charge to toss into the canal, but the quarter stick of dynamite went off in his hand. His hand was gone, and he had a big hole in his chest. As I ran back to him, I could smell burnt flesh. He was screaming, 'Let me go in the water. I'm burning up! I'm burning up!' The medics came and jabbed him with morphine. He was all blown up, but this guy was so tough he never even passed out," Kochanski said.

A helicopter was summoned to evacuate Murray. Kochanski asked his lieutenant if he could accompany his buddy back to the rear, but the request was denied. The lieutenant said he needed every troop he had in the field, and Kochanski couldn't be spared. Then fate intervened.

"I carried him to the chopper, but before I could get out, it took off with me inside. I was holding his IV tube and tried to keep the stretcher stable during the ride. Over the radio, the lieutenant said to come back out on the next supply chopper. We got him to the hospital, and these majors and colonels came out to work on him," Kochanski said.

Kochanski waited for word as long as he could, but he obeyed orders and flew back to his unit. He had to rustle up a new helmet to replace the one that Murray had borrowed.

Meanwhile, back in Murray's hometown of Carbondale, two Army officers arrived at the family residence with the news that Billy Murray had been wounded. A short time later, two ROTC candidates from the University of Scranton went to the house to notify the family that Billy's wounds had been fatal. Murray had died in the hospital in Vietnam.

"They went in and they sat for the longest time and talked with my parents," Leo Murray said. "I knew, but I didn't want to know. It stung."

The official notice attributed the cause of death to "explosives prematurely detonated."

About two weeks after the explosion that took Murray's life, a small helicopter landed at the Hoc Mon Bridge to find Kochanski. Through the intercession of Congressman Joe McDade, whose district included Carbondale, Kochanski received orders to accompany Murray's body back home. It's a sacred duty, one that requires the escort to be in the presence of the corpse at all time. The trip began at the military morgue in Saigon.

"I had to identify him. We put him in a rubber body bag, then an aluminum coffin," Kochanski said.

Kochanski was provided with a dress uniform for a melancholy flight to Dover Air Force Base in Delaware, which was the home of a mortuary for fallen soldiers who lived in the eastern half of the country. At Dover, Kochanski was looking forward to a steak dinner when he was called to identify Murray again. Once all the procedures were followed, Murray's coffin and Kochanski were placed in a hearse for the trip to northeastern Pennsylvania. The orders stipulated that the coffin remain sealed. If the family insisted on opening the casket, the orders stated that a doctor and priest had to be present in case someone in the family had a heart attack.

"I remember it like it was yesterday. The coffin was draped in an American flag, and we were in a hearse driving back to Scranton. Pennsylvania's traffic laws say to keep right except to pass, but the driver was in the left lane. A state trooper pulled us over, and after I explained to him what was going on, he let us go with a warning," Kochanski said.

At the funeral home in Carbondale, Kochanski met Murray's family for the first time. The casket was closed, but like so many families who lost a loved one in Vietnam, the Murrays wanted assurance that Billy's body was really inside. Leo Murray pulled Kochanski to the side.

"Eddie, the only thing I want to know is if that's my brother," Leo said.

"That's your brother's remains. I was with him the whole time," Kochanski assured him. Then he hugged Leo Murray.

"It was heartbreaking. Heartbreaking. You have to bring somebody home to their family, and they have to trust you that's him in the casket," Kochanski said.

A complication arose in advance of the December 2 funeral. Through the grapevine, Leo Murray heard that war protesters planned to show up at the service. He went to the local police chief for help.

"That's my brother. They can oppose the war if they want to. I defend with my life their right to speak up, but they don't have the right to spoil my brother's memory," Leo told the police chief.

Uniformed policemen were assigned to funeral detail to make sure there were no disruptions. The service, complete with an honor guard, was held without incident at St. Rose of Lima Catholic Church. Burial followed in Our Mother of Sorrows Cemetery.

William Joseph Murray, 20, was remembered as a two-way football player for the Ben Franklin High School Pioneers. Having volunteered to join the Army, the solider who was trained to be a cook served instead as an Airborne infantryman. He had taken part in long range recon missions, overcame malaria, insisted on returning to Vietnam and risked his own life in an attempt to save a drowning comrade.

Having completed the mission of taking his friend home to his final resting place, Ed Kochanski caught a long, lonely flight back to Vietnam. A lame-ass sergeant had insisted that Kochanski return by Christmas or he would be declared Absent Without Leave and subject to military discipline.

"I got off this air conditioned plane into the 130 degree heat of Vietnam. It was so humid I was gasping for air," Kochanski said.

He was back in the war at Christmastime. Guarding the Hoc Mon Bridge was far from the last duty he performed.

"I never thought I was coming out of this alive," Kochanski said.

As the years passed, Leo Murray became a journalist for The Scranton Times but never spoke about his brother outside the family. When the Vietnam Memorial Wall was dedicated in Washington, D.C., his editor assigned him to cover the event.

"My brother's name is on that Wall," Leo said. He found it on Panel 38 West, Line 7.

Years later, on September 26, 2015, a memorial was dedicated to the 55 veterans from Lackawanna County who died in Southeast Asia. The name of William J. Murray Jr. of Carbondale is on that memorial placed at Courthouse Square in Scranton. Ed Kochanski attended the dedication to honor his friend.

"Ed comes from a solid, solid family. And he became part of our family," said Leo Murray. "I was thrilled they did the memorial. Better late than never. These guys went out and sacrificed. How they were treated when they came home was really, really wrong. I take pride in having my brother's name. He lived life the way he wanted to. He could have easily gotten out on a medical, but he went back because he said his friends needed him."

Every August 3, Leo Murray visits his brother's grave. That's the day he last saw Billy alive, the day he left Carbondale to return to Vietnam.

"I lost a brother and a best friend. There's just no way you ever forget about it. There's not a day goes by that I don't think about him," Leo Murray said. "The thing I want people to remember is that he was a 20-year-old kid who made the supreme sacrifice for his country in a war that even today we don't know why we were there. He died doing what he loved. He believed in his country so much that he sacrificed his life for it."

Chapter 37
THANKSGIVING

Sharp-eyed infantrymen provided the last line of defense against Russian-made rockets that were transported on an arduous journey of hundreds of miles to get to within striking distance of Saigon. The weaponry entered North Vietnam through seaports or a railroad line originating in China, then were put into the supply chain at the source of the Ho Chi Minh Trail. From there, the cargo bypassed the Demilitarized Zone and moved down a network of pathways concealed by triple-canopy cover through Laos and Cambodia. If the supply line survived attempts by American bombers to stop the flow, which it stubbornly did, the payloads reached the Viet Cong in South Vietnam. The guerrillas then buried stockpiles of rockets capable of reaching Saigon, firing them under cover of darkness at a time of their choosing. Launch procedures were amazingly simple. A rocket could be placed on a tripod or leaned against an embankment, with wooden aiming sticks aligning it on the proper angle.

Responsibility for finding the hidden stockpiles belonged to the 82nd Airborne in the area north and west of Saigon. In November, near a village named Ap Tay, one such mission was assigned to Charlie Company of 1st of the 505. A battalion is the smallest Army unit with a headquarters staff, and the battalion intelligence officer, Captain Elton Parrish, accompanied the unit on a foot patrol. He probed a suspicious area and felt a metal object buried in the ground. An electronic mine detector confirmed the find, and soldiers began to dig. Uncovered was a 122-millimeter rocket complete with fuse, motor and warhead. Then another metal object was detected, and another, and another. In all, 37 complete rockets of the same size and 11 fully assembled smaller rockets had been uncovered, some of them still packed in their waterproof shipping crates. The haul was one of the largest ever found, and Charlie Company merited a letter of appreciation from higher command.

All day, every day, under the tropical sun or drenched by monsoon downpours, rifle companies of the Golden Brigade performed similar tasks. Daily existence was never routine, but it did have a sameness. Patrol during the day, cordon off a village before performing a sweep, ambush at night. Put one foot in front of another to get to a destination, ride into an area aboard a helicopter on what were called eagle flights or popper missions, or board boats powered by outboard motors or air foils. Take malaria pills, slather on the bug repellant, endure the jungle rot feasting on the flesh of wet feet, purify canteen water with iodine pills, keep weapons clean and oiled, stay constantly alert for booby traps, attempt to win the hearts and minds of a local population that wasn't exactly greeting U.S. troops as liberators, open a can of C Rations for sustenance.

On one day that seemed indistinguishable from all the others, Don Behm and the soliders of Charlie Company, the unit that that uncovered the big haul of rockets at Ap Tay, were brought in from the field. It was November 28, the fourth Thursday of the month, 333 days into the year with 33 more remaining, Thanksgiving Day.

On that most American of holidays, Uncle Sam—or Uncle Sugar as the drill sergeants called the bearded symbol of the country—took on the tough logistical problem of serving his soldiers the best meal possible under war-time conditions. Cooks in their field kitchens prepared roast turkey, which was shipped out to the grunts in insulated cans called Mermite Tactical Military containers. In a reversal of roles that is an Airborne tradition, officers and senior sergeants ladled out the meal to the grunts as a way of showing appreciation to the guys at the tip of the bayonet.

Behm and his orphan-like brethren, all of them dirty, filthy, wet, stinky and unshaven, shuffled through the chow line to be served their Thanksgiving feast. Appetites were large, and if anybody had a wishbone, it was dedicated to the thought of Mom's cooking and family gathered around a table back home. Nobody appreciates America's blessings more than a soldier away at war. But in the otherworldly realm of Vietnam, a steady downpour doused those about to dine.

"It was raining like hell, and we were served our turkey dinner right out in the rain. The water was a half-inch deep on my tray," Behm said.

A soggy meal was just one more indignity to bear. Because all of the grunts were subject to the same conditions, they leaned on each other to get through. If they were separated from their families, they were surrounded by their military family. Brothers could care less if they didn't use the right salad fork, if anyone in the field got a salad or a fork. They were alive and could still offer a prayer of thanks for the waterlogged bounty they were about to receive—roast turkey, mashed potatoes, vegetables and whatever trimmings were available. It was just another day to get through, another day closer to going home.

Away from his own wife and family, Brigadier General Bud Bolling gave thanks to his boys. His holiday message to his All Americans noted that Thanksgiving Day, 1968, was one that few would ever forget.

"Almost every man in the brigade will put in a full day's work, and most of that work will take place in the rice paddies and river mud of our area of operations," Bolling said. "Though there may appear to be little to be thankful for, I think we can all be more than grateful that we are citizens of a great nation built on the principle of freedom. When you return home, you will all realize that there is no greater honor, no greater feeling of accomplishment, than being part of the citizen group that must defend that freedom. Every man in this brigade will be able to stand tall with pride as he remembers the hardships of his tour in Vietnam. I shall do everything I can to make your Thanksgiving Day as pleasant as the tactical situation will permit. During the day, I shall give thanks for the honor of serving with the All American troopers of the Third Brigade, 82nd Airborne Division. I shall also give thanks for the knowledge that your effort this year will guarantee a happy Thanksgiving for you next year—and for your children in the years to come. ALL THE WAY."

War doesn't stop for American holidays, however. Out in the field on Thanksgiving Day, the Golden Brigade suffered the loss of Private First Class Dwayne Jefferson Whorton, 20, of McKinleyville, California, who was killed by an enemy mortar in Gia Dinh Province. An infantryman who had been drafted into the Army, Whorton was a member of Alpha Company of the 1st of the 505. He was six months into his tour.

Back in The World, four televised professional football games were played on Thanksgiving. Although the NFL and the American Football League had already agreed to merge, they were still playing separate schedules. In the NFL, Cleveland defeated Detroit, and the Dallas Cowboys rallied to beat the Washington Redskins. In the AFL, the Oakland Raiders beat the Buffalo Bills by a field goal, and the Kansas City Chiefs defeated a Houston team then called the Oilers.

In Vietnam, a football game was played between the 82nd Airborne and the Air Force. The All American football team got its start when a couple of guys, looking for a diversion in a combat zone, started tossing around a ball that had been mailed from home.

"A guy named David Studebaker had a football and asked me if I wanted to play some catch. It grew from there. Someone would see us and ask if they could play too, then another, and another, until we had enough guys to have a scrimmage. It really started as an escape. These guys would come back from living hard in the field and needed a diversion. We played maybe one day a week. And for 60 minutes or so, while they were playing a game, they weren't in Vietnam anymore. It took their minds off things," said John Bell.

The field was a humble patch of ground just off a small Post Exchange at Phu Loi near Ford's photo lab. Some loose gravel had been strewn on the ground to keep down the dust and the mud. Then somebody from the Air Force spotted troops playing football and inquired about playing a friendly game.

The Air Force had its own team at the Tan Son Nhut Air Base, and well, it might be fun to let off a little steam with a little inter-service competition. The challenge was accepted.

On game day, the Air Force team showed up, and Mark Markiewicz, a member of the public affairs unit who had played some football back home in Pennsylvania, ran in to see Bell.

"John, John, we're going to get killed. They have their own bus. They have uniforms. They're huge," Markiewicz told Bell.

"Hold on, hold on. Are any of them as fast as you? Can any of them turn on a dime and give you a nickel's change like you can? Let's play and see what happens," Bell replied.

The Airborne team wore jungle fatigues and combat boots. The Air Force players had jerseys with numbers on them, along with football pants and athletic shoes.

"They looked like professionals. I don't know if they were on steroids or not, but they sure looked like it," Bell said.

The game lacked a scoreboard, spectators and referees. No Commander-In-Chief Trophy was at stake. Instead of playing tackle, the game was flag football. A play ended when a defender snatched a strip of material worn by the guy with the ball. The Air Force had plastic flags that snapped into place. The grunts had strips of rope in their belts.

The outcome was indeed lopsided, but the score favored the All Americans.

"We beat those guys so bad. Really bad. I mean, we beat the crap out of them. When they got on their bus to go home, Markiewicz went running after them and said, 'Come on back any time you want to play us and get your butts whipped!' We never saw or heard from them again," Bell said.

In addition to being the star of the game, Markiewicz was the person who came up with the words inscribed on the Golden Brigade's membership coin. Those words are also inscribed on the brigade's monument at Fort Bragg and a plaque at Arlington National Cemetery: "Nothing is dearer than life, but nothing is more precious than to live it in freedom.

Chapter 38
HELPING A NEW GUY

Rick Dalton's first days in Vietnam were rough in more ways than one. A product of America's Heartland, he wore sergeant's stripes for having completed the 12-week Noncommissioned Officer's school and was derisively called a shake and bake, or 90-day wonder, by old-school NCOs who earned their rank in the field.

"There were 165 of us on one of those commercial airlines that was a front for the CIA. When we landed in Vietnam, I got to the door, and the smell was as if somebody hit me in the face with a dead fish. I picked up my equipment and noticed it was all used stuff. That was not a comforting thought," said Dalton, who grew up in a small town near Bloomington, Illinois.

After two days of orientation, he was told he was assigned to the 101st Airborne and looked on the bulletin board for confirmation. He was reminded of what other Army units said about the Airborne: the three things that drop from the sky are rain drops, bird shit and fools. When he couldn't find his name, he found that he had been assigned to the 82nd Airborne.

"Wow! Out of the frying pan and into the fire. God had decided that I was going to be Airborne something," Dalton thought to himself. "There was another saying that was popular at the time—If you ain't infantry, you ain't. I take a great deal of pride in being an Eleven Bravo."

Now part of the Golden Brigade, Dalton was assigned to Alpha Company of the 2nd of the 505. Another icy reception awaited, and not just because he was a leg.

"Guys were really stand-offish. One guy even took a swing at me. I thought I was going to get fragged right off the bat," Dalton said.

Just then, a sergeant in Dalton's platoon stepped forward to explain the details of a prickly situation. Benjamin Benton, a draftee from rural North Carolina, told Dalton that the outfit was supercharged with anger because the company commander had been removed from his duties to face allegations in front of a military court. The charges stemmed from an incident Up North.

"Benton told me that everyone thought I was working undercover for the Criminal Investigation Division to dig up dirt, which was absurd. I don't know what I would have done without Benton," Dalton said. "He was kind of the glue that held everybody together. I was just getting my feet wet. Everybody who knew him would put him up for soldier of the year."

An instant bond developed between Dalton and Benton. The court martial was resolved in a timely manner too.

Just after Thanksgiving, an eight-man court headed by General Walter T. (Dutch) Kerwin convened at Long Bihn. After a day of testimony, the military jury took 30 minutes to acquit the accused on two charges of premeditated murder. The court martial, which is part of the public record, still riles those who served in Alpha Company. Anger stemmed from the fact that the case got that far, that it was a disservice to Captain John Kapranopoulos and that the allegations were leveled by junior officers who were in disfavor within the company.

"I'm still pissed off about it. It was a bunch of crap. I know I was in the right," Kapranopoulos said.

Captain K was held in the highest regard by both the troopers under his command and by his superiors within the Golden Brigade. His combat experience paid off in saving the lives of many of his men on several missions, including the assault on Nui Ke, operations in a gnarled area of jungle called the Salad Bowl and the sapper attack on Fire Base Panther III.

"He was a one-of-a-kind troop leader. He had that confidence, that winning spirit. The troops loved him. They would go to the ends of the earth to fight for him," said Jim Littig, who was Alpha Company's executive officer.

Keith Bell served as a platoon leader for a time under Captain K and had similar impressions.

"He had a certain charisma about him. If it was raining, he'd say, "Don't worry, it'll be sunny soon.' He knew what he was doing," Bell said.

As the trooper who carried the company radio and was always within arm's length of his company commander, Carl Bludau was as close to Captain K as any soldier could be.

"He had an aura about him. Everybody in the company loved him. He was a guy that everybody trusted, a guy you could trust with your life," Bludau said.

The lieutenant who brought the charges was Ralph Loomis, a self-described anti-intellectual redneck from northern Kentucky who grew up fighting, drinking and playing football. His journey to Vietnam began when he had an argument with his father, which led him to drop out of the University of Kentucky and join the Army. After completing Officer's Candidate School, Loomis went off to war with the 82nd Airborne and became a platoon leader in Alpha Company. However, he had been relieved of his duties in the field for what Captain K called ineptitude and was placed in charge of the motor pool at Camp Rodriguez. Later, when the company was short-handed, he returned to the field.

Once again, he drew Captain K's ire. An ambush was being set up and Loomis was told to keep an eye on a jittery Cherry. But what happened, according to members of the company, was that the new guy shot and killed one of his own comrades in a friendly fire incident. Captain K berated Loomis and told him, "A mother's son is dead because of your incompetence," according to those who witnessed the incident.

The engagement that led to the charges occurred on September 22. Versions differ, but the consensus was that four Vietnamese were seen carrying packs into the jungle and then emerged without them. It was a tactic commonly used by the Viet Cong, and Captain K called in an artillery strike. Two survivors, including one who was wounded, were taken into custody. The wounded man was bleeding profusely but refused medical care, and if he wanted to die out in the bush, that was his business. Timing was critical. It was getting darker and darker, and Alpha Company was making plans for an assault the next day. At his command post, Captain K stayed in touch by radio with those handling the captives, including Loomis.

The wounded VC tried to bite a trooper. The other made a lunge for the medic's weapon. Both were killed. Loomis then filed criminal charges.

Given that the matter was now in the hands of the military justice system, Colonel Bud Bolling confronted the issue head-on and pushed for a speedy resolution. He wanted to get it off the books as quickly as possible, even though some in the brigade questioned why the case had to be pursued at all.

In the absence of any physical evidence, the trial boiled down to testimony. In a small air conditioned courtroom, Loomis said that he radioed in word that the wounded prisoner was unarmed. He said the reply from Captain K was: "Damn it. I don't care about prisoners. I want a body count. I want that man shot."

Another prosecution witness was Joe Harris, a first lieutenant who served as an artillery forward observer. Harris said he heard all the radio transmissions and watched through his binoculars as one of the captives was shot and killed. He said he told Captain K: "If I were you, I'd untie him."

But Harris had his own issues with his company commander. Captain K was in the process of removing him from the field because he couldn't read a map, and a forward observer who can't give proper grid coordinates was of little value.

During testimony, it was brought out that Alpha Company's slogan was Wine, Women and Body Counts, a twist on a popular song and a dark reference to the strategy of measuring progress in the war by the number of enemy killed.

The first defense witness was Colonel Bolling. Under oath, he said that Kapranopoulos was "one of the most outstanding company commanders I've ever had in my command."

Robert Hurley, the lieutenant colonel who commanded the battalion, testified that Captain K was "the best company leader I've seen in my 19 ½ years of military service." Hurley also indicated that Loomis was unfit for combat duty. "He wasn't sure he could kill anyone or have anyone killed," Hurley said.

Kapranopoulos took the stand in his own defense, denying that he ever said a word to Loomis or anyone else about killing prisoners. He said Loomis "was a lousy platoon leader."

Several troopers also were defense witnesses, including John Thieleman, a medic who held the equivalent rank of sergeant. He said he had fumbled his weapon just before one of the men in custody lunged for it. Joseph Mattaliano of New Jersey, a radio operator with the third platoon, said he was the one who fired his M-16 to protect the medic. He also testified that there had been no radio transmission from Captain K, and that there had been no order to kill any prisoner.

In half a hour of deliberations, the jury cleared Kapranopoulos of the two specifications of premeditated murder. No charges were pursued against Mattaliano, although he was reduced two grades in rank to private first class. He was subsequently given an honorable discharge from the Army.

Forty-seven years after the court martial, Loomis told the story of what he called his "conversion experience" in an online testimonial given to Church of the Redeemer of St. Paul, Minnesota. After completing his tour in Vietnam, Loomis said he returned "as a bitter man" to the University of Kentucky. He became a leading spokesman for the Students for a Democratic Society, a radical leftist group that promoted the overthrow of the U.S. government by any means necessary, including by use of force. Shortly after four unarmed students at Kent State were killed by the Ohio National Guard in 1970, he favored burning an ROTC building at Kentucky because provoking the National Guard could result in the killing of more students. More killings would fuel rebellion against the government.

Then in June of 1970, Loomis said he suddenly became aware of the presence of God and heard the words: "Judge not that ye be not judged!" Paralyzed by fear, he experienced a moment of clarity, saying he understood what it meant to be saved by grace through faith. He said he dropped to his knees and asked Jesus to forgive him for what he had become.

After graduating from Kentucky and a Bible college in Pensacola, Florida, Loomis received a Master of Theology degree from Gordon-Conwell Theological Seminary in Massachusetts. He later received a Doctor of Theology degree with a major in ethics from Harvard. He remained convinced that the men in Alpha Company lied to protect their captain.

Kapranopoulos stayed in the Army and retired as a lieutenant colonel. Before he left Vietnam, the troopers of Alpha Company pitched in to buy a plaque of appreciation for Captain K's leadership. It is hung on the wall of his office at home.

Meanwhile, fate had something else in store for Rick Dalton and Benjamin Benton in the abyss of Vietnam.

Chapter 39
'TIS THE SEASON

Like an unseen courier who delivers an annual package, a flashback returns every year just before Christmas for Frank Cunane. Anniversaries trigger memories, and the strongest echo from Cunane's past transports him back to a night ambush and fierce firefight when his battalion delivered on its mission of providing security for the Bob Hope USO Christmas Show.

"I wake up in the middle of the night with the shakes. I can't help but think about it," Cunane said 50 years after the fact.

Two days before Hope and his entourage were scheduled to do a big Christmas show for the troops at Long Binh, Cunane was among those from the Golden Brigade placed under the operational control of the 720th Military Police Battalion. Security was a major concern because of the high profile of the performers and because 30,000 U.S. troops were expected to attend the December 23 event. A rocket attack or any other disruption would have been a major psychological blow. Located 20 miles northwest of Saigon. Long Binh was the largest American installation in Vietnam, home to 50,000 troops based in an area that covered 25 square miles. Assigned to help keep the peace were the Red Devils of the 1st Battalion of the 508th Parachute Infantry Regiment, organized for the occasion under the name Task Force Devil. Headquarters and combat support elements of the 508th set up inside Long Binh, while Alpha and Delta Companies operated outside the wire in areas designated Satan and Devil.

As a member of fourth squad in the fourth platoon of Alpha Company, Cunane and his element set up a night ambush on the banks of a canal along one of the numerous waterways southeast of Long Binh. The Viet Cong used the channels to move men and equipment aboard sampans, often inserting a rocket-firing crew during high tide and then withdrawing covertly when the tide ebbed. Those on ambush had to be aware of the rising and falling water for practical reasons as well. A squad might establish a position on dry ground but be knee-deep in water when the tide came in. While the nine other soldiers in his squad racked out, Cunane took the first watch. It was sometime after 9 o'clock at night when he spotted movement.

"To my right, there were breaks in the vegetation along the canal. I looked straight ahead, and there was nothing. But as I was rubber-necking to my left, I spotted the front of a sampan and saw two guys aboard. I could hear my heartbeat," Cunane said.

Sampans were prohibited from moving at night, and anything that stirred was suspected of transporting bad guys. This particular one ferried a tripod that the guerrillas could use as a stand to fire a rocket.

Cunane broke the silence by yelling: "La de!" which is Vietnamese for "Come here!" The occupants froze but refused to obey as the boat continued on. Cunane opened up with his rifle.

"It all happened so quick. Once the wheels get in motion, they just roll," Cunane said.

Just as he fired up the two guys in the sampan, a second boat carrying three men rode in on the tide. Cunane starting chucking grenades. He was the quarterback on his Haddon Township High School football team in New Jersey, and he was a pretty good baseball player too. The grenades landed right where he wanted them to.

"I know I got the three of them. Then a third sampan comes into view, and I hit them with more grenades. Everybody's up by now. Mike Milton, the platoon sergeant, got hit in the first 20 seconds. The radio's barking. Within minutes, there are choppers above us, and the gunships are firing too," Cunane said.

The fight raged all night. At some point, Cunane waded into the water to take on what was a whole string of boats, emptying magazine after magazine.

"I must have went through my whole bandolier. I didn't let up. Just kept firing," Cunane said. "The sampans were bumping into each other like it was an amusement park."

The company command post, located about 700 yards from the initial contact, ordered everyone in the unit to move up and engage. Overhead, the airplane the grunts called Puff appeared and dropped illumination flares to light up the darkness. The artillery battery at Bien Hoa was alerted to fire in support.

"One of the gunships got on the radio and says, 'I want you guys to get down. You got gooks behind you.' I never saw anyone on land, but the next thing you know, three Cobras are making passes and firing their rockets right over our heads. Holy shit, you couldn't get close enough to the ground," Cunane said.

An air ambulance arrived to evacuate Milton, and Cunane helped him into the chopper. Forty-five years later, Cunane was relaxing by the pool at his New Jersey home when he received a phone call from California. It was Milton, thanking him for getting him out of there.

As the gunships fired up the area, pilots spotted 15 additional sampans about three-quarters of a mile away. They went into action and expended all of their ordnance, then went back to reload. The targets were so numerous that they repeated the same cycle four more times.

According to the Pacific Paraglide, the night's action resulted in a body count of 19, with a total of 29 sampans sunk or captured, and only one man wounded. Cunane has no idea how many enemy he killed, but the memory never faded of guerrillas getting hit and flipping over backwards into the water.

"It's easy to kill someone in a war. You tell yourself you do it for your country, or for self-preservation, or for the guys you're with. The bitch is living with it for 50 years," Cunane said. "One time, we searched a body and found a picture of the guy we had killed. He was sitting in a chair and holding a child. We thought to ourselves, 'We just took out that family's father.' Then somebody says, 'Yeah, but look at the AK-47 on him. Would he have felt bad about killing you?' "

Afterwards, Cunane learned that the flotilla of sampans intended to land men and rockets into position to fire up Bob Hope's show. No one can say how close the bad guys came to wrecking Christmas, but Cunane and his unit saved a lot of American blood.

For its part in Task Force Devil, and for what it had done Up North in thwarting the ambush along Highway 547 and its role in Operation Mot, the Red Devil Battalion and its attached units—Batteries A, C and D of the 321st Artillery—received a Valorous Unit Award for "extraordinary heroism." The Department of the Army cited the exceptional bravery and combat proficiency of the officers and men of the 1st Battalion, 508th Parachute Infantry Regiment, Third Brigade, 82nd Airborne Division. The award cited the battalion's "determination and incomparable fighting spirit."

Meanwhile, Bob Hope performed without incident. With an All American crest adorning one of the telephone poles ringing the stage, the wisecracking comedian brought laughter to 30,000 troops away from home at Christmas.

Hope, known as a one-man morale boost, described Long Binh as "Vietnam's answer to Disneyland." He also alluded to the turmoil, riots and unrest back in The World. "I planned to spend Christmas in the States, but I can't stand violence," Hope deadpanned.

Actress Ann-Margaret, wearing a mini-skirt and white go-go boots, pranced around the stage to the song *Dancing in The Streets* while flashing the peace sign. Creighton Abrams, who was attending his first Christmas event since becoming the top commander in Vietnam, gave the peace sign too.

Abrams distributed Christmas cards to men at war during a season of peace. The text read: "Christmas has a special meaning for American soldiers in Vietnam. Amid the tragedy and ugliness of war, the Holy Season reminds us of the joy and beauty of peace. In a land whose people struggle for a better life, the Christmas message brings cheer and hope for the future. We who serve in this distant land may be justly proud. On this Christmas Day, no finer gift may one provide than to give of his own that his brother might share what he himself enjoys. This is what we are doing as we assist in supporting the Vietnamese in their struggle to maintain independence. My best wishes to each of you and to your families on this Christmas Day. As we face a coming new year, may we each pray for success in our mission, peace on earth, and good will for all mankind."

The Golden Brigade held a contest to determine the best idea for its Christmas card. The winning entry depicted two hands folded in prayer against the backdrop of a parachute. The card, adorned with the All American crest, listed the names of the units that made up the brigade.

Meanwhile, Christmas arrived early for Bud Bolling, but it came with mixed emotions. He was granted a leave to return home to the States, where he could spend the holidays with a family he last saw 11 months earlier. He would also have to say goodbye to the Golden Brigade because he had been promoted. Upon his return to Vietnam, he would become the chief of staff of an Army corps headquartered Up North near Phu Bai. The change was expected. Under the Army way of doing things, a brigade commander keeps his job for two years and then moves on. This policy of rotation made no exceptions for the brigadier general who was the heart and soul of the All Americans in Vietnam. On December 17, in a short ceremony at Camp Red Ball, the formal passing of the baton was completed. Headquarters personnel and all troops not on combat missions in the field formed up to say farewell to Night Rider.

"There wasn't a dry eye in the whole formation. The troops absolutely loved this guy," said photographer John Bell.

The brigade colors were transferred to Brigadier General George W. Dickerson, a jungle fighter from World War II who had taken part in such Southwest Pacific campaigns as the assault landings that liberated the Philippines. A native of Warrenton, Virginia, he had received the Silver Star for valor and the Combat Infantryman's Badge. At the request of the Army, which was fully expecting a repeat of the Tet Offensive around Saigon, Bolling stayed in Vietnam for five extra days to make sure Dickerson was fully briefed.

Dickerson, whose call sign was Bold Strike, bore a passing resemblance to Hollywood actor Kirk Douglas, a comparison he didn't mind. A scholar/soldier, Dickerson had taught strategy at the U.S. Army War College and had earned master's degrees in industrial management and business administration. A capable leader, Dickerson had his own way of doing things. On trips to the field, for example, he wore heavily starched fatigues fresh out of the camp laundry.

At the same time, a meaningful symbol arrived in the mail to correct an oversight at Fire Base All American, the headquarters of 1st of the 505. Sergeant Donald McPhail of Macon, Georgia, had noticed that there was no U.S. flag flying over the post, so he wrote a letter requesting one from Senator Herman Talmadge. Talmadge delivered the gift of the Stars and Stripes—a piece of fabric that not only symbolized America but had once flown over the White House. Raised on Christmas Eve, Old Glory flew in tandem with the flag of the Republic of Vietnam.

Unexpected presents arrived in various forms, like when the field phone rang at the military intelligence unit. It was as if invisible reindeer were flying through the skies delivering a morale boost.

"There was a female voice on the other end, and she asked to speak to one of the guys who was from Hawaii. It was his mother," said Dickie Keaton. "While we were tracking him down, I asked her how she was getting this call through. She said she was a switchboard operator in Hawaii, and she had priority on phone calls. Well, she talked to her son for maybe 15 or 20 minutes. Then I asked her if she could patch us through to the States. Sure enough, she could. Everybody got a chance to call home. A call would last for five or 10 minutes, and we tied up the line for two hours. For a lot of these kids, it was there first time away from home. Naturally, their parents were worried about them."

The grunt work of war continued unabated. Infantry officer Keith Bell was out with part of his platoon on night ambush near the Hoc Mon Bridge when startling sights and sounds interrupted the stillness.

"It gets dark very early in Nam, and it was pitch black. All of a sudden, a Huey helicopter hovered over our ambush point. Lights under the fuselage formed the shape of a cross. Over the loudspeaker, *Silent Night* was playing. I was pissed because I thought it would give away our position. Fortunately, it was a quiet night. Later on, I realized it was a nice moment, a real moment of humanity in that war," Bell said.

Christmas packages arrived from The World. Pete Watkins received 19 different parcels from his family, and he shared the contents with his adopted family in the field.

Rick Dalton received a Christmas package too, but it didn't catch up to him until three weeks later. "When I opened the package, there were two dozen cookies reduced to crumbs. There was a broken hot sauce bottle and deck of playing cards soaked with the hot sauce. Everything was destroyed. The package looked like it was used as a football, but it was still a great package," Dalton said.

Evergreens don't grow in Vietnam, so Christmas trees were imported. Rod Snodgrass recalls that his unit was guarding the Hoc Mon Bridge and living in a water-logged bunker made of sandbags.

"We had one guy, Billy DeWitt of Detroit, whose dad rented a lot every year back home and sold Christmas trees. Well, he gets sent this wooden crate in the mail and out comes a three-feet tall Christmas tree with all the decorations on it. We put the tree on our bunker, and all the G.I.'s riding up and down Highway One would blow their horn when they saw it. Some major came over and offered to buy it for $300. We told him, 'It ain't for sale.' But we gave that tree away for nothing when we moved out the next day," Snodgrass said.

"On Christmas Day, we were taken to an ARVN compound in a deuce-and-a-half for a stand down. We had been out in the field for so long that we hadn't used our ration cards in a while, so we were eligible for back rations. Turns out, we had like 70 cases of beer coming to us. One guy drank his fill and was looking for a place to sleep. There was a life-sized Nativity scene set up at this compound, and he takes the baby

Jesus out of the crib and falls asleep in the manger with all the Magi adoring him. We got him out of there before anybody noticed," Snodgrass said.

One Christmas tree was placed outside the firing pit of an artillery battery, which continued shelling whenever the big guns were needed.

Over in Charlie Company of the 307th Engineers, Glenn McGhie said an aluminum tree was on display, courtesy of First Sergeant James Wallace, whose family had shipped it from The World. The tree was green and had little bulbs on it for ornaments, and McGhie placed his presents from home beneath its branches.

"I have a picture of it, and if you look closely, there's a Playboy calendar among the gifts. I had just became a father in November, and I had some explaining to do with my wife when she saw it. It turns out, my mother sent it to me as a gag gift. I could count down how many days I had left by consulting the different Playboy bunnies of the month," McGhie said.

"There was another amazing thing. Some chocolate chip cookies arrived in a sealed tin. By the time they got to us, they were all crumbs. And even if they were in a sealed container, the ants somehow got into it. I remember Christmas as being away from family. Here I am in a war zone. It was a tough time. We leaned on each other to get through. New Year's was bad too, but at least I could see the end by then," McGhie said.

Tom Wallace's infantry unit also had a tree. "That Christmas would be hard to forget. It was the only one I was away from home. I do remember us getting a hot meal of turkey for Christmas," he said.

Peter Henderson remembers December 25 because he was promoted to the pay grade of sergeant. "That was my Christmas present. It was one of those days that the sooner you got past it the better. It was probably the most depressing day," Henderson said.

Throughout history, any American on any battlefield feels an especially strong tug from home at Christmastime. In Vietnam, Christmas of 1968 was unlike any other experience.

The cost of war kept growing. George Lubomyr Tataryn, who had been with the brigade for seven months, was killed in a vehicle crash on Christmas Eve. A mechanic in Charlie Company of the 82nd Support Battalion, he was listed as being from Chicago. Tataryn was born in Augsburg, Germany, at a displaced person's camp because his parents were uprooted for their native Ukraine during World War II.

Back in The World, America's attention focused on a celestial event. Apollo 8, the first manned spacecraft ever to leave Earth's orbit, circled the far side of the Moon and re-established communications with mission control. The crew of William Anders, James Lovell and Frank Borman, an Air Force fighter pilot, took turns reading from Genesis. Apollo 8 also took the picture of Earthrise, which showed a bright blue planet floating in the dark void of space. The astronauts, who were named *TIME* magazine's persons of the year, concluded with these words from Borman aboard a cramped command module 240,000 miles from home: “And from the crew of Apollo 8, we close with good night, good luck, a Merry Christmas—and God bless you all, all of you on the good Earth.” The message brought relief from the forces tearing the country apart in the bloody year of 1968.

Chapter 40
CHRISTMAS WITHOUT JOY

Sergeant Kenny Bryant's Christmas present was being able to return to his unit, easing the guilt he felt about being away while he was in the hospital. Although some remember that he needed time to recover from a shrapnel wound in his leg, others said he had to have his ears lanced for an ailment common in Vietnam. Bryant had been around so many shellings, explosions and thunderous booms that fluid had built up inside his ears. Doctors in Saigon immobilized his head and inserted needles to drain the built-up fluid and thereby relieved the pressure.

At the time, because of attrition and troop rotations, Bryant's platoon in Delta Company of the 2nd of the 505 was down to two squads. Between them, they alternated ambush duty—one night out, one night in. It just so happened that Bryant's seven-man squad was scheduled to be in the field on Christmas Eve. Because Bryant's face was still ashen and gray as he recovered, others in the unit volunteered to go in his place.

"No, no, I'll go. I'm all right. Nobody wants to be out on a night like this. It's Christmas Eve. I'll probably sleep most of the night anyway," Bryant insisted.

Since the warring sides had agreed to a Christmas truce, no enemy activity was expected, but nobody took anything for granted either. John Szczepanski, the man everyone called Ski, took the point as he led Bryant and the squad to their ambush point.

"I realized it was Christmas. There wasn't supposed to be any shooting. We were going to just set up and wait for daylight. But it was never that easy," Ski said. "Every time I walked out, I'd ask myself, 'Am I going to bring them all back and not walk into an ambush or a booby trap?' My responsibility was to get everybody back safely. I knew nobody else wanted to take the point."

Kenneth Mark Bryant was an easy-going country boy who was liked by all. A draftee from Cold Spring, Kentucky, he always talked about two things—his fiancé and his muscle car, a 1967 Chevrolet Chevelle SS 396. He had gotten engaged to Donna Lange on Christmas Day of 1967, and he had written her name on his combat helmet. He also kept a photo of her standing by that car, one of the most popular high performance machines of the day.

Having arrived in Vietnam on March 23, Bryant had less than 90 days left on his tour. He and his squad set up an ambush in a field of tall grass near a rice paddy. The view ahead was clear, which meant they could spot anybody coming toward it. There was brush behind them so they would have cover if they needed to pull back. Bryant was asleep with three of his men. Ski and the others had the watch. The calendar had flipped to Christmas, and it was about 2 o'clock in the morning.

"All of a sudden, I saw the helmet of this guy. He didn't see us at first. I just saw him. Ken was asleep, and I saw a motion, like Ken was going to get up. I turned real quick to cover his mouth and keep him down, but it was too late," Ski said.

Ski remembers seeing the muzzle flash of an assault rifle. He put his right hand out instinctively, and he was shot through his middle finger. Bryant had been hit too.

"My motion must have caught the corner of the shooter's eye, and the next thing I know Kenny was laying there. I had my hand on him, and I was literally watching the flash coming out of the end of the rifle. I didn't know I was shot, but I just knew Ken was dead. I glanced at him. He didn't have a chance," Ski said.

Overtaken by rage, Ski stood up, which was the most dangerous thing he could have done on ambush. Then he fired in the direction of the muzzle flash. He emptied the 20-round magazine, and after the silence that followed, he heard English being spoken. The shot that killed Bryant and wounded Ski came from a South Vietnamese Army unit that wasn't supposed to be where it was. They were one kilometer away from the grid square they were responsible for. Ski ordered a soldier to call for a medevac. Three other soldiers were also wounded and were too shaken to move.

"My hand felt funny because it was burning. It's like somebody had a torch in there. I shook it, and my finger is dangling, and blood is coming out. The helicopter came, but the pilot didn't want to land. I told him I'd shoot him out of the sky if he didn't. The Vietnamese soldier wanted to come over and help and I told him I didn't need his help and I picked Ken up. I don't know how I carried him. All I can remember is carrying him through a rice paddy and putting him down on the helicopter. Then I sat next to him and I couldn't think anymore. Everything just kind of stopped," Ski said. "I think the thing that bothered me was that he was dead, and I couldn't do anything about it. That was the worst thing. I couldn't do anything and I'm thinking, 'You let your friend die.' I just felt so terrible that it was him, and I'm sorry that it happened. I didn't mean for it to happen to him."

The rest of the platoon was stunned that Bryant had been killed on Christmas by soldiers of the country they were defending.

"The South Vietnamese unit walked right up one them. They should not have been in that area," said John Koons, an Oklahoma native who was the platoon sergeant. He, too, had offered to take Bryant's place on ambush that night. He never got a chance to say goodbye or tell Bryant how much he appreciated the job he was doing as a squad leader.

"Kenny was an excellent solider. He was my right hand. No, check that. He was my brother," said Koons, who had joined the unit the day after it had been overrun in August on Panther III. "It was pretty sad. It really pissed us off."

On Christmas Day, radio operator Robert Zeeman accompanied Delta Company's commander to the military hospital in Saigon where Ski and the wounded soldiers were taken. They also visited the morgue to identify Ken Bryant.

"They took us downstairs where all the bodies were kept. There were so many of them, some missing big chunks of flesh. There are some things you just can't un-see. They stay with you for life," Zeeman said.

Later, on Christmas Day, an officer from the Golden Brigade who had dressed up like Santa Claus visited the unit to share some holiday cheer. He was accompanied by some Doughnut Dollies, who were young female college graduates working in conjunction with the American Red Cross. Not every female wore flowers in her hair or wore love beads in 1968. This particular cohort shared the hardships and privations of American soldiers at war. Most of the time, they were a big morale boost. Not on this day.

"There wasn't any joy," said John Koons. "The next day, they had an empty boots memorial service for Kenny. It was very rough, very somber. Our company commander was from Kentucky, and he escorted Kenny's body back to the States. He never returned to the company. We lost the Old Man too."

Bryant's death was especially hard to take for platoon-mate Ernest Roach of Lewisburg, West Virginia. He had also offered to take Bryant's place on ambush that night, even though he had been on ambush the night before. Roach drew the unpleasant but necessary duty of boxing up Bryant's belongings and shipping them back to Kentucky.

"It was the toughest thing I ever did," Roach said. "Me and Kenny were real close. I remember him showing me the picture of the girl he was going to marry when he got back to The World. I was mad for a long time."

At the hospital in Saigon, doctors surgically removed the knuckle at the base of the middle finger of John Szczepanski's right hand. What was left was a digit about the size of a pinkie finger. Ski was bandaged and placed in a ward surrounded by the fellow soldiers who had also been shot up. Because this was the second time he had been wounded, he was headed back to The World. After two weeks of recuperation, he was on his way home. Part of Vietnam came home with him.

The metal transfer case containing Ken Bryant's arrived in Kentucky on New Year's Eve.

Chapter 41
STRONGER THAN WAR

John Szczepanski's way of knowing his return date was that it coincided with the upset victory by Joe Namath and the New York Jets over the Baltimore Colts in Super Bowl III. It was Sunday, January 12, 1969, but professional football's biggest spectacle was background noise.

Ski and a planeload of wounded from Vietnam landed at the military transfer center in San Francisco to be taken to the appropriate Bay Area hospitals. Military Police directed the returnees to where they were bound—burn victims to one place, amputees to another. The reception was as jarring as an earthquake.

"There was a cyclone fence surrounding the area. War protestors on the other side of the fence were yelling stuff. The MPs said, 'Don't pay any attention to them,' but it angered me. Some of the wounded were on stretchers and had to be carried. There were guys with IVs in their arms, and some of them weren't going to make it. It's one thing to shout something to a soldier, but to treat the wounded like that…," Ski said, unable to complete the sentence.

For a split second, he contemplated doing something about it.

"I looked at an MP's sidearm and figured I could get to it before he could stop me, but my right hand was my strong hand and it was wrapped in bandages. I couldn't have done anything anyway," Ski said.

After all the physical pain from doing what his country had asked him to do, and after the emotional loss of two of his closest friends in a war like no other, the shameful reception was one more cross for Ski to bear. He returned home to Indiana to mend. In time, his hand healed, and he picked up his life the best he could.

Using benefits available to him through the G.I. Bill, Ski majored in philosophy at Calumet College of St. Joseph, a private Roman Catholic school in Whiting, Indiana. He got married, and he and his wife Maria Dolores had a son while he embarked on a career with White Lodging Services Corp. in the hotel industry. He also worked through some of his demons at group therapy sessions for veterans, but not a day passed without recollections of Kenny Bryant and David Alicea.

Driven by a need to pay proper respects and to say goodbye to brothers-in-arms, Ski searched phone directories but never could locate their families. Then again, he wore a medallion of St. Jude, the patron saint of hopeless causes, and was never one to give up.

"I carried those two guys all these years. Someone had hands on them," Ski said. "There's something about when you are with someone when they pass on. In a sense, they don't die. They are always with you."

One breakthrough came just before Memorial Day in 1999. Ski had a chance encounter with Rick Miller, a staff writer with *The Indiana Post-Tribune*, a newspaper serving northern Indiana and the southern suburbs of Chicago. The subject of Vietnam came up, and Ski mentioned something about his quest to find the grave of a buddy. Using his skills as an investigative reporter, Miller made some phone calls and located Ken Bryant's fiancé, Donna Lange of Cold Spring, Kentucky.

Ski placed a nervous call to find that, at 49, Donna was married and had a son, but she was still in contact with Ken's mother. She recognized the name Ski from the letters that Bryant had written from Vietnam, and a road trip was arranged.

"It's almost like she knows me already and I know her. She said on the phone she always knew that I would get in touch with her. She never had any doubt," Ski said.

For the five-hour drive, Ski was accompanied by his wife and their 15-year-old son Jonathan. His Honda Accord was packed with items for a family excursion—sandwiches, chips and fruit packed in a cooler. Reporter Rick Miller traveled along to document the experience. As an All American, Ski knew he had to reach Kenny Bryant's family.

"I have a part of him they need to know about. They need to know I was with him. I feel like I've got to take this message to them, like I'm carrying something for them," Ski told the reporter. "I didn't want it to seem I was doing it just for me. But I figured there are people who are still alive who may want to know about what happened to their son and how their son really was at the time he died. You always think about why him and not me, and I'm right next to him. That's the thing, and you feel a responsibility for that person and you actually sometimes feel guilty. You end up living with that other person. The other person is dead, but he really doesn't die for you. I think this will give peace to his mother and to Donna. But most of all, Kenny can rest. This is when he can really rest in peace. His soul is not settled until this is done."

The plan was to meet Donna first. She and her husband Rick arranged to have a Saturday morning breakfast at a family restaurant with Ski and his entourage. In the parking lot, Donna and Ski hugged each other for the longest time.

Once inside, Ski pulled out stack of color photos of Ken and the rest of the guys in Delta Company. In one snapshot, Donna noticed that Ken was wearing a blue sapphire ring she had given him. She told the story about how they had met at the county fair when she was 16. In front of a concession stand, Ken's opening line to the crowd was, "Let the little lady get a drink." The couple started to date and began making plans. They picked a plot of land near Ken's family farm where they would build a house. They had even chosen names for future children. Wedding invitations had come back from the printer when she learned Ken had been killed.

"I was actually saying a novena to St. Jude and the prayer was supposed to be answered at midnight on Christmas. Of course, my prayer was that Kenny would come home safely. And when they told me that he was killed, probably right about that time, I told God I didn't think that was funny. But He took him all the way home, so now I make my prayers more specific," Donna said.

She reached across the restaurant table to take John's right hand. The company commander who had escorted Ken's body back home had told her that another soldier had been wounded trying to save him. All she knew was the wounded solider was called Ski. She never knew how seriously he was hurt, or whether he was dead or alive.

"So, is this where you were injured?" she asked.

"That's where they took the knuckle off. Actually, the bullet went right through here," Ski replied.

The memories of what happened flooded back. When Ken's body returned from Vietnam, the paperwork said that he had been killed by friendly fire and that the body was not viewable. Donna wanted to have the casket opened, hoping against hope that it wasn't him.

"We went down and we walked to the funeral home," she told Ski. "A soldier had accompanied the body home and I was hoping it would be you. For some reason, I thought it might be you, but it wasn't. So, we were walking through a narrow door. I had Kenny's brother on one side and his cousin on the other, and something stopped me, and I couldn't go any further. I felt it was Kenny's spirit. It was God. It was something, because I just couldn't move. It was hard in a way because there wasn't really any closure. But I don't think I could have seen him."

She couldn't bring herself to look at the corpse.

"That's why I think it's probably better that it works out that I come down here. It's probably a better closure that way. You don't want to have that image. The one thing about war is that you get these images in your mind and they don't come out," Ski said.

After breakfast, the group proceeded to Evergreen Cemetery in South Gate, where Kenneth Bryant is buried under the branches of a maple tree. Next to a family headstone is a plaque listing Bryant's rank, years of service and medals received, including the Purple Heart.

Ski walked up and gently touched the headstone as if he were reaching out for his buddy's hand. He placed a single red rose on the stone, got down on his knees and prayed. After a silent conversation, Donna joined Ski in kneeling by Ken's marker and placed more flowers. Knowing that Ski was with Ken when he was killed brought some solace.

"When there's somebody you love so much, you hate to think of them dying so far away from home with no family around. I always felt bad...But I knew you were there. He wrote about you and I knew you were good friends. I just wanted to say thank you," Donna said.

She hugged Ski again and made a request. "Tell me how it happened," she said.

Ski took her back to the wee hours of a Christmas morning to relate the details of what was supposed to be a quiet night but turned out to be the last hours of Ken Bryant's life. The details were not meant to rip open a scar but to heal a wound.

With that part of the mission completed, the group departed the cemetery for the visit to the Bryant farm. Donna led the way, her car turning onto a gravel driveway shaded by a canopy of trees. At the end of the country lane was a one-story house with white aluminum siding. A small American flag flew proudly over the property of a family that lived off the land. Greeting the visitors at the door was Ruth Bryant, 74, who had been a widow for 20 years. She kept up appearances by getting her hair done every Saturday, and this day was no exception. Wearing a polka dot apron, she invited the group to sit around her kitchen table. Mrs. Bryant wasn't sure at first if she wanted to meet Ski, but she made him feel at ease.

"It seemed like it had been so long that maybe it was fading or something. I don't know how to explain it. But then I thought about it and I was glad to see him, glad to know him," Mrs. Bryant told the reporter.

She had baked a cake, the white frosting topped with an American flag crafted into the shape of a heart. A prayer was said before the cake was cut. Mrs. Bryant warmed up to her company as the afternoon wore on. At one point, she brought out a box of letters her son had written from Vietnam, the memories flooding back as the correspondence was read aloud. Ski produced his photo album to enhance the remembrances. Reluctant at first, Mrs. Bryant agreed to take them when Ski offered them to her. The overriding message was what a good soldier her son had been.

"Your son, he didn't suffer. He was dead immediately from the gunshot wounds," Ski told her.

Mrs. Bryant was thankful that Ski had contacted her after so much time had passed, but she still mourned the loss of her son in that far-off war. "To me, it was just uselessness, and it broke his father's heart. He never got over it," she said. Then Mrs. Bryant asked the question that had been on her mind ever since she first heard the news. "What really happened? Are you allowed to tell?" she asked.

Once more, Ski told the story of how her son volunteered to go out that night, of the dreadful circumstances that turned an ambush into a tragedy, of seeing the muzzle flash and of carrying Ken to the helicopter.

"No one predicted it?" Mrs. Bryant asked.

"Kenny never even knew. Actually, Kenny was sleeping," Ski replied. "Every Christmas I'd think about you and pray for you because I knew it had to be terrible."

In the end, Mrs. Bryant found solace in the fact that other people cared that much about her son. She was glad that Ski had gone to all of the trouble of finding her, and she hoped that he would find healing too.

At one point, Donna went outside and moved around the farm, recalling a recurring dream she would have. She would see Ken near a clearing, and then he would leave.

"I remember it would hurt so bad. Why wouldn't he tell me he was alive?" she said.

Then Donna would awake and cry.

Meeting Ski was like having part of Ken around again. She even wondered if their blood had intermingled when Ski, his hand bleeding from his own wound, carried Ken's bloody body to the chopper.

"It's been really good to be able to talk about it again and to hear stuff like how much he loved me and how much he talked about me. Rick and I really love each other obviously, or he wouldn't be here. But there is something about that first love," Donna told the reporter. "I didn't know that he was actually asleep at the time, so he really didn't know what happened. That's really good, that he didn't suffer. And you know what I thought, when I found out he was sleeping, maybe he was dreaming about me. Maybe that's how he died."

The morning after visiting the grave and the Bryant farm, Donna and Rick stopped by to say goodbye before Ski and his family began the drive back home. There were hugs all around and promises to meet again. A friendship was just beginning.

"It's hard to put into words what it has meant meeting you, because it is a dream come true. It sort of brought closure and gave me peace about it," Donna told Ski.

Ski looked for the greater meaning in the visit, just the way a philosopher would.

"Now I feel like it's just not one experience that happened in a war. It's real life now. For me, it's stronger than the war was. It's almost like we defeated it now. Whatever happened there has been defeated by us all coming together," he said.

A mission had been accomplished. A burden had been lifted. Healing chased away nightmares.

Ski wanted to do the same for David Alicea's family, but for decades, he was never able to locate them or find his friend's grave. He searched cemetery records in New York City, rummaged through newspaper archives for any pertinent articles and reached out to the Latino community for information. Five decades of searching proved futile, but Ski never gave up.

Then on November 21, 2019, a relative of David Alicea made contact with Ski through a third party that the family had found through social media. The breakthrough had come at last. The family had been searching for answers for as long as Ski had been searching for them. As it turned out, David Alicea had been buried in a New York City cemetery, but within a couple of years, his family had the body exhumed and took it to Puerto Rico to be buried in a family plot next to his grandfather. At the time Alicea was killed, his sister was pregnant, and she named her son David to honor her brother. Ski spoke by phone to the man named after his friend.

"I never met my uncle, and part of my heart was empty," David told Ski. "Thank you for being there for my uncle, and thank you for your service."

Ski promised to go to Puerto Rico to visit the grave, just like he had gone to Kentucky to visit Ken Bryant's final resting place. David agreed to accompany him. As plans were discussed, it occurred to Ski that the last time he saw David Alicea was in the morgue at Da Nang. His nephew had electronically sent him a picture of his uncle in uniform. The soldier in the photo looked so young. Forever young.

"I had tears in my eyes when I spoke with David," Ski said. "Chills ran through my body. I told David that, in my heart, that his uncle never died. His memory lived in my heart. At that moment, I felt my soul at peace."

Chapter 42
TWO-WAY VISION

Paratrooper Ernie Garrahan, at the age of 19, had taken part in every major event involving the 82nd Airborne since it left Fort Bragg. Following the engagements Up North and the movement Down South, Garrahan and his company were headquartered at a South Vietnamese Army compound on Highway One about 14 miles northwest of Saigon. There, he got word to lead his squad on a night ambush in the rice paddies just south of the village of Cu Chi, a Viet Cong stronghold that was notorious for a tunnel complex originally dug by insurgents in their fight to evict the French in the First Indochina War.

A native of the Ozone Park neighborhood of the New York City borough of Queens, Garrahan had made the transition from being a Cherry to a veteran leader. Now a sergeant, he and his squad left the compound under cover of darkness to avoid detection by the prying eyes of enemy forces, a common precaution. But before reaching their ambush site, they were surprised by an attack.

With bullets filling the air, Garrahan fired back from the prone position behind a rice paddy dike while directing his men into position. In the inky night, the muzzle flashes from his rifle alerted the enemy to his location. A rocket-propelled grenade exploded, killing Garrahan instantly. A member of Alpha Company of the 1st of the 505, Garrahan was 19 days shy of his 20th birthday and six weeks short of completing his one-year tour in Vietnam. He died on December 31 in the last hours of 1968.

His parents and two sisters back in The World received word of his death but without any details about what had happened. In the cold calculus of war, Ernest Edward Garrahan became the 111th member of the 82nd Airborne to have been killed in Vietnam. For that price in blood, the All Americans had compiled a body count of 1,043, including 267 Viet Cong, and took 17 prisoners during 1968, according to the unit history.

The same night that Garrahan was killed, streaks of fiery crimson flashed through the night, followed by more and more flaring trails until the whole sky appeared to be ablaze. The extraordinary volume of fire seemingly came from everywhere, all of it shooting up from the ground. The shade of red was the kind produced by tracers—magnesium projectiles with an oxidizer that can mark a target or warn a soldier his clip was about to run out of ammo. Tracer rounds burn bright enough to be visible during daylight. In the dark, they look like pyrotechnics.

"The whole damn sky lit up with tracers, long streams of tracers. It was the damnedest fireworks display you ever saw," said Ron Snodgrass.

The shower of tracers began just as the clock struck midnight and rumbled on for a while. The page on the calendar had been imperceptibly flipped to a new month in a fresh year. It was a time to drive on and a time to reflect.

The ancient military superpower of Rome had a religious figure with the ability of doing two things at the same time, especially on the first day of a new month in a new year. A god named Janus, depicted with two faces peering in opposite directions, symbolized the duality of looking to the future and glancing back at the past. In Roman culture, Janus was the mid-point between war and peace or the gateway between barbarism and civilization. The 82nd Airborne's vehicle for taking stock while peering ahead to 1969 was *The All American Magazine*, an illustrated publication produced as a keepsake.

The role of looking back belonged to outgoing commander Bud Bolling. He wrote this farewell message that appeared on the magazine's inner flap: "Every man can take personal pride in what this unit has accomplished during its first year of Vietnam duty. After deploying 10,000 miles, engaging and defeating North Vietnamese forces west of Hue, completely reorganizing and moving 400 miles south to defend Saigon, the All Americans have begun a major pacification effort in this area. This could not have been achieved without the aggressiveness, imagination and will to win of the individual soldier. I regret that I must leave, but I am certain your future accomplishments will exceed those of the past. I will always consider myself part of the brigade, for serving with the All Americans has provided me the finest years of my military career. All the way, and Godspeed."

Gazing ahead was the new commander, Brigadier General George W. Dickerson. His message was: "You have defeated the enemy at every turn in battles with your successful night operations and numerous patrols. You have completely confused the local guerrillas. You have made it difficult for them to recruit, propagandize, tax and terrorize the people in the hamlets. You have worked effectively with regional and popular forces enforcing security and defeating the enemy. Villagers now work and live in a safety they have not enjoyed for years. But while we're combating the enemy, let's remember that we are the men of the All American Brigade and just what that means. We are operating in a densely populated area, in daily contact with the Vietnamese people. To the ARVN soldier with whom you go out on patrol, to the housewife in the marketplace, to the child who pesters you for candy, you are America. By what you do, by how you act, America is judged in the eyes of the Vietnamese. Let's behave toward these people in a way that will make the notion of 'the ugly American' nothing but an empty, worn out idea; and let's continue to soldier so well that in the years to come we can be proud not only of the job we came here to do, but also of the fact that we did it better than anybody else!"

The war Down South, with a few notable exceptions on big operations, was waged against small bands of guerrillas and sympathizers living stealthily among the local population. The foe could be the villager who farmed by day and fought by night to support the shadow government of the National Liberation Front. Dickerson saw the mission as being more akin to that faced by security police than troops fighting along an established line against massed formations. If the enemy could be found and fixed, the superior mobility and fire power of the American military usually insured his destruction. But he had to be found first. Dickerson thought of Vietnam as being an intelligence war.

Meanwhile, the narrative in the 82nd Airborne magazine was written by Captain St. Elmo P. (Step) Tyner, who had shaken Lyndon Johnson's hand before departing for Vietnam and who had been wounded by a rocket explosion at the Battle of the Lazy W in which John Plunkard was killed. Now assigned to staff duties after recovering from his wounds, Tyner had experienced war first-hand from the point of view of the grunts. He shared this insight: "The solider loves war as little as any man, and the men of the brigade had seen war at its dirtiest…in Vietnam."

Particular attention was paid to the unique role of the 82nd Airborne in being able to respond to trouble, and about how the unit had been transformed into a separate light infantry brigade, or Fire Brigade.

"Sadly, for many, we lost our airborne status," the text said. "Despite the large number of non-airborne replacements we received, the old spirit continued to be very much in evidence. The new men proved themselves to be airborne in all but the strictest technical sense, displaying a particular brand of aggressiveness and the same esprit that characterized division troopers in the trenches of France and the flak-filled skies of Italy."

It continued: "We like to think that we have done more with less than any other unit in Vietnam, and it's a contention that would be hard to deny in terms of statistics…We have been fried and frozen. We've trembled with fever and shaken with fatigue. We've breathed in pounds of dry, red dust, and choked on brackish paddy water. We've been persecuted by mosquito and leech. There have been times when we would have traded our (return date) for a can of warm beer or a dry smoke. We've gone without sleep, dry clothes and hot food. Many of us have attained the heights of heroic accomplishment… most of us have experienced pain, fear and bitter despair…some of us have died. But all have displayed the quieter courage in accomplishing impossible tasks in the presence of a crafty enemy and a hostile climate. All of us have added to the honor of our brigade. And we can rest easy, for the crew that takes our places is every bit as good as we think we are. When we rotate, we will leave behind a fighting unit that we helped develop, one that we will always proudly associate ourselves with. We have been there, All The Way."

The magazine cover was designed by Private First Class John Chuldenko, who grew up in the tough western Pennsylvania steel town of Midland, about an hour's drive from Pittsburgh. The son of a Serbian father and a Russian mother, he had won a national award for high school artistry given out by *Scholastic Magazine*. His plans for a career as a commercial illustrator, however, were put on hold when he was drafted into the Army in 1968. With a military occupation in reconnaissance, he was sent to Vietnam and assigned to the 82nd Airborne.

"I never jumped out of any damn plane. I'm not qualified to jump," Chuldenko said at the conclusion of Proficiency Training.

"Don't worry about it. Nobody's jumping in Vietnam," he was told.

At first, Chuldenko served in the cavalry troop, conducting ambushes, clearing roads of mines, patrolling and acting as a scout in his armored personnel carrier. A stroke of good luck brought him in from the field to the base camp where the public affairs unit was quartered.

"I got a taste of everything in Nam—the heat, the snakes, the bugs. Unfortunately, death was part of it too," Chuldenko said. "One morning, I just came off ambush. It wasn't dawn yet, so you could barely see. I heard the lieutenant's voice say, 'Can anybody draw?' And I answered, 'Yes, I have a background in drawing.' The next thing you know I was producing the magazine."

For illustrations, Chuldenko selected a cross-section of graphics and photographs depicting the brigade in action. He also included a number of images of Vietnamese villagers receiving assistance from the All Americans during the program called pacification. Even at this stage of the war, the American military was still trying to persuade the locals to build a nation that was non-communist.

"I didn't want it to look like we were just shooting up the whole place. I told my sergeant, 'Look, we're here to help these people. I want the magazine to go in that direction,' " Chuldenko said.

Indeed, villagers received medical and dental care from the brigade's Civil Affairs Unit. As one example, the locals were inoculated against the bubonic plague, a medieval scourge spread by the fleas of rats but one that still existed in this Third World country.

Also, part of the pacification effort, which was aimed at eliminating Viet Cong presence and trying to instill confidence in the central government, was the building of a telephone system. In addition, television sets were distributed. Villagers may not have had indoor plumbing, but they could watch the news programs produced in Saigon.

Chuldenko also created another piece of 82nd Airborne history. A Golden Brigade Association had already been formed in Vietnam, and Chuldenko advanced the idea of a distinctive coin to be given to everyone who served in the unit. The coin is a physical symbol that serves the same kind of purpose as a secret handshake. It identifies the holder as having been with the Golden Brigade in Vietnam.

"We were sitting around bullshitting one day. The thought was, that after all this, wouldn't it be neat to have something all the troops can carry around, something to give us an identity," Chuldenko said. "I was proud of being part of the 82nd. That coin unites us. We went through a difficult time. People lost their lives."

Fifty years after the first coins were stamped, Chuldenko keeps one on his person at all times. He also has one on his mantel, one in the bedroom and one in his car. Through the passing of the years, he has separated the sacrifice of the warriors from the policies of the war.

"We were there to kick ass. We'd fight on some ground, then we'd leave, and the enemy would move back in again. In a war, you either kick ass or get out of Dodge. I was married when I went, but the letters from home started becoming less frequent and I got divorced when I got back. This country frowned on me when I got back too. I remember being in an airport terminal and was interacting with a little child. The mother went crazy and told the child to stay away from me, like I had leprosy or something. Another guy tried to cuss me out. You go over there and do you job, and then when you come back, you get treated like shit. You have choices. I could give up or keep fighting and do the best I can. That's what I chose to do, to make the best of life. I went out of my way to make things better. I didn't talk about Nam. I got remarried and have two kids, and I made a career of being a commercial illustrator. I thank God I'm alive. I have a lot to be grateful for."

Chuldenko added: "We shouldn't have been there. Our government killed 58,000 of us for nothing."

Meanwhile, New Year's Day was the day Sergeant Rick Dalton was wounded and knocked out of the war when his own unit mistakenly fired on him. It began when Dalton and his squad, accompanied by a lieutenant, were picked up by helicopter and inserted into a landing zone in the general vicinity of the Hoc Mon Canal. Dalton found an officer's map showing eight ambush locations along the road he and his men were to march, and he turned it in. His dinner that day was the kind of freeze-dried rations the long range recon units had introduced as an improvement over canned food—chili with meat sauce, made edible by adding water.

"We were supposed to go two klicks and set up, but we walked from 4 p.m. to 8 p.m. along a road overgrown with brush. I tried to tell the lieutenant we were walking too far. He pointed to a tree line up ahead and said we'd set up our ambush there. Mike Tolbert was walking point all that time, so I told him to take a break and take the slack. I took over the point from then on," Dalton said. "I had seen that map. I knew there were more ambushes out there. I knew we were going to run into our own people if we kept walking."

Up ahead was a five-foot wide crater in the road, most likely made by a mortar. Because the VC commonly placed booby traps on the edges of such craters, Dalton decided to walk straight on through. Then a blast went off. Dalton was hit below the waist. Although both of his legs were broken in three places, he somehow remained upright.

"Then I got shot. Bullets don't whiz. They break the sound barrier as they go by. They were snapping like the sound of Rice Krispies," Dalton said. "I somehow flung myself to the side into a rice paddy. I landed with the barrel of my M-16 down in the mud, so it was jammed. I figured everybody else in the squad got killed, and I'm out there all by myself. I carried four grenades and was set to throw three. The fourth I would keep for myself. I wasn't going to let Charlie cut me to pieces."

The next thing he heard was an American voice saying, "Halt! Who goes there?"

Anger flared. Dalton had been hit by the explosion of a claymore detonated by a different squad in the same company. He wasn't supposed to be near that location, and in the gloaming, he had been mistaken for an enemy soldier.

"I don't remember hearing any sound. It felt like somebody slammed a door that impacted every part of the front of my body. I'm 6 feet tall and weigh 205 pounds wearing a steel pot helmet with a rucksack, and how somebody can mistake that for a VC, I'll never know. It was dark. I yelled for a medic. They told me to keep my voice down, but my yelling for a medic is not going to make it any more dangerous after an explosion just went off. The medic came up with the battalion chaplain. Every other word the medic said was mother- this and mother- that. I told him to calm down, but the medic says, 'Oh, don't worry. The chaplain's heard it all before.' Then the chaplain says, 'Don't worry, son, all your parts are still there.' By the time they got there, I had stopped bleeding," Dalton said.

As the medevac chopper was being summoned, Dalton was placed on a poncho. He was in shock and had been given a shot of morphine to dull the pain. Four comrades each grabbed a corner to carry him across the rice paddy, but each one seemed to be pulling in a different direction.

"I said, 'Stop, goddamn it. Put me down. Everybody take a breath. Now move out with your left foot forward.' I didn't count cadence, but I got them working together," Dalton said. "I had so many pellets in me they couldn't count them all."

Dalton was whisked to a hospital at Tan Son Nhut for what he called the five most terrifying days of his life. He threw up that chili he ate before going on that patrol. Although he liked chili, it took him about 10 years before he could eat it again.

"They had Vietnamese construction crews working in and out of the hospital. When you're 21 years old and all shot up, they looked like candidates to be Viet Cong. I reached for my M-16 and didn't have it," Dalton said.

Later, he was transferred to a hospital in Japan.

"It's a miracle I lived. I still got a pellet in my right ankle from that claymore," Dalton.

The worst part for him that he was away from Alpha Company of the 2nd of the 505 when it got into a big fight three weeks later.

Chapter 43
DEATH FROM ABOVE

At the fire base where the brigade's artillery unit was headquartered, troops worked 12-hour shifts. Those on duty monitored the radios to relay fire missions or humped shells to the fire pits where the cannons thundered. Off-duty troops rested, as in the case of Wayne Henry Fischer and Ronald Lewis Morris. Fischer, 21, was a radio teletype operator from Summit, Illinois, and Morris, three weeks shy of his 21st birthday, was a field wireman from Louisa, Virginia. Both were draftees. Both had the pay grade of corporal. Both of them were assigned to the 82nd Airborne during the fighting Up North and were now involved in the defense of Saigon. Their home away from home was Fire Base Copperhead, where artillery was on call whenever it was needed, providing a steel umbrella for friendly troops while raining down death and destruction on the bad guys.

Copperhead, named for a venomous snake that delivered a nasty bite, had grown into a fairly developed camp. Officers and enlisted men were quartered in separate tents, and those stationed there had the relative comfort of a canvas roof over their heads. They slept on cots instead of the ground. A battalion aid station had been built. On the base perimeter, sentries provided 24-hour security.

Late in the afternoon of January 7, Fischer and Morris were in the enlisted man's area, which was adjacent to where the officers bunked. A Vietnamese woman performed housecleaning chores for the officers, earning money to feed her family by serving as a maid.

Less than five miles to the south of Copperhead was the bustling Tan Son Nhut Air Base, which handled military as well as civilian air traffic. The base had undergone an amazing transformation since its creation. Begun as an unpaved strip built by the French in the 1920s, Tan Son Nhut became a transport base for the Japanese in World War II and later as a point of entry for French forces in the First Indochina War. It had been expanded and improved by the Americans in 1961, and it was the headquarters for the South Vietnamese officers who overthrew President Ngo Dihn Diem in the 1963 coup. During the Tet Offensive, Tan Son Nhut was a major target because its warplanes delivered incredible firepower. Like the artillery at Copperhead, the U.S. Air Force was on call 24 hours a day to bomb targets or to provide close air support for the grunts.

On the afternoon of January 7, an F-4 Phantom roared down the runway and lifted into the sky, its two-man crew on its way to a bombing mission. A supersonic interceptor and fighter-bomber, the Phantom was a workhorse equipped with after-burners for the twin engines attached to its fuselage. Originally developed for the Navy, the Phantom was a triumph of thrust over aerodynamics. Its ungainly appearance earned it the nickname the Flying Brick, but it was also called the world's largest distributor of MiG parts because of its air-to-air successes.

Something went terribly wrong just after takeoff. A fire broke out aboard the Phantom, and its crew put it on a path toward open ground to the West before ejecting safely. The structural integrity of the plane had been compromised, however. The tail section broke off in flight and tumbled without warning toward Copperhead.

"I saw that plane on fire. Something told me I had better look for cover," said James (Doc) Slavin, who was assigned to the medical aid station.

Herb Hassel, a solider with the pay grade of corporal, knew something was wrong because of what his ears told him.

"We heard the whine of a jet, but instead of hearing it pass, it got louder and louder. Then I knew we were going to get hit, and I dove for the ground," Hassell was quoted as saying in the Pacific Paraglide.

The flaming chunk of debris crashed into the officers' area near the camp perimeter. Fire engulfed the barracks where the Vietnamese woman was busy tidying up the place. Flames quickly spread to where Fischer and Morris spent their off-duty hours. Both were killed. So was the Vietnamese maid.

Flames also threatened the battalion aid station, and wounded men were evacuated to a central point. Medical supplies were also moved away from the fire. In the chaos and confusion, those stationed at Copperhead grabbed fire extinguishers to douse the flames. Soldiers from all over the base rushed to help, and a bucket brigade was quickly formed. Answering an emergency call, a South Vietnamese unit from the nearby Quang Trung Training Center raced toward the conflagration in fire trucks. Working side by side with their American allies, they managed to minimize the damage.

The fire burned for 90 minutes. If not for quick thinking and fast reaction, the incident could have been a lot worse. In addition to the three dead, one soldier was injured badly enough to require evacuation by helicopter to a larger medical facility. The episode underscored the grim reality that there was no safe place in Vietnam. According to Murphy's Laws of Combat, anything you do in a combat zone can get you killed, including doing nothing.

Two days later, after most of the debris had been cleared away, the 2nd Battalion of the 321st Field Artillery Regiment (Motto: Don't Tread On Me) held a memorial service for its fallen comrades. Separately, all the officers who lived where the Vietnamese woman had perished attended her funeral and expressed their sympathy to her family.

Back in The World, the families of Fischer, who was white, and Morris, who was black, received official notification that their loved ones had been killed. Neither one had left the fire base or left the ground, but the military informed the families that they had been killed in a fixed wing air crash. Technically, the explanation was correct. The reality was far different. They died when the flaming debris of a fighter jet crashed into the spot where they were off duty.

Fischer was buried at Fairmount Cemetery in Willow Springs, Illinois. Morris was buried at the Wayland Baptist Church Cemetery in Trevillians, Virginia, site of the largest all-cavalry battle of the Civil War. Both are together on Panel 35 West of The Wall.

Chapter 44
DEATH DOWN BELOW

Carl Gulas reported for duty at Fire Base All American and was taken to meet his company commander. A native of Cleveland, Ohio, Gulas volunteered to join the Army, fully aware he was destined for Vietnam to fight his generation's war. The son of a World War II veteran who earned his Combat Infantryman's Badge serving in the U.S. Army 96th Infantry Division, Gulas went through boot camp at Fort Knox and received jungle training at Tigerland. "I just didn't want to miss out. I wanted a CIB too," he said.

Then Captain James Callahan introduced him to the realities of war.

"The first time I met him, he had his feet up on a table inside a tent," Gulas said. "He slid a Polaroid picture across the desk of a dead Viet Cong with his guts hanging out. Captain Callahan said, 'Fuck up, and you won't look any different than this guy. You're in the big leagues now.' It was like a punch in the stomach for me. But Callahan's primary job was to keep as many of us alive as he could. He was my mentor. This guy was the real deal. This is the kind of guy they make movies about."

Indeed, Callahan initiated all the soldiers in the Delta Dragons of the 1st of the 505 with either a photograph or the body of a dead enemy combatant.

"I wanted to be sure the new guys understood this wasn't Hollywood or TV land, and that when the shooting stopped, the extras weren't going to just get back up and go for a coffee and a Danish. This was real. One minute you're a living, breathing human being with hopes and dreams, the next you're just so many kilos of rapidly cooling dead meat. The difference was training, discipline and luck," said Callahan.

"What I truly respected in the kids I commanded was that most of them were there simply because life dealt them that hand. Unlike me, they did not ask for Nam, but they got it while their middle class contemporaries found one way or another to skip out. I owed it to those kids to see that as many of them as possible made it home in one piece or another. I loved every one of them. Still do," he added.

Then 29, Callahan was on the third of his four tours of duty in Indochina when he became commander of a rifle company in the 82nd Airborne. Fifty years later, he was a grandfather living in the French countryside as a retired lieutenant colonel and foreign service operative. In an unpublished memoir, Callahan preserved what Vietnam was like in Delta Company, including the remarkable events leading up to and including January 8, 1969, when the war was waged in underground tunnels.

Like Gulas, Callahan had a Cleveland connection. Although he was born Irish tough in South Boston, Callahan had spent his formative years in that gritty industrial city on the shores of Lake Erie. Undersized but scrappy, Callahan had above average smarts, so much so that he earned a scholarship to a private high school in Cleveland. He parlayed that into another scholarship to Georgetown University, where he graduated from the school of foreign service. With a college degree in hand, he was offered a commission in the U.S. Army and volunteered for Special Forces. Having undergone the tough training needed to earn his Green Beret, he then volunteered for Vietnam.

On his first tour in 1965, Callahan was an advisor to a South Vietnamese Army battalion. As an American, he had a radio that could call in U.S. attack jets or summon a helicopter for the wounded. Callahan described that experience as "a myriad of small actions, death in small doses, brother on brother, your counterpart a Vietnamese captain who had already spent 20 years fighting the Communists." That captain, whose name was Diyen, led the 3rd Battalion of the 51st Independent Infantry Regiment of the Army of the Republic of Vietnam. Diyen was killed in the war.

On his second tour, Callahan commanded a Special Forces detachment working with a tribe of Montagnards, or the Mountain People, who resisted communist ideology to maintain their own self-sufficient lives in the rain forest along the border with Laos. Those partisans taught him to shed the veneer of civilization and revert to being a hunter-gatherer in the image of the earliest humans.

"From time immemorial, survival in the jungle has always been a matter of reverting to animal instinct. You are a hunter, but never forget, you are also the hunted," Callahan said.

Ingrained into Callahan were the responsibilities of his unique assignment. "When a tribal partisan was killed, you carried his savaged body the last five yards to place it in the arms of his mother. Your duty as *le chef* (the chief). If not, the tribe lost respect for you, for the resistance and for the United States of America which you represented," Callahan noted.

Conversant in French and able to speak Vietnamese, Callahan was a staff officer when first assigned to the 82nd Airborne, but a job at headquarters is a bad fit for a man who by one friend's reckoning should be frozen in a cryogenic chamber and unthawed only in time of war. Callahan ruffled some feathers when, in enforcing the rules, he filed a legal action under the Uniform Code of Military Justice against a soldier who went into Saigon without authorization. That soldier happened to be Bud Bolling's jeep driver. Not long after, the position of company commander of the Delta Dragons came open, and Callahan became responsible for the 120 or so lives of the Delta Dragons.

"By this time, I was more Vietnamese than American. I must have seemed like a strange bird to those 19-year-olds in the ranks," Callahan said. "Together, officers and NCOs must earn the respect of their men. If they succeed, the men themselves will create that unique bond which is the brotherhood of arms. Service, sacrifice and suffering are life's norm for a professional officer. He must set the example, to include, if necessary, showing the men how to die well."

If he stood out in a crowd, it was because he was smaller than most soldiers. Yet the heart of a lion can beat inside a tenacious terrier.

"Size is relative," wrote Callahan. "In peacetime, it matters. You're my size, best avoid a bar room brawl with a guy who plays rugby. On the battlefield, it's different. God made man, but Sam Colt made all men equal. You have to master the fear of death, a fear present in every man, whether he knows it or not, and do so before it jumps out in front of you for the first time. After that, it's a return to basics. Bring a gun to a knife fight. Bring a long gun to a gun fight. Place your shots. Do that, keep your wits about you, (which is) the hardest part, and you'll be OK. Unless, of course, Lady Luck makes an appearance. But then, why worry? The lady will do whatever the lady wants, one way or the other, and nothing you do will change the fact."

Fully aware that an Airborne battalion was historically made of up of three companies, Callahan surmised that the regular line units kicked in all their presumed misfits to form what he called the "bastard company" known as the Delta Dragons. This was the company created Up North on July 29 at Col Co Beach, the unit comprised of Stanley Dodson, Felix Conde, Les Hayes, Pete Watkins and Ron Vitale, et al. Whatever their origins, Callahan noted the company possessed an Airborne spirit created by the core of officers and sergeants who remained from the original deployment. By Callahan's reckoning, Delta had the highest number of enemy killed versus the lowest number of friendly losses of any unit in the Golden Brigade.

"It retained sufficient Airborne cadre to ensure a degree of discipline and dedication down through the ranks. It is such qualities, far more than any listing of structure and equipment, that creates the vital aspect by which good units surpass themselves in battles. It got the job done, which was killing, while keeping as many of its men alive as the mission allowed, the cruel ratio by which combat units are judged," Callahan noted.

Fire Base All American was just outside the gates of Saigon, which offered every temptation of the flesh a 19-year-old male could fantasize about. Callahan kept his troops in the field and away from temptation. The realities of an infantryman's homeless existence were soon mastered—no roof, no toilet, no bath, no heating or air conditioning, no change of clothes, and most of the time, no hot meals, just what can be gobbled cold from a can, all the while staying on the lookout for adversaries and booby traps.

Under Callahan, Delta's mission was simple—find the enemy and kill him. Standard procedure was to place three of his four platoons out on operations, each platoon fielding multiple squads of five or so men waiting silently in the dark to ambush forces that moved at night. The remaining platoon was positioned at Callahan's company command post as a reaction force in case of contact.

"We had no problem with drunks, drugs or fragging," Callahan said. "We stayed grounded in the reality of our own deadly bubble."

One thing Callahan brought with him from Special Forces was his choice of headgear, especially for night work. Callahan believed in the advantages of the cloth boonie hat over the steel pot helmet.

"There is a reason why special operations forces often go without a helmet. It's a metal pot on your head that makes noise brushing against vegetation or other objects, endangering stealth. Worse, it is a metal sounding board that causes incoming sound to reverberate, seriously complicating the ear's ability to quickly identify directional source. If you are hunting other lethal game, those two defects of the helmet could prove fatal. Need protection? Wear a helmet. Want to go hunting other armed men over difficult terrain, or at close quarters, or at night? Calculate the additional risk the helmet represents versus the protection it offers. There is no simple answer," Callahan said.

An unorthodox war called for unorthodox strategies. Callahan made sure his troops never stayed in one place too long while ceding nothing to the forces operating against him.

"Charlie always knew our daylight movements. How could he not? He had passive but observant agents through the countryside. Accordingly, I bedded the company down through the day, changing the laager site regularly, then slipped a dozen heavily armed small ambush teams out at dusk, blanketing a zone. The key was in keeping the ambush teams well-armed but still small enough to escape detection as they moved into position, then ensuring everybody stayed in communication. Once the kids got the hang of it, we began to clean up. Charlie thought he owned the night. He didn't expect to meet any Americans when out and about tripping through the countryside after dark. It cost him dearly," Callahan noted.

On one particular night, an ambush team was en route to a new position, moving down the dike of a rice paddy in the dark, when it ran headlong into a group of enemy coming the other way. Callahan said the enemy moved fast and exercised little caution, almost as if they were running late to an appointment. Delta's command staff figured later that they had missed a turn or something and were likely behind schedule. Only a few more hours remained before first light, not much time to cover the remaining distance to the outskirts of Saigon, if that was their objective. The result was what the military refers to as a meeting engagement.

"We came out on top. My guys were better trained, better disciplined, and finally quicker. We opened up first, cutting down the Viet's lead element before the rest fled. The fact that my men were wearing bush hats, thus giving them a different outline in the star-lit night than that of a standard helmeted American troop, may have temporarily confused the Viets. The timing was extremely close. Check the wound on the hand of their point man, the individual with the bandaged leg, and the condition of the magazine in the M-16 rifle he was carrying. He was cut down the very second he was about to open fire," Callahan noted.

The dead man's right arm bore a tattoo that said "Killer of Americans." Given that his backup sidearm was an American .45 caliber handgun, he might well have been, but not on this night. The All Americans killed him.

Another VC, armed with an officer's Chinese-made Makarov pistol, was seriously wounded. Callahan radioed for a medical helicopter to evacuate him. Les Hayes overheard the captain's call and said it was an authentic request.

"He called in a medevac for a wounded VC, and he was told on the other end that they didn't take wounded gooks. So, he called in a medevac for a wounded American," Hayes recalled. "He cried for that man to live. (The wounded man) was fighting for a cause he believed in. He was the enemy, but I didn't hate them. I knew that was somebody's son."

The VC died within an hour. Callahan tried to explain his empathy for the bleeding man.

"Even before intelligence confirmed he was a senior officer from the documents he was carrying, I had seen he was different. Older, more distinguished looking than the average ambush kill. He had the ascetic, disciplined look of a hardened field officer. I wanted him to live. Instead, he died next to me in the still dark night at an impromptu landing zone on Highway One as we were waiting for a dust-off to get him to hospital. Strangely, I felt closer to him than to the people back home. He went down in a hail of American automatic weapons fire, but still, whatever else he was, he was one of us. One prepared to accept the risk inherent in his mission. One who had an objective beyond his own self-interest. One of the committed. He killed, we killed, but in a sense, we were all one of a kind, and you could not understand us unless you too had played the killing game," Callahan noted.

One consequence of the ambush was the taking of a prisoner who would have a big impact on Delta Company. The prisoner had been recruited by the district military leader who was tattooed with the words Killer of Americans. Captain Callahan coaxed the prisoner to work for the Americans.

"I'd questioned enough die-hard Viet Cong to see immediately that he was just a peasant kid who wanted to ensure he ended up on the winning side. I respected his initiative and understood his reasoning. The war was a huge burden on the average Vietnamese, and for the simple folk, what mattered was not this or that side, but family and ancestors," Callahan noted.

Callahan handed the defector an M-16 rifle to replace his communist-made weapon and promptly convinced him to become the captain's shadow. The defector served as bodyguard, interpreter and reader of any signs that indicated "something is wrong here." He also helped the Americans know who might be friend or foe.

"No way for an American to tell a good guy from a bad guy in daylight. Checking IDs was a joke. Any Charlie worth his salt had good papers, often as not valid ones depending on the level of local corruption," Callahan noted.

Then came the events of January 8, initiated by a piece of info provided by the battalion intelligence officer. Callahan said the officer came from a family of New York City cops and, like him, was Irish. The officer cultivated sources, and not necessarily among the right people, but battalion didn't put much credence into what he had learned. Undeterred, the intelligence officer made an urgent radio call to Callahan. A meeting of local Viet Cong leaders at such and such a location was planned.

"At some point, all your battle contacts begun to run into each other. The only ones that stick with you forever are the ones where you lost one of your own," Callahan said. "In the infantry, there is no free lunch. Each loss is a lesson to be learned. If you survive, you get good."

At the time, Delta Company was in its usual ambush configuration in an area of scrub brush just off Highway One, 15 miles northwest of Saigon and just south of Cu Chi. The company had been in the field for two weeks and was due to be extracted that morning. But when the tip was received about a possible Viet Cong meeting at dawn, plans changed. Callahan wasn't going to ignore this tip just to keep an administrative schedule.

The squad closest to the location was led by Staff Sergeant Billy Smith, who was instructed to swing by the site after he pulled up his ambush at first light. Bingo! The info was solid. Smith and his men surprised the Viet Cong and opened fire. Offering little resistance, the VC ran for their lives and disappeared into a nearby hole. Without hesitating, Sergeant Smith and one of his squad mates pursued them underground.

When Captain Callahan arrived at the location 15 minutes later, the squad mate had surfaced but Smith was still down below. The unfolding events were one more thing that made Vietnam unlike any other war.

"Battalion is calling, wanting to know where the hell we are and when to expect us as the extraction site. I tell them the plan for the day has changed, I'm engaged at such and such location, then kiss them off and drop down the hole with the squad mate. Nothing else for it. I can't ask anyone else to go down there when it was my decision to launch this game in the first place," Callahan wrote.

The surface war had its own rigors, with fighting taking place everywhere from rice paddies to royal tombs to rain forests. The tunnels took the war to a darker place. Like Alice in Wonderland entering a rabbit hole, a special breed of volunteers called tunnel rats ventured into the surreal realm of the underworld, relying on touch, sound, smell and pure guts to guide them.

Although tunnels were everywhere in Vietnam, the immense network at Cu Chi was particularly notorious. Insurgents began digging by hand through the red laterite clay in 1945 to foil French forces intent on again making Vietnam their colony. If intruders ventured into the area, the tunnel-dwellers would avoid contact by disappearing into the maze, where they stored food, weapons and ammo. On the other hand, they could surface when least expected to launch hit-and-run attacks. In 1966 and 1967, the American Army had conducted a couple of big operations at Cu Chi, one involving 30,000 men, but never could eliminate the tunnel threat. Carpet bombing of the surface was as ineffective as trying to blow them up or burn them out.

Some tunnels were so long that enemy troops could crawl all the way to Saigon, and the enemy had used the Cu Chi tunnels as a staging area before the Tet Offensive. Tunnel entrances were so well concealed that a soldier could be standing next to one and never know it was there. Passageways almost never ran in a straight line, the twists and turns and drops providing a way of foiling any pursuers. Booby traps, such as pits of punji sticks coated with animal urine, added a layer of defense. The tunnels were also home to pests such as biting ants, venomous centipedes, scorpions, snakes and spiders. With concealed ventilation holes providing air, underground cities flourished. Deep below the surface were war rooms, sleeping quarters, kitchens, hospitals and ammo dumps.

The confined space of a tunnel offered no room to maneuver. A tunnel rat could only inch forward holding a handgun and a flashlight, but a flashlight could also give away one's position and the noise accompanying the firing of a weapon assaulted the ears. A tunnel rat's only lifeline was the rope tied to one of his ankles. If he tugged on the rope, comrades knew to drag him out.

Callahan gave this account about going in after Billy Smith: "I'm scared shitless. It's narrow, pitch black, and practically airless down there. I've got a .45 and a flashlight and I'm inching my way forward in the dark. If I use the flashlight, I light myself up. If I have to use the .45, I may hit what's in front of me, but I'll likely blow out my ear drums at the same time. Plus, presumably, my missing sergeant is somewhere in front of us. I pray there will be no side tunnels to confuse the issue or permit a Viet to slip in behind us. If something happens, I have no Plan B. I have no contact with the surface. I'm living my worst nightmare. As a kid, I cried out in fear in the darkened movie theater throughout the film sequence where Tom Sawyer was lost in the caves. I'm only doing marginally better at the moment. Then I sense it. There is an object just up ahead. I inch further forward, the .45 cocked and my thumb on the safety. The object isn't moving. In the narrow confines of the tunnel, my arms are extended anyway, helping me to scrabble forward. I reach out and touch the obstruction. Boots! G.I. jungle boots. I use the flashlight and confirm that I have found my sergeant. At least, I have found a body wearing a G.I. issue field uniform. No sound from him. I can't get a response. Wounded, dead, temporarily asphyxiated? I try pulling him backward, but even as skinny as I am, my shoulders are too wide for the tunnel width. I can't get any traction. In fact, I'm stuck. Maybe that's what happened to my sergeant as well. The tunnel has narrowed down at this point, and I am wedged in and immobilized. It a tough shit G.I. situation. Nobody said the Viet Cong were stupid. They built these tunnels for the average Viet, not for some big boned American. I'm physically and emotionally drained, running strictly on adrenaline, ready to lose it. No sense crying out, however.

I'd just use up what little oxygen was left in the fetid air. The survival instinct kicks in. A lot of gasping and scraping of shins, and I extract myself. I tell the sergeant, in the event he can hear, that help will be there soon, and begin inching my way backward, doing everything by feel since I am unable to turn around. I'm gasping for every breath of oxygen I can manage. When I'm finally back out, I brief the situation to the trapped sergeant's anxious squad and have no problems getting a relief crew, to include my Viet scout, to go down and pull out their fellow soldier. The next hour or so is a bit of a blur. I was going through some kind of decompression. We got our man out, that I know, but until these memoirs I couldn't have told you his condition. My man died."

Sergeant Billy Eugene Smith, a draftee who had begun his tour in Vietnam on June 28, was killed inside a tunnel, shot through the head. A graduate of Baker High School in Columbus, Georgia, Smith was brought home in an aluminum transfer case to be buried at Parkhill Cemetery in his hometown. Forty-six years after his death, his sister Donna left this online tribute to her hero: "I truly miss you, Billy. I remember all the times you babysat us. Will never forget you. I know you are in heaven with Mom and Dad. I know Mom is at peace with you. Love you forever."

The operation continued at the tunnel site.

"Meanwhile, battalion is in an uproar," Callahan wrote. "I eventually talk to the battalion commander direct. He is torn between court-martialing me for not respecting the extraction schedule and congratulating me for cornering some of the enemy. To his credit, he finally goes with the latter option. We're into the afternoon by this time, and I am determined to get as much back on the investment of my sergeant as possible. I ask for smoke generators and explosives. The material arrives late afternoon. We begin pumping smoke into the tunnel complex, all the while staying spread out to spot the tell-tale smoke plumes indicating an air hole or another tunnel opening. A half hour or so of this, and sure enough, out pops a Viet from an opening. Just one. It's a beginning. Night is coming on by now, so I convince battalion to leave the guy with us until morning. He is mute but doesn't look too hard core to me. With my Vietnamese bodyguard, I squat down and we have a talk. It's all psycho-drama on my part, but I have learned this bit from Vietnamese past masters in the art. I explain to the young man, in a gentle but assured tone, that the war is over for him, that it is time he thinks of his family—past, present and future—and of his eventual grave site. That I will give him until dawn to reflect. At dawn, I will ask him to aid us in convincing any of his compatriots still underground to surface. If he accepts to do so, he and they will live. If not, I will execute him and will put his remains into an unmarked grave. He will be forever lost to his family. No one will be able to honor his grave. This is all total bluff, but between Viet Cong propaganda concerning the fierceness of Americans, and with the assistance of my bodyguard, we make a fearfully believable pitch. I then leave him in isolation through the night to communicate with his ancestors. Come morning, he thinks of his family, and with a hand-held loudspeaker at various tunnel openings we have located, exhorts his compatriots to surrender. Some dozen of them do so.

For those that don't, it's a few brief firefights in which my Viet scouts demonstrate exemplary courage before we place explosives and blow the tunnels. In addition to a significant weapons haul, to include light machine guns and RPGs, we also garner a couple of sacks of Vietnamese documents. The whole operation is wrapped up by mid-morning without the injury or loss or a single additional G.I. We check out the captured weapons and send the dozen Viets and the documents back to battalion. It's an intelligence bonanza. The intel officer is vindicated. Good on him. He deserved every bit of credit that came his way. Like I said, in all my years in Indochina, I never saw another American with sufficient moxie to pick up local intelligence."

In retrospect, Callahan said Smith's actions probably saved the lives of a number of his fellow soldiers, given the significant loss of Viet Cong operatives, plus the documents, weapons and explosives retrieved from the tunnel. When weapons were stacked and inspected, Delta troopers kept the Chinese or Soviet bloc pistols for themselves.

"Then we'd select the best of the rest to use as trading material with the rear echelon for better chow, like steaks, or for non-regulation operational field necessities, such as shotguns. None would henceforth be used to kill American troops, a small but important recompense for the sergeant who gave his life," Callahan noted.

The captain also wrote this postscript: "Two weeks later, the company was running night ambushes along a waterway. Sometime around midnight a sampan comes gliding down the river. It pulls abreast of one of our ambush sites and the three-man ambush team lights it up with an M-60 machine gun and close range shotgun blasts. One thoroughly holed sampan and two KIA. More interesting, a document bag. The KIA were couriers. Among the documents translated, there is an account detailing the destruction south of Cu Chi two weeks previously of a local Viet Cong command element captured or killed at the time they were holding a regional meeting. The blow is attributed to an American Special Forces Commando Unit. We all get a good laugh out of the report. Nothing like getting your press clippings directly from the enemy."

The story was remarkable enough to make it into the 82nd Airborne's in-house newsletter. Years later, the publication occupied a spot in Callahan's footlocker of personal military effects.

Cu Chi is now a tourist destination and a place of pilgrimage for Vietnamese school children and Communist Party bigwigs. At a welcome center, a video documents what the tunnel complex is like. Those with claustrophobia are advised not to underground for a tour. Maps and displays describe an underground wonder that existed as a parallel city.

Troopers from the 82nd Airborne ventured so often into the subterranean world that a certificate of distinction for the tunnel rats was created. It was presented to those who survived their adventures below ground and did combat with "snakes, rats, bats, bugs and other vermin to perform his mission." The certificate wryly came with the wish that may the tunnel rat "wear his layers of Republic of Vietnam dirt proudly, and may he never suffer from a loud ringing noise in his ears."

Doc Slavin, the battalion surgeon, was once out on an operation during which smoke was pumped into a tunnel complex, and it is likely it was the time Sergeant Smith was killed. Smoke started coming out of concealed openings located 50 to 60 yards away, and soon after, Viet Cong began to surface. Slavin had a camera in his pocket and snapped pictures of the emerging VC, who were quickly apprehended.

"I don't know how many other doctors captured a VC," Slavin said with a touch of pride. He also noted with an air of certainty: "The bravest guys in Vietnam were the freaking tunnel rats."

Because space was confined in a tunnel, only smaller, wiry guys could venture inside, such as 5-foot-2 paratrooper Salome Beltran.

"You go in with only a .45 and a flashlight. You got to be real careful. The bad guys have the upper hand. It takes a lot of guts," Beltran said.

At 5-foot-9 and 130 pounds, cavalryman Reid Lyon had the physique to be a tunnel rat. It is noteworthy that Lyon, after the war, earned a doctorate degree and became one of the nation's leading experts on Post Traumatic Stress Disorder. Being a tunnel rat took an emotional toll.

"If I smell dirt, I think of the tunnels. It takes you back," said Lyon. "It was a terrifying job. I never got used to it. Why did I do it? I'm a paratrooper. I was also cautious. The tunnels are pretty narrow. They're also serpentine, which was actually good. You could chuck a grenade around a bend and be protected from the blast. It's a slow process of feeling your way through."

One incident that stuck with him began when a comrade who had entered a tunnel failed to respond to tugs of the rope tied to his leg. Lyon and cavalrymen Don Dittenhoff and Charlie Severino went in to get him.

"That was a real terrifying time," Lyon said. "As we moved through the tunnel, we found that it was blocked by dirt and debris, and we dug through it. When we came to the guy we were looking for, we realized his rope had become stuck as he had turned a corner. Then we heard more dirt falling behind us, and we knew we could not go back the same way we had entered. We were isolated in a very small space several feet underground. So we had to claw our way out straight up to the surface. All of us were deeply traumatized by this experience, as we all felt fear we never thought possible. It was much worse than getting shot at."

What was amazing were the types of weapons Lyon would sometimes retrieve from underground. There were just as many M-16s as communist-made assault rifles, not to mention American grenades, C Rations and even a grenade launcher. The military hardware that the U.S. supplied to its South Vietnamese allies ended up in the hands of adversaries who used American weapons to kill Americans.

"It reinforced our developing realization that the war was un-winnable," Lyon said.

In Vietnam, there never was a light at the end of the endless tunnels.

Chapter 45
MIKE FOXTROT

When Private First Class Larry Dobson was still Up North, he learned first-hand that anything could happen at any time in Vietnam. In the process of moving from one fire base to another, he was in the back of a deuce and a half as the workhorse truck pulled a trailer and kicked up red dust that was as fine a talcum powder. The vehicle hit a land mine, or an improvised explosive device as it was called in future wars. Dobson and two other troopers were ejected by the blast, and Dobson was run over by the trailer. He suffered a dislocated hip and back injuries that were severe enough to land him in the hospital at Cam Ranh Bay for 38 days. A native of Phoenix, New York, Dobson had enlisted in the Army right out of high school and knew he would end up fighting for South Vietnam's independence.

"I had this idea that there was a big guy picking on a little guy, and I was going to do something about it. I thought I knew what I was getting into. Turns out, I didn't. Everybody at some point crossed that bridge when you ask yourself, 'How am I going to survive this?' " Dobson said.

In January of 1969, Dobson had rejoined Bravo Company when it and the entire 2nd Battalion of the 505 were sent on a joint operation all the way out to the Cambodian border. It was the 82nd Airborne's bloodiest fight against North Vietnamese regulars in all of 1969, but it wasn't the last. "They kept putting us out farther and farther as feelers. It's hard for people to grasp how thick that jungle was. Then all of a sudden, beneath the triple canopy of the black mahogany trees, there was a road that went on for miles and miles. I couldn't believe it. It was the Ho Chi Minh Trail. We weren't officially allowed to cross the border, but we were in Cambodia. When you pick on somebody in their backyard, they have an awful advantage on you," said Dobson.

In a limited war, Cambodia was off limits to American ground forces, a point of frustration given that it was the southern terminus of North Vietnam's major supply route and a sanctuary for enemy fighters. U.S. warplanes did drop tons of bombs on Cambodia in a futile attempt to stop the flow of men and supplies, but ground forces always felt like their flank was open. Others in Dobson's battalion also say with matter-of-fact certainty that they had reached the Ho Chi Minh Trail and knew a savage fight was brewing.

"It looked like a two-lane highway. We knew were in Cambodia," said machine-gunner Ed Kochanski of Alpha Company.

"Right in the middle of this thick jungle was a road that looked like one you would find in front of your house," said an incredulous John Koons of Delta Company.

On the books, the big push toward Cambodia was named Operation Sheridan-Sabre, which was mounted after military intelligence concluded that a North Vietnamese division was massing in a staging area about 70 miles north of Saigon for a possible assault on the South Vietnamese capital. The area was located in the northern edge of Phuoc Long Province, from which the Song Be and Saigon Rivers flowed on a southerly course. It was north and east of the Fish Hook, named for a feature on aerial maps of the Cambodian-Vietnamese border.

In a bid to disrupt enemy plans, the 1st Cavalry Division (Airmobile) planned a helicopter assault by one of its brigades. For additional punch, it requested a battalion of 600 or so orphans from the Golden Brigade.

Just before things kicked off, Lieutenant Don Paquin arrived as a forward artillery observer in Captain Tom Hennessey's Bravo Company, and troopers still talk about their first impression of him. A native of the industrial town of Lowell, Massachusetts, where textile mills churned out fabric with mind-numbing regularity, Paquin had joined the Army as an enlisted man in June of 1960.

"Lowell was the armpit of the world. I was 17, and it was either work in the mills or take a chance on getting shot. For me, getting shot was the better option," Paquin said.

While in the Army, Paquin encountered a group of paratroopers leaving the States on various assignments and was impressed by their sharp-dressed professionalism. Thus inspired, he volunteered for jump school, then went on to take Special Forces training where he specialized in demolition. He made sergeant by the time he was 21. Paquin had a top secret security clearance when his Special Forces unit went to Vietnam in the early 1960s in an advisory role while the American military was building bases in advance of the ground war. After what he called a "wonderful assignment," Paquin hoped to become a helicopter pilot, but he never could master the flying machine.

"I was really a terrible pilot. I couldn't even hover," he laughed.

While in the air on a bumpy training flight, Paquin's agitated instructor ordered him to put the bird down even though they were some distance from the operations center.

"Cadet, I've got two tours in Vietnam," the instructor told him. "I've been awarded the Distinguished Flying Cross and the Silver Star. Nobody can accuse me of being a coward, but you scared the shit out of me today."

Undaunted, Paquin qualified for Officer Candidate School and was minted as a lieutenant with a specialty in field artillery. At the artillery center in Fort Sill, Oklahoma, the home of the big guns, he learned the power of cannons. Newcomers were taught the basics of how to aim, load and pull the lanyard to fire an artillery piece that sends a shell down range on an arc. Additional lessons are learned when artillerymen move to a forward observation post to witness what happens when the rounds actually reach their target, and how a forward observer can radio back to adjust fire and make them even more effective.

"On a clear June day, we were down range to observe an impact zone. I heard a boom, boom, boom and looked up for thunderclouds. Then 100 rounds started exploding on the ground we were observing, and an officer adjusted fire to bring the rounds closer to the target. From that day on, I knew that a forward artillery observer has in his hands the Hammer of Thor," Paquin said.

Subsequently, Paquin was serving with the 101st Airborne in Vietnam when word came that the Golden Brigade needed forward observers.

"They must have been really hard up, because they sent me," Paquin said with self-deprecating humor. Paquin reported to artillery headquarters at Fire Base Copperhead before hooking up with Bravo Company.

"We left the hardball of Highway One and drove over roads that were essentially the dikes of rice paddies. We were in moderate jungle by then and got behind a truck driven by a South Vietnamese soldier. It was moving slowly, so we honked the horn and tried to go around. Every time we turned to get around him, he turned to get in our way. This happened a couple of times, so I fired a warning shot over his head as he sat in the cab," Paquin said.

As a witness to the episode, Bravo Company's first sergeant gasped, "Holy shit!" Upon Paquin's arrival at company headquarters, the new forward observer was called before Captain Hennessey for an explanation.

"Lieutenant Paquin, did you shoot at an ARVN?" the captain asked.

"I used the M-16 horn," Paquin replied.

The newcomer was reminded that soldiers in the Army of the Republic of Vietnam were America's allies, and although there were frustrations in working at their pace sometimes, the alliance could not be jeopardized by shooting at them.

At the same time, Paquin had made a mark on the troops in his new unit. The first sergeant spread the word to the rest of the company: "Do not fuck with this guy. That son of a bitch is crazy." Paquin had either acquired instant credibility or a reputation as someone to be feared. He fit right in with the 82nd Airborne.

"Hennessey and I got along very well," Paquin said. He was defined not so much by that incident but by how well he could do his job of placing steel on target when it was desperately needed.

Operation Sheridan-Sabre kicked off on January 11. Dozens of giant, twin-rotor Chinook helicopters, loaded with troopers carrying rucksacks and rifles, took to the air. The thundering machines overcame the obstacles of time and terrain, dropping the grunts off at a landing zone at the edge of the jungle. The infantry also brought along their protective steel umbrella—artillery pieces slung from the bellies of the helicopters.

"Our battalion was on the right flank of the 1st Cav, and Bravo Company was on the right flank of the battalion," Captain Hennessey said. "They dropped us off, and we were somewhere in between three regiments of what we learned later was the 9th NVA Division. We pin-balled back and forth at first."

Underscoring the thickness of the undergrowth was the fact that the individual companies could not see each other as they moved forward. They kept in touch with each other by radio, and overall movement was coordinated by battalion commander James Irons, a lieutenant colonel who flew over the terrain in his command and control helicopter.

Six days into the operation, a reconnaissance in force located enemy troops outside of Fire Support Base Jill, described as little more than a brown scar in the jungle. At 8:30 in the morning of January 17, Hennessey's Bravo Company made a combat assault across the Song Be River and touched down in a flooded field. The grunts named it Landing Zone Mike Foxtrot, code words taken from the military alphabet. Troops knew that MF had a saltier and ominous meaning. The fight ahead of them was a real MF-er. With their feet wet, and with snipers shooting at them, troopers pushed into the tangled wilderness.

"It was a nasty, nasty place to move around in. It was so thick in there that you could never see from one end of the column to the other. You hung on to the pack of the guy in front of you, and the guy behind you was hanging on to yours. The triple canopy didn't even let in the sun, except for periodic shafts of light that made it through. They looked like telephone poles, and we ran our hands through them just to see if they were real. I wish everybody could see the rain forest. It's beautiful, as long as you're not sleeping in it. It's just no place for a human being to live," said Larry Dobson, whose neck was adorned with a medal of Saint Christopher, the patron saint of travelers. "We were constantly wet from the rain, mist and sweat. We carried a ridiculous amount of weight. You tried to get water in you early, but the water was always hot and went through you without making things much better. You end up doing it for the guy next to you. The world gets very narrow. All that stuff about Mom and apple pie goes right out the window when people start dying."

At one point, a main trail junction off what was believed to be the infiltration route was discovered. The point platoon moved up one of the trails and received accurate sniper fire from four or five enemy perched in trees. Artillery was called in. Exploding shells were walked in as the company rolled back the hostile force.

Another platoon maneuvered around to the left and came upon a clearing. Beyond the open area were enemy bunkers and fighting positions, plainly visible. These weren't hastily dug holes surrounded by sandbags. They were World War II-style bunkers constructed of logs piled three or four feet high. Built with reinforced ceilings, the bunkers were also arranged to provide interlocking fields of fire and mutually supporting gun positions.

Along the trail, at about one o'clock in the afternoon, Hennessey's men discovered a telephone wire on the ground. To take advantage of a direct source of information, troops spliced into the wire to eavesdrop. A Vietnamese operative assigned to Bravo Company as a guide and interpreter listened in. What he heard made him drop suddenly to the ground.

"We never saw anybody dig a foxhole so fast and so deep. He seemed to have dug himself in up to his eyes," Hennessey said. "That's how we found out we were in the middle of three NVA regiments."

According to information obtained from the wire before it went dead, the All Americans were close to a rice storage area. The enemy massed rockets and mortars to protect it. This was what was called *Injun Country*, a place infested with hostiles. The pucker factor kicked in.

At the same time, Lieutenant Don Paquin was on his way to join the fight. With him on a helicopter was Sergeant Jimmy Greene, an enlisted man who was also a forward artillery observer. Eleven months earlier, the 18-year-old Greene had been with the 2nd of the 505 when it arrived at Hue while the fighting was still going on. Paquin and Greene arrived at Landing Zone Mike Foxtrot, and while under fire, asked the whereabouts of Captain Hennessey's Bravo Company. Forward observers aren't much use if they're not forward.

"Sergeant Greene and I hit that hot landing zone," Paquin said. "We dropped our packs and crawled ahead. Along the way, we kept asking for the location of the point of the company, and we kept being told, 'It's up there.' Eventually, we came to this hummock to find two soldiers behind a tree while this ferocious firefight was going on. I asked where the point of the company was, and they said, 'This is the point.' I said to myself that I didn't mean to get that close!"

A short while later, while patrols were trying to locate enemy positions, Hennessey sipped some C Ration coffee and Paquin had a cup of cocoa.

"We were sitting on our helmets when we heard the distinctive plop, plop, plop of mortar rounds leaving their tubes. We looked at each other and together said, 'That ain't ours,' " Hennessy said.

With their steel pots now on their heads, and with shells impacting around them, both men consulted their compasses and shot azimuths toward the sound of the tubes. Having gotten a fix on where the mortars were, Paquin called in an artillery strike. Several mortars were eliminated, and their crews were killed by the accurate fire. Hennessey said one of his troopers perished and four others wounded by enemy fire. Bravo's list of killed in action that day included Specialist Norman Louis Cates, 21, of Hampton, Virginia. Nicknamed Tim, he was the oldest of seven children.

The battle reached a crescendo. All four of Bravo Company's platoons took heavy fire and were effectively pinned down. While attempting to maneuver, Lieutenant Greg Ellison, 22, of Bellmore, New York, who led Tiger Platoon and had been with the 82nd Airborne since the original deployment, was cut down. Also killed was Lieutenant Stanley K. Rykaczewski, leader of Panther Platoon and a native of Natrona Heights, Pennsylvania.

Sergeant Jim Greene was right next to Rykaczewski, who was known as Rock by those who had trouble pronouncing his last name. "Me and Rock were shoulder to shoulder. He was in a squatting position, pointing out targets to his men. He was saying, 'They're in there! They're in there!' Then a sniper got him. He was hit right above the eye. He said two words, 'Help me.' There was nothing I could do, so I hollered for the medic. He died right next to me," Greene said. "They kept trying to flank us. There were a whole lot of them out there."

The grunts placed their rucksacks in front of them for cover. The fighting was so vicious that the packs were riddled with bullets. Enemy troops were 10 feet away in spots. It was the very definition of a situation called "danger close." Troops were so near to the enemy that they could be hit by their own artillery if the big guns fired.

"One of the troops, who was scared shitless, asked me, 'Captain, are they all around us?' I said, 'Yeah, we got them right where we want them. It's a target-rich environment.' Then the trooper asked, 'What are we going to do, surrender?' And I said, 'No, we're going to fix bayonets and charge.' I meant it facetiously, but people thought I was serious," Hennessey said. "You get so focused on doing the job, you don't have time to worry when you're in the moment. Your whole universe becomes that which you can see around you. After things are over is when you say to yourself, 'Oh, shit, that was pretty hairy.' "

Don Paquin heard the words to fix bayonets, along with the soldier's question about giving up.

"Surrender? Under no circumstances can a Special Forces officer be allowed to surrender. I would have died before I did that," Paquin said.

Hennessey considered the possibility of calling in artillery and air power on his own position. One piece of radio equipment he had was called the Silent Sam, which was encrypted to send secure messages back to battalion headquarters. Surrounded by a force later determined to number 800 men, he had no room to maneuver. Ammo was running short. The only officers who had avoided death or wounds were him and Paquin. The company had 70 men still in action, down from the original number of 112 who went in. It was truly a tactical emergency. To this day, Paquin believes that Hennessy called in a Broken Arrow, a code used only in a worst-case scenario when an American unit is in a hopeless situation. It means to direct all available firepower on a friendly position that has been overrun, thereby creating a high probability that American forces would be hit while blowing the crap out of the enemy. Hennessey said he called in only to alert higher-ups that a Broken Arrow was within the realm of possibility.

"Actually, I got on the secure radio to battalion and was thinking, 'What if?' There was a possibility of declaring a Broken Arrow, but we weren't broken. We were still fighting. All artillery and air assets were coming to us. The Air Force was dropping loads of steel in the jungle around us. It was 'danger close' on more than one occasion. I never had to call Broken Arrow. I was ready, though," Hennessey said.

As the savage fight raged, Paquin did what a forward observer is trained to do. With the Hammer of Thor in his hands, and using his call sign Bravo2Bravo, he called for fire missions from the artillery battery, located at Fire Base Jill. The first rounds landed behind the enemy bunkers to seal off any escape, right where Paquin had wanted.

"Good shooting!" the forward observer radioed back to the battery.

An NVA lieutenant who later surrendered said the first two rounds of the initial volley killed 30 troops, including his battalion commander. Then Paquin walked the artillery forward into the bunker complex. Battery B of the 321st Field artillery fired 700 rounds in three hours— a shell exploding, on average, every four seconds. Artillery controlled by a higher command also blasted the area.

"We were fighting for our lives. I did not think we were going to get out of the place we were, but we hit them with everything except the kitchen sink," Paquin said. "I killed a lot of dinks with artillery. I didn't think of them as human beings. They were there to kill me. I have no regrets."

As daylight faded, Bravo Company formed a circle in a night defensive position. The prospect of a Last Stand ran through more than one mind. Critically short ammunition was re-distributed so that troopers could shoot back. One of them, Stephen Hinds of King City, California, recalled: "This day seemed like the closest I ever came to being in Hell."

At one point, Bravo Company's executive officer, Lieutenant Robert Haddock of Wilmington, Delaware, rushed toward the sound of the guns even though he was within weeks of completing his tour. He had been in a rear area, responsible for seeing to it that the company was adequately supplied, when he heard that Ellison and Rykaczewski had been killed.

"He knew that we had lost half of our leadership, and he came out on the next available chopper. Then he was wounded too," Hennessey said.

The fight reignited the morning of January 18 when enemy mortars opened up on Bravo's position. Urgently needed were helicopters to fly in ammo and to remove the wounded, but the choppers faced a heavy volume of fire each time they attempted to land.

"We had a number of wounded. Several of them were dying. Two birds tried to come in, but with the volume of fire directed at them, the best they could do was kick out boxes of ammo. I thought we were all dead ducks," Paquin said.

The pilot of one of the birds, codenamed Medevac 5, said he would attempt to land. The original landing zone was too hot, but a hole in the jungle canopy had been blasted open by aerial bombs. A skilled helicopter pilot who was brave enough or crazy enough might be able to descend straight down, but it would be like flying in an elevator shaft.

"Medevac 5 said to mark a landing spot. The fire was intense, but Sergeant Greene took a smoke grenade and marked the location. The pilot skidded over trees, turned the tail of the bird to the bad guys and started to land. His crew chief, who was right behind the pilot, was shot. He fell out, but he had his safety harness on. He only fell as far as the skids. The pilot put the bird down. Then Sergeant Greene went to help load the wounded," Paquin said.

Greene put his own life on the line to guide the chopper.

"Tracers were whizzing through the air. Us shooting at them, them shooting at us. I wondered at the time, 'What are you saving me for, God?' " Greene said.

Now it was decision time. Paquin wanted Greene to board the helicopter and get out while he still had the chance. Greene insisted on staying.

"I told Sergeant Greene, 'That's your Freedom Bird, son. You gotta get out of here. You're going back.' He started crying because he wanted to stay in the fight," Paquin said. "Here's the order I gave him. 'Sergeant Greene, one of two things is going to happen. You're going to get on that fucking helicopter and get out of here, or I'm going to have you court-martialed and shot for willful disobedience of a commissioned officer in combat.' " Reluctantly, Greene obeyed.

Protected by the umbrella of awesome American firepower, Bravo Company survived to fight another day. When the shooting stopped, the unit spent a day or so combing over the battlefield. What they had been up against was a virtually impregnable complex of 30 bunkers. Now reduced to rubble, the bunkers yielded a body count of 200 NVA soldiers, and blood trails indicated that the toll was even higher, according to Captain Hennessey. From the weapons and documents that were seized, it was determined that the 9th NVA Division was combat ineffective for the next 12 months, and that any designs of moving on Saigon had been thwarted. Bravo Company took 30 casualties over a 10-day period. Tom Hennessey was awarded a Silver Star for valor, and three other members of the company also received Silver Stars. Seven Commendation Medals with V device and six Bronze Stars were also awarded.

Finally, Bravo Company was extracted and air-lifted back to base camp. Fresh off an adrenaline-fueled fight for their lives, and still in their battle gear, Hennessey took five of his officers to lunch at the stately Air Force Officer's Club at Tan Son Nhut Air Base.

"We had been in the field for two weeks and were in our stinking jungle fatigues—half a dozen of the most heavily armed troops you've ever seen, with bandoliers of ammo strapped on them. We looked like the Dalton Gang walking into a saloon. You could have heard a pin drop," said Don Paquin.

A startled waiter attempted to usher the gang to a side room, out of sight from the rear echelon patrons who frequented the club. In the main dining hall, however, was a big table covered with a white tablecloth and marked with a sign that said reserved. Hennessey commandeered that table, and he and his men plopped themselves down.

"We stowed our helmets under our chairs and slung our weapons on the back of the chairs," Hennessey said. "Not long after that, the base commander, I believe he was a full colonel, came in and started for our table. He turned and talked with the NCO who had first approached us. For some reason, they agreed that we would keep the commander's table for lunch. We enjoyed the break and especially the reaction of the rear detachment folks who weren't real sure what to make of the fully locked and loaded officers from the 82nd Airborne. Bravo Company's officers still talk about that lunch and the 'balls' we had to take over the base commander's table."

As a postscript, Don Paquin had written up Jimmy Greene for a Bronze Star for his valor in guiding down that rescue chopper. Greene left the unit in March when his 12-month tour was up, and the certificate for the medal, but not the Bronze Star itself, arrived in the mail at his house. Greene volunteered to go back to Vietnam in 1970 with the 101st Airborne, and four days into his second tour, he was wounded and sent home for good. Paquin and Greene met again at a reunion of the Golden Brigade nearly 50 years after the vicious battle, and the subject of the Bronze Star came up. Greene replied that he had received the paperwork but not the actual medal. That's when Paquin began pulling some strings to correct the oversight.

At the 82nd Airborne Division Association's annual convention in Orlando, Florida, in 2017, a ceremony was arranged. The current division commander, Major General Erik Kurilla, and active paratroopers who did a demonstration jump as part of the convention, entered the hospitality room of the Panther Association. Paratrooper-for-life Jimmy Greene awaited their arrival.

Paquin retold the story of what Greene had done during Operation Sheridan-Sabre, and the official citation for a Bronze Star with V device was read. Secretary of the Army John W. McHugh had signed the papers, which noted that Greene had acted without regard for his own safety to help rescue his wounded brothers and that he had gone above and beyond the call of duty in the finest traditions of the United States Army. General Kurilla then personally pinned on the Bronze Star that Greene should have received a half-century earlier.

"We want to do it right. Paratroopers take care of paratroopers," the division commander said. "We are honored to recognize your valor, because you can't teach valor."

The two-star general had to bend at the waist to pin the medal on Greene's lapel. Due to the ravages of age, Greene was unable to stand at attention. Instead, he sat in his wheelchair, his left hand trembling involuntarily. The general saluted him, and the white-haired Greene saluted back, lifting the bent, bony fingers of his right hand to the brim of his cap. The gleam in his moistened eyes was a snapshot of what makes a man proud. Paquin had accomplished his mission.

"I have a tremendous amount of affection for Jimmy Greene. He taught me more about being a forward observer by accident than the Army ever taught me on purpose. This guy is the real deal, and America is a better place for his service," Paquin said.

Meanwhile, Alpha and Charlie Companies of the 2nd of the 505 were accomplishing their own harrowing missions in their battles against NVA sanctuaries along the Cambodian border during Operation Sheridan-Sabre.

Chapter 46
WATER AND BLOOD

Arthur Kellogg's first platoon leader was West Point graduate Thomas Schwartz, who was wounded when he backed into a log and triggered a booby trap that sent shrapnel into his back during an operation along the Saigon River. Lieutenant Schwartz was awarded the Silver Star, the Bronze Star and Purple Heart while serving in the Golden Brigade. One reason that Kellogg remembered him so vividly was that in 1999, four-star General Thomas Schwartz was named to command all the troops in Korea.

Anyway, in January of 1969, Kellogg and his comrades in Alpha Company assembled on the flight line in full battle gear for an air assault that marked the beginning of their part in Operation Sheridan-Sabre. Boarding a flying machine was an everyday occurrence for a grunt in Vietnam, but it was never routine.

"We were ready to go anywhere on moment's notice. We were always combat ready at all times," said Kellogg, who carried a Bible and wore a crucifix around his neck for spiritual protection. "I think we can all look back at situations, whether it was in civilian life or in the Army, where we can say only by the grace of God am I alive. I believe with all my heart that one reason I survived was prayer. If anyone has ever seen combat, it makes you appreciate all the freedoms you have in this country."

Alpha Company was bound for Fire Base June, which was built in a single day by combat engineers of the 1st Cavalry Division. A sign bearing the crest of the 2nd of the 505 of the 82nd Airborne was placed at the entrance. The fire base was north of a village named Phuoc Vinh out toward the Cambodian border, and the territory only got more hostile as the troops moved out to find the North Vietnamese Army camp that threatened Saigon.

For seven days, the company patrolled the terrain and established night ambushes as it advanced. It was on the left flank but out of visual range of Bravo Company. In a January 16 letter home, Kellogg wrote that the ground was mostly flat but thick with vegetation. Carrying what they needed on their backs, the troops chopped their way through the tangle. Unshaven, Kellogg figured his whiskers made him look like Santa Claus. The company was due for fresh clothes, and Kellogg said soldiers stunk so bad that the enemy could smell them. He had slept out in the rain without cover for two straight nights and was losing the battle to keep his feet dry.

"We lived like animals for those seven days," Kellogg said.

At least the mail system was working. Kellogg received a care package from home and shared fudge and cookies with his buddies. Included in the package was a Case knife and a Zippo lighter engraved with the crest of the 82nd Airborne. Both were manufactured in Bradford, Pennsylvania, not too far from Kellogg's hometown. His brother had sent the items as gifts. Also sent was a copy of his hometown newspaper from Titusville. In addition to the local news, the publication carried stories of the anti-war protests and civil unrest roiling the nation.

"We were out sacrificing every day, not knowing if you're going to live or die from day to day, and then you'd read about what's happening in the States. It makes you angry. It was only natural to ask, 'What am I doing here? Where's our support?' Our country was not behind us anymore," Kellogg said. "I felt it was my duty, my obligation to serve. I live in a free country because someone was willing to die to make it free. We wanted to put in our time and come back alive."

He tucked that folded newspaper into his back pocket. Before too long, that newspaper would have a bullet hole through it, but Kellogg would be unscathed. That's how close life or death could be in Vietnam.

Also with Alpha Company was Juan Blaz, a platoon sergeant who was from the U.S. territory of Guam in the western Pacific Ocean. At 22, Blaz had already distinguished himself as a peacetime soldier. Having joined the Army in 1964, he had been selected to serve in the elite Presidential Honor Guard, which appeared at White House functions attended by foreign dignitaries. He was also part of the U.S. Army Drill Team, which toured the country and led to Blaz's TV appearance on the *Ed Sullivan Show*. In addition, he was a member of the unit that oversees the ceremonies at Arlington National Cemetery—the Old Guard of the 3rd Infantry Division headquartered at Fort Meyer, Virginia. He even made soldier of the year for the military district of Washington in 1967.

Sent to Vietnam to serve with the 82nd Airborne, Blaz was also known as the luckiest solider in Alpha Company. He earned that status while on a patrol seven miles north of Saigon near the hamlet of Ap Lan Tay. When the detail came to a ditch, a lieutenant told Blaz to split up the men to cross at different points. Taking the lead, Blaz leaped over the ditch and landed on a hastily hidden Soviet-made rocket. A subsequent search uncovered a cache of weapons that included 112 similar rockets, 70 mortar rounds, three cases of propellant charges, one land mine and a booby-trapped grenade.

"Really, it was an accident. All I did was jump across the ditch and there I was—right in the middle of all those rockets!" Blaz said at the time. His fortuitous discovery earned him a pass into Saigon.

Now out on the big operation, one of Alpha Company's ambush points heard and observed about 100 North Vietnamese soldiers pushing bicycles laden with bags of rice along the Ho Chi Minh Trail. The force was too large to engage, but after the procession had moved a safe distance away, the squad called for artillery to light them up.

Machine-gunner Ed Kochanski knew from personal experience that the NVA was close. Out in the middle of nowhere, he had spotted four outdoor latrines made out of bamboo, including one so new that the wood was still green.

"They're in here. We're going to make contact," Kochanski told his comrades. "Then the shit hits the fan."

As the sun came up on the morning of January 18, Alpha Company was out of water, and a soldier can't live for long without water in the tropics. Because the vegetation was too tangled for re-supply helicopters to land, a detail was organized to fill empty canteens from a stream about 400 yards away. Leading that detail was Sergeant Benjamin Benton, a squad leader in Blaz's first platoon.

A short-timer, Benton was 10 months into his one-year tour of duty with the Golden Brigade. He was in line to run a program designed to make sure that replacement troops were physically fit to be in the field. But Benton's presence was required for this operation, and that new assignment at a base camp would have to wait. At 23, Benton had his parents, two younger sisters and a girlfriend awaiting his return in South Mills, North Carolina. As one who always placed the needs of his men first, Benton volunteered for the water run. He and a half dozen men strung the empty canteens together and headed out.

"It was so quiet it was eerie," said Carl Bludau, the company radioman. He had been asked by Benton to be an usher in his wedding when they got back to The World.

Ten to 15 minutes later, the deep-throated grumble of a Chinese-made machine gun shattered the silence. In a bamboo thicket near the stream, Benton's detail was ambushed. Even basic needs were fraught with peril in a war zone, where dying for a drink of water took on its own grim meaning. Troopers from Alpha Company instinctively dropped their rucksacks and raced toward the sound of the guns.

"We just ran as fast as we could to see what was going on," said Arthur Kellogg. "We had no clue about what we were up against. We were all scared, but we couldn't leave our guys down there. We went on the run."

The ambush site was on the perimeter of an NVA bunker complex. One hundred or so men of Cold Steel Alpha found themselves up against roughly 800 enemy soldiers of the 9th NVA Division.

"There was a trench around their machine gun. They pinned us down. Your old heart just pounds. We'd shoot and shoot and shoot. The ground was red with blood," Kellogg said.

Upon reaching the site, Ed Kochanski dropped to a firing position and opened up with his machine gun, 40 yards away from the NVA gun pit. His helmet was pushed down so tight that it almost covered his ears. Two rounds from the enemy gun dinged his steel pot, but he didn't realize that until later. He also didn't realize that he was set up atop a nest of red ants, which bit and stung the whole battle through. In the moment, nothing mattered but the gunfight.

"I was in second platoon, which was on the right flank of the whole company. I know I killed a guy, then another guy would jump on the gun and fire. *Buh-buh-buh-buh-buh.* They must've had some underground network. Every time I killed a guy, another would pop up and take over," said Kochanski. "Then I see two tracers out of the corner of my eye coming down. So I yell, 'They're in the trees! They're in the trees! Shoot the trees!' Branches and limbs were falling down. Those snipers tied themselves to the trees. They tied their weapons too."

Off to his left was Staff Sergeant Juan Castro, a cook who had volunteered to go on the big operation. A native of Costa Rica, the 30-year-old Castro was married and had two children.

"He got up and shouted, 'Airborne!' Then he went down," Kochanski said. "A guy opened up his spider hole with his helmet and fired a rocket propelled grenade. I took a piece of shrapnel in my right shoulder, but what saved me was a bamboo tree that absorbed the blast. That RPG sheared off the front of the barrel of my M-60 though. I no longer had a front sight, so I fired by following my tracers."

Mike Gamble, who served in Benton's squad within Blaz's platoon, came across three soldiers from the water detail. They were hit, but their wounds were not life-threatening.

"I asked where Benton was, and they told me he had gone up the hill," Gamble said, a reference to a knoll where the sergeant had gone in pursuit of enemy troops. Gamble took off to find Benton. The knoll was about 50 yards from a virtually impregnable complex of 30 NVA bunkers that were protected by overhead cover and impossible to see from the air through triple-canopy jungle.

"He was lying on his left side, and I asked him if he was OK. He said, 'I just got grazed in the shoulder.' Then he said, 'Mike, get down. They're in the trees. They're everywhere!' Those are the last words I ever heard him say," Gamble said. "I was going for help when I heard one shot from a sniper in a tree. Benton rolled over and looked at me. I'll never forget that. I wanted to get him, but the medic told me to stay away. He even hit me to make sure I pulled back. Bullets were impacting into the ground and kicking dirt up on my legs. Benton's warning likely saved my life that day."

At first, troopers had just reacted and returned fire. Then Lieutenant Jim Littig, Alpha's executive officer, organized the company into a combat formation. That's when Sergeant Juan Blaz went into action, leading 11 men against the bunkers that were endangering his comrades.

Blaz made the first of his five charges against enemy positions that day. While some of what he did remains a blur, his actions were cobbled together from his own sworn statement, eyewitness accounts, an article in the 82nd Airborne's in-house publication and an interview Blaz gave 47 years after the battle with the Pacific Daily News of Guam. Things happened so fast that he didn't have time to think. As Blaz approached an enemy position on his first charge, an adversary in a bamboo grove opened fire and felled a soldier in his platoon.

"I recall one of my men screaming in pain from a six-inch gaping hole in his back," Blaz said. "I dashed toward him to render first aid. When I reached him, I discovered that the standard gauze bandage I had was much smaller than his wound. I managed to dress it and gave him reassurance and comfort that he would make it. At that moment, I received a burst of automatic gunfire. I immediately covered the wounded man's body with mine. None of the bullets hit either of us, but it angered me. In response, I charged ahead with a pulled-pin grenade."

He tossed the grenade into the bunker, killing the two occupants. Then he took on a second bunker and was wounded in the process.

"Out of the corner of my eye, I saw an NVA with a lit device, which he threw at me. I was approximately 15 feet from him. I fired a burst from my M-16, hitting him in the forehead. I still remember his front skull exploding. The device he threw at me exploded about three feet from my position. A fragment hit me, and I saw blood oozing from my right shoulder. The wound did not bother me at all. It only infuriated me more," Blaz said.

Anger helps explain why a soldier ignores the bullets coming at him and continues to charge. He was enraged that the men under his care were being horribly wounded. The only way to stop the carnage was to eliminate the people doing the shooting. He had to take lives to save lives.

"My only concern was to eliminate the enemy and the saving of lives of the men in my unit," Blaz said. "Something happened to me that caused me to be so darned brave, even though in the beginning I'm scared. And if I were to die on the battlefield, I would accept that. I remember making another solo charge to the front, but I cannot recall the circumstances which prompted this act. As I charged, I remember shouting profanities at the enemy and the sound of Lieutenant Littig's voice telling the rest of the unit, 'Don't shoot up front. Sergeant Blaz is up there.' "

The point man in weapons platoon, Darron Sharp of San Diego, California, witnessed some of what Blaz did.

"Everything slowed down. I was pinned down and trying not to breathe. If you inhaled, you made yourself a bigger target. The medic was tending to two of our guys who had blood spurting out of them. Blaz was up and running through the most outrageous shit even though he was hit himself. He had a wild look in his eye. He was a real bad ass. A soldier's soldier," Sharp said.

As the fight continued, Blaz charged across a ravine toward another fortified position occupied by an unsuspecting NVA, who was startled at the sight of an American soldier having penetrated so deep into what was considered a safe haven.

"I came across a bunker with a dazed enemy soldier staring at me. Why didn't he shoot me? I don't know, but my grenade exploded in his bunker," Blaz said.

"About 10 minutes later, I was hit by an AK-47 round, again on my right shoulder. This time, I felt like I had been hit with a baseball bat. My medic wanted to treat my wound. However, I refused and requested that he treat the other wounded men first," Blaz said. "Painful, but I could still move. It didn't damage any organ. So it was OK. No big thing. I was already wounded twice and still charging."

Automatic weapons fire came from yet another bunker, hitting Blaz's platoon leader, a lieutenant, four times. Blaz was now in command of first platoon. He sent the wounded back and led the remaining members of his element back up the hill.

"In retrospect, what I did on that day is really an unorthodox way for a platoon sergeant to act because what happens if I die? Who's the leader of the platoon? My platoon leader was severely wounded, so he's out of the mission already, so now I'm in charge. I took over the platoon and my attitude (is) I'm not afraid to die. I tell you that much. I'm single, 22 years old, and because some of my men were wounded, that kind of infuriated me."

As he maneuvered, Blaz came up on a wounded soldier who he recognized immediately. It was one of his squad leaders, Sergeant Benjamin Perry Benton, the man who had led the water run.

"He was seriously wounded but still breathing. I yelled for my platoon medic. I was in a sitting position on the ground with Sergeant Benton in my arms while the medic was administering mouth-to-mouth. At this precise moment, our position received an immense volume of automatic fire. It was a miracle that the bullets kicked dirt all around and had missed me completely. Sergeant Benton's body had absorbed three rounds and had actually saved my life," Blaz said.

Those shots were fatal. Benton died right there in the middle of the fight. The machine gun fire from the bunkers was returned with everything that Alpha troopers had, including the M-79 grenade launcher known as The Blooper.

"I saw an NVA pop his head in and out of a (spider hole). He hadn't spotted me. My grenadier was nearby. I took the grenade launcher and fired about four or five rounds at the NVA's position. I continued to fire until I scored a direct hit on the last round," Blaz said.

One of the scariest moments of the battle unfolded when Blaz received a radio call from his company commander, who was positioned about 100 meters back to the right rear. While Blaz was out front of everyone else and pinned down by a machine gun, he was told to direct fire from a Cobra helicopter gunship that was inbound. Blaz radioed his position to the gunship, which belonged to the 1st Cav. The pilot couldn't see him through the triple canopy jungle. Blaz knew that if he and his men failed to receive help, they would be wiped out. Blaz radioed back and popped smoke to mark the target. Again, the pilot radioed to say that, under his rules of engagement, he was not authorized to fire so close to a friendly position. The best he could do was fire 70 meters from the location marked by smoke, and the danger to Blaz and his men was much closer than that. Directing the battle from his own helicopter, battalion commander James Irons heard Blaz's request.

"And fortunately for me, the battalion commander circling overhead and monitoring the situation heard me. He said to the pilot, 'Give Sergeant Blaz what he wants, and I'm giving you authorization to fire based on where he wants you to fire,' " Blaz said.

Blaz and his men tucked in while the helicopter opened up with rockets and machine guns. Some rockets in the opening volley impacted so close that Blaz radioed back to adjust the fire. On the third pass, the bunker was eliminated. Then the steel umbrella of artillery from Fire Base June began blasting the NVA complex. Two prisoners taken later—a lieutenant and a sergeant major—said 30 NVA were killed and 40 wounded in the barrage.

At last, an opportunity arose for Blaz to receive medical treatment for his wounds. As dusk approached, Alpha's battle-weary soldiers secured an emergency landing zone for helicopters dispatched to evacuate the wounded. Juan Blaz had to be ordered onto the last chopper out.

"I refused to be medevaced. I felt that my remaining men needed me. I did feel weak from the loss of blood. However, I still wanted to fight. My company commander ordered me out on the last ship. I reluctantly complied," Blaz said.

At the same time, Alpha Company was ordered to fall back and take up a night defensive position at the spot where everything had started.

"I looked around and everyone's gone. There was a guy stuck between the trunks of two trees, so I unlocked his web belt and dragged him back 100 yards or so. I was exhausted. That's when I found out I was covered with fire ants. They had been biting me all over, and I didn't even know it," Kochanski said.

The troopers made their way back to where they had dropped their rucksacks. No one had remained behind to guard the packs, and there was a real concern that the gear could have been booby-trapped during the battle. The NVA had used the tactic before. Nerves were taut as men picked up their packs. Fortunately, no booby traps had been planted. The enemy, however, was still all around them, and Alpha Company formed a defensive circle. Then came an order given only when the situation is desperate.

"Word spread that the company ran out of ammo. The company commander said to fix bayonets. That was the first time in Vietnam I had heard that order. That was a surprise. Kind of scary. I didn't have a bayonet, but I had this big buck knife that I carried," said Mike Gamble.

"Now it's dark. It's so black, you can't see a thing. Then boom! They hit us again. You try to find anything to hide behind. We could have been overrun. That was the longest night of my life," Ed Kochanski said.

Arthur Kellogg said the grunts were saved by guardian angels in the helicopter gunships, but it took coordination from below to make it work.

"The gunships came in but didn't know where our position ended and where the enemy's began. A pilot told us to hold our strobe lights straight up in the air. They circled and fired at everything outside the lights. Their rounds came within feet of us. I never felt such a feeling of relief. That was the hairiest night I spent in Vietnam," Kellogg said.

"That's a night I'll never forget. I put a case of C Rations in front of me for cover," said Carl Bludau. "The wounded were taken out by medevac, but the dead stayed with us. We couldn't do anything for them. If it wasn't for Jim Littig and Juan Blaz, the whole company could have been wiped out."

With gunships firing and the artillery blasting away, Darron Sharp couldn't sleep. Seared into his mind was the sight of the cherry lieutenant who had been shot in the face, his nose blown off and his tongue hanging by a thread in the bloody mess that once was his throat.

"I felt like there were a couple of thousand eyes on me. We were lying there, shoulder to shoulder, thirsty and tired after a day-long firefight, with a cold, cold rain coming down," said Sharp. "The only way to get away from a mini-gun was to go down a hole or move left or right. Ain't no place to run. God was involved. You know that expression that there aren't any atheists in foxholes? God spoke to me that night and said you're going to have to work at staying alive. We made it through the night."

When dawn came, troopers who considered themselves lucky to be alive prepared for what was to come by cleaning and oiling their weapons. Supply helicopters were unable to land at Alpha's position, but crews kicked out boxes of ammo. The grunts loaded up right on the spot. Then the marching orders came to go take the hill again. But first, the fast movers roared overhead and blasted the NVA complex with bombs and napalm.

"That air strike lasted 20 minutes. It was sweet music to us. I was blowing kisses at those pilots. That's how happy I was to seem them," said Ed Kochanski. "There wasn't much left of the bunkers. We found chunks of hair and lots of body parts, but no bodies. The NVA believed in reincarnation and dragged off their dead. They would do anything to make sure the bodies were buried. Still, I'll never forget that putrid smell of burning flesh. We stayed out there for quite a while."

Said Darron Sharp: "We found fires still smoldering that the enemy used to cook their rice and fish heads."

The abandoned complex consisted of 44 bunkers, 13 mess halls, a large classroom and a central command post. The bunkers were so well camouflaged that they could not be detected from the ground or the air.

At that very moment, guided by a hand-held compass, Charlie Company slithered through the let-me-go bushes and the wait-a-minute vines to sweep toward the site of Alpha Company's fight. On the way, troops came across a remarkable complex of 19 abandoned defensive bunkers protecting a hospital compound that had been built in the jungle. Capable of treating up to 200 wounded, the field hospital had two operating rooms and 10 wards. The last patients had been evacuated on January 19, just before Charlie Company reached it. All surgical equipment had been removed too, but a large quantity of medical supplies was captured. What amazed Ron Snodgrass was that the NVA had built the hospital with American-made materials.

"They were using our shit to make operating tables. They took the wood from the boxes used to ship our artillery shells. They even used the hinges. One spot looked like a regular doctor's office. It was elaborate. We found an area where crutches were being made for their wounded out of the wood from our supply system," Snodgrass said.

Also seized were eight to nine tons of rice and a regimental-sized radio network. Combat engineers were called in to blow up the compound.

In the beginning of the big operation, Charlie Company had air-assaulted into hostile territory and suffered its own losses while pushing toward the Ho Chi Minh Trail.

"We saw lots of action. We were all in line, going through a bamboo thicket that had four-foot high termite mounds. There was a freshly cut tree stump, and I'm thinking, 'We're in the middle of nowhere, and someone was cutting trees?' I told my squad leader, 'Oh shit,' " Snodgrass said.

He said the company reached the Ho Chi Minh Trail and promptly set out listening posts and night ambushes. They encountered NVA troops pushing bicycles laden with big bags of supplies and rice.

"They were so close I could hear them talking. We were surrounded and outnumbered. We knew they were all around us. We knew they were watching us. It was intense," Snodgrass said.

At one point when the company paused for a chow break, two troopers from Minnesota were digging C Rations out of their packs when an NVA soldier popped out from concealment and killed them both. They were Sergeant Richard Bruce Apland, 23, of Herman, who was one of seven children and was married with a son and a daughter; and Private First Class Richard Arnold Carlson, 24, of Wabasha. Charlie Company carried their bodies through the bush before they could be evacuated.

At another point, Specialist Ken Micloskey was preparing to take the point on a patrol, exchanging small talk with his squad.

"We used to kid each other that we were going home with a chest full of medals and get elected to office. Ken says, 'Hey, I got 60 days left.' We all laughed. He was gone five minutes later," Snodgrass said.

Three days after his 21st birthday, Micloskey was killed while walking point. A native of Plymouth, Connecticut, he was described as an excellent soldier and a smart, all around good guy.

"He never flinched," Snodgrass said. "Ken had taken the exam for sergeant so he could get out early to go to college. What a waste, a damn waste. He could have gone home, went to school and found a cure for cancer. We'll never know. Who knows what they all would have become? It was a tough time. Some bad, bad days. My squad went out on that op with 10 to 12 guys. We came back with three. The others were killed, wounded or out of action. I got amoebic dysentery out there and spent three weeks in the hospital."

Fifty years later, Snodgrass was still processing the experience.

"I think about it every day. What impact did we have? What difference were we making? What a senseless, useless war," he said.

Records also show that Specialist Thomas Edward Draughn, 21, of Baton Rouge, Louisiana, was killed by small arms fire the same day as Micloskey.

One helicopter insertion that stuck with John Koons of Delta Company was when the gunships cleared a landing zone by firing their mini-guns and rockets. The purpose was to make sure no enemy were around, but there were unintended consequences.

"We had been trying to get guys in there for three months. The gunships busted up hornet's nest, and the hornets attacked us. We all got bit. Guys' faces swelled up so bad they couldn't see. It's amazing any of us survived," Koons said.

At another point, Delta was patrolling in the rain forest when it encountered an enemy force.

"They were building bunkers. We could hear them talking. My blood was running cold. We opened up with an M-60, but we got off only one round before the gun jammed. They heard the shot and took off. That's the only thing that really saved our lives," Koons said.

Early on in the operation, Delta lost Private First Class Alec Henry Horn, 21, a draftee from New Berlin, Wisconsin. Five months into his tour, he was killed by small arms fire.

The 2nd of the 505 continued to look for base camps out along the border. Companies were repositioned to various landing zones in support of the 1st Cav. Some stayed out on the operation until the middle of February.

"We were supposed to be there for 12 days, but we were out for 50 days straight. We had a contest to see who could grow the best beard. I won. There was no re-supply of uniforms. Everybody looked like they were wearing shorts because our pants were shredded away. Our jungle fatigues were white from all the dried salt from the sweat. Dirt was the only thing holding them together. We were rag tag," Koons said.

On Operation Sheridan-Sabre, the 2nd of the 505 took on the NVA on ground the enemy considered to be safe. Base camps, supply points, a hospital and a regimental headquarters had been destroyed. Bloodied and bruised, unable to mount an attack against Saigon, the NVA melted away to the West. It was the same old story. Having no intention of holding what they just took, the All Americans were air-lifted out, leaving the NVA to slink back into the area.

The names of those from the battalion who were killed are together on Panel 34 West of The Wall—Alec Horn, Norman Cates, Greg Ellison, Stanley (Rock) Rykaczewski, Benjamin Benton, Juan Castro, Richard Apland, Richard Carlson, Larry Martin, Thomas Draughn and Ken Micloskey among them.

As an aside, Juan Blaz was sent to a 1st Cav field hospital to be treated for his wounds. Sometime in February, when he had healed enough to return to Alpha Company, Blaz was called to a ceremony at Fire Base All American. Brigade commander George

Dickerson pinned a Silver Star on his chest and told him, "Sergeant, this is just an interim award. You have something higher coming to you."

So remarkable were Blaz's actions on the water run that Jim Littig wrote them down on the cardboard of a C Ration box. His recommended Blaz for the Medal of Honor, the country's highest award for valor, because he had risked his life to save others. The cardboard citation was given to a medic, Doc Thieleman, who was evacuated with shrapnel wounds in his legs. Thieleman had the papers in the right pocket of his jungle fatigues, and at the hospital, an orderly with the equivalent rank of a staff sergeant cut off Thieleman's trousers.

"You got a safe place to put this? I gotta turn it in to the brigade or the 1st Cav," Thieleman told the orderly. With that, he was taken away for treatment.

When Thieleman returned to retrieve the paperwork, he couldn't find the orderly or the original citation. The paperwork was lost. Events were later reconstructed, and Blaz did receive the Distinguished Service Cross. Years later, at Fort Lewis, Washington, Blaz ran into his battalion commander. He asked if Blaz had ever received the Medal of Honor. It was the first Blaz had heard about it.

"I did whatever I was told or expected of me and never questioned top to bottom directives. My attitude at the time was, if they wanted me to get it, they would give it to me," Blaz said.

The 82nd Airborne later ran a tracer action through the Awards and Decoration Branch at the Department of the Army, but no record of Blaz's actions was on file. Again, the paperwork was reconstructed, including a sworn statement given in 1987 by Blaz, who stayed in the Army and retired as a sergeant major. It is still possible for him to receive the Medal of Honor if the Department of Defense reopens the file for review.

"Blaz deserves the Medal of Honor," said Darron Sharp. "But in the moment, who cared about anything except staying alive?"

Back in The World on January 20, Richard Nixon took the oath of office as the 37th president of the United States. As the new commander in chief, Nixon had promised to end America's involvement in the war and turn over the fighting to the South Vietnamese. "The greatest honor history can bestow is the title of peacemaker," Nixon said in his inauguration address. "We are caught in war, wanting peace. We are torn by division, wanting unity…After a period of confrontation, we are entering an era of negotiation. I shall consecrate my office, my energies, and all the wisdom I can summon, to the cause of peace among nations." Nixon also told the nation: "The American dream does not come to those who fall asleep." America's combat role in Vietnam dragged on for four more years. Nixon was re-elected before all U.S. combat troops had been brought home.

Chapter 47
AN ACT OF LOVE

At the hospital in Japan where Rick Dalton was recovering from his wounds, word spread that Joe Namath, the quarterback of the New York Jets who was the MVP of Super Bowl III, was coming on a USO tour to visit the troops. Dalton was shipped home an hour before Broadway Joe arrived. But the disappointment of missing out on a chance to meet Joe Namath paled in comparison to the awful news he got in a letter from a buddy. His friend, Benjamin Benton, had been killed in action.

"I felt guilty because I would have been in charge of the squad if I hadn't been hit," Dalton said. "Benton had taken my place. I felt guilty for coming back alive."

In the back of his mind, Dalton promised that someday he would visit Benton's grave to say a proper goodbye. It became a lifelong mission.

Meanwhile, on a Monday morning in February of 1969, a government sedan carrying two men in military uniforms stopped at a gas station in rural South Mills, North Carolina, to ask for directions to the Benton farm. Word spreads like wildfire in a small town where everybody knows everybody else and where everyone knew Benjamin Perry Benton was in Vietnam with the 82nd Airborne.

Unwelcome news had reached a slice of small-town America that, come spring, would be surrounded by fields of potatoes, soybeans and sage. Mr. and Mrs. Cecil Benton had lost their oldest child and only son. Lois and Vivian Benton had lost their beloved brother.

"The car pulled up to the house, and I stood on the couch to look out the window. I will never forget that cry my mother let out," said Vivian, who was in the eighth grade at the time. "My mother and dad never did recover. It rained the whole week. It poured rain on the day of the funeral, but the cemetery was packed."

Benton's headstone in West Lawn Cemetery, located in the Pasquotank County community of Elizabeth City in the northeastern corner of North Carolina, bears the carvings of SS, for Silver Star, an award he was given posthumously, along with the Bronze Star medal and the Purple Heart. He was buried in the family plot, next to an uncle who had fought in World War II. Both he and his uncle shared the name Benjamin, which was also the name of both his maternal and paternal grandfathers.

The entire community grieved the loss of a sharp-dressed young man who had attended Camden High School and had a promising life ahead of him. The loss particularly pained R.W. Byrum, who had grown up about a mile away from the Bentons and who had attended the same high school as Benjamin. Byrum had done his part in Vietnam, being wounded while serving with the Army's 25th Infantry Division at Cu Chi.

"He was one of the nicest persons you could ever meet," Byrum said.

The two soldiers had agreed to stay in touch through the mail. The final letter Byrum wrote was the one that stayed with him through the years. "The last letter got sent back because it couldn't be delivered. He had been killed in action," Byrum said. "I was shocked."

History may not linger long, but the bonds forged by brothers-in-arms last forever. After returning from Vietnam and getting on with his life, Carl Bludau embarked on his own quest to find Benton. A locomotive engineer with the Southern Pacific Railroad, Bludau knew Benton was from North Carolina but didn't know what part. In the days before computers, Bludau combed the phone books of every town he visited, spending a fortune calling operators. After searching for some time, Bludau's efforts paid off in March of 1982 when he found a phone number for Benjamin Benton. It turned out to be the family of the uncle who had served in World War II, but Bludau was able to track down his friend's family. He made the pilgrimage to North Carolina to say goodbye, something he was unable to do in Vietnam. In so doing, he brought solace to a family burdened with unanswered questions.

Benton was a sole surviving son and could have appealed the draft notice that plucked him from civilian life and into the Army. He chose to report as ordered and wound up in Vietnam. The uncertainty surrounding his son's death haunted Mr. Benton.

"I really need to ask you something," Mr. Benton told Bludau.

The fatal wounds had entered through Benton's back, and without knowing any of the particulars, the father wondered if his son had been running away from a fight. Bludau quickly disabused him of that notion. He related the facts of how Benton's team was ambushed, about how he had had been hit by a sniper in the trees as he pursued the ambushers and about how he had been slung over the shoulders of Juan Blaz when machine gun bullets tore through his back.

"Rest assured, your son was a hero," Bludau said.

As the years passed and America moved on from the war, two other comrades who had served with Benton in Alpha Company were driven by their own need to pay their final respects. In 2015, Mike Gamble and Rick Dalton found each other on the internet. In the subsequent exchange of emails, they pledged to find Benton's gravesite.

"Mike and I made a promise that this was something we had to do before we died. It was Mike's idea, but I told him don't dare go without me," Dalton said.

A retired prison guard, Dalton never forgot how Benton had helped him become accepted into the unit. He also carried the guilt of being away from his squad on the day Benton's water detail was ambushed.

"When I was just getting my feet wet over there, he was kind of the glue that held everybody together," Dalton said. "He wasn't a super man or a super human. He was just so steady. He was a guy you could always count on to do the right thing. And he was my friend."

To Gamble, Benton was a soldier's soldier, a leader who made sure the men in his rifle squad were cared for before he looked out for himself.

"He was very unselfish. Always looking out for us. We'd get a box C Rations, which weren't very good to begin with, and he would hand the best of them out to us and take what was left. He always kept his composure. Never got mad. If a guy was afraid, he'd say, 'I'm scared too.' He would take the point when he didn't have to. He put his people first," Gamble said. "Only by the grace of God did I come home. Benjamin saved my life. I have never forgotten that day and will never forget him. The best compliment I can give him is that he was a good solider. He wore that uniform proudly. When you're in a position to lead, you have to accept that responsibility. As in any family, you do whatever you have to do."

Finding the burial place took time and research. After a number of frustrating dead ends, Dalton learned through a third party that Benton was buried in West Lawn Cemetery. A phone call confirmed the location of his grave, and the call also led to a contact with Benton's surviving sister, Vivian Benton Bridgers.

When word spread that two soldiers who served with Benton were arranging a visit, the Veterans of Foreign Wars Post 6060 in Elizabeth City got involved. In conjunction with Memorial Day, the post annually honored a hometown veteran who had been killed overseas. Dalton and Gamble made plans to be in town on May 20, 2018, and a larger memorial service for Benton was arranged.

Friends and family met on a Sunday at the VFW, then formed a procession of cars to the cemetery. At the grave, a motorcycle group called the Patriot Guard Riders of North Carolina stood in formation to greet visitors. The leather jackets and vests of the Patriot Guard Riders were emblazoned with the emblems of military units and the American flag. One of the group's slogans is: Standing For Those Who Stood For Us.

A crowd of 65 people gathered. Some were war veterans in motorized scooters or wheelchairs. Some were veterans of Benton's second family, the 82nd Airborne Division. Also attending was Kerry Jones, the young woman who had been Benton's girlfriend. She had married but had never forgotten, and she and her husband drove for three hours to attend the service.

"He was just a good fellow. He loved his family. We loved to go to dances. Then he got plucked by the Army and sent to Vietnam," said Kerry.

She had saved all the letters Benjamin had written to her and, years earlier, had given them to Vivian.

The VFW provided an empty boots memorial, also known as a battle cross. The tribute consisted of a pair of polished combat boots and a military rifle stuck into the ground with a bayonet, a combat helmet resting on the butt stock. Daniel Serik, a retired U.S. Army sergeant and a member of Post 6060, spoke from a portable dais placed at Benton's grave. He introduced Mike Gamble and Rick Dalton.

"They did not receive the best welcome home back in those days, but we're here today to welcome them home once again," Serik said.

Gamble and Dalton spoke, recounting stories of the man they had served with. At Benton's grave, with heads bowed, they said their own private farewells. Selma Parron, the post bugler, sounded "Taps".

"It was my honor. It was very emotional. It was the hardest one I've ever done," she said. "Ben was raised in South Mills, and I was too."

After the graveside service, family and friends were invited to Post 6060 for a reception. As food and drink were served, the juke box played songs from the Sixties, including *Fortunate Son* by Credence Clearwater Revival.

"I wish my parents had been alive to see this," said Vivian Benton Bridgers when asked about the day's events. What would she want people to remember about her big brother? "That he loved his family. He loved his country. It wasn't his choice to go into the Army, but he served and did what he thought was his obligation as a citizen."

Ken Sandridge, a Navy submariner and commander of Post 6060, told Gamble and Dalton: "I hope my friends are as good to me as you have been to your friend."

It was pointed out to Rick Dalton that he had fulfilled that part of the contract to remember those who didn't come back, to shoulder some of the grief on behalf of a fallen brother's family.

"It's more than a duty. It's an act of love," Dalton said.

When the time came to leave, Mike Gamble reflected on the events.

"It was something I needed to do. Something Rick needed to do," Gamble said. "It fixed things. Closed the circle. It was kind of like the last chapter. I can close the book, but I'll never forget the contents. We won't ever forget. I have the same feeling now as I had when we were at the cemetery. I don't want to leave."

Chapter 48
BAPTISM BY BOAT

The time had come, as it did for every lieutenant who was new to combat in Vietnam, for Jerald Dewveall to lead his first independent patrol. At 23, the fresh-faced officer from Fort Worth, Texas, had been in country for 25 days, long enough to have had a backup role in the tunnel operation at Cu Chi but still learning. Eager to prove his worth, he had lobbied for the assignment of plying the Hoc Mon Canal network feeding off the Saigon River in an area of marshland just north of the South Vietnamese capital. He volunteered to lead a handful of soldiers aboard a flat-bottomed, aluminum boat powered by an outboard motor.

At his side was an experienced hand, Staff Sergeant Ramon Felix Ortega Jr. of Tucumcari, New Mexico. Ortega, also 23, was on his second combat tour and had been with the Golden Brigade for seven months and one day.

Also in Dewveall's boat was radio man David Roberts of Bridgeport, Connecticut. His father had fought as a Marine at Tarawa and in other Pacific battles in World War II, and Roberts wanted to do his part too. He had asked his local draft board to call his name shortly after his graduation from Warren Harding High School in 1967.

The mission took place on January 25, 1969, a day that Roberts said, "is forever burned into my mind."

All three were part of Captain James Callahan's Delta Dragons. As part of the 1st of the 505 of the Golden Brigade, Delta Company had scored some earlier successes in the same area with night ambushes on land. On one such mission, a squad lying in wait in the thick vegetation of a canal bank had engaged a sampan moving along the waterway in the dead of night. The sampan was sunk, and its three occupants killed. They were Viet Cong couriers carrying papers that included a report of a Special Forces commando unit that annihilated a VC element near Cu Chi, a mistaken reference to the Delta Company action during which Billy Smith was killed.

Although the top talent of the Viet Cong had been sacrificed in the Tet Offensive in 1968, the insurgents still maintained a stubborn presence in Binh Duong Province, which abuts the northern city limits of Saigon. They used rivers and canals as watery highways to ferry troops and supplies. As a countermeasure, some tactical genius at a higher command thought it would be worthwhile to place troops in boats to get a view of the shoreline from the water. Although river patrols were nothing new to the Golden Brigade, going out in boats was a relative novelty for Delta Company. There was skepticism about placing infantrymen in watercraft that lacked armor and were propelled by a noisy engine in broad daylight.

The way Callahan remembered it, the brigade had the use of some boats for the day and passed them down to battalion with instructions to "use them or lose them." The boats were given to Callahan, who thought it was a dumb idea and countenanced the thought of telling battalion what to do with its boats. Reluctantly, he accepted the mission, partly because he intended to give it to one of his experienced lieutenants. Dewveall, however, requested a meeting with the captain the night before the mission and volunteered. Callahan thought about his own learning curve during his first tour in Vietnam, and since Sergeant Ortega would be on the boat, he relented and granted Dewveall's request.

"War is a cruel master. You have to start learning sometime, and real learning comes from doing," Callahan said. He did caution Dewveall: "No John Wayne stuff. A dead lieutenant is of no use to me or to the U.S. Army."

On the morning of January 25, with Callahan and much of the company aboard a U.S. Navy boat that would patrol the Saigon River, Dewveall and five troopers in battle gear squeezed into a Boston Whaler skimmer that looked like a bass fishing boat.

"I followed orders and did what I was told," said radio man Dave Roberts. "But in retrospect, the boats were a dumb idea. No stealth involved, which was what we did best with our roving night patrols. They could hear you coming and could see you clearly as well."

From his vantage point in a different part of Delta Company, Les Hayes said: "It was a suicide mission. The canals were narrow, and the banks were thick with jungle on both sides. Perfect for the gooks to fire us up without ever being seen. Stupid plan. We were sitting ducks."

At some point, the squad in Dewveall's boat spotted a lone Vietnamese man on shore. The vessel was beached, and the man was questioned. Claiming to be a rice farmer, the man had no uniform, no weapons or anything else that indicated he was an enemy combatant. Without grounds to detain him, he was let go. Roberts disagreed with the decision and voiced his objections to Lieutenant Dewveall, who was only four years older than him but was still referred to as the Old Man.

"I knew the gook we caught was not right. He was too fit. Too military looking. My gut knew that. This guy was no farmer. His hands weren't calloused. I wish I had been much more forceful about that," Roberts said. Fifty years of hindsight later, Roberts said they should have just shot the guy.

There are different takes about the initial encounter. One version was that the squad radioed for guidance about the detainee before letting him go. Callahan said he received no such message. He was of the mind that one prisoner who was a potential source of information was worth more than two dead adversaries. Because he spoke Vietnamese, he would have relished the opportunity to interrogate the detainee. No one mentioned the initial encounter in a debriefing called a "hot wash" later that day, Callahan said.

At any rate, the boat resumed its journey up a canal that was about 30 yards wide. By mid to late afternoon, the patrol was on its way back to link up with the company. Then, at the very spot where the detainee had been released, some Vietnamese were observed running along the bank, and Dewveall ordered the skimmer to shore. Sergeant Ortega wanted to get his men out of the boat and into combat formation to advance on foot, a prudent recommendation in the event they were being led into a trap.

Just as they reached land, an explosion came from the type of Chinese grenade the Viet Cong used in booby traps. Gunfire also erupted in the opening of what grunts called the "Mad Minute." Grenade fragments hit Dave Roberts, who was knocked silly for a few seconds by the blast. Also wounded was the medic, Beauford (Doc) Rosselot, a Seventh Day Adventist from Beaumont, Texas, who packed emergency medical gear but went into the field without a weapon.

The first one out of the boat was Lieutenant Dewveall. Attempting to advance toward the gunfire, he was shot in the head and crumpled to the ground. Having shaken off the effects of the grenade, Roberts followed and tried to lay down suppressing fire. His radio was hit and knocked out of action, the piece of equipment likely shielding him from a mortal wound. Before Sergeant Ortega could exit the boat, he was also shot through the head. Everybody on the boat had been hit except for the motor operator.

While taking fire and returning fire, everyone returned to the boat, either under their own power or with assistance. The skimmer sped away and linked up with another patrol boat. On that boat's radio, an urgent call was made for an air ambulance. During the wait, the medic worked in vain to revive Dewveall and Ortega. Both were mortally wounded.

"The lieutenant was doing what he was trained to do. He was the first one out of the boat," Roberts said. "He was a likeable sort and a good officer. He certainly wasn't one of those cocky know-it-all lieutenants that we saw a lot. He listened. I guess it's true that only the good die young."

The medevac chopper arrived within minutes, although under the circumstances, it seemed like hours. The flying ambulance raced to the nearest military hospital. Roberts and Doc Rosselot had bandaged each other up as best they could, and they looked like a sight.

"When we got off the chopper, pretty much carrying each other, some guy was on his way to the tennis court all dressed in tennis whites with nice white shoes and carrying his racket. It was such a contrast from where we had come. He looked at us like we had just come from the Moon," Roberts said.

An hour later, a nurse came out and confirmed the worst. Lieutenant Dewveall, on his first independent patrol, and Sergeant Ortega, on the last of many ambushes, had been pronounced dead. Doc Rosselot's wounds were serious enough that he was sent home. He received a Silver Star for valor for his actions that day. Roberts spent 30 days recuperating before he was sent out to the field again.

Meanwhile, except for the medevac helicopter, no lift choppers were available to pursue the enemy forces responsible for the ambush. In hindsight, Captain Callahan said he should have just refused the boat mission or should have been much more explicit with Dewveall about not getting caught in the open on "a piss ant little canal." He lived with the command decision for the rest of his life.

Reflecting on the events of that day years later, Callahan wrote of Ortega: "His loss hit hard. He was an older hand."

Of Dewveall, Callahan wrote: "A very brave young man, he did not survive that cruelest of learning curves—an infantry officer's first 30 days in combat, when you learn the dirty tricks of war not taught at the infantry school. Jerald was smart, really driven. Had he survived, he would have been one of the best. The problem is you first have to survive…Combat is wonderfully direct. You do or you don't. Fuck up and you're dead. Just get unlucky and you're dead. Every day above ground is a good day. Everything else is secondary. Grasping that reality was the ultimate learning curve. If you survived, it stayed with you for life. It also forever marked you off from the rest of your generation. It was a secret you could only really share with a fellow member of the brotherhood, be he alive, or like Lieutenant Dewveall, be he dead. We all still talk to our dead."

Dewveall is buried in Mount Olivet Cemetery in Fort Worth, Texas. Ortega was interred at Tucumcari Cemetery in his hometown. Their names are listed on Panel 34 West, Line 75, of The Wall.

During its next rotation in the same area, Delta Company operated on land and flooded the zone with night ambushes usually comprised of five men each.

"It paid off," Callahan wrote. "A pocket ambush on a clear night spotted a significant column of enemy, some 15 to 20 plus, on the move through a wide swath of marshland. Enemy was too distant and too numerous to engage, but battalion supplied some night gunships. They were given the ambush team leader's frequency, and he then vectored the birds in on multiple gun runs to hose down the zone. The next day, aerial recon reported numerous blood trails, a sign the enemy unit was hard hit. Battalion couldn't cough up a bird for a quick ground search, however, and with no surviving enemy POWs to interrogate, it could never be confirmed if the unit was the same that had ambushed Dewveall's patrol. Working assumption was it was the same."

Delta Company continued its mission of finding and fighting the forces threatening to topple the South Vietnamese government. The resilient and resourceful adversary was worthy of respect, according to Callahan.

"He had the three essentials for fighting a limited war—presence, patience and persistence. That's why we came to call him Mister Charlie," he said.

By March, and in accordance with Big Army policy of rotating combat officers every six months, Callahan was promoted to major and was required to take a staff job as the operations officer in the 1st of the 508. He wanted to stay with the company and tried to turn down the promotion, but to no avail.

In his reflections on having commanded Delta Company, Callahan wrote: "The soldiers are not there to further this or that officer's career. They are there to kill, to get the job done, and to go home. They have signed on to do the job, but expect you to ensure it is done with the minimum of friendly losses in keeping with the job at hand. Everything else is secondary. Keep it simple. Above all, leave them with the conviction that if the job at hand is bloody, no life will be sacrificed for glory. Glory isn't even a whore. A whore at least puts in a hard day's work. Soldiering is for professionals. The only thing that counts at the end of the day is getting the job done, protecting each other, keeping the faith. When it's over, that's all you'll have. The world will move on, your sacrifice will be forgotten, but you'll be able to live with yourself."

Callahan had relinquished control to a new commander when Delta Company participated in a big operation Out West near the Cambodian border in mid-March and early April.

Chapter 49
SUPPORTING ROLES

Although Ron Lane spent most of his time in the field with the grunts, his mission centered on morale and the spiritual needs of troops rather than combat. A draftee from Murphreesboro, Tennessee, he was a chaplain's assistant, or Charlie Alpha, with the job of helping the Catholic and Protestant clergy provide aid and comfort to those doing the fighting.

"When I was assigned to the 82nd Airborne at Tan Son Nhut, I was told, 'Here's your jeep. Get to work.' I put 13,000 miles on that jeep, driving out to the troop locations and the field hospitals," Lane said. "I didn't have a hard job, but it was dangerous. The thing that got me through was I wasn't worth killing. The bad guys weren't going to risk giving away their presence to fire up one jeep."

Lane doesn't recall meeting any atheists on his travels. "If there were any, they didn't walk around bragging about it," he said. Because he drove from unit to unit, he became a primary source of information for soldiers looking for scraps of information about the war in general or the location of buddies in the various rifle companies.

"I usually knew where everybody was. I was 25 with a receding hairline, and I'd show up out of nowhere," Lane said. "One of the things that made the job bearable was interactions with the soldiers. They were isolated. They'd come up to me and ask me questions like where's Charlie Company this week, or what's going on with the war. Then one time, one of the troops said to me, 'Guess where I was last week?' "

The answer, later confirmed by one of the chaplains, was that a platoon of infantry from one of the rifle companies had been pulled into Saigon on a secret mission. About 30 or so members of the Golden Brigade were placed atop the roof of the U.S. Embassy as extra security in case there was a repeat of the Tet Offensive. Several tracked vehicles from the cavalry unit were also moved into the capital city as a contingency. At the highest levels of command, the American military's major concern was that the local insurgency and the North Vietnamese Army would attempt a repeat of their 1968 attack on Saigon. No such coordinated offensive materialized, however, due in no small part by the presence of the All Americans.

Troops had neutralized the rocket belt in the northwest quadrant outside of Saigon. The tactics of saturating the area of operations with aggressive patrols prevented, for the foreseeable future at least, a second psychological blow against the government allied with the United States. "No rocket fired at Saigon was launched from the brigade's area of operations, testimony to its effectiveness and its pacification and security programs," the unit history said with justifiable pride.

Based on lunar cycles observed for 46 centuries, Tet is a movable holiday and a days-long celebration of the first morning of the first day of the new year. In 1969, the first day of Tet was February 17 and heralded in the Year of the Rooster with a celebration of family and the welcoming of spring. It was also another year of change for the 82nd Airborne. Those who had been part of the original deployment and who had elected to complete their required 12-month tour had rotated back to The World. Replacements filled the gaps in the constant churn of manpower.

"Tet of 1968 got everybody's attention. It was a big pivot in history for the America that came out of World War II. It marked the beginning of a new era for this country," Lane said.

With a perspective gained over five subsequent decades, Lane added: "Ain't no monuments to us in Vietnam. If you win a war, they put up monuments to you."

Another unique perspective on the war belonged to Bruce Andrews of Sheridan, Wyoming. Commissioned as a second lieutenant in the Army's Medical Service Corps, Andrews had been granted status as a conscientious observer and wasn't slotted for Vietnam. He volunteered. By his count, he spent 10 months, five days, three hours and 46 seconds in the combat zone while he was based at a logistics center at the 7,000-foot mark off the noisy runway of Tan Son Nhut.

"I didn't believe in war. Never have, never will. And I certainly didn't believe in this war. I was 23 when I went over. I had never been tested in my life. I figured that if I went to war, I might get tested," Andrews said. "Just because I hate war doesn't mean I hate the warriors. They're my brothers and sisters. I decided that if I was going to kill, the only one who would make that decision was me, not somebody else."

A cherry lieutenant who didn't carry a weapon still played a role in a combat unit. One duty for Andrews was running the morgue at Third Field Hospital, identifying the bodies brought in from the field and preparing them for their final journey back to the United States.

"The one I remember still had a wet uniform on with grass in his boots and a tag on his chest. This one major—I called him Daffy Duck—says to me, 'Okay, lieutenant, doesn't the sight of this dead American kid make you want to kill a lot of gooks?' If you're a conscientious observer, they think they can walk all over you. I saluted the rank, but I had no respect for Daffy Duck. He did tell me once, 'At least you're not a chicken shit. You're over here.' People asked me all the time, 'If you don't have a weapon, what about your patients? What would you do if the enemy attacked your hospital?' And I answered, 'I'd pick up a weapon and blow them away.' Like I said, the only reason for being a conscientious objector is that I was going to make the decision to pull a trigger, not somebody else."

At times, Andrews accompanied his medics on combat missions.

"I don't want them going where I wouldn't go. I should do whatever one of my men is asked to do," Andrews said.

He also left base camp for the rice paddies and the forward operating bases to pay the troops once a month, often carrying $50,000 worth of military pay certificates in ammo boxes. Troops weren't paid in cash because American greenbacks fueled the black market, and the images on military pay certificates were changed routinely to thwart the war profiteers. Andrews also was pressed into service as a defense counsel in court martial proceedings.

"Guys hung over from the night before at the Officer's Club sat in judgment of enlisted men charged with smoking weed. I knew some of my medics smoked, but I never knew it to be done on patrol," he said.

Andrews said that on the whole, he has no regrets about his service.

"I learned about myself, learned about life and death. I still don't like war, but it was important for me to find out what my principles are and live them. Own your stuff and deal with it," Andrews said.

In civilian life, he became a licensed professional marriage counselor and spent a career listening to guys and their struggles.

Meanwhile, Captain Robert Anderson was the assistant supply officer in the 82nd Support Battalion that supported the troops in the Golden Brigade. Unofficially, he went by several names. Higher-ups in the overall supply system called him "the biggest crook in the Republic of Vietnam," a title he wore with pride because he would beg, borrow and steal on behalf of the trigger-pullers doing the fighting. Because he was stationed at a base camp in Phu Loi, the grunts referred to him as a REMF—one who is in the rear with the gear, or a Rear Echelon Mother Fucker.

"I was a REMF, and I'm not ashamed of it. I did my job the best I could, and I hope I saved some peoples' lives," Anderson said. "The supply system in Vietnam was basically paralyzed. Everything was back ordered, from T-shirts to shorts to socks. We made the system work in spite of itself. If you have thousands of troopers fighting a war, they shouldn't want for anything they really need. Anything we needed, I got. I could find just about anything, anywhere, if it was still in the supply system."

Anderson was stationed at Fort Bragg with the 82nd Airborne when it was sent in an emergency to Vietnam. A native of Chicago, Illinois, he majored in history and English with a minor in philosophy at DePaul University, where he attended on an ROTC scholarship. Once in the Army, he volunteered for the Airborne.

"I was afraid of heights, but if I learned to cope with my fear of parachuting, I figured I could contain my fear when people are shooting at me," he said.

Supply officers may not get much love in the history books, but they are vital in a war zone. Although a modern army may not march on its stomach as it did in the days of Napoleon, it can't function for long without bullets, beans and benzene.

"I used to tell my guys, hey, you can go weeks with little or no food, you can go days without water, but you can only go a few minutes without ammo in a firefight," Anderson said.

What he found in Vietnam was a jury-rigged supply system with an unworkable computer network run by civilian employees of the Department of Army. Some of those administrators were really good at what they did. Others were the dregs of the departmental system raking in tons of overtime, Anderson said. For example, one computer network kept track of everything in the inventory. A separate computer network kept track of location, but the two computers didn't talk to each other. It was indicative of a supply effort that started small and then escalated as more and more units were sent off to war. Red tape nearly suffocated the whole effort.

One example of necessary pilferage was an item critical for keeping the artillery firing. Because the big guns blasted away so often to support the grunts, the recoil mechanisms on the cannons wore out. Anderson found out that an entire load of recoil mechanisms was arriving on an Air Force Starlifter, and he dispatched his trucks to pick them up right off the plane while it was still on the runway. He bypassed the system to deliver the goods for his unit.

Delivery was a separate issue that required midnight requisitions, which was another term for thievery. The 82nd Airborne has always been heavy on combat might but light on logistics, and an orphan brigade always has problems getting supplies because larger organizations with higher-ranking generals got their stuff first. As a way of keeping the supplies flowing, Anderson said he stole a deuce-and-a-half truck from the Air Force and another from the Marines. He created his own transportation system with what he could find. American factories produced a flood of trucks coming in for the South Vietnamese Army, but the vehicles were part of an arrangement that lined a whole lot of pockets.

"We gave the South Vietnamese a whole bunch of five-ton trucks worth about $12,000 each. But their government also imposed a 100 percent import tariff, so we also gave the government $12,000 for each truck we brought in. They were making double on each truck," Anderson said. "Another time, one guy offered me $5,000 for a truck engine with a turbocharger. He was a Philippine national who owned a truck company. There was so much stuff going on it was incredible."

Drivers for the 82nd Support Battalion were the walking wounded—troopers who were recuperating after being shot up in firefights but were not yet healthy enough to return to the field.

"We didn't have our own chow hall, so I took the drivers to a Chinese restaurant at Long Binh. The place had hot and cold running water with a flush toilet. The walking wounded who had been out in the field with no amenities whatsoever would hit the flush lever, again and again, just to watch the water swirl before it flushed down. They'd do this over and over. Some of them would take a complete bath in the sink," Anderson said.

On one occasion, Anderson located a quantity of poncho liners, one of the most needed pieces of equipment in the field. To guard the precious commodity, one of his soldiers slept on the beach next to the crates that had arrived at a Vietnamese seaport before they were transferred to a Landing Ship Tank for shipment to the Saigon area.

"I was at the dock when it landed. A Vietnamese civilian with a forklift took a pallet holding one of the crates and started to drive away with it. I put a 12 gauge shotgun against his head and got my poncho liners back," Anderson said.

The absurdity of the system knew no bounds. Even body counts could be used for barter. Anderson said he traded 10 Viet Cong killed in action to a unit that hadn't met its quota of KIAs for 20 communist assault rifles. He traded half of the rifles to the Navy for steaks and ice cream. The 10 remaining weapons were sold on the black market to procure aviation gloves required by helicopter pilots. Vietnamese civilians could obtain these Nomex gloves and wear them when riding their motor bikes, but U.S. helicopter pilots had to rely on the ingenuity of a supply officer to get what should have been theirs in the first place.

Another time, infantrymen sent on missions in the Pineapple Plantation southwest of Saigon needed something solid to stand on so their feet wouldn't be constantly in water. Anderson traded some captured assault rifles for three truckloads of wood.

"We couldn't get 2-by-4s or 4-by-4s, but we could get 12-by-16s. So, we built our own sawmill at Phu Loi to cut them down so the troops would have something to stand on," Anderson said.

Jungle boots were rationed out by the program manager of the Military Assistance Command, Vietnam. The 82nd Airborne averaged six pairs of boots per man for a year, but the bean counters failed to understand why so many boots were being allotted. It was like pulling teeth to get combat boots for the guys who really needed them.

On the other hand, the brigade still had wood-burning stoves in its inventory in Vietnam. Those stoves were on the books because the brigade had been alerted to go to North Korea in January of 1968.

If there was one image that illustrated the lunacy of it all, it was a memory that Anderson never could get out of his mind—a Vietnamese woman nursing a baby as she sat on a pile of garbage while taking a dump.

"It was like Alice in Wonderland. We fell through the rabbit hole when we went to Vietnam, found this totally bizarre world that bore no resemblance to real life, where weirdness became normal, where you don't think like you normally think. Like, hey, the base is being rocketed, wouldn't that make a cool picture? Then we popped back out of the hole when we went home, and everything was weird in the United States," Anderson said.

Chapter 50
CONDE'S CREW

The surefire way of knowing a platoon sergeant like Felix Conde was to walk a mile in his combat boots, or in the surreal bubble of Vietnam, follow him through the daily and nightly slog of shared stress and communal misery. Set up a night ambush in a rice paddy. Patrol a canal. Probe the tunnels. Guard a bridge. Air assault into an area aboard a helicopter. March with wet feet. Learn to urinate while walking because a column can't be held up for a call of nature. Spray bug juice on the ground to repel leeches and scorpions before bedding down on a poncho liner.

"When you face death together, there's an unbreakable bond that forms. You look out for each other," said machine-gunner Pete Watkins, who served in Conde's first platoon in the Delta Dragons. "Sometimes it was terrifying. Sometimes it was peaceful. Any time we left the wire, we were at war, and we were almost always out in the field. Even the biggest bases could be rocketed or mortared. There were no front lines. We had no final destination, just get out there and look for the bastards. Hump to new spot or get lifted in by helicopter, then leave. With all of our firepower, we always won, then we'd leave, and they'd take back the ground. Whose idea was that? When you let politicians run a war, you're bound to fail."

The bond is strongest between the platoon sergeant and his radio man, as in the case of Les Hayes. His duties put him within arm's reach of the man in charge, 24 hours a day, in case a call for fire support or a medevac was needed. Hayes and Conde slept up against each other, a tangible example of what it means to have your buddy's back.

"We'd get rained on and have that wet dog smell. Then the rain would stop, and it would be cold. We would lay back to back just to stay warm, out of mud," Hayes said.

In such close proximity, Conde might mention his two children, 3-year-old Little Richard and 2-year-old Little Jeannie. The two men got so tight that they knew each other's smells.

"He farted a lot," Hayes deadpanned.

Well, flatulence was a byproduct of canned Army food. What's more, Conde sometimes cooked up a mulligan stew, a dish made of various offerings from the C ration menu. In his unique recipe, however, he would toss in some insects and spiders. Hayes would pass on the final product, then Conde would pick out the bugs and have more for himself.

"I was down to 120 pounds, but he seemed to keep his weight up," Hayes said.

Sometimes, what keeps a man going is the thought of actual food, and Hayes would fantasize about the Golden Arches that went up in his Kentucky home just before he was drafted into the Army.

"I could buy a cheeseburger for 15 cents, fries for ten cents and a Coke for 10 cents. I could eat a full meal for 35 cents, plus two cents for the sales tax. Like a gift from heaven. I dreamed of living to eat at McDonald's again. Despite the kind of lifestyle we were living, a cheeseburger and fries was my greatest craving," he said.

Such anecdotes always elicit a chuckle in the retelling, and those who have never lived an infantryman's life might wonder what was so funny. But anything that broke the stress could produce a laugh, although the one being pranked or victimized never saw it as funny.

"One time, we were in an old burned out church. It was once a beautiful structure, but it was all blown up. Conde was sacked out on his back. Well, nearby, some local citizens had drained a lake. They went into the mud with cups and pans, sifting through the mud for snails and other edible critters. They also killed a six-foot long snake, which was probably was going to be their dinner. We took the snake, and someone comes up with a piece of string that we tied to the snake's head. We coiled the dead snake on Conde's chest, and using the string, waved its head right under Conde's nose. Then Conde's eyes came open and there's this snake right in front of his face. He didn't realize it was dead. He went into a dying cockroach position, laying on his back with his arms and legs spread. His mouth was open, but no sound was coming out. It was like he was paralyzed. He turned blue in the face, and we hopped out of there, trying to control our laughter. When he regained his senses, he came looking for the guys who did it. He never asked any questions. Never said a word. He came to my area and looked at each one of us while carrying his loaded M-16. If I'd have looked guilty, he probably would have shot me," Hayes said.

On another occasion, Conde called his patrol to a halt for a chow break. Hayes plopped himself down on a dry patch.

"I saw what I thought was a stone, and I sat on it to get off the wet earth. Conde comes over and says, 'What the hell are you guys doing?' I told him I was sitting on a rock. And he says, 'That's a bomb. You want to get blown to smithereens?' It turned out that the object was a 500-pound bomb dropped by our Air Force that had failed to detonate," Hayes said.

If humor can be found in the darkest of times, anything can be funny, even fire ants and hornets.

"Those fire ants would leap at you from the trees. They attacked the ears, nose, eyes or any opening on the body. The only hope of escaping them was to get under water. One time, one of our guys was walking along a canal when the ants got him. He dove into water and emerged on the other bank. Just as he was getting out, his head hit a hornet's nest in another tree. As he was being stung, he jumped back in water. It's not funny if your head swells to twice the size of what it was because of all the bites, but we couldn't control ourselves," Hayes said.

Leeches were the least amusing of critters, but when asked once what was the funniest thing that happened to him, Hayes said: "We were coming off an ambush patrol when I stopped to take a leak. Apparently, a four-inch leech had attached itself to my tool during the night. My buddy spotted it first. Not so funny to me, but my comrades sure had a good laugh."

There was also the time one sergeant almost incinerated his private parts in a self-inflicted incident. The sergeant neglected to put the safety cap back onto his pop-up flares. As he was putting the devices back into his pack, a flare went off and lit a fire right into his crotch.

Field hygiene was another matter. "Living conditions were horrendous, plus the fact there was constantly someone out there trying to kill us. We were plum nasty. We were in the field so long that one Italian guy's hair grew so long and curly that he could barely get his helmet on. Conde threw me a dull, rusty bayonet and told me to cut his hair. He looked ragged, but it was best we could do, and there weren't any mirrors around for him to see what he looked like. Appearance was secondary in our line of work," Hayes said.

More often than not, a night ambush would pass without incident. After one such night, Hayes found himself in a state of distress because he needed to take a dump. He stepped out of the bush into a farmer's rice field and was just about to squat down.

"I went out a few feet into the dry paddy to relieve myself. During the process, I saw a gook walking toward me who I thought was a local farmer. He was dressed in black, wearing a big straw hat and carrying a bundle of rice stalks. He stopped at an intersection of two dikes, squatted down and laid the bundle of straw on the ground. He started talking to me and pointed to the bundle of straw. I looked and saw a rifle barrel sticking out of it. I took my gun off safe and approached him. He wanted to surrender to our side without getting shot. That is why he camouflaged his gun. A few days later I was surprised to receive credit for capturing a gook with a weapon. This gook was sent to the rear to be re-educated and later joined our company as a scout. I was given a pass into Saigon," Hayes said.

Mail arrived on the helicopters, and there was no bigger boost in morale than a letter or package from home. Pete Watkins got a lot of mail. After reading the letters, he'd burn them so Charlie wouldn't happen to find a return address and write harassing letters to his folks. He'd also get luxury items like cookies, cake frosting in a can, Tang to improve the iodine water or Jiffy Pop Popcorn. Everything was shared with his buddies.

"He got a can of cake frosting once. I personally never saw a drug in Vietnam, and we never had a problem with drugs in our unit, but we passed that can around like it was a marijuana cigarette. Everybody used the same spoon too," Hayes said.

Soldiers learned to run to the re-supply helicopters, which sometimes carried ice. It was unwise to put ice made of contaminated water directly into a drink, but by spinning a can of soda or beer in ice for a minute or too, the beverage would cool.

One never knew what a helicopter might bring.

"We were in an old burned out area when a Huey flew in and landed. Who gets out but Sebastian Cabot, the actor who played Mister French on that TV show, *Family Affair.* Then a cute little blonde in a mini-skirt got out too. We set up some ammo crates, and she played the guitar and sang. One of our guys apparently went to the same high school as her in Shelby, North Carolina. She got up and kissed him right on top of his nasty forehead. Then Sebastian gives each man a gallon of vanilla ice cream. Remember those flat wooden spoons? We used them and ate the ice cream fast before it melted. Every guy got a freeze headache. It damn near killed us," Hayes said.

Any well-meaning gesture was appreciated, even if it failed to serve a practical purpose. Although it rained all the time, Conde's men never wore ponchos. The sound of droplets hitting a poncho was loud enough to give away a position. Then one platoon member wrote his home church to asked for a shipment of windbreakers. The pullovers arrived, but they were bright yellow—not a good color when trying to look inconspicuous.

Situations in Vietnam didn't exist anywhere else. One image that stayed with Hayes occurred in a village, where a man wearing a collar was chained to something that looked like a doghouse.

"Apparently, he was crazy, and that was the Vietnamese way of dealing with the mentally ill," Hayes said.

For eight months or so, the leader of first platoon was Lieutenant Stanley Dodson. He set the tone by insisting that his soldiers avoid fraternization with the local population, including buying cans of Coca-Cola from little Vietnamese girls. He was a stickler for making sure that weapons were clean and functional.

"We tried to focus on one thing, doing our jobs without wasting a whole bunch of kids," Dodson said.

The day-to-day details fell upon the shoulders of Sergeant Conde, and he was all business when bullets were flying. Take the time Conde's unit was supposed to get a good night's sleep for once while holing up in a relatively secure compound run by the South Vietnamese Army. An ambush was sprung less than a mile away, and Conde's crew went to investigate.

"When we arrived at the scene, we went on line behind a rice paddy dike. Someone yelled fire, and we opened up on the tree line to our front. Then Conde jumped up and yelled, 'Charge!' We had never heard that order before, but we all followed him and fired as we went," Hayes said.

"Another night, we heard fire erupt, and Conde says, 'Let's go!' I had taken the radio off, and by the time I put it back on, he was gone with the others. I figured I'd better stay put rather than wander around alone in the dark," Hayes said. "Then I heard running, and we didn't run at night. My heart was pounding so hard. I heard that drum beating in the back of my mind. I was plum scared. Just then, I saw four soldiers silhouetted, talking in Vietnamese, probably arguing about which way to go. I pulled the pin on a grenade and set my rifle to full auto. I was just about to open up when they ran away and disappeared. Sure enough, Conde and the others came back to get me."

Platoon member Ron Vitale said of Conde: "He was all serious when it came to being the field. He had a saying that he repeated over and over again, 'It's a privilege to shed blood for your country.' "

The grunts never really knew exactly where they were or where they would be going the next time a helicopter arrived. But there was a sense that something out of the ordinary was in store in mid-March when Conde and the Delta Dragons joined the entire 1st Battalion of the 505 on a big operation to the Cambodian border. Troops were air-lifted to an area near the Parrot's Beak and the Angel's Wing, named for the shapes that man-made lines formed on a map. The grunts called it going Out West. Officially, the move was made in conjunction with Operation Atlas Wedge. Instead of smaller groups taking on the shadowy Viet Cong, this confrontation involved multiple Army units searching for the North Vietnamese Army in base camps off the Ho Chi Minh Trail.

The main thrust involved the 11th Armored Cavalry Regiment and the 1st Infantry Division in the Michelin Rubber Plantation. On the left flank was the 25th Infantry Division, which had operational control of the All Americans and placed them to their left. The 82nd Airborne's role, which got scant recognition, was to probe an area of the border to prevent NVA troops from massing for an attack on Saigon.

Troops rode helicopters to a place called Fire Support Base Tracy, which had been built by the 1st Cavalry Division in an earlier operation. Located 22 miles northwest of Saigon in Hau Nghia Province, Tracy was a rudimentary camp carved out of the jungle.

"They didn't push us off the choppers. We went. It was part of the job," said Pete Watkins. In fact, having completed 10 months of his 12-month tour, Watkins began to feel that he just might make it home alive.

Troops remember Tracy as having one four-hole latrine, which got a lot of use one morning after some contaminated eggs were served at breakfast. A soldier with food poisoning would run to the latrine and relieve himself, get off his hole to allow another soldier to use it and then get right back into line behind others in the same miserable condition to go again.

The remote landscape was mostly flat and overgrown with high grass dotted with stands of bamboo and rubber trees, but it was also saturated with booby traps emplaced to discourage U.S. forces from finding NVA positions. Tracy sat on the east bank of the Vam Co Dong River, a waterway that originated in Cambodia and was used as an infiltration route to Saigon. The river fed a canal network, and to beat back the vegetation choking the banks, crews aboard barges manned devices that looked like deluge guns to spray the undergrowth with Agent Orange. The dead stuff was then burned off with flame throwers. The Gates of Hell could not have been less welcoming.

The first contact with enemy forces was made by Bravo Company. Just after 2 o'clock in the morning on March 21, the NVA fired rockets and mortars into Bravo Company's command post as a prelude to an attack. The attackers were beaten back, and a sweep at first light turned up seven NVA bodies. Bravo Company came away from that fight unscathed, but Fire Base Tracy was hit by rockets, killing two Americans and wounding six.

One of the dead was a medic, Specialist Thomas Jackson Grindstaff of Maryville, Tennessee. His presence there was a mystery because Grindstaff, 23, was supposed to be on a Freedom Bird back to The World. The last anyone knew, he was about to board a flight at Tan Son Nhut. But he had come down with an infection from a recent tattoo, and he showed up at a battalion aid station at Tracy. Why he went back to the field is a secret he carried with him to his grave at Memorial Park Cemetery in St. Petersburg, Florida.

Later in the day on March 21, Bravo Company made additional contact and paid a price in blood. Troops encountered a North Vietnamese bunker complex, and in the battle to dislodge their adversaries, six All Americans lost their lives.

"We took the fighting positions of the NVA. That was a mistake because the enemy that dug them knows how they work. We took it to them in that fight, but a reasonable estimate is we were outnumbered by 100 to 1," said John Carney, the platoon leader who later became a priest. "That was a bad night for us."

Among the dead were Specialist Barry Wade Graf, 20, of Texarkana, Arkansas; Sergeant Herman Earl Lassiter, 22, of Holland, Virginia; Staff Sergeant Adger Moody, four days shy of his 32nd birthday, of Hartsville, South Carolina; Private First Class Billy Dan Murphy, 20, of Santa Clara, California; and Private First Class Anthony Souza, 22, of Lakewood, California, who liked to talk about his muscle car, a Chevrolet Chevelle Super Sport with a 396 cubic inch engine. All of them are listed on Panel 29 West of the Wall excepted for Souza, whose name is on Panel 28.

Elsewhere that same day, the highest ranking member of the Golden Brigade to lose his life in Vietnam died of natural causes. Lieutenant Colonel William Malcolm Church, 44, of Chicago, Illinois, suffered a heart attack while on his cot at headquarters. He is buried in Arlington National Cemetery.

Meanwhile, after arriving at Fire Base Tracy, Conde and the Delta Dragons were transported to the west of the Vam Co Dong River to search for the enemy. Part of their welcome was the sight of a cobra as big as a fire hose that was killed by the first sergeant. Although there were no markings to identify the border, Les Hayes believes the unit was inside Cambodia. The mission was to intercept any enemy forces attempting to infiltrate from Cambodia into Saigon.

"We were attached to the 25th Division at the time. We became their little bastards," said Les Hayes. "That place was booby trap city. We were losing a man a day to booby traps. They weren't meant to kill but to wound because it tied us up while evacuating the wounded. We were always under stress. First platoon was greatly under strength. Normally, it had 40 or so men. We were down to about 15 but the workload remained the same. A full squad ambush should be eight to 10 soldiers. Now the ambushes were three to four men, which greatly reduced our efficiency to successfully engage and neutralize a larger enemy force."

As the calendar turned to April, Captain James Callahan was long gone as company commander, and first platoon leader Stanley Dodson had been promoted to command Headquarters and Headquarters Company of the 1st of the 505. He was positioned at FSB Tracy while his old outfit was out in the boonies.

"No one knows how they're going to react the next time they're shot at," Dodson noted.

Chapter 51
GRIM FRIDAY

Almost three weeks after the initial air assault into Fire Support Base Tracy, fourth platoon of the Delta Dragons toughed out an uneasy night in the middle of hostile territory. Their ears told the soldiers that danger lurked.

"All night, we had heard digging and voices," said Carl Gulas.

At daybreak, the platoon formed up according to plan and lit out to link up with the rest of the company. Sergeant David Harold McDonald, a squad leader from Hialeah, Florida, led the way.

"We encountered an NVA sitting on top of a bunker, and our guys started sniping at him. McDonald was walking point, and then he was shot point blank in the head. If there was anyone who you thought would survive Vietnam, it was this guy. He was our safety net, always did his job. When he was killed, it was devastating," Gulas said.

Also killed in the exchange of gunfire was Private First Class Douglas Wayne Richards, 20, of Granite City, Illinois.

The platoon had reached the outer perimeter of a staging area for a battalion of NVA soldiers, who had built a complex of 35 bunkers in the wilderness. The opening exchange was just the start of a bloody, exhausting 10 hours of mayhem. Artillery and air strikes were called in to pound that position.

"How anybody could survive that air show, I don't know," Gulas said.

At the same time, Staff Sergeant Felix Conde and the dozen or so members of first platoon were spaced out at 15-yard intervals on the bank of a canal off the Vam Co Dong River. They had just come off an uneventful night of ambushes that had been set astride an infiltration corridor. While waiting for fourth platoon to link up, some jokesters tossed pebbles off the helmet of radio operator Les Hayes.

"The sun was up already, and it was hotter than hell. All of a sudden, we heard intense small arms fire and explosions, which appeared to be about a half mile directly in front of our position. My radio came alive, and I was attempting to monitor the traffic to determine what was happening. I yelled at the rock-pingers to stop as we had a major problem," Hayes said.

The radio delivered word that fourth platoon was under fire and pinned down. Conde's platoon saddled up to relieve the pressure.

Under the circumstances, nobody knew or much cared that the date was April 4, 1969. Back in The World, it was Good Friday, the most solemn day for Christians around the globe. According to Christian beliefs, this prelude to resurrection marked the suffering and crucifixion of Jesus Christ, the Son of God, who washed away the sins of the human race with his blood. It was also the one-year anniversary of the single deadliest day of the Golden Brigade in Vietnam.

"Our first obstacle was to cross the canal, which was quite deep and about fifty feet wide. It was impossible to swim due to our gear, plus some of us were non-swimmers, me being one of them. By some miracle, one of our men had a long rope. I have wondered for years why a light weapons infantryman would be carrying a rope. One of our swimmers strung it across the canal and we were able to walk it across. This took about half an hour, and the distant firing was continuing," Hayes said.

Among the soldiers who crossed the waterway was machine gunner Ron Vitale, who had nicknamed his M-60 the Ass Kicker. In water almost up to his neck, he gripped the rope as he walked along the muddy bottom.

"When we got to the other side, I broke down weapon and cleaned it. Maybe it was fate," Vitale said.

Now across the canal, the hard-charging Conde and his men then came upon a protective dike behind fourth platoon's position. Troopers went on line and opened up with a stream of fire into the enemy bunkers. The cacophony of combat bellowed from assault rifles, machine guns, grenade launchers and a rocket launcher called the Light Anti-Tank Weapon that packed a punch similar to a bazooka.

"We had the dike as good cover and proceeded to call in air and artillery support on the enemy bunker complex. Our support consisted of a squadron of Cobra gunships armed with mini-guns and rockets. They strafed the enemy complex and withdrew. We then called in a bomber group, and they blasted the enemy with 500-pound bombs. After this devastation, the enemy fire became very light and erratic," Hayes recalled.

One bunker put up a stubborn and remarkable resistance. A bomb had landed 10 feet from it, turning the ground to jelly, but the occupant kept firing away with his heavy machine gun. Then the commander of the 1st of the 505, who was directing the fight while hovering overhead in a light observation helicopter, eliminated the threat. Lieutenant Colonel Grace G. Thomas, whose call sign was Master Blaster, leaned out the cockpit of the helicopter and dropped a hand grenade through the bunker entrance. The explosion silenced the machine gun. For that bit of quick thinking, Master Blaster was awarded the Distinguished Flying Cross.

With the pressure eased, evacuation helicopters thundered in to extract the dead and wounded. Conde's platoon then moved forward to mop up. Bombs and napalm dropped by Phantom jets had devastated the bunker complex. Burned bodies littered the ground.

"By this time, it was probably four or five in the afternoon. We took about a half hour break and dined on some good old C rations. Thinking our mission was completed for the day, we reformed and started to leave to rejoin the company," Hayes said.

Conde's platoon split up into tactical formation along the opposite banks of a small canal. Shortly after moving out, they were targeted.

"We had walked probably about 100 meters along this canal when we once again came under heavy enemy fire. Myself and Conde had hit a heavy patch of bamboo on our side of the canal and could not pass through to get to the enemy positions. We hit the ground and started getting small arms fire over our heads. It appeared we had become pinned down in the same spot from which we had just rescued the fourth platoon. Conde yelled at me to stay in position and call in a medevac chopper as he knew we had wounded. He called some men forward and they started crawling around the bamboo thicket in an attempt to flank the enemy. I stayed where I was attempting to make radio contact, but my radio was dead. I later discovered a hole in the battery pack where something had hit it, either shrapnel or a bullet," Hayes said. The radio likely spared Hayes from a gruesome wound.

On his side of the canal, Pete Watkins walked point, unaware that Conde's column had been held up by the bamboo thicket.

"I was concentrating on the bunkers ahead of me and watching for any enemy in front of us. When I realized that the bamboo thicket had slowed their progress, that's when the enemy opened fire on me," Watkins said.

He didn't hear the shot that got him, but his comrades said it was a burst. All they heard was a groan that sounded like, "Uuhhnn." They figured Watkins had been shot dead. As it turned out, only one round found its mark, and it struck Watkins in the right buttock, tearing through muscle but not smashing any bone. A half-step quicker, and the burst would have missed him. A half-step slower, and the rounds may have been fatal. It turned out to be a million dollar wound, the kind that merits a ticket home.

"Maybe it was shock, but I never felt any pain. About that time is when everything broke loose on the opposite side of the canal. I took time to assess my wound and realized that it was not life-threatening. I crawled back to my slack man, Bruce King, who was about 20 to 30 feet behind me. All the time I was calling out that it was me coming back and not an enemy so I would not get fired up by my own men. Bruce said, 'We knew you had been hit. All we heard was a groan. We thought you were dead.' "

During the chaos, Watkins had lost his helmet, in which he had carried his wallet and the $15 he kept each payday while sending the rest of his money home. A helicopter was on the way to fly out the wounded, and Watkins had to reach the emergency landing zone. Assisting him was the Vietnamese scout who had surrendered to Hayes some weeks earlier.

"Everything seemed to be happening fast," Watkins said. "The medevac was coming, and I had to get across the canal, which was about eight feet wide. After making my way across, I came upon Les and asked if I could borrow $15 because I lost my helmet with my wallet in it. Les told me, 'You better get down. There's bullets flying over here.' And he was right. I got down."

Asking for money may have seemed like an odd request for a bleeding man in the middle of a firefight. But Watkins had the presence of mind to know he was going back to the rear, and he would need money to buy sodas and other goodies.

"I really didn't expect Les to give me all of his money, but I'm glad he had $15. I told him, 'When this is over, if you can get across that canal and find my helmet, all my money is in there.' And he told me, 'Hell, no. I'm not going over there. They're shooting at people over there.' I guess I really wasn't thinking clearly. The main thing on my mind was that I had the million-dollar wound and I was going home alive. I had 60 days left. I knew it was over for me," Watkins said.

In the midst of all the noise and confusion, Sergeant Conde reacted. His goal was to eliminate the bunker complex that was threatening the lives of his men.

"He came over to me, Bill Simmons and Charlie Richardson and said, 'You, you and you. Come on. Follow me!' I'll never forget the expression on his face. We were going to flank them," said Ron Vitale.

What happened next was pieced together by soldiers involved or those who witnessed the events. It occurred at an extensive bunker complex, later identified as a battalion command post, in Hau Nghia Province. The closest village was Ap Tan Hoa, but nobody remembers seeing a village.

After positioning the three men with him, Conde moved ahead on his own and heaved grenades as he assaulted a bunker. Even though the volume of enemy fire increased, Conde crawled to the blind side of an entrenched position. He jumped to the roof and tossed a grenade into an opening, eliminating that threat. In short order, Conde took on two additional bunkers, both of which he destroyed in the same manner as the first. He then rejoined Vitale, Simmons and Richardson just as an intense volume of fire erupted.

"We were in grass, a wide open area of four-foot tall grass. As I was crawling up, I got heat cramps in my legs and couldn't move. Sergeant Conde took my M-60 and gave me his rifle and a bandolier of ammunition. He was pulling out grass to stick onto his helmet as camouflage. To be honest, a lot of that day goes blank, but I did fire a couple of magazines from where I was," Ron Vitale said.

Using the machine gun called Ass Kicker, Conde maneuvered toward the enemy's flank. He single-handedly assaulted the nearest fortification, killing the enemy inside. But having exhausted all the ammo for the machine gun, Conde returned to Vitale. He exchanged the machine gun for his M-16, then took off for the next bunker. Within 10 meters of his objective, Conde was shot by an enemy soldier firing from a concealed position. Conde went down, felled by two slugs that hit his midsection.

"It haunts me in my mind. That could've been me," Vitale said. "He was incredible that day. Fearless. He exposed himself many, many times. He was a leader. He took the initiative. It was way above and beyond what anybody would do. He stuck his neck out for us. But it was anything but a Good Friday."

Vitale had gotten back into the fight when something slammed into his hip.

"It felt like a slap. I got mad. I'm wondering, 'Who the hell is slapping me?' It turned out to be a shard of shrapnel. My military belt took the brunt of it, but I had to get that shrapnel out. I burned my hand in doing so, and Charlie Richardson poured water on it," Vitale said.

Conde had been dragged back to the grassy area from which he had started. At the same time, Les Hayes moved up to the sounds of the guns.

"Somewhere up front, someone yelled that Conde had been hit. I started crawling and found Conde and a couple of men. Conde had two holes in his stomach area and was bleeding from his mouth. His last words were, 'God, don't let me die.' That was the last breath he took," Hayes said.

Felix Conde, the dreamer who wanted to be a baseball player, the man who had joined the Army and was married with two kids, was dead.

Conde's body was placed on a poncho. Four men, each holding a corner, carried him to a landing zone. A helicopter whisked him and the most severely wounded back to the battalion aid station. Because there was no more room on the air ambulance, a wounded Ron Vitale walked back to his position and stayed in the field.

Meanwhile, laying on the ground where the helicopter had landed was a shoulder holster that belonged to Conde. It was left behind during the pandemonium. Without being consciously aware of it, Hayes placed the leather holster into his rucksack.

"Having been basically joined at the hip, 24 hours a day, seven days a week, with this man for 10 months, we became very close. I made myself a promise that if I stayed alive, I would get in touch with his widow and his two small kids and tell them what a great man he was and how he sacrificed his life for his country and fellow soldiers," Hayes said. "I knew that his actions that day saved a lot of our lives, and had he not taken the offensive, I most likely would not have been around to tell this."

Although he never said it directly, Hayes had come to think of Conde as a father figure, a surrogate to his own father who had died before Hayes went into the Army. Conde's loss hit just as hard, but there was no time to process what happened. The survivors had to stay in the moment and continue the fight.

"Since I had no radio contact, I had no idea what was going on. I heard someone yell that our artillery was on its way. Being that we were close to the enemy positions, we knew we had to get the hell out of there. We ran like hell. A machine gunner running ahead of me was hit by a piece of shrapnel in his upper right shoulder and went down. He managed to get up to run, and I carried his M-60 to the protective dike we had been on when we first got there. We went on line and started firing on the enemy positions. I fired the M-60 until I wore all the skin off my right elbow," Hayes said.

At Fire Base Tracy, Stanley Dodson and his first sergeant loaded ammo and water aboard a re-supply helicopter bound for Delta Company's position. Radio chatter brought word that troops had been hit and killed. The casualties arrived late in the day.

"I saw Pete (Watkins) lying face down on a helicopter. He was waving at me. By that time, he had been juiced up by the medics," Dodson said.

Dodson helped unload the casualties.

"Conde was one of the ones I identified," Dodson said. "When I heard what he did, that's what I would have expected him to do." Conde's name appears on Panel 27 West of The Wall, which also includes the names of Delta Company comrades Sergeant David Harold McDonald and Private First Class Douglas Wayne Richards. A swimmer and a basketball coach, McDonald had a water park named after him in his hometown of Hialeah, Florida. His fiancé, Thelma Gilbert, wrote a heartbreaking letter to the men of the fourth platoon who served with him. Richards was survived by a son and two brothers.

As Good Friday came to a close, Delta Company was still engaged.

"By now it was almost full dark, and we managed to get back to our company and set up a night defensive perimeter. Our artillery continued to fire on the enemy complex all night," Les Hayes said.

At first light on Holy Saturday, operations continued.

"Our entire company did a helicopter assault back into the enemy positions and found them to be totally abandoned. We blew up the undamaged bunkers, and that was basically the end of this particular action," Hayes said.

The task of policing up the battlefield remained. Troopers sifted through the rubble for the obligatory body count.

"In that dark humor that soldiers have, while we were digging out dead bodies, somebody said sarcastically that this was what an Easter Egg hunt was like in Vietnam," said Carl Gulas.

On its operation Out West, the 1st of the 505 killed 81 enemy, wounded 12 more and captured one prisoner along with three suspects. Over 10 tons of enemy equipment were captured. The Delta Dragons, who suffered 30 percent casualties, were credited with discovering the largest single cache. Two tons of enemy equipment were found buried along canal banks near the Vam Co Dong River, including 530 mortar rounds, 38 rockets, 42 land mines, 72 assorted booby traps, nine Bangalore torpedoes, nine cases of Chinese-made grenades, 25 pounds of plastic explosives, 8,000 rounds of rifle ammo and 16 pounds of assorted documents.

Having lost his platoon sergeant, and without realizing it, Les Hayes slipped into a state of shock. He has no memory of his remaining 40 days with Delta Company in Vietnam. Somewhere deep in his soul was that promise he had made to Felix Conde. It smoldered like an ember for years.

Chapter 52
ONE FAMILY'S GRIEF

Pete Watkins had what was called a through-and-through wound, the projectile entering and exiting without hitting bone or vital organs. Such bullet holes can't heal properly in the tropics, however, and there was fear of infection. Accordingly, he was transferred to a military hospital in Japan, where the climate and level of care was better suited to mending soft tissue torn up by a bullet. The wound had to heal from the inside before doctors could sew him up.

"The most painful part of the whole ordeal was in the mornings when they'd come through and tear off the bandage after it had seeped and dried at night," Watkins said.

Within a week of being shot in a vicious firefight, Watkins received word that Felix Conde had been killed.

"I have often wondered if he didn't advance on those bunkers knowing that he had at least one of his men down. I guess we'll never know. The Army lost a good man on April 4, 1969," Watkins said.

Back in Texas, Lydia Conde and her two toddlers were accompanied by other family and friends as they attended a festival on Easter Monday. The six-week period of Lent was over, having given way to the celebration of resurrection. In addition to spiritual renewal, trees awoke from their winter's dormancy and sprouted new buds. Then the dreaded word arrived that ended the world as the Conde family knew it. Lydia's husband, the father of her children, had been slain in Vietnam.

Hysterics brought on by heartbreak caused family members to take her to see a doctor. A short time later, Conde's remains arrived at the funeral home in Rogers, Texas. Lydia never got to see her husband's face again. Morticians partially unwrapped the cotton gauze surrounding the body. She identified her husband by his hands and feet.

Conde had taken precautions in the event he didn't return. He had purchased a house for his family, and he had acquired eight plots in the Rogers Cemetery, which is surrounded by pastures for horses and cattle on the wind-swept Texas plain. Conde made it clear that he wanted to be buried in America. His father flew in from Puerto Rico for his son's funeral.

At the mid-April internment, an honor guard from Fort Bliss fired a three-volley salute, 21 shots in all. A bugler sounded the mournful 24-notes of "Taps" as the casket was lowered into the Texas soil about 10 minutes away from the place where Felix first met Lydia Layton. Lorenzo and Maria Layton comforted their grieving daughter.

Relatives wrapped their arms around Richard and Jeannie, too young to comprehend a pain that cut through the community like a jagged piece of glass. The American flag that had been draped over the casket was folded with white-glove care and presented to a war widow with the thanks of a grateful nation, a nation torn apart by Vietnam and dealing with the price families pay when civilian authorities send America's sons and daughters off to fight.

"Lydia truly never recovered," said family member Sandra Esqueda. "He would always be a part of her. There wasn't a whole lot of time to grieve because she had to care for her children. She made do and moved on, but she never recovered emotionally or psychologically. That scar never really healed. It was so raw. She had it rough. A single parent, with two kids, at a time when women didn't work, at the most vulnerable period of life..."

About three months after the funeral, Lydia received her husband's military awards in the mail. One was the Distinguished Service Cross, the nation's second highest award for valor. Although the prevailing feeling was that Felix Conde had merited the Medal of Honor, the DSC acknowledged that Conde had sacrificed his own life for his men. Lydia already knew deep down in her heart that her husband was a hero. She picked up her life as best she could, working odd jobs to earn extra money.

"She was a good mother. She took care of those kids and gave them whatever they needed, all the while telling them what a great man their father was," Sandra Esqueda said.

As the years passed, Lydia dated other men, but she never remarried.

"There's only one man I ever loved. Nobody can ever take his spot," she would tell her suitors.

She found solace in the big family gatherings she organized at Thanksgiving and other holidays. Her table might have 15 to 20 people gathered for her dishes, such as her signature salad made with olive oil, avocado and tomatoes. But there was always something missing for two children who were too young to understand but old enough to know sorrow.

"She was a tough, tough lady. She was very proud," said daughter Jeannie. "I'd see her crying and I'd ask what was wrong. And she would say, 'I just miss your dad.' God, I was angry. I'd ask God, 'Why did you do this to us?' We were on our own."

The struggles were particularly overpowering when there would be a father/daughter dance at school and Jeannie had no one to take her. Because it was a dreadful anniversary, Easter was a time to be hated. She met her future husband when she was a freshman in high school, all the while knowing in the back of her mind how important it is to have a father in her life. Without realizing it, she also provided comfort to a brother who was a year older than her.

"Jeannie the one who helped me through all this. She was a rock," Richard said. "It was an understanding that we had each other's backs. She's the stronger of the two."

Rico, as he was called, was the miracle baby, the son of a father who fought to save his life when his mother had such a difficult pregnancy. He too dreamed of being a baseball catcher, but he never had a father to play catch with or to guide him on life's path.

"I was a mama's boy, and she was phenomenal, but I didn't have a dad to relate to. I didn't even know he existed. I didn't know I had an empty bucket," Rico said. "There were times at night when I would be crying, arguing with God. Father's Day would come around and I'd ask myself what story I would make up this time to explain to my friends why my father wasn't around."

When he was 17, Rico started getting letters from the Reserve Officer Training Corps about a possible career in the Army. He sat down at the kitchen table to discuss things with his mother. She nixed the idea outright.

"She would look at me, without ever changing the tone in her voice, and say, 'Over my dead body will I let them take another man from my life. You're all I have.' She was fiercely protective. She had given enough," Rico said.

A young man doesn't know what he doesn't have. Rico would always feel a little bit lost as he entered adulthood. He was unaware that Les Hayes, a man who considered Felix Conde to be a father figure in their time together in the 82nd Airborne, was searching for him. Likewise, the final chapter on his father's Distinguished Service Cross had yet to be written. Those records were subject to review.

Chapter 53
OF THEIR OWN ACCORD

I wanna be an Airborne Ranger; Live me a life of guts and danger. – Airborne Cadence.

High school buddies Bailey Stauffer and Walter Foote of Safford, Arizona, were college roommates at the University of Arizona at a time when full-time students were deferred from the draft. Yet in October of 1967, with ground troops committed to Vietnam, they jointly decided to quit school and volunteered to join the Army.

"We just wanted to do it," said Stauffer, whose father was Army infantry in World War II and would have been on the force that invaded Japan until two atomic bombs forced a surrender.

With their college backgrounds, the two friends could have had any Army career they wanted. They chose to be the best of the best by becoming Airborne Rangers. Both of them also wanted to be in the Special Forces. While Foote did become a Green Beret and went to Vietnam, Stauffer was terminated from the program because an eye test revealed his vision fell short of standards. The Army gave him a choice between Officers Candidate School or Vietnam. He opted for Vietnam, where he deployed in July of 1968 as a Ranger specializing in long range recon.

Stauffer was part of a six-man unit that operated deep into enemy territory with a mission to "out-guerrilla the guerrilla," to see without being seen while tracking enemy movements.

Then the Big Army ordered a restructuring that altered the course of the war for these highly trained volunteers. Long range recon units were folded into various companies of the 75th Infantry Regiment (Ranger), which adopted the Latin motto *Sua Sponte*—Of Their Own Accord. Overall commander Creighton Abrams saw to it that they received jump pay even if they were not parachuting into battle. Accordingly, each company in the regiment was assigned to an Army unit in South Vietnam. In Stauffer's case, he was placed in Oscar Company and assigned to the Golden Brigade.

Wearing fatigues with tiger stripes, the fighters in Oscar Company carried five-quart canteens and ate freeze-dried rations that were the forerunner of the modern-day Meal, Ready To Eat. Inserted mostly by helicopter but sometimes by river boat, the Rangers operated in the flat, marshy terrain west and north of Saigon where cover was much more sparse than in other areas of Vietnam.

"We sure missed the jungle," Stauffer said. "We were pretty well trained. We did a lot of in-house training before missions. We'd go out and set up recon. We'd be out so far at times that a communications plane would do figure eights overhead to maintain radio contact. A lot of times, they used us as bait to see if larger units were around. There were supposed to be 70 of us in the company, but we were down from that number."

Then came a mission north of Saigon in Binh Duong Province. The team leader was Staff Sergeant Jerry Don Beck, 20, of Dallas, Texas, an infantry operations and intelligence specialist who had been in Vietnam for five months. He was a shake and bake from NCO school and got his sixth stripe after completing Ranger school. Also, on that mission was Sergeant Daren Koenig, 20, of Hannibal, Missouri, who had been in Vietnam for six months and was assigned to Oscar Company's communications section. Koenig, considered by his buddies to be the best soldier in the outfit, had volunteered for the mission. Numbers were needed in the field, and besides, it afforded him the opportunity to qualify for the coveted Combat Infantryman's Badge.

The team was inserted into an area of rice paddies, with earthen dikes providing the only cover. It was April 6, which was Easter Sunday back in The World.

"Beck says to Koening, 'You go with me. Let's earn you your CIB,' " Stauffer recalled.

As the team moved to its location, a sniper opened up from a tree line. Beck was killed instantly, and Koenig suffered a sucking chest wound. Like he was trained to do, Stauffer tried to seal the wound with a poncho. He held Koenig in his arms while waiting for the medevac, which took some time to arrive because the air ambulances weren't used to working with small patrols sent out to remote areas.

"I wished I could have done more. I remember this day forever. He's been in my thoughts every day since," said Stauffer.

Koenig was eventually flown to a field hospital, where he was pronounced dead. One of the rounds had nicked his heart. His Combat Infantryman's Badge was presented posthumously. Both Beck and Koenig are listed on Panel 27 West on The Wall.

Stauffer was also on Oscar Company's next mission on April 15. The Rangers were set up in a rice paddy in the same area of operations and suffered another fatality. Staff Sergeant John Anthony LaPolla, 20, of Frankfort, New York, was killed by a sniper, six weeks after he began his tour in Vietnam. He is also listed on Panel 27 West of The Wall.

Then at the end of April, Private First Class Michael Joseph Kelly Jr., 20, of Syracuse, New York, was out on a Ranger mission as the eyes and ears of the Golden Brigade. He was due to come in from the field, but because Oscar Company was under strength, the team that came out to relieve him was short on numbers. Kelly, who had a dry wit and was nicknamed The Professor, volunteered to stay and went over to the helicopter to get water. As he did so, he was shot by a sniper and died instantly. A medic, Fred (Doc) Merry, later honored his Ranger brothers by naming a son John Michael in honor of John LaPolla and Michael Kelly.

It was not the last of Oscar Company's casualties.

The Rangers had their share of characters in the ranks. One was Specialist Phillip Ward of Georgetown, Guyana, in South America.

"I joined the Airborne Rangers so I could fight for America in Vietnam," he said. He used his combat service as a stepping-stone to apply for American citizenship at the end of his tour.

Specialist Tony Quinata was noted for opening soda cans and beer cans with his teeth, much to the amusement of his fellow Rangers.

Also in the unit were a father and son who hadn't seen each other for five years until they were reunited in Oscar Company. Staff Sergeant Carl Robinson, who had spent two previous tours with the 173rd Airborne and six months as an advisor in the Mekong Delta, arrived for additional duty on June 16. While processing in, he was asked if he had any relatives serving in Vietnam. He answered that his son Victor was serving in Oscar Company, now attached to the 82nd Airborne. Within four hours, Sergeant Robinson was on his way to join the All Americans, where Private First Class Vincent Robinson of Paris, Arkansas, was a radio operator. Sergeant Robinson became the supply officer in his son's unit, taking the concept of the 82nd Airborne as family to an actual reality. The father also had two other sons serving in the Army. Jack Robinson was with the 1st Air Cavalry Division in Vietnam, and son Robert was stationed in Korea awaiting his 18th birthday so that he could be assigned to Vietnam.

Meanwhile, Bailey Stauffer completed his tour and was finishing out his enlistment at Fort Riley, Kansas. In a phone call home, his father told him that his high school and college buddy, Walter Bruce Foote, had been killed in action. Sergeant Foote, 21, was serving on Special Forces A Team 413 as an advisor to a South Vietnamese company operating in the Mekong Delta near Moc Hoa. Of his own accord, he asked to go out on a mission into the dark of night on March 6, 1970. Those along for the mission were fired up at a landing zone by a company-sized force, and Foote was killed. His last message radio message to his company commander was, "Help me! I'm hit."

Stauffer was assigned to escort his buddy back to Safford, Arizona, for burial at Resthaven Cemetery. Foote, an Eagle Scout, was awarded the Silver Star, Bronze Star, Purple Heart and Combat Infantryman's Badge. Every year on Memorial Day, Green Berets from all over Arizona gather to place an American flag on his grave. He rests next to his father and mother.

"We have reunions every two years," Stauffer says of his comrades in Oscar Company in the 75th Rangers. "We're brothers. That bond is still there, especially among the ones who went on missions together when everybody had to depend on the other person. We can look at each other and know what the other is thinking without saying a word. I really can't explain it. There's no other feeling like it. We try to live in ways that honor the sacrifice of the fallen. And we cry together."

Chapter 54
DEAD DUCKS AND LOOSE ENDS

Five decades after his time in Vietnam with the 82nd Airborne, Les Museus opened up for the first time to talk about experiences he had buried. He volunteered to join the Army in time of war, taking basic training at Fort Campbell and advanced training at Fort Lewis before he arrived in Vietnam.

"When I got off the plane, I was 19 years old. Right from the start, I never knew if I'd have to run and shoot. But in the 82nd, the camaraderie was terrific. A guy from North Carolina took me under his wing," said Museus, a native of Brainerd, Minnesota.

As part of Bravo Company in the 2nd of the 505, Museus was in a four-man ambush squad set up on the south side of the Hoc Mon Canal one night in 1969. Just before midnight, when it was darker than the inside of a coal mine, he received a rather unusual radio message from the company command post.

"I got a call that said, 'There's something coming your way, and it's big,' " Museus said. "I told everybody to tuck in. We were not going to light them up because we were outnumbered."

The American military had turned to technology in the quest to find and destroy hostile forces that operated clandestinely at night. The Golden Brigade established its own Surveillance Task Force to centralize all of its assets, including a ground radar system known was the AN/TPS 25, or Tipsy 25, also known as the eye in the night. Any movement would show up as a blip on a radar screen, and appropriate artillery units would be alerted. At the Hoc Mon, a Tipsy 25 was installed on an island in the middle of the canal network. A blip may not be what it appears to be, however.

At headquarters, forward artillery observer Donald Paquin, who had survived the big fight at Landing Zone Mike Foxtrot during Operation Sheridan-Sabre, monitored the radar for any indication of suspected activity. Around midnight, a big blob showed up on radar, and it was moving south.

"That thing lit up like a Christmas tree," Paquin said.

A radio operator alerted Captain Tom Hennessey to come quick. After some hurried discussions about what appeared to be a target of opportunity, Paquin got the green light to order a fire mission. He requested all available artillery to zero in on the coordinates he provided. With six guns in each battery, two batteries of 105-millimeter howitzers and one battery of 155-millimeter howitzers opened fire. At the same time, a higher headquarters was monitoring the radio traffic. The corps that had operational control of the Golden Brigade joined in and started shelling with more and bigger guns. Helicopter gunships took off to add the firepower of rockets and mini-guns. Mortar squads also joined the effort. Then the air base at Tan Son Nhut got wind of the artillery strikes and scrambled some attack jets to drop their bombs on the target as a force multiplier. What a show of light and sound that was. Around three o'clock in the morning, the radar was unable to detect any more movement.

"Daylight came, and an observation helicopter pops up on the eastern horizon. It flew over the impact area. We turned on the speakers of our radios so the men could hear," Paquin said. "The call came back, 'They're all dead ducks.' In the artillery section, we all cheered. Then he said dead ducks a couple of more times. I got on the radio and said, 'You mean dead dinks, don't you?' And the pilot replied, 'No. Ducks. The kind with feathers."

What had happened was that a large flock of Vietnamese waterfowl had wandered into the area, and the blips returned by the radar were mistaken for enemy soldiers. All of the artillery and air strikes had fallen on a thousand unlucky ducks.

From his position outside the kill sack, Les Museus said: "I was so relieved to learn it was ducks. It was crazy. We never did see any enemy."

A political problem arose. U.S. military command determined that the local villagers should be reimbursed for the loss of their ducks, which were their commissary on the wing. The bill was $5 per duck. What's more, the duck carcasses had to be disposed of, lest they rot and reek in the tropical environment.

"One of the combat engineers came out, and I asked him if he had bulldozers to dig a mass grave. He said, 'Yeah, we got that. But they weigh 47 tons each, and that's a rice paddy. They'll sink,' " Paquin said. "So, I asked him if he had five-ton trucks with flame throwers, the kind of equipment that was used to burn off the dead vegetation along trails and canals. He says, 'Yeah, we got that.' The trucks show up, and a stream of fire was trained on the ducks. The intent was to incinerate them, but some ducks were just wounded, and they started flying when the fire was turned on them. Some of the flaming ducks took to the air and crashed into a local village, and the ducks set some of the hooches on fire. You can't make this stuff up."

The fallout worsened.

"Captain Hennessey says to me, 'I do not understand how we went from killing a few ducks to killing a thousand ducks. I've heard of Buffalo Bill. Now we have the fucking Duck Hunter!' " Paquin said.

From that moment forward, Paquin's radio call sign was changed to Duck Hunter.

"If you can't live it down, you have to live it up," said Paquin, able to chuckle about the whole episode 50 years later. "Laughing is therapy. I prefer to remember the funny stuff."

On a serious note, Paquin noted: "I'm glad to have served with the guys I did. They were brave to a man. But people paid a terrible price. Our politicians sent us into a war that, under the rules of engagement, we couldn't win. We could have won that war the same way we beat the Japanese and the Germans."

Meanwhile, West Pointer Bob Murrill completed an odyssey that took him out of the field to a hospital in Japan and then back to Vietnam. Stricken with a medical condition known as mal-absorption syndrome, Murrill was unable to digest nutrients, and he lost roughly one-fourth of his body weight. At 6-foot-3 and 142 pounds, he looked like a scarecrow and lacked the energy needed for combat.

Ordered to an Army hospital in Da Nang in September of 1968, he saw a nurse, the first female he had seen in about eight months. He thought he had died and gone to heaven. He was then flown to Japan and admitted to Camp Drake, an American hospital in Asaka, about 30 miles outside of Tokyo. An old runway used by kamikaze planes in World War II was part of the grounds.

Convalescing in an open bay, Murrill got to know the soldier next to him, an enlisted man from Arkansas who was wrapped in bandages and had both legs and an arm in traction. Murrill guessed that he had stepped on a booby trap or land mine, but the reality was quite different. The solider had been in Saigon on an in-country R&R (Rest and Recreation).

"He visited an unauthorized whore house, which was raided by the Military Police. He knew how much trouble he would be in if caught, so he jumped out a back window. Just as he hit the ground, he was hit by a truck. That was going to be a hard one to explain back home, especially since his injuries did not provide justification to award him with a Purple Heart. He told me he already was thinking of another story that he could use for his family," Murrill said.

Three of Murrill's buddies came through Camp Drake. One was Al Nahas, a fellow Ranger who had been shot twice in the leg. An infantry platoon leader in the 101st Airborne, Nahas later authored a book of about Vietnam Veteran Memorials titled *Warriors Remembered.*

The second was Buz Altshuler, a West Point classmate who had a temporary plate implanted in his head as the result of a severe shrapnel wound that took out part of his skull. Murrill and Altshuler had gone to Ranger School together, but Altshuler was unable to recognize him.

"Years later, Buz achieved the rank of major general. His wife jokingly told me at our 40th West Point reunion, 'Buz is proof that anyone with half a brain can become a general.' I laughed, but inside I was just glad he recovered," Murrill said.

The third friend was Bill Haneke, an upper classman in Murrill's West Point company. Having been an usher for Haneke's wedding a few years before, Murrill said the sight of his comrade in the intensive care unit was unnerving.

"He had lost one leg, part of his other leg, an arm, a lot of his other hand, an eye and sight in his other eye was questionable. I didn't recognize him and knew he had a long recovery to endure," Murrill said. Haneke's story is included in the book *The Long Gray Line* about the West Point Class of 1966.

"He was one of those casualties who never should have survived, but he did. He returned home to Richmond, Virginia, and was told by his doctors that he would not be able to have kids. He had three. He was told he would not be able to walk again. He did, using only a cane. He was told he probably would not be able to see. He saw enough to return to school and obtain a master's degree in hospital administration. Bill became the Director of the Veterans Administration Hospital in Richmond. He will continue to be one of my personal heroes," Murrill said.

After three months in which he regained most of his lost weight, Murrill received orders to return to the States. Instead, he asked to be reassigned to the 82nd Airborne in Vietnam. He returned to the Golden Brigade early in 1969.

"I didn't want to be with any other unit. Those were my brothers," Murrill said.

He didn't know until years later that Bud Bolling had written several letters to his parents while he was recuperating. During Murrill's time in Japan, the brigade had moved Down South. His unit spent a lot of time in the Cu Chi area.

"The brigade sustained many more injuries and deaths from booby traps instead of direct combat. As we learned years later, Cu Chi possessed one of the most intricate systems of underground tunnels ever created. The Viet Cong had tunnels right below our feet and none of us knew it," Murrill said.

He also recalled the night his base camp was hit with mortars, and one of the shells hit the ammo storage dump.

"The concussion from the explosion of the ammo dump was horrendous. It was so strong that I looked up after diving behind some sandbags to see a naked U.S. soldier flying through the air with his pants trailing behind him. I learned later that he had been sitting on an uncovered outdoor latrine when the explosion occurred. The force blew him into the air and almost out of his pants. His only injury was a broken arm. Explain that war wound, when you get home! It wasn't funny to that soldier, but the rest of us couldn't hold back our laughter," Murrill said.

Crazy things happen in a crazy place.

Draftees had their own way of finding humor in the absurdities of Vietnam. One example was a letter on official-looking stationery that was a spoof on the unfairness of Selective Service. Written by a fictional official from an unspecified draft board, it read: "In reviewing our records, we have discovered a slight error. According to our files, you were drafted by mistake. Arnold Shirker should have been drafted instead of you. However, since you have already been inducted, and are probably enjoying the military life, we see no reason to go through all the necessary red tape to make a correction. Besides, my nephew Arnold has a very good job, and it would be somewhat of a hardship to make any change at this time. We certainly appreciate what you are doing for your country. Your draft board sends its best regards—as does Arnold."

Chapter 55
LOST IN THE WOODS

One reason why Dwaine Selk joined the U.S. Army was to ease his path to becoming an American citizen. A native of the prairie province of Alberta, Canada, Selk was naturalized in 1954 after he had earned a Combat Infantryman's Badge in Korea. Now a resident of Lolo, Montana, a town of 4,000 residents seven miles south of Missoula, Selk began the first of his three tours in Vietnam in July of 1965. As a member of Advisory Team 61 of the Military Assistance Command, Vietnam, his first year was spent running a training center for South Vietnamese Army recruits. Then as a first sergeant, he returned to Vietnam in January of 1969 and was assigned to Bravo Company of the 1st of the 508 of the Golden Brigade.

"I wanted a rifle company. If I was going again, I wanted it to be for something worthwhile," Selk said. "I was 40. The troops were my kids. I took it on as my goal to bring as many of those kids home as I could."

But even the best intentions of a top kick were subject to the vagaries of Vietnam and that inexplicable condition known as the fog of war.

At the beginning of May, Bravo Company and the entire battalion of Red Devils were lifted by helicopter to Fire Support Base Patton in the Ho Bo Woods, once a plantation of rubber trees located west of the Saigon River about 34 miles northwest of South Vietnam's capital city. The Woods were just west of the Iron Triangle in Binh Duong Province, about 12 miles north of Cu Chi. The area was infamous for being a political and military headquarters of the Viet Cong, and while the region was a new area of operations for the Golden Brigade, it bore the scars of previous battles. In 1966 and 1967, the U.S. Army had mounted some big operations in these woods, which guerrilla forces used as a staging area for the Tet Offensive. The ground was pockmarked with craters from earlier B-52 strikes. The rubber trees had been knocked down, replaced by scrub brush and undergrowth that concealed enemy bunkers. Beneath the surface was a maze of multi-tiered tunnels that provided sanctuary for hostile forces.

Although the Rangers of Oscar Company operated for only a short time in the Ho Bo Woods, they were productive. On a mission of reconnaissance and surveillance, the Rangers killed four Viet Cong while locating and monitoring a major infiltration route. Specialist Herbert Tortice, who was part Apache Indian, set up in the same area for two days only to discover that he had been sitting on a VC tunnel entrance the whole time. A search led to the capture of a number of documents and weapons.

Meanwhile, the Red Devils achieved initial success against bunker complexes with the support of artillery, helicopter gunships and air strikes. The battalion found and destroyed a 60-foot high observation tower, complete with a fire direction control center built into coconut trees. A concrete command bunker was also knocked out. According to the 82nd Airborne's records, the Red Devils killed more than 130 enemy combatants, captured 22 tons of rice, eliminated 88 booby traps and blew up 156 bunkers.

Dwaine Selk's Bravo Company had been in the Hobo Woods for 12 days, patrolling during the day and setting ambushes at night, all the while searching for the elusive enemy and the places where ammo and food were concealed. On May 13, the company was waiting for food, water, ammo, radio batteries and other essentials being brought out by helicopters. In the ranks was a machine gun team consisting of Specialist Robert Susumu Masuda, 21, a Japanese-American from San Jose, California, and David Munoz, 21, a Mexican-American who was born in Fresno but grew up in Los Angeles. Both were draftees but were at opposite ends of their tours of duty. Masuda was short, with 34 days left before he could return to The World. Munoz had been in Vietnam for 23 days.

The re-supply helicopter was late, the first of a series of seemingly innocuous developments that set in motion a tragic series of events. When the company was told to stay in place, troops took advantage of the down time to rest and sack out. At about 6 o'clock in the evening, Bravo Company saddled up to march to its re-supply point. On the company radio net, a message was sent that all troops were present and accounted for, and the march began. About 15 minutes later, however, the second platoon radioed the company commander with disturbing news. Despite the earlier assurance that everybody was accounted for, Masuda and Munoz were not in the formation. Bravo Company retraced its steps to find them.

"We only walked a quarter of a mile, and we turned around and went back into the area that we had just left," Selk said.

At a well that had recently been filled in with dirt, shell casings from enemy rifles and scattered bits of blood-soaked sand were discovered, but Masuda and Munoz were nowhere to be found. Further excavation of the well, and searches in other areas, stopped as night fell.

In the meantime, the pilot of the re-supply Chinook helicopter ordered Bravo Company by radio to get to where it was supposed to be as soon as possible. The argument was made that they couldn't leave without locating the two missing troopers, but to no avail. The message was: "You better get there, or you aren't going to get your stuff."

A horrible dilemma faced Bravo Company.

"Either we made the chopper, or we went without supplies," Selk said. "We tried our best to find those guys, but I had 140 other men to look after."

Despite the Airborne code that no one gets left behind, the company again moved out. It was decided to alert Alpha Company, a nearby sister unit, to resume the search for Masuda and Munoz in the morning.

"It bothered me a lot. It still bothers me," Selk said. "Maybe if I had argued a little harder…"

When dawn broke on May 14, troopers from Alpha Company headed toward the last known location of the two missing soldiers. Among them were fourth platoon members Frank Walenga and his squad leader, Ronnie Johnson. Both of them were short-timers and had already figured the Ho Bo Woods would be their last mission in the field. Johnson, a farm boy who had a wife and family waiting for him in Burke, South Dakota, had two weeks remaining on his tour. His replacement hadn't shown up yet, however, and because the company needed all the men it could get into the field, he was out on the mission. He had already received a Bronze Star for an earlier action in Vietnam. Walenga, a Polish-American from Chicago, had a month to go in Vietnam.

When they had first arrived in Nam, Johnson and Walenga were in different squads in the same platoon. Their relationship really solidified when Walenga joined Johnson's squad.

"We just got along great. Those last two or three months, we were together every day. We slept next to each other. If mortar rounds came in, we'd jump in the same hole. If nobody got hit, we'd laugh and tell each other we were lucky," Walenga said. "What I liked about Ronnie, he led. Even though he was the squad leader, he'd jump in and do a job. He was on the quiet side unless you talked to him and brought up something. He talked with a little bit of South Dakota twang. I'm a big-mouthed, Polish-American from Chicago. That's what war does. It takes people from completely different backgrounds and makes them into brothers. We had to depend on each other."

Alpha Company had seen its share of contact in the Ho Bo Woods.

"It was a much different area than we had been used to. That was the most tunneled and booby trapped area in South Vietnam. It was infested with VC, but we never saw them because they lived in the tunnels. We always had the feeling there were eyes on us. We never went out without a platoon-sized force. If we did make contact, we'd have a firefight, then call in napalm strikes or drop grenades into the tunnels and spider holes. We were always on alert for booby traps and ambushes. Charlie would almost always kiss us good night with a few mortar rounds."

Fourth platoon was tasked with searching a village that was closest to where the missing men were last seen, just in case the missing men had ventured there.

"The closer you were to Saigon, the safer the villages were. It was a different story out in the boonies. The VC had family there. This village was creepy. Creepy and weird. There were inhabitants there, but they stayed in their hooches. We wanted to find those boys. That was our job. To this day, I don't know why that company moved out and left two boys behind, but they did. When we arrived in the ville, we noticed almost immediately AK-47 casings all over the floor of a hut with a trap door. Directly across was another hut that had blood on the floor and a blood trail leading to a dry well in the middle of the ville. Our conclusion was that the two soldiers may have been ambushed by VC coming up from the trap door of one hut and firing into the other hut, killing the two soldiers and dragging their bodies to the dry well and burying them. Our squad was picked to dig up the well and hopefully find their bodies."

Ronnie Johnson took charge to explore a well that was maybe four feet wide and eight feet deep.

"I was going to jump in, but Ronnie stopped me. He said, 'I'll start, Frank.' Both of us had taken off our steel pots and used them as scoops. He'd dig and hand me a helmet full of dirt to dispose of. In turn, I'd hand him an empty helmet," Walenga said. "All of a sudden, he said, 'Frank, look. I think I found a cache.' We used to find weapons, mortar rounds and grenades all the time. I was three feet away. I looked and Ronnie was cradling a mortar round. Then it just blew up. I remember the earth just rising. All I heard was a sharp ping, like a super-loud ringing in my ears. Ronnie took almost the whole blast. It blew off his leg and arm and he got shrapnel through the midsection."

Walenga yelled for a medic. He and two other comrades had been peppered with shrapnel, but their thoughts focused solely on Johnson. "When that explosion went off, our wounds meant nothing to the three of us. We were all crying because of what happened to Ronnie. He took in that whole blast. Whether he cradled that mortar round at the last minute, or just because he volunteered to jump in there and started digging, it was heroic. He gave his life to save mine," Walenga said.

As the medic worked feverishly, a helicopter arrived. Walenga accompanied Johnson on the chopper and then to an emergency aid station.

"The medic was still working on him, but he wasn't making a sound," Walenga said.

Walenga didn't know what a concussion was, but having been so close to the blast, he had suffered a traumatic brain injury. One side effect of being concussed is having hallucinations.

"I was in the aid station, and I swore I saw Ronnie. I said to him, 'You're alive! You made it!' It turned out it was a different soldier who had lost the same arm and leg," Walenga said.

Unbeknownst to him, Johnson had already been pronounced dead. Meanwhile, on May 18, Bravo Company returned to the area to look for Masuda and Munoz, who were still unaccounted for. According to various accounts, searchers found an All American patch in a deck of cards that may have belonged to Masuda. Another version is that searchers found bloody shirts and trousers. Selk said that troopers found two pieces of scalp and 82nd Airborne shoulder patches nailed to a tree.

Masuda and Munoz were never found, and what happened to them forever remains a mystery. The best guess is that they fell asleep and failed to fall in when the company left the area, and something terrible happened to them while they were on their own. What is certain is that they were the only two members of the 82nd Airborne listed as Missing In Action during the Vietnam War.

The war was already over when the Secretary of the Army approved a presumptive finding of death for Masuda on March 16, 1976. He had been promoted to staff sergeant in the interim. A similar finding was issued for Munoz on July 31, 1978. He had been promoted to sergeant first class. Both men were honored with a memorial ceremony at the Courts of the Missing in Honolulu. Both are listed on Panel 25 West of The Wall.

Munoz's father, who had served in the Navy in World War II, had written hundreds of letters in an attempt to find out what happened to a son who felt it was his duty to serve his country in Vietnam. He never got a satisfactory answer. The oldest of six children, David Munoz was married and had a two-year-son when he went missing in action in the Hobo Woods.

Meanwhile, Frank Walenga was flown back to The World and spent six months recuperating at an Army Hospital in Fort Knox, Kentucky. He promised himself that he would one day say a proper goodbye to the squad leader who saved his life.

"Right when it happened, I knew I'd pay my respects before I died," Walenga said. "If you knew Ronnie, you had to love him. He was just such a giver. It was Ronnie who volunteered to lead and jumped into that well and started digging. It was Ronnie who discovered the booby trapped mortar round. It was Ronnie who gave his life for us. I live and breathe today because of him. I will never forget him. He was my friend, my brother and my hero."

In addition to Masuda, Munoz and Johnson, the Red Devils also suffered seven men lost in the Ho Bo Woods operation. They were:

– Delta Company Sergeant Armand Dominic Masten, 20, of Cleveland, Ohio, who was president of his high school class. His father, a veteran of the Battle of the Bulge, was the mayor of Lindale, Ohio. Masten was supposed to return from Vietnam on May 5, but he extended his tour in order to hasten his discharge from the Army. He and Specialist Ronald Ree Somes, 21, of Sault Sainte Marie, Michigan, who was described by his platoon sergeant as "the kid everyone liked," were riding in the same jeep when it struck a land mine. Also killed from Delta Company was Specialist Charlie C. Williamson Jr., 21 of Memphis, Tennessee. The oldest of eight children, he was 22 days short of completing his tour. He had already told his family he was looking for some good home cooking, and the family bought a big country ham for his homecoming and a family reunion. Williamson never got that meal. He was killed by a mortar while out on night ambush.

– Private Leroy James Gentry, 24, of Asheville, North Carolina, who was married and had a son. He served in Charlie Company.

– Sergeant Arthur T. Mallinckrodt, 20, of New Franklin, Missouri, a member of Alpha Company. The son of Mr. and Mrs. Arthur T.H. Mallinckrodt Sr., he had attended the Nashville Automotive Diesel College.

– Private First Class Joel R. Kelly, 26, of Columbus, Georgia. A member of Bravo Company, he was married.

– Specialist Donald William Vallen Jr., 20, of New Hyde Park, New York. He served in Echo Company. The son of Mr. and Mrs. Donald W. Vallen Sr., he was a graduate of Holy Cross High School in Bayside, Queens. He had two sisters, Mary and Alice, and a brother John. Vallen frequently wrote to his parents to say that he served with "a great bunch of guys." Said his father at the time of his death: "He loved his country and never complained, but he had rough times over there throughout his stay." All are listed on Panels 24, 25 and 26 West of The Wall.

Back in The World, President Richard Nixon spoke to the nation on May 14 and called Vietnam "the most difficult war in American history, fought against a ruthless enemy…Never have America's fighting men fought more bravely for more unselfish goals than our men in Vietnam. It is our responsibility to see that they have not fought in vain." At the time of his speech, U.S. combat deaths in Vietnam exceeded the 33,629 killed in the Korean War.

Chapter 56
GOLDEN PROMISE

Ronnie Wayne Johnson was originally rejected by the Army because he had flat feet. He was reclassified after a second physical but didn't have to go to Vietnam because a younger brother was already serving there. Then having volunteered to go to Vietnam, he was two weeks short of coming home. Yet he was killed in Southeast Asia while serving with Alpha Company of the 1st of the 508 in the Golden Brigade of the 82nd Airborne, leaving a young wife and a grieving family to untangle his All American story.

A child of America's Heartland, Johnson was from the farm country around Burke, South Dakota, a town with fewer than 1,000 residents that consisted of little more than a community center, bank, hardware store and granary hugging its main drag. Born December 30, 1946, he was the oldest of four boys of Charles L. and Neva Johnson, who raised milk cows and livestock on their self-sufficient farm.

Johnson attended Burke High School but opted to leave school after six weeks to take a job so that he could help support his family. He didn't much care for books anyway. He was more interested in construction work, tinkering with cars and hunting pheasant and deer in the southeastern part of his home state. He met his future wife, Annie Preslicka, in 1965 when life seemed simple and filled with promise.

"He was quiet and one of the nicest guys you could meet. He was caring," Annie said.

On dates when the couple took in a movie, Johnson's younger siblings—Allen, Gene and Roger—went with them.

"We took all the kids with us. He'd never tell them no," Annie said.

At other times, Ronnie took Annie to the Saturday night dances in nearby Herrick, just to take in the teen scene and listen to the music of their generation—from rock and roll to soul and Motown, to the British invasion of The Beatles and Rolling Stones. Instead of dancing, they would sit and talk or just enjoy being in the company of friends their age.

"We liked to watch the other couples," Annie said.

As required by law, Ronnie registered for Selective Service when he turned 18. Not long afterwards, he received a notice from his local draft board to report by bus to Sioux Falls for a physical. There, it was determined that his feet were flat, and the Army sent him home. One essential thing an infantryman needs is a sound pair of feet. He was classified as 4F, or unfit for service.

With military service seemingly out of the way, Johnson got on with his life. He married Annie on May 20, 1967, in Sacred Heart Church, with Father James Tunnissen presiding at the altar.

Seven months later, at Christmas time, Johnson received a notice to report to Sioux Falls for a second evaluation. With the Army needing soldiers for Vietnam and other postings, local draft boards were under pressure to meet quotas set by higher authorities. His draft board, without explanation, determined that Johnson merited a second look. Annie offered to go with him, but Ronnie said no. The condition of his feet hadn't changed, and he figured he'd be back as soon as he was rejected again. He kissed his wife goodbye and boarded a bus on January 2, 1968.

This time, Johnson passed the physical. Not only that, he was handed an airplane ticket to report immediately to boot camp at Fort Lewis, Washington. Before boarding the plane, he called home to break the news to his wife that he was in the Army.

"Basically, I was in shock," Annie said.

Not that a farm boy from rural South Dakota had much political pull, but Johnson never considered filing an appeal with the draft board, never tried to get a doctor's excuse, never thought of calling his congressman. When his country called, he thought it was his duty to serve.

"We're raised different out here. You go because you keep everybody else safe," Annie said.

The next time his wife saw him was after basic and advanced infantry training. Johnson returned to South Dakota on a 21-day leave, taking advantage of the time to celebrate his first wedding anniversary with his wife. A younger brother, Allen, was also in the service by this time and was serving in Vietnam. Under Army regulations, Ronnie was not required to serve in the same war zone. But he volunteered for Vietnam because combat pay meant an extra $100 a month in salary, according to his brother. He left home for the last time on June 1, and once in Vietnam, he was assigned to the 82nd Airborne as an infantryman. Annie moved their trailer to a spot across from her mother in Burke.

Instead of writing letters, Ronnie and Annie exchanged reel-to-reel audio tapes. He would talk about the friends he had made in his unit, seldom mentioning the dangers he faced or even the Bronze Star for valor he was awarded on March 11, 1969. Halfway through his 12-month tour, Johnson was eligible for a leave known as rest and recreation, or R & R. He chose to go to Hawaii, where married personnel were most often sent. Annie couldn't afford to join him, however. She had just started a new job and couldn't take time off work. Besides, Ronnie would be home soon enough. The couple had even discussed where they would live after Ronnie came home from Vietnam, and it didn't matter much to Annie if her husband finished out his Army contract in Kansas, Colorado or Washington State.

Then on the Saturday morning of May 17, 1969, a government sedan arrived at Annie's place. Accompanying the solemn members of the notification team was Father Tunnissen, the priest who had presided over her wedding. The awful news was delivered that Ronnie had been killed in action. Details were scant. The family was told only that he had been killed by a land mine.

"Nobody believed it was Ronnie, because he was supposed to be on his way home," Annie said. "He was supposed to be home in two weeks."

Ronnie's body was flown from Vietnam in an aluminum transfer case to the military morgue in Oakland, California. His flag-draped casket arrived there on May 20, which coincided with his second wedding anniversary.

As it turned out, Ronnie's brother Allen was then stationed in San Francisco as a finance clerk in a Military Police company. Annie requested that Allen escort the body back to South Dakota, but complications arose. On the Saturday night that the casket touched down on American soil, Allen was on guard duty and was told nothing about his brother's death. He didn't find out until the following Monday when he phoned home. His mother delivered the news. The last time Allen had seen Ronnie was in Vietnam. In August of 1968, Ronnie was guarding a bridge over a river Up North, and Allen spent a night with that unit before he moved out the next day.

Once the situation was straightened out, Allen brought Ronnie's casket back to the place of their youth. Father Tunnissen presided over the funeral services on Sunday, May 25, and full military honors were given to the fallen soldier. Ronnie was laid to rest in ZCBJ Cemetery in Gregory, South Dakota.

A few months later, a shadow box arrived containing his medals. Presented to the family at a ceremony at the Burke Veterans of Foreign Wars Post were his Bronze Star, Army Commendation Medal, Purple Heart, Army Good Conduct Medal, National Defense Service Medal, Vietnam Service Medal, Republic of Vietnam Gallantry Cross with Palm, Vietnam campaign ribbon and the Vietnamese Quan Cong Boi Tinh Military Merit Medal.

Ronnie Johnson's loss wasn't the only grief shouldered by the community of Burke. Within weeks of his death, word arrived that Sergeant Darwin Lyn Labahn, who served with C Troop of the 1st Squadron in the 11th Armored Cavalry Regiment, was killed on June 3. Annie Johnson had gone to school with him. Then Sergeant John Paul Beckers, of Company A, 65th Engineer Battalion, 25th Infantry Division, was killed on June 6. Each loss was a jolt.

Annie and the Johnson family picked up the pieces as best they could and tried to move on. She went to beauty school and then worked in a local hospital. Every Memorial Day, she placed flowers on her husband's grave.

Meanwhile, 39 years after the action in the Ho Bo Woods, Frank Walenga was in the process of moving from Chicago to Albuquerque, New Mexico. Before leaving, he told his wife about some unfinished business.

"I have to go to South Dakota. If I don't do it now, it'll break my heart. I have to pay my respects to a soldier who saved my life in Vietnam," Walenga told his wife. "He was like a brother. I have to do this."

Walenga had pored over telephone directories in South Dakota and found a number for the Johnson family. He made contact with one of Ronnie's brothers, and a visit was arranged.

After driving to Burke, Walenga met Annie and Ronnie Johnson's brothers at a local pub. With patrons coming and going, Walenga told stories about Vietnam in general terms.

"I want to talk to you privately," Annie told Walenga.

They agreed to have coffee the following morning before visiting the cemetery. She had one burning question.

"Did he suffer?" she asked.

"No, Ronnie did not move or make a sound. He did not suffer," Walenga reassured her.

The trip did bring some closure to the Johnson family.

"It's nice to know somebody loved him as much as we did. I'm glad he was surrounded by the guys he was with," Annie said. "Frank is like family now. There were parts of the story we didn't know about. We found out the details of how it happened. It cleared up some things, but it always leaves more questions. It isn't any easier, no matter how long it's been."

His promise kept, Walenga found peace of mind.

"This was important for me to do before I died. I'm so glad I was able to bring some closure. On that score, it was the best feeling I ever had in my life," said Walenga said.

Somewhere around 2012, the combat veterans of Alpha Company met for a reunion and have been meeting ever since.

"We know what happened. We share amongst ourselves," Walenga said.

Having retired to New Mexico, Walenga underwent two medical operations to have cancerous tumors removed from his tongue and his kidney, the after-effects of being exposed to Agent Orange.

"You serve, you fight, you bleed for your country, and the nightmare never ends," Walenga said. "But if I die tomorrow, I won't have a complaint. I got 50 years of life because of Ronnie. He saved my life. I should've been in that hole. I should've been dead at 20, but 50 years later, I'm still here. I'm a survivor, and I have Ronnie to thank for that. I'm a lucky, blessed person. If it wasn't for him, I wouldn't be here. I live and breathe because of him. Ronnie was gold."

While hiking the trails of the Sandia Mountains, Walenga heals physically and spiritually.

"I made three promises to myself—to visit his gravesite to pay my respects, to donate 100 pints of blood and to donate bone marrow. I got to pay my respects 39 years later," Walenga said. "I served in the 82nd Airborne, the most renowned and respected organization in all the services. Looking back on it, we just did our job for our country. Now vets are getting the treatment and respect they deserve."

Chapter 57
BIRTHDAY WITHOUT JOY

Hollis Crowder joined the Golden Brigade in August of 1968 and served in long range recon in the 1st of the 508, spending extended periods of time in the field to spy on enemy movements. Instead of engaging hostile forces, Crowder's relatively small but quiet element would stay in touch with higher headquarters, which could apply long-range firepower.

"You had to be sharp. You couldn't be a half-stepper. If you couldn't do the job, they'd yank you from the unit," said Crowder, a member of Echo Company. "We did see a lot of action. We were always going somewhere. We did everything on 30-minute notice. You want to be the best. I'm so proud to have been with the 82nd."

Half-steppers, or those who talked tough but couldn't hack it, never qualified for Army commendations like the Silver Star for valor, which Crowder received following one fight. His platoon ran into a company-sized force of North Vietnamese Army regulars, which opened up on Crowder's unit with a machine gun. Crowder left his position to retrieve one wounded soldier, then crawled over an earthen bank to retrieve a second man. Superior firepower was a radio call away.

"We always had air support—Puff, Phantoms, Cobra gunships. That always gave me a sense of security in a life or death situation. Or we could walk the artillery in. You could hear it coming," Crowder said. "It was like the highest high, something you never get in civilian life. Some things in life have to be experienced."

Like the time a higher ranking platoon member called for assistance after an enemy force was spotted.

"Ever spend $20,000?" Crowder was asked.

"No, I've never even seen $20,000," he replied.

"Watch this."

A Phantom attack jet soon appeared and zapped the enemy position.

The occupational hazards of his job included the kind of nasty things all grunts were exposed to—Agent Orange, mosquitoes, spiders, snakes and leeches. Oh, the leeches. On one mission Down South, Crowder's unit encountered another friendly group wearing tiger-stripe fatigues. Panty hose was hanging off their rucksacks.

"We were wet the whole time, and we'd hang our socks out to dry. But panty hose was something new," Crowder said.

On missions, soldiers routinely checked each other for leeches and then burned the bloodsucking pests off with lit cigarettes or bug juice. But some genius, and who knows how this particular piece of knowledge came about, had discovered that leeches couldn't attach through the tightly woven synthetic fibers of a garment that covered the wearer from waist to toes. Prevention was better than the cure.

"The next time I called in for re-supply, I asked for two gallons of water, some iodine tablets, a pair of boots for a guy who had worn his out and six pairs of panty hose," Crowder said.

"Say again, sergeant?" the supply clerk replied.

When the order for panty hose was repeated, it could not be filled. The item wasn't in the inventory. Even the women serving in Vietnam didn't have a ready supply on hand. So, one guy wrote to his wife and asked her to send some from home. Another guy said he'd write his mother. She would still love him, even if a request for panty hose seemed unmanly.

The day the hosiery arrived in the mail, a major happened to be in the field for a debriefing. He was astonished to see soldiers taking off their jungle fatigues and putting on nylon leg wear.

"The major was listening to me talk but watching this scene unfold. He looked at me and said, 'I better not see this behavior in the rear.' I assured him he wouldn't. That was our leech abatement program. The next time we made a run to the big Post Exchange at Tan Son Nhut, we bought a whole case of panty hose," Crowder said. "The things G.I.s come up with."

Vietnam could make you laugh one moment and tear your heart out the next. One time, Crowder's unit was under the operational control of the 1st Infantry Division, and he befriended a radioman named Timothy Ballinger. They may have seemed like an odd couple, a black man from the South and a red-haired man from Michigan, but they hit it off right away.

"He was just a good person. We could talk about anything. We shared a common interest in history, and we talked about history a lot," Crowder said.

Ballinger found out that Crowder's birthday was May 27, and he took it upon himself to come up with something special for the occasion. Sifting through boxes of C Rations, or trading with other soldiers, Ballinger squirreled away two pound cakes and two cans of peaches, the most popular items a grunt could get in the way of Army rations.

"Soldiers do it right in the field," Crowder said.

Three days before the planned party, Crowder and Ballinger went on a mission together. Crowder's recon element wore boonie hats, but Ballinger didn't have one. Instead, he tied a bandana around his head while carrying the radio linked to battalion.

"We were in line on a roving patrol. He was right behind me when a machine gun went off and we got fired up. He just dropped. During my time in Vietnam, I may have been with 15 or 16 guys when they got killed. You could be here today and gone tomorrow. His loss hit me the hardest. He was truly a brother and my best friend," Crowder said. "But we were in a firefight. We had to keep going."

When the shooting stopped, Ballinger's body was flown to the morgue.

"I was the last person he was with. I took him to the chopper. That could have been me. I never had a chance to process it. I never had a chance to mourn, didn't have a chance to grieve. I was angry about that," Crowder said. "We were just solemn the next day. I gave away the peaches and the pound cake. The birthday celebration never happened."

Like a lot of guys, Hollis Crowder stored his experiences and memories of Vietnam somewhere in the recesses of his own mind when he came home. He went back to school, earned a master's degree in psychology from Pepperdine University, got married and went to work to support his family without ever really sharing what he had gone through. Then 20 years or so after the fact, after he went to see the dentist because he was grinding his teeth at night, he started to open up.

"Something comes over you one day. I came out of the closet. Vietnam is very much a part of me—the good, the bad and the ugly," Crowder said.

One thing he had to do was go to Panel 24 West, Line 92 of The Wall to find the name of Timothy J. Ballinger of Springport, Michigan, who had spent less than two months in Vietnam before he was killed. It's part of the same code by which he served. Complete the mission. *All The Way.* Make it matter by remembering the sacrifice, not burying it.

"He's still with me," Crowder said 50 years later. "He inspired me all my life. A lot of what I'm doing in life I dedicated to him. I truly believe he is still looking down on me. Sometimes when I find myself in a spot where I need to check my bearings, I ask him, 'Am I doing OK?' I owe him. He is my friend for life. I live my life to do right by him.

"Our time together was so short, but the relationship was so intense. He wasn't in the Golden Brigade, but he was out there with us. He didn't have a chance to have a full life, to go all the way in life. He never had a chance to have a family," Crowder continued. "In the big picture, there weren't that many of us in the 82nd Airborne who served in Vietnam, and there were even less who served on long range recon. If you served your country with honor, if you did what you were asked to do, be proud of it. That's the essence of the brotherhood. I trust these guys more than I trust people from my own church. We have a bond you can't break."

Chapter 58
RANDOM FATE

Two young men who arrived in Vietnam in May of 1968 were introduced to each other during in-country orientation, only to discover they had grown up about 60 miles apart in Michigan. They were then assigned to the 82nd Airborne and placed in the same unit, Bravo Company of the 2nd of the 505, which designated its platoons as Cougar, Leopard and Tiger instead of using numbers. As fate would have it, both soldiers were placed in Tiger Platoon. On May 28, the eve of their first mission, both stood in formation with five other new guys while a lieutenant assigned them to one of two squads. James Wilson Clay of Waterford was assigned to Tiger One. Robert Szilagyi of Owosso went with Tiger Two. Before dawn the next day, Clay and seven other members of his 11-man squad were killed at their ambush site. Szilagyi's squad, which saw and heard the shooting that broke out in the wee hours of the night, moved to the scene when Tiger Two failed to answer urgent calls over the radio. The first soldier Szilagyi found was Clay, hit in the head by a rocket propelled grenade but identifiable by the weapon he carried. In Vietnam, or in any other war, life or death was a random proposition.

"That could've been me," Szilagyi said. "It was just pure luck of the draw when the lieutenant moved down the line and put us into squads."

The lieutenant, platoon leader Richard Lee Patterson of Harriman, Tennessee, was among those killed. So was Private First Class Herman Leroy Judy Jr. of Alexandria, Virginia, who helped square away Szilagyi's gear before the squads moved out.

Szilagyi's squad was led by Gerald Schaefer, a buck sergeant from San Francisco who was a product of the Army's Non-Commissioned Officer's school. He had been in Vietnam for five months. A student at the University of San Francisco, Schaefer became eligible for the draft after his grades dipped below the minimum required to maintain his deferment, but his college schooling qualified him for the accelerated leadership course.

"I didn't know the 82nd Airborne was in Vietnam until I was in it," Schaefer said.

Schaefer felt the hand of destiny that night too. The movie *Gone With The Wind* was playing at the fire base, but Schaefer didn't care to watch. He took Tiger Two out and established its ambush site.

"If I had decided to stay in to watch the movie, I would've had the ambush position that got hit," Schaefer recalled. "None of us was all that experienced. It was a quiet area. Buddha's birthday was being observed. Nobody expected anything to happen."

As the new guy, Szilagyi took the point and led the squad over a rickety old bridge that spanned the Hoc Mon Canal near the spot where it branched off from the Saigon River in Binh Duong Province. Squad members arrayed in ambush position, taking turns on watch during the night. The spot overlooked a rice paddy along a dike, which was used by the farmers in a nearby village to walk their water buffaloes out to the field. Nearby was a line of scraggly trees that divided one rice paddy from another. Through radio communications, they knew that Tiger One had set up a distance of about six football fields away. Sometime between midnight and 2 a.m. on May 29, streams of enemy tracers and the sound of gunfire interrupted the stillness at Tiger One's position.

"We could hear them getting hit. It sounded like claymores going off, and some rocket propelled grenades. It didn't last long," Szilagyi said.

Added Schaefer: "I don't think it lasted over a minute. It was that quick. When they didn't answer their radio, we loaded up and went to see what was up. We may have only been a couple hundred yards apart, but it took us maybe 45 minutes to get there in the dark."

At headquarters, Darrell Criswell of York, Pennsylvania, monitored the radio frequencies of three ambush squads that were out that night. The last transmission from Tiger One was: "We're under attack! We're under attack!"

Said Criswell, "I could hear gunfire and screaming. It was like all Hell broke loose. That was the most horrible night I spent in Vietnam."

Criswell summoned the company commander, and Forward Observer Don Paquin of the artillery section assembled a team to investigate.

Meanwhile, Szilagyi scrambled to find his Army-issued eyeglasses that he had somehow misplaced in the dark. He never did find them. Still, he walked point again, constantly on the lookout for trip wires as he led his squad to the ambush site. To avoid being shot at, he called out, "Tiger One, this is Tiger Two." There was no response.

"I'm the first one in, and I saw a guy laying across the dike. He was hit in the head with an RPG and barely alive. I recognized him because he was carrying the grenade launcher," Szilagyi said.

The soldier was his buddy from his home state, Jimmy Clay, who was armed with the M-79. Clay held the rank of private, the lowest enlisted rank.

Schaefer reached the scene at about the same time as Don Paquin.

"I heard a faint voice from someone who was lying face down in the rice paddy. It was very traumatic. Heartbreaking. The place had been shot up," Schaefer said.

By this time, a helicopter with search lights hovered over the area. Illumination rounds from a four-deuce mortar also pierced the darkness. The extent of the carnage began to reveal itself. Schaefer went out looking but could find no trace of the attacking force. Szilagyi recalled that the Tiger One solider carrying the M-60 machine gun was found dead in the rice paddy as if he had been giving chase. Szilagyi was told to hunker down and stand guard. On his first night out, with his buddy among the dead, he took cover behind the dike in the muck and mire of the rice paddy. Those hours seemed like days.

"We had to stay during the night to guard the bodies. I was just scared. I thought to myself, 'Oh, no. I'm probably not to make it out of Vietnam alive.' Daylight was a relief," he said.

Daylight also revealed a grisly scene. The highest ranking man, Lieutenant Richard Lee Patterson, was found dead in the nearby tree line. At 25, he was married and had a stepson.

"I wish I could have done more to help him. He and his soldiers were brave men who got into a bad spot," said Don Paquin.

One of the lifeless bodies was Private First Class Craig Edward Yates, 18, of Sparta, Michigan. Like Patterson, he had been in Vietnam for about six weeks. The casualties also included Private First Class Herman Leroy Judy Jr., 23, of Alexandria, Virginia, the soldier who had looked after Szilagyi before the squads had moved out; Private First Class Robert James Rosenow, 20, of La Farge, Wisconsin; Private First Class Joe Rodriguez, 21, of Austin, Texas; and Private First Class Cris Holliday, a black man from Meridian, Mississippi, who had turned 24 on Christmas Day and who was the radio operator on the mission. Holliday had been in Vietnam for six months. Judy, Rosenow and Rodriguez had been in country for four months.

Found nearby was Private Harry Massey, 23, of Bridgeport, Connecticut. From the clues that could be pieced together, Massey was present when the shooting started but went to get help. In the dark, he wandered into the kill zone of the third ambush out that night. In the fog of war, he was killed by fratricide.

No one knows what exactly happened except the people who were in Tiger One, but something went terribly wrong. Theories abounded that a squad of Viet Cong had been tipped off or had spotted the position, or that someone in the squad fell asleep on guard duty. One of the dead had been killed by the blast of a claymore, which meant the Viet Cong had triggered a device that it had stolen, or that they turned the claymore around and targeted the squad, a practice that was known to happen in Vietnam.

"Every G.I. in Nam has a different tale. I was there, but I was not taking notes. I have no explanation for it," Schaefer said.

An American television network reported that the eight dead had been assassinated as they slept, and no other unit came to their aid. But in an article published in the Pacific Stars & Stripes dated June 8, 1969, the U.S. military in Saigon strongly denied the report. Based on accounts given by the three surviving members of Tiger One, military headquarters said the squad was attacked on three sides. It issued a statement that said: "There is no indication that any personnel were killed by a bullet in the back of the head, as alleged." The military also denied reports that the squad had been asleep, but it did confirm that Massey tried to get help and was killed when he wandered into an ambush set by another American unit. The assertion that no units came to assist the squad was flat out incorrect. Tiger Two and headquarters had reacted as fast as the circumstances allowed.

At first light, Ed Kochanski and a team from Alpha Company of the 2nd of the 505 arrived via helicopter to recover the eight bodies.

"It was pouring, pouring, pouring rain. What struck me, and it was so profound, they were laying in a row covered by their ponchos. One had the radio still by his side," Kochanski said. "I'm almost positive they were all shot in the head."

A short time later, *LIFE* magazine published a piece entitled "One Week's Dead: May 28—June 3, 1969." Lieutenant Patterson was among those pictured in the display, which is how some of his buddies from Officer Candidate School found out that he had been killed.

"It was like a punch in the gut. Dick was the best," said Richard Hill, who went to OCS with Patterson and later retired as a lieutenant colonel. Hill posted these comments online 39 years after his friend's death: "As I get older, I often think of him and so many others, always young. Such men are still out there serving and giving the ultimate sacrifice on behalf of people who fail to understand such sacrifice. We should salute each of these heroes."

A gifted athlete who graduated from Tennessee Tech University with a degree in business, Patterson was remembered as an avid fisherman and hunter who took his responsibilities seriously. "One of the sharpest officers I had ever met," said John Kieffer, who went through OCS with Patterson and posted an online tribute to his friend 32 years later. "He was a no-nonsense, by-the-book officer that with great effort prepared us physically, emotionally and intellectually for the rigors of combat as future infantry platoon leaders."

Patterson's stepson, Troy Rice, posted this message on the 30th anniversary of his death: "Although I was only five when you entered my mother's life and mine, I have vivid memories of our brief time together. I want to thank you for the tremendous love that you gave to us. It will never be forgotten, and neither will you."

Kay Patterson Austin, the lieutenant's widow, left this message on the 38th anniversary of her husband's death and referenced the words at his burial site in Roane Memorial Gardens, Rockwood, Tennessee: "I think it is important to remember the life well lived. His legacy of respect is reflected on his grave marker. 'Leadership is the privilege of a few. A man as a leader embraces a privileged position endowed upon him by other men because of his attributes visible to them in mind, heart and soul... He inspired and led his men with the courage and training of a devoted individual. But most importantly, he cared about his men.' In death as well as life, his example lives in our country, a stimulus and encouragement to all who have the soul to adopt it."

The names of all of those in Tiger One who perished in that ambush are together on Panel 23 West of The Wall.

Bravo Company suffered an additional casualty in the same province on June 2. He was John Hensley, 20, an American Indian from North Fork, California. His name also appears on Panel 23 West.

Back in The World on Friday, May 30, 1969, America marked Memorial Day to honor the men and women who died while serving in the U.S. Armed Forces. Every Memorial Day since, Gerald Schaefer reflects on the eight All Americans from Tiger One whose lives were taken that awful night. As far as his own service in Vietnam, Schaefer said: “I’d do it again. Reluctantly, but I’d do it again.”

Chapter 59
SMALL DOSES

Born and raised in the San Francisco area, Rick Talioaga lived up to what he thought were his responsibilities as an American male when he received his draft notice on his 20th birthday—March 27, 1968. He stepped forward at induction, swore his oath to his country and reported to boot camp to begin the process of becoming an American soldier. While there, his drill sergeant asked him to stand up in front of his fellow trainees in order to make a point.

"This is what your enemy looks like," the drill sergeant said.

The racially insensitive comment by an instructor in a Smokey Bear hat was all about appearances. Talioaga was of Filipino descent. His dark hair, slight build and facial features bore a passing resemblance to the foe and friend in Vietnam, but fidelity cannot be judged by appearances. In the Sixties, the operative phrase was not to put labels on people.

Undaunted, Talioaga brushed off the stereotype and trusted that his buddies would not see him as an enemy. Six months to the day after his induction, he was standing on Vietnamese soil and destined to become part of Alpha Company of the 1st of the 505 in the Golden Brigade of the 82nd Airborne.

"One minute you're a trainee, and the next thing you know you're in a war. I had never been on an airplane before. Had never seen dead people either. It was quite a shock," Talioaga said. "I've shown my photo album to friends who ask, 'How did you survive? You're a city kid. You hate bugs.' I look at the pictures of me when I first arrived and after I had been there a while. My eyes are so different. They had seen a lot. It's like two different faces."

Talioaga had experienced losses—Dwayne Whorton on Thanksgiving Day and Ernest Garrahan on New Year's Eve—and wondered how their families felt when receiving word their sons had been killed on holidays. He also knew a medic, Ralph Judson Mears of Norfolk, Virginia, who had been part of the original deployment and had extended his tour in Vietnam. A one-time paperboy whose favorite C Ration item was a can of sliced peaches, Mears was seriously wounded just south of the tunnel complex at Cu Chi and went into a coma. During his prolonged stay in a hospital, Mears succumbed to his head injuries. Talioaga didn't know that Mears had died on May 30, 1969, until he saw Mears' picture in the June 27 issue of *LIFE* Magazine, which published the powerful photo essay of 242 Americans who lost their lives in a single week.

Then in July, Talioaga was on patrol with his trusted squad leader, Sergeant David Gormican of Fort Lauderdale, Florida, who was on his second tour of duty in Vietnam.

"You would follow him anywhere. He was that good," Talioaga said. "He's basically the reason why I'm still here."

In the rice paddy region northwest of Saigon, Gormican's squad was searching for signs of the Viet Cong, all the while alert for booby traps and land mines. During the mission, someone discovered a big Chinese-made grenade planted to harm the unwary. The fuse that could detonate it was removed.

"We were in line on a dike and were pressing around to look at this thing. I held it in my hand and gave it to Gormican, who gave it to another guy. We're maybe 20 feet apart, and this thing has a kill range of 30 feet. We were all inside the kill range," Talioaga said.

Then, boom! The grenade exploded. Although one fuse had been removed, the device had a second fuse.

"Gormican was between me and the explosion. He took most of the blast," Talioaga said. "I landed in the bushes. I had a real bleeder on my arm, and I panicked at first. Gormican did make it to the hospital. A medic was working on me, talking, when he said, 'Oh by the way, your buddy didn't make it.' That's how I found out he was killed."

A paratrooper, Gormican, 24, was one of eight children born to Leo and Helena Gormican. He is buried in Our Lady Queen of Heaven Cemetery in North Lauderdale, Florida. Before he left for his second tour in Vietnam, a niece remembered that they went down to the beach to listen to his favorite song—*A Whiter Shade of Pale* by Procol Harum. Another niece named her firstborn son after him. Yet another niece, Kathy McIntyre, wrote in an online post in 2013: "David was the sweetest person ever to influence my young life. I was 17 when he was killed in Vietnam. I am in my 60's now and still don't understand why mankind uses war to solve problems. I also understand that my uncle was dedicated and loyal to his country. It was always the right thing to do, to serve your country. His picture keeps his youth captured, in our memories and in our hearts. Forever young, forever beautiful. God bless you, Uncle David."

Forty-six years after Gormican was killed, Rick Talioaga posted a picture of his squad leader on the Wall of Faces and left this tribute: "He knew his job and he did it well. Wherever he led us, we would follow willingly with no questions asked. Best of all, he was a good friend to all of us. We will never forget David Gormican, Forever Young."

To mend from his own wounds, Talioaga was admitted to Third Field Hospital and was visited by brigade commander George Dickerson.

"I tried to get out of my bed and stand at attention. He said that wasn't necessary," Talioaga said.

As a footnote, Talioaga volunteered to extend his tour by another seven months if he could be a door gunner. Instead, he was flown home after completing his 12 months was finished out his enlistment at Fort Ord, California. While there, he and a friend went to an Army-Navy Store to purchase the medals he had received commendations for, including the Purple Heart, but had never received.

"When I was checking out, the guy in the store said those awards are for the American Army," Talioaga said without a trace of bitterness. "I guess he assumed by the way I looked I was part of someone else's army."

Stereotypes die hard.

Down South, most of the casualties came not in pitched battles but in singular incidents. A soldier could be blown up by a booby trap, hit by a mortar round or take a bullet while he walked point. Others died in accidents. When a sudden rain started to fall, one soldier tried to close the hatch on his armored personnel carrier and accidentally pulled the pin on one of his own grenades. He died in the blast.

Mike Gamble, who had taken over his squad in Alpha Company of the 2nd of the 505 when Benjamin Benton was killed, vividly remembers two buddies.

"There was a kid named Spencer from South Carolina. He'd ask me, 'Mike, are we going to make it today?' And I'd say, 'Of course, we are.' He would tell me, 'I gotta get back. I'm the only thing my Mom has.' It rips my heart out to think about that," Gamble said.

Gamble finished his tour and was serving out his enlistment in Fort Benning, Georgia, when he got a letter from one of his comrades in the 82nd Airborne. The letter said that Specialist James Albert Spencer Jr., 24, of Gaffney, South Carolina, 13 days shy of coming home, and Sergeant James Harold Autrey, 21, of Dallas, Texas, a platoon leader that everyone could count on, were killed. Autrey always carried a picture of his wife and his little daughter. Both are listed on Panel 26 West of The Wall.

"I have often thought that I should have been there with them to take care of them," Gamble said. "I think of them all the time. They were my guys. I will never forget them. America's heroes."

In 2012, Gamble located Autrey's family and visited the grave of his buddy in Grove Hill Cemetery in Dallas.

"Me and my wife met his brother and his wife. Autrey's widow got remarried and moved on, but she never got over losing him. She said that when James got on the plane to go to Vietnam, she knew she'd never see him again. Autrey's grave has an American flag on it, and fresh flowers are placed there periodically," Gamble said. "If it hadn't been for God, I wouldn't have come home either."

Gamble has a son and a daughter, five grandchildren and two great-grandchildren. They call him Papa and are grateful he made it back alive.

"You can't live in the past, but the older you get, the more you reminisce," Gamble said.

In Vietnam, as in any war, nothing can explain why one guy is killed and another survives. In Norse mythology, maiden spirits who served the god Odin were called the Valkyrie, the chooser of the slain. They accompanied the fallen to the warrior heaven of

Valhalla. The French explained the unexplainable with the saying, *C'est la guerre.* That's war. Stuff happens. There is no rational explanation. It don't mean nothing.

For example, Alpha Company of the 1st of the 508 was on a search and destroy mission in Long An Province when it lost Private First Class Eric Allan Ream, of Schaefferstown, Pennsylvania, three days past his 21st birthday, and Lieutenant Richard Alfred Gwinn, 21, of Miami, Florida. Ream was walking point and was killed first. Gwinn, his platoon leader, was also fatally hit when an enemy force opened up on them. One of twin boys, Ream lettered three times in soccer at Eastern Lebanon High School and held a couple of records in the broad jump on the track team. The son of Morris and Josephine Ream, he was a Boy Scout and, as a member of the Richland Fire Company, he rushed toward blazing fires. His buddies called him Turtle Man because he was so baby-faced, and his undersized head seemed to be encased in the shell of his combat helmet. Gwinn, who was born on Christmas Eve in 1947, was described as soft-spoken, dedicated leader who was liked and respected by his men. He had attended North Georgia College and was an instructor in Ranger School before shipping out to Vietnam. Both of them were decorated with the Bronze Star, and both are together on Panel 17 West of The Wall.

A 39-year-old father of six children was among the Golden Brigade's casualties. He was Sergeant First Class Rudolph Swoope, a former drill instructor from Chicago, Illinois. A member of the Delta Dragons, he was killed by small arms fire. What he was doing in Vietnam and the circumstances around his death are secrets he took with him to his grave in Chattanooga National Cemetery.

Fatalities around a man's 21st birthday were especially poignant, largely because soldiers would say they were old enough to die but too young to vote. Medic Robert Theodore Hamilton, who had the equivalent rank of corporal, died in an explosion the day before his 21st birthday. He was from South Ozone Park, New York, and is buried at Long Island National Cemetery.

Private First Class George Thomas (Tex) Gibner of Spearman, Texas, was killed by an explosive device the day after he turned 21. Described as the nicest guy in his platoon, Gibner carried pictures of his family and his fiancé with him. Before his last patrol, someone congratulated him on his birthday, and Gibner spoke of a premonition: "Last night, I dreamed I got blown away."

Killed in a mortar attack was an officer with a college degree who quarterbacked his high school football team, ran track and competed in the boxing ring. He was Lieutenant Johnny F. Davis, 24, an infantry unit commander from Waldron, Arkansas. A 1963 graduate of Walnut Ridge High School, Davis earned his college degree from Arkansas State University before joining the Army.

Gerald Stephen Powlistha, 21, of Maquoketa, Iowa, was providing bridge security aboard an airboat along the Hoc Mon Canal network when he was killed. An infantryman with the equivalent rank of corporal, he was in the reconnaissance company of the 1st of the 505.

Vietnam was a watery world of rivers, canals and marshes, some of which were deadly. Eight members of the Golden Brigade drowned Down South. They included: Private First Class Lloyd Kenneth Turner, 24, an infantryman from Glasgow, Virginia; Staff Sergeant Larry Joe Mason, 25, an infantryman from Louisville, Kentucky; Lieutenant Victor Reid Landes, 24, an infantry unit commander from Cowley, Wyoming; Private First Class James Allen Lee, 18, an infantryman from San Diego, California; Private First Class Foster Earl Harrison, 21, of Los Angeles, California; Sergeant Dennis Lee Henry, 20, a personnel specialist in the 58th Signal Company who was from Bellevue, Kentucky; Sergeant Willie James Smith, 21, of Greenwood, Mississippi, an intelligence assistant in the field artillery; and Private First Class Nicholas Pierre Lannoye, 19, an infantryman from Thief River Falls, Minnesota.

Tropical pests could be fatal too, even for those who prepared meals at a base camp. Staff Sergeant Maryus Napoleon Jones, 33, a cook from Lackey, Virginia, succumbed to a fever of unknown origin.

A member of the Peace Corps who was drafted into the Army was among the 82nd Airborne's fallen. He was Private First Class Gary Edward Reynolds, 26, an infantryman from Clinton, Illinois.

Specialist Francis Mark Samz's military occupation was wheel vehicle repairman in the artillery unit. He died in a vehicle crash. An altar boy from Argonne, Wisconsin, Samz was 21.

One appropriate passage from *The Fallen,* a poem by British writer Laurence Binyon penned after World War I, reads: "They shall not grow old, as we that are left to grow old: Age shall not weary them, nor the years condemn. At the going down of the sun and in the morning/ We will remember them."

On one night, four members of the same squad who had set up an ambush became the ambushed. Killed were Private First Class Michael Donald Hughes, 24, of Salt Lake City, Utah; Private First Class David Carl Tobie, 19, of Livonia, Michigan, where a Veterans of Foreign Wars post is named after him; Private First Class Michael Joseph Troyan Jr., 20, of Dearborn, Michigan, one of a family of five and an altar boy at St. Clement Parish, who played chess and the piano, and who received a cake for his 20th birthday and packets of Kool-Aid to make the water taste better; and Staff Sergeant John Morascini, three days shy of his 27th birthday, from North Windham, Connecticut. They served in the 2nd of the 505.

At the same site of those four deaths, a plan was hatched to get some payback. From details contained in a declassified after-action report, elements of Delta Company set out on "a dummy ambush" in which a patrol would appear to be lax and a relatively easy push over. Those on the seven-man patrol dressed sloppily to play the part. In order to appear undisciplined, they also played transistor radios at high volume and took an obvious route to the site. As part of a ruse that was rehearsed four times, the ambushers stuffed clothing to make it look like soldiers were wrapped in poncho liners as they slept, and helmets were arranged to look like heads. One transistor radio continued to play. In reality, the ambushers had set up 20 claymore mines that could be detonated from a mile away. Movement sensors were emplaced before the squad lit out after dusk to a different location to wait. Artillery units had been alerted to fire on the pre-plotted coordinates. However, no enemy movement was detected that night, and the site was cleaned up the next morning to keep the enemy from learning anything about the deception. Three other dummy ambushes at the same site were attempted without success. The guerrillas never took the bait.

Back in The World, the groundwork was laid to withdraw U.S. troops from the war and turn the fighting over to the South Vietnamese Army. President Richard Nixon met South Vietnamese President Nguyen Van Thieu on Midway Island and announced on June 8 the first stage of his plan to disengage from the war. About 25,000 American troops were slated to come home. One month later, a battalion from the 9th Infantry Division assembled on the tarmac of Tan Son Nhut Air Base for a two-hour sendoff ceremony officiated by General Creighton W. Abrams and South Vietnamese President Thieu. Nine Starlifters flew the troops back to U.S. soil. On a rainy July 10, the returning soldiers, wearing jungle fatigues and carrying rifles with fixed bayonets, paraded in Seattle. A banner prepared by the G.I.-Civilian Alliance For Peace read: Welcome Home—We'll Stay In The Streets Until All The G.I.s Are Home.

Between then and the withdrawal of the last U.S. troops on March 29, 1973, more than 28,200 Americans were killed in Vietnam.

Chapter 60
DEAR JOHN AND OTHER LUNACY

Among the snapshots Jerald Manning kept from Vietnam is a picture of him and a fellow soldier from the same company standing in front of a tent. Although they went to war together and lived the same existence, Manning knew the tall man with the unassuming smile only as Dum Dum.

"I asked him his real name, but he would never tell me. He said he knew he wasn't going to make it out of there, so I should just call him Dum Dum. If you think like that, you're not going to make it. Dum Dum didn't make it," Manning said.

The soldier's real name, stamped onto his dog tags, is somewhere on the 82nd Airborne's list of casualties and is etched on The Wall. It is still unknown to Manning and others in Bravo Company of the 2nd of the 505. In the prosecution of the war, the turnover of troops was so great and so constant that people in the same unit might not know each other's names.

Married and the father of a baby daughter, Manning was a draftee from rural Wattsville, Alabama. After training at Fort Benning and Fort Polk, he landed at Bien Hoa and remembers that one of his buddies in orientation was shot in the leg by a Viet Cong sniper before he was ever assigned to a unit.

As a 60-gunner, Manning carried an extra barrel for his machine gun, plus a glove that resembled an oven mitt so he could switch barrels when the thing glowed cherry red from extended firing. He also packed a .45 caliber sidearm with three or four extra clips, one canister of red smoke and one of white smoke to signal helicopters, four frag grenades, some sticks of C4 plastic explosive and some detonation cord in case he needed to blast out a landing zone. At 6-foot-3, he weighed 130 pounds. His combat gear weighed half that. In Vietnam, Manning never slept in a bed. He once went a month without a bath and once was down to his last can of peanut butter before his unit received more supplies. He slathered on the bug juice but couldn't put it on his lips, so that's where the mosquitoes bit him. Each week, he took the malaria pills. He remembers one guy who was assailed by a leech that was three inches long and engorged with blood. With too little fresh water to be found, his biggest issue was drinking the rough-tasting stuff in his canteen.

"I don't regret being in Vietnam," Manning said. "I fought for my country, and I'll die for it. Those troops I served with were really good people for the most part."

Not all the burdens were the ones in a soldier's pack. Not all the wounds are inflicted by the enemy. Not everything in the mail was good news, such as the dreaded Dear

John letter from a wife or girlfriend informing the recipient she was done with him, often because she had taken up with another man. The Dear John letter was one of the most destructive explosive devices in Vietnam, a cold-blooded dagger that could rob a man of hope and cut him with an internal wound. Manning had first-hand knowledge of the heartbreak.

"My wife divorced me while I was over there. Got the divorce papers in the mail. I still wrote letters to my daughter. Still have a good relationship with her," Manning said. "You gotta get a hold of yourself. You gotta be strong. Gotta keep going."

One young soldier in Manning's company wasn't as fortunate. After receiving a Dear John letter, he descended into a personal hell and never climbed out. Although he was listed as having drowned, his comrades say he actually committed suicide one day on patrol. Weighted down by his own gear, he slipped beneath the waters of the Saigon River and ended it.

"He just went under. We found him a mile downstream. He didn't have nothing to live for," Manning said.

Les Museus knew the same tortured soul.

"He was getting letters from his girl back home saying she was sleeping around with this guy and that guy. That was about the dirtiest thing you could do to a soldier in Vietnam. He'd read them and cry. He was walking around like a dead man," Museus said.

Soldiers in the field live by the code of watching out for each other. Comrades tried to console the Dear John recipient, but nothing worked.

"It makes you bleed inside. I spent hours each week talking to him. I couldn't do anything to help him. She was hurting him, and I was watching it happen, and I couldn't do anything about it. The Army said he drowned, but he just jumped in the water one day and was gone," Museus said.

The preventable tragedies cut the deepest. Manning witnessed one unfold when a shake and bake staff sergeant showed up from the States. During the constant churn of personnel during Vietnam, the biggest shortage in the 82nd Airborne was competent staff sergeants—those unsung leaders serving between the officers who give orders and the grunts who carry them out. This particular one thought he knew more than anybody with a lower rank, even among those who were experienced in the realities of Vietnam.

"One of the first things he said to me was, 'I can't wait to kill me some gooks.' I said, 'You'll get your chance, but you may not be the one who fires the first shot.' I tried to warn him, but he insisted he knew what he was doing. Did he think they fired rubber bullets?" Manning said.

In fact, Manning had once been out on ambush with the sergeant in the watery world of Long An Province west of Saigon. He considered himself lucky to have survived.

"I went in to see the captain and said, 'I don't care if you court martial me. I'm not going out with him again. He's going to get himself killed and other people killed too,'" Manning said.

Les Museus, a squad leader who operated the patrol boats along the canal and river networks, knew the same sergeant and had a similar unfavorable impression.

"I called him Mussolini. You know, Hitler's friend. He was a talker, not a listener. He did everything wrong. It cost him his life. He got some other people killed too," Museus said.

Mussolini's unit operated out of Fire Base Rock, named for Stanley Rykaczewski, the officer killed during the Mike Foxtrot battle in January. The place was equipped with artillery and mortars to support the infantry squads, which routinely boarded boats powered by twin 40-horsepower Johnson outboard engines. One evening, Manning saddled up with his squad in his boat and Mussolini went out with another.

"One thing about the 82nd Airborne, we knew how to set ambushes. We'd get dropped off in one location, and then to throw off anyone who might be watching us, move to the actual spot under cover of darkness so we wouldn't be observed. It's serious business. Life or death," Manning said. "Well, this sergeant couldn't wait to get there. He went out too early."

As Manning recalled, nightfall was approaching but daylight hadn't faded completely. He and his squad were riding on the Saigon River when he saw the sergeant waving to him from shore. In the area were two sampans, which Manning knew from experience could be Viet Cong scouts. Manning pointed at the sampans as a warning to the sergeant. Then he continued on to his position, which was about 300 meters away. After being dropped off, he proceeded to his location with his Starlight scope and four claymores. He placed his squad on 100 percent alert all night.

"I just had a feeling. I knew he was going to get it. With the ambush spot he picked, he had nowhere to go," Manning said.

At about 3 o'clock in the morning, Manning's worst fears were realized. Gunfire erupted at the sergeant's location. From the telltale sound, none of weapons that fired were from the U.S. arsenal. It was all one-sided.

At base camp, Les Museus was concerned because Mussolini's squad hadn't checked in by radio during the night. At first light, he put a boat in the water and proceeded to the ambush point to investigate.

The first indication that something was wrong was the realization that a cardinal rule had been violated. The ambush site was right next to a canal or a tributary. Experienced soldiers knew never to set up an ambush next to running water because the noise could mask the enemy's movements.

"When I got there, nobody was moving. They were all on the ground. Their weapons and radio were gone. They must've been sleeping, or they got snuck up on," Museus said.

Meanwhile, Jerald Manning and his squad had moved to the sergeant's location and found the grisly scene.

"I pulled the sergeant out of the water. He was shot right between the eyes. I'll never forget the look on his face. They were all dead. Every one of them. The radio and all their weapons were gone," Manning said. "The water looked like it was all blood. We said our prayers and said goodbye. It was horrible. I knew some of the guys who were with him. I felt really bad for them."

Museus had called for a medevac helicopter, but the pilot balked at landing because the ambush site had yet to be secured. The bad guys might still be lurking in the area.

"He wouldn't come down unless the perimeter was secure. There were six or seven of us there, but not enough to secure the perimeter. I begged him like a two-year-old would. I was so angry. Tears were coming down my face. He still wouldn't come down. A gunship was overhead, and that pilot said, 'Fuck that guy.' He came down and evacuated the bodies. That gunship pilot deserved a medal," Museus said.

Meanwhile, marijuana became a worsening problem as the war dragged on, and the self-policing code of abstaining from weed in the field was eroding. Proof came in the form of an article in the May issue of the Pacific Paraglide, the 82nd Airborne's in-house publication, which spun the war in the best possible light. The article said at least 15 classes called "Military vs. Marijuana," an idea begun with Major David Stem of the Provost Marshal's unit, were given at Phu Loi, Camp Red Ball and the battalion fire bases. In some cases, a Military Police unit ended the classes with a controlled burn of marijuana to familiarize the attendees with the pungent odor of weed. The article concluded with the advice: "Possession and use of marijuana is a serious offense. Stay away from it."

Les Museus had his own story to tell about the night he was out on ambush and detected the telltale aroma of someone smoking pot.

"I didn't want any heroes. I just wanted to get through the night," Museus said. "Then I inhaled a big whiff of marijuana, and I told the soldier who was smoking it to put it out. That smell could be detected from a half a mile away on a still night. If I could smell it, the enemy could too. I told the guy, 'I don't give a shit if you smoke marijuana all day tomorrow. You're not going to give away our position by getting high.' Then I put my .45 up against his temple. I told him, 'If you ever smoke marijuana out in the field again, I'm going to blow your brains out.' He never did it again. He just wasn't a good soldier."

Decades later, Museus struggles to justify the blood, sweat and sacrifice by those who upheld their end of the contract and did the best they could under the worst of circumstances.

"After 50 years, I still can't rationalize it. There was no reason for us to be there, no reason for us to be laying in that mud getting shot at," Museus said. "We were brainwashed 19-year-olds. What the hell were we doing there? The college kids turned out to be right."

Back in The World, on July 18, Massachusetts Senator Edward M. Kennedy and Mary Jo Kopechne, who worked on Robert F. Kennedy's presidential campaign, left a party on Chappaquiddick Island near Martha's Vineyard. The car driven by Kennedy went off a rickety bridge. The senator escaped to safety, but the 28-year-old woman drowned. A week after the incident, Kennedy pleaded guilty to a charge of leaving the scene of an accident after causing injury. He received a two-month suspended sentence. Mary Jo Kopechne was buried in her hometown of Wilkes-Barre, Pennsylvania.

Chapter 61
MOONSTRUCK

With a degree in graphic design and illustration from the Maryland Institute College of Art, Darrell Criswell had yet to decide on his career. Then three months after graduation, Uncle Sam interceded and put him on a path to Vietnam. A native of York, Pennsylvania, Criswell received a telegram ordering him to take his physical for Army service.

"If your country asks you to go, you go. That's the way I was brought up. I was 23. Everybody called me the Old Man," Criswell said.

The way things worked, Criswell was mailed a bus ticket to Harrisburg, where he took his Army physical. Like all the others who were deemed physically fit, he was immediately sent to Philadelphia and then on to Fort Dix, New Jersey, for boot camp. On that same journey was Richard Larry Davis from the York County community of Red Lion. The two became fast friends and were in the same company in basic training. They also took jungle training together at Fort Polk. Before departing for Vietnam from San Francisco, they went on leave together. During the last free time they had before going to war, they took in the sights of the Bay Area and had a grand time frequenting the bars and clubs.

After their flight to Southeast Asia, they bunked together at P School but received different assignments and parted ways. The last time they saw each other was when Criswell went to the Golden Brigade of the 82nd Airborne while Davis was placed in a different unit.

"Two weeks later, I got a letter from a buddy that Davis was dead. It was a devastating blow. I wrote a letter to his parents. That was tough," said Criswell, who lives a life in retirement in Glendale, Arizona.

Private First Class Richard Davis was killed in a vehicle crash on February 7, 1969. He had turned 22 four days earlier. He was one of a dozen soldiers riding in a truck when it was struck by a U.S. Army vehicle towing a disabled American tank. The son of Edgar C. and Nell L. Davis, he was survived by seven siblings. Through the years, Criswell has visited his name on Panel 33 West of The Wall and has visited his grave at St. Jacobs Stone Church Cemetery in York County.

"I have thought of him so many times. I still see his face and his smile, a guy who liked to have fun and had so much life ahead of him," Criswell said.

As a member of Bravo Company in the 2nd of the 505, Criswell received the letter of his friend's death while taking part in the Mike Foxtrot operation in February.

The way he remembers it, his unit reached the Ho Chi Minh Trail in Cambodia. Criswell described it as "a black-topped road through the jungle, about the width of a Volkswagen, with the jungle so thick you couldn't see anything on either side."

Originally a mortarman and later a map-maker because of his degree in graphic design, Criswell and his unit saw its share of war in Vietnam, including the ill-fated ambush around Memorial Day that killed eight of his comrades.

"Our whole mission was to protect Saigon from a second Tet, which never materialized. We were either on the front end for bigger units like the Big Red One or the 9th Infantry Division, or we were a rear guard for bigger units," Criswell said. "The 82nd Airborne is an elite unit. My whole thing was do your job and get out. Get back to civilian life and move on. I was blessed to get through it. South Vietnam was a Third World country of dirt floors and no indoor toilets. It was an eye opener."

Oddities were commonplace. Criswell remembers the time a captain started shooting at water buffalo in a rice paddy. He also recalled the time a master sergeant at base camp got the crazy idea of having troops run around the compound every morning in the 95-degree heat and high humidity of the tropics. One of the stranger incidents involved an action at a village near the Hoc Mon Bridge.

"We were taking fire from this village and had it surrounded, but we couldn't light it up. The mayor or the chief elder had a relative in Saigon. It was a political war. You had to get permission to do stuff. But if you flew a helicopter over the village and it took fire, you could shoot back. Well, we sent a Huey over it, and sure enough, it was shot at. We just let loose. We found one body and a bunch of blood trails. They took their dead with them down a rat hole," Criswell said.

The otherworldly nature of Vietnam reached its zenith the day two American astronauts in a lunar module named Eagle touched down in the Sea of Tranquility on the Moon, fulfilling a mission begun with President John F. Kennedy. The same nation engaged in a hot conflict against Communist expansion won the Space Race with the Soviet Union, attaching a plaque to the first spacecraft to deliver men to a celestial body other than Earth. The plaque said: "We came in peace for all mankind."

To get reaction of the historic event, a *CBS News* crew sought and was granted permission by Golden Brigade headquarters to visit soldiers in the field.

"I know the men of your unit whom we interview will represent the highest standard of soldiers fighting here," CBS correspondent Don Webster wrote in a letter to brigade commander George Dickerson.

The landing occurred at 4:17 a.m. on July 21, Saigon time, and Criswell was among those assembled in the darkness for the event.

"We were out at night in a rice paddy. Nobody ever made a sound or shined a light at night in a rice paddy. Hell, a lit cigarette could get you killed. This CBS crew came out and turned on a battery-powered transistor television. I moved as far away from it as I could. A bright light from a TV set in the middle of a rice paddy? That was the worst thing you could do. No one with any common sense would be out there with a bright light at night," Criswell said.

"I thought to myself that I might was well be on the Moon myself. It was the most bizarre thing I had ever gone through. The only way to get through it is to talk about it," he added.

A light observation helicopter provided by the brigade rushed the film to Tan Son Nhut Air Base, where it was placed on a jet bound for the Philippines and then transmitted by satellite from Manila to New York for broadcast around the globe.

Six hours after the lunar landing, Naval aviator and test pilot Neil Armstrong descended a ladder to leave the first human boot prints on a surface other than Earth, calling it a giant leap for mankind. Buzz Aldrin, a West Point graduate and Air Force fighter pilot, followed him down as the American flag was planted on the Moon. Speaking to the astronauts by phone from the Oval Office, President Richard Nixon told them: "And as you talk to us from the Sea of Tranquility, it inspires us to redouble our efforts to bring peace and tranquility to Earth."

Those efforts came too late for two members of the 1st of the 505 who were killed on July 21. They were Specialist James Michael Cox, 20, a squad leader in Bravo Company from Willis, Virginia, and Private First Class Duncan Albert Warwick, 22, of Leesville, Louisiana, who served in Alpha Company.

Warwick's loss was noted in a journal kept by Lieutenant William P. Gunter, who was informally referred to as Willie Peter, a code for white phosphorous. Bravo Company was out in the boonies near the Parrot's Beak, with dead bodies all over the place.

Gunter's diary passage dripped with irony: "Today they walked on the Moon and everyone cheered and paid no attention to PFC Duncan Warwick, who walked upon a booby trap and died—a two inch hole in his throat, the blood spurting out, his upper teeth pushed straight out of his mouth in a grotesque smile, the eyes rolled straight up into his brain and the place in his head where the brains were. The brains were lying out in the grass. I sure am glad they got to walk on the Moon."

Meanwhile, 10 days after the Apollo 11 landing, the Golden Brigade was handed a special security mission. In the middle of an eight-nation trip that was codenamed Moonglow, President Nixon landed in Saigon to discuss further U.S. troop withdrawals with South Vietnamese President Nguyen Van Thieu. Nixon had made eight previous visits to Vietnam, but this was his first and only one as president. During his nearly six-hour stay, Nixon visited troops of the 1st Infantry Division at their base camp in Di An, about 12 miles northwest of Saigon. The 82nd Airborne had an infantry battalion aboard helicopters the whole time, ready to strike at anybody or anything that posed a threat to the president.

"I was the brigade's officer in charge of planning air operations, and we had the outer security of Saigon. I was given three helicopter companies. We had the whole battalion in the air running out of Saigon," said Tom Hennessey.

Elsewhere, on the same day that astronauts descended the ladder of the Eagle, infantryman Michael Benedict of Columbus, Nebraska, exited an orange Braniff International jet and walked down the steps to plant his combat boots in Vietnam. In his words, he had stepped "into the shit."

"I was so scared, I thought to myself, 'I ain't even going to be make it down the steps,' " Benedict said.

While units disengaged from the war and were being sent home under the program of Vietnamization, fresh troops were still being deployed during the transition. Having volunteered for the draft, Benedict took basic and advanced training at Fort Ord, California. Once in country, he was assigned to Bravo Company of the 1st of the 505 of the Golden Brigade, a leg in an Airborne unit.

"We combat-assaulted out of Hueys, so the jump was not that far. I did not have time to go to jump school, so I want to get that up front." Benedict said.

At first, Benedict was an assistant machine gunner, which meant he humped ammo and fed belts of bullets into the M-60. He later served as a rifleman, a grenadier on the Blooper and finally as the 60-gunner.

One highlight of Benedict's tour was when Miss America 1969, Judy Ann Ford of Illinois, visited his unit while on a USO tour. She autographed the camouflaged cover of his steel pot helmet, but a subsequent monsoon rain soon erased what she wrote.

While his company operated along the Hoc Mon Canal network, Benedict remembers being picked up by Navy PBRs (Power Boat, River) and ferried to various locations. From a roadblock at the rickety East Bridge over the canal, Benedict and his unit rode motorboats to overnight sites, pulling what was known as three-day, stay-behind ambushes. On such missions, troops would conduct a reconnaissance in force to make sure no bad guys were around, and then a squad would filter into the bush, lying in wait to spring surprise attacks on enemy forces that used the trails and crossings at night. Getting to such locations was perilous, however, and Benedict owes his life to his platoon leader, Lieutenant William Peter Gunter, the officer who kept a diary.

"We were crossing a rain-swollen creek when I slipped off the air mattress and sunk down under the weight of my ammo. I could not get back up. Lieutenant Gunter dove in, pulled me up and saved my life," Benedict said.

The same lieutenant once unified all his squads into a single ambush to take advantage of strength in numbers and combined firepower. On one operation, Benedict was among 20 or soldiers who surrounded and searched the village of Phu Hoa Duong, then stayed behind in case any Viet Cong filtered in during the night.

"We were in rice paddies, and the lieutenant decided we would stay dry that night. We set up the ambush in an open-air pagoda that had four-foot high walls from the floor to the top. It had something like big picture windows, but the window glass was gone," Benedict said.

Among the equipment the troops carried were hand flares—a silver cylindrical tube about 12 inches long and two inches around. Troops also had white parachute flares for illumination and a couple of red star clusters, which were usually popped to signal trouble. To set off a flare, a soldier would remove the safety cap at the bottom and bang it against something solid. Ideally, the flare would fire upwards. But with the unit that night was a Cherry named Sam Stuart from Tribune, Kansas.

"Sam would not mind relaying this. He was clumsy and tripped on someone's bag and knocked a couple of flares down and in. They shot off inside that pagoda and ricocheted around until they were smothered. Ambush blown. God's honest truth, one of the flares landed on some M-79 grenade rounds inside a butt pack and started the pack on fire. If memory serves, we put out the fire with urination. You never move around at night in the Nam unless you absolutely have to. We did and relocated," Benedict said.

The difference between disaster and an episode to laugh at later sometimes depended on the amount of urine in a soldier's bladder.

Fortune was not so kind on other ambushes, and Mike Benedict received a Purple Heart and still has a Communist-made slug in his body as proof. Benedict's squad had cordoned off and searched a village during the day, then waited in the dark to monitor any enemy activity. Sure enough, some bad guys tried to break out at night. In the ensuring firefight, Benedict's rifle jammed. He got out of his fighting hole in an attempt to fetch some LSA oil (lubricant, small arms) to get it working again.

"My rucksack was out of the hole behind me, and there was a good firefight going on. I got hit and went down, and the medic and the others put me in a poncho and half-dragged me to where the dust-off chopper was coming in. Remember, this was at night. It takes a special person to risk their lives to fly into a hot LZ to pick up wounded. When they threw me on the medevac and it lifted off, all I remember was the tracers bouncing everywhere. The medic had given me morphine, and I got really nauseous. When I was wheeled into the operating room, I remember the surgeon saying he was going to try mosquito clamps (a small hemostat) one last time, or they'd just leave the bullet in," Benedict said. "They left the bullet in, and to this day, my x-ray shows about where it was 50 years ago."

Benedict was hit in the left buttocks, kind of like the Forest Gump wound, when it felt that something just reached up and bit him. The bullet lodged near his pelvis. He had been taken to the 12th Evacuation Hospital at Cu Chi, the base camp of the 25th Infantry Division (Electric Strawberry) that sat atop 200 miles or so of enemy tunnels. After a short stay, Benedict went back into the field. His unit moved to the Iron Triangle north of Saigon, and he remembers the sight of Black Virgin Mountain, or Nui Ba Den in Tay Ninh Province.

"At night, every night, it looked like the Fourth of July on steroids—tracers, mini-guns from Spooky gunships and parachute flares dropped from C-130 Hercules planes, the big flares that burned for 15 minutes coming down," Benedict said.

Elsewhere, after the Good Friday battle in which Felix Conde was killed, Carl Gulas and Delta Company continued their missions with the 1st of the 505. Guys would joke about date night back in The World and remind themselves that they were looking at the same Moon and the same stars that were seen by people back home. Their links to The World were letters, the Stars and Stripes newspaper and Armed Forces Radio. Gulas had received a pleasant surprise on May 6, his birthday. His fiancé sent him a birthday cake from Hough Bakery in Cleveland, and it had survived the trip to Vietnam without being smashed. He cut the cake with a bayonet and shared it with his buddies.

Around the time the Eagle landed on the Moon, Gulas and Delta Company made what was called an eagle flight—a combat assault aboard helicopters into the Pineapple Plantation in Long An Province. He recalled the destination as Fire Base Barbara, built by the 9th Infantry Division in a world of water dotted with sporadic fingers of land that were covered with nipa palm trees and gnarly brush. It was common for ambush teams to sit in water all night. On July 18, Delta was set up in a palm tree grove on a night so dark he couldn't see his hand in front of his face. As dawn broke, Gulas' fourth platoon was set up as a blocking force.

"All morning, we heard guns being fired and grenades exploding. About noon, my squad saddled up. I was the point man. As we moved forward through the swamp, automatic fire came from a bunker complex," Gulas said. "A Loach (helicopter) was right above us. The blades were kicking up mud and stuff. The mud was so thick and gluey that nobody could move to the flank. The palm trees were like a picket fence," Gulas said.

Crawling under machine gun fire, Gulas inched forward to eliminate the threat. With hand grenades, he destroyed five bunkers and forced the occupants to flee. He was later awarded the Bronze Star for valor.

Then on July 25, another eagle flight transported Gulas and his unit to a different location in a bid to find the enemy. In a quirk of fate, one of his buddies snapped a picture of Gulas in full battle gear, kneeling in a growth of thick weeds against a background of scraggly trees. Two hours later, his time in Vietnam ended.

"I hit a trip wire. An explosion blew me into the air. I got it in the legs—broke my heel bones and shin bones. Hey, my number was up. The war was over for me. The adrenaline must've been so high that all I could think about was the theme music from *Combat!,*" Gulas said.

He was rushed to a military hospital in Saigon for emergency surgery, then flown to Japan for more advanced care.

"The eye opener for me was Japan. There were lots of guys worse off than me," Gulas said.

After a period of recovery, he boarded a plane for a flight back to The World, stopping first in Alaska and then on to Andrews Air Force Base in New Jersey for a one-night stay in Fort Dix. Then came a bus ride to Valley Forge outside of Philadelphia, home of a Veterans Administration hospital where the severely wounded were warehoused in ward after ward.

"We were on litters on the bus. The driver dressed up like a clown to cheer us up," Gulas said. "I remember seeing ice cream vendors and fruit stands along the road. This was late August, and people were going on vacation. Most of them smiled and waved. Some gave us the finger. One person mouthed, 'Fuck you.' "

Gulas was released in November and went home to Cleveland.

"There were no exit interviews. No nothing. Just like a door slamming shut. You know what you had done. You know you took the right path. You know you didn't cop out. But it was like nobody cared. You're home? Great. Pass the potatoes," Gulas said. "My biggest regret is I didn't do more. I felt like I abandoned the guys in my platoon. Felt like I didn't finish the job. At one point, my father says to me, 'You miss your guys, don't you?' "

Gulas healed up and became a police officer, a position he held for 33 years. The relationships he built, especially among those who didn't return, never waned.

"My job is to not forget and live a full life. They got cheated out of theirs. Those names are in my heart forever," Gulas said. "I'm very blessed. Every day is a gift."

In 2006, Carl Gulas was inducted into the Ohio Military Hall of Fame.

Back in The World, on August 9, pregnant actress Sharon Tate, the daughter of an Army officer, was butchered at her Los Angeles home with four other people. Dipping a cloth into Tate's blood, the killers wrote the word "pig" on her front door. Demonic cult leader Charles Manson and his "family," who lived in a commune where drug use and orgies were common, were later convicted of the murders. Manson became known as one of the most notorious murderers in U.S. history.

Chapter 62
DOGS OF WAR

One thing about war is how keenly the adrenaline rush puts the brain on hyper alert and sharpens the senses. Eyes pick up the slightest movement or spot the smallest of things that are out of place. Ears zero in on any sound or notice when everything gets quiet. Noses detect odors in an almost superhuman way.

"I never realized before that I had an amazing sense of smell," Robert Murrill said. "My sensory capability came in handy on several occasions. I could literally smell the enemy. When that happened, I would warn my soldiers. Almost always, I was right on. The North Vietnamese possessed a unique odor—a combination of poor hygiene and the type of food and spices they ate. I couldn't describe it, and still can't, but I recognized the smell immediately."

Other Vietnam veterans swear they know of a good point man who could smell a fart from 100 yards away. If humans have the capacity to sniff out trouble, imagine the ability of creatures designed by Mother Nature to perceive the environment through their snouts, creatures such as man's best friend. Among the 82nd Airborne's new assets Down South was the 37th Infantry Platoon (Scout Dogs), a marriage of human handlers and specially trained canines.

A limited number of dogs on loan from bigger units had worked with the Golden Brigade Up North, but the 37th was dedicated solely to the All Americans. Although the critters don't show up on rosters, the likes of Thor, Ranger, Prince, Bodo and others held up their end of the contract too. Commendation medals were invented to recognize their work. They also paid a price in blood or, wearing a fur coat in the tropics, died of heat stroke. At least two of them were killed, two more were wounded and an undetermined number suffered the same long-term, debilitating side effects from Agent Orange and other defoliants.

Thirty German Shepherds, or similar breeds known as Military Working Dogs, joined the Golden Brigade with their human handlers at the beginning of 1969. The dogs were chosen for their intelligence, keen sense of smell and fierce loyalty. Some were donated by civilians while others were purchased by the Army. Most were three years old, which in dog years, made them roughly the same age as the grunts they worked with. While a soldier's serial numbers were stamped on a dog tag, each dog had an identifying number tattooed inside the left ear. Each scout dog team took 13 weeks of training at Fort Benning, Georgia, plus another five weeks of exercises after arriving in Vietnam.

A dog and handler worked as one. The mission was to sniff out booby traps, detect sites where the enemy stored food and ammo, spot tunnel openings and point out trails. Teams worked with each of the three maneuver battalions along with the Rangers of Oscar Company. They also complemented the cavalry and the combat engineers in their never-ending quest to find road mines.

The dogs went out on both day and night patrols, most often taking the point. It was easier to read their reactions during the day, but the dogs picked up scents more readily at night. Before each patrol, the dogs would sniff each soldier going into the field so that it could recognize the good guys from the bad guys. But as with all things in Vietnam, the enemy had countermeasures. The Viet Cong and North Vietnamese spread red pepper around tunnel entrances to throw the dogs off their scent. No critter, no matter how well trained, could find every booby trap, some of which had lurked silently in wait for years in the underbrush.

Don Behm of the 1st of the 505 kept a photograph of a dog named Bodo. It was a black and tan shepherd capable of amazing feats, but it also came down with cancer from the defoliants.

"When he sniffed out a booby trap, he would lay down, wagging his tail and pointing his nose right at the danger," Behm said. "Bodo also barked to keep away the villagers and the kids who sometimes tried to mingle with us. That way, we could concentrate on our jobs. It was a kind of hyper vigilance."

As with all the other dogs, Bodo got a can of dog food a day. His handler carried the rations and extra water for the dog on extended stays in the field. Almost always, the dog was watered first before the handler slaked his thirst.

As one indication of the dogs' importance, the furry critters bedded down in air conditioned environments when they were off duty. In the rear, they were penned up at what was called the Ahern Kennels, named for a dog handler who was killed on March 30.

Robert P. Ahern, who held the equivalent rank of sergeant, had one of the more unique backgrounds in the Golden Brigade. A college graduate who enlisted in the Army, he was a lawyer who passed the New Hampshire bar exam while he was in the service. The only son of Stephen and Hilda Glennon Ahern of Laconia, New Hampshire, he graduated in 1960 from Laconia High School. A gifted athlete, he played quarterback and defensive end on the football team, was a member of ski team and was a pole vaulter on the track team. Ahern also received a Bachelor of Arts degree in 1964 from Bates College, where he lettered in tennis. His post-graduate studies included the successful completion of courses in 1967 from Columbia Law School, and he served as an intern for U.S. Senator Tom McIntyre before he volunteered to join the Army. Ahern, 27, had been in Vietnam for two months when he was killed in an accident. Buried in St. Lambert Cemetery, he is listed on Panel 28 West of The Wall.

Scout dogs hunted on every piece of terrain patrolled by the grunts—the Hoc Mon Canal network, the Parrot's Beak out on the Cambodian border, the Iron Triangle, the

Pineapple, the An Son Valley and elsewhere. When the 1st of the 508 was sent to the Hobo Woods in May, Private First Class Jim Teller and his dog Thor went too.

"The dogs work well and have saved us from many casualties in this area," said Captain William G. Carter, commander of Delta Company.

On that same operation, Specialist Jim Frantz and his dog Prince were with Alpha Company when they were both wounded. Under a hot sun that turned jungle fatigues dark with sweat and induced heavy panting in the dog, someone tripped a booby trap. Frantz and Prince were knocked to the ground. Both were evacuated by helicopter. Shortly thereafter, an impact ceremony was held at brigade headquarters. General George Dickerson presented Frantz with a Purple Heart. Prince received a decoration that was the first of its kind. Created in the spirit of the Purple Heart, it was made of metal and cardboard and named the Honorable Woof Award. It was hung around Prince's neck for bravery under fire and in recognition of his wounds.

"I cannot praise too highly the courage and good sense displayed on combat operations by you men and the dogs you have trained so well," Dickerson said. "You have been instrumental in using your dogs to uncover many of Charlie's deadly surprises in the form of mines and booby traps. I am proud to have you in the All American Brigade."

While working with Echo Company of the 1st of the 508, a dog named Ranger was not as lucky. He and his handler were both wounded by a grenade. Crazed by his injuries, Ranger attacked a radio operator who tried to help. The dog had to be destroyed.

The dogs protected their handlers under any and all circumstances. Carl Gulas found that out after his platoon sprung an ambush that killed two Viet Cong. During a subsequent sweep of the area, one of the dogs was on point as the unit walked along a river or a canal.

"I was the slack man, right behind the point. The dog got into a hornet's nest, and the handler was stung. I went up to help the handler, and the dog latches onto my collar. All three of us tumbled into the water," Gulas said.

One member of the 37th Infantry Platoon killed in action was Private First Class John Alan Kuefner, 20, of Duluth, Minnesota. A draftee trained as an infantryman, Kuefner and his dog triggered a booby trap out near the Parrot's Beak and suffered multiple fragmentation wounds. Kuefner's name appears on Panel 19 West of The Wall.

Man's best friend saved lives in the 82nd Airborne and paid a price doing so, but not even the best-trained dog could sniff out every trouble spot or prevent his master's death. Kuefner was killed on August 14, 1969.

Back in The World, a concert known as Woodstock attracted 400,000 free spirits and curiosity-seekers between August 15-18 in upstate New York. Although the concert-goers were stereotyped as dope-smoking, long-haired Hippies, plenty of young people attended to take in the freak show or ogle the maidens who went skinny-dipping.

Officially known as "An Aquarian Exposition: 3 Days of Peace & Music," the event was held on Max Yasgur's 600-acre dairy farm near White Lake in Bethel, New York, 43 miles southwest of Woodstock. Among the 32 performers was guitarist Jimi Hendrix, a veteran of the 101st Airborne. Country Joe and The Fish performed a dark satire about Vietnam called *I Feel Like I'm Fixin' To Die.*

Chapter 63
DELTA DIARY

Fifty years after he left Vietnam, Stuart Simonson can say with certainty that Vietnam never left him. One universal truth about war is that it's such an intense personal experience that it forever imprinted on the psyche. Memories of firefights do return in the wee hours of the morning, but what stayed with Simonson over the decades is not necessarily a nightmare, just a recurring memory of the most intense moments of his life at a time when he was 19 years old.

"I can close my eyes right now and envision it. It's like a constant video loop, playing over and over," said Simonson, a family man who became a certified public accountant after the war. "Vietnam veterans can get together at a bar, sit down and drink a beer and not say a word for hours. There's just a comfort zone in being together again. It's phenomenal. You get a good feeling just being around one another. There's a bond that can't be broken. You just know. You don't have to talk about it."

One of seven children raised on an Iowa farm, Simonson learned the hard work of self-sufficiency at an early age by milking cows, tending cattle and feeding chickens. He didn't know he was poor, but the very first time he got a new suit of clothes was for the Catholic sacrament of Confirmation when he was in the eighth grade. His mother's brother had served in World War II and was killed. Answering the country's call was a given.

"We just grew up knowing we were going to serve our country. Not going was not an option. The red, white and blue, apple pie and motherhood—all of that was in our DNA," Simonson said. "We did what everyone who went before us did. We served proudly and sacrificed. We did what we were asked to do."

Drafted in February of 1969, Simonson was keenly aware that service comes at a price. His brother Steven, two years his elder, had been killed during training at Fort Lewis when a hand grenade exploded prematurely. Simonson trained at the same fort following boot camp.

"I wanted to finish what he started," Simonson said. "I wanted to know if I could cut the mustard, to find out if I had the stamina to do this. I didn't want to bail on my buddies."

In Vietnam, where he was assigned to Alpha Company of the 1st of the 508, he vividly recalls the first time his unit was ambushed. A Chinese-made machine gun was shooting out chunks of lead an inch long and a half-inch in diameter.

"I was behind the radio with my butt down. I was in the third or fourth line of the Lord's Prayer before I realized what was happening. Then training kicks in and you do what you gotta do," he said.

Some years after the fact, Simonson wrote down his experiences as a keepsake for his sons. His words shed light on life in the 82nd Airborne in the late summer and early fall of 1969. What follows is the good, the bad and the absurd of his personal recollections:

First Night

I'm in 82nd Airborne, down in the Delta. Oh My God, they're going to be throwing me out of perfectly good airplanes and I'm not jump-qualified. I've been in Nam maybe a week, go through processing and in-country orientation, and now I'm on a truck headed to join up with my company. I don't have a clue where we are, but I'm all eyes, and I have a death grip on my M-16.

We are going to some fire support base, and I'm thinking, "All right, another base camp. How bad can this place be?"

Finally, the fire support base comes into view. This place can't be much larger than a football field. It has a half dozen rolls of wire around it and claymores everywhere. Mostly tents on the inside with bunkers along the berm. There is a USO show going on. No, not Bob Hope, but several American girls singing on a makeshift stage, which consisted of some planks on 55-gallon barrels. We jump off the back of the deuce and some guy yells, "Hey, Cherry Boys, you best watch this show as it will be the last fucking show you'll see for some time." Just what I needed, to feel worse that I already did.

Some guys say, "Hey, you new guys, follow me." He takes us over to one of the tents where another guy asks if there is anyone from Iowa. I say, "You bet!" And he says, "Follow me." His RTO (radio telephone operator) is from Iowa. He takes me to another tent and tells me to take an empty cot. Everyone else is at the USO show, so I'll meet them later. He tells me to drop my gear and take in the rest of the show, but I'm just not up to it and prefer to be by myself.

Nightfall comes and everyone has to pull his watch. Being the Cherry Boy, I get the worst hours. I haven't really slept soundly, and some guy is poking me, "You're up." I grab my M-16 and head for the bunker on the berm. He tells me there is a Starlight scope up there and asks if I know how to work claymores. He says if I see anything out there, shoot it. And wake up so and so in two hours. So, I sit there on top of that bunker, all alone, scared as hell, and ready to shoot anything, Starlight scope in one hand and M-16 in the other. The scope seldom leaves my eye.

A voice from nowhere startles the hell out of me. It scared me so that I didn't even understand what was said. Shortly afterwards, there it is again. "Give me your Sit Rep." It's coming from the radio. What the hell is this? No one said anything about this. What the hell am I supposed to do? A few more times it comes over the radio and then it stops. It's not five minutes when the same guy that first asked if there was anyone from Iowa shows up. He asks if anyone explained radio procedure to me, and I told him no. He proceeds to tell me that Sit Rep is short for Situation Report, and I needed to respond over the radio that all was OK. So, he got me squared away and off he went. The rest of my watch was uneventful. Thank God, I survived the first night with my company.

One would never have thought then that I would end up serving a full tour of duty and part of another. I would soon become an RTO and end up humping that Prick 25 for 10 out of the 12 months that I would be in the bush. I would serve as RTO for squad leaders, platoon lieutenants and the Old Man. I would be a lot more scared than I was that first night, and for damned good reason. That small fire support base would soon seem like a five-star hotel compared to life in the bush. One more thing. That soldier was right. I should have watched that USO show because it was one long fucking time before I would get to see another.

First Contact

I don't remember every time we had contact, as there got to be too many times. However, I do remember the first time distinctly. I had not been in country very long. Our platoon was working out of a small ville pulling sweeps, patrols and ambushes. We were on patrol through grassy and brushy terrain, and we spotted some gooks right at the same time they spotted us. We immediately exchanged some small arms fire, and the gooks turned and started to run away. We pursued them, also at a run. They were trying to lose us in the grass and brush, and we were trying to stay close enough to keep them in our sights. We are firing M-16s and M-79s at them on the run. I can visualize the two I kept my sight on. I would lose them for a second or two in some tall grass or brush, but I would not change my focus and then they would reappear back in my sight. I'd yell, "There they are. Eleven o'clock!"

Someone's M-16 rounds made contact with one of them. Even with them at a full run, I could tell when each round hit the body. First hit, his body jerks. Second hit, his body jerks again and he starts to go down. The force of the rounds and his body in motion from running cause him to hit the ground hard and tumble and roll a little before all motion stopped and he lay still on the ground with clouds of dust rising around him. Within seconds, the second gook gets hit, and it is an exact repeat of the first. We reach both dead bodies within a few more seconds. Man, am I PUMPED. Our squad just nailed two dinks, and none of our guys got killed or wounded. What a rush. My heart was racing a hundred miles per hour. Hueys picked up us and the two dead dinks and took us back to the small ville we were working out of. The Huey that had the dead dinks hovered four to six feet off the ground at the edge of the ville along the road, and the door gunner pushed the two dead bodies out. They hit the ground with a thud, and there they lay for all passers-by to see. Some of my buddies knelt beside them and had their pictures taken. Some lifted the dead dinks' heads and a more posed picture was taken, like a proud hunter with his recent kill. I don't recall posing or taking any pictures, not that I was opposed to it or felt it was in poor taste. I was probably a little overwhelmed by it all. The bodies were on display there until the next day, and then they were gone. I don't have a clue what happened to them. Years later, I do not consider the posing and picture-taking in poor taste or feel sorry for it. However, before my tours would be over, there would be some things done that I regret now. My first combat, everything would go our way. That great hunter with his prize game feeling would be damned short-lived, and within days, I would experience buddies being wounded and killed, and that would continue throughout my tour.

Surviving the Delta

I got there in July of 1969 during the monsoons. Water, mud, rain, heat, swamps, mosquitoes, snakes and leeches were the environmental enemies. The Viet Cong and booby traps were the other enemies. Surviving the elements was a form of combat itself, and coupled with the fighting, it took its toll on the human spirit very quickly. We lived in the field most of the time, so everything you owned, you carried on your back. You latched onto a small waterproof ammo can to keep writing papers, letters, valuables and smokes dry. We operated out of small villes and small fire support bases, but most of the time just existed in the field. We would secure a location for what we called a Day Area. Here we would rest, clean weapons, possibly get mail, have a hot meal flown in, dry out clothes, boots and feet, take a shower if a well or stream was close, try to unwind and prepare ourselves for the next patrol, sweep or ambush. Sometimes a week, sometimes two to three weeks, could go by between clean uniforms. They would bring out a big stack of jungle fatigues, and it was a luck of the draw on the size and condition of what you got.

I recall being on watch at an ambush site and the huge mosquitoes buzzed relentlessly around my face and ears. I was drenched, cold, filthy and tired. I wanted to scream as if insane. We spent the entire night in a sweep providing a blocking force as part of a larger mission. We had both enemy fire and friendly fire zinging over our heads. We had short rounds from friendly artillery hitting trees dangerously close to our position. The next morning, once we got to some dry ground, we had to strip and do a de-leeching for one another. No part, and I mean no part, of your anatomy would escape from the attachment of a leech. I got jungle rot on my feet, and they got so sore and swollen that I could not walk. I had to go to the rear for a few days to heal up. I got a two inch cut on my leg, and again, I had to go to the rear for a few days due to the infection and swelling. Existence was so miserable that some guys quit taking their malaria pills in hopes of contracting malaria so they could get out of the field. It got so bad that I had to go along with the medic as he distributed the malaria pills to make sure the guys actually swallowed them in front of us. We all hated the Delta, but there was no way I would risk malaria as my ticket out.

Booby traps were the norm versus the exception. They were everywhere and could be made out of anything. You stayed off the trails. You touched nothing. Everything was suspected of being bobby-trapped, and you left absolutely nothing behind for the gooks to use, including trash.

One night on our way to our ambush site, a horrendous thunderstorm arrived. The lightning was intense, and it seemed like daylight when it flashed. It would destroy our night vision, and so as not to get separated from each other, we grabbed hold of the guy's rucksack in front of you. Before my tours in Vietnam were over, I would serve farther north in different types of terrain and different types of warfare. I would never propose to another grunt that the Delta was worse than anywhere else in Vietnam. I just know that when a grunt tells me he served in the Delta, I know where he is coming from. It rained for the first eight weeks. I think I was there three days before I finally saw the mountains due to fog and overcast skies. Anyway, I think it would have been better if we had gone to Fort Polk so as to help us better prepare for the Delta. I'm not big on clichés but you had to be there, and I mean you really had to be there. IT SUCKED!

New Lieutenant

I don't know what happened to the previous LT. He was gone already when I joined the platoon, and I don't recall any of the guys ever talking about him. A buck sergeant was in charge of the platoon. He was well-liked and really seemed to care for our safety. We had a guy in our platoon who was our goof-off. He was taking more advantage of the fact that we did not have an LT than he should have been. As a disciplinary measure, the sergeant made him carry the radio as RTO most of the time. I thought that being the RTO and humping that radio must be one suck-ass duty as the sergeant used it as punishment.

Being the Cherry, I got the duty of walking point a lot. It was only by the grace of God and not my skill that I survived doing that. Nothing in basic or advanced training prepared me for walking point. It required on the job training, and hopefully you survive long enough to get skilled at it. We had been working out of this tiny ville, which had a dirt road down the center with six to ten huts on each side. Our bunkers consisted of two to three metal rings, the kind you would use to make a culvert for a road. At least it helped keep some of the rain off you. One day, the buck sergeant came around. He says, "Inspection formation on the road in five minutes." A what in five minutes? You have to be kidding. Who the hell's brainstorm is this? There we are on the road in a two-column formation. Being only 5' 7 ½" tall, naturally I was in front of the column. Standing in front of us is this first lieutenant, our new platoon leader, complete with new and clean boots and fatigues. He told us his name and in the same breath said he was a graduate of officer candidate school. He started at the end of the first column, stopping in front of each soldier, checking him out and asking his name. Soon, it is my turn. "Stuart Simonson, sir," I reply to his question. Standing there with his index finger extended poking me hard in the bread-basket of my chest, he says, "Simonson, you are my RTO, and that radio is more important than your life." I'm thinking, "Fuck, not RTO, that is punishment duty. More important than my life? There isn't anything more important than my life."

I don't know how the existence of a grunt in Vietnam could be made worse, but our new LT did just that. He constantly did the things you were never supposed to do, like use the trails and kick or pick up items that could very easily be booby-trapped. He had everyone awake all night on ambush. You were supposed to sleep during the day, but that was impossible with cleaning weapons and reconning that night's ambush site, along with whatever else had to be done during the day. We were soon totally exhausted, and the tension among us was growing. He was labeled with the nickname Doofus, and there was talk of fragging him. As his RTO, he instructed me that he never wanted me more than an arm's-length away from him when we were on a mission. I was certain that one of his antics would get me killed. On the whole, I had excellent lieutenants, excellent company commanders, excellent officers. But this Doofus, he could not read a map. He would order us to charge a wood line without ever calling in artillery prep or air strikes. That's not how it works. When he ordered the charge, one of the other RTOs started choking him. Six of us would have said, "We didn't see a thing." He would break all the rules. You just didn't feel safe around him. It was as if he wanted our platoon to win the war all by ourselves, and we were his expendable resources to accomplish that. Within a month of his arrival, he would have us completely exhausted, morale depleted, and the guys talking about taking him out.

As the RTO for the platoon sergeant too, we were the only two that were close to the LT, and this closeness was only due to our direct working relationship with him, but there was no personal friendship. I had orders to never be more than several footsteps behind him so that the radio was accessible at all times. I would cringe when he would spot something that could be easily booby-trapped, and he would fiddle with it. It was an existence in unnecessary fear.

We were on patrol one day and came across this stream that was more like a raging river due to the monsoons. The guys had only had their M-16 and a small pack but were having a hell of a time getting across. As I waited for my turn, I thought, "I'm going to drown with this damned radio on." I started across with my M-16 in one hand and the handset of the radio in the other, keeping both above the water to keep them dry. I got about three-quarters of the way across when I hit a deep spot, and I went down. I recalled trying to swim and gasping for as much air as I could take in during my brief moments of popping up above the water. It seemed like forever, and I'm not sure how many times I popped up. The last vivid memory I have is outstretching my arm holding the M-16 in hopes someone would see it and grab it. LT saw I was in trouble and dived in after me. He spotted my M-16 and grabbed it and started pulling me to shore. Thank God for solid ground. As my buddies pulled me on shore, I spit up water and gasped for air. I lost my helmet in the ordeal, and LT dived in again and found it. How does one listen to buddies talking about fragging the same LT that just saved me from drowning? Anyway, LT never got fragged. Maybe his diving in to save me saved him. I don't know. The number of days that LT had in the field were numbered anyway.

It was a large mission, involving the entire company. We were performing a search and destroy. Our platoon had split into two groups, and naturally I was RTO for the LT's group. We hear an explosion, and within seconds, the other RTO with the platoon sergeant's group is reporting one of our guys was wounded from setting off a booby trap along a stream. The LT had a bad habit of wandering off by himself. What made it a really bad habit was that he wanted the radio and thus me along with him. We went wandering off that day and came across a trail. Despite my urgings not to, we proceeded on the trail, and we both stopped at the exact same time. We both spotted a trip wire about waist high that ran between some brush on each side of the trail. Despite much stronger urgings by me this time, he proceeded to approach the trip wire and naturally I followed. He turned to me and said that I could hang back. I got off the one side of the trail in the brush but was still able to see the trail, the wire and the LT. He walked up to that wire and very gently tapped it with his finger as if to check to see how tight it was. I couldn't believe what I had just seen. Very shortly, there is this explosion, lots of dirt, and LT is thrown into the air. It seemed liked he went 10 feet high. I immediately started calling for a Dust Off as I headed for the LT. He was bleeding very little, but he was missing one of his boots. Hanging in a tree, about 10 feet up, was his boot, completely intact, laced and tied. The trip wire was a decoy, and he stepped on a small mine. It crushed the bones in his foot and blew his boot right off. It took a few minutes for the other guys to find us. The Dust Off was called in, and I had done all I could to care for LT. We finished our search and destroy, joining up with the rest of the company late in the day. As we sat around, we told each other what happened to each group. We were all bummed about our wounded buddy, but no one was bummed about LT. Quite frankly, I was greatly relieved, and I think everybody else was, but we did not say it. I felt bad for him, but I was thankful he had only taken himself out and no one else, especially me.

Dusk came, and the area took on a desolate appearance. The trees had been stripped of all leaves and smaller branches from artillery rounds, and there was no brush or grass from the same. We were not far from where choppers kept landing and taking off. The last Dust Off came in to pick up the dead. I didn't know any one of them as they were from different platoons. As they loaded the last guy, his head fell back, and I could see his face. His eyes were wide open. I wish I could erase those cold, glassy eyes from my memory. I got up to go over to the chopper to close them, but it lifted off. What a day. I will never forget that day even though we have had many worse days. I don't remember all the combat experiences. Don't remember all the different times we made contact even. Then why can I remember that specific day? It was my mother's birthday, September 25. I've never heard from LT since and don't have a clue how he came out. I remember what he did for me, and I'm grateful. However, I did, and we all did, feel safer with him gone and with the platoon sergeant back in charge. Did a lot of fragging take place in Nam? Don't know. But before my tours would be over, I would have buddies talk again about taking out their commanding officer.

You Are Expendable

Another day, another search and destroy mission. So goes the existence of a grunt. The area was mostly jungle with small clearings here and there. We never knew where we were, but this was out on the Cambodian border. The chopper dropped us off, and we proceeded into the jungle. Chopping a path through thick jungle in extreme heat is a real chore for the point man. It is difficult to maneuver due to the large packs on our backs, weapons, ammo and radios.

We had not been at it for a long time, nor had we gone a long distance, when we were ambushed. We have several guys wounded. We cannot maneuver and do not even see the dinks that are ambushing us. We blindly return fire, and their firing stops. We call in the contact, request medevacs and request artillery. We grab our wounded and return to the clearing so they can be dusted off.

I am now one of the company commander's RTOs. I recall sitting in that clearing and watching the first artillery rounds come in. There was no second series of rounds. That's it. Didn't look to me like they landed in the right spot. Orders followed from battalion to proceed back into the jungle. We do just that, get back to about the exact same location and we are ambushed a second time. Again, we retrieve our wounded and call battalion for dust off and artillery. Sitting in the clearing, I watch artillery rounds come in. We give the instructions on needed adjustments and soon another set of rounds hit in the jungle, followed by orders from battalion to proceed with our mission. I'm a seasoned grunt by now, and I possessed good judgment on distance and accuracy of artillery. I kept track of my steps to count klicks, and this was very useful for our forward observer when determining our location. I knew that those two sets of artillery rounds did not hit the ambush location yet. I voice my concerns to the company commander while we prepare to go back into the jungle. For the third time, we get about to the same spot in the jungle, and for the third time we are ambushed. You know the routine. Once again, we are back in the clearing. No artillery support at all is received, and I believe that the only thing that saved us from being ordered in a fourth time was the lateness of the day.

The artillery in the area was committed to a larger mission going on elsewhere, and thus was not about to spare us very many rounds. You find these things out when you are the Old Man's RTO. We got choppered out of there and were dropped off at a fire support base we had been operating out of. We were rationed several beers, and I traded some smokes for several more beers. We had a mission debriefing, and I went to it loaded for bear.

I told the CO what I thought about the brilliance of the military. I told him what I thought about our artillery support. I told him I thought human lives were less expendable than an artillery round, and that any SOB who didn't should get their fucking ass out there. There are probably guys that have gotten busted for saying less than what I did at the debriefing. I think why I didn't get busted is because I was the Old Man's RTO and in his gut he knew I was right. The debriefing was never brought up to me afterwards. We spent a month in Cambodia and suffered 25 to 30 percent losses. We found food, weapons, ammo, you name it. We were finding stuff faster than the engineers could blow it up. I said to myself, "We're not going to lose this war, but we're going to turn it over to the South Vietnamese, and they're going to lose it."

There were guys who drank beer and guys who smoked marijuana. But when it came time to go out in the field, we were all about each other. I searched for a joint once. I wondered what it tastes like, what's it do? Never found one, though. I think it was a sign from God.

Postscript

When I came home, the whole town of 650 people welcomed me with a big party. You couldn't ask for anything more. I have no animosity toward anybody. If I see a guy who deserted to Canada, I forgive him. My dad would always say, that anger in your gut eats away at you but the guy you're angry at doesn't feel a thing.

Meanwhile, back in The World, word was received that Ho Chi Minh, the personification of North Vietnam's struggle for self-determination, had died of heart failure on September 2. He was 79. Any thought that his absence would have an impact on the war was pure fantasy, however. Other leaders had already taken over the day-to-day prosecution of the fighting. Uncle Ho, as he was called, had read Vietnam's Declaration of Independence back in 1945. He didn't live to see it, but the capital of South Vietnam was changed from Saigon to Ho Chi Minh City in 1976 and his picture appears on Vietnamese paper currency. He called himself a nationalist inspired by patriotism, not communism. One of his most famous quotes was: "It is better to sacrifice everything than to live in slavery." He is also quoted as saying about the war: "You can kill 10 of our men for every one we kill of yours. But even at those odds, you will lose, and we will win."

Chapter 64
LAST BLOOD

Ted Mathies grew up in the village of Hartville in northeastern Ohio, far from the social upheaval of the Sixties but hardly immune from the trouble overseas. Drafted into the Army, he was being molded into a soldier in basic training when his name came up on the Big Army's list of needs. He was selected to be a medic. In Vietnam, Mathies served in Bravo Company of the 1st of the 505, pulling missions everywhere from the Pineapple to the Parrot's Beak, from the rice paddies to the rain forest.

"They moved us around quite a bit, usually by helicopter. Sometimes we'd have three popper missions in a day. At night, we set up ambush positions and night patrols," Mathies said. "A rice paddy would extend for a couple of hundred yards to a tree line, then there would be another rice paddy with a tree line, and another rice paddy with a tree line, as far as you could see. The jungle was thick, but it was flat. It was a big culture shock to go from the U.S. to Vietnam."

Along the way, Doc Mathies befriended Sergeant Charles Emil Miller, a blue-eyed, blonde-haired squad leader from western Pennsylvania. Both men talked about their families, and Miller often mentioned his younger sister Cheryl.

"Charlie went into the Army to get money to help his sister go to college," Mathies said.

Also in Miller's inner circle was Mike Benedict of Nebraska.

"He was there before I was," Benedict said. "We just seemed to hit it off. He was a close buddy of mine. One thing that stood out about him was that he had been stationed with the Army in Korea, but he couldn't take the cold. Instead, he volunteered for Vietnam."

Beginning on September 10, Bravo Company and the entire 1st Battalion of the 505 were repositioned to a forested area known as the Iron Triangle, located on the east side of the Saigon River and adjacent to the Ho Bo Woods.

Airlifted from the battalion base at Fire Support Base All American, troops established a new camp. It was built atop a slight hill three kilometers south of the village of Ben Cat in Binh Duong Province about 20 miles north of Tan Son Nhut along a highway known as Thunder Road. The new home was called Fire Base All American II.

The Iron Triangle was a Viet Cong stronghold and supply point. The ground was the site of bloody fighting in the earliest days of the Vietnam War, but the guerrillas maintained a stubborn presence there. In place of a forest that had been blasted away were fields of elephant grass, eight-feet tall with stalks as thick as bamboo saplings.

The Iron Triangle was a nasty place, undermined with an elaborate tunnel system and polluted with booby traps ranging from handmade devices to captured American artillery shells hidden in the undergrowth.

The mission in the Iron Triangle was to root out a unit called the 83rd Rear Service Force, which supplied food and ammo to the Viet Cong in the Golden Brigade's area of operations. A declassified after-action report described the unit as "almost mythical." It went on to say: "Although the brigade captured substantial weapons and sufficient documents attributed to the (group), the location of this group had never been fixed, nor could intelligence precisely determine their method of operation." Higher headquarters mounted another attempt to clear out the Iron Triangle, and the 1st of the 505 fell under the operational control of the U.S. 1st Infantry Division and South Vietnamese Army forces.

Accompanying the battalion were elements of the Scout Dog Platoon and the Airborne Rangers of Oscar Company, which was given the eyes-and-ears mission of locating hostile forces referred to in an after-action report as "the phantoms of the forest." Enemy positions were so well concealed that they avoided detection even if U.S. forces were right on top of them.

Using time-tested tactics, the rifle companies of the 1st of the 505 cordoned off and sealed villages prior to searches. Body counts piled up, and the Golden Brigade history noted matter-of-factly that All American patches were placed on the enemy dead. In addition to capturing tons of weapons and supplies, the battalion also uncovered an elaborate network of hiding places. Troops found 59 separate tunnels that were an amazing example of underground engineering. Tunnel rats detected trap doors leading to a lower level of passages that led to supply rooms, aid stations and storage areas. In addition, troops found 124 above-ground bunkers guarded by scores of booby traps. Bulldozers were brought into level the ground. Artillery, napalm and flame throwers incinerated the vegetation.

While the fighting in the Iron Triangle was going on, word leaked out that Golden Brigade was going home. Under the policy of pulling out American troops and having South Vietnamese units take over their role in the war, the All Americans were ordered to redeploy to the United States. At first, only a select few knew the score, and those who did were prohibited from saying anything for security reasons.

"I was in the communications section when we got the word," said Robert Pearson, based at Fire Support Base Hard Core with the 1st of the 508. "That was great, but we couldn't put it out on the net. Over a multi-channel radio, I was talking to my wife back home. She asked me, 'When are you coming home?' Someone said, 'He can't answer that, ma'am.' So I started humming, *I'll Be Home For Christmas.* That's how she found out."

Official notification came September 17 from Defense Secretary Melvin Laird through U.S. high command. One group of soldiers, huddled in anticipation around a transistor radio, heard the announcement over the Armed Forces Radio Network.

In a scene that was made part of the documentary film *Dear America: Letters Home From Vietnam,* troops erupted in cheers and hugged each other with an exuberance reminiscent of men whose death sentence had just been commuted. They shouted, danced and paraded around with Vietnamese children on their shoulders. They took rides on the backs of motorbikes or climbed atop the roofs of civilian's vans. But as with all things Vietnam, reality was something different. A total of 1,835 soldiers had enough time in-country to qualify to go home with the brigade colors. Another 2,784 would be assigned to other Army units to complete their one-year tour of duty. Most of the cheering, jubilant troops shown in the video were among them. Even those who were going home remained on combat operations for at least another month. There was still a war to fight.

After the announcement that the Golden Brigade had been ordered to withdraw from Vietnam, a name was given to the combat in the Iron Triangle. It was designated as Operation Yorktown Victor, with Yorktown referring to the climactic battle of the American Revolution, when British troops surrendered to George Washington's Colonial Army and its French allies. The operation was the last major one mounted by the 82nd Airborne in Vietnam.

Two days after the announcement, an Airborne Ranger in Oscar Company who had been in Vietnam for 10 weeks was killed on a night ambush. He was Private First Class Charles Herman Wright, 22, of Beckley, West Virginia. The timing and the circumstances made Wright's death especially heartbreaking, according to Don Carson, the Canadian citizen who served as Bud Bolling's bodyguard before volunteering to join Oscar Company.

"Our mission was to observe two tons of rice that had been rigged with explosives. We were not supposed to make contact, but to gather intel and send it back. If Charlie did come, we could detonate the explosives by remote control," Carson said.

On the night of September 19, a civilian photographer received permission from higher command to accompany the ambush. The Rangers argued against bringing along an outsider, but their concerns went unheeded.

"A team works as a single unit. Well, this outsider shows up with a canteen and a camera as if was going to Disneyland," Carson said. "We did have contact that night. Wright says to me, 'Don, there's eight of them. Move!' Then this media puke stands up to take a picture. He gave away our position."

The shadowy figures in the dark opened up on the Rangers, killing Wright. As the radio operator, Carson called for a medevac while the Rangers blew up two spider holes and were about to destroy a third.

"This guy jumps out, and I was hit in the side of the head. I shot him. He died on top of me," Carson said.

Carson was grazed in the scalp. As an example of the speed of medical care in Vietnam, Carson was at an aid station in eight minutes and was undergoing surgery 14 minutes after that. After a short stay in the hospital, Carson was back in the field.

Wright's named is carved on Panel 18 West of The Wall. In 2015, Carson's son, Paul, visited the shrine and posted this on-line tribute: "I am alive today because of Charles Wright. My father was with him when the enemy approached. He told my father to move, and in doing so, my father was shot, and the bullet went alongside his helmet. If my dad didn't move, it would have hit him straight on and more than likely killed him. On a trip to Washington in April 2014, I went to the Charles H. Wright portion of The Wall to thank him. I took a few pictures and was overcome with emotion, seeing my reflection on The Wall and his name across my heart, knowing I am alive because he told my father to move. I am thankful for his actions and just want to let his family know that I am very appreciative."

A remembrance of Wright appears in the book *Soul Patrol* by Ed Emanuel, which was published in 2003.

Casualties continued to mount in the 1st of the 505. Alpha Company Sergeant Kenneth Neal Hatch of Pensacola, Florida, was killed on September 24. Born on the 4th of July in 1948, he played trombone in the band at J.M. Tate High School. In Delta Company, Private First Class Alton Leon Ellison of LaGrange, Georgia was killed on October 3, ten days before his 20th birthday.

Meanwhile, Bravo Company's bloody work continued during Yorktown Victor, and two men lost their lives and four others were badly wounded in a firefight on October 16. Killed were Staff Sergeant Robert Nicholas Demgen, a 27-year-old draftee from Detroit, Michigan, and Private First Class Raymond Albert Gibson, 20, of Pinconning, Michigan. A draftee, Gibson had been in Vietnam for 34 days.

Lieutenant William P. Gunter wrote about the casualties in his diary: "The war is supposed to be over…They're a bunch of brave bastards. I wish there was some way for me to pay them tribute."

Less than two weeks later, Sergeant Charlie Miller was pulling security at Fire Base All American II. He was part of an element that went out at night, setting up claymore mines and remaining ever vigilant against anything that might be sneaking up on the base. The night passed quietly, and those who had gone out returned to their bunker inside the wire. Their claymores supposedly had been disarmed and were stacked for future use.

At seven in the morning on October 28, Doc Mathies was resting in front of the protective sandbags of his hooch.

"To my left, guys were sitting on a bunker. There was a line at the mess hall," Mathies said. "All of a sudden, an explosion knocked me over. Somehow, the claymores exploded. A whole bunker was blown up. Guys were blown 25 yards in a radius from the bunker. Charlie Miller was blown farthest away. I grabbed my stuff and started tending to the wounded."

Mathies reached Miller and applied a tourniquet. He then administered first aid to other wounded men, including a trooper named Rocky Poore. The last time Mathies saw Miller, the sergeant was on a stretcher awaiting evacuation by helicopter. He learned later that Miller died on the flight to the hospital. The news stunned his comrades.

"We were standing there, face to face, looking at each other, speaking more with expressions than words. What just happened? There was total disbelief. It was a very sobering time," Mathies said.

As fate would have it, Mike Benedict was away at the time. He had come down with a toothache and caught a log bird back to the rear area at Phu Loi to have it treated. A sergeant came to him with the news that his friend Charlie Miller had been killed.

"I would have been there with them but for my toothache. It hit me very hard," Benedict said. "If only he had stayed in Korea..."

Charles Emil Miller, who had been in Vietnam for five months, died eight days after his 19th birthday. It was 41 days after word came that the 82nd Airborne was going home, and 20 months since Joe Rodriguez died in a booby trap explosion when the Golden Brigade first arrived in country. Lieutenant William Gunter wrote in his diary: "Sgt. Miller killed today. Poore's face ripped apart. Accident with claymores. I cried for a few minutes. Why? I searched my mind for someone to hate. There is no one."

At least 10 members of the Golden Brigade lost their lives between the time of the withdrawal announcement and the time the colors left Southeast Asia. Sergeant Charles Miller is believed to be the last of the 227 All Americans killed in Vietnam.

Miller was flown home in an aluminum transfer case. He was buried in a cemetery named for St. Michael, the patron saint of the Airborne, in the Pittsburgh neighborhood of Mount Oliver. His name is on Panel 17 West of The Wall. Decades later, Doc Mathies remembered a brother who dreamed of going to school after the Army. "When his country needed him, he was there. His dreams are my memories. He covered my ass every day. I live his last day everyday as I do with the others. People should know he was one of America's best. I would serve with him anywhere," Mathies said.

Left to cherish Miller's memory were his parents and sister. Thirty-eight years after that dark day, Charles and Dorothy Miller of Jamestown, Pennsylvania, left this online tribute to their son: "No words can express the depth of our love for you. From the day you were born, you were such a joy to us. Always a happy baby. Watching you grow up, we realized what a precious gift God had bestowed upon us. When your sister came into this world and was so very ill as a child, you were always kind to her and were a tremendous help. Your loss has devastated all who knew you. You had a greatness about you. You were wise beyond your years. We took comfort in knowing the tremendous love you had for your fellow man and your country, the pride you took in serving in the United States Army, especially the 82nd Airborne. You died doing what you wanted to do, defending the country that you loved with your whole heart and soul. You made the ultimate sacrifice. We as your family are very proud of you. You were the bravest of the brave."

Cheryl Miller also remembered her older brother by penning these words: "My wonderful, loving, caring brother. You left us when I was only 15 years old. I did not fully realize the magnitude of this war. I never thought for a moment when you got on that plane you would never come back alive. I mourn for you every day of my life. It has taken me a long time to realize what it really meant for you to serve your country and your loved ones. You are the bravest person I know and were more of a man at the age of 19 than most of the men two and three times your age are now. I will always love you and cherish the short time we had together on the Earth, only to meet again in heaven."

Operation Yorktown Victor continued into November. One ceremonial part of it involved General George Dickerson pulling the lanyard on the last of the 370,000 artillery rounds fired by the Golden Brigade in its 22 months in Vietnam.

Bravo Company continued to lose men to wounds, sometimes three or four at a time, mostly to booby traps. The unit was ground down so badly in the Iron Triangle that all of its officers were wounded and out of action. The acting company commander when it pulled out to go home was Staff Sergeant John Moore of Duluth, Georgia.

"I know we didn't have any officers left. We were down to two platoons, with two squads in each platoon, maybe a total of 60 guys left in the company," Doc Mathies said. He still had time left in Vietnam. Instead of returning home, he was assigned to a rifle company in the Army's 1st Infantry Division.

Before Operation Yorktown Victor was over, the 2nd of the 505 and the 1st of the 508 also operated in the Iron Triangle. The Golden Brigade fought right up to the time it was told to stop.

Back in The World in November of 1969, the first story and first pictures of the My Lai Massacre were published. That stain on the Army's honor unfairly tarred every G.I. with the same broad brush. At the same time, anti-war protests in a number of cities were organized by the Vietnam Moratorium Committee, which was dissatisfied with the speed at which America was withdrawing from Southeast Asia. Future president Bill Clinton, then a Rhodes scholar at Oxford University, participated in a demonstration in England. The largest of the demonstrations, held in Washington, D.C., on November 15, drew an estimated crowd of 500,000, roughly the number of Americans serving in Vietnam. Folk singer Pete Seeger performed John Lennon's new song *Give Peace A Chance.* President Richard Nixon, whose timetable for withdrawal was unaffected by the marchers, said he watched college football on television during the event.

Chapter 65
UNKINDEST CUT

In the process of turning over the war to the South Vietnamese, a ceremony involving the 82nd Airborne was staged at a floating dock along a waterway. Top brass from the American army and the host country, as well as government officials from Saigon, gathered as four air boats were donated to the local forces. Units of the Golden Brigade had roared up and down the marshy areas on the outskirts of the South Vietnamese capital on those watercraft. The Hurricane Cats, as they were known, were powered by an airplane motor that drove a huge rear fan. In essence, a Cat was a sampan with a propeller on the back. Capable of operating in as little as two feet of water, the boats were used by the All Americans to reach Viet Cong safe havens inaccessible by land. The air boats could reach speeds of 50 miles per hour, but they weren't built for stealth. The engines were so noisy that the operator couldn't hear if anyone was shooting at him. Having been with one of the units that patrolled the wetlands, Les Museus was there when a South Vietnamese soldier sat in the control seat and revved the engine.

"He thought it had a reverse gear, and he goosed it. He put that boat right up on that floating dock. He put all those officers and officials right into the water," Museus said.

To paraphrase President Lyndon Johnson, getting out of a war was a lot tougher than getting in.

The Army moves with urgency when it sends a unit into combat. Pulling troops out takes time. More than 128,000 items of equipment were turned over or turned in during the transition period between the announcement that the Golden Brigade was going home and the final departure date. Brigade headquarters was moved from Camp Red Ball to Phu Loi to ease the process. Under an established schedule, each infantry battalion and its artillery battery would stand down every 15 days. The first one, the Panthers of 2nd of the 505, came out of the field on October 15. Next came the Red Devils of the 1st of the 508 and then the Nightfighters of the 1st of the 505, who stood down on November 14. Busy clerks processed the paperwork of those going home as well as those who were transferred to other units to complete their tours of duty. The fire bases were vacated and either turned over to other units or boarded up.

While all this was going on, supply officers directed the building of the All American Swimming Pool at Phu Loi for troops transitioning from Vietnam to The World, according to supply officer Robert Anderson.

"We borrowed an Air Force drilling rig to dig a well and got the plumbing from somewhere," Anderson said. "It was so weird. As we shut down one battalion at a time to go home, we wanted to give them something to do, to make them as comfortable as possible. They could get a real suntan, not a field suntan."

The pool required an additional 3,000 gallons of potable water per day over and above the 10,000 gallons per day the brigade was allotted. It was one of the biggest morale boosts during the stand down, but nothing compared to getting on a Freedom Bird.

Dwaine Selk of the Red Devils was aboard a plane with infantrymen, support personnel, engineers and communications specialists on his flight back to The World.

"We were the second unit to stand down. We had closed up the fire bases. It was just our time to come home," Selk said.

His Starlifter landed for refueling at 3 o'clock in the morning at Clark Air Force Base in the Philippines, where a breakfast was served to the hungry troops. Then it was off to Elmendorf Air Force Base in Alaska.

"They had dress uniforms laid out for us, with name tags and everything. We had all new clothes. I never saw anything like it," Selk said.

Hollis Crowder's battalion was the last to be pulled out of the Iron Triangle. Wounded three days prior to the official announcement that the 82nd Airborne was being redeployed, he had been hit in the side by jagged shards of shrapnel from a rocket propelled grenade, and he had been concussed. After a medic shot him up with morphine, he was choppered to a hospital in Saigon and spent a couple of days recovering before he lobbied to return to the field.

"I told them I had to get back to my unit. It was my job. I still had stitches in when I went back out on the supply chopper. They told me a medic could take the stitches out," Crowder said.

Then one night, at ten minutes to midnight when he was out on ambush, Crowder was told to return to the rear.

"I didn't think much of it. The fire bases got rocketed all the time. We felt safer in the field," Crowder said. "They told me I had orders to return to the States. I didn't get a stand down. Just a bottle shower and a hot meal and some clean socks."

Aboard his plane, Crowder said a sober mood prevailed as the big jet powered up and thundered down the runway.

"It wasn't festive. I mean, we were glad to be going home. We were really proud. We never lost a battle. Who can duplicate that? We were a tight unit. If you served your country with honor, if you did what you were asked to do, be proud of it," Crowder said. "But we lost some good men. We lost some of the best. I do remember that when the plane was in the air, we all said, 'Hoo-ah!' "

Hoo-ah is a soldier's word that has more than one definition, but in this case, it meant the mission was over. Imagine, then, what he felt about the reception that greeted the flight when it touched down in San Francisco, which had the dual role of being a pivotal military installation and the epicenter of the counter-culture revolution.

"We got off the airplane, and a bus on the runway took us to the terminal. Protesters were there. We got spit on. I got spit on," Crowder said. "The MP's said to the officer in charge of our detail, 'Major, get these men out of the terminal.' I'll admit, I wanted to take out those protesters. I heard a lot of name calling. I never thought I'd come home and be spit on. It was a shameful time. So much had changed between 1968 and 1969."

The final farewell ceremony was held on December 11 for the 188 men in the Guard of Honor, the last members of the Golden Brigade to depart. The brigade colors that had flown Up North and Down South were packed up for the journey. Of the 5,000 or so soldiers who had served in the brigade during its 22 months stay, only 13 were with the unit the entire time, according to Don Carson.

While it had taken 161 Starlifters to ship the entire brigade in 10 days to Vietnam, two flights departed Tan Son Nhut on December 12, 22 months to the day that the 82nd Airborne received its emergency deployment orders. One president had ordered them to Vietnam. A different commander-in-chief ordered them out.

"We did our jobs so well that they decided to bring us home," said General George Dickerson.

The after-action report concluded with two words: Mission Accomplished. The last item on the last page was an illustration of a road sign that said: "Fort Bragg: 13,137 Miles."

Bruce Potts, the first sergeant of Alpha Company of the 82nd Support Battalion, was on the last flight. He carried the brigade colors.

"The plane wasn't fully loaded. From the air, my last view of Vietnam was of the four-hole latrines at Tan Son Nhut. They were probably burning shit. I said to myself, 'I hope I never see this damn place again,' " said Potts, who had earned a Combat Infantryman's Badge in the Korean War. "We landed at Pope, got off the plane and took a bus to a processing center at Bragg. My wife and son drove up from Atlanta. There was no big celebration. A lot of our people had been killed."

At Pope Air Force base, a sign said: "Welcome Home Third Brigade." A reception and dinner were held at one of the clubs on Fort Bragg. One way to mark the exact moment a war begins is when a soldier's plane goes wheels up on takeoff. The time it ends is when his plane touches down. The era of the Golden Brigade had come to a close. While the unit was in Vietnam, a new brigade had been formed to help the 82nd Airborne fulfill its role of being able to respond to any emergency anywhere in the world. Now that the colors had returned, the new unit was folded in to the Third Brigade.

One measure of an organization is how it remembers its dead, especially an organization that considers itself family. A memorial to those who were killed in Vietnam had been rushed to completion before the brigade colors returned. It was primarily paid for by the donations of Vietnam veterans. In keeping with Airborne tradition, a pair of bronzed Corcoran jump boots was placed atop a four-sided base of granite, and an M-16 rifle with bayonet was thrust into the stone to support a combat helmet. Names of the dead were chiseled into the granite, which had room for later additions after all the records were checked. The Vietnam Memorial at Fort Bragg went up 13 years before The Wall was dedicated in Washington, D.C.

In reality, coming home was an individual experience for most of those who wore All American patches in Vietnam. Under the rotation system, troops returned not with a unit but as individuals. While investing a year of their lives to Vietnam, they had all thought of little else but doing their jobs and returning to The World. The feeling was far from mutual when they returned home.

"That left some of the deepest scars," said Larry Dobson, who touched down in San Francisco on his birthday, November 4, 1969. "We had to walk about a half a mile to the processing center. People were standing on the other side of a chain link fence, and you could see their mouths moving. They weren't smiling. They were snarling. It really caught you by surprise. It left such a bad taste in your mouth."

Battalion surgeon James (Doc) Slavin of Waterbury, Connecticut, who jumped once with an Airborne unit in the South Vietnamese Army, was among the fortunate returnees.

"The Army gave me everything I asked for. I don't regret serving in Vietnam for one second. It was the most worthwhile, most memorable thing I ever did, the most remarkable year of my life. I proved to myself I was worthy. I didn't shirk from any of my responsibilities. It was a huge, huge honor to serve in the 82nd Airborne," Slavin said. He resumed practicing medicine in civilian life.

Pete Watkins, who was wounded in the same battle that claimed the life of Sergeant Felix Conde, was justifiably proud of his service too, but it took him decades before he even mentioned Vietnam to anyone outside his immediate family.

"We were treated like shit, and if you put that in the book, that's S-H-I-T," Watkins said.

Returning soldiers with military haircuts and wearing the uniform of their country were visible symbols of the establishment and a war that became unpopular. Separating the war from the warrior was a rarity.

"You had to wear your military uniform to get an airline discount for a ticket for home. I got a lot of funny looks. The war wasn't popular, and people were not behind us," said Darrell Criswell. "All you wanted to do was get out, get back to civilian life and move on. I was blessed to get through it, but it took three years to get my head back."

Art Kellogg of Franklin, Pennsylvania, was among the many who felt so ostracized or overlooked that he never spoke of Vietnam.

"I was in an airport bar on my way home, and people didn't even want to sit beside you. They looked at you as if you were scum. That's why Vietnam was such a disaster.

We got a bad rap. But even knowing the outcome, I would do it again for my country," Kellogg said. One item that Kellogg brought home from Vietnam was a transistor TV set. It was the first TV his family owned, and he had it in his attic 50 years later.

For Don Behm, homecoming was one last battle for those who fought the North Vietnamese Army, the Viet Cong, the tropical pests of lizards and bugs and snakes, the mud and the rain, the Army bureaucracy, the politicians and finally public opinion. Through all the hard times of Vietnam, he had come home without a scratch when everybody he knew of in his original company had either been killed or wounded. After his plane landed in Seattle, the final trip-wire awaited when he went to a restaurant inside the airport.

"The worst part was when we came home," Behm said. "I was told to grab a steak and get the hell out of there because demonstrators would arrive. Hell, they were there at one o'clock in the morning. When I got to the airport in Toledo, Ohio, on my last leg home, I just sat on a curb thinking, 'What the hell happened?' I went into the Army because I thought I owed it to my country. I had a contract with America, but my whole contract with America was broken. Everything was against us."

That kind of thing makes the bond even stronger among Vietnam vets. They leaned on each other over there, and all they had was each other back home. Silver Star recipient Salome Beltran, who survived vicious firefights Up North and crawled through the tunnels Down South, came back through Hawaii with a buddy. They wore their jungle fatigues, which violated Army travel regulations, and were arrested by the Military Police.

"They put us in a holding area, and I said to my buddy, 'Let's get the fuck out of here. What are they going to do, send us back to Vietnam?' We just left and went on our way," Beltran said.

He caught the next flight to the West Coast and made another decision. Instead of flying to Fort Bragg and then doubling back for home, he got off the plane in California, caught a bus to Santa Cruz and went into a bar to wait for his sister to pick him up. Attitudes had changed.

"People didn't like us. I was getting dirty looks. These long-haired Hippies were talking shit. Those cowards. At least I did something. They don't know what it was like. Fuck them. I'm proud of the things I did, but there were some terrible things that happen in war. I was strong enough to do the right thing. I had the support of my family. That was a blessing. I took the uniform off and never talked about Vietnam. Nobody knew I was in the service," Beltran said.

Like Beltran, Andrew Blais was part of the original deployment and was still processing the loss of his buddy, Johnny Plunkard, when he returned.

"We didn't go home to any parades, that's for sure. It was like Vietnam never happened," Blais said.

Ed Kochanski gave everything he had to give and then received the shock of his life when he got home.

"Eight days left in country and I was still out on ambush. They squeezed every drop out of us they could," Kochanski said.

Back in the States, Kochanski completed the terms of his enlistment at Fort Benning and was selected for the Honor Guard, a duty reserved for the best troops. He shaved twice a day to look his best, spit-shined his boots to a high gloss and polished his chrome helmet. He went home for good to Scranton, Pennsylvania, only to receive the unkindest cut of all.

"When I came home, I was so proud to be wearing the uniform. Then people spit on me," Kochanski said, his voice cracking with emotion.

Pete Henderson remembers returning to Oakland, California, at 9:30 at night.

"Protesters were throwing garbage at us. Somebody asked me later how that made me feel, and I said, 'Well, they weren't shooting bullets at us, so I didn't care.' Most of us tried not to think about Vietnam. Nobody talked about it. I didn't have anybody to talk to about it anyway."

As part of the reception, returning soldiers were given dress uniforms for their flights home. Before he left, Henderson remembers being fed all the steak and French fries he could eat.

"Every September 25 from that point on, I have a dinner with all the steak and French fries I can eat," he said.

Intelligence officer Dickie Keaton extended his tour for six months to serve with a South Vietnamese Airborne Division. When he did come home, he was in the company of two Special Forces sergeants at the airport in San Francisco and on his way to a connecting flight to Atlanta.

"Protesters were shouting, 'Baby killers!' The Green Beret sergeants said, 'Captain, you might want to use the restroom. You don't need to see this.' These guys had been to Vietnam four or five times for six months at a time. So, I went in and heard this God-awful commotion. I came out to find that the protestors were out cold. They had been decked. As we walked to our gate, other people in the airport were cheering us," Keaton said.

Keaton remained in the service and married an Army nurse. Their son David was born at Clark Air Force Base in the Philippines. About his service in Vietnam, Keaton said, "I lost friends over there, but I would do it all over again. I don't regret any of it."

Infantry officer Keith Bell also landed in San Francisco.

"I was walking through the airport with a Russian carbine. Try that today. A bunch of long-haired kids, maybe 15 or 20 of them, surrounded me and called me baby killer. Before I could butt-whip them, the MPs came along and dispersed them. I sat down at a bar and had a Scotch," Bell said. "Forty some years later, I was on a barge trip to France with Jim Littig and John Kapranopoulos. There were only 14 passengers on board, so we got to know a little bit about them. The others knew we were Vietnam vets from the 82nd Airborne. Someone wanted to know what we did, what combat was like. One night at dinner, we were asked what homecoming was like. I told my story. The next day, a lady from San Francisco told me that she might have been in the group that was harassing me. She had tears in her eyes and quietly apologized. I told her that it was a long time ago and most of us had gone on with our lives."

Other returnees were greeted with the cold shoulder of apathy, which was no less of an injustice than being greeted with scorn.

"When I got home, a guy told me you need to get out of that uniform because protesters were in the airport. I didn't know what was happening back home. I got angry. I wanted to rip the guy's face off," said Darron Sharp of San Diego. "I told my mother I'd be home but didn't say what time, so I took a taxi to the house. My mother hugged me, but one of her friends was crying hysterically. She had broken a fingernail. That's what she was worried about. A broken nail. I said to myself, 'This is Disneyland. We live in Disneyland.' Nobody cared."

Ron Snodgrass of Marietta, Georgia, remembers hostile glances instead of the thanks of a grateful nation.

"We wanted to go home and be left alone. I couldn't adapt to civilian life. My family had a barbeque for me as a welcome home picnic. People were talking about the high price of hamburger when guys were dying in Vietnam. I just couldn't relate," Snodgrass said.

All soldiers in all wars face a period of adjustment when their battles end. But Purple Heart recipient Rick Dalton felt abandoned by the older generation when he went for a beer at a Veterans of Foreign Wars post near his hometown in Indiana.

"Guys would be telling their war stories, and you just knew they were full of shit. They would say that Vietnam was just a conflict, that it wasn't a real war, that we were the first ones ever to lose a war. Paying ten cents less for a beer wasn't worth it to have to listen to that," Dalton said. "We have to fight. Sometimes, we have to die. We should not be treated the way some people were."

Added Mike Benedict: "A lot of us felt betrayed, by our government, by our countrymen, by the older generation. The World War II guys at the VFW would say, 'You don't know what a real war is.' "

If the 82nd Airborne was an orphan brigade in Vietnam, Rich O'Hare had his own story to tell about being made to feel like an outcast at home. Like Jim Littig, Mike Hood, John Carney, Joe Mays, Dwaine Selk and others, O'Hare volunteered to serve another tour in Vietnam.

"My mother told me before I left that no mother wants to bury a son," O'Hare said.

On his second stint, he served as an advisor to a South Vietnamese Army airborne unit and even did a training jump. The unit awarded him a red beret, the headgear of a French peasant that serves as the international symbol for paratroopers. O'Hare also remembers going to the big Post Exchange at Tan Son Nhut and seeing a poster that read: "Will the last person to leave Vietnam please turn out the lights?"

O'Hare ultimately returned home, completed his Army commitment and took a job driving a UPS delivery truck. He later returned to school at the State University of New York at Oneonta to pursue a dual major in economics and American history. In attempting to recapture the adrenaline rush of Vietnam, he also bought a Plymouth muscle car with a four-barrel carburetor and a Kawasaki motorcycle, the fastest road bike on the market. He joined the 82nd Airborne Division Association and also sought membership in the association representing the 505th Parachute Infantry Regiment, which did multiple combat jumps in World War II.

"They told me, 'We only take winners.' I don't want this to sound like a whine, but it definitely hurt. Our fathers and our families were proud of us, but the World War II guys didn't embrace us. People say we weren't joiners, but we weren't asked to join anything," O'Hare said. Small wonder that guys gravitated to the only organization they could relate to, the Golden Brigade Association that had been founded in Vietnam.

The hardest part of homecoming for Mark Robertson of Concord, North Carolina, happened when he had been home a couple of months. He reconnected with Reid Lyon, a fellow cavalryman, and talked about friends that had been killed.

"I just broke down and started to really cry. It was the first time I expressed fucking grief for the whole year. It flipped some kind of switch," Robertson said. "We never did any dishonorable stuff there. We never mutilated corpses. It was just the insanity of it all. There was so much anger about our guys being killed. The adrenaline was another thing. I did a lot of reckless stuff after the war trying to get the adrenaline back. The other thing was not having a weapon after carrying one for a whole year. I felt naked. Vulnerable. No longer protected."

As one who had done his duty and had every right to speak his mind, Robertson got involved in the anti-war movement. He was among the founders of the Veterans For Peace at North Carolina State University and marched against the war in Washington, D.C. He also campaigned for Democratic presidential candidate George McGovern in the next election.

"We were not winning that war. There was no reason for us to be there. We were not making a damn bit of difference, and we were losing people to compound the tragedy of it," Robertson said.

Reid Lyon, Airborne cavalryman and tunnel rat, returned to pursue a career in higher education as a way of dealing with Vietnam and as a way of helping others who struggled with the invisible wounds of war. In earlier wars, internal scars were described as soldier's heart, shell shock or combat fatigue. The Vietnam version was called Post Traumatic Stress Disorder.

"It was a tough thing to be a Vietnam veteran. I never told anybody I was there, never talked about it. I'm pissed at myself now for doing that. It was a great honor to have served my country as a paratrooper in the 82nd Airborne. They were all life-changing experiences. The way I handled coming back, I worked my ass off, studying 15 to 18 hours a day at school," Lyon said.

Using the benefits of the G.I. Bill, Lyon received a doctorate in neuroscience from the University of New Mexico and became one of the nation's pre-eminent experts on Post Traumatic Stress Disorder. He headed research programs at the National Institutes of Health and worked at the Lee County Veterans Administration Health Center in Cape Coral, Florida. Years later, Lyon served as an advisor to George and Laura Bush on the importance of reading in childhood education. Vietnam left an indelible mark.

"Going there, I was a kid. I looked at the world in a very naive way. I used to be a blabbermouth. I'm a lot more quiet now. My Vietnam experience gave me the desire to push through to get to where I am. It taught me to focus and make decisions under difficult circumstances. Keep going. Drive on. When I would start to feel sorry for myself, I would tell myself at least I'm not getting shot at," Lyon said. "I carry with me a lot of lousy memories. If I smell dirt, I think of being a tunnel rat. It takes you back. There is no cure for Post Traumatic Stress Disorder, but it can be managed. You may always walk with a limp, but you can walk straight and tall. In a minute, I would do it again, if it was with same guys."

Elsewhere in America, in the same month as the colors of the 82nd Airborne returned home, a music concert billed as Woodstock West was held on December 6 at the Altamont Speedway in northern California. It drew 300,000 attendees, but bloodshed gave it an entirely different vibe from the New York event held four months earlier. As the Rolling Stones performed as the final act, an unruly concert-goer, 18-year-old Meredith Hunter, attempted to climb on stage. He was stabbed to death by a member of Hells Angels, which provided concert security in return for $500 worth of beer. In some circles, the violence at Altamont symbolized the end of the Sixties. Some called it the day the music died. One of the final songs played by The Stones was *(I Can't Get No) Satisfaction,* the anthem of the Sixties.

Chapter 66
RECKONING

Homecoming for Leslie Hayes felt a lot like his arrival in Vietnam. When he touched down on U.S. soil, he boarded a green Army bus and noticed that protective screens had been welded onto the outside of the windows.

"What are these for?" he asked the driver.

"That's so protesters don't throw garbage into the bus," came the reply.

"That just don't sound right," said Hayes, recalling the bus that had been modified to prevent grenades from being tossed through the windows in Vietnam.

Like a lot of guys, Hayes picked up his life as best he could without ever mentioning Vietnam. He got a job at an oil refinery in Russell, Kentucky, got married and started a family. And yet, something inside gnawed at him, subconsciously reminding him he still had some unfinished mission to accomplish. While the human brain may try to block out an intense experience as one way of coping, the subconscious operates on a different level. A switch that turns off a war has yet to be invented. Besides, on that awful day that Felix Conde had been killed, Hayes had made a promise to himself to look up the family of his platoon sergeant.

His wife Diane, sensing that peace of mind might never come until Conde's family was found, embarked on a quest of her own. She searched for the Conde name in Chicago, because that's where Conde said he had joined the Army after failing to make it as a professional baseball player.

"I called or wrote to every Conde in Chicago. I only got one response. The guy said he was sorry he was not the one we were looking for, but he wished us well in our search," said Diane, who had worn a bracelet inscribed with the name of a Prisoner Of War during Vietnam.

As one sure sign that he didn't just forget the whole thing, Hayes bought a boat for fishing and recreation. He christened it *Conde*, painting the name on the hull.

Hayes was hardly alone in sorting out the emotions of what was then America's longest war. If anything, public attitudes worsened after the 82nd Airborne came home in 1969. President Nixon authorized incursions into Cambodia as a way of preventing an attack on Saigon, but the move in 1970 was interpreted as widening a war that was supposed to be winding down. Nixon's orders led to demonstrations across the country, including one at Kent State University in which four unarmed college kids were killed by Ohio National Guardsmen. A commission headed up former Pennsylvania Governor William Scranton, a moderate Republican, concluded that the only way to end public unrest was to end the war. To that end, the Paris Peace Accords of 1973 ceased direct U.S. military involvement in the war, but the agreement allowed North Vietnamese troops to remain in the south. A little more than two years later, the final outcome was as inevitable as it was unconscionable. Without America's combat support, Saigon fell and was renamed Ho Chi Minh City.

Seven years later, the Vietnam Veterans Memorial in Washington, D.C., was dedicated. Some referred to the panels of granite as a black scar. To the Vietnam veterans who paid for it out of their own pockets, The Wall was the most fitting way to honor the 58,300 Americans who died in Southeast Asia, including 227 names from the Golden Brigade.

Members of the Golden Brigade reassembled as a group was on Veterans Day in 1984 for the dedication of an addition to The Wall, a bronze statue called The Three Soldiers. A trooper named David Stits of Riverside, California, bought an ad in the Vietnam Veterans of America newsletter advocating for a reunion, and a dozen or so Vietnam veterans from the 82nd Airborne joined the ranks of 150,000 or so people who participated. Among them was Carl Bludau, who in the years after the war had become commander of the Disabled American Veterans of Texas.

"I was standing in a group in the hotel lobby when the elevator came down," Bludau said. "I heard one guy ask another, 'Sir, do you think the Dallas Cowboys will beat the Washington Redskins this Sunday?' The answer was, 'Yes, they're going to beat them.' So, I tapped the older guy on the shoulder and said, 'You from Texas?' He answered yes, and I told him I was from Victoria. It was Bud Bolling. He said, 'Son, what is your name?' I told him, and he remembered immediately that I was the RTO for John Kapranopoulos. Everything just kind of clicked."

The bond of brotherhood has a healing quality. Soldiers who have been through a shared experience, especially one as unique as Vietnam, just felt at ease in each other's presence. For many, it was the first time they had visited the Vietnam Memorial, also known as The Wall That Heals. Its polished black granite reflects as a mirror reflects. Those who search and find a name see their own image looking back at them. In dedicating the statue that day, President Ronald Reagan chose a theme of reflection. In his role as The Great Communicator, the commander-in-chief uttered words that needed to be said, words that should have been said long before. As a way of binding up the nation's wounds, Reagan embraced the Vietnam veterans as part of America's story who deserved better than to be treated as outcasts. Those who died in Vietnam are part of America's family, Reagan said. He added that they fought as well and as bravely as as any Americans in any war, and that they reflected the best in all of us.

"Today we pay homage not only to those who gave their lives but to their comrades present today and all across the country. You didn't forget. You kept the faith. You walked from the litter, wiped away your tears, and returned to the battle. You fought on, sustained by one another and deaf to the voices of those who didn't comprehend.

You performed with a steadfastness and valor that veterans of other wars salute, and you are forever in the ranks of that special number of Americans in every generation that the nation regards as true patriots," Reagan said.

"The war in Vietnam threatened to tear our society apart, and the political and philosophical disagreements that animated each side continue to some extent. It's been said that these memorials reflect a hunger for healing. Well, I do not know if perfect healing ever occurs, but I know that sometimes when a bone is broken, if it's knit together well, it will in the end be stronger than if it had not been broken. I believe that in the decade since Vietnam, the healing has begun," the president added.

Rather than sweeping aside the moral and philosophical disagreements about whether the war was just or not, Reagan confronted them. No wisdom can be gained by forgetting, he said.

"And let me say to the Vietnam veterans gathered here today. When you returned home, you brought solace to the loved ones of those who fell, but little solace was given to you. Some of your countrymen were unable to distinguish between our native distaste for war and the stainless patriotism of those who suffered its scars. But there's been a rethinking there too. And now we can say to you, and say as a nation, thank you for your courage. Thank you for being patient with your countrymen. Thank you for continuing to stand with us together," Reagan continued. "Many sacrificed their lives in the name of duty, honor and country. All were patriots who lit the world with their fidelity and courage. They were both our children and our heroes. We will never forget them. We will never forget their devotion and their sacrifice. They stand before us, marching into time and into shared memory forever. May God bless their souls."

Recognition of sacrifice is the least a country can do after sending its sons and daughters off to a foreign battlefield. It means the world to those who held up their end.

More than any other individual, Bud Bolling was responsible for preserving the bonds formed by his soldiers in Vietnam. In 1987, he was the keynote speaker at the 82nd Airborne Division Association's convention in Houston, where for the first time, the Golden Brigade had its own hospitality suite as its command post. As a combat veteran in two wars, Bolling understood that unit associations, forged in the mud and blood of combat, grow in importance as the years go by.

"We were the 82nd Airborne Division in Vietnam. We carried the division colors, and we wore the patch. It was a proud outfit, and the troopers of the Golden Brigade added much glory to an already glorious history," Bolling said.

One of the most profound legacies of Vietnam was evident when the fourth generation of All Americans went to war in 1990-91. The Soviet Union had disintegrated, and the communist dominoes had fallen the other way. With a cadre of sergeants and officers who were veterans of Vietnam, the rebuilt U.S. military applied overwhelming force to evict Saddam Hussein's Iraqi army from Kuwait. The Second Brigade of the 82nd Airborne drew a line in the sand as the vanguard of the largest military buildup since Vietnam, and the entire division deployed. While two All Americans were killed in accidents, the division did not have a single combat casualty in the ground war. Public support for the war was evident, and America welcomed home its troops with parades and open arms. In the aftermath, President George H.W. Bush said the Vietnam syndrome had been kicked once and for all. Desert Storm was the shortest war in U.S. history.

Meanwhile, as the years passed and attitudes changed, Diane Hayes continued her mission of helping her husband find peace. Plagued by nightmares, Les sometimes slept outside on the porch or in the woods near his Kentucky home. It was his way of building a bridge back to the time when he slept so many nights an arm's length away from the platoon sergeant and father figure who had made such a big impact on his life. To further strengthen Diane's intuition that something was amiss, her husband experienced what she called a mini-breakdown. Having worked 60 straight days at the refinery, he came down with the flu. Doctors at the Veterans Administration thought it might be related to Post Traumatic Stress Disorder. Hayes insisted it had nothing to do with Vietnam, but Diane thought otherwise.

"We should contact some of your friends," she said.

"They're probably dead," Les would reply.

One who was very much alive was Pete Watkins. After finding the address, Les wrote Watkins a letter at the turn of the century in what became a breakthrough.

"It was in the year 2000, and I went out to the mailbox to find this letter with a return address from Les Hayes. It was only one paragraph, with an email address and a phone number. I had a big smile on my face. I answered immediately," Watkins said.

Having spoken for the first time in 30 years, the two Army buddies took the logical next step. Les and Diane Hayes agreed to meet Pete and Peggy Watkins in Morgantown, West Virginia, a location that was halfway between their residences. The rendezvous point was a restaurant.

"We got there first. And when Pete and Peg walked in, Les said, 'There he is. That's Pete,' " Diane said.

When the server brought drinks to the table, the wives noticed that both men swirled their glasses, causing the ice cubes to make an audible sound. Ice was something they lacked in Vietnam. Both men appreciated the little things others take for granted.

"That was the first time either of us talked about Vietnam in front of our wives," Pete said. "The first thing Les said to me was, 'Where's my $15?' "

That was the amount of money a wounded Pete Watkins borrowed on Good Friday of 1969, just before he was taken to an aid station by a helicopter. Both men could laugh about the memory now, and Pete made good on his debt.

"I work in construction, and he makes me go to work for him around the house when we visit Kentucky every year. I owe him that," Watkins chuckled.

After the meal, the couples checked into their hotel rooms and the reunion became even livelier.

"I never heard such carrying on in my life. The front desk called twice to tell them to keep it down. It was like they had been together yesterday. It's like they had not missed a beat. It blew my mind," Diane said.

Les and Pete were brothers-in-arms. But from that moment, Diane and Peg became like sisters. Two families became one.

The next plot twist came four years later. Word spread through the grapevine that some members of the Golden Brigade Association were planning a trip back to Vietnam, and that Bud Bolling would be leading the delegation. Relations between America and Vietnam had changed in the years after the war. Two countries that once traded bullets with each other had become trading partners in 1995.

"We talked it over. Our wives were all for it. All four of us decided to go," Hayes said.

"Our wives had lots of questions. When we were at war, we never had the opportunity to see the culture of Vietnam. I wanted to go back to the places I had been, like Birmingham and Bastogne, but never knew where I really was. In the war, I spent three or four nights across the river from Hue and never knew there was a city there. We didn't have to worry about anybody shooting at us, but the Vietnamese always had somebody following us. Their job was to watch us," Watkins said.

Acting as a guide, Bolling explained the mission—to cut off the avenues the North Vietnamese soldiers used to threaten Hue, and to cut off their adversary's food supplies. Bolling also made a gesture that buried any possible friction between jump-qualified troops and the infantrymen shipped to Vietnam as replacements in his unit. He presented official Golden Brigade challenge coins to Hayes, Watkins and others on the trip.

"Whenever a two-star general hands you a coin, you take it," Hayes said. "Besides, I never felt any resentment. The Airborne guys have treated us like champs."

At one point, the group stayed at a beautiful resort hotel on the South China Sea at Da Nang. The country was at peace. Old animosities were gone. Former enemies were now friends.

"I never slept better in my life," Hayes said.

Among other Vietnam veterans who returned was Don Behm. Admittedly, he had gone through a low point after the war and was being counseled for Post Traumatic Stress Disorder.

"I lost something there. I was going to go back and have a battle with the Devil, and only one of us was going to come back alive. I did it out of anger. It was either going to be the Devil or me," Behm said.

He revisited the old battle sites, remembering buddies who would say before a mission: "If I don't make it, drink my share of beer for me when you get back." He even made it to Hanoi to visit the places that once housed American prisoners, including one who was a friend of Behm's.

"Our interpreter was a former NVA officer who fought against us on the Cambodian border. I don't know if we talked for 30 minutes or three hours. But when we finished, we cried and hugged each other," Behm said. "It was really amazing. I knew right then that my job now is to live for those who didn't come back. Until then, I had been dead within."

Through conciliation, he had beaten the Devil. Through healing, he had restored his faith.

"Going back made it all worthwhile. Based on what I know now, I wouldn't change a thing. I wouldn't have said that 10 years ago," Behm said. In addition, Behm returned to Fort Bragg during one All American Week and ate in the chow hall of his old unit, Charlie Company of the 1-505. The company commander was a Vietnamese-American from Los Angeles. Behm and the captain had a nice lunch together.

Reid Lyon, by now a leading authority on the PTSD that afflicted him, also found some measure of solace in his return. He visited places from Hue to the village of Chau Chu, from Birmingham to Bastogne.

"It was just amazing. I came to terms with it, came to peace with it. It's a beautiful country. What really helped was the kindness of the Vietnamese," Lyon said.

One of his guides was a former captain in the North Vietnamese Army. Once formidable enemies, they discovered that they shared much in common as soldiers.

"I told him about that ambush outside of Hue when the steering wheel in my jeep was shot out of my hands. He said that the army should have taught that soldier how to shoot better. We both laughed. There were no hard feelings," Lyon said.

Paul Davin, the former commander of a rifle company involved in some vicious fighting, also made it back to the places where he had lost so many men.

"There was a little old lady, whose face looked like she was 100 years old, and she was selling things in Hue. I hugged her. Bought everything she was peddling. And I told her, 'I'm sorry. Sorry for what we did.' I had to say it. We should never have been in Vietnam," Davin said.

John Carney, the infantry officer who became a priest, revisited Vietnam with a fellow clergyman. He was amazed that Saigon, renamed as Ho Chi Minh City, had tripled in size from the 2 million residents there during the war. He also toured Hue and Hanoi, having a vehicle and a guide at each stop.

"It's a beautiful, beautiful country. The people are kind and gentle, but when they get agitated, they're ferocious. In Hanoi, they had a nickname for us. They called us Russians with money," Carney said.

At the Hanoi War Museum, Carney lingered at an exhibit for Operation Babylift, which was an effort to bring to America the 2,000 or so illegitimate children fathered by American G.I.s during the war. The first flight of the operation crashed on April 4, 1975. Of the 300 people on board, 78 children and 50 others, including U.S. Air Force personnel, were killed.

"I think every guy has a desire to return. There's a bit of nostalgia, especially the war places. You get to see it again, touch it, feel it. When I was there for the war, I didn't have a brain in my head. I didn't know what introspection was," Carney said.

Richard O'Hare went back more than once. He discovered that Camp Rodriguez, once the headquarters for the Golden Brigade, had become a municipal cemetery for the city of Hue.

Meanwhile, the search for Felix Conde finally bore fruit. Diane Hayes enlisted her daughter's help to do computer searches. One nugget was that Felix Conde had been buried in Texas, and Diane found the funeral home that had arranged the services. A short time later, a representative of the Sheffield Funeral returned a call, confirmed the information and provided an address for Conde's son, Richard. During the holiday season in 2004, Diane told her husband: "Guess what I got you for Christmas?"

Les penned a short letter and sent it off. He was at work when Richard called the first time, but Diane arranged for him to call Les the next day. She also suggested to her husband that he jot down the things he wanted to talk about on a yellow legal pad.

"It would have been easy to give up over the years, but I'm obsessive-compulsive," said Diane, the unsung hero of the follow-up story. "There was something missing, always something missing, with Les. There was something he needed to tell somebody."

Loose ends were about to be interwoven.

Chapter 67
RESOLUTION

With his mind racing and his hand shaking involuntarily, Richard Conde picked up the phone in his Texas home and dialed the number for Leslie Hayes. What would the voice on the other end be able to tell him? What would he ask? It was 4 o'clock in the afternoon on New Year's Day of 2005, a time for a new beginning and a time to look back into the past. "Mister Hayes, this is Little Richard," Conde said.

Les got straight to the point.

"Do you want to know how your dad died?" Hayes asked.

"Yes, Les, I want to know."

With that, Hayes recounted the events of Good Friday in 1969, explaining that he was the radio operator for his father. During a battle out near the Cambodian border against soldiers of the North Vietnamese Army, Richard's father reacted and advanced against a series of bunkers that endangered the lives of his men. During the fight, Sergeant Felix Conde was mortally wounded. His last words had been about his two young children, Little Richard and Little Jeannie.

"Your dad saved my life so many times. Your dad was my hero. I wouldn't be here today if it wasn't for him," Hayes told him.

Once the ice was broken, the two talked and talked and talked. Other than knowing that his father was a soldier who had been killed in Vietnam, Richard knew next to nothing about the man who brought him into the world.

"I had no idea anyone was looking for us. I had no idea that my life was an empty bucket, and now I wanted to fill it. I couldn't get enough," Richard said. "I was hungry for knowledge, just wanting to know everything. Opening up that letter was like opening up a bottle of vintage wine. You take one sip, savor it, and you want more of it and more of it. I can't say Les gave me my father back, because I never knew my father. He gave me my father for the first time."

The initial call opened a portal to the past. Richard, or Rico as he was known, phoned his sister with the news that a man who had been with their father the day he was killed had connected with the family after searching for decades. This stranger had even named his boat after their father.

"I didn't believe Richard at first. Then it sunk in that this was real," Jeannie said. "Who looks up a family after all these years? Who names their boat after another man? My dad must've impacted him in some way. It was such a relief to know that Les was with my father. All these years, I thought he was all alone in the jungle when he died. It gave me a sense of closure."

Every day for the next two weeks, Richard called Les or Diane, looking for any scrap of information. After decades in the dark, after all the darkness of Vietnam, a light had emerged.

The story took another turn on January 15. Terri Conde's water broke at three o'clock in the morning, and she gave birth to a daughter. Terri had already picked out a name, but her husband had a last-minute suggestion.

"How about naming her Leslie?" Richard asked.

Terri laughs at her initial reaction.

"You want me to name my baby after some guy I don't even know? You're crazy. Now I'm very glad we did," she said.

The baby was named Payten Grace Leslie Conde, a tribute to the RTO of first platoon of the Delta Dragons.

"I have lots of nieces and nephews, but not one of my brothers or sisters ever named a baby after me," Leslie Hayes said in his deadpan manner. He was as proud of the honor as he could be.

At first, Richard didn't want to tell his terminally ill mother about Les Hayes. He feared it might tear open an old scar or cause her distress as she languished in a hospital. When he finally told her about what he had learned, Lydia Layton Conde broke into a smile.

"See? I told you your father was a good man," she told her son.

Lydia died on March 10, 2005, at the age of 69. She was survived by her two children, three brothers and seven grandchildren, including Payten Grace Leslie Conde. Following a Mass at St. Mary's Catholic Church in Temple, Texas, she was buried next to her husband in the plot he had purchased in Rogers Cemetery before he left for Vietnam. She rests in eternal peace, knowing that the life of her husband and soul mate had been resurrected for her children.

The next step was a face-to-face meeting between Rico and Les later that spring. As a representative of a company called Wilson Arts Countertops, Richard Conde was coming to Louisville, Kentucky, for a trade show. He made arrangements to visit. Les then invited his buddy, Pete Watkins, to join them. It was then that Les retrieved Felix Conde's shoulder holster, which he had picked up off the bloody ground and placed in his rucksack 36 years prior. Hayes presented the holster to Richard, who now had something tangible that belonged to his father. That holster had been stained with the sweat and DNA of Vietnam.

"I spent three or four hours at the house. Les gave me the holster and all the pictures and told me more stories. It was like I knew them my whole life," Richard said. "In essence, I built a relationship with my dad through Les. I think of Les as my father. I call him Papi, and Diane is Mimi. Les is the guy I'd want a father to be."

A question kept recurring. Why? Why search all these years to find Richard and Jeannie? What compelled him to look?

"Les said, 'It was something I just had to do. I just knew Little Richard and Little Jeannie were out there. With his final breath, Sergeant Conde said to go find my kids and let them know I loved them and cared for them.' I can't express what that means to me," Rico said.

Les Hayes had kept his promise. He had lived up to the 82nd Airborne code—All The Way.

"It was an Oprah moment," said Diane Hayes, who had made the breakthrough that healed her husband and brought peace to a family. "It was meant to be. It was just meant to be."

Fifteen minutes after he left the house, Richard called back with more questions. He also called Jeannie to tell her about their father's holster.

Meanwhile, members of the Golden Brigade found resolution in their own ways. Forty-two years after he returned from war, Tom Ladwig attended a 2010 event called LZ Lambeau, Wisconsin's way of welcoming home Vietnam veterans with a ceremony in the stadium where the Green Bay Packers play. The three-day event culminated with a display of 1,241 white folding chairs placed on the turf, each chair representing a Wisconsin resident killed in the war. Once a hotbed of anti-war sentiment, Wisconsin welcomed home its warriors.

"When we came home, we weren't respected, weren't treated well. Even at the VFWs, we were told we weren't in a real war," Ladwig said. "LZ Lambeau was my welcome home. It was so impressive. You couldn't buy a meal at the local restaurants. People picked up the check. During that ceremony on the field, the Wisconsin National Guard marched in and encircled the folding chairs. They came to attention and saluted the chairs. Then they did an about face and saluted us. Wow! I just started crying," Ladwig said.

Other members of the Golden Brigade found solace through a gesture made by the latest generation of All Americans. Carl Bludau, chairman of the Golden Brigade Association, was aware that the 101st Airborne had embraced its Vietnam veterans with organized events. He wanted the same for the All Americans. Bludau contacted Major General James Huggins, commander of the 82nd Airborne Division, and requested a homecoming for those who had fought in Vietnam.

"I ain't no hero, but I sure served in the company of guys who were," Bludau said. "It's not because we have been spit on. It's not because we ever whined. It's not because we never got a welcome home. It's just that none of our people ever asked for anything, and I wanted to do something for them. We spent tons of time in that jungle. We were tight. They are just so proud of who they are. These are the toughest sons of bitches in the world."

At the time, Huggins and his Fourth Brigade Combat Team were deployed to Afghanistan, which has supplanted Vietnam as the longest war in American history. He was the right man at the right time. For one thing, Huggins came from a paratrooper family. He remembers as a child that he woke up one morning to find that his father was away. He left in the middle of the night on a secret mission. A few days later, Huggins saw on TV that the 82nd Airborne was in the Dominican Republic on Operation Power Pack. That told him where his father was. In addition, Huggins' father had served in Vietnam with the 7th Special Forces Group, but he had never talked about the experience. Huggins could relate to what the Golden Brigade had gone through.

"It was an easy call on my part. Carl and his guys deserve 99 percent of the credit," Huggins said. "We were trying to correct a wrong. That was unfathomable how people were treated from that war. None of us can make up for the sins of the past, but at least some of us appreciate their sacrifice. None of those guys ever asked for anything. They just did it. This was a way of closing that chapter."

One of the things Huggins tried to do as a commander was infuse modern day troops with the essence of All American history, that they stand on the shoulders of those who fought in two world wars, Vietnam, Panama, Desert Storm and beyond. In his own experience, he had once commanded the 505th Parachute Infantry Regiment, the same one led by James Gavin when it did combat jumps in World War II. When Gavin died in 1991 and was buried at the cemetery in West Point, Huggins served as the funeral officer and met Gavin's daughter, Barbara Gavin Fountleroy. Outside of the events in his own family, Huggins considered it to be the greatest honor of his life. Honoring Vietnam veterans with a homecoming was the least he could do.

"We do it because we're paratroopers. I just wish we could have done more," Huggins said.

The general directed Bludau to have his group in place at Fort Bragg in the first week of September in 2012, when the 82nd Airborne returned from one of its multiple deployments Sure enough, 43 members of the Golden Brigade assembled. With veterans carrying the guidons of their individual units, the formation marched onto the tarmac to greet the plane. The veterans of Southeast Asia welcomed those who had just completed a combat tour in Southwest Asia. Leading the formation was John Kapranopoulos, the former company commander in the Golden Brigade.

"It was a tear-jerker for me. I remember the shitty treatment we got. That's still on my mind," Kapranopoulos said.

Rick Talioaga, holding the guidon of the 1st Battalion of the 505th Parachute Infantry Regiment, was in the handshake line as Huggins and the troops got off the plane.

"The commanding general shook our hands. I didn't even know he was a general," Talioaga said.

One of the promises that Vietnam veterans had made to themselves was that no generation of Americans would ever be forgotten by another. The old soldiers led the returning troops into a hangar similar to the one the 82nd Airborne had departed from when it went to Vietnam in 1968. Two separate generations mingled for a bit before the returning troops reconnected with family, loved ones and friends. Various banners lined the hangar walls. One sign welcomed home the troopers from Afghanistan. Another said: Welcome Home Golden Brigade.

"That was a special moment. We kept telling them to go see their families, and they kept talking to us to thank us for our sacrifice," Richard O'Hare said.

The Golden Brigade led the way to where families waited.

"When we marched into the hangar, the crowd welcomed us and them home. There really wasn't a dry eye in the place. All of us old guys were crying," said Bob Gaddi, who had served in Vietnam with the 82nd Support Battalion. "For a lot of guys, it was their own welcome home."

Off to the side during all this was a retired Special Forces sergeant major who had served in Vietnam but did not fall in with the Golden Brigade. He was James Huggins' father.

"Maybe he didn't do such a bad job in raising a son," General Huggins said. "I got dozens of letters from the guys in the Golden Brigade who offered their sincere thanks me for including them in the homecoming. That had been missing for them."

Two other events made the homecoming even more special. One was the naming of the Third Brigade dining facility in honor of Bud Bolling. Having retired from the Army as a two-star general, Bolling had died the previous year. He likely would have objected to the ceremony, according to Mike Hood, the former company commander who delivered the eulogy at Bolling's funeral and spoke at the dedication of the dining hall. The place where active soldiers ate their meals became an everlasting legacy of an officer who put the needs of generic Joe Tentpeg above all else.

"We're up here because of General Bolling's love and respect for the American paratrooper. He has done it again. He has honored us by allowing us to be here in his name," Hood said.

The other event was the placing of a wreath at the Vietnam Veterans Memorial, located at the 82nd Airborne Museum among the monuments dedicated to all generations of All Americans. The speaker was Bob Murrill, former company commander in Vietnam.

"You can leave the 82nd Airborne, but the 82nd Airborne never leaves you," Murrill began.

Murrill drew inspiration from the commander of Darby's Rangers, the unit his uncle was a part of. Colonel William Darby said the ideals for which they fought would forever reflect the memory of the fallen. "Our hearts join in sorrow for their loss, but also, our hearts swell with pride to have fought alongside such valiant men. They will never be considered dead, for they live with us in spirit," Darby said.

Quoting William Shakespeare, Murrill also gave a nod to the "eternal band of brothers" who shed their blood together. The bond defined all those who fought in Vietnam, and in a larger sense, all the generations who have been part of the 82nd Airborne.

"This monument is a constant reminder that young men and young women give their lives, knowing full well the consequences of personally confronting the evils and horrors of war. They made the ultimate sacrifice for something greater than themselves. Their legacy endures in every All American soldier in the 82nd Airborne Division. Most important, their legacy endures in our hearts," Murrill said. "We veterans of the Golden Brigade are part of the brotherhood. We can look into the eyes of young as well as experienced soldiers and know in our collective hearts that all of us have an unbreakable and eternal bond, especially with those fallen warriors with whom we served."

Then roughly 18 months after that homecoming, another chapter was added to the Felix Conde saga. Rico answered the phone and heard the person on the other end identify himself as President Barack Obama, calling from the White House. His initial reaction was disbelief.

"Am I getting played here?" Richard said.

"Do you recognize my voice?" the president replied. "Your father has been awarded the Medal of Honor, and I want you and your family to attend the ceremony."

What had happened was, Congress had authorized a review of military records of those who had received the Distinguished Service Cross and may have been overlooked on the basis of nationality or creed for the nation's highest award for valor. The review opened the files of 6,505 veterans from three wars. Twenty-four of them, including Felix Conde, were selected to receive the Medal of Honor. The ceremony was slated for March 18, 2014. The first thing Richard did was call his sister.

"Jeannie, you ain't gonna believe this," he began.

Then he phoned Les and Diane Hayes, who were vacationing in Florida. Upon hearing the news, they dropped their cell phone into the ocean. Rico figured that Les had something to do with this latest twist. He didn't, but he insisted that it should have been awarded years before.

"It's about time," Les said.

At the ceremony, the Conde family was joined by Les and Diane Hayes along with Pete and Peggy Watkins. The big event included police escorts and a stay at a swank hotel in the nation's capital.

The Medal of Honor, with 13 white stars adorning an accompanying light blue ribbon, came in a glass-enclosed case. The president handed the award to Rico with the thanks of a grateful nation. Two of Rico's children from a previous marriage, both of whom are in the service, watched the ceremony via closed circuit television. The lone regret for Rico and Jeannie was that their mother wasn't alive to witness it.

The wheel of life had come full circle. Les Hayes had lost his own father but found a father figure in Felix Conde, and then lost him too. In contacting Conde's children, he had presented the gift of a father to a son and daughter who grew up in a fatherless void. Rico then found a father figure in Les, who came to look upon Richard as a son. When Richard named his daughter after Les, family ties were solidified. What's more, Conde's children discovered they had a second family they never knew—the 82nd Airborne Division, their father's unit.

About 80 members of the Golden Brigade traveled to Washington for the Medal of Honor ceremony. Such an award is a reflection on the entire 82nd Airborne, and a reception for the Conde family was held. Rico called it the highlight of the whole affair.

"There was so much energy, so many stories being told. The 82nd Airborne is like a family to me. These guys are so tight-knit. It truly is a band of brothers," Richard said. "I had once closed that book. I never wanted to open it again. But ever since Les reached out to us, I've had a relationship with my dad that I never had before. For 40 years I didn't have anything. Now I have this big huge family filled with people who care. There was a price to pay but look at what I gained."

One wounded warrior from the 82nd Airborne, who had prosthetics instead of legs because of war wounds, shook Rico's hand and thanked him.

"I said, 'I'm the one who should be thanking you because you paid such a high price.' He told me, 'You paid a price too, because you grew up without a father,' " Rico recalled.

Jeannie Conde Holland was overwhelmed by it all.

"The 82nd Airborne gave our dad back to us. They'd introduce us by saying, 'These are Conde's kids.' They treated us like royalty. The whole time I was saying, 'Please pinch me. Is this really happening?' They're part of our family, and we're part of them. I have never been prouder. My mom told me before she died, 'You don't have cry anymore.' Well, I cried, but they are tears of joy for once."

Among the Golden Brigade veterans in attendance was Carl Gulas, who was a member of the Delta Dragons and was engaged in the same Good Friday firefight that claimed Conde's life. He purchased a commemorative book from the Medal of Honor ceremony and gave it to Jeannie. She keeps it in her home in Waxahachie, Texas, next to the American flag that was draped over her father's coffin.

"It was the greatest feeling in the world," Gulas said. "They had no recollection of their father growing up. We gave them the stories that brought a good man back to life. Who could possibly do that other than the guys who were with him when he died?"

More honors would be bestowed. An engraved sidewalk panel dedicated to Sergeant Conde was placed outside the Airborne and Special Operations Museum in Fayetteville, North Carolina. Attending that ceremony were 82nd Airborne veterans from Puerto Rico, who had named their chapter after Conde. Conde's name was also affixed to the classroom of the 1st Battalion of the 505th Parachute Infantry Regiment at Fort Bragg. His jungle uniform and a pair of combat boots are displayed inside a glass case, and the room is ringed with pictures from Vietnam.

"This has been a long time coming," said Lieutenant Colonel Marcus W. Wright, then the battalion commander. "We acknowledge the pain a family feels at the loss of a loved one. The man whose name is on this room is a hero of ours because of his sacrifice."

Cade Perry, the battalion's command sergeant major, told the Vietnam veterans in attendance: "You guys are our heroes."

At the monument to the Golden Brigade's dead, Conde's name was flecked with gold paint, an honor accorded to him because of the Medal of Honor. He was also part of the inaugural class of the 82nd Airborne's Hall of Heroes, a galaxy of luminaries that includes the names Ridgway, Gavin and Alvin York. Duke Dewey was subsequently added to the Hall of Heroes.

All the while, Payten Grace Leslie Conde was transformed by the outpouring of affection for a grandfather she never knew except through the soldiers who were with him when he died. In time, she sensed the presence of a higher power.

"She told me that she did not believe in God until all that happened with her grandfather," said Terri Conde.

When he returned to Texas, Rico Conde drove on a stretch of road that one day would be named the Felix Modesto Conde-Falcon Highway. With the case housing the Medal of Honor in hand, he visited the cemetery where his parents are buried. He had a silent, private conversation with the man he had come to know.

"Dad, I brought this home to you. I will always try to live up to you," he said.

With tears in his eyes, with all the stories about his father fresh in his mind, he knelt in front of the tombstone to pay his father the highest Airborne compliment there is.

"Damn, Dad, you were a real bad ass," he said.

Epilogue
GOLDEN DEVOTION

In the rugged splendor of New York's Hudson Valley, the survivors of the last man's club from the Golden Brigade reunited to mark the golden anniversary of their time together with the 82nd Airborne in Vietnam. Organizers called it Operation West Point, a nod to the military academy located a few short miles away. A wall-sized welcome banner in the headquarters hotel, a testament to brotherhood and remembrance, greeted attendees proudly decked out in All American shirts, hats and other regalia.

Paddy Barry and Richard O'Hare approached the planning of the event, held the second week of June in 2018, as if it were a last hurrah. Tom Hennessey, holder of a doctorate degree in public policy from George Mason University, handled the registration of 200 or so brigade veterans who reunited after 50 years. Duke Dewey of Vermont held court with Dickie Keaton of Texas. Les Hayes of Kentucky and Pete Watkins of Pennsylvania showed off photo albums that included snapshots of Sergeant Felix Conde. Salome Beltran brought his wife and kids from California. In keeping with the theme of a family gathering, Richard Davidson of Montreal, wounded in war, was accompanied by his wife, two children and seven grandkids along with motorcycle riders representing the Vietnam Veterans of Canada. The wonder of it all was how easily they all reconnected.

A week of special events began with a chartered bus trip into Manhattan, located 50 miles to the south. One hint of the extraordinary experience that awaited flashed from the blinking lights of New York State police cruisers that escorted them on an hour-long drive. The motorcade zipped down the Palisades Parkway, through the bottleneck of commuters at the George Washington Bridge and into Manhattan. Inside the city limits, the New York Police Department picked up the procession and led it to the West Side wharf of the Circle Line, the company that offers luxury cruises on New York City's waterways. On an idyllic sunny day, the veterans and their guests boarded a World Yacht luxury vessel named *Duchess.* The crew at the top of the gangway welcomed each passenger with a flute of champagne or a glass of wine. The classy gesture was only the start. As Golden Brigade chairman and retired NYPD detective Paddy Barry said, "I called in every favor I was ever owed to make this happen." He was owed a lot of favors.

River cruises are a staple of the tourist industry for a city surrounded by water, a popular way for visitors to see the panorama of a metropolitan area crammed with cathedrals of capitalism. On this voyage down the Hudson River, the *Duchess* journeyed toward the Statue of Liberty, which grew larger and larger in the background with each elapsed minute.

When the yacht reached the point where it was nearly perpendicular to Lady Liberty, a police fireboat pulled alongside. Seven NYPD officers in orange life vests lined up on deck, snapped to attention and saluted the veterans. In the background was a New York Fire Department vessel. Its water cannons spewed out graceful arcs of spray, which with the addition of dye, became flowing streams of red, white and blue. Then a police helicopter appeared. The pilot banked at precisely the proper angle for him to salute the Golden Brigade. All of them appreciated those who run toward danger. Police and firefighters had performed the same act of courage on the September 11, 2001, terrorist attack on New York City.

At that same moment, the sound system aboard the *Duchess* played songs appropriate to the occasion. One was *America* by Ray Charles, and the line "may God thy gold refine" wafted from the speakers just as the yacht, the water arcs, the saluting policemen and the helicopter aligned with Lady Liberty in the background. The soldiers of liberty, lumps in their throats and mist in their eyes, came to attention and saluted back. Over the loudspeaker, the captain of the *Duchess* said, "Thank you for your service. Our freedom is intact because of men like you."

The moment was transformative. Unlike Jason and the Argonauts of ancient Greece who embarked on a quest to find the golden fleece, this gilt-edged moment materialized as something better than treasure. After the acid test of Vietnam and the trials of the Sixties, those who went to fight in Vietnam basked in the glow of a solid gold moment.

John Kelsey of Missouri struggled to find words. "That was about as patriotic as you can get. It was my welcome home. That fulfilled the mission for me," Kelsey said. "A person would have to linger over his vocabulary for a long time to explain the feeling correctly. It was like an epiphany."

Scott Carroll of Tryon, North Carolina, called it closure. "It took 50 years. All it takes is a little respect," he mused.

Catharsis came to mind for James (Doc) Slavin of Waterbury, Connecticut. The release of emotions resulted in a sense of restoration. "A once in a lifetime experience," Slavin said. "You couldn't buy that feeling if you had 10 million bucks."

Ed Kochanski of Scranton, Pennsylvania, savored the scene. "Going from being spit on when I got home 50 years ago to this, it was overwhelming," he said.

Stuart Simonson of Iowa felt like he had never felt before. "It made me feel appreciated. What a way to be treated. How could you not feel good?" he said.

Cristobal Garcia of San Antonio, Texas, was like a man who had found gold at the end of a rainbow following a bad storm. "I'll never forget that," he said. "No eraser or medication can ever take away Vietnam, but it feels like there's a different light on it now."

The veterans moved below decks for a grand lunch aboard the yacht. Bruce Potts, who had carried the brigade colors home from Vietnam, gave the benediction and referenced the 227 Forever Young listed on the memorials.

"Thank you for being here when our brothers could not," Potts told the attendees.

Two days later, chartered buses with their police escorts returned to Manhattan to tour the 9-11 Memorial where the twin towers of the World Trade Center were brought down in the worst terrorist attack on U.S. soil. Amid the exhibits salvaged from the rubble was this quote from the poet Virgil: "No day shall erase you from the memory of time."

Afterwards, the veterans were whisked to a dinner held at Clyde Frazier's Restaurant on 10th Avenue. Food and drink were provided courtesy of Walter Rauscher, a former 82nd Airborne paratrooper who participated in the Dominican Republic operation. Rauscher had enjoyed a lucrative career built on his management of Tavern on the Green in Central Park and the Sequoia Restaurant in Washington, D.C. The meal was his tribute to those who had once been overlooked.

"We are the lost generation. Here's to the guys that stayed together all these years. You are our heroes," Rauscher said, raising his glass.

After the meal, members of the Golden Brigade formed up outside on the sidewalk for a picture. Aging soldiers cleared their throats and sang *The All American Soldier.* No one could have ever envisioned that scene in the immediate years after Vietnam. The wheel of history had definitely turned.

To conclude the reunion with a final flourish, the Golden Brigade held a dressy dinner at Eisenhower Hall on the campus of the U.S. Military Academy. A color guard had been sent from Fort Bragg. The 82nd Airborne Chorus performed as well.

An empty table was set aside to honor those who had died in the war. Also, on display was the Legacy Bowl that the Vietnam veterans had financed out of their own pockets. One guest of honor was artist in residence Wendy Yothers, a professor at the Fashion Institute of Technology in New York City, who had helped in the design. Roughly the same age of those who fought in Vietnam, Yothers was a college student at the University of Michigan during the time of the Tet Offensive but did not comprehend what it all meant or understand what young Americans did in Vietnam. Years later, she was working at Tiffany & Co. in Manhattan when a Golden Brigade veteran walked in and asked about a silver bowl in the window. An object like that, if donated to the 82nd Airborne Museum at Fort Bragg, would preserve the memory of those who did their jobs under very trying circumstances. To get a better feel for the concept, Yothers even went to All American Week at Fort Bragg and hung out with members of the Golden Brigade.

"The project is about their devotion," Yothers said. "Every artist and craftsman is a historian. The object tells a story. What happens when you make art is that the vision becomes very clear. When those who wrote the story are gone, the object is still there. Melted into this ornament are aspects of all those guys. They did what they had to do. They did what they were supposed to do."

Wendy Yothers never took a dime for her services.

Mark Frankel, a master silversmith from MJF Silversmiths in Williamsburg, Virginia, crafted the Legacy Bowl.

Made of sterling silver laced with gold inlets, the bowl comes with two serving ladles that honor the brigade's two commanders, Bud (Night Rider) Bolling and George (Bold Strike) Dickerson. Enhancing the concept are 15 silver toasting cups adorned with the crests of the 15 individual units that made up the brigade. The All American patch and the motto All The Way are etched into the metal as well as a map of Vietnam. Two red rubies mark the sites of Hue and Saigon, the two cities defended by the brigade.

The Legacy Bowl was blessed by Father James Sanner, the chaplain who had served in Vietnam. At the age of 85, he was still active in the Catholic Church, and he figured he still had a chance to inherit the bottle of whiskey in the last man's cabinet.

Toasts were made to the wives of the men who served, to the commanders, to the fallen and to the band of brothers who remained true to each other.

Richard O'Hare lifted his glass "to the 82nd Airborne, the best damn outfit in the United States Army."

Paddy Barry offered a final tribute with the highest compliment one All American can pay to another: "To the best men I know. You guys were, and still are, the baddest asses I ever knew."

By any measure, the moment was precious. May it inspire the final survivor of the last man's club when he toasts all the brothers who went before him. Salute!

INDEX

A

A Shau Valley, 51, 135–137, 186, 187
Abrams, Creighton W., *461*
    counterattack planning, 38
    jump pay policy, 351
    letter of condolence, 134
    meeting with Bud Bolling, 54
    new orders for the 82nd, 225
    replacement of William Westmoreland, 152–153
    restructuring of the 82nd, 173
    sendoff ceremony, 384
    at USO Christmas Show, 259
accidental deaths
    Ahern, Robert, 400
    Davis, Richard, 391
    examples of, 381, 383
    F-4 Phantom accident fire, 282–283
    Miller, Charlie, 416–417
    Murray, Billy, 245–246
    Simonson, Steven, 403
    See also "friendly fire" incidents
Adams, Barbara, 72
Adams, James, 10, 65, 66, 68, 72
Agent Orange, 130, 133, 245, 368, 399
Ahern, Robert P., 400
aid station
    building and supplying of, 53–54
    F-4 Phantom accident fire, 282
air support
    during attack on Camp Rodriguez, 145
    Candy Stripe battle, 71
    Hollis Crowder on security of, 369
    Operation Mot, 201
    Thon Chau Chu mission, 157
    Three Ville battle, 125
Airborne and Special Operations Museum, 443
Aldrin, Buzz, 393
Alicea, David, 210–211, 212, 213, 214, 273–274
The All American Magazine, 276–277
The All American Soldier (song), 26, 56, 235, 447
All American Swimming Pool, 419–420
All Americans. *See* 82nd Airborne
Allport, James Sherwood, 127
Alpha Company of the 1st of the 505
    Candy Stripe, Battle of the, 63–67, 70–71
    return to the front, 123–124
    Rick Talioaga's joining of, 379
    Three Villes, Battle of the, 125, 126, 127
Alpha Company of the 1st of the 508
    deaths of Eric Ream and Richard Gwinn, 382
    dog scouts and handlers, 401
    Highway 547 ambush, 131, 132–133
    Ho Bo Woods casualties, 364
    Operation Mot, 200, 201, 202–204, 205
    reunions, 368
    search for two missing Bravo Company soldiers, 361–362
    Stuart Simonson's diary account of, 403–411
Alpha Company of the 2nd of the 505
    Billy Murray's experiences in, 221–224
    Fire Base Panther III attack, 211–214
    Hock Mon Bridge accident, 245–246
    Jim Littig's position in, 116
    Kapranopoulos court martial, 253–256
    Mike Gamble on losing men of, 381–382
    Nui Ke Mountain mission, 151–152
    Operation Sheridan-Sabre, 305–312, 314–315, 318–319
    recovery of Tiger Platoon bodies, 376

Robert Gary Owen's death, 221
search for downed helicopter, 226
Altamont Speedway concert, 427
Altshuler, Buz, 357
ambush tactics, 58–59
American Red Cross, 267
amoebic dysentery, 169
Anders, William, 262
Anderson, John Harrison, Jr., 150, 151
Anderson, Robert, 44, 329–331, 419–420
Anderson, Viola, 151
Andrews, Bruce, 328–329
Ann-Margaret, 259
antiwar movement, veterans in the, 426
antiwar protesters, 175–176, 247, 269, 418, 421–425, 430
Ap Nam Phu, Vietnam, 85–92, 95, 103
Ap Tay, Vietnam, 249, 250
Apland, Richard Bruce, 313, 314
Apollo 8 flight, 262–263
Apollo 11 moon landing, 392–393
Arlington National Cemetery, 127, 160, 161, 252, 338
Armed Forces Radio Network, 169, 414–415
Armstrong, Neil, 393
Army Commendation Medal, 367
Army Good Conduct Medal, 367
Army of South Vietnam, atrocities by, 160
Army Post Office (APO), 54
Austin, Kay Patterson, 376
Autrey, James Harold, 381
AWOL soldiers, 28, 42, 44

B

B-52 aircraft, 180, 199
B Troop, 17th Cavalry, 48, 56–57, 135, 139–141, 155–159, 228
Babinsack, John, 169
Ballinger, Timothy, 370–371
Barnes, Jimmy, 22, 82, 104–109, 174–175
Barrimond, Errol Michael, 127
Barry, Paddy, *514*
ambush tactics of, 59
on attack on Camp Rodriguez, 144
Detroit race riots deployment, 11, 13
golden anniversary of 82nd's time in Vietnam, 445, 448
on living with danger, 137
on reception upon returning home, 175
on the rioting after King's death, 94
on travel through Hai Van Pass, 49
Barsanti, Olinto, *460, 470, 476*
body counts and, 70, 71
Carroll Guthrie's Silver Star ceremony, 146
greeting of Bud Bolling, 37
request for immediate airlift of Bolling's brigade, 38
Silver Star ceremony for Ronald Frazer, 149
battle cross. *See* Empty Boots ceremonies
Battle of Michigan Avenue, 207
Battle of the Bulge, 5, 10, 37, 130
Battle of the Candy Stripe, 63–72
Battle of the Schoolhouse. *See* Battle of the Candy Stripe
Battle of the Three Villes, 124–128
Baumann, Bluette, 134
Baumann, Rene Georges, 129–134
Baxter, John, 205
Beard, Alexander, 223–224
Beatty, Cindy, 156
Beatty, Don, 156
Beck, Jerry Don, 352
Beckers, John Paul, 367
Beckwith, Charlie, 229
beheadings, 159, 160
Behm, Donald, 184–185, 250, 400, 423, 433–434
Bell, John, 206–207, 236, 237, 251–252, 260
Bell, Keith
on combat conditions, 165, 166
on "firsts," 26
on John Kapranopoulos, 254
on the massacre at Hue, 57
on Nui Ke Mountain mission, 152
on the playing of *Silent Night,* 261
on return home, 424–425
search for downed helicopter, 226–227
Belliott, Ron, 90–91
Beltran, Salome, *507*

at Ap Nam Phu, 85–86, 88–89, 91
on Bud Bolling, 233
golden anniversary of 82nd's time in Vietnam, 445
on return home, 423
as tunnel rat, 294
Benedict, Michael, 394–396, 413, 417, 425
Bennett, Anthony, 155–156, 157
Benton, Benjamin, *506*
Operation Sheridan-Sabre, 307, 308, 310, 314
Rick Dalton and, 253–254, 317–320
Bien Hoa air base, 174, 227, 230
Bird Dogs (aircraft), 179–180
Bishop, Roger Earl, 205
black market goods, 76–79
Blais, Andrew
on being held back from Lazy W engagement, 103–104
on John Plunkard, 55, 81–82, 106–107, 113
on return home, 423
on soldiers returning to Vietnam, 22
on travel through Hai Van Pass, 49
Blaz, Juan, 306, 308–312, 314–315, 318, *507*
Bludau, Carl
dedication of The Three Soldiers, 430
on John Kapranopoulos, 152, 254
Operation Sheridan-Sabre, 307, 311–312
pack weight of, 165–166
on race relations, 94
talk with Benjamin Benton's father, 318
Vietnam veterans homecoming request of, 439–440
blue-on-blue fire incidents. *See* "friendly fire" incidents
boat patrols, 321–324
Bodo (scout dog), 400, *510*
body count
of the 82nd, 275
bartering with, 331
Candy Stripe battle, 70, 71, 72
The Donnybrook, 141
emphasis on, 44, 70
Good Friday battle, 346
Highway 547 ambush, 132
night ambush of sampans, 258–259
of the 101st Airborne, 109
Operation Mot, 220
Operation Sheridan-Sabre, 302
Three Ville battle, 128
war strategy change and, 153
body escorts, 111, 246, 267
Bold Strike. *See* Dickerson, George W.
Bolling, Alexander (Bud)
on 82nd Airborne identity, 37, 431
on aborted *Pueblo* mission, 17
The All American Magazine piece, 276
in armored personnel carrier, *479*
on arriving in Chu Lai, 30
attack on Camp Rodriguez, 146
background of, 4–5, 7
brigadier general promotion, *478*
building of camp outside Hue, 51–54
Camp Rodriguez address to troops, *473*
Candy Stripe battle, 70
counterattack planning, 38
court martial trial of John Kapranopoulos, 255
departure from Pope Air Force Base, 25–26
Detroit race riots deployment, 11–12
on drug use by soldiers, 77
Duke Dewey on, 8
farewell ceremony for, 260
in field with another officer, *471*
Fire Base Panther III attack and, 213
greeting a new arrived officer, *474*
jammed guns and, 62–63
Lazy W battle, 108
Legacy Bowl as honor to, 448
letters to parents of Bob Murrill, 358
on Mike Hood, 128
with Olinto Barsanti, *460, 470, 476*
Operation Durango City, 18–19
Operation Golden Sword, 225, 229, 230–231
Operation Mot, 197, 205–206, 220
post-war return to Vietnam, 433
release of confined Special Forces soldiers, 39
replacement soldiers and, 180

request for volunteers to return to the front, 123
restructuring of the 82nd, 173–174
retrieval of fallen soldiers, 72
reward for troops after Operation Mot, 206–207
on Ronald Frazer's death, 150–151
Ronald Frazer's relationship with, 149
sacking of Charlie Company commander, 44
Saigon defense plan, 230–231
soldiers' regard for, 233–239
tent caper and, 119
Thanksgiving message to troops, 250–251
Third Brigade dining facility named for, 441
at The Three Soldiers dedication, 430
William Porter's convoy assignment, 135
with William Westmoreland, *461*

Bolling, Fran, 25–26
Bolling, Kathryn, 149, 150
Borman, Frank, 262–263
Bottan, Daniel Jacques, 213
Bracken, Donald W., 111
Bravo Company of the 1st of the 505
Candy Stripe battle, 69, 70–71
Iron Triangle mission, 413–418
at Lazy W River, 103–109
Mike Benedict's wounding, 395
Operation Atlas Wedge, 338
Phu Hoa Duong ambush, 394–395
Bravo Company of the 1st of the 508
Ho Bo Woods, 359–361, 362–364
Operation Mot, 200, 201, 202–203
September 9th ambush of, 220
Bravo Company of the 2nd of the 505
attachment to the 101st, 229
battle for Hue, 39
Donald Paquin on, 356–357
Jerald Manning on turnover in, 385
Operation Sheridan-Sabre, 295, 297–304
shooting down of ducks, 355–356
Thon Chau Chu mission, 159
Tiger Platoon, 373–377
transport to Bien Hoa, 229–230
Bravo2Bravo. *See* Paquin, Donald
Brenson, Johnny, 238
Bridgers, Vivian Benton, 317, 319, 320
Brocker, Thomas George, 132
Broken Arrow call, 300
Bronze Star recipients
Baumann, Rene, 134
Benton, Benjamin, 317
Foote, Walter Bruce, 353
Greene, Jimmy, 303
Gulas, Carl, 396
Gunning, Leo, 98
Gwinn, Richard Alfred, 382
Headley, Paul, 68
Johnson, Ronnie, 361, 366, 367
Kennedy, Gerald, 68
Ream, Eric Allan, 382
Schwartz, Thomas, 305
brotherhood in combat, 195
Bryant, Kenneth, 265–267, 270–273, 274
Bryant, Ruth, 272
Bunker, Ellsworth, 16
Bush, George and Laura, 427
Bush, George H.W., 432

C

C-rations, 166–167, 183, 238, 319, 333, 370
Cabot, Sebastian, 336, *507, 508*
Callahan, James, *498*
background of, 285–287
boat patrol mission, 321–324
at Cu Chi tunnels, 291–293
on Delta Company command, 325
on Delta's mission, 287–288
on night ambush, 288–289
on Viet Cong defector, 289–290
Calley, William, 58
Cambodia, incursions into, 429
Cambodian border, fighting at the. *See* Operation Atlas Wedge; Operation Sheridan-Sabre
Camp Drake, 357
Camp Eagle, 53, 144, 145, 146, 227
Camp Evans, 86
Camp Red Ball, 228, 238, 239, 260, 419
Camp Rodriguez

82nd Airborne's departure from, 227
attack on, 143–145, 146–147
Bud Bolling's promotion ceremony, 234
capers and practical jokes, 118–119
Empty Boots ceremony, 73
fate of, 435
movie night, 194
POW treatment, 198
setup, 51–54
Campbell, Andrew, 132
Canadian veterans, 97–98
Canadian Vietnam Veterans Memorial, 98
Canadian Vietnam Veterans of Quebec, 95, 98
Candle Prayer, 99
Candy Stripe, Battle of the, 63–72
capers and practical jokes, 117–121, 334, 358
care packages, 306–307
Carlos, John, 231
Carlson, Richard Arnold, 313, 314
Carney, John, 177–178, 218, 338, 425, 434–435
Carpenter, Archie, 13
Carroll, James Nathan, III, 132
Carroll, Scott, 446
Carson, Don, 144, 147, 233, 415–416, 421
Carson, Paul, 416
Carter, William G., 401
Cassidy, Joseph J., Jr., 66–67, 68
Castro, Juan, 314
Cates, Norman Louis, 299, 314
Caton, Douglas, 139–140, 158–159, 160
Caton, Gerald Lewis, 160
Cavalry. *See* 11th Armored Cavalry Regiment; 1st Cavalry Division; 17th Cavalry
CBS News, 392–393
Central Intelligence Agency, 158
chain of command, 37, 230
Chappaquiddick Island, 389
Charlie Company of the 1st of the 505
at Ap Nam Phu, 85–92
Candy Stripe battle, 63–65, 67, 69, 71
casualties in, 174
Col Co Beach stand down, 75–76
death of Joe Rodriguez, 42–44
Donald Behm on, 184, 434
finding of enemy rocket stockpile, 249
Lazy W battle, 107–108
Paul Davin's command of, 61
Three Ville battle, 124–125, 126
Charlie Company of the 1st of the 508
Highway 547 ambush, 130–131, 132
Ho Bo Woods casualties, 363
mission to secure Highway 547 near Nui Ke, 149–150
Operation Mot, 200, 201–202, 204
post-Operation Mot sweep, 206
Charlie Company of the 2nd of the 505
Operation Sheridan-Sabre, 312–313
Ron Snodgrass's assignment to, 182
search for downed helicopter, 226–227
Charlie Company of the 82nd Support Battalion, 262
Charlie Company of the 307th Engineers, 262
Chau Chu mission, 155–159
Chicago Democratic National Convention protests, 207
Christmas, 1968, 261–263, 265–267
Chu Lai, Vietnam, 30–35, 48
Chuldenko, John, 277–279
Church, William Malcolm, 338
Cincotti, Joseph, 106
civilians
Candy Stripe battle casualties, 64
displaced, 124
goods sold by, 76–77
massacres, 57–58
medical care for, 76, 91, 278
Clark, Vincent Allen, 205
Clay, Frank Butner, 127
Clay, James Wilson, 373, 374
claymore explosion accident, 416–417
Clemente, Roberto, 3
climate and weather, 164–165, 168, 215–219
Clinton, Bill, 418
clothing, combat, 165, 166, 331
Col Co Beach stand down, 75–76
Collins, Louis (Rip), 38
combat, brotherhood formed in, 187, 195
combat boots, 331
combat engineers, 135, 137, 147, 236–237, 356
Combat Infantryman's Badge recipients

Davidson, Richard, 95
Dickerson, George W., 260
Foote, Walter Bruce, 353
Gulas, Carl, 285
Headley, Paul, 42
Koenig, Daren, 352
Koons, John, 188
Potts, Bruce, 421
Rodriguez, Joe, 43
Selk, Dwaine, 359
commemorative coins, 151, 252, 278–279
computers, supply system, 330
Conde, Felix, *478, 509*
background of, 3–4
behavior in the field, 336–337
daily life of crew of, 333–336
death of, 344–345
fellow Delta Dragons on, 191, 192
funeral of, 347–348
Good Friday battle, 341, 342, 343
honors for, 442–444
Leslie Hayes's letter to son of, 1
Leslie Hayes's quest to honor, 349, 429, 435, 437–439
Stanley Dodson on, 346
on Typhoon Bess, 218
Conde, Lydia, 4, 347, 348, 349, 438
Conde, Payten Grace Leslie, 444
Conde, Richard, 1, 348–349, 435, 437–439, 442–443, 444
Conde, Terri, 444
Connors, Jimmy, 158
conscientious observer status, 328
Coor, Anthony, 146
Cornelius, Amanda, 116
Country Joe and the Fish, 402
court martial trial of John Kapranopoulos, 253–256
Cox, James Michael, 393
Criswell, Darrell, 374, 391–393, 422
Cronin, Phil, 35
Crowder, Hollis, 93–94, 369–371, 420–421
Cu Chi tunnel system, 275, 290–293, 358
Cunane, Frank, 178–179, 205, 218–219, 257–259

D

daily life
of Felix Conde's crew, 333–336
Jerald Manning's recollections of, 385
of Joe Tentpeg, 163–171
of rifle companies, 249–250
Robert Zeeman on, 187
Stuart Simonson's diary account of, 404–411
Dalton, Rick
Benjamin Benton's death and, 317, 318–320
Christmas package for, 261
first days in Vietnam, 253–254
on return home, 425
wounding of, 279–280
Darby, William, 34, 441
Davidson, Richard, *473*
on arrival in Chu Lai, 32
background, 8–9
on bridge security duty, 55–56
Candy Stripe battle, 67–68
commerce with villagers, 76–77
on drug use in Vietnam, 77
on finding out about Vietnam deployment, 20
golden anniversary of 82nd's time in Vietnam, 445
honoring of Leo Brent Gunning, 95, 98–99, 101
on Leo Gunning's premonition, 79
on stand down, 75
on travel through Hai Van Pass, 49
wounding and aftermath, 89, 95–97
Davin, Paul
at Ap Nam Phu, 87, 89, 90, 91
arrival at Camp Rodriguez, 61
Candy Stripe battle, 67, 71
Highway 547 ambush and, 132
Lazy W battle, 107–108
post-war return to Vietnam, 434
on Three Ville battle, 124–125
Davis, Johnny F., 382
Davis, Richard Larry, 391
Day, Gordon

background of, 21
Candy Stripe battle, 69
on combat clothes, 166
honoring of John Plunkard, 113
on John Plunkard, 83, 107
on Lazy W battle, 104, 105
Louis Pigeon, relationship with, 103
Day, John Lee, 113
Dear America: Letters Home From Vietnam (documentary), 416
Dear John letters, 385–386
Delta Company of the 1st of the 505. *See* Delta Dragons
delta diary, 404–411
Delta Dragons
boat patrol mission, 321–324
Carl Gulas's wounding, 396–397
Christmas Eve, 1968, 265–267
at Cu Chi tunnels, 290–293
daily life of Felix Conde's crew, 333–336
dog scouts and handlers, 401
"dummy ambush" set-up, 383–384
Fire Base Panther III attack, 209–214
Good Friday battle, 341–346
Ho Bo Woods casualties, 363
James Callahan's command of, 287–288, 325
Operation Atlas Wedge, 338–339
Operation Mot, 199–200, 202, 204
Operation Sheridan-Sabre, 314
soldiers of, 191–195
Demgen, Robert Nicholas, 416
Detroit race riots, 11–13, 31, 135
Dewey, Gordon (Duke)
on attack on Camp Rodriguez, 146
background of, 7–8
on Bud Bolling, 235
capers of, 117–118, 119
on convoy on Highway One to, 47
on danger zone, 51–52
Detroit race riots deployment, 13
golden anniversary of 82nd's time in Vietnam, 445
Hall of Heroes, 444
naming of the Golden Brigade, 25
on Operation Mot, 197, 199
on the paratrooper mindset, 29
on replacement soldiers, 180
on travel time, 30
on Wesley Ford, 56
DeWitt, Billy, 261
Dewveall, Jerald, 321–324
diarrhea, 169, 195
Dickerson, George W., *479, 501, 507, 512, 514*
CBS News remote broadcast and, 392
on dog scouts and handlers, 401
Golden Brigade command, assumption of, 260
Legacy Bowl as honor to, 448
Operation Yorktown Victor, 418
on orders for withdrawal, 421
piece for *The All American Magazine,* 276–277
Silver Star ceremony for Juan Blaz, 314–315
visit with Rick Talioaga, 380
Diem, Ngo Dinh, 5, 6
Dillon, James Dale (Doc), 47, 115–116
disease. *See* illness and disease
displaced civilians, 124
Distinguished Flying Cross
Purser, Thomas, 72
Thomas, Grace G., 342
Distinguished Service Cross
Blaz, Juan, 315
Conde, Felix, 348
Edwards, James L., 204
Fleener, Larry, 203
Harrell, Ronnie, 106
Trotty, Henry, 122
Dittenhoff, Don, 294
divorce papers, 386
Dobson, Larry
on Operation Sheridan-Sabre, 298
on returning home, 422
wounding of, 295
Dodson, Stanley, 218
on brotherhood of combat, 195
on Felix Conde, 191
as leader of first platoon, 336
promotion of, 339

on unloading Operation Atlas Wedge casualties, 346
dogs, scout, 399–401
Dominican Republic, 9
Doughnut Dollies, 267
Dover Air Force Base, 246–247
draftees, 181, 358
Draughn, Thomas Edward, 314
drinking water, 166, 194, 195, 215
drivers, 330–331
drownings, 383, 386
drug use, 77–79, 147, 388–389, 411
Duchess river cruise, 445–446
Duck Hunter. *See* Paquin, Donald
ducks, shooting of, 355–356
"dummy ambush" set-up, 383–384
Duncan, Al, 111
Dunn, Claud, 35, 136–138
dysentery, 103, 123, 169, 238, 313

E

Eagle Dustoff. *See* Caton, Gerald Lewis
Ealum, Carrel Gorum, 220
Echo Company of the 1st of the 508, 401
Edwards, James L., 203–204, 206
82nd Airborne
The All American Magazine, 276–277
relationship to the 101st Airborne Division, 37
reorganization of, 173–174
82nd Airborne Division Association, 95, 303, 426, 431
82nd Airborne Division Museum, 132, 447
83rd Rear Service Force, 414
Eisenhower, Dwight, 6, 178
11th Armored Cavalry Regiment, 337, 367
Elgin, Robert Gerald, 90, 91
Ellison, Alton Leon, 416
Ellison, Greg, 299, 301, 314
Emanuel, Ed, 416
emperor's tomb mission, 139–140
Empty Boots ceremonies, 73, 234, 319–320, 2667
enemy weapons recovery, 249, 293, 294, 346
entertainment and diversions, 119, 121, 143–145, 194, 251–252
environment, jungle, 167–169, 185, 186, 187, 406–407
escorts, body, 111, 246, 267
Esqueda, Sandra, 348

F

F-4 Phantom accident, 281–283
The Fallen (Binyon), 383
Farmer, Michael Lee, 90, 91
Fedro, James Ray, 123–124, 125
"fillers," 20–22
fire ants, 311, 334–335
Fire Base All American, 227–228, 260, 287, 314
Fire Base All American II, 413, 416
Fire Base Bastogne, 130, 135–136, 186, 187–188, 193, 218
Fire Base Birmingham, 130, 199, 218
Fire Base Boyd, 130, 149, 155, 218
Fire Base Copperhead, 281–283
Fire Base Hardcore, 228
Fire Base Jill, 298, 301
Fire Base June, 305, 311
Fire Base Panther I, 145
Fire Base Panther III, 178, 199, 207, 210–214, 216
Fire Support Base Harrison, 229
Fire Support Base Patton, 359
Fire Support Base Tracy, 337–338
First Indochina War, 5, 50, 275, 281
1st Cavalry Division, 20, 33, 296, 305, 337
Fischer, Wayne Henry, 281–283
fist fighting, emperor's tomb, 140–141
505th Parachute Infantry Regiment. *See* specific units
508th Parachute Infantry Regiment. *See* specific units
fix bayonet orders, 11, 202, 203, 300, 311
flag football games, 251–252
flare accident, 395
Fleener, Larry, 202–203
Flint, Billy, 103, 107
food
C-rations, 166–167, 183, 238, 319, 333,

370
at Col Co Beach, 75
ice cream, 75, 198, 207, 219, 233, 238, 336
supplied by Marion Foster, 216–217
thoughts of, 334
football games, 251–252
Foote, Walter, 351, 353
Ford, Judy Ann, 394
Ford, Wesley, 56
Fort Benning, 78, 188, 399
Fort Bragg
All American Week, 138, 434, 447
day care center named for Joe Rodriguez, 43
deployment from, 11, 24
82nd Airborne Division Museum, 132, 447
Felix Conde, honoring of, 443–444
homecoming ceremony, 2012, 439–442
President Johnson's visit to, 27–28
Vietnam Memorial, 421–422
Foster, Marion, 139, 216–217
Frankel, Mark, 448
Fransen, Ronald Clifford, 71
Frantz, Jim, 401
fratricide, 127, 375
Frazer, Ronald, 10, 149–150
Frazer family, 151
"Frenchy," 210, 213
"friendly fire" incidents, 204–205, 244–245, 266, 271, 279–280, 375. *See also* accidental deaths
Fritz, Franklin D., 140, 141
Froidevaux, Raymond, 134
Frye, Gerald, 89

G

Gamble, Mike, 187–188, 308, 311, 318–320, 381–382
Garcia, Cristobal, 446
Garrahan, Ernest, 275, 379
Gavin, James, 10, 16, 444
gear, combat, 165–166
Gehron, Bill, 228
Gentry, Leroy James, 363
Get Smart (television show), 117
Ghais, Ahman, 92–93
Ghais, Taher, 92–93, 103
G.I.-Civilian Alliance For Peace, 384
Gibner, George Thomas (Tex), 382
Gibson, Raymond Albert, 416
Gilbert, Thelma, 346
Glines, Michael, 111
golden anniversary of 82nd's time in Vietnam, 100, 445–448
Golden Brigade. *See* Third Brigade of the 82nd Airborne
Golden Brigade Association, 426, 433–435, 439
Golden Brigade commemorative coins, 151, 252, 278–279
Good Friday battle, 341–346
Goodheart, William, 69
Goodwin, Doris Kearns, 84
Gormican, David, 380
Graf, Barry Wade, 338
Grant, Willie, Jr., 69
Green, Gerald, 111
Greene, James T., 39, 299–300, 301–302, 303, *506*
Griffin, Abron, 155
Grindstaff, Thomas Jackson, 338
grunts. *See* Joe Tentpeg
Guard of Honor, 421
Guardado, Daniel, 87, 91
Guasp, Gary Arnaldo, 133
Gulas, Carl, *510*
on David McDonald's death, 341
on dog scout and handler, 401
Felix Conde's Medal of Honor ceremony, 443
Good Friday battle, 346
on James Callahan, 285
on wounding and return home, 396–397
Gunning, Colleen, 99
Gunning, Irene LaBrake, 98
Gunning, Leo Brent, 67, 79, 89, 91, 95, 98–101
Gunning, Steve, 100
Gunter, William P., 393, 394, 416, 417

Guthrie, Carroll, 145, 146, *470*
Gwinn, Richard Alfred, 382

H

Haddock, Robert, 301
Hai Van Pass, 47–49
Haines, Ralph, 134
Hale, Glynn, 128
Hall, Gary, 131, 132
Hall of Heroes, 444
hand-to-hand combat, 88, 211, 212
Haneke, Bill, 357–358
Hanoi War Museum, 434
Harrell, Ronnie, 106
Harris, Joe, 255
Harrison, Foster Earl, 383
Hartman, Howard John, 214
Hatch, Kenneth Neal, 416
Hayes, Diane, 1, 429, 432–433, 435, 438–439, 442
Hayes, Leslie, *478*
    background of, 192–193
    on Delta Company boat mission, 322
    on Felix Conde, 333, 336–337, 345
    Felix Conde's Medal of Honor ceremony, 442–443
    golden anniversary of 82nd's time in Vietnam, 445
    Good Friday battle, 341, 342, 343, 344, 346
    on James Callahan, 289
    letter to Richard Conde, 1
    memories of, 194
    Operation Atlas Wedge, 338–339
    Pete Watkins's reconnection with, 432–433
    post-war return to Vietnam, 433
    practical jokes, 334
    quest to honor Felix Conde, 349, 435, 437–439
    on return home, 429
Hayman, Jack, 131–132
Headley, Paul
    on Ap Nam Phu, 86, 87, 88
    Candy Stripe battle, 64, 67, 68
    death of Joe Rodriguez and, 42–43
    on death of Larry Kocher, 90
    on reassignment in Vietnam, 32–33
health issues. *See* illness and disease
Heaukulani, Charles, 200, 202–203
helicopter downing, 226–227
Hells Angels, 427
Henderson, Peter, 179–180, 262, 424, *477*
Hendrix, Jimi, 402
Hennessey, James (Tom)
    flock of ducks incident, 355, 356
    golden anniversary of 82nd's time in Vietnam, 445
    Operation Sheridan-Sabre, 297, 299, 300, 301, 302–303
    on presidential security mission, 393
    on transport to Bien Hoa, 229–230
Henry, Dennis Lee, 383
Hensley, John, 377
Herbert, Richard, 132
Hernandez-Carrion, Gilbert, 71
Highway 546, 155
Highway 547, 130, 135–137, 149–150, 179
Highway One, 47–50, 56
Hill 66, 131
Hill 90, 130
Hill 224, 220
Hill 618, 149–150, 151–152
Hinds, Stephen, 301
Ho Bo Woods, 359–364, 401
Ho Chi Minh, 5, 73, 151, 411
Ho Chi Minh City, 430, 434
Ho Chi Minh Trail, 295, 313, 392
Hoc Mon Bridge, 245–246, 261, 392
Hoffay, William, 140, 141
Holland, Jeannie Conde, 348, 437, 439, 442–443
Holliday, Cris, 375
homecoming ceremony, 2012, 439–441
Honorable Woof Award, 401
Hood, Michael, *474*
    on arriving in Chu Lai, 33
    attendance at John Carney's ordination, 177
    background of, 10
    on being relieved by the Marines, 73

on Bud Bolling, 236, 441
Candy Stripe battle, 63, 64–66, 67
on finding out about Vietnam deployment, 23–24
photo of medics, 124
on Sherman Hussey volunteering to return to the front, 123
Silver Star award, 128
on Three Ville battle, 125, 127
volunteering for another tour, 425
Hope, Bob, 257, 259
Horn, Alec Henry, 314
Hudson, Arthur, 55
Hue, Vietnam
Bud Bolling's original visits to, 5
civilian massacre at, 57
convoy on Highway One to, 47–50
Operation Carentan, 54
Operation Carentan II, 83–84
plan for 505th Parachute Infantry to join battle for, 38
Huggins, James, 439–440, 441
Hughes, Earl, 226
Hughes, Michael Donald, 383
human waste, burning of, 169
Hunter, Meredith, 427
Hurley, Robert, 255
Hussey, Sherman, 33, 123, 125, 127, 128
Hussey, Shirley Mae, 128
hygiene, 167, 335

I

I Corps, 51
ice cream, 75, 198, 207, 219, 233, 238, 336
illness and disease
deaths from, 383
diarrhea, 169, 195
dysentery, 103, 123, 169, 238, 313
malaria, 169, 188, 222, 223, 406–407
venereal disease, 237
In Retrospect (McNamara), 45
incompetent leadership, 386–388, 407–408, 409–410
infantry life. *See* daily life
insects, jungle, 168–169, 185, 187, 334–335, 406
intelligence
from Cu Chi tunnels, 293
in Operation Sheridan-Sabre, 298–299
in post-Operation Mot sweep, 206
from The Professor, 197–198
Iron Triangle mission, 413–418
Irons, James, 298, 310

J

James, Washington, 205
Jameson, John G.
on Bud Bolling, 235–236
Candy Stripe battle, 66
on Col Co Beach, 75–76
command of the 1st Battalion, 61
departure from Fort Bragg, 28
on Joe Rodriguez, 42
on Joseph Cincotti, 106
"Joe Tentpeg," 163–171, 236
Johnson, Allen, 366, 367
Johnson, Annie, 365–367, 368
Johnson, Harold K., 26
Johnson, Lyndon, *456*
on campaign trail, 8
Detroit race riots and, 11
letter of, on death of Rene Baumann, 134
optimism of, at end of 1967, 16
renunciation speech of, 84
sending off of troops, 26–27
visit to Womack Army Hospital, 27–28
Johnson, Raymond (Doc), 76, 87, 91
Johnson, Ronnie, 361–362, 363, 365–368, *507*
Jones, Kerry, 319
Jones, Maryus Napoleon, 383
journals, soldiers', 170–171
Joyce, Walter Edward, Jr., 107
Judy, Herman Leroy, Jr., 373, 375
jungle boots, 331
jungle environment, 167–169, 185, 186, 187, 406–407

K

Kapranopoulos, John
on 2012 Fort Bragg homecoming

ceremony, 440
command of Alpha company, 151–152
court martial trial of, 253–256
on Fire Base Panther III attack, 211, 212
Keith Bell's barge trip with, 424–425
search for downed helicopter, 226
Keaton, Dickie, 118–120, 197–198, 261, 424, 445
Kellogg, Arthur, 238–239, 305–307, 311–312, 422–423
Kelly, Joel R., 364
Kelly, Michael Joseph, Jr., 352
Kelsey, John, 181–182, 446
Kendra, George, 241, 242–243
Kendra, Steve, 243
Kennedy, Edward M., 389
Kennedy, Gerald, 17, 53, 68, 144–145, 157
Kennedy, Robert, assassination of, 161, 175
Kernoelje, Michael, 212, 213
Kerwin, Walter (Dutch), 230, 254
Kieffer, John, 376
killed in action
after Golden Brigade withdrawal notice, 415–418
Alpha Company, 379–380, 381–382
at Ap Nam Phu, 86–87
Ballinger, Timothy, 370–371
Beatty, Don, 156
Bryant, Kenneth Mark, 266–267
from Burke, South Dakota, 367
Candy Stripe battle, 65, 66–67, 68–69, 71
Cassidy, Joseph J., Jr., 66–67
Conde, Felix, 344–345
on day of moon landing, 393
in Delta Company boat mission, 323–324
in Fire Base Panther III attack, 211, 212, 213–214
Fire Base Tracy attack, 338
Foote, Walter Bruce, 353
Garrahan, Ernie, 275
in Good Friday battle, 341
in Highway 547 ambush, 131, 132–133
in Ho Bo Woods, 362, 363
Johnson, Ronnie, 362, 363
on May 25, 1968, 151
Murray, Billy, 245–248
in Operation Mot, 201, 202, 205
in Operation Sheridan-Sabre, 299, 301, 313, 314
Oscar Company, 352–353
Owen, Robert Gary, 221
Plunkard, John, 111–113
retrieval of, 72, 90, 91
Smith, Billy, 291, 292, 293, 294
in Thon Chau Chu mission, 156, 157, 159
Three Ville battle, 125, 127
Tiger Platoon, 373, 374, 375–376
Whorton, Dwayne Jefferson, 251
King, Martin Luther, assassination of, 93–94, 185, 209
Klein, James, 157, 183, 219, 229
Kline, Steve, 156
Kochanski, Ed, *493*
on death of Robert Gary Owen, 221
on Fire Base Panther III attack, 211
golden anniversary of 82nd's time in Vietnam, 446
on Ho Chi Minh Trail, 295
Hoc Mon Bridge accident, 245–248
on meeting William Murray, 222
Operation Sheridan-Sabre, 306–308, 311, 312
recovery of Tiger Platoon bodies, 376
on return home, 424
on Typhoon Bess, 219
on William Murray's rescue attempt, 223–224
Kocher, Karen, 90
Kocher, Larry, 86, 87, 90, 91
Koenig, Daren, 352
Koons, John, 188–189, 266, 267, 295, 314
Kopechne, Mary Jo, 389
Krobetzky, Raymond, 202, 205
Kuefner, John Alan, 401
Kurilla, Erik, 303, *506*

L

Labahn, Darwin Lyn, 367
Ladwig, Tom, 53, 133, 146, 175–176, 439

Laird, Melvin, 414–415
Landes, Victor Reid, 383
Landing Zone Mike Foxtrot, 297, 299, 391–392
landscape, 231, 337–338
Lane, Ron, 327, 328
Lange, Donna, 265, 270–273
Lannoye, Nicholas Pierre, 383
LaPolla, John Anthony, 352
Lassiter, Herman Earl, 338
Layton, Lorenzo, 3–4, 347
Layton, Maria, 347
Lazy W, 84, 103–109
Lee, James Allen, 383
leeches, 168, 195, 335, 369–370
Legacy Bowl, 447–448
legs' experience, 177–189
letters of condolence, 150, 151
Levendis, William McNamara, 150
LIFE magazine, 376, 379
Littig, Jim, *462*
- on ambush tactics, 58
- attempt to revive Taher Ghais, 92
- background of, 8
- on Doc Dillon and, 47, 115, 116
- on finding out about Vietnam deployment, 24
- on John Kapranopoulos, 254
- Keith Bell's barge trip with, 424–425
- on Nui Ke Mountain mission, 152
- Operation Sheridan-Sabre, 308, 309, 312, 315
- volunteering for another tour, 425
- on William Murray, 223

local villagers, 76–77, 278
Locastro, Thomas
- on Ap Nam Phu, 87, 91
- on Battle of Three Villes, 126, 128
- bridge security duty memories, 55
- on Camp Evans, 86
- Candy Stripe battle, 63, 64, 67, 68, 69
- on day after combat, 75
- on destruction of villages, 50
- on marijuana use, 77
- on meeting President Johnson, 28
- orders to go home, 174
- on Raymond Johnson, 76
- on volunteering to return to the front, 123

The Long Gray Line, 358
Long Range Recon
- Hollis Crowder's memories of, 369–371
- makeup of, 58
- restructuring of units, 351
- role of, 47
- Taher Fahti Ghais's death, 92
- at Yado, 115–116

Loomis, Ralph, 254–255, 256
Lovell, James, 262
Lukas, John, 31–32, 50, 57, 78
Lyon, Reid
- on Fire Base Panther III attack, 145
- on Hai Van Pass, 49
- on post-Army life, 426–427
- post-war return to Vietnam, 434
- on taking enemy fire, 56–57
- Thon Chau Chu mission, 156–157, 158, 159
- as tunnel rat, 294

LZ Lambeau, 439

M

MacArthur, Douglas, 138
mail, 54, 167, 238, 306–307, 335, 385–386
malaria, 169, 188, 222, 223, 406–407
Malcor, Dennis, 49, 56
Mallinckrodt, Arthur T., 364
Manning, Jerald, 385–388
Manson, Charles, 397
Manuel, Willie S., 139–141
maps, 452–455
Marcon, John, 228
marijuana use, 77–79, 147, 388–389, 411
Marines
- assistance in setting up camp, 52
- in battle for Hue, 38, 39
- at Col Co Beach, 76
- at Phu Bai, 51
- prisoner of war of, 197
- relief by after Candy Stripe battle, 72–73

Markiewicz, Mark, 251–252

Martin, Larry, 314
Mason, Larry Joe, 383
Massey, Harry, 375
Masten, Armand Dominic, 363
Master Blaster. *See* Thomas, Grace G.
Masuda, Robert Susumu, 360–361, 362–363
Mathies, Ted, 413, 416–417, 418
Mattaliano, Joseph, 256
Mays, Joe
  background of, 15–16
  bridge security duty memories, 55
  Candy Stripe battle, 66
  flight to Vietnam, 33–34
  on marijuana use, 78
  on Vietnamese life view, 73
  volunteering for another tour, 425
  wounding of, 126
McCollum, David Vernon, 214
McDade, Joe, 223, 246
McDonald, David Harold, 341, 346
McGee, Charles Edward, 71
McGhie, Glenn, 120–121, 262
McHugh, John W., 303
McIntyre, Kathy, 380
McIntyre, Tom, 400
McNamara, Robert, 44–45, 70, 152
McPhail, Donald, 260
Mears, Ralph Judson, 379
Medal of Honor, 315, 348, 442–443, 444
Medevac 5, 301–302
medic shortages, 123–124
Medical Service Corps, 328–329
medical supply problems, 54
Meeker, Thomas, 129, 133–134
Memorial Day, 319, 353, 377
Merry, Fred (Doc), 352
Mexico City Olympics, 231
Michelin Rubber Plantation, 337
Michigan Avenue, Battle of, 207
Micloskey, Ken, 313, 314
Military Assistance Command, Vietnam, 331, 359
Military Intelligence Unit, 179
Military Police, 144, 145, 227, 228
Military Working Dogs, 399–401
Miller, Charles and Dorothy, 417
Miller, Charles Emil, 413, 416–418
Miller, Cheryl, 417–418
Miller, Rick, 270
Milton, Mike, 258
Miss American visit, 394
Missing in Action, 360–363
Mitchell, Jerry, 76
Mollick, Charles, 111–112
Moody, Adger, 338
moon landing, 392–393
Moonglow (Nixon's trip to Saigon), 393
Moore, John, 418
Moore, Louis Charles, 212, 214
Moore, Robert Joseph, 86, 91
Morascini, John, 383
Morning, Larry, 56
Morris, Ronald Lewis, 281–283
mosquitoes, 168–169
Mott (NVA commander). *See* Operation Mot
movies, 119, 121, 143–145, 194
Munoz, David, 360–361, 362–363
Murphy, Billy Dan, 338
Murphy, Don, 140
Murray, Leo, 222–223, 246, 247–248
Murray, William, 221–224, 245–248
Murrill, Robert (Bob), *471*
  on bailing out a soldier prior to deployment, 24
  on beheadings, 160
  Camp Drake, stay in, 357–358
  letter of condolence to John and Viola Anderson, 151
  North Vietnamese soldier's journal and, 170
  on opening sealed orders, 34
  Operation Mot, 199–201
  recollections of, 358
  on replacements, 189
  on sense of smell in combat, 399
  as supply officer, 17
  on Typhoon Bess, 216
  on Typhoon Bess aftermath, 219
  U.S. Military Academy class of 1967, 10
  wreath placement at Fort Bragg Vietnam Veterans Memorial, 441–442
Museus, Les, 355–356, 386, 387, 388–389, 419

My Lai massacre, 57–58, 418

N

Nahas, Al, 357
Namath, Joe, 317
Nance, Paul, Jr., 124, 127
napalm, 67–68, 133, 158–159
National Defense Service Medal, 367
National Liberation Front, 170, 277
Neary, John Runyon, II, 127
Night Rider. *See* Bolling, Alexander (Bud)
Nightfighters, 191, 419
Nimphie, Max Edward, Jr., 133
9th Infantry Division, 384, 396
Nixon, Richard
  on antiwar protest, 418
  Cambodia, incursions into, 429
  election of, 207
  moon landing, 393
  promise to end the war, 315
  speech of May 14, 1969, 364
  troop withdrawal plan, 384
  visit to Saigon, 393
Noel, Chris, 169
non-airborne replacements, 177–189, 277
Non-Commissioned Officer's School, 188, 253
Normandy Invasion, 5, 37, 54
North Korea, 17
North Vietnamese Army
  concealment ability, 41
  hospital complex of, 312–313
  John Therrien on, 50
  local villagers and, 155
  soldier's journal, 170–171
  Tet Offensive, 18
  war crimes at Hue, 54, 57
  See also body count; Viet Cong
The North Wall. *See* Canadian Vietnam Veterans Memorial
Nui Ke Mountain mission, 149–150, 151–152

O

Obama, Barack, 442
observation helicopter, downing of a, 226–227
O'Donnell, David, 65
O'Hare, Richard
  arrival in Chu Lai, 35
  background of, 13–15
  on combat conditions, 164
  on diversionary attacks, 144
  emperor's tomb mission, 140
  on finding out about Vietnam deployment, 23
  on food, 167
  golden anniversary of 82nd's time in Vietnam, 445, 448
  homecoming ceremony, 2012, 441
  post-Army life, 426
  post-war returns to Vietnam, 435
  on replacement soldiers, 180
  Thon Chau Chu mission, 158–159
  on Typhoon Bess, 216, 217–218, 219
  as volunteer for another tour, 425–426
Ohio Military Hall of Fame, 397
101st Airborne
  A Shau Valley, 130–134, 186, 229
  Ap Nam Phu, 85, 86
  birthday celebration, 235
  Bravo Company's attachment to, 229
  82nd's relationship to, 37
  killing of NVA battalion commander, 109
  Operation Golden Sword, 226, 227
  suicide attack against, 144, 145–146, 147
  supply system, 38, 166
Operation Atlas Wedge, 337, 338–339, 341–346
Operation Babylift, 434
Operation Carentan, 54–56
Operation Carentan II, 84–85
Operation Durango City, 18
Operation Golden Sword, 225, 227–231
Operation Mot, 197–207, 220
Operation Out West. *See* Operation Atlas Wedge
Operation Power Pack, 9–10
Operation Sheridan-Sabre
  Alpha Company, 305–312, 314–315, 318–319
  Bravo Company, 295, 297–304
  Charlie Company, 312–313
Operation West Point, 445–448

Operation Yorktown Victor, 415–418
Ortega, Ramon Felix, Jr., 321–324
Oscar Company of the 75th Infantry, 351–353, 359, 414, 415
Owen, Robert Gary, 221

P

P Training, 41, 182, 183, 186, 188, 193, 206
Pacific Paraglide newsletter, 203, 258, 282, 388
pacification effort, 276, 278
panty hose for leech control, 369–370
Paquin, Donald
    Jimmy Greene's Bronze Star and, 303
    Operation Sheridan-Sabre, 296–297, 299, 300–301, 302
    on shooting down of ducks, 355, 356
    Tiger Platoon casualties and, 374, 375
paratrooper mindset, 29
Paris Peace Accords of 1973, 430
Parrish, Elton, 249
Parron, Selma, 320
Passavanti, Joseph, 150
Patriot Guard Riders, 319
Patterson, Richard Lee, 373, 375, 376
Patton, George S., 233
pay, 206–207, 329, 351
Payne, Ernest, 131, 132
Pearce, John, 25, *461*
Pearson, Robert, 414
Perfume River bridge security details, 54–56
Perry, Cade, 444
Perry, Robert Conroy, 214
Pharis, Ronald, 205
phone calls home, 261
Phu Bai, convoys arrival at, 50
Phu Hoa Duong ambush, 394–395
Phu Loc, Vietnam, 225–226
Phu Loi, Vietnam, 228, 237, 251–252, 331, 419–420
Phuoc Long Province. *See* Operation Sheridan-Sabre
Phuoc Vinh, Vietnam, 305
Pigeon, Louis, 103, 106
Plunkard, Joe, 111, 112
Plunkard, John, *472*
    Andrew Blais on, 104, 106–107
    attempted water rescue of marine, 55
    background, 20–21
    as Blais's replacement, 104
    Candy Stripe battle, 69–70, 73
    comrades' memories of, 81–83
    funeral and memorials to, 111–113
    Jimmy Barnes on the death of, 109
    letters home from, 83, 84, 105
    pact with Gordon Day, 22
    travel through Hai Van Pass, 49
Plunkard, John L. and Frances Everhart, 112
police riot of 1968, 207
Poore, Rocky, 416, 417
Porter, William R., 135–136
Posey, Charles, 105
post-war return to Vietnam, 433–435
postal operation. *See* mail
Potts, Bruce, 421, 446–447
Powlistha, Gerald Stephen, 382
practical jokes and capers, 117–121, 334, 358
presidential security mission, 393
Price, Billy, 109
Prince (dog), 401
prisoners of war
    court martial trial over killing of, 255
    at Cu Chi tunnels, 292
    interrogation of, 158
    Leslie Hayes's capture of, 335
    movies and, 121
    "Professor," 197–198
    Viet Cong defectors, 289–290
Privette, Jake, 38, 62
professional football, 251, 269
The Professor, 197–198, 201
Proficiency School. *See* P Training
prostitution, 237
protesters. *See* antiwar protesters; Chicago Democratic National Convention protests
Provisional Reconnaissance Unit (PRU), 158
psychological warfare, 207
public opinion in America, 243
Pueblo incident, 17
Puff the Magic Dragon (airplane), 145
Purple Heart
    Barsanti, Olinto, 37

Benedict, Mike, 395
Benton, Benjamin, 317
Bryant, Kenneth, 271
Dalton, Rick, 425
Davidson, Richard, 95, 96
Dunn, Claud, 136, 137–138
Foote, Walter Bruce, 353
Frantz, Jim, 401
history of, 137–138
Johnson, Ronnie, 367
Locastro, Thomas, 28
Plunkard, John, 21
Rodriguez, Joe, 43
Schwartz, Thomas, 305
Taher Ghais, 92
Talioaga, Rick, 381
Walls, Carlton, 95
Weddle, Randy, 111
Purser, Thomas, 72
Pyle, Ernie, 164, 165

Q

Quinata, Tony, 353
Quinones, Juan Manuel, 202, 205

R

race relations, 93–94, 185
radio, Armed Forces, 169, 414–415
radio intelligence unit, 53
Ragsdale, Daniel, 89, 96
Ramirez, Edgar, 205
Ramos, Manuel, 169
Randall, Robert Bruce, 214
Ranger (dog), 401
Rangers. *See* Oscar Company of the 75th Infantry
Rasmussen, Ollie, 96
rations. *See* C-rations
rats, 168, 186, 217–218
Rauscher, Walter, 447
Reagan, Ronald, 430–431
Ream, Eric Allan, 382
Red Devils
extraction of, 220
Highway 547 ambush, 129–131
Ho Bo Woods, 359–360, 363
new base of, 228
night ambush of sampans, 257
Operation Mot, 198–199, 200, 201, 202, 205
Valorous Unit Award, 259
religious services, 119–120
Renaud, Carmine Francis, 127
reorganization of the 82nd Airborne, 173–174
replacements, non-airborne, 177–189, 277
Republic of Vietnam Gallantry Cross with Palm, 367
Reynolds, Barbara Pharis, 205
Reynolds, Gary Edward, 383
Reynolds, Peter LaBrake, 100
Rice, Troy, 376
Richards, Douglas Wayne, 341, 346
Richardson, Charlie, 344, 345
Ridgway, Matthew, 6, 444
rifle companies, daily life of, 249–250
Risseeuw, Dean, 10, 30–31, 149, 150
Rivera, Willie, 94
Roach, Ernest, 267
road guards, 135–137
Roane Memorial Gardens, 376
Roberts, David, 321–324
Robertson, Mark
background of, 22–23
on blowing up a water tower, 228–229
on emperor's tomb fist fight, 141
on marijuana use, 78
on return home, 426
on Thon Chau Chu mission, 156, 157
travel through Hai Van Pass, 49
on Typhoon Bess, 215–216
Robinson family, 353
rocket stockpile, discovery of, 249
Roderick, Craig, 111
Rodriguez, Joe, 42–44, 375, 417
Rosenow, Robert James, 375
Rosselot, Beauford (Doc), 323–324
Rykaczewski, Stanley K., 299–300, 301, 314, 387

S

Saigon
    fall of, 430
    Operation Golden Sword, 225, 227–231
    Richard Nixon's visit to, 393
    U.S. Embassy in, 327
sampans, night ambush of, 257–259
Samz, Francis Mark, 383
Sandridge, Ken, 320
Sanner, James, *470*
    on attack on Camp Rodriguez, 146
    background of, 24–25
    on Bud Bolling, 233
    last rites for Joe Rodriguez, 44
    Legacy Bowl blessing, 448
    religious services of, 119–120
Sautter, Susan Nance, 127
Schaefer, Gerald, 373, 374, 375, 377
Schoolhouse Battle. *See* Battle of the Candy Stripe
Schwartz, Thomas, 10, 305
Scout Dog Platoon, 399–401, 414
Seabees, 50, 52, 53, 76, 120
security for USO Christmas show, 257–259
Seeger, Pete, 418
Seitz, Richard, *456*
    background, 10
    departure of troops and, 25
    Detroit race riots deployment, 12, 13
    orders for the 82nd to deploy to Vietnam, 18–19
    visit to Womack Army Hospital with President Johnson, 27–28
Selective Service, 181
Selk, Dwaine, 359, 360–361, 362, 420, 425
Serik, Daniel, 319–320
Sevarn, Allen, 214
720th Military Police Battalion, 257
17th Cavalry, 48, 56–57, 136, 139–141, 155–159, 228
75th Rangers. *See* Oscar Company of the 75th Infantry
Severino, Charlie, 294
Shain, Jerry, 88, 91
"shake and bakes," 188, 253, 386
Sharp, Darron, 309, 312, 315, 425
Signett, James Guerdon, 90, 91
Silver Star
    Adams, James R., 65
    Barsanti, Olinto, 37
    Beltran, Salome, 88
    Benton, Benjamin, 317
    Blaz, Juan, 314–315
    Bolling, Bud, 234
    Cassidy, Joseph J., Jr., 66
    Cincotti, Joseph, 106
    Crowder, Hollis, 369
    Dickerson, George W., 260
    Elgin, Robert Gerald, 90
    Farmer, Michael Lee, 90
    Foote, Walter Bruce, 353
    Frazer, Ronald, 149
    Guardado, Daniel, 87
    Guthrie, Carroll, 146
    Hennessey, Tom, 302
    Hood, Mike, 128
    Johnson, Raymond, 87
    Kernoelje, Michael, 213
    Kocher, Larry, 90
    Moore, Robert Joseph, 86
    Pearce, John, 25
    Plunkard, John, 111, 112
    Rosselot, Beauford (Doc), 324
    Schwartz, Thomas, 305
    Small, Eugene, 68–69
Simmons, Bill, 344
Simonson, Steven, 403
Simonson, Stuart, 403–411, 446
Sirhan Sirhan, 161
Skyraiders, 71
Slavin, James (Doc)
    on arriving in Chu Lai, 34
    building of aid station, 53
    on experience in Vietnam, 422
    on F-4 Phantom accident, 282
    golden anniversary of 82nd's time in Vietnam, 446
    on marijuana use, 77–78
    on medic shortage, 124
    on soldiers' ailments, 169
    on tunnel rats, 294
    on Typhoon Bess, 218

Small, Eugene, 68–69
Smith, Billy, 290, 291, 292, 293, 294, 321
Smith, Blaine, 111
Smith, John, 100–101
Smith, Tommie, 231
Smith, Willie James, 383
snakes, 168, 338
sniper attacks, 155–156
Snodgrass, Ron, 182–183, 227, 261–262, 275, 312–314, 425
Somes, Ronald Ree, 363
Song Bo River, 83–84
Soul Patrol (Emanuel), 416
Souza, Anthony, 338
Spencer, James Albert, Jr., 381
Spooky (airplane), 145
Springer, Gerald Wayne, 187
staff sergeant shortages, 386
stand down at Col Co Beach, 75–76
Stauffer, Bailey, 351–353
Stem, David, 388
Stephenson, J. V., 53, 197, 206, 233
stereotypes, 379, 381
Stewart, James Adams, 72
Stits, David, 430
Stone, Jerry Michael, 159
Straza, David, 241–243
Street Without Joy, 50
Stuart, Sam, 395
Studebaker, David, 251
suicide, 386
suicide attacks, 209–214
Summer Olympics, 231
Summers, William, 66
sundry packs, 217–218
supply officers, 329–331
support personnel, 327–331
Surveillance Task Force, 355
Swoope, Rudolph, 382
Szczepanski, John (Ski), 209–214, 265, 266, 269, 270–274
Szilagyi, Robert, 373–375

T

Tabor, Jessie, 87
Talioaga, Rick, 379–381, 440, *494, 496*
Talmadge, Herman, 260
Tan Son Nhut Air Base, 251, 280, 281, 384
tanker trucks, 135–136
Task Force Devil, 257, 259
Tataryn, George Lubomyr, 262
Tate, Sharon, 397
Taylor, Darrell, 111
Taylor, Kenneth, 66–67
Taylor, Maxwell, 6–7
team-building, need for, 41
tear gas use, 133
Teller, Jim, 401
Tet of 1968, 328
Tet Offensive
  America's strategy and, 18
  Andrew Blais on, 22
  Cu Chi tunnel use before, 291
  Hoc Mon bridge, 245
  Phu Vang village, 61–62
  Tan Son Nhut Air Base as target in, 281
  Viet Cong, broken cover of the, 159–160
  William Westmoreland's plan to counterattack, 173
Thanksgiving, 1968, 250–252
Therrien, John, 50, 140, 159
Thieleman, John, 256, 315
Thieu, Nguyen Van, 384, 393
Third Brigade of the 82nd Airborne
  All American Week, 138
  Chu Lai, arrival in, 30–35
  Combat Team picnic, 138
  commemorative coins, 151, 252, 278–279
  Detroit race riots and, 11–13, 31
  farewell ceremony, 421
  fill-ins, 19
  first combat loss in Vietnam, 42–44
  George Dickerson's assumption of command, 260
  golden anniversary of time in Vietnam, 445–448
  Golden Brigade name, 25
  naming of dining facility after Bud Bolling, 441
  Operation Golden Sword, 225, 227–231

orders for Vietnam deployment, 17–18
presidential security mission, 393
reorganization of, 173–174
replacements' experience, 177–189
scout dogs in, 399–401
supplies deliveries, 135–136
support personnel, 327–331
withdrawal schedule, 419
See also Camp Rodriguez; specific units
37th Infantry Platoon, 399–401
Thomas, Grace G., 342
Thomas, Joseph Harold, 169
Thon Chau Chu mission, 155–159
Thor (dog), 401
The Three Soldiers (statue), 430
Three Villes, Battle of the, 124–128
Thua Thien Province, 51
Tiger One, 373–376, 377
Tobie, David Carl, 383
Tran Ninh Nguyen, 170–171
travel time, 29–30
troop strength, 19–20, 173, 174
troop withdrawal, 384, 414–415, 419, 421
Trotty, Henry, 132
Troyan, Michael Joseph, Jr., 383
trucks, supply of, 330
Trusko, Pete, 163
tunnel systems, 275, 290–294, 358, 361, 414
Tunnissen, James, 366, 367
Turner, Lloyd Kenneth, 383
Tyner, Elmo P. (Step), 21, 104–105, 112, 277
Typhoon Bess, 215–219, 228

U

Underwood, Richard
on Ap Nam Phu, 85, 87, 91–92
on burden of command, 33
Candy Stripe battle, 64
on death of Joe Rodriguez, 44
on setting up camp, 54
U.S. Air Force
football team, 251–252
Operation Babylift, 434
Skyraiders, 71
U.S. Embassy, 18, 327
U.S. Military Academy class of 1967, 10, 65, 72
U.S. Navy Col Co Beach, 75–76
USO shows, 257, 259, 317, 394, 404

V

Vallen, Donald William, 364
Valley Forge Hospital, 96–97
Valorous Unit Award, 259
Van Co Dong River mission. *See* Operation Atlas Wedge
Van Gorp, Phillip, 202
Vance, Cyrus, 12
Vera, Abelardo, 69
Veterans For Peace, 426
Veterans of Foreign Wars, 319–320, 425
Viet Cong
American financing of, 76
beheadings of, 159
in Binh Duong Province, 321, 359
Creighton Abrams's war strategy, 153, 225
defectors, 62, 158, 289–290
identifying, 41
in the Iron Triangle, 413–414
local villagers and, 155
National Liberation Front poem, 170–171
Operation Mot results, 206
pacification effort, 278
prisoners, killing of, 255
spies, 146
supply line, 249
Tet Offensive, 18
tunnel systems, 140, 290–294, 358
war strategy change and, 153
weapons stockpiles, 231
See also body count; North Vietnamese Army
Vietnam, post-war return to, 433–435
Vietnam campaign ribbon, 367
Vietnam Memorial at Fort Bragg, 421–422
Vietnam Moratorium Committee, 418
Vietnam Service Medal, 367
Vietnam Veterans Memorial
Ahern, Robert, 400

Anderson, John Harrison, Jr., 151
Ap Nam Phu deaths, 91
Ballinger, Timothy, 371
Candy Stripe battle deaths, 72
Davis, Richard, 391
dedication of, 430
Delta Company boat mission deaths, 324
Dillon James Dale, 116
F-4 Phantom accident deaths, 283
Fire Base Panther III attack deaths, 214
Ghais, Taher, 93
Good Friday battle deaths, 346
Hensley, John, 377
Highway 547 ambush deaths, 133
Kuefner, John, 401

PHOTO CREDITS AND ACKNOWLEDGMENTS

Photos provided courtesy of the 82nd Airborne Museum, including combat pictures taken by Bernie Manigboyat, who was attached to the brigade and was wounded during the course of his work. Other pictures were taken by John Bell and Bob Schoenecker of the 45th Public Information Detachment. Donated to the museum were the Individual albums of General George Dickerson, Bill Bonser, Bill Culp, Bob Amos, Bob Engel, Bruce Eihlers, Burnis Eades, Chip Bell, Dave Robertson, Don McPhail, Dave Straza, Craig Forrester, Don Carson, Nick Castoro, Ray Wilson, Rick Talioaga, Robert McKenna, Roy Baker, Ted Mathies, Thomas Ladwig, Tim Sprouse and Tom Faucher. Photos were also provided by Jim Littig, Bob Murrill, Joe Plunkard, Tom Wilson, Les Hayes, Pete Watkins, Ray Henry, Ed Kochanski, Paddy Barry, Jerald Manning, Glen McPhie, Pete Henderson, Frank Walenga, Don Behm, Larry Dobson, Tommy Locastro, Reid Lyon, John Lukas, Darrell Criswell, John Marcon and Rich O'Hare, among others. The author acknowledges the contributions of Rich O'Hare for providing video interviews with General Alexander R. Bowling Jr. and providing historical documents and declassified information. Personal journals and recollections were shared by Stuart Simonson, Tommy Locastro, Jim Littig, Bob Murrill, Tom Hennessey, Raymond Froidevaux and William Gunter, among others. The author also acknowledges the contributions made by members of the Golden Brigade and the families and friends of the fallen, without whom this book would not be possible. Special thanks, also, to literary agent Gayle Wurst of the Princeton International Agency for the Arts.

ABOUT THE AUTHOR

Robert J. Dvorchak worked as a journalist for nearly fifty years, including eight years as a New York City–based national writer for the *Associated Press*. During the First Iraq War, he was a war correspondent assigned to the 82nd Airborne Division, whose commanding general called him the "Ernie Pyle of Desert Storm."

A 1972 graduate of California University of Pennsylvania with a degree in English literature, Dvorchak has covered such stories as the original outbreak of Legionnaires' disease, the Three Mile Island accident, the 1989 earthquake in San Francisco, the Jeffrey Dahmer serial killings, the first World Trade Center bombing, the Oklahoma City bombing, three Super Bowls, two Stanley Cup finals, and two World Series.

An Army veteran, Dvorchak has authored five books, including *Drive On*, a journal about his personal experiences in Desert Storm. The recipient of numerous writing awards, he is a native of Uniontown, PA, and was inducted into the inaugural class of the Uniontown Area High School Hall of Fame in 2013. Now residing in Penn Hills, he is married and has two daughters and five granddaughters.

MAPS AND PHOTOGRAPHS

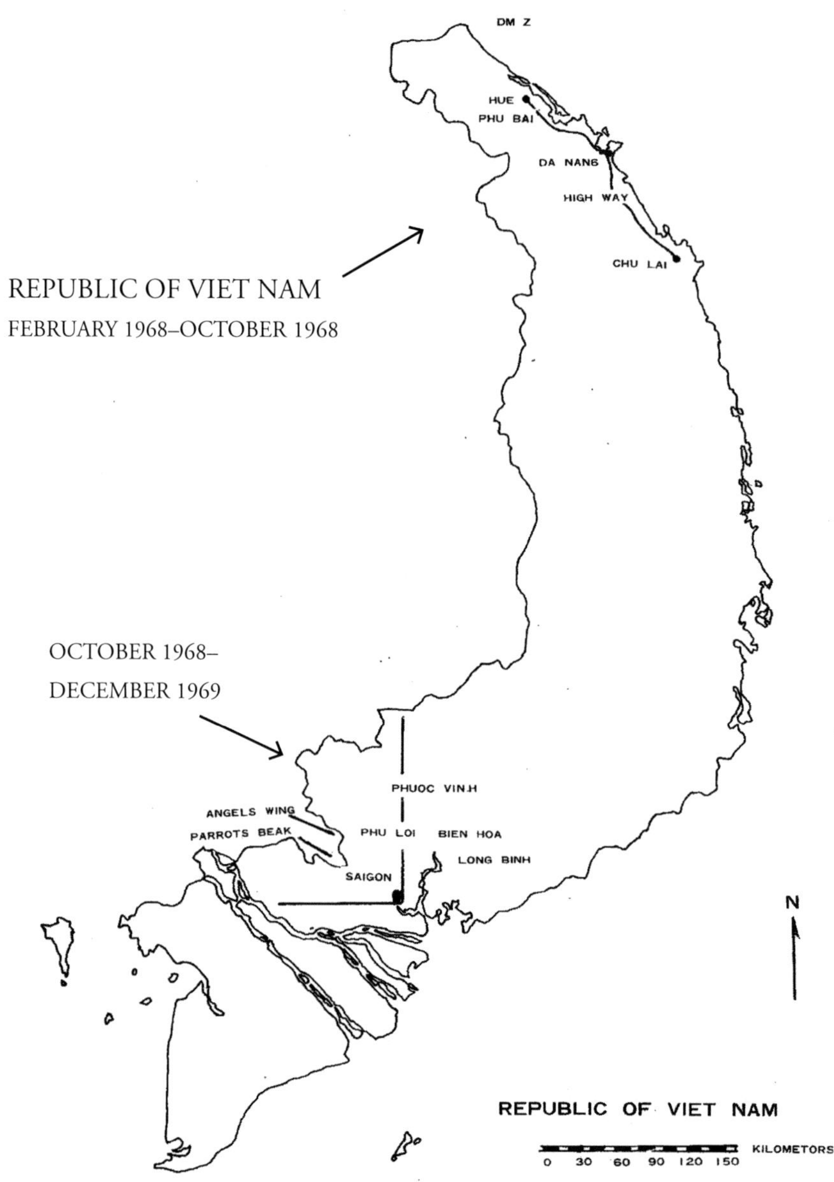

Map of South Vietnam taken from brigade archives shows the two major areas of operation over the 22-month deployment. Up North, the Airborne arrived at Chu Lai, then moved by truck convoy on Highway One through Da Nang and over the Hai Van Pass to reach Phu Bai and the Imperial City of Hue. The brigade then was ordered to redeploy Down South to defend the area north and west of Saigon. Combat operations were mounted all the way out to the Cambodian border at features marked as the Parrot's Beak and the Angel's Wing.

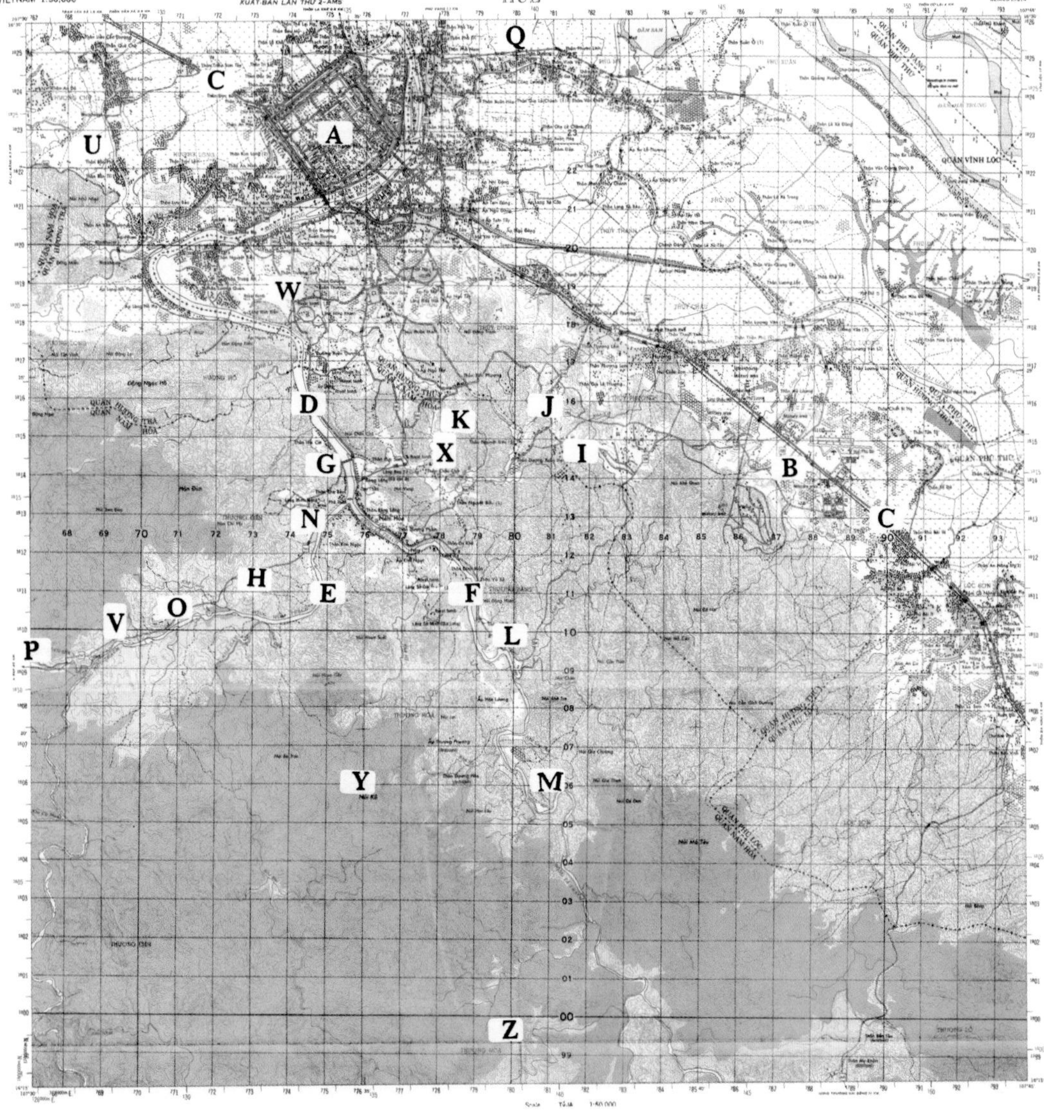

Area of operations, February to October 1968, Hue and Thua Thien Province.

Alphabet code:

- A. Hue City, with bridges over the Perfume River connecting the Old and New City
- B. Phu Bai Military complex
- C. Highway One, Vietnam's major road
- D. Perfume River
- E. West Branch, Perfume River
- F. East Branch, Perfume River
- G. Nam Hoa Bridge
- H. Highway 547 from Hue to the A Shau Valley
- I. Camp Rodriguez, Headquarters of 82nd Airborne
- J. Camp Eagle, Headquarers of 101st Airborne
- K. Fire Support Base Panther I, artillery position
- L. Fire Support Base Panther II, artillery position
- M. Fire Support Base Panther III, artillery position, site of suicide attack August 29
- N. Fire Support Base Boyd
- O. Fire Support Base Birmingham
- P. Fire Suport Base Bastogne
- Q. Battle of the Candy Stripe, March 20
- U. Battle of the Three Villes, May 1
- V. Ambush on Highway 547, May 5
- W. Donnybrook inside a Buddhist shrine, May 19
- X. Battle of Thon Chau Chu, May 29
- Y. Nui Ke Mountain, a.k.a. Landing Zone Greek
- Z. Operation Mot

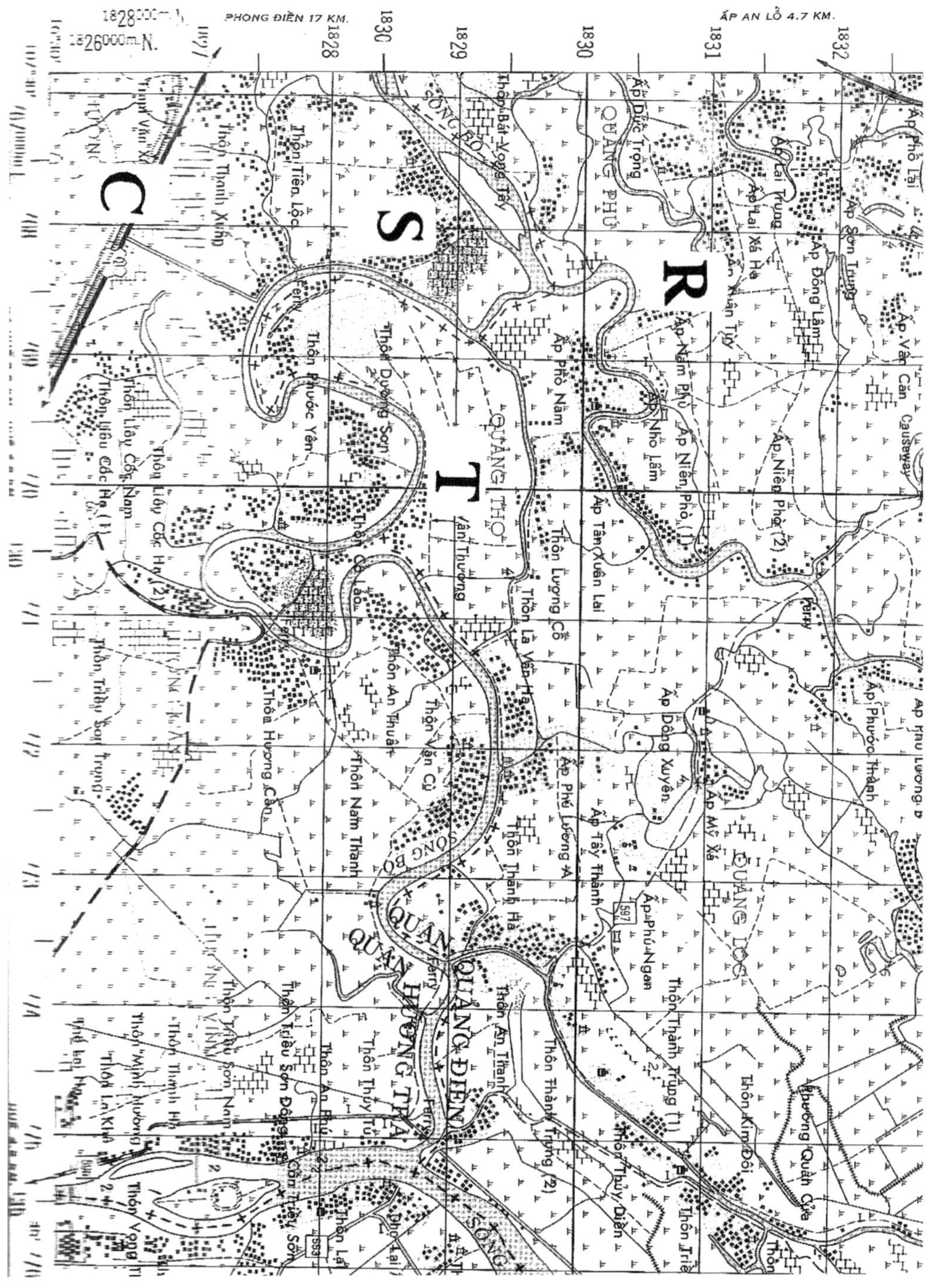

Battles along the Song Bo River, five miles northwest of Hue, just north of Highway 1.

C. Highway One

R. Village of Ap Nam Phu, April 4, deadliest single day in Vietnam for the 82nd Airborne

S. Battle of the Lazy W, April 5 thru April 9

T. Song Bo or Lazy W River

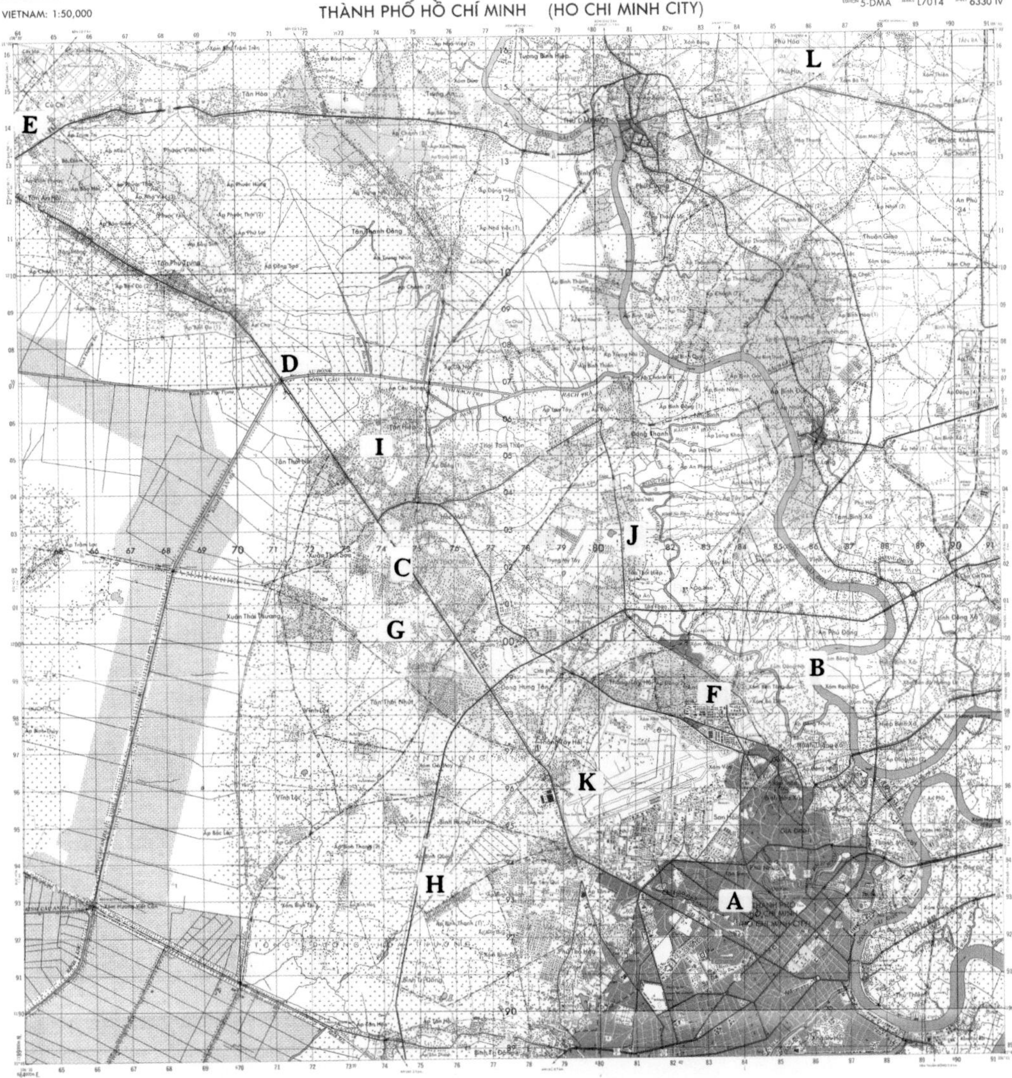

Area of operations, October 1968 to December 1969, Fire Bases on the approaches to Saigon from the northwest.

Alphabet code:

A. Northwest quadrant of Saigon
B. Saigon River
C. Highway One, Vietnam's major road
D. Bridge over the Hoc Mon Canal
E. Cu Chi tunnel complex
F. Camp Red Ball, headquarters of the Golden Brigade
G. Fire Support Base All American, headquarters of 1st Battalion, 505th Parachute Infantry Regiment.
H. Fire Support Base Hardcore, headquarters of 1st Battalion, 508th Parachute Infantry Regiment
I. Fire Support Base Harrison, headquarters of the 2nd Battalion, 505th Parachute Infantry Regiment
J. Fire Support Base Copperhead, headquarters of the 321st Artillery Regiment
K. Brigade logistics area, Tan Son Nhut Air Base
L. Phu Loi, headquarters of 82nd Support Battalion

(Top) Troopers from the Third Brigade of the 82nd Airborne Division guarding a bridge during Operation Power Pack in the Dominican Republic. The operation began in April of 1965.

(Center) President Lyndon Johnson is escorted by 82nd Airborne Division commander Richard Seitz after arriving at Fort Bragg to meet with paratroopers he had ordered to Vietnam in February of 1968.

(Bottom) As commander-in-chief, President Johnson shakes hands with paratroopers he ordered to Vietnam, pledging in a speech that he and the country would support them until their duty was done. Six weeks later, Johnson announced he would not seek re-election would devote his efforts to end the war.

(Top) Troopers from the Golden Brigade arrive aboard Air Force C-141 Starlifters at Chu Lai in response to attacks by the Viet Cong and North Vietnam army during the Tet Offensive.

(Center) Airborne infantry arriving at Chu Lai with the duffel bags they carried with them from Fort Bragg.

(Bottom) Arriving troopers loading their gear onto trucks while awaiting orders to move north to meet their adversaries.

(Top) The arrival of Bravo Company of the 1st Battalion of the 505th Parachute Infantry Regiment, one of three infantry battalions in the Golden Brigade.

(Bottom) Infantry moving out on exercises for detecting booby traps during Proficiency Training, which was a five-day orientation program for arriving troops.

(Top) The early phase of construction of Camp Rodriguez, the headquarters of the Third Brigade. South Vietnamese civilians helped fill sand bags used as defensive measures.

(Bottom) Construction of the fortified Tactical Operations Center, the nerve center of the brigade inside the perimeter of Camp Rodriguez. The camp was named for Sergeant Joe Rodriguez, the brigade's first combat casualty.

(Upper left) Completed Tactical Operations Center adorned with the All American symbol.

(Upper right) A different view of the TOC. Note the forested mountains in the background that mark the border with Laos.

(Center left) Airborne headquarters emerging from what was empty ground.

(Center right) Infantrymen posing in front of the sign proclaiming the ground as Camp Rodriguez, along with the U.S. flag and the Third Brigade battle flag.

(Lower left) A caution sign erected on the perimeter of base camp, proclaiming it to be Airborne Country.

(Lower right) Brigade commander Alexander R. Bolling Jr., at far right, conferring with Olinto M. Barsanti, commanding general of the 101st Airborne Division.

(Upper left) Colonel Bolling, at right, with overall commander William Westmoreland.

(Upper right) Command Sergeant Major John Pearce, the highest ranking enlisted man in the brigade and the non-commissioned officer who carried the brigade battle flag to Vietnam.

(Large photo in the lower left) A combat ready Colonel Bolling heading out on a mission, followed by three-star general Creighton W. Abrams, who succeeded Westmoreland as overall commander.

(Two photos in the lower right) Two infantrymen from the brigade out on combat patrol. The ammunition belts carried by the trooper in lower right photo is extra ammo for the M-60 machine gun.

(Clockwise from upper left) Faces of brigade soldiers at the ready on combat operations. Color photo is Second Lieutenant Jim Littig, commander of the Long Range Recon element, wearing the red, white and blue All American shoulder patch. Picture at lower right shows soldiers humping up a challenging hill while shouldering their 70-pound packs.

(Clockwise from upper left) A soldier takes a water break while wearing the green Army towel around his neck. Photos show the thick vegetation encountered by those seeking to make contact with their adversaries. (Lower left) A soldier stands guard over a convoy on Highway 547 leading from Hue to the western mountains.

(Top) Soldiers operating in one of the many villages outside of Hue.

(Bottom) Soldiers engaged in fighting in a village.

The brigade positioned its artillery at various fire support bases to assist the infantry in combat operations. The canons were part of the 321st Artillery Regiment.

(Top) Soldier on guard behind a .50 caliber machine gun.
(Bottom) Soldier on lookout at a fortified observation post.

Part of the daily routine for combat engineers was clearing roads of booby traps and land mines, known in future wars as improvised explosive devices. The dangerous work could be done by hand, as in top photo, or by a modified tank provided by the 101st Airborne.

Water was everywhere in Vietnam, but fresh water was a precious commodity. Rain water gathered in bomb craters but had to be treated with Halazone or iodine tablets before troops could drink it. Troops tried to take care of their feet to ward off jungle rot and other jungle pests, or they bathed in waterways such as the Perfume River.

(Clockwise from upper left) Troops engaged in the unpleasant but necessary duty of burning off the human waste from the latrines. Helicopters provided new-found mobility in whisking troops from one area to another. The Nam Hoa Bridge over the Perfume River was vital in keeping supplies flowing to fire bases west of Hue.

(Lower right) The entrance to Fire Base Bastogne. Lower left is the view from a helicopter cockpit over Fire Base Birmingham.

(Center left) Billows of napalm, a jellied gasoline dropped in canisters from aircraft.

(Clockwise from top left) A soldier seeks spiritual solace in a bombed out church. Chaplain James Sanner officiates at Mass in the boonies, using the hood of his jeep as an altar. An infantry patrol heads into the mists that hung eerily in the valleys of the western mountains. Colonel Bolling, whose call sign was Night Rider, discusses battle plans with one of his subordinates. Major General Olinto Barsanti pins the Silver Star for valor on Lieutenant Carroll Guthrie following a sapper attack on the base camps of the 82nd Airborne and the 101st Airborne.

(Top) Colonel Bolling, at right, in the field with one of his officers.

(Bottom) Second Lieutenant Robert Murrill with a boa constrictor captured by the locals. Note the red, white and blue All American shoulder patches. Bolling preferred the colors over the subdued patches because he wanted his adversaries to know who was fighting them.

(Top) Sergeant John Plunkard, on his second tour of duty in Vietnam, on stand down at Col Co Beach on the South China Sea. He was later killed in action in the Battle of the Lazy W.

(Bottom) An Empty Boots memorial service at Camp Rodriguez for troopers killed in action. A three-volley salute, or 21 shots in all, honored the fallen.

(Top) Colonel Bolling addresses a formation of troops at Camp Rodriguez.

(Bottom) Richard Davidson, a Canadian who volunteered to join the 82nd Airborne, visiting the grave of Leo Brent Gunning of Potsdam, New York, on April 4, 2018, 50 years to the day that Gunning was killed trying to save Davidson's life.

(Clockwise from upper left) Second Lieutenant Mike Hood, commanding a combat company less than a year after his West Point graduation, assists a wounded South Vietnamese ally from the battlefield. Top right shows Highway 547 after Agent Orange was used to kill the jungle undergrowth as a way of deterring ambushes. Troopers carrying a wounded comrade on a stretcher race toward a medical evacuation helicopter like the one shown in the center right picture. Colonel Bolling greets a newly arrived artillery officer. At lower left, helicopters insert infantrymen in an operation near the western mountains.

Medevac helicopters landing in jungle battlefields to rush wounded troopers to aid stations for emergency care. Helicopter pilots risked life and limb during the extractions, which were often done under fire.

(Top) Colonel Bolling presents an 82nd Airborne plaque of appreciation to Major General Barsanti of the 101st Airborne. Bolling's brigade was under the operational control of Barsanti's division but maintained its All American identity.

(Bottom) Troopers ready to fire a 106-millimeter recoilless rifle, a big bore gun that was most often mounted on a gun jeep.

(Top) Pete Henderson, who served the brigade by flying in the backseat of an observation airplane called the O1-Bird Dog. He was connected by radio to the brigade artillery.

(Bottom) The identification card given to the Nightfighters of the 1st Battalion of the 505th Parachute Infantry Regiment, The unit adopted the owl as a symbol and operated under the motto: Travel Light, Fight At Night.

(Clockwise from top left) Bud Bolling after his promotion to brigadier general. Leslie Hayes of Kentucky, pictured in the upper right, was the radio operator for Sergeant Felix Modesto Conde-Falcon, a native of Puerto Rico who is pictured in lower left. Both of them, along with Pete Watkins of Pennsylvania, pictured in the lower right, were in the same platoon in the original Delta Company of the 1st of the 505.

(Clockwise from top left) Brigadier General George Dickerson, call sign Bold Strike, who took over the brigade in December of 1968 when Bud Bolling was promoted to serve in a higher command. Top right shows Bolling in an armored personnel carrier, which replaced the gun jeeps in the cavalry unit. Center right shows General Dickerson on a helicopter mission. Lower right is General Dickerson conducting a briefing. Lower left is General Dickerson.

(Top) Infantrymen disembarking from a Navy vessel to conduct patrols Down South.
(Bottom) A soldier with canteen in the watery world of Vietnam.

(Top) The terrain outside of Saigon featured a network of rivers, streams and canals, which infantrymen had to cross during combat operations.

(Bottom) Grunts helping each other across a waterway.

In the rice-growing culture of Vietnam, farmers raised livestock and relied on water buffalo to till the marshy ground.

PHOTOGRAPHS

(Top and center) Vietnamese men and women worked the rice paddies, which were separated by earthen dikes and bordered by lines of scraggly trees.

(Bottom) An infantry unit setting up in a graveyard. The mounds and walls offered some protection for troops on the ground. No disrespect was intended. In Vietnam, the dead protected the living.

(Top) A different view of the graveyard.

(Center) The impact of tides Down South. Water levels would rise and fall on the tides. At low tide, infantrymen struggled through the muck to get to where they were going.

(Bottom) A soldier eats a meal of C Rations while immersed in swamp water. Dry land was a luxury.

(Clockwise from upper left) Troops sped to trouble spots aboard helicopters. Soldiers also plied the waterways in the search for their adversaries, whether it was in a sampan propelled by oar, or in flat-bottomed boats powered by outboard engines. At lower left, a soldier wades through the deep muck at low tide.

(Clockwise from upper left) Elements of the brigade operated in boats powered by air foils or saw this view from the bow of one of the flat-bottomed boats. Picture at lower left shows soldiers seizing haul of ammunition and supplies buried in the ground. Middle left photo shows soldiers burning off vegetation on the banks of waterways. The banks would be sprayed with Agent Orange or other defoliants to kill the vegetation, then deluge guns of flame would burn back the dead stuff. Given enough time, the undergrowth always grew back.

Brigade troopers making an inventory of weapons and supplies seized from hidden stockpiles.

(Clockwise from upper left) Buried in pre-positioned caches were mortar rounds and other tools of war. Bottom right photo shows an infantry squad resting in a day area before heading out on night ambush.

An ingenious enemy buried supplies in some of the most out of the way places, including swamps and marshes. Soldiers form a relay system to haul out the stores.

(Top) The main bridge over the Hoc Mon Canal along Highway One. The bridge was guarded 24 hours a day.
(Center) One of the many off-shoots of the canal.
(Bottom) Civilian traffic like this bus operated from the outer provinces over the bridge and into Saigon.

(Clockwise from upper left) Vietnamese peddlers known as Coke girls drove around on motor bikes to sell goods to soldiers. Bunker at the Hoc Mon Bridge where off-duty guards could rest. Damaged Navy vessel that ran aground on the banks of the canal. Soldiers often strung ropes over the water to help each other across. Soldiers often were submerged in water even in their bunkers. Center left is the rickety East Bridge over the Hoc Mon Canal.

(Left from top to bottom) Machine gunner Ed Kochanski of Scranton, Pennsylvania, with his pack and his weapon prior to a patrol. Bottom picture shows Kochanski with his gear on.

(Right from top to bottom) In photos on the right, crews in a mortar pit respond to a fire mission. Every morning, soldiers would check themselves for leeches, which thrived in the tropical environment.

(Clockwise from upper left) Leaders stayed in contact with higher command via the PRC-25 radio, with the radio operator always within arm's length. Military Police in a jeep head out to patrol roads. Photo at lower left show Rick Talioaga in fighting position with his jungle clothes rotted away. Center left is artillery crew responding to a fire mission.

(Clockwise from upper left) An Army truck got stuck in the mire of South Vietnam, then a rescue vehicle got bogged down trying to free it. Jeeps could also sink into the wet ground. Two South Vietnamese fishermen in sampan encountered by an American patrol. Soldiers cross a waterway with a napalm explosion in the background. Center left photo is aftermath of a jeep that detonated a mine.

(Top) Rick Taglioaga with a humble Christmas tree adorning a tent at base camp.

(Bottom) A Christmas tree also adorned the fire pit of an artillery position.

(Clockwise from upper left) A brigade officer dressed up as Santa Claus moved from place to place aboard a light observation helicopter. Christmas tree in a tent. Volunteers called Doughnut Dollies visited troops in the field to boost morale. Santa visited Vietnamese children too.

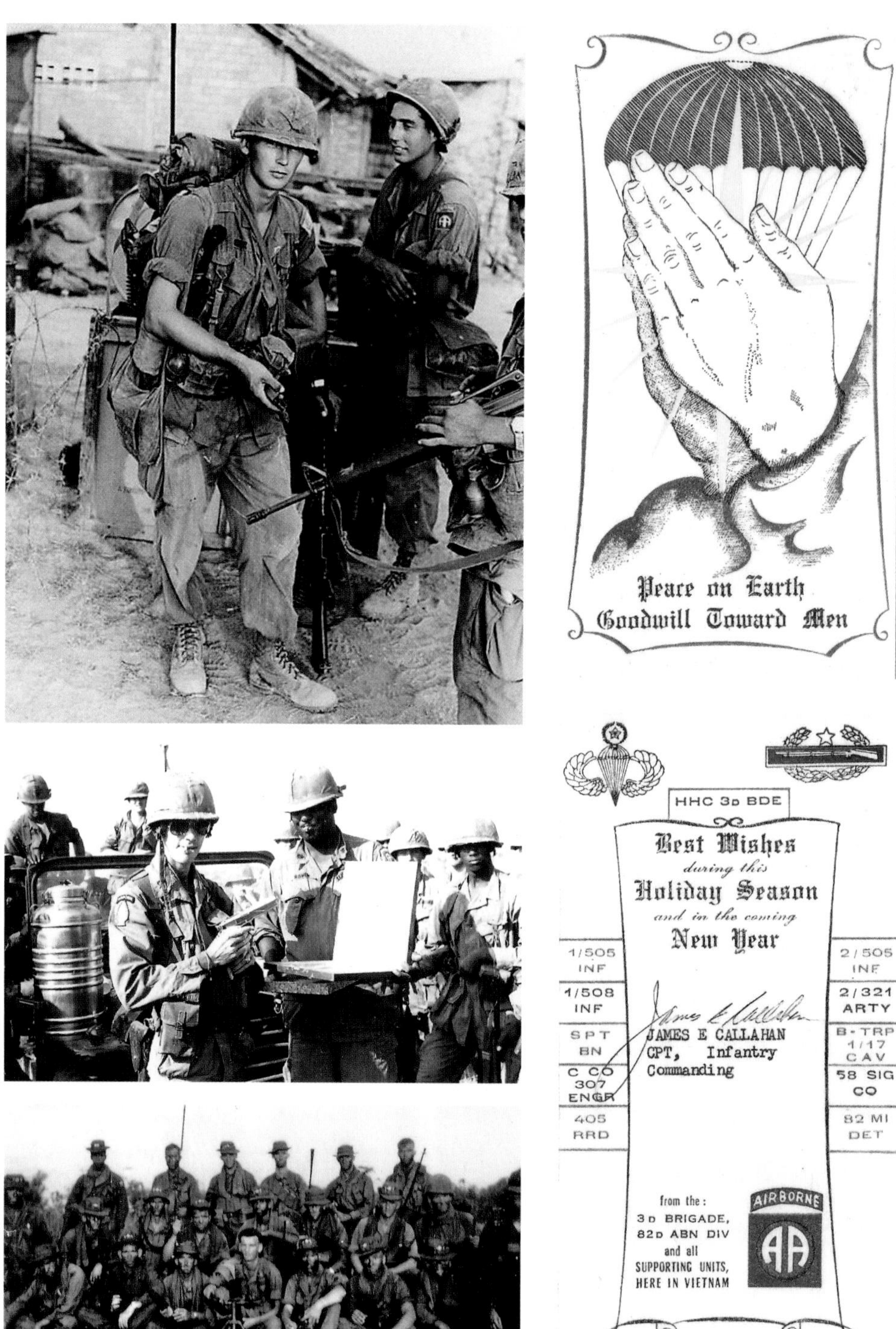

(Left from top to bottom) Captain James Callahan, who commanded Delta Company following two tours of duty as a Special Forces operative. Part of the Delta Dragons, wearing soft-cover boonie hats.
(Right top and bottom) The brigade's Christmas card from Vietnam, signed by Captain Callahan.

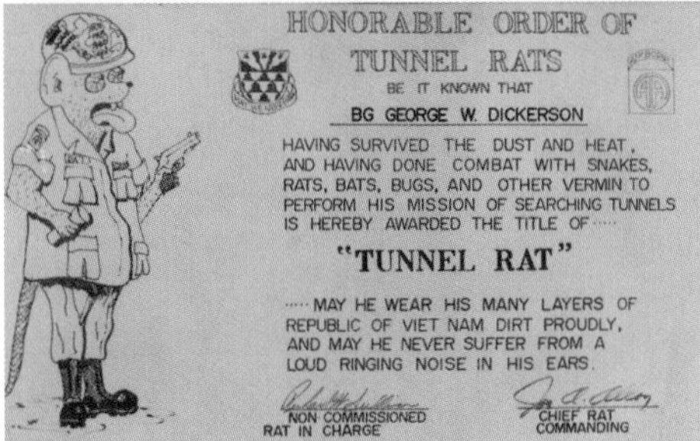

HONORABLE ORDER OF
TUNNEL RATS
BE IT KNOWN THAT
BG GEORGE W. DICKERSON
HAVING SURVIVED THE DUST AND HEAT, AND HAVING DONE COMBAT WITH SNAKES, RATS, BATS, BUGS, AND OTHER VERMIN TO PERFORM HIS MISSION OF SEARCHING TUNNELS IS HEREBY AWARDED THE TITLE OF·····
"TUNNEL RAT"
·····MAY HE WEAR HIS MANY LAYERS OF REPUBLIC OF VIET NAM DIRT PROUDLY, AND MAY HE NEVER SUFFER FROM A LOUD RINGING NOISE IN HIS EARS.

NON COMMISSIONED RAT IN CHARGE

CHIEF RAT COMMANDING

(Clockwise from upper left) The war sometimes went underground into a maze of tunnels. Volunteers called Tunnel Rats went into the dark passages and were tethered to the surface by a length of rope tied around an ankle. Middle left shows a Tunnel Rat certificate given to brigade commander George Dickerson. Photo at bottom left shows the kind of boat used to patrol rivers, streams and canals.

(Upper left) An Empty Boots memorial service for troopers killed in action Down South.

(Upper right) Artillery fires in support of the infantry.

(Center left and right) A mortar firing in daytime and the visual effect of a mortar shell leaving the tube at night.

(Lower left and right) Chaplains administering to the spiritual needs of troops. An ammo crate could be used as an altar. Vestments could be made from camouflage material.

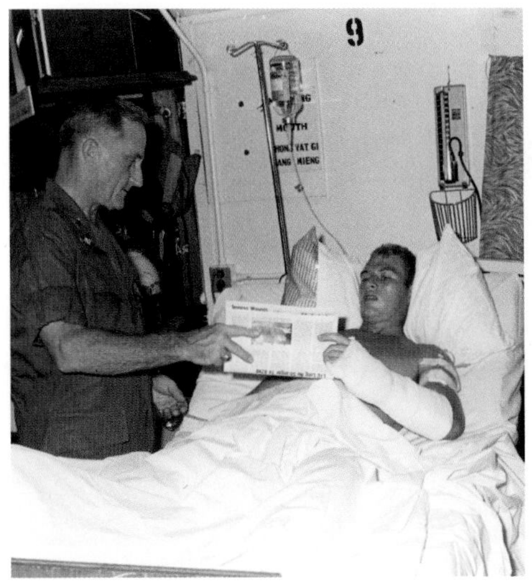

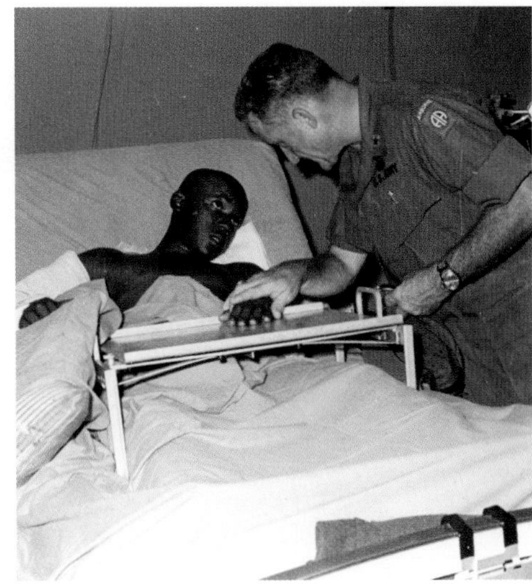

(Clockwise from upper left) Brigade commander George Dickerson visiting wounded troops in the hospital. Combat engineers in their up-armored bulldozers carving out a fire base in the boonies. Chaplain conducting services in the field.

The twin-rotor Chinook helicopter was used extensively to haul troops to operating areas near the Cambodian border, which soldiers called going Out West. In addition to moving troops, the flying machines lifted artillery into forward positions.

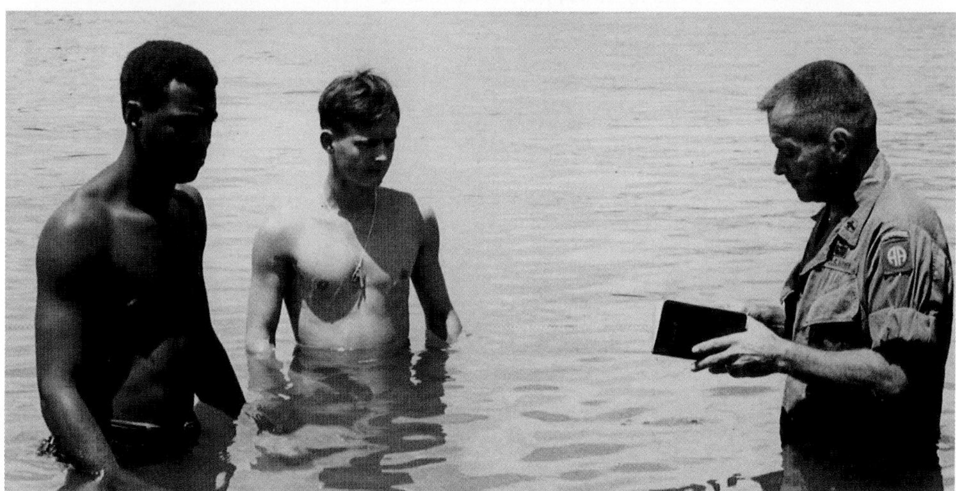

(Top) Helicopters arrive to lift troops to wherever they were needed.
(Center and bottom) A brigade chaplain baptizing a convert with river water.

(Upper left) Chaplain giving Communion to combat troops at a fire base.
(Upper right) Troops saddling up for an operation out on the Cambodian border.
(Center left) Soldier at center left patrols in the water surrounded by dense vegetation.
(Center right) A foot patrol entering a village.
(Bottom left and right) Foot patrols .

(Top) A radio operator standing guard within arm's length of an officer communicating with headquarters. (Clockwise from center left) A soldier with the M-79 grenade launcher. Soldiers negotiating the waterways while on patrol, gear placed atop an air mattress to keep it dry during the crossing of a waterway. Lower left, a squad finds daytime cover in a clump of scraggly trees off an open field.

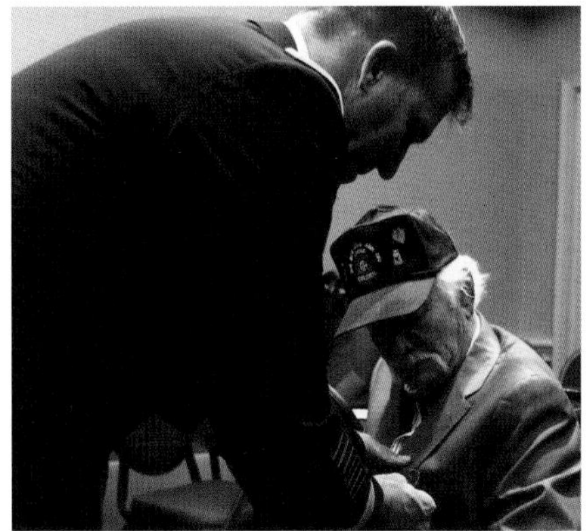

(Clockwise from upper left) 82nd Airborne Division commander Erik Kurilla pins the Bronze Star on paratrooper-for-life Jimmy Greene 50 years after a battle. Greene was unable to stand during the 2017 ceremony but returned the two-star general's salute from his chair. He had received the citation 50 years earlier but had never received the actual medal. His face is the very picture of paratrooper pride. Photo at lower left is Sergeant Benjamin Perry Benton, killed in action in Operation Sheridan-Sabre.

(Clockwise from upper left) Sergeant Juan Blaz, who received the Distinguished Service Cross for his valor during Operation Sheridan-Sabre. A soldier outside a base camp. Soldiers add sand bags to fortify an observation bunker. Bottom right is actor Sebastian Cabot flanked at left by brigade commander George Dickerson. Cabot visited troops in the field as a morale boost. Salome Beltran, recipient of the Silver Star for valor at the Battle of Ap Nam Phu. Ronnie Johnson of Burke, South Dakota, a squad leader who was killed in action in the Ho Bo Woods.

(Clockwise from upper left) Sebastian Cabot in the field with the troops. Cabot receiving All American shoulder patches, which he wore into the field. Photo of the Delta Dragons. Soldiers washing off layers of grime by using their steel pot helmets as wash bowls.

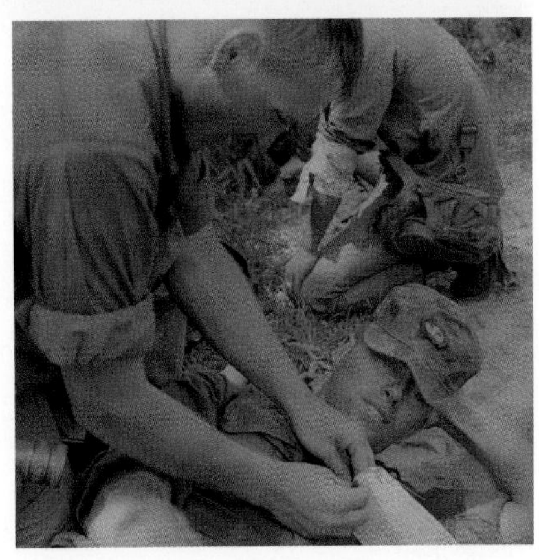

(Clockwise from upper left) As part of the effort to pacify the villages, the brigade's Civil Affairs unit administered medical care, including inoculations to ward off bubonic plaque. Soldiers did their part by befriending village children. Picture at center left is Sergeant Felix Modesto Conde-Falcon, killed in action on Good Friday of 1969 and posthumously awarded the Medal of Honor 45 years after the fact.

(Clockwise from upper left) Artillery supports infantry operations. Down South, the brigade was augmented by the addition of the 37th Scout Dog Platoon. The animals and their handlers worked in concert with the infantry to sniff out booby traps or to find tunnel entrances. Pictured at lower left is Carl Gulas of Cleveland, Ohio. Picture was taken two hours before he was wounded. Picture at center left is the scout dog named Bodo.

(Clockwise from upper left) Combat engineers probe the ground for booby traps. Troopers assess the haul retrieved from a buried stockpile. A trooper is shown against the backdrop of the thick vegetation out near the Cambodian border. Captured weapons seized in a search. A foot patrol leaves a fire base. A handler and his scout dog ready for action.

(Clockwise from upper left) Troopers receive word over the radio that the brigade colors are being withdrawn because the war was being turned over to the South Vietnamese. Searches continue for buried supplies. Troopers examine items found in a cache. Troops board a truck before departing Vietnam. General George Dickerson poses in front of a ceremonial artillery round, the last of 370,000 shells fired by the brigade during its 22 months in country.

(Clockwise from upper left) Returning troops arrive in Fort Bragg. U.S. troops and a Vietnamese interpreter question a captured Viet Cong. Center, Soldiers load up on trucks to go home. Sign outside Fire Base All American. The Honor Guard carrying the brigade's battle flag receives a final salute before boarding a plane for home.

(Clockwise from upper left) Returning troopers are welcomed home at Pope Air Force Base. The 82nd Airborne Vietnam Memorial honors the 227 brigade members who lost their lives in Vietnam. Paddy Barry, center, and veterans of the Golden Brigade were invited to welcome home a new generation of paratroopers returning from a deployment in Afghanistan in 2012. Veterans of the Golden Brigade snap to attention and return a salute with the Statue of Liberty in the background. The Legacy Bowl and its 15 toasting cups were on display at a reunion marking the 50th anniversary of the brigade's deployment. General George Dickerson speaking to a formation upon the brigade's return to Fort Bragg.